THE COLLECTED WORKS
OF W. B. YEATS

VOLUME I

THE COLLECTED WORKS OF W. B. YEATS

Richard J. Finneran and George Mills Harper, *General Editors*

W. B. YEATS

The Poems

SECOND EDITION

EDITED BY
Richard J. Finneran

Scribner

SCRIBNER
1230 Avenue of the Americas
New York, NY 10020

SCRIBNER and design are trademarks of Macmillan Library Reference USA, Inc.,
used under license by Simon & Schuster, the publisher of this work.

Designed by Jenny Dossin
Set in Adobe Sabon

Manufactured in the United States of America
5 7 9 10 8 6

Library of Congress Cataloging-in-Publication Data
Yeats, W. B. (William Butler), 1865–1939.
The poems/W. B. Yeats: edited by Richard J. Finneran.—2nd ed.
p. cm.—(The collected works of W. B. Yeats; v. 1)
Includes bibliographical references (p.   ) and indexes.
I. Finneran, Richard J. II. Title. III. Series: Yeats, W. B. (William Butler),
1865–1939. Works. 1989; v. 1.
PR5900.A3   1997
821'.8—dc21   97–23065
CIP

ISBN 0-684-83935-0

CONTENTS

THE WIND AMONG THE REEDS (1899)

IN THE SEVEN WOODS (1904)

Narrative and Dramatic

PART TWO

Additional Poems

PREFACE

The main purpose of this volume is to provide accurate texts of all poems by Yeats published in his lifetime or scheduled for publication as of his death on 28 January 1939. Part One of this edition is, in effect, a reconstruction of the expanded version of *The Collected Poems* (1933) which as of 22 June 1937 Yeats had planned to publish 'in about two years' time.' To the 1933 volume have been added the poems from *A Full Moon in March* (1935), except 'Three Songs to the Same Tune,' later revised; from *New Poems* (1938); and from a manuscript table of contents for a volume of poems and plays Yeats had projected during the last few weeks of his life (published posthumously as *Last Poems and Two Plays*, 1939). Part Two offers the remainder of Yeats's published poems, bringing together works from a disparate variety of sources: not only those lyrics which Yeats published one or more times but then excluded from his collected editions, but also poems from other sources, such as essays, plays, and stories. The song 'Come ride and ride to the garden' from Lady Gregory's play *The Travelling Man* has been included on the bases of her ascription of it to Yeats and of the existence of a holograph draft of the poem in his hand. The unpublished poem 'Reprisals' has been included because in December 1920 it was in press and was withdrawn only at the request of Lady Gregory. For further information on these and other editorial matters, interested readers are referred to this writer's *Editing Yeats's Poems: A Reconsideration* (1990).

With two exceptions, this volume does not offer early versions of poems which Yeats later revised. Thus, for example, 'Song of the Faeries' (*Dublin University Review*, March 1885) is excluded because it was later incorporated into 'The Island of Statues,' and 'In a Drawing-Room' (*Dublin University Review*, January 1886) because both stanzas reappear with little change in 'Quatrains and Aphorisms.' However, 'The Hero, the Girl, and the Fool' and 'Three Songs to the Same Tune' have been included in Part Two, despite the presence in Part One of 'The Fool by the Roadside' and 'Three Marching Songs.' In the first instance, Yeats had printed the poem in two separate collections of his verse before deciding to use only 'The Fool by the Roadside,' a shorter version first published in *A Vision* (1925), in the *Collected Poems*. The two works seem sufficiently distinct as to justify the inclusion of both in this edition. The question of 'Three Songs to the Same Tune' is more problematical. The decision to offer both it and its revision, 'Three Marching Songs,' in *Poems* (1949) was made by Mrs. W. B. Yeats, who ten years earlier had consulted 'various poets' and found 'unanimous agreement that *both* versions should be printed, as they are, on the whole, so different.' As I have argued elsewhere, such a choice does not accord with Yeats's usual practice. Nevertheless, Mrs. Yeats's recommendation gave 'canonical' status to 'Three Songs to the Same Tune' for over three decades, and thus it is included in Part Two of this volume (likewise, the 1949 *Poems* improperly offered 'The Hero, the Girl, and the Fool' rather than 'The Fool by the Roadside').

The textual policy for this edition has been to present the final versions of the poems authorized by Yeats. The copy-texts therefore consist of printed editions (some with corrections by Yeats), manuscripts, typescripts, and corrected proofs. Emendation has been held to a minimum. For example, there has been virtually no attempt to regularize Yeats's unorthodox punctuation, nor has the spelling of Gaelic names been corrected or made uniform unless Yeats himself established a standard spelling (as with 'Cuchulain' or 'Oisin'). The Textual Notes provide a full record of the copy-texts employed and the emendations admitted.

The Explanatory Notes attempt to elucidate all *direct* allusions in the poems. Attention is directed to the headnote, which explains the principles of annotation.

This edition was first published in New York in 1983 and in London in 1984 as *The Poems: A New Edition*. The discovery by John S. Kelly of three fugitive early poems was the primary reason for the publication in 1989 of *The Poems,* revised edition, in which I also took the opportunity to include "Reprisals." The discovery of a corrected copy of *The Wanderings of Oisin* (1889) in the Pierpont Morgan Library resulted in additional changes to *The Poems* in 1990. The most significant revisions in the present volume (which has been reset) are derived from James Pethica's forthcoming edition of the manuscripts of [*Last Poems*] in the Cornell Yeats. In each printing, any significant errors or misprints which have come to light have been corrected.

As this chronology suggests, and as I argued in *Editing Yeats's Poems: A Reconsideration* and in a chapter in *Representing Modernist Texts: Editing as Interpretation,* edited by George Bornstein (1990), the notion of a "final" or "definitive" text of Yeats's poems is fundamentally illusory. This is especially true for those works which Yeats did not see into print, where any editor must struggle with the difficulty of distinguishing between the hands of Yeats and that of his wife, as well as with uncertainty about the date and authority of revisions which are clearly in Mrs. Yeats's hand. Thus, for example, a close reader of the Cornell Yeats [*Last Poems*] will notice several places where the archival materials offer alternative readings to those provided herein, such as the possibility that the line "The soul's perfection is from peace;" should be added between the present lines 55–56 of "Under Ben Bulben." An electronic edition of the poetry projected by myself and others will be able to present both the alternative texts and the manuscript materials from which they derive.

Any project of this scope is of course impossible without the assitance of many individuals. In the years since 1983, I have relied most on the assistance and advice of George Bornstein, Mary FitzGerald, and William H. O'Donnell. More recently I am indebted to James Pethica for discussions about the textual problems in [*Last Poems*] and for the opportunity, in my role as Series Editor for the Poems in the Cornell Yeats, to review his work prior to publication. I am also grateful to Scott Moyers and Jennifer Chen at Scribner for their care in seeing the second edition through the press. The acknowledgments from the 1983 edition are reprinted below.

I should first like to thank Anne Yeats and Michael B. Yeats, not only for authorizing me to undertake this project but also for giving me free access to their collections of Yeats's books and manuscripts, without which its completion would have been quite impossible.

Of the many scholars who contributed to this edition, my greatest debt by far is to Brendan O Hehir, who not only provided me with much of the information on Irish materials in the Notes but also saved me from numerous errors. His combination of precise knowledge and generosity in sharing it is a rare virtue. I should also like to give special thanks to George Bornstein, whose advice on many matters I have valued, as I have his friendship.

I am also indebted to the following: the late Russell K. Alspach; Charles Bowen; Maureen Brown; Francis John Byrne; Edward Callan; Eamonn R. Cantwell; Andrew Carpenter; David R. Clark; Rosalind E. Clark; Peter Connolly; Kevin Danaher; Istvan Deak; Eilís Dillon; Clive E. Driver; Michael Durkan; the late Oliver Edwards; the late Richard Ellmann; Julia Emmons; Richard Fallis; T. M. Farmiloe; Ian Fletcher; Richard Garnett; the late James Gilvarry; Warwick Gould; Maurice Harmon; George Mills Harper; Carolyn Holdsworth; M. C. K. Hood; Walter Kelly Hood; Michael Horniman; K. P. S. Jochum; John Kelleher; John Kelly; Hugh Kenner; Dan H. Laurence; A. Walton Litz; Seán Lucy; the late F. S. L. Lyons; Phillip L. Marcus; Vivian Mercier; William M. Murphy; William H. O'Donnell; James Olney; Edward O'Shea; Mícheál Ó Súilleabháin; Thomas Parkinson; Edward B. Partridge; Richard F. Peterson; Donald Pizer; Elizabeth Poe; Raymond J. Porter; J. A. V. Rose; M. L. Rosenthal; Ann Saddlemyer; Ronald Schuchard; Paula Scott-James; Charles Seaton; David Seidman; Linda Shaughnessy; Colin Smythe; Gerald Snare; John Sparrow; Jon Stallworthy; Donald E. Stanford; Thomas R. Starnes; Julia Tame; Mary Helen Thuente; Donald T. Torchiana; and Karen Wilcox.

I am also indebted to the following institutions and libraries: The Berg Collection, New York Public Library; British Library; Henry E. Huntington Library and Art Gallery; Houghton Library, Harvard University (Rodney G. Dennis); Humanities Research Center, University of Texas at Austin (Ellen S. Dunlap and Cathy Henderson); National Library of Ireland; Pierpont Morgan Library; Princeton University Library (Nancy N. Coffin and Richard Ludwig); Southern Illinois University Library (Kenneth W. Duckett); University College, Dublin, Library (Norma Jessop); William Andrews Clark Memorial Library; and the Yeats Archives, State University of New York at Stony Brook (Narayan Hegde, Lewis Lusardi, Peggy McMullen, and Arthur Sniffin).

For the financial support which enabled me to undertake and to complete this volume, I am most grateful to the American Council of

Learned Societies; the American Philosophical Society; the Graduate Council on Research, Tulane University; the Henry E. Huntington Library and Art Gallery; and the National Endowment for the Humanities.

I would like to rededicate this second edition to Mary, as always.

Mandeville, Louisiana   R.J.F.
10 December 1996

PART ONE

LYRICAL

Crossways

1889

'The stars are threshed, and the souls are threshed from their husks.'

WILLIAM BLAKE

TO

A.E.

The Song of the Happy Shepherd

The woods of Arcady are dead,
And over is their antique joy;
Of old the world on dreaming fed;
Grey Truth is now her painted toy;
Yet still she turns her restless head:
But O, sick children of the world,
Of all the many changing things
In dreary dancing past us whirled,
To the cracked tune that Chronos sings,
Words alone are certain good.   10
Where are now the warring kings,
Word be-mockers?—By the Rood
Where are now the warring kings?
An idle word is now their glory,
By the stammering schoolboy said,
Reading some entangled story:
The kings of the old time are dead;
The wandering earth herself may be
Only a sudden flaming word,
In clanging space a moment heard,   20
Troubling the endless reverie.

Then nowise worship dusty deeds,
Nor seek, for this is also sooth,
To hunger fiercely after truth,
Lest all thy toiling only breeds
New dreams, new dreams; there is no truth
Saving in thine own heart. Seek, then,
No learning from the starry men,
Who follow with the optic glass
The whirling ways of stars that pass—   30

Seek, then, for this is also sooth,
No word of theirs—the cold star-bane
Has cloven and rent their hearts in twain,
And dead is all their human truth.
Go gather by the humming sea
Some twisted, echo-harbouring shell,
And to its lips thy story tell,
And they thy comforters will be,
Rewarding in melodious guile
40　　　Thy fretful words a little while,
Till they shall singing fade in ruth
And die a pearly brotherhood;
For words alone are certain good:
Sing, then, for this is also sooth.

I must be gone: there is a grave
Where daffodil and lily wave,
And I would please the hapless faun,
Buried under the sleepy ground,
With mirthful songs before the dawn.
50　　　His shouting days with mirth were crowned;
And still I dream he treads the lawn,
Walking ghostly in the dew,
Pierced by my glad singing through,
My songs of old earth's dreamy youth:
But ah! she dreams not now; dream thou!
For fair are poppies on the brow:
Dream, dream, for this is also sooth.

2

The Sad Shepherd

There was a man whom Sorrow named his friend,
And he, of his high comrade Sorrow dreaming,
Went walking with slow steps along the gleaming
And humming sands, where windy surges wend:
And he called loudly to the stars to bend

From their pale thrones and comfort him, but they
Among themselves laugh on and sing alway:
And then the man whom Sorrow named his friend
Cried out, *Dim sea, hear my most piteous story!*
The sea swept on and cried her old cry still, 10
Rolling along in dreams from hill to hill.
He fled the persecution of her glory
And, in a far-off, gentle valley stopping,
Cried all his story to the dewdrops glistening.
But naught they heard, for they are always listening,
The dewdrops, for the sound of their own dropping.
And then the man whom Sorrow named his friend
Sought once again the shore, and found a shell,
And thought, *I will my heavy story tell*
Till my own words, re-echoing, shall send 20
Their sadness through a hollow, pearly heart;
And my own tale again for me shall sing,
And my own whispering words be comforting,
And lo! my ancient burden may depart.
Then he sang softly nigh the pearly rim;
But the sad dweller by the sea-ways lone
Changed all he sang to inarticulate moan
Among her wildering whirls, forgetting him.

3

The Cloak, the Boat, and the Shoes

'What do you make so fair and bright?'

'I make the cloak of Sorrow:
O lovely to see in all men's sight
Shall be the cloak of Sorrow,
In all men's sight.'

'What do you build with sails for flight?'

'I build a boat for Sorrow:
O swift on the seas all day and night

Saileth the rover Sorrow,
10   All day and night.'

'What do you weave with wool so white?'

'I weave the shoes of Sorrow:
Soundless shall be the footfall light
In all men's ears of Sorrow,
Sudden and light.'

4

Anashuya and Vijaya

*A little Indian temple in the Golden Age. Around it a garden;
around that the forest. Anashuya, the young priestess, kneeling
within the temple.*

Anashuya. Send peace on all the lands and flickering corn.—
     O, may tranquillity walk by his elbow
     When wandering in the forest, if he love
     No other.—Hear, and may the indolent flocks
     Be plentiful.—And if he love another,
     May panthers end him.—Hear, and load our king
     With wisdom hour by hour.—May we two stand,
     When we are dead, beyond the setting suns,
     A little from the other shades apart,
10   With mingling hair, and play upon one lute.

Vijaya [*entering and throwing a lily at her*]. Hail! hail, my
     Anashuya.

Anashuya.   No: be still.
     I, priestess of this temple, offer up
     Prayers for the land.

Vijaya.   I will wait here, Amrita.

Anashuya. By mighty Brahma's ever-rustling robe,
     Who is Amrita? Sorrow of all sorrows!
     Another fills your mind.

Vijaya.   My mother's name.

Anashuya [*sings, coming out of the temple*].
   A sad, sad thought went by me slowly:
   Sigh, O you little stars! O sigh and shake your blue apparel!
   The sad, sad thought has gone from me now wholly:
   Sing, O you little stars! O sing and raise your rapturous carol   20
   To mighty Brahma, he who made you many as the sands,
   And laid you on the gates of evening with his quiet hands.
                 [*Sits down on the steps of the temple.*]
   Vijaya, I have brought my evening rice;
   The sun has laid his chin on the grey wood,
   Weary, with all his poppies gathered round him.

Vijaya. The hour when Kama, full of sleepy laughter,
   Rises, and showers abroad his fragrant arrows,
   Piercing the twilight with their murmuring barbs.

Anashuya. See how the sacred old flamingoes come,
   Painting with shadow all the marble steps: 30
   Aged and wise, they seek their wonted perches
   Within the temple, devious walking, made
   To wander by their melancholy minds.
   Yon tall one eyes my supper; chase him away,
   Far, far away. I named him after you.
   He is a famous fisher; hour by hour
   He ruffles with his bill the minnowed streams.
   Ah! there he snaps my rice. I told you so.
   Now cuff him off. He's off! A kiss for you,
   Because you saved my rice. Have you no thanks?   40

Vijaya [*sings*]. *Sing you of her, O first few stars,*
   Whom Brahma, touching with his finger, praises, for you hold
   The van of wandering quiet; ere you be too calm and old,
   Sing, turning in your cars,
   Sing, till you raise your hands and sigh, and from your
      car-heads peer,
   With all your whirling hair, and drop many an azure tear.

Anashuya. What know the pilots of the stars of tears?

Vijaya. Their faces are all worn, and in their eyes
   Flashes the fire of sadness, for they see
   The icicles that famish all the North,   50

Where men lie frozen in the glimmering snow;
And in the flaming forests cower the lion
And lioness, with all their whimpering cubs;
And, ever pacing on the verge of things,
The phantom, Beauty, in a mist of tears;
While we alone have round us woven woods,
And feel the softness of each other's hand,
Amrita, while—

Anashuya [*going away from him*].
                      Ah me! you love another,
                               [*Bursting into tears.*]
And may some sudden dreadful ill befall her!

60   *Vijaya.* I loved another; now I love no other.
Among the mouldering of ancient woods
You live, and on the village border she,
With her old father the blind wood-cutter;
I saw her standing in her door but now.

Anashuya. Vijaya, swear to love her never more.

Vijaya. Ay, ay.

Anashuya.   Swear by the parents of the gods,
Dread oath, who dwell on sacred Himalay,
On the far Golden Peak; enormous shapes,
Who still were old when the great sea was young;
70   On their vast faces mystery and dreams;
Their hair along the mountains rolled and filled
From year to year by the unnumbered nests
Of aweless birds, and round their stirless feet
The joyous flocks of deer and antelope,
Who never hear the unforgiving hound.
Swear!

Vijaya.   By the parents of the gods, I swear.

Anashuya [*sings*]. *I have forgiven, O new star!*
Maybe you have not heard of us, you have come forth so newly,
You hunter of the fields afar!
80   *Ah, you will know my loved one by his hunter's arrows truly,*

Shoot on him shafts of quietness, that he may ever keep
A lonely laughter, and may kiss his hands to me in sleep.

Farewell, Vijaya. Nay, no word, no word;
I, priestess of this temple, offer up
Prayers for the land.

　　　　　　　　　　　　　　　　　[*Vijaya goes.*]
　　　　　　　O Brahma, guard in sleep
The merry lambs and the complacent kine,
The flies below the leaves, and the young mice
In the tree roots, and all the sacred flocks
Of red flamingoes; and my love, Vijaya;
And may no restless fay with fidget finger　　　　　　90
Trouble his sleeping: give him dreams of me.

5
The Indian upon God

I passed along the water's edge below the humid trees,
My spirit rocked in evening light, the rushes round my knees,
My spirit rocked in sleep and sighs; and saw the moorfowl pace
All dripping on a grassy slope, and saw them cease to chase
Each other round in circles, and heard the eldest speak:
Who holds the world between His bill and made us strong or weak
Is an undying moorfowl, and He lives beyond the sky.
The rains are from His dripping wing, the moonbeams from His eye.
I passed a little further on and heard a lotus talk:
Who made the world and ruleth it, He hangeth on a stalk,　　10
For I am in His image made, and all this tinkling tide
Is but a sliding drop of rain between His petals wide.
A little way within the gloom a roebuck raised his eyes
Brimful of starlight, and he said: *The Stamper of the Skies,*
He is a gentle roebuck; for how else, I pray, could He
Conceive a thing so sad and soft, a gentle thing like me?
I passed a little further on and heard a peacock say:
Who made the grass and made the worms and made my feathers
　gay,

He is a monstrous peacock, and He waveth all the night
20   *His languid tail above us, lit with myriad spots of light.*

6

The Indian to his Love

The island dreams under the dawn
And great boughs drop tranquillity;
The peahens dance on a smooth lawn,
A parrot sways upon a tree,
Raging at his own image in the enamelled sea.

Here we will moor our lonely ship
And wander ever with woven hands,
Murmuring softly lip to lip,
Along the grass, along the sands,
10   Murmuring how far away are the unquiet lands:

How we alone of mortals are
Hid under quiet boughs apart,
While our love grows an Indian star,
A meteor of the burning heart,
One with the tide that gleams, the wings that gleam and dart,

The heavy boughs, the burnished dove
That moans and sighs a hundred days:
How when we die our shades will rove,
When eve has hushed the feathered ways,
20   With vapoury footsole by the water's drowsy blaze.

7

The Falling of the Leaves

Autumn is over the long leaves that love us,
And over the mice in the barley sheaves;
Yellow the leaves of the rowan above us,
And yellow the wet wild-strawberry leaves.

The hour of the waning of love has beset us,
And weary and worn are our sad souls now;
Let us part, ere the season of passion forget us,
With a kiss and a tear on thy drooping brow.

8

Ephemera

'Your eyes that once were never weary of mine
Are bowed in sorrow under pendulous lids,
Because our love is waning.'
                    And then she:
'Although our love is waning, let us stand
By the lone border of the lake once more,
Together in that hour of gentleness
When the poor tired child, Passion, falls asleep:
How far away the stars seem, and how far
Is our first kiss, and ah, how old my heart!'

Pensive they paced along the faded leaves,   10
While slowly he whose hand held hers replied:
'Passion has often worn our wandering hearts.'

The woods were round them, and the yellow leaves
Fell like faint meteors in the gloom, and once
A rabbit old and lame limped down the path;
Autumn was over him: and now they stood
On the lone border of the lake once more:
Turning, he saw that she had thrust dead leaves
Gathered in silence, dewy as her eyes,
In bosom and hair.
                    'Ah, do not mourn,' he said,   20
'That we are tired, for other loves await us;
Hate on and love through unrepining hours.
Before us lies eternity; our souls
Are love, and a continual farewell.'

9

The Madness of King Goll

I sat on cushioned otter-skin:
My word was law from Ith to Emain,
And shook at Invar Amargin
The hearts of the world-troubling seamen,
And drove tumult and war away
From girl and boy and man and beast;
The fields grew fatter day by day,
The wild fowl of the air increased;
And every ancient Ollave said,
While he bent down his fading head,
'He drives away the Northern cold.'
*They will not hush, the leaves a-flutter round me, the beech
    leaves old.*

I sat and mused and drank sweet wine;
A herdsman came from inland valleys,
Crying, the pirates drove his swine
To fill their dark-beaked hollow galleys.
I called my battle-breaking men
And my loud brazen battle-cars
From rolling vale and rivery glen;
And under the blinking of the stars
Fell on the pirates by the deep,
And hurled them in the gulph of sleep:
These hands won many a torque of gold.
*They will not hush, the leaves a-flutter round me, the beech
    leaves old.*

But slowly, as I shouting slew
And trampled in the bubbling mire,
In my most secret spirit grew
A whirling and a wandering fire:
I stood: keen stars above me shone,
Around me shone keen eyes of men:
I laughed aloud and hurried on

10

20

30

By rocky shore and rushy fen;
I laughed because birds fluttered by,
And starlight gleamed, and clouds flew high,
And rushes waved and waters rolled.
*They will not hush, the leaves a-flutter round me, the beech
   leaves old.*

And now I wander in the woods
When summer gluts the golden bees,
Or in autumnal solitudes
Arise the leopard-coloured trees;   40
Or when along the wintry strands
The cormorants shiver on their rocks;
I wander on, and wave my hands,
And sing, and shake my heavy locks.
The grey wolf knows me; by one ear
I lead along the woodland deer;
The hares run by me growing bold.
*They will not hush, the leaves a-flutter round me, the beech
   leaves old.*

I came upon a little town
That slumbered in the harvest moon,   50
And passed a-tiptoe up and down,
Murmuring, to a fitful tune,
How I have followed, night and day,
A tramping of tremendous feet,
And saw where this old tympan lay
Deserted on a doorway seat,
And bore it to the woods with me;
Of some inhuman misery
Our married voices wildly trolled.
*They will not hush, the leaves a-flutter round me, the beech
   leaves old.*   60

I sang how, when day's toil is done,
Orchil shakes out her long dark hair
That hides away the dying sun
And sheds faint odours through the air:

When my hand passed from wire to wire
It quenched, with sound like falling dew,
The whirling and the wandering fire;
But lift a mournful ulalu,
For the kind wires are torn and still,
70   And I must wander wood and hill
Through summer's heat and winter's cold.
*They will not hush, the leaves a-flutter round me, the beech
    leaves old.*

I O

The Stolen Child

Where dips the rocky highland
Of Sleuth Wood in the lake,
There lies a leafy island
Where flapping herons wake
The drowsy water-rats;
There we've hid our faery vats,
Full of berries
And of reddest stolen cherries.
Come away, O human child!
10   *To the waters and the wild*
With a faery, hand in hand,
For the world's more full of weeping than you
    can understand.

Where the wave of moonlight glosses
The dim grey sands with light,
Far off by furthest Rosses
We foot it all the night,
Weaving olden dances,
Mingling hands and mingling glances
Till the moon has taken flight;
20   To and fro we leap
And chase the frothy bubbles,

While the world is full of troubles
And is anxious in its sleep.
Come away, O human child!
To the waters and the wild
With a faery, hand in hand,
For the world's more full of weeping than you
    can understand.

Where the wandering water gushes
From the hills above Glen-Car,
In pools among the rushes   30
That scarce could bathe a star,
We seek for slumbering trout
And whispering in their ears
Give them unquiet dreams;
Leaning softly out
From ferns that drop their tears
Over the young streams.
Come away, O human child!
To the waters and the wild
With a faery, hand in hand,   40
For the world's more full of weeping than you
    can understand.

Away with us he's going,
The solemn-eyed:
He'll hear no more the lowing
Of the calves on the warm hillside
Or the kettle on the hob
Sing peace into his breast,
Or see the brown mice bob
Round and round the oatmeal-chest.
For he comes, the human child,   50
To the waters and the wild
With a faery, hand in hand,
From a world more full of weeping than he can
    understand.

I I

To an Isle in the Water

Shy one, shy one,
Shy one of my heart,
She moves in the firelight
Pensively apart.

She carries in the dishes,
And lays them in a row.
To an isle in the water
With her would I go.

She carries in the candles,
And lights the curtained room,
Shy in the doorway
And shy in the gloom;

And shy as a rabbit,
Helpful and shy.
To an isle in the water
With her would I fly.

I 2

Down by the Salley Gardens

Down by the salley gardens my love and I did meet;
She passed the salley gardens with little snow-white feet.
She bid me take love easy, as the leaves grow on the tree;
But I, being young and foolish, with her would not agree.

In a field by the river my love and I did stand,
And on my leaning shoulder she laid her snow-white hand.
She bid me take life easy, as the grass grows on the weirs;
But I was young and foolish, and now am full of tears.

13

The Meditation of the Old Fisherman

You waves, though you dance by my feet like children at play,
Though you glow and you glance, though you purr and you dart;
In the Junes that were warmer than these are, the waves were
    more gay,
When I was a boy with never a crack in my heart.

The herring are not in the tides as they were of old;
My sorrow! for many a creak gave the creel in the cart
That carried the take to Sligo town to be sold,
When I was a boy with never a crack in my heart.

And ah, you proud maiden, you are not so fair when his oar
Is heard on the water, as they were, the proud and apart,   10
Who paced in the eve by the nets on the pebbly shore,
When I was a boy with never a crack in my heart.

14

The Ballad of Father O'Hart

Good Father John O'Hart
In penal days rode out
To a shoneen who had free lands
And his own snipe and trout.

In trust took he John's lands;
Sleiveens were all his race;
And he gave them as dowers to his daughters,
And they married beyond their place.

But Father John went up,
And Father John went down;   10
And he wore small holes in his shoes,
And he wore large holes in his gown.

All loved him, only the shoneen,
Whom the devils have by the hair,
From the wives, and the cats, and the children,
To the birds in the white of the air.

The birds, for he opened their cages
As he went up and down;
And he said with a smile, 'Have peace now';
And he went his way with a frown.

But if when anyone died
Came keeners hoarser than rooks,
He bade them give over their keening;
For he was a man of books.

And these were the works of John,
When, weeping score by score,
People came into Coloony;
For he'd died at ninety-four.

There was no human keening;
The birds from Knocknarea
And the world round Knocknashee
Came keening in that day.

The young birds and old birds
Came flying, heavy and sad;
Keening in from Tiraragh,
Keening from Ballinafad;

Keening from Inishmurray,
Nor stayed for bite or sup;
This way were all reproved
Who dig old customs up.

15

The Ballad of Moll Magee

Come round me, little childer;
There, don't fling stones at me
Because I mutter as I go;
But pity Moll Magee.

My man was a poor fisher
With shore lines in the say;
My work was saltin' herrings
The whole of the long day.

And sometimes from the saltin' shed
I scarce could drag my feet,
Under the blessed moonlight,
Along the pebbly street.

I'd always been but weakly,
And my baby was just born;
A neighbour minded her by day,
I minded her till morn.

I lay upon my baby;
Ye little childer dear,
I looked on my cold baby
When the morn grew frosty and clear.

A weary woman sleeps so hard!
My man grew red and pale,
And gave me money, and bade me go
To my own place, Kinsale.

He drove me out and shut the door,
And gave his curse to me;
I went away in silence,
No neighbour could I see.

10

20

The windows and the doors were shut,
One star shone faint and green,
The little straws were turnin' round
Across the bare boreen.

I went away in silence:
Beyond old Martin's byre
I saw a kindly neighbour
Blowin' her mornin' fire.

She drew from me my story—
My money's all used up,
And still, with pityin', scornin' eye,
She gives me bite and sup.

She says my man will surely come,
And fetch me home agin;
But always, as I'm movin' round,
Without doors or within,

Pilin' the wood or pilin' the turf,
Or goin' to the well,
I'm thinkin' of my baby
And keenin' to mysel'.

And sometimes I am sure she knows
When, openin' wide His door,
God lights the stars, His candles,
And looks upon the poor.

So now, ye little childer,
Ye won't fling stones at me;
But gather with your shinin' looks
And pity Moll Magee.

16

The Ballad of the Foxhunter

'Lay me in a cushioned chair;
Carry me, ye four,
With cushions here and cushions there,
To see the world once more.

'To stable and to kennel go;
Bring what is there to bring;
Lead my Lollard to and fro,
Or gently in a ring.

'Put the chair upon the grass:
Bring Rody and his hounds,
That I may contented pass
From these earthly bounds.'

His eyelids droop, his head falls low,
His old eyes cloud with dreams;
The sun upon all things that grow
Falls in sleepy streams.

Brown Lollard treads upon the lawn,
And to the armchair goes,
And now the old man's dreams are gone,
He smooths the long brown nose.

And now moves many a pleasant tongue
Upon his wasted hands,
For leading aged hounds and young
The huntsman near him stands.

'Huntsman Rody, blow the horn,
Make the hills reply.'
The huntsman loosens on the morn
A gay wandering cry.

10

20

Fire is in the old man's eyes,
His fingers move and sway,
And when the wandering music dies
They hear him feebly say,

'Huntsman Rody, blow the horn,
Make the hills reply.'
'I cannot blow upon my horn,
I can but weep and sigh.'

Servants round his cushioned place
Are with new sorrow wrung;
Hounds are gazing on his face,
Aged hounds and young.

One blind hound only lies apart
On the sun-smitten grass;
He holds deep commune with his heart:
The moments pass and pass;

The blind hound with a mournful din
Lifts slow his wintry head;
The servants bear the body in;
The hounds wail for the dead.

The Rose

1893

'*Sero te amavi, Pulchritudo tam antiqua et tam nova! Sero te amavi.*'

S. AUGUSTINE

TO

LIONEL JOHNSON

17

To the Rose upon the Rood of Time

Red Rose, proud Rose, sad Rose of all my days!
Come near me, while I sing the ancient ways:
Cuchulain battling with the bitter tide;
The Druid, grey, wood-nurtured, quiet-eyed,
Who cast round Fergus dreams, and ruin untold;
And thine own sadness, whereof stars, grown old
In dancing silver-sandalled on the sea,
Sing in their high and lonely melody.
Come near, that no more blinded by man's fate,
I find under the boughs of love and hate,   10
In all poor foolish things that live a day,
Eternal beauty wandering on her way.

Come near, come near, come near—Ah, leave me still
A little space for the rose-breath to fill!
Lest I no more hear common things that crave;
The weak worm hiding down in its small cave,
The field-mouse running by me in the grass,
And heavy mortal hopes that toil and pass;
But seek alone to hear the strange things said
By God to the bright hearts of those long dead,   20
And learn to chaunt a tongue men do not know.
Come near; I would, before my time to go,
Sing of old Eire and the ancient ways:
Red Rose, proud Rose, sad Rose of all my days.

18

Fergus and the Druid

Fergus. This whole day have I followed in the rocks,
　　And you have changed and flowed from shape to shape,
　　First as a raven on whose ancient wings
　　Scarcely a feather lingered, then you seemed
　　A weasel moving on from stone to stone,
　　And now at last you wear a human shape,
　　A thin grey man half lost in gathering night.

Druid. What would you, king of the proud Red Branch kings?

Fergus. This would I say, most wise of living souls:
10　Young subtle Conchubar sat close by me
　　When I gave judgment, and his words were wise,
　　And what to me was burden without end,
　　To him seemed easy, so I laid the crown
　　Upon his head to cast away my sorrow.

Druid. What would you, king of the proud Red Branch kings?

Fergus. A king and proud! and that is my despair.
　　I feast amid my people on the hill,
　　And pace the woods, and drive my chariot-wheels
　　In the white border of the murmuring sea;
20　　And still I feel the crown upon my head.

Druid. What would you, Fergus?

Fergus. 　　　　　　　　　　Be no more a king
　　But learn the dreaming wisdom that is yours.

Druid. Look on my thin grey hair and hollow cheeks
　　And on these hands that may not lift the sword,
　　This body trembling like a wind-blown reed.
　　No woman's loved me, no man sought my help.

Fergus. A king is but a foolish labourer
　　Who wastes his blood to be another's dream.

Druid. Take, if you must, this little bag of dreams;
30　　Unloose the cord, and they will wrap you round.

Fergus. I see my life go drifting like a river
    From change to change; I have been many things—
    A green drop in the surge, a gleam of light
    Upon a sword, a fir-tree on a hill,
    An old slave grinding at a heavy quern,
    A king sitting upon a chair of gold—
    And all these things were wonderful and great;
    But now I have grown nothing, knowing all.
    Ah! Druid, Druid, how great webs of sorrow
    Lay hidden in the small slate-coloured thing!   40

19

Cuchulain's Fight with the Sea

A man came slowly from the setting sun,
To Emer, raddling raiment in her dun,
And said, 'I am that swineherd whom you bid
Go watch the road between the wood and tide,
But now I have no need to watch it more.'

Then Emer cast the web upon the floor,
And raising arms all raddled with the dye,
Parted her lips with a loud sudden cry.

That swineherd stared upon her face and said,
'No man alive, no man among the dead,   10
Has won the gold his cars of battle bring.'

'But if your master comes home triumphing
Why must you blench and shake from foot to crown?'

Thereon he shook the more and cast him down
Upon the web-heaped floor, and cried his word:
'With him is one sweet-throated like a bird.'

'You dare me to my face,' and thereupon
She smote with raddled fist, and where her son
Herded the cattle came with stumbling feet,
And cried with angry voice, 'It is not meet   20
To idle life away, a common herd.'

'I have long waited, mother, for that word:
But wherefore now?'
                    'There is a man to die;
You have the heaviest arm under the sky.'

'Whether under its daylight or its stars
My father stands amid his battle-cars.'

'But you have grown to be the taller man.'

'Yet somewhere under starlight or the sun
My father stands.'
                    'Aged, worn out with wars
On foot, on horseback or in battle-cars.'

'I only ask what way my journey lies,
For He who made you bitter made you wise.'

'The Red Branch camp in a great company
Between wood's rim and the horses of the sea.
Go there, and light a camp-fire at wood's rim;
But tell your name and lineage to him
Whose blade compels, and wait till they have found
Some feasting man that the same oath has bound.'

Among those feasting men Cuchulain dwelt,
And his young sweetheart close beside him knelt,
Stared on the mournful wonder of his eyes,
Even as Spring upon the ancient skies,
And pondered on the glory of his days;
And all around the harp-string told his praise,
And Conchubar, the Red Branch king of kings,
With his own fingers touched the brazen strings.

At last Cuchulain spake, 'Some man has made
His evening fire amid the leafy shade.
I have often heard him singing to and fro,
I have often heard the sweet sound of his bow.
Seek out what man he is.'
                    One went and came.
'He bade me let all know he gives his name
At the sword-point, and waits till we have found
Some feasting man that the same oath has bound.'

Cuchulain cried, 'I am the only man
Of all this host so bound from childhood on.'

After short fighting in the leafy shade,
He spake to the young man, 'Is there no maid
Who loves you, no white arms to wrap you round,
Or do you long for the dim sleepy ground,   60
That you have come and dared me to my face?'

'The dooms of men are in God's hidden place.'

'Your head a while seemed like a woman's head
That I loved once.'
                 Again the fighting sped,
But now the war-rage in Cuchulain woke,
And through that new blade's guard the old blade broke,
And pierced him.
              'Speak before your breath is done.'

'Cuchulain I, mighty Cuchulain's son.'

'I put you from your pain. I can no more.'

While day its burden on to evening bore,   70
With head bowed on his knees Cuchulain stayed;
Then Conchubar sent that sweet-throated maid,
And she, to win him, his grey hair caressed;
In vain her arms, in vain her soft white breast.
Then Conchubar, the subtlest of all men,
Ranking his Druids round him ten by ten,
Spake thus: 'Cuchulain will dwell there and brood
For three days more in dreadful quietude,
And then arise, and raving slay us all.
Chaunt in his ear delusions magical,   80
That he may fight the horses of the sea.'
The Druids took them to their mystery,
And chaunted for three days.
                     Cuchulain stirred,
Stared on the horses of the sea, and heard
The cars of battle and his own name cried;
And fought with the invulnerable tide.

20

The Rose of the World

Who dreamed that beauty passes like a dream?
For these red lips, with all their mournful pride,
Mournful that no new wonder may betide,
Troy passed away in one high funeral gleam,
And Usna's children died.

We and the labouring world are passing by:
Amid men's souls, that waver and give place
Like the pale waters in their wintry race,
Under the passing stars, foam of the sky,
Lives on this lonely face.

Bow down, archangels, in your dim abode:
Before you were, or any hearts to beat,
Weary and kind one lingered by His seat;
He made the world to be a grassy road
Before her wandering feet.

21

The Rose of Peace

If Michael, leader of God's host
When Heaven and Hell are met,
Looked down on you from Heaven's door-post
He would his deeds forget.

Brooding no more upon God's wars
In his divine homestead,
He would go weave out of the stars
A chaplet for your head.

And all folk seeing him bow down,
And white stars tell your praise,
Would come at last to God's great town,
Led on by gentle ways;

And God would bid His warfare cease,
Saying all things were well;
And softly make a rosy peace,
A peace of Heaven with Hell.

22

The Rose of Battle

Rose of all Roses, Rose of all the World!
The tall thought-woven sails, that flap unfurled
Above the tide of hours, trouble the air,
And God's bell buoyed to be the water's care;
While hushed from fear, or loud with hope, a band
With blown, spray-dabbled hair gather at hand.
Turn if you may from battles never done,
I call, as they go by me one by one,
Danger no refuge holds, and war no peace,
For him who hears love sing and never cease,   10
Beside her clean-swept hearth, her quiet shade:
But gather all for whom no love hath made
A woven silence, or but came to cast
A song into the air, and singing passed
To smile on the pale dawn; and gather you
Who have sought more than is in rain or dew,
Or in the sun and moon, or on the earth,
Or sighs amid the wandering, starry mirth,
Or comes in laughter from the sea's sad lips,
And wage God's battles in the long grey ships.   20
The sad, the lonely, the insatiable,
To these Old Night shall all her mystery tell;
God's bell has claimed them by the little cry
Of their sad hearts, that may not live nor die.

Rose of all Roses, Rose of all the World!
You, too, have come where the dim tides are hurled
Upon the wharves of sorrow, and heard ring
The bell that calls us on; the sweet far thing.
Beauty grown sad with its eternity
30   Made you of us, and of the dim grey sea.
Our long ships loose thought-woven sails and wait,
For God has bid them share an equal fate;
And when at last, defeated in His wars,
They have gone down under the same white stars,
We shall no longer hear the little cry
Of our sad hearts, that may not live nor die.

2 3

A Faery Song

*Sung by the people of Faery over Diarmuid and Grania,
in their bridal sleep under a Cromlech.*

We who are old, old and gay,
O so old!
Thousands of years, thousands of years,
If all were told:

Give to these children, new from the world,
Silence and love;
And the long dew-dropping hours of the night,
And the stars above:

Give to these children, new from the world,
10   Rest far from men.
Is anything better, anything better?
Tell us it then:

Us who are old, old and gay,
O so old!
Thousands of years, thousands of years,
If all were told.

24

The Lake Isle of Innisfree

I will arise and go now, and go to Innisfree,
And a small cabin build there, of clay and wattles made:
Nine bean-rows will I have there, a hive for the honey-bee,
And live alone in the bee-loud glade.

And I shall have some peace there, for peace comes dropping slow,
Dropping from the veils of the morning to where the cricket sings;
There midnight's all a glimmer, and noon a purple glow,
And evening full of the linnet's wings.

I will arise and go now, for always night and day
I hear lake water lapping with low sounds by the shore;   10
While I stand on the roadway, or on the pavements grey,
I hear it in the deep heart's core.

25

A Cradle Song

The angels are stooping
Above your bed;
They weary of trooping
With the whimpering dead.

God's laughing in Heaven
To see you so good;
The Sailing Seven
Are gay with His mood.

I sigh that kiss you,
For I must own   10
That I shall miss you
When you have grown.

26

The Pity of Love

A pity beyond all telling
Is hid in the heart of love:
The folk who are buying and selling,
The clouds on their journey above,
The cold wet winds ever blowing,
And the shadowy hazel grove
Where mouse-grey waters are flowing,
Threaten the head that I love.

27

The Sorrow of Love

The brawling of a sparrow in the eaves,
The brilliant moon and all the milky sky,
And all that famous harmony of leaves,
Had blotted out man's image and his cry.

A girl arose that had red mournful lips
And seemed the greatness of the world in tears,
Doomed like Odysseus and the labouring ships
And proud as Priam murdered with his peers;

Arose, and on the instant clamorous eaves,
A climbing moon upon an empty sky,
And all that lamentation of the leaves,
Could but compose man's image and his cry.

10

28

When You are Old

When you are old and grey and full of sleep,
And nodding by the fire, take down this book,
And slowly read, and dream of the soft look
Your eyes had once, and of their shadows deep;

How many loved your moments of glad grace,
And loved your beauty with love false or true,
But one man loved the pilgrim soul in you,
And loved the sorrows of your changing face;

And bending down beside the glowing bars,
Murmur, a little sadly, how Love fled   10
And paced upon the mountains overhead
And hid his face amid a crowd of stars.

29

The White Birds

I would that we were, my beloved, white birds on the foam of
    the sea!
We tire of the flame of the meteor, before it can fade and flee;
And the flame of the blue star of twilight, hung low on the rim of
    the sky,
Has awaked in our hearts, my beloved, a sadness that may not die.

A weariness comes from those dreamers, dew-dabbled, the lily
    and rose;
Ah, dream not of them, my beloved, the flame of the meteor
    that goes,
Or the flame of the blue star that lingers hung low in the fall of
    the dew:
For I would we were changed to white birds on the wandering
    foam: I and you!

I am haunted by numberless islands, and many a Danaan shore,
Where Time would surely forget us, and Sorrow come near us
10	no more;
Soon far from the rose and the lily and fret of the flames would
we be,
Were we only white birds, my beloved, buoyed out on the foam of
the sea!

30

A Dream of Death

I dreamed that one had died in a strange place
Near no accustomed hand;
And they had nailed the boards above her face,
The peasants of that land,
Wondering to lay her in that solitude,
And raised above her mound
A cross they had made out of two bits of wood,
And planted cypress round;
And left her to the indifferent stars above
10	Until I carved these words:
*She was more beautiful than thy first love,
But now lies under boards.*

31

The Countess Cathleen in Paradise

All the heavy days are over;
Leave the body's coloured pride
Underneath the grass and clover,
With the feet laid side by side.

Bathed in flaming founts of duty
She'll not ask a haughty dress;
Carry all that mournful beauty
To the scented oaken press.

Did the kiss of Mother Mary
Put that music in her face?   10
Yet she goes with footstep wary,
Full of earth's old timid grace.

'Mong the feet of angels seven
What a dancer, glimmering!
All the heavens bow down to Heaven,
Flame to flame and wing to wing.

3 2

Who goes with Fergus?

Who will go drive with Fergus now,
And pierce the deep wood's woven shade,
And dance upon the level shore?
Young man, lift up your russet brow,
And lift your tender eyelids, maid,
And brood on hopes and fear no more.

And no more turn aside and brood
Upon love's bitter mystery;
For Fergus rules the brazen cars,
And rules the shadows of the wood,   10
And the white breast of the dim sea
And all dishevelled wandering stars.

3 3

The Man who dreamed of Faeryland

He stood among a crowd at Drumahair;
His heart hung all upon a silken dress,
And he had known at last some tenderness,
Before earth took him to her stony care;
But when a man poured fish into a pile,
It seemed they raised their little silver heads,
And sang what gold morning or evening sheds

Upon a woven world-forgotten isle
Where people love beside the ravelled seas;
That Time can never mar a lover's vows
Under that woven changeless roof of boughs:
The singing shook him out of his new ease.

He wandered by the sands of Lissadell;
His mind ran all on money cares and fears,
And he had known at last some prudent years
Before they heaped his grave under the hill;
But while he passed before a plashy place,
A lug-worm with its grey and muddy mouth
Sang that somewhere to north or west or south
There dwelt a gay, exulting, gentle race
Under the golden or the silver skies;
That if a dancer stayed his hungry foot
It seemed the sun and moon were in the fruit:
And at that singing he was no more wise.

He mused beside the well of Scanavin,
He mused upon his mockers: without fail
His sudden vengeance were a country tale,
When earthy night had drunk his body in;
But one small knot-grass growing by the pool
Sang where—unnecessary cruel voice—
Old silence bids its chosen race rejoice,
Whatever ravelled waters rise and fall
Or stormy silver fret the gold of day,
And midnight there enfold them like a fleece
And lover there by lover be at peace.
The tale drove his fine angry mood away.

He slept under the hill of Lugnagall;
And might have known at last unhaunted sleep
Under that cold and vapour-turbaned steep,
Now that the earth had taken man and all:
Did not the worms that spired about his bones
Proclaim with that unwearied, reedy cry
That God has laid His fingers on the sky,
That from those fingers glittering summer runs

Upon the dancer by the dreamless wave.
Why should those lovers that no lovers miss
Dream, until God burn Nature with a kiss?
The man has found no comfort in the grave.

34

The Dedication to a Book of Stories
selected from the Irish Novelists

There was a green branch hung with many a bell
When her own people ruled this tragic Eire;
And from its murmuring greenness, calm of Faery,
A Druid kindness, on all hearers fell.

It charmed away the merchant from his guile,
And turned the farmer's memory from his cattle,
And hushed in sleep the roaring ranks of battle:
And all grew friendly for a little while.

Ah, Exiles wandering over lands and seas,
And planning, plotting always that some morrow   10
May set a stone upon ancestral Sorrow!
I also bear a bell-branch full of ease.

I tore it from green boughs winds tore and tossed
Until the sap of summer had grown weary!
I tore it from the barren boughs of Eire,
That country where a man can be so crossed;

Can be so battered, badgered and destroyed
That he's a loveless man: gay bells bring laughter
That shakes a mouldering cobweb from the rafter;
And yet the saddest chimes are best enjoyed.   20

Gay bells or sad, they bring you memories
Of half-forgotten innocent old places:
We and our bitterness have left no traces
On Munster grass and Connemara skies.

35

The Lamentation of the Old Pensioner

Although I shelter from the rain
Under a broken tree,
My chair was nearest to the fire
In every company
That talked of love or politics,
Ere Time transfigured me.

Though lads are making pikes again
For some conspiracy,
And crazy rascals rage their fill
At human tyranny;
My contemplations are of Time
That has transfigured me.

There's not a woman turns her face
Upon a broken tree,
And yet the beauties that I loved
Are in my memory;
I spit into the face of Time
That has transfigured me.

36

The Ballad of Father Gilligan

The old priest Peter Gilligan
Was weary night and day;
For half his flock were in their beds,
Or under green sods lay.

Once, while he nodded on a chair,
At the moth-hour of eve,
Another poor man sent for him,
And he began to grieve.

'I have no rest, nor joy, nor peace,
For people die and die';
And after cried he, 'God forgive!
My body spake, not I!'

He knelt, and leaning on the chair
He prayed and fell asleep;
And the moth-hour went from the fields,
And stars began to peep.

They slowly into millions grew,
And leaves shook in the wind;
And God covered the world with shade,
And whispered to mankind.

Upon the time of sparrow-chirp
When the moths came once more,
The old priest Peter Gilligan
Stood upright on the floor.

'Mavrone, mavrone! the man has died
While I slept on the chair';
He roused his horse out of its sleep,
And rode with little care.

He rode now as he never rode,
By rocky lane and fen;
The sick man's wife opened the door:
'Father! you come again!'

'And is the poor man dead?' he cried.
'He died an hour ago.'
The old priest Peter Gilligan
In grief swayed to and fro.

'When you were gone, he turned and died
As merry as a bird.'
The old priest Peter Gilligan
He knelt him at that word.

'He Who hath made the night of stars
For souls who tire and bleed,
Sent one of His great angels down
To help me in my need.

'He Who is wrapped in purple robes,
With planets in His care,
Had pity on the least of things
Asleep upon a chair.'

37

The Two Trees

Beloved, gaze in thine own heart,
The holy tree is growing there;
From joy the holy branches start,
And all the trembling flowers they bear.
The changing colours of its fruit
Have dowered the stars with merry light;
The surety of its hidden root
Has planted quiet in the night;
The shaking of its leafy head
10 Has given the waves their melody,
And made my lips and music wed,
Murmuring a wizard song for thee.
There the Loves a circle go,
The flaming circle of our days,
Gyring, spiring to and fro
In those great ignorant leafy ways;
Remembering all that shaken hair
And how the wingèd sandals dart,
Thine eyes grow full of tender care:
20 Beloved, gaze in thine own heart.

Gaze no more in the bitter glass
The demons, with their subtle guile,
Lift up before us when they pass,
Or only gaze a little while;
For there a fatal image grows
That the stormy night receives,
Roots half hidden under snows,
Broken boughs and blackened leaves.

For all things turn to barrenness
In the dim glass the demons hold,   30
The glass of outer weariness,
Made when God slept in times of old.
There, through the broken branches, go
The ravens of unresting thought;
Flying, crying, to and fro,
Cruel claw and hungry throat,
Or else they stand and sniff the wind,
And shake their ragged wings; alas!
Thy tender eyes grow all unkind:
Gaze no more in the bitter glass.   40

38

To Some I have Talked with by the Fire

While I wrought out these fitful Danaan rhymes,
My heart would brim with dreams about the times
When we bent down above the fading coals
And talked of the dark folk who live in souls
Of passionate men, like bats in the dead trees;
And of the wayward twilight companies
Who sigh with mingled sorrow and content,
Because their blossoming dreams have never bent
Under the fruit of evil and of good:
And of the embattled flaming multitude   10
Who rise, wing above wing, flame above flame,
And, like a storm, cry the Ineffable Name,
And with the clashing of their sword-blades make
A rapturous music, till the morning break
And the white hush end all but the loud beat
Of their long wings, the flash of their white feet.

39

To Ireland in the Coming Times

Know, that I would accounted be
True brother of a company
That sang, to sweeten Ireland's wrong,
Ballad and story, rann and song;
Nor be I any less of them,
Because the red-rose-bordered hem
Of her, whose history began
Before God made the angelic clan,
Trails all about the written page.
10 *When Time began to rant and rage*
The measure of her flying feet
Made Ireland's heart begin to beat;
And Time bade all his candles flare
To light a measure here and there;
And may the thoughts of Ireland brood
Upon a measured quietude.

Nor may I less be counted one
With Davis, Mangan, Ferguson,
Because, to him who ponders well,
20 *My rhymes more than their rhyming tell*
Of things discovered in the deep,
Where only body's laid asleep.
For the elemental creatures go
About my table to and fro,
That hurry from unmeasured mind
To rant and rage in flood and wind;
Yet he who treads in measured ways
May surely barter gaze for gaze.
Man ever journeys on with them
30 *After the red-rose-bordered hem.*
Ah, faeries, dancing under the moon,
A Druid land, a Druid tune!

While still I may, I write for you
The love I lived, the dream I knew.
From our birthday, until we die,
Is but the winking of an eye;
And we, our singing and our love,
What measurer Time has lit above,
And all benighted things that go
About my table to and fro, 40
Are passing on to where may be,
In truth's consuming ecstasy,
No place for love and dream at all;
For God goes by with white footfall.
I cast my heart into my rhymes,
That you, in the dim coming times,
May know how my heart went with them
After the red-rose-bordered hem.

The Wind
Among the Reeds

1899

40

The Hosting of the Sidhe

The host is riding from Knocknarea
And over the grave of Clooth-na-Bare;
Caoilte tossing his burning hair,
And Niamh calling *Away, come away:*
Empty your heart of its mortal dream.
The winds awaken, the leaves whirl round,
Our cheeks are pale, our hair is unbound,
Our breasts are heaving, our eyes are agleam,
Our arms are waving, our lips are apart;
And if any gaze on our rushing band,   10
We come between him and the deed of his hand,
We come between him and the hope of his heart.
The host is rushing 'twixt night and day,
And where is there hope or deed as fair?
Caoilte tossing his burning hair,
And Niamh calling *Away, come away.*

41

The Everlasting Voices

O sweet everlasting Voices, be still;
Go to the guards of the heavenly fold
And bid them wander obeying your will,
Flame under flame, till Time be no more;
Have you not heard that our hearts are old,
That you call in birds, in wind on the hill,
In shaken boughs, in tide on the shore?
O sweet everlasting Voices, be still.

42

The Moods

Time drops in decay,
Like a candle burnt out,
And the mountains and woods
Have their day, have their day;
What one in the rout
Of the fire-born moods
Has fallen away?

43

The Lover tells of the Rose in his Heart

All things uncomely and broken, all things worn out and old,
The cry of a child by the roadway, the creak of a lumbering cart,
The heavy steps of the ploughman, splashing the wintry mould,
Are wronging your image that blossoms a rose in the deeps of
   my heart.

The wrong of unshapely things is a wrong too great to be told;
I hunger to build them anew and sit on a green knoll apart,
With the earth and the sky and the water, re-made, like a casket
   of gold
For my dreams of your image that blossoms a rose in the deeps of
   my heart.

44

The Host of the Air

O'Driscoll drove with a song
The wild duck and the drake
From the tall and the tufted reeds
Of the drear Hart Lake.

And he saw how the reeds grew dark
At the coming of night-tide,
And dreamed of the long dim hair
Of Bridget his bride.

He heard while he sang and dreamed
A piper piping away,   10
And never was piping so sad,
And never was piping so gay.

And he saw young men and young girls
Who danced on a level place,
And Bridget his bride among them,
With a sad and a gay face.

The dancers crowded about him
And many a sweet thing said,
And a young man brought him red wine
And a young girl white bread.   20

But Bridget drew him by the sleeve
Away from the merry bands,
To old men playing at cards
With a twinkling of ancient hands.

The bread and the wine had a doom,
For these were the host of the air;
He sat and played in a dream
Of her long dim hair.

He played with the merry old men
And thought not of evil chance,   30
Until one bore Bridget his bride
Away from the merry dance.

He bore her away in his arms,
The handsomest young man there,
And his neck and his breast and his arms
Were drowned in her long dim hair.

O'Driscoll scattered the cards
And out of his dream awoke:
Old men and young men and young girls
Were gone like a drifting smoke;   40

But he heard high up in the air
A piper piping away,
And never was piping so sad,
And never was piping so gay.

45

The Fish

Although you hide in the ebb and flow
Of the pale tide when the moon has set,
The people of coming days will know
About the casting out of my net,
And how you have leaped times out of mind
Over the little silver cords,
And think that you were hard and unkind,
And blame you with many bitter words.

46

The Unappeasable Host

The Danaan children laugh, in cradles of wrought gold,
And clap their hands together, and half close their eyes,
For they will ride the North when the ger-eagle flies,
With heavy whitening wings, and a heart fallen cold:
I kiss my wailing child and press it to my breast,
And hear the narrow graves calling my child and me.
Desolate winds that cry over the wandering sea;
Desolate winds that hover in the flaming West;
Desolate winds that beat the doors of Heaven, and beat
10   The doors of Hell and blow there many a whimpering ghost;
O heart the winds have shaken, the unappeasable host
Is comelier than candles at Mother Mary's feet.

47

Into the Twilight

Out-worn heart, in a time out-worn,
Come clear of the nets of wrong and right;
Laugh, heart, again in the grey twilight,
Sigh, heart, again in the dew of the morn.

Your mother Eire is always young,
Dew ever shining and twilight grey;
Though hope fall from you and love decay,
Burning in fires of a slanderous tongue.

Come, heart, where hill is heaped upon hill:
For there the mystical brotherhood   10
Of sun and moon and hollow and wood
And river and stream work out their will;

And God stands winding His lonely horn,
And time and the world are ever in flight;
And love is less kind than the grey twilight,
And hope is less dear than the dew of the morn.

48

The Song of Wandering Aengus

I went out to the hazel wood,
Because a fire was in my head,
And cut and peeled a hazel wand,
And hooked a berry to a thread;
And when white moths were on the wing,
And moth-like stars were flickering out,
I dropped the berry in a stream
And caught a little silver trout.

When I had laid it on the floor
10   I went to blow the fire aflame,
But something rustled on the floor,
And some one called me by my name:
It had become a glimmering girl
With apple blossom in her hair
Who called me by my name and ran
And faded through the brightening air.

Though I am old with wandering
Through hollow lands and hilly lands,
I will find out where she has gone,
20   And kiss her lips and take her hands;
And walk among long dappled grass,
And pluck till time and times are done
The silver apples of the moon,
The golden apples of the sun.

49

The Song of the Old Mother

I rise in the dawn, and I kneel and blow
Till the seed of the fire flicker and glow;
And then I must scrub and bake and sweep
Till stars are beginning to blink and peep;
And the young lie long and dream in their bed
Of the matching of ribbons for bosom and head,
And their day goes over in idleness,
And they sigh if the wind but lift a tress:
While I must work because I am old,
10   And the seed of the fire gets feeble and cold.

50

The Heart of the Woman

O what to me the little room
That was brimmed up with prayer and rest;
He bade me out into the gloom,
And my breast lies upon his breast.

O what to me my mother's care,
The house where I was safe and warm;
The shadowy blossom of my hair
Will hide us from the bitter storm.

O hiding hair and dewy eyes,
I am no more with life and death,   10
My heart upon his warm heart lies,
My breath is mixed into his breath.

51

The Lover mourns for the Loss of Love

Pale brows, still hands and dim hair,
I had a beautiful friend
And dreamed that the old despair
Would end in love in the end:
She looked in my heart one day
And saw your image was there;
She has gone weeping away.

52

He mourns for the Change that has come upon Him and his Beloved, and longs for the End of the World

Do you not hear me calling, white deer with no horns?
I have been changed to a hound with one red ear;
I have been in the Path of Stones and the Wood of Thorns,
For somebody hid hatred and hope and desire and fear
Under my feet that they follow you night and day.
A man with a hazel wand came without sound;
He changed me suddenly; I was looking another way;
And now my calling is but the calling of a hound;
And Time and Birth and Change are hurrying by.
I would that the Boar without bristles had come from the
    West
10   And had rooted the sun and moon and stars out of the sky
And lay in the darkness, grunting, and turning to his rest.

53

He bids his Beloved be at Peace

I hear the Shadowy Horses, their long manes a-shake,
Their hoofs heavy with tumult, their eyes glimmering white;
The North unfolds above them clinging, creeping night,
The East her hidden joy before the morning break,
The West weeps in pale dew and sighs passing away,
The South is pouring down roses of crimson fire:
O vanity of Sleep, Hope, Dream, endless Desire,
The Horses of Disaster plunge in the heavy clay:
Beloved, let your eyes half close, and your heart beat
10   Over my heart, and your hair fall over my breast,
Drowning love's lonely hour in deep twilight of rest,
And hiding their tossing manes and their tumultuous feet.

54

He reproves the Curlew

O curlew, cry no more in the air,
Or only to the water in the West;
Because your crying brings to my mind
Passion-dimmed eyes and long heavy hair
That was shaken out over my breast:
There is enough evil in the crying of wind.

55

He remembers forgotten Beauty

When my arms wrap you round I press
My heart upon the loveliness
That has long faded from the world;
The jewelled crowns that kings have hurled
In shadowy pools, when armies fled;
The love-tales wrought with silken thread
By dreaming ladies upon cloth
That has made fat the murderous moth;
The roses that of old time were
Woven by ladies in their hair, 10
The dew-cold lilies ladies bore
Through many a sacred corridor
Where such grey clouds of incense rose
That only God's eyes did not close:
For that pale breast and lingering hand
Come from a more dream-heavy land,
A more dream-heavy hour than this;
And when you sigh from kiss to kiss
I hear white Beauty sighing, too,
For hours when all must fade like dew, 20
But flame on flame, and deep on deep,
Throne over throne where in half sleep,
Their swords upon their iron knees,
Brood her high lonely mysteries.

5 6

A Poet to his Beloved

I bring you with reverent hands
The books of my numberless dreams,
White woman that passion has worn
As the tide wears the dove-grey sands,
And with heart more old than the horn
That is brimmed from the pale fire of time:
White woman with numberless dreams,
I bring you my passionate rhyme.

5 7

He gives his Beloved certain Rhymes

Fasten your hair with a golden pin,
And bind up every wandering tress;
I bade my heart build these poor rhymes:
It worked at them, day out, day in,
Building a sorrowful loveliness
Out of the battles of old times.

You need but lift a pearl-pale hand,
And bind up your long hair and sigh;
And all men's hearts must burn and beat;
And candle-like foam on the dim sand,
And stars climbing the dew-dropping sky,
Live but to light your passing feet.

5 8

To his Heart, bidding it have no Fear

Be you still, be you still, trembling heart;
Remember the wisdom out of the old days:
Him who trembles before the flame and the flood,

And the winds that blow through the starry ways,
Let the starry winds and the flame and the flood
Cover over and hide, for he has no part
With the lonely, majestical multitude.

59

The Cap and Bells

The jester walked in the garden:
The garden had fallen still;
He bade his soul rise upward
And stand on her window-sill.

It rose in a straight blue garment,
When owls began to call:
It had grown wise-tongued by thinking
Of a quiet and light footfall;

But the young queen would not listen;
She rose in her pale night-gown;   10
She drew in the heavy casement
And pushed the latches down.

He bade his heart go to her,
When the owls called out no more;
In a red and quivering garment
It sang to her through the door.

It had grown sweet-tongued by dreaming
Of a flutter of flower-like hair;
But she took up her fan from the table
And waved it off on the air.   20

'I have cap and bells,' he pondered,
'I will send them to her and die';
And when the morning whitened
He left them where she went by.

She laid them upon her bosom,
Under a cloud of her hair,
And her red lips sang them a love-song
Till stars grew out of the air.

She opened her door and her window,
And the heart and the soul came through,
To her right hand came the red one,
To her left hand came the blue.

They set up a noise like crickets,
A chattering wise and sweet,
And her hair was a folded flower
And the quiet of love in her feet.

30

60

The Valley of the Black Pig

The dews drop slowly and dreams gather: unknown spears
Suddenly hurtle before my dream-awakened eyes,
And then the clash of fallen horsemen and the cries
Of unknown perishing armies beat about my ears.
We who still labour by the cromlech on the shore,
The grey cairn on the hill, when day sinks drowned in dew,
Being weary of the world's empires, bow down to you,
Master of the still stars and of the flaming door.

61

The Lover asks Forgiveness
because of his Many Moods

If this importunate heart trouble your peace
With words lighter than air,
Or hopes that in mere hoping flicker and cease;
Crumple the rose in your hair;
And cover your lips with odorous twilight and say,
'O Hearts of wind-blown flame!

O Winds, older than changing of night and day,
That murmuring and longing came
From marble cities loud with tabors of old
In dove-grey faery lands; 10
From battle-banners, fold upon purple fold,
Queens wrought with glimmering hands;
That saw young Niamh hover with love-lorn face
Above the wandering tide;
And lingered in the hidden desolate place
Where the last Phoenix died,
And wrapped the flames above his holy head;
And still murmur and long:
O Piteous Hearts, changing till change be dead
In a tumultuous song': 20
And cover the pale blossoms of your breast
With your dim heavy hair,
And trouble with a sigh for all things longing for rest
The odorous twilight there.

62

He tells of a Valley full of Lovers

I dreamed that I stood in a valley, and amid sighs,
For happy lovers passed two by two where I stood;
And I dreamed my lost love came stealthily out of the wood
With her cloud-pale eyelids falling on dream-dimmed eyes:
I cried in my dream, *O women, bid the young men lay*
Their heads on your knees, and drown their eyes with your hair,
Or remembering hers they will find no other face fair
Till all the valleys of the world have been withered away.

63

He tells of the Perfect Beauty

O cloud-pale eyelids, dream-dimmed eyes,
The poets labouring all their days
To build a perfect beauty in rhyme
Are overthrown by a woman's gaze
And by the unlabouring brood of the skies:
And therefore my heart will bow, when dew
Is dropping sleep, until God burn time,
Before the unlabouring stars and you.

64

He hears the Cry of the Sedge

I wander by the edge
Of this desolate lake
Where wind cries in the sedge:
Until the axle break
That keeps the stars in their round,
And hands hurl in the deep
The banners of East and West,
And the girdle of light is unbound,
Your breast will not lie by the breast
Of your beloved in sleep.

65

He thinks of Those
who have spoken Evil of his Beloved

Half close your eyelids, loosen your hair,
And dream about the great and their pride;
They have spoken against you everywhere,

But weigh this song with the great and their pride;
I made it out of a mouthful of air,
Their children's children shall say they have lied.

66

The Blessed

Cumhal called out, bending his head,
Till Dathi came and stood,
With a blink in his eyes, at the cave-mouth,
Between the wind and the wood.

And Cumhal said, bending his knees,
'I have come by the windy way
To gather the half of your blessedness
And learn to pray when you pray.

'I can bring you salmon out of the streams
And heron out of the skies.'   10
But Dathi folded his hands and smiled
With the secrets of God in his eyes.

And Cumhal saw like a drifting smoke
All manner of blessed souls,
Women and children, young men with books,
And old men with croziers and stoles.

'Praise God and God's Mother,' Dathi said,
'For God and God's Mother have sent
The blessedest souls that walk in the world
To fill your heart with content.'   20

'And which is the blessedest,' Cumhal said,
'Where all are comely and good?
Is it these that with golden thuribles
Are singing about the wood?'

'My eyes are blinking,' Dathi said,
'With the secrets of God half blind,
But I can see where the wind goes
And follow the way of the wind;

'And blessedness goes where the wind goes,
And when it is gone we are dead;
I see the blessedest soul in the world
And he nods a drunken head.

'O blessedness comes in the night and the day
And whither the wise heart knows;
And one has seen in the redness of wine
The Incorruptible Rose,

'That drowsily drops faint leaves on him
And the sweetness of desire,
While time and the world are ebbing away
In twilights of dew and of fire.'

67

The Secret Rose

Far-off, most secret, and inviolate Rose,
Enfold me in my hour of hours; where those
Who sought thee in the Holy Sepulchre,
Or in the wine-vat, dwell beyond the stir
And tumult of defeated dreams; and deep
Among pale eyelids, heavy with the sleep
Men have named beauty. Thy great leaves enfold
The ancient beards, the helms of ruby and gold
Of the crowned Magi; and the king whose eyes
Saw the Pierced Hands and Rood of elder rise
In Druid vapour and make the torches dim;
Till vain frenzy awoke and he died; and him
Who met Fand walking among flaming dew
By a grey shore where the wind never blew,
And lost the world and Emer for a kiss;

And him who drove the gods out of their liss,
And till a hundred morns had flowered red
Feasted, and wept the barrows of his dead;   20
And the proud dreaming king who flung the crown
And sorrow away, and calling bard and clown
Dwelt among wine-stained wanderers in deep woods;
And him who sold tillage, and house, and goods,
And sought through lands and islands numberless years,
Until he found, with laughter and with tears,
A woman of so shining loveliness
That men threshed corn at midnight by a tress,
A little stolen tress. I, too, await
The hour of thy great wind of love and hate.   30
When shall the stars be blown about the sky,
Like the sparks blown out of a smithy, and die?
Surely thine hour has come, thy great wind blows,
Far-off, most secret, and inviolate Rose?

68

Maid Quiet

Where has Maid Quiet gone to,
Nodding her russet hood?
The winds that awakened the stars
Are blowing through my blood.
O how could I be so calm
When she rose up to depart?
Now words that called up the lightning
Are hurtling through my heart.

69

The Travail of Passion

When the flaming lute-thronged angelic door is wide;
When an immortal passion breathes in mortal clay;
Our hearts endure the scourge, the plaited thorns, the way
Crowded with bitter faces, the wounds in palm and side,
The vinegar-heavy sponge, the flowers by Kedron stream;
We will bend down and loosen our hair over you,
That it may drop faint perfume, and be heavy with dew,
Lilies of death-pale hope, roses of passionate dream.

70

The Lover pleads with his Friend for Old Friends

Though you are in your shining days,
Voices among the crowd
And new friends busy with your praise,
Be not unkind or proud,
But think about old friends the most:
Time's bitter flood will rise,
Your beauty perish and be lost
For all eyes but these eyes.

71

The Lover speaks to the Hearers
of his Songs in Coming Days

O women, kneeling by your altar-rails long hence,
When songs I wove for my beloved hide the prayer,
And smoke from this dead heart drifts through the violet air
And covers away the smoke of myrrh and frankincense;
Bend down and pray for all that sin I wove in song,

Till the Attorney for Lost Souls cry her sweet cry,
And call to my beloved and me: 'No longer fly
Amid the hovering, piteous, penitential throng.'

72

The Poet pleads with the Elemental Powers

The Powers whose name and shape no living creature knows
Have pulled the Immortal Rose;
And though the Seven Lights bowed in their dance and wept,
The Polar Dragon slept,
His heavy rings uncoiled from glimmering deep to deep:
When will he wake from sleep?

Great Powers of falling wave and wind and windy fire,
With your harmonious choir
Encircle her I love and sing her into peace,
That my old care may cease;   10
Unfold your flaming wings and cover out of sight
The nets of day and night.

Dim Powers of drowsy thought, let her no longer be
Like the pale cup of the sea,
When winds have gathered and sun and moon burned dim
Above its cloudy rim;
But let a gentle silence wrought with music flow
Whither her footsteps go.

73

He wishes his Beloved were Dead

Were you but lying cold and dead,
And lights were paling out of the West,
You would come hither, and bend your head,
And I would lay my head on your breast;
And you would murmur tender words,

Forgiving me, because you were dead:
Nor would you rise and hasten away,
Though you have the will of the wild birds,
But know your hair was bound and wound
10   About the stars and moon and sun:
O would, beloved, that you lay
Under the dock-leaves in the ground,
While lights were paling one by one.

74

He wishes for the Cloths of Heaven

Had I the heavens' embroidered cloths,
Enwrought with golden and silver light,
The blue and the dim and the dark cloths
Of night and light and the half-light,
I would spread the cloths under your feet:
But I, being poor, have only my dreams;
I have spread my dreams under your feet;
Tread softly because you tread on my dreams.

75

He thinks of his Past Greatness
when a Part of the Constellations of Heaven

I have drunk ale from the Country of the Young
And weep because I know all things now:
I have been a hazel-tree, and they hung
The Pilot Star and the Crooked Plough
Among my leaves in times out of mind:
I became a rush that horses tread:
I became a man, a hater of the wind,
Knowing one, out of all things, alone, that his head
May not lie on the breast nor his lips on the hair

Of the woman that he loves, until he dies.   10
O beast of the wilderness, bird of the air,
Must I endure your amorous cries?

76

The Fiddler of Dooney

When I play on my fiddle in Dooney,
Folk dance like a wave of the sea;
My cousin is priest in Kilvarnet,
My brother in Mocharabuiee.

I passed my brother and cousin:
They read in their books of prayer;
I read in my book of songs
I bought at the Sligo fair.

When we come at the end of time
To Peter sitting in state,   10
He will smile on the three old spirits,
But call me first through the gate;

For the good are always the merry,
Save by an evil chance,
And the merry love the fiddle,
And the merry love to dance:

And when the folk there spy me,
They will all come up to me,
With 'Here is the fiddler of Dooney!'
And dance like a wave of the sea.   20

In the Seven Woods

1904

77

In the Seven Woods

I have heard the pigeons of the Seven Woods
Make their faint thunder, and the garden bees
Hum in the lime-tree flowers; and put away
The unavailing outcries and the old bitterness
That empty the heart. I have forgot awhile
Tara uprooted, and new commonness
Upon the throne and crying about the streets
And hanging its paper flowers from post to post,
Because it is alone of all things happy.
I am contented, for I know that Quiet   10
Wanders laughing and eating her wild heart
Among pigeons and bees, while that Great Archer,
Who but awaits His hour to shoot, still hangs
A cloudy quiver over Pairc-na-lee.

August 1902

78

The Arrow

I thought of your beauty, and this arrow,
Made out of a wild thought, is in my marrow.
There's no man may look upon her, no man,
As when newly grown to be a woman,
Tall and noble but with face and bosom
Delicate in colour as apple blossom.
This beauty's kinder, yet for a reason
I could weep that the old is out of season.

79

The Folly of being Comforted

One that is ever kind said yesterday:
'Your well-belovèd's hair has threads of grey,
And little shadows come about her eyes;
Time can but make it easier to be wise
Though now it seems impossible, and so
All that you need is patience.'
                              Heart cries, 'No,
I have not a crumb of comfort, not a grain.
Time can but make her beauty over again:
Because of that great nobleness of hers
The fire that stirs about her, when she stirs,
Burns but more clearly. O she had not these ways
When all the wild summer was in her gaze.'

O heart! O heart! if she'd but turn her head,
You'd know the folly of being comforted.

80

Old Memory

O thought, fly to her when the end of day
Awakens an old memory, and say,
'Your strength, that is so lofty and fierce and kind,
It might call up a new age, calling to mind
The queens that were imagined long ago,
Is but half yours: he kneaded in the dough
Through the long years of youth, and who would have thought
It all, and more than it all, would come to naught,
And that dear words meant nothing?' But enough,
For when we have blamed the wind we can blame love;
Or, if there needs be more, be nothing said
That would be harsh for children that have strayed.

81

Never give all the Heart

Never give all the heart, for love
Will hardly seem worth thinking of
To passionate women if it seem
Certain, and they never dream
That it fades out from kiss to kiss;
For everything that's lovely is
But a brief, dreamy, kind delight.
O never give the heart outright,
For they, for all smooth lips can say,
Have given their hearts up to the play.　　　　10
And who could play it well enough
If deaf and dumb and blind with love?
He that made this knows all the cost,
For he gave all his heart and lost.

82

The Withering of the Boughs

I cried when the moon was murmuring to the birds:
'Let peewit call and curlew cry where they will,
I long for your merry and tender and pitiful words,
For the roads are unending, and there is no place to my mind.'
The honey-pale moon lay low on the sleepy hill,
And I fell asleep upon lonely Echtge of streams.
No boughs have withered because of the wintry wind;
The boughs have withered because I have told them my dreams.

I know of the leafy paths that the witches take
Who come with their crowns of pearl and their spindles of wool,　　10
And their secret smile, out of the depths of the lake;
I know where a dim moon drifts, where the Danaan kind
Wind and unwind dancing when the light grows cool
On the island lawns, their feet where the pale foam gleams.

No boughs have withered because of the wintry wind;
The boughs have withered because I have told them my dreams.

I know of the sleepy country, where swans fly round
Coupled with golden chains, and sing as they fly.
A king and a queen are wandering there, and the sound
20   Has made them so happy and hopeless, so deaf and so blind
With wisdom, they wander till all the years have gone by;
I know, and the curlew and peewit on Echtge of streams.
No boughs have withered because of the wintry wind;
The boughs have withered because I have told them my dreams.

8 3

Adam's Curse

We sat together at one summer's end,
That beautiful mild woman, your close friend,
And you and I, and talked of poetry.
I said, 'A line will take us hours maybe;
Yet if it does not seem a moment's thought,
Our stitching and unstitching has been naught.
Better go down upon your marrow-bones
And scrub a kitchen pavement, or break stones
Like an old pauper, in all kinds of weather;
10   For to articulate sweet sounds together
Is to work harder than all these, and yet
Be thought an idler by the noisy set
Of bankers, schoolmasters, and clergymen
The martyrs call the world.'

                              And thereupon
That beautiful mild woman for whose sake
There's many a one shall find out all heartache
On finding that her voice is sweet and low
Replied, 'To be born woman is to know—
Although they do not talk of it at school—
20   That we must labour to be beautiful.'

I said, 'It's certain there is no fine thing
Since Adam's fall but needs much labouring.
There have been lovers who thought love should be
So much compounded of high courtesy
That they would sigh and quote with learned looks
Precedents out of beautiful old books;
Yet now it seems an idle trade enough.'

We sat grown quiet at the name of love;
We saw the last embers of daylight die,
And in the trembling blue-green of the sky   30
A moon, worn as if it had been a shell
Washed by time's waters as they rose and fell
About the stars and broke in days and years.

I had a thought for no one's but your ears:
That you were beautiful, and that I strove
To love you in the old high way of love;
That it had all seemed happy, and yet we'd grown
As weary-hearted as that hollow moon.

84

Red Hanrahan's Song about Ireland

The old brown thorn-trees break in two high over Cummen
   Strand,
Under a bitter black wind that blows from the left hand;
Our courage breaks like an old tree in a black wind and dies,
But we have hidden in our hearts the flame out of the eyes
Of Cathleen, the daughter of Houlihan.

The wind has bundled up the clouds high over Knocknarea,
And thrown the thunder on the stones for all that Maeve
   can say.
Angers that are like noisy clouds have set our hearts abeat;
But we have all bent low and low and kissed the quiet feet
Of Cathleen, the daughter of Houlihan.   10

The yellow pool has overflowed high up on Clooth-na-Bare,
For the wet winds are blowing out of the clinging air;
Like heavy flooded waters our bodies and our blood;
But purer than a tall candle before the Holy Rood
Is Cathleen, the daughter of Houlihan.

85

The Old Men admiring
Themselves in the Water

I heard the old, old men say,
'Everything alters,
And one by one we drop away.'
They had hands like claws, and their knees
Were twisted like the old thorn-trees
By the waters.
I heard the old, old men say,
'All that's beautiful drifts away
Like the waters.'

86

Under the Moon

I have no happiness in dreaming of Brycelinde,
Nor Avalon the grass-green hollow, nor Joyous Isle,
Where one found Lancelot crazed and hid him for a while;
Nor Ulad, when Naoise had thrown a sail upon the wind;
Nor lands that seem too dim to be burdens on the heart:
Land-under-Wave, where out of the moon's light and the sun's
Seven old sisters wind the threads of the long-lived ones,
Land-of-the-Tower, where Aengus has thrown the gates apart,
And Wood-of-Wonders, where one kills an ox at dawn,
10   To find it when night falls laid on a golden bier.
Therein are many queens like Branwen and Guinevere;

And Niamh and Laban and Fand, who could change to an otter
    or fawn,
And the wood-woman, whose lover was changed to a blue-eyed
    hawk;
And whether I go in my dreams by woodland, or dun, or shore,
Or on the unpeopled waves with kings to pull at the oar,
I hear the harp-string praise them, or hear their mournful talk.

Because of something told under the famished horn
Of the hunter's moon, that hung between the night and the day,
To dream of women whose beauty was folded in dismay,
Even in an old story, is a burden not to be borne.   20

87

The Ragged Wood

O hurry where by water among the trees
The delicate-stepping stag and his lady sigh,
When they have but looked upon their images—
Would none had ever loved but you and I!

Or have you heard that sliding silver-shoed
Pale silver-proud queen-woman of the sky,
When the sun looked out of his golden hood?—
O that none ever loved but you and I!

O hurry to the ragged wood, for there
I will drive all those lovers out and cry—   10
O my share of the world, O yellow hair!
No one has ever loved but you and I.

88

O do not Love Too Long

Sweetheart, do not love too long:
I loved long and long,
And grew to be out of fashion
Like an old song.

All through the years of our youth
Neither could have known
Their own thought from the other's,
We were so much at one.

But O, in a minute she changed—
O do not love too long,
Or you will grow out of fashion
Like an old song.

89

The Players ask for a Blessing
on the Psalteries and on Themselves

Three Voices [together]. Hurry to bless the hands that play,
The mouths that speak, the notes and strings,
O masters of the glittering town!
O! lay the shrilly trumpet down,
Though drunken with the flags that sway
Over the ramparts and the towers,
And with the waving of your wings.

First Voice. Maybe they linger by the way.
One gathers up his purple gown;
One leans and mutters by the wall—
He dreads the weight of mortal hours.

Second Voice. O no, O no! they hurry down
Like plovers that have heard the call.

Third Voice. O kinsmen of the Three in One,
  O kinsmen, bless the hands that play.
  The notes they waken shall live on
  When all this heavy history's done;
  Our hands, our hands must ebb away.

Three Voices [*together*]. The proud and careless notes live on,
  But bless our hands that ebb away.   20

9 0

The Happy Townland

There's many a strong farmer
Whose heart would break in two,
If he could see the townland
That we are riding to;
Boughs have their fruit and blossom
At all times of the year;
Rivers are running over
With red beer and brown beer.
An old man plays the bagpipes
In a golden and silver wood;   10
Queens, their eyes blue like the ice,
Are dancing in a crowd.

The little fox he murmured,
'O what of the world's bane?'
The sun was laughing sweetly,
The moon plucked at my rein;
But the little red fox murmured,
'O do not pluck at his rein,
He is riding to the townland
That is the world's bane.'   20

When their hearts are so high
That they would come to blows,
They unhook their heavy swords
From golden and silver boughs;
But all that are killed in battle

Awaken to life again.
It is lucky that their story
Is not known among men,
For O, the strong farmers
30   That would let the spade lie,
Their hearts would be like a cup
That somebody had drunk dry.

The little fox he murmured,
'O what of the world's bane?'
The sun was laughing sweetly,
The moon plucked at my rein;
But the little red fox murmured,
'O do not pluck at his rein,
He is riding to the townland
40   *That is the world's bane.'*

Michael will unhook his trumpet
From a bough overhead,
And blow a little noise
When the supper has been spread.
Gabriel will come from the water
With a fish-tail, and talk
Of wonders that have happened
On wet roads where men walk,
And lift up an old horn
50   Of hammered silver, and drink
Till he has fallen asleep
Upon the starry brink.

The little fox he murmured,
'O what of the world's bane?'
The sun was laughing sweetly,
The moon plucked at my rein;
But the little red fox murmured,
'O do not pluck at his rein,
He is riding to the townland
60   *That is the world's bane.'*

The Green Helmet and Other Poems

1910

His Dream

I swayed upon the gaudy stern
The butt-end of a steering-oar,
And saw wherever I could turn
A crowd upon a shore.

And though I would have hushed the crowd,
There was no mother's son but said,
'What is the figure in a shroud
Upon a gaudy bed?'

And after running at the brim
Cried out upon that thing beneath   10
—It had such dignity of limb—
By the sweet name of Death.

Though I'd my finger on my lip,
What could I but take up the song?
And running crowd and gaudy ship
Cried out the whole night long,

Crying amid the glittering sea,
Naming it with ecstatic breath,
Because it had such dignity,
By the sweet name of Death.   20

92

A Woman Homer sung

If any man drew near
When I was young,
I thought, 'He holds her dear,'
And shook with hate and fear.
But O! 'twas bitter wrong
If he could pass her by
With an indifferent eye.

Whereon I wrote and wrought,
And now, being grey,
I dream that I have brought
To such a pitch my thought
That coming time can say,
'He shadowed in a glass
What thing her body was.'

For she had fiery blood
When I was young,
And trod so sweetly proud
As 'twere upon a cloud,
A woman Homer sung,
That life and letters seem
But an heroic dream.

93

Words

I had this thought a while ago,
'My darling cannot understand
What I have done, or what would do
In this blind bitter land.'

And I grew weary of the sun
Until my thoughts cleared up again,
Remembering that the best I have done
Was done to make it plain;

That every year I have cried, 'At length
My darling understands it all,   10
Because I have come into my strength,
And words obey my call';

That had she done so who can say
What would have shaken from the sieve?
I might have thrown poor words away
And been content to live.

94

No Second Troy

Why should I blame her that she filled my days
With misery, or that she would of late
Have taught to ignorant men most violent ways,
Or hurled the little streets upon the great,
Had they but courage equal to desire?
What could have made her peaceful with a mind
That nobleness made simple as a fire,
With beauty like a tightened bow, a kind
That is not natural in an age like this,
Being high and solitary and most stern?   10
Why, what could she have done, being what she is?
Was there another Troy for her to burn?

95

Reconciliation

Some may have blamed you that you took away
The verses that could move them on the day
When, the ears being deafened, the sight of the eyes blind
With lightning, you went from me, and I could find
Nothing to make a song about but kings,
Helmets, and swords, and half-forgotten things
That were like memories of you—but now
We'll out, for the world lives as long ago;
And while we're in our laughing, weeping fit,
Hurl helmets, crowns, and swords into the pit.
But, dear, cling close to me; since you were gone,
My barren thoughts have chilled me to the bone.

96

King and no King

'Would it were anything but merely voice!'
The No King cried who after that was King,
Because he had not heard of anything
That balanced with a word is more than noise;
Yet Old Romance being kind, let him prevail
Somewhere or somehow that I have forgot,
Though he'd but cannon—Whereas we that had thought
To have lit upon as clean and sweet a tale
Have been defeated by that pledge you gave
In momentary anger long ago;
And I that have not your faith, how shall I know
That in the blinding light beyond the grave
We'll find so good a thing as that we have lost?
The hourly kindness, the day's common speech,
The habitual content of each with each
When neither soul nor body has been crossed.

97

Peace

Ah, that Time could touch a form
That could show what Homer's age
Bred to be a hero's wage.
'Were not all her life but storm,
Would not painters paint a form
Of such noble lines,' I said,
'Such a delicate high head,
All that sternness amid charm,
All that sweetness amid strength?'
Ah, but peace that comes at length,   10
Came when Time had touched her form.

98

Against Unworthy Praise

O heart, be at peace, because
Nor knave nor dolt can break
What's not for their applause,
Being for a woman's sake.
Enough if the work has seemed,
So did she your strength renew,
A dream that a lion had dreamed
Till the wilderness cried aloud,
A secret between you two,
Between the proud and the proud.   10

What, still you would have their praise!
But here's a haughtier text,
The labyrinth of her days
That her own strangeness perplexed;

And how what her dreaming gave
Earned slander, ingratitude,
From self-same dolt and knave;
Aye, and worse wrong than these.
Yet she, singing upon her road,
20   Half lion, half child, is at peace.

99

The Fascination of What's Difficult

The fascination of what's difficult
Has dried the sap out of my veins, and rent
Spontaneous joy and natural content
Out of my heart. There's something ails our colt
That must, as if it had not holy blood
Nor on Olympus leaped from cloud to cloud,
Shiver under the lash, strain, sweat and jolt
As though it dragged road metal. My curse on plays
That have to be set up in fifty ways,
10   On the day's war with every knave and dolt,
Theatre business, management of men.
I swear before the dawn comes round again
I'll find the stable and pull out the bolt.

100

A Drinking Song

Wine comes in at the mouth
And love comes in at the eye;
That's all we shall know for truth
Before we grow old and die.
I lift the glass to my mouth,
I look at you, and I sigh.

101

The Coming of Wisdom with Time

Though leaves are many, the root is one;
Through all the lying days of my youth
I swayed my leaves and flowers in the sun;
Now I may wither into the truth.

102

On hearing that the Students of our New University have joined the Agitation against Immoral Literature

Where, where but here have Pride and Truth,
That long to give themselves for wage,
To shake their wicked sides at youth
Restraining reckless middle-age?

103

To a Poet, who would have me Praise certain Bad Poets, Imitators of His and Mine

You say, as I have often given tongue
In praise of what another's said or sung,
'Twere politic to do the like by these;
But was there ever dog that praised his fleas?

104

The Mask

'Put off that mask of burning gold
With emerald eyes.'
'O no, my dear, you make so bold
To find if hearts be wild and wise,
And yet not cold.'

'I would but find what's there to find,
Love or deceit.'
'It was the mask engaged your mind,
And after set your heart to beat,
Not what's behind.'

'But lest you are my enemy,
I must enquire.'
'O no, my dear, let all that be;
What matter, so there is but fire
In you, in me?'

105

Upon a House shaken by the Land Agitation

How should the world be luckier if this house,
Where passion and precision have been one
Time out of mind, became too ruinous
To breed the lidless eye that loves the sun?
And the sweet laughing eagle thoughts that grow
Where wings have memory of wings, and all
That comes of the best knit to the best? Although
Mean roof-trees were the sturdier for its fall,
How should their luck run high enough to reach
The gifts that govern men, and after these
To gradual Time's last gift, a written speech
Wrought of high laughter, loveliness and ease?

106

At the Abbey Theatre

(Imitated from Ronsard)

Dear Craoibhin Aoibhin, look into our case.
When we are high and airy hundreds say
That if we hold that flight they'll leave the place,
While those same hundreds mock another day
Because we have made our art of common things,
So bitterly, you'd dream they longed to look
All their lives through into some drift of wings.
You've dandled them and fed them from the book
And know them to the bone; impart to us—
We'll keep the secret—a new trick to please.   10
Is there a bridle for this Proteus
That turns and changes like his draughty seas?
Or is there none, most popular of men,
But when they mock us, that we mock again?

107

These are the Clouds

These are the clouds about the fallen sun,
The majesty that shuts his burning eye:
The weak lay hand on what the strong has done,
Till that be tumbled that was lifted high
And discord follow upon unison,
And all things at one common level lie.
And therefore, friend, if your great race were run
And these things came, so much the more thereby
Have you made greatness your companion,
Although it be for children that you sigh: 10
These are the clouds about the fallen sun,
The majesty that shuts his burning eye.

108

At Galway Races

There where the course is,
Delight makes all of the one mind,
The riders upon the galloping horses,
The crowd that closes in behind:
We, too, had good attendance once,
Hearers and hearteners of the work;
Aye, horsemen for companions,
Before the merchant and the clerk
Breathed on the world with timid breath.
Sing on: somewhere at some new moon,
We'll learn that sleeping is not death,
Hearing the whole earth change its tune,
Its flesh being wild, and it again
Crying aloud as the racecourse is,
And we find hearteners among men
That ride upon horses.

109

A Friend's Illness

Sickness brought me this
Thought, in that scale of his:
Why should I be dismayed
Though flame had burned the whole
World, as it were a coal,
Now I have seen it weighed
Against a soul?

110

All Things can tempt Me

All things can tempt me from this craft of verse:
One time it was a woman's face, or worse—
The seeming needs of my fool-driven land;
Now nothing but comes readier to the hand
Than this accustomed toil. When I was young,
I had not given a penny for a song
Did not the poet sing it with such airs
That one believed he had a sword upstairs;
Yet would be now, could I but have my wish,
Colder and dumber and deafer than a fish.   10

111

Brown Penny

I whispered, 'I am too young,'
And then, 'I am old enough';
Wherefore I threw a penny
To find out if I might love.
'Go and love, go and love, young man,
If the lady be young and fair.'
Ah, penny, brown penny, brown penny,
I am looped in the loops of her hair.

And the penny sang up in my face,
'There is nobody wise enough   10
To find out all that is in it,
For he would be thinking of love
That is looped in the loops of her hair,
Till the loops of time had run.'
Ah, penny, brown penny, brown penny.
One cannot begin it too soon.

Responsibilities

1914

'*In dreams begins responsibility.*'

OLD PLAY

'*How am I fallen from myself, for a long time now
I have not seen the Prince of Chang in my dreams.*'

KHOUNG-FOU-TSEU

Pardon, old fathers, if you still remain
Somewhere in ear-shot for the story's end,
Old Dublin merchant 'free of the ten and four'
Or trading out of Galway into Spain;
Old country scholar, Robert Emmet's friend,
A hundred-year-old memory to the poor;
Merchant and scholar who have left me blood
That has not passed through any huckster's loin,
Soldiers that gave, whatever die was cast:
A Butler or an Armstrong that withstood   10
Beside the brackish waters of the Boyne
James and his Irish when the Dutchman crossed;
Old merchant skipper that leaped overboard
After a ragged hat in Biscay Bay;
You most of all, silent and fierce old man,
Because the daily spectacle that stirred
My fancy, and set my boyish lips to say,
'Only the wasteful virtues earn the sun';
Pardon that for a barren passion's sake,
Although I have come close on forty-nine,   20
I have no child, I have nothing but a book,
Nothing but that to prove your blood and mine.

January 1914

113

The Grey Rock

Poets with whom I learned my trade,
Companions of the Cheshire Cheese,
Here's an old story I've re-made,
Imagining 'twould better please
Your ears than stories now in fashion,
Though you may think I waste my breath
Pretending that there can be passion
That has more life in it than death,
And though at bottling of your wine
Old wholesome Goban had no say;
The moral's yours because it's mine.

When cups went round at close of day—
Is not that how good stories run?—
The gods were sitting at the board
In their great house at Slievenamon.
They sang a drowsy song, or snored,
For all were full of wine and meat.
The smoky torches made a glare
On metal Goban'd hammered at,
On old deep silver rolling there
Or on some still unemptied cup
That he, when frenzy stirred his thews,
Had hammered out on mountain top
To hold the sacred stuff he brews
That only gods may buy of him.

Now from that juice that made them wise
All those had lifted up the dim
Imaginations of their eyes,
For one that was like woman made
Before their sleepy eyelids ran
And trembling with her passion said,
'Come out and dig for a dead man,
Who's burrowing somewhere in the ground,

And mock him to his face and then
Hollo him on with horse and hound,
For he is the worst of all dead men.'

We should be dazed and terror-struck,
If we but saw in dreams that room,
Those wine-drenched eyes, and curse our luck
That emptied all our days to come. 40
I knew a woman none could please,
Because she dreamed when but a child
Of men and women made like these;
And after, when her blood ran wild,
Had ravelled her own story out,
And said, 'In two or in three years
I needs must marry some poor lout,'
And having said it, burst in tears.

Since, tavern comrades, you have died,
Maybe your images have stood, 50
Mere bone and muscle thrown aside,
Before that roomful or as good.
You had to face your ends when young—
'Twas wine or women, or some curse—
But never made a poorer song
That you might have a heavier purse,
Nor gave loud service to a cause
That you might have a troop of friends.
You kept the Muses' sterner laws,
And unrepenting faced your ends, 60
And therefore earned the right—and yet
Dowson and Johnson most I praise—
To troop with those the world's forgot,
And copy their proud steady gaze.

'The Danish troop was driven out
Between the dawn and dusk,' she said;
'Although the event was long in doubt,
Although the King of Ireland's dead
And half the kings, before sundown
All was accomplished.

70   'When this day
    Murrough, the King of Ireland's son,
    Foot after foot was giving way,
    He and his best troops back to back
    Had perished there, but the Danes ran,
    Stricken with panic from the attack,
    The shouting of an unseen man;
    And being thankful Murrough found,
    Led by a footsole dipped in blood
    That had made prints upon the ground,
80 Where by old thorn-trees that man stood;
    And though when he gazed here and there,
    He had but gazed on thorn-trees, spoke,
    "Who is the friend that seems but air
    And yet could give so fine a stroke?"
    Thereon a young man met his eye,
    Who said, "Because she held me in
    Her love, and would not have me die,
    Rock-nurtured Aoife took a pin,
    And pushing it into my shirt,
90 Promised that for a pin's sake,
    No man should see to do me hurt;
    But there it's gone; I will not take
    The fortune that had been my shame
    Seeing, King's son, what wounds you have."
    'Twas roundly spoke, but when night came
    He had betrayed me to his grave,
    For he and the King's son were dead.
    I'd promised him two hundred years,
    And when for all I'd done or said—
100 And these immortal eyes shed tears—
    He claimed his country's need was most,
    I'd saved his life, yet for the sake
    Of a new friend he has turned a ghost.
    What does he care if my heart break?
    I call for spade and horse and hound
    That we may harry him.' Thereon
    She cast herself upon the ground

And rent her clothes and made her moan:
'Why are they faithless when their might
Is from the holy shades that rove   110
The grey rock and the windy light?
Why should the faithfullest heart most love
The bitter sweetness of false faces?
Why must the lasting love what passes,
Why are the gods by men betrayed?'

But thereon every god stood up
With a slow smile and without sound,
And stretching forth his arm and cup
To where she moaned upon the ground,
Suddenly drenched her to the skin;   120
And she with Goban's wine adrip,
No more remembering what had been,
Stared at the gods with laughing lip.

I have kept my faith, though faith was tried,
To that rock-born, rock-wandering foot,
And the world's altered since you died,
And I am in no good repute
With the loud host before the sea,
That think sword-strokes were better meant
Than lover's music—let that be,   130
So that the wandering foot's content.

I I 4

To a Wealthy Man who promised a second Subscription to the Dublin Municipal Gallery if it were proved the People wanted Pictures

You gave, but will not give again
Until enough of Paudeen's pence
By Biddy's halfpennies have lain
To be 'some sort of evidence,'
Before you'll put your guineas down,
That things it were a pride to give
Are what the blind and ignorant town
Imagines best to make it thrive.
What cared Duke Ercole, that bid
His mummers to the market-place,
What th' onion-sellers thought or did
So that his Plautus set the pace
For the Italian comedies?
And Guidobaldo, when he made
That grammar school of courtesies
Where wit and beauty learned their trade
Upon Urbino's windy hill,
Had sent no runners to and fro
That he might learn the shepherds' will.
And when they drove out Cosimo,
Indifferent how the rancour ran,
He gave the hours they had set free
To Michelozzo's latest plan
For the San Marco Library,
Whence turbulent Italy should draw
Delight in Art whose end is peace,
In logic and in natural law
By sucking at the dugs of Greece.

Your open hand but shows our loss,
For he knew better how to live.

Let Paudeens play at pitch and toss,
Look up in the sun's eye and give
What the exultant heart calls good
That some new day may breed the best
Because you gave, not what they would,
But the right twigs for an eagle's nest!

                              December 1912

115

September 1913

What need you, being come to sense,
But fumble in a greasy till
And add the halfpence to the pence
And prayer to shivering prayer, until
You have dried the marrow from the bone;
For men were born to pray and save:
Romantic Ireland's dead and gone,
It's with O'Leary in the grave.

Yet they were of a different kind,
The names that stilled your childish play,   10
They have gone about the world like wind,
But little time had they to pray
For whom the hangman's rope was spun,
And what, God help us, could they save?
Romantic Ireland's dead and gone,
It's with O'Leary in the grave.

Was it for this the wild geese spread
The grey wing upon every tide;
For this that all that blood was shed,
For this Edward Fitzgerald died,   20
And Robert Emmet and Wolfe Tone,
All that delirium of the brave?
Romantic Ireland's dead and gone,
It's with O'Leary in the grave.

Yet could we turn the years again,
And call those exiles as they were
In all their loneliness and pain,
You'd cry, 'Some woman's yellow hair
Has maddened every mother's son':
They weighed so lightly what they gave.
But let them be, they're dead and gone,
They're with O'Leary in the grave.

30

116

To a Friend whose Work has come to Nothing

Now all the truth is out,
Be secret and take defeat
From any brazen throat,
For how can you compete,
Being honour bred, with one
Who, were it proved he lies,
Were neither shamed in his own
Nor in his neighbours' eyes?
Bred to a harder thing
Than Triumph, turn away
And like a laughing string
Whereon mad fingers play
Amid a place of stone,
Be secret and exult,
Because of all things known
That is most difficult.

10

117

Paudeen

Indignant at the fumbling wits, the obscure spite
Of our old Paudeen in his shop, I stumbled blind
Among the stones and thorn-trees, under morning light;

Until a curlew cried and in the luminous wind
A curlew answered; and suddenly thereupon I thought
That on the lonely height where all are in God's eye,
There cannot be, confusion of our sound forgot,
A single soul that lacks a sweet crystalline cry.

118

To a Shade

If you have revisited the town, thin Shade,
Whether to look upon your monument
(I wonder if the builder has been paid)
Or happier-thoughted when the day is spent
To drink of that salt breath out of the sea
When grey gulls flit about instead of men,
And the gaunt houses put on majesty:
Let these content you and be gone again;
For they are at their old tricks yet.
                         A man
Of your own passionate serving kind who had brought   10
In his full hands what, had they only known,
Had given their children's children loftier thought,
Sweeter emotion, working in their veins
Like gentle blood, has been driven from the place,
And insult heaped upon him for his pains,
And for his open-handedness, disgrace;
Your enemy, an old foul mouth, had set
The pack upon him.
                 Go, unquiet wanderer,
And gather the Glasnevin coverlet
About your head till the dust stops your ear,   20
The time for you to taste of that salt breath
And listen at the corners has not come;
You had enough of sorrow before death—
Away, away! You are safer in the tomb.

September 29, 1913

119

When Helen lived

We have cried in our despair
That men desert,
For some trivial affair
Or noisy, insolent sport,
Beauty that we have won
From bitterest hours;
Yet we, had we walked within
Those topless towers
Where Helen walked with her boy,
Had given but as the rest
Of the men and women of Troy,
A word and a jest.

10

120

On Those that hated
'The Playboy of the Western World,'
1907

Once, when midnight smote the air,
Eunuchs ran through Hell and met
On every crowded street to stare
Upon great Juan riding by:
Even like these to rail and sweat
Staring upon his sinewy thigh.

121

The Three Beggars

'Though to my feathers in the wet,
I have stood here from break of day,

I have not found a thing to eat,
For only rubbish comes my way.
Am I to live on lebeen-lone?'
Muttered the old crane of Gort.
'For all my pains on lebeen-lone?'

King Guaire walked amid his court
The palace-yard and river-side
And there to three old beggars said,   10
'You that have wandered far and wide
Can ravel out what's in my head.
Do men who least desire get most,
Or get the most who most desire?'
A beggar said, 'They get the most
Whom man or devil cannot tire,
And what could make their muscles taut
Unless desire had made them so?'
But Guaire laughed with secret thought,
'If that be true as it seems true,   20
One of you three is a rich man,
For he shall have a thousand pounds
Who is first asleep, if but he can
Sleep before the third noon sounds.'
And thereon, merry as a bird
With his old thoughts, King Guaire went
From river-side and palace-yard
And left them to their argument.
'And if I win,' one beggar said,
'Though I am old I shall persuade   30
A pretty girl to share my bed';
The second: 'I shall learn a trade';
The third: 'I'll hurry to the course
Among the other gentlemen,
And lay it all upon a horse';
The second: 'I have thought again:
A farmer has more dignity.'
One to another sighed and cried:
The exorbitant dreams of beggary,

40   That idleness had borne to pride,
               Sang through their teeth from noon to noon;
               And when the second twilight brought
               The frenzy of the beggars' moon
               None closed his blood-shot eyes but sought
               To keep his fellows from their sleep;
               All shouted till their anger grew
               And they were whirling in a heap.

               They mauled and bit the whole night through;
               They mauled and bit till the day shone;
50   They mauled and bit through all that day
               And till another night had gone,
               Or if they made a moment's stay
               They sat upon their heels to rail,
               And when old Guaire came and stood
               Before the three to end this tale,
               They were commingling lice and blood.
               'Time's up,' he cried, and all the three
               With blood-shot eyes upon him stared.
               'Time's up,' he cried, and all the three
60   Fell down upon the dust and snored.

               'Maybe I shall be lucky yet,
               Now they are silent,' said the crane.
               'Though to my feathers in the wet
               I've stood as I were made of stone
               And seen the rubbish run about,
               It's certain there are trout somewhere
               And maybe I shall take a trout
               If but I do not seem to care.'

122

The Three Hermits

               Three old hermits took the air
               By a cold and desolate sea,
               First was muttering a prayer,

Second rummaged for a flea;
On a windy stone, the third,
Giddy with his hundredth year,
Sang unnoticed like a bird:
'Though the Door of Death is near
And what waits behind the door,
Three times in a single day   10
I, though upright on the shore,
Fall asleep when I should pray.'
So the first, but now the second:
'We're but given what we have earned
When all thoughts and deeds are reckoned,
So it's plain to be discerned
That the shades of holy men
Who have failed, being weak of will,
Pass the Door of Birth again,
And are plagued by crowds, until   20
They've the passion to escape.'
Moaned the other, 'They are thrown
Into some most fearful shape.'
But the second mocked his moan:
'They are not changed to anything,
Having loved God once, but maybe
To a poet or a king
Or a witty lovely lady.'
While he'd rummaged rags and hair,
Caught and cracked his flea, the third,   30
Giddy with his hundredth year,
Sang unnoticed like a bird.

1 2 3

Beggar to Beggar cried

'Time to put off the world and go somewhere
And find my health again in the sea air,'
Beggar to beggar cried, being frenzy-struck,
'And make my soul before my pate is bare.'

'And get a comfortable wife and house
To rid me of the devil in my shoes,'
Beggar to beggar cried, being frenzy-struck,
'And the worse devil that is between my thighs.'

'And though I'd marry with a comely lass,
10   She need not be too comely—let it pass,'
Beggar to beggar cried, being frenzy-struck,
'But there's a devil in a looking-glass.'

'Nor should she be too rich, because the rich
Are driven by wealth as beggars by the itch,'
Beggar to beggar cried, being frenzy-struck,
'And cannot have a humorous happy speech.'

'And there I'll grow respected at my ease,
And hear amid the garden's nightly peace,'
Beggar to beggar cried, being frenzy-struck,
20   'The wind-blown clamour of the barnacle-geese.'

124

Running to Paradise

As I came over Windy Gap
They threw a halfpenny into my cap,
For I am running to Paradise;
And all that I need do is to wish
And somebody puts his hand in the dish
To throw me a bit of salted fish:
And there the king is *but as the beggar.*

My brother Mourteen is worn out
With skelping his big brawling lout,
10   And I am running to Paradise;
A poor life, do what he can,
And though he keep a dog and a gun,
A serving-maid and a serving-man:
And there the king is *but as the beggar.*

Poor men have grown to be rich men,
And rich men grown to be poor again,
And I am running to Paradise;
And many a darling wit's grown dull
That tossed a bare heel when at school,
Now it has filled an old sock full: 20
And there the king is *but as the beggar.*

The wind is old and still at play
While I must hurry upon my way,
For I am running to Paradise;
Yet never have I lit on a friend
To take my fancy like the wind
That nobody can buy or bind:
And there the king is *but as the beggar.*

125

The Hour before Dawn

A cursing rogue with a merry face,
A bundle of rags upon a crutch,
Stumbled upon that windy place
Called Cruachan,[1] and it was as much
As the one sturdy leg could do
To keep him upright while he cursed.
He had counted, where long years ago
Queen Maeve's nine Maines had been nursed,
A pair of lapwings, one old sheep,
And not a house to the plain's edge,   10
When close to his right hand a heap
Of grey stones and a rocky ledge
Reminded him that he could make,
If he but shifted a few stones,
A shelter till the daylight broke.

[1]Pronounced as if spelt 'Crockan' in modern Gaelic.

But while he fumbled with the stones
They toppled over; 'Were it not
I have a lucky wooden shin
I had been hurt'; and toppling brought
20   Before his eyes, where stones had been,
A dark deep hollow in the rock.
He gave a gasp and thought to have fled,
Being certain it was no right rock
Because an ancient history said
Hell Mouth lay open near that place,
And yet stood still, because inside
A great lad with a beery face
Had tucked himself away beside
A ladle and a tub of beer,
30   And snored, no phantom by his look.
So with a laugh at his own fear
He crawled into that pleasant nook.

'Night grows uneasy near the dawn
Till even I sleep light; but who
Has tired of his own company?
What one of Maeve's nine brawling sons
Sick of his grave has wakened me?
But let him keep his grave for once
That I may find the sleep I have lost.'

40   'What care I if you sleep or wake?
But I'll have no man call me ghost.'

'Say what you please, but from daybreak
I'll sleep another century.'

'And I will talk before I sleep
And drink before I talk.'
                      And he
Had dipped the wooden ladle deep
Into the sleeper's tub of beer
Had not the sleeper started up.

'Before you have dipped it in the beer
50   I dragged from Goban's mountain-top

I'll have assurance that you are able
To value beer; no half-legged fool
Shall dip his nose into my ladle
Merely for stumbling on this hole
In the bad hour before the dawn.'

'Why, beer is only beer.'
         'But say
"I'll sleep until the winter's gone,
Or maybe to Midsummer Day,"
And drink, and you will sleep that length.'

'I'd like to sleep till winter's gone   60
Or till the sun is in his strength.
This blast has chilled me to the bone.'

'I had no better plan at first.
I thought to wait for that or this;
Maybe the weather was accursed
Or I had no woman there to kiss;
So slept for half a year or so;
But year by year I found that less
Gave me such pleasure I'd forgo
Even a half-hour's nothingness,   70
And when at one year's end I found
I had not waked a single minute,
I chose this burrow under ground.
I'll sleep away all time within it:
My sleep were now nine centuries
But for those mornings when I find
The lapwing at their foolish cries
And the sheep bleating at the wind
As when I also played the fool.'

The beggar in a rage began   80
Upon his hunkers in the hole,
'It's plain that you are no right man
To mock at everything I love
As if it were not worth the doing.
I'd have a merry life enough
If a good Easter wind were blowing,

And though the winter wind is bad
I should not be too down in the mouth
For anything you did or said
If but this wind were in the south.'

'You cry aloud, O would 'twere spring
Or that the wind would shift a point,
And do not know that you would bring,
If time were suppler in the joint,
Neither the spring nor the south wind
But the hour when you shall pass away
And leave no smoking wick behind,
For all life longs for the Last Day
And there's no man but cocks his ear
To know when Michael's trumpet cries
That flesh and bone may disappear,
And souls as if they were but sighs,
And there be nothing but God left;
But I alone being blessèd keep
Like some old rabbit to my cleft
And wait Him in a drunken sleep.'
He dipped his ladle in the tub
And drank and yawned and stretched him out,
The other shouted, 'You would rob
My life of every pleasant thought
And every comfortable thing,
And so take that and that.' Thereon
He gave him a great pummelling,
But might have pummelled at a stone
For all the sleeper knew or cared;
And after heaped up stone on stone,
And then, grown weary, prayed and cursed
And heaped up stone on stone again,
And prayed and cursed and cursed and fled
From Maeve and all that juggling plain,
Nor gave God thanks till overhead
The clouds were brightening with the dawn.

126

A Song from 'The Player Queen'

My mother dandled me and sang,
'How young it is, how young!'
And made a golden cradle
That on a willow swung.

'He went away,' my mother sang,
'When I was brought to bed,'
And all the while her needle pulled
The gold and silver thread.

She pulled the thread and bit the thread
And made a golden gown,   10
And wept because she had dreamt that I
Was born to wear a crown.

'When she was got,' my mother sang,
'I heard a sea-mew cry,
And saw a flake of the yellow foam
That dropped upon my thigh.'

How therefore could she help but braid
The gold into my hair,
And dream that I should carry
The golden top of care?   20

127

The Realists

Hope that you may understand!
What can books of men that wive
In a dragon-guarded land,
Paintings of the dolphin-drawn
Sea-nymphs in their pearly wagons
Do, but awake a hope to live
That had gone
With the dragons?

128

I. The Witch

Toil and grow rich,
What's that but to lie
With a foul witch
And after, drained dry,
To be brought
To the chamber where
Lies one long sought
With despair?

129

II. The Peacock

What's riches to him
That has made a great peacock
With the pride of his eye?
The wind-beaten, stone-grey,
And desolate Three Rock
Would nourish his whim.
Live he or die
Amid wet rocks and heather,
His ghost will be gay
Adding feather to feather
For the pride of his eye.

10

130

The Mountain Tomb

Pour wine and dance if manhood still have pride,
Bring roses if the rose be yet in bloom;
The cataract smokes upon the mountain side,
Our Father Rosicross is in his tomb.

Pull down the blinds, bring fiddle and clarionet
That there be no foot silent in the room
Nor mouth from kissing, nor from wine unwet;
Our Father Rosicross is in his tomb.

In vain, in vain; the cataract still cries;
The everlasting taper lights the gloom;   10
All wisdom shut into his onyx eyes,
Our Father Rosicross sleeps in his tomb.

131

I. To a Child dancing in the Wind

Dance there upon the shore;
What need have you to care
For wind or water's roar?
And tumble out your hair
That the salt drops have wet;
Being young you have not known
The fool's triumph, nor yet
Love lost as soon as won,
Nor the best labourer dead
And all the sheaves to bind.   10
What need have you to dread
The monstrous crying of wind?

132

II. Two Years Later

Has no one said those daring
Kind eyes should be more learn'd?
Or warned you how despairing
The moths are when they are burned?
I could have warned you; but you are young,
So we speak a different tongue.

O you will take whatever's offered
And dream that all the world's a friend,
Suffer as your mother suffered,
10 Be as broken in the end.
But I am old and you are young,
And I speak a barbarous tongue.

133

A Memory of Youth

The moments passed as at a play;
I had the wisdom love brings forth;
I had my share of mother-wit,
And yet for all that I could say,
And though I had her praise for it,
A cloud blown from the cut-throat north
Suddenly hid Love's moon away.

Believing every word I said,
I praised her body and her mind
10 Till pride had made her eyes grow bright,
And pleasure made her cheeks grow red,
And vanity her footfall light,
Yet we, for all that praise, could find
Nothing but darkness overhead.

We sat as silent as a stone,
We knew, though she'd not said a word,
That even the best of love must die,
And had been savagely undone
Were it not that Love upon the cry
20 Of a most ridiculous little bird
Tore from the clouds his marvellous moon.

134

Fallen Majesty

Although crowds gathered once if she but showed her face,
And even old men's eyes grew dim, this hand alone,
Like some last courtier at a gypsy camping-place
Babbling of fallen majesty, records what's gone.

The lineaments, a heart that laughter has made sweet,
These, these remain, but I record what's gone. A crowd
Will gather, and not know it walks the very street
Whereon a thing once walked that seemed a burning cloud.

135

Friends

Now must I these three praise—
Three women that have wrought
What joy is in my days:
One because no thought,
Nor those unpassing cares,
No, not in these fifteen
Many-times-troubled years,
Could ever come between
Mind and delighted mind;
And one because her hand   10
Had strength that could unbind
What none can understand,
What none can have and thrive,
Youth's dreamy load, till she
So changed me that I live
Labouring in ecstasy.
And what of her that took
All till my youth was gone
With scarce a pitying look?
How could I praise that one?   20

When day begins to break
I count my good and bad,
Being wakeful for her sake,
Remembering what she had,
What eagle look still shows,
While up from my heart's root
So great a sweetness flows
I shake from head to foot.

136

The Cold Heaven

Suddenly I saw the cold and rook-delighting heaven
That seemed as though ice burned and was but the more ice,
And thereupon imagination and heart were driven
So wild that every casual thought of that and this
Vanished, and left but memories, that should be out of season
With the hot blood of youth, of love crossed long ago;
And I took all the blame out of all sense and reason,
Until I cried and trembled and rocked to and fro,
Riddled with light. Ah! when the ghost begins to quicken,
Confusion of the death-bed over, is it sent
Out naked on the roads, as the books say, and stricken
By the injustice of the skies for punishment?

137

That the Night come

She lived in storm and strife,
Her soul had such desire
For what proud death may bring
That it could not endure
The common good of life,
But lived as 'twere a king
That packed his marriage day

With banneret and pennon,
Trumpet and kettledrum,
And the outrageous cannon,   10
To bundle time away
That the night come.

138

An Appointment

Being out of heart with government
I took a broken root to fling
Where the proud, wayward squirrel went,
Taking delight that he could spring;
And he, with that low whinnying sound
That is like laughter, sprang again
And so to the other tree at a bound.
Nor the tame will, nor timid brain,
Nor heavy knitting of the brow
Bred that fierce tooth and cleanly limb   10
And threw him up to laugh on the bough;
No government appointed him.

139

The Magi

Now as at all times I can see in the mind's eye,
In their stiff, painted clothes, the pale unsatisfied ones
Appear and disappear in the blue depth of the sky
With all their ancient faces like rain-beaten stones,
And all their helms of silver hovering side by side,
And all their eyes still fixed, hoping to find once more,
Being by Calvary's turbulence unsatisfied,
The uncontrollable mystery on the bestial floor.

140

The Dolls

A doll in the doll-maker's house
Looks at the cradle and bawls:
'That is an insult to us.'
But the oldest of all the dolls,
Who had seen, being kept for show,
Generations of his sort,
Out-screams the whole shelf: 'Although
There's not a man can report
Evil of this place,
The man and the woman bring
Hither, to our disgrace,
A noisy and filthy thing.'
Hearing him groan and stretch
The doll-maker's wife is aware
Her husband has heard the wretch,
And crouched by the arm of his chair,
She murmurs into his ear,
Head upon shoulder leant:
'My dear, my dear, O dear,
It was an accident.'

141

A Coat

I made my song a coat
Covered with embroideries
Out of old mythologies
From heel to throat;
But the fools caught it,
Wore it in the world's eyes
As though they'd wrought it.
Song, let them take it,
For there's more enterprise
In walking naked.   10

142

While I, from that reed-throated whisperer
Who comes at need, although not now as once
A clear articulation in the air,
But inwardly, surmise companions
Beyond the fling of the dull ass's hoof,
—Ben Jonson's phrase—and find when June is come
At Kyle-na-no under that ancient roof
A sterner conscience and a friendlier home,
I can forgive even that wrong of wrongs,
Those undreamt accidents that have made me   10
—Seeing that Fame has perished this long while,
Being but a part of ancient ceremony—
Notorious, till all my priceless things
Are but a post the passing dogs defile.

The Wild Swans at Coole

1919

The Wild Swans at Coole

The trees are in their autumn beauty,
The woodland paths are dry,
Under the October twilight the water
Mirrors a still sky;
Upon the brimming water among the stones
Are nine-and-fifty swans.

The nineteenth autumn has come upon me
Since I first made my count;
I saw, before I had well finished,
All suddenly mount   10
And scatter wheeling in great broken rings
Upon their clamorous wings.

I have looked upon those brilliant creatures,
And now my heart is sore.
All's changed since I, hearing at twilight,
The first time on this shore,
The bell-beat of their wings above my head,
Trod with a lighter tread.

Unwearied still, lover by lover,
They paddle in the cold   20
Companionable streams or climb the air;
Their hearts have not grown old;
Passion or conquest, wander where they will,
Attend upon them still.

But now they drift on the still water,
Mysterious, beautiful;
Among what rushes will they build,
By what lake's edge or pool
Delight men's eyes when I awake some day
To find they have flown away?   30

144

In Memory of
Major Robert Gregory

I

Now that we're almost settled in our house
I'll name the friends that cannot sup with us
Beside a fire of turf in th' ancient tower,
And having talked to some late hour
Climb up the narrow winding stair to bed:
Discoverers of forgotten truth
Or mere companions of my youth,
All, all are in my thoughts to-night being dead.

II

Always we'd have the new friend meet the old
And we are hurt if either friend seem cold,
And there is salt to lengthen out the smart
In the affections of our heart,
And quarrels are blown up upon that head;
But not a friend that I would bring
This night can set us quarrelling,
For all that come into my mind are dead.

III

Lionel Johnson comes the first to mind,
That loved his learning better than mankind,
Though courteous to the worst; much falling he
Brooded upon sanctity
Till all his Greek and Latin learning seemed
A long blast upon the horn that brought
A little nearer to his thought
A measureless consummation that he dreamed.

IV

And that enquiring man John Synge comes next,
That dying chose the living world for text
And never could have rested in the tomb
But that, long travelling, he had come
Towards nightfall upon certain set apart
In a most desolate stony place,   30
Towards nightfall upon a race
Passionate and simple like his heart.

V

And then I think of old George Pollexfen,
In muscular youth well known to Mayo men
For horsemanship at meets or at racecourses,
That could have shown how pure-bred horses
And solid men, for all their passion, live
But as the outrageous stars incline
By opposition, square and trine;
Having grown sluggish and contemplative.   40

VI

They were my close companions many a year,
A portion of my mind and life, as it were,
And now their breathless faces seem to look
Out of some old picture-book;
I am accustomed to their lack of breath,
But not that my dear friend's dear son,
Our Sidney and our perfect man,
Could share in that discourtesy of death.

VII

For all things the delighted eye now sees
Were loved by him; the old storm-broken trees   50
That cast their shadows upon road and bridge;
The tower set on the stream's edge;

The ford where drinking cattle make a stir
Nightly, and startled by that sound
The water-hen must change her ground;
He might have been your heartiest welcomer.

VIII

When with the Galway foxhounds he would ride
From Castle Taylor to the Roxborough side
Or Esserkelly plain, few kept his pace;
At Mooneen he had leaped a place
So perilous that half the astonished meet
Had shut their eyes; and where was it
He rode a race without a bit?
And yet his mind outran the horses' feet.

IX

We dreamed that a great painter had been born
To cold Clare rock and Galway rock and thorn,
To that stern colour and that delicate line
That are our secret discipline
Wherein the gazing heart doubles her might.
Soldier, scholar, horseman, he,
And yet he had the intensity
To have published all to be a world's delight.

X

What other could so well have counselled us
In all lovely intricacies of a house
As he that practised or that understood
All work in metal or in wood,
In moulded plaster or in carven stone?
Soldier, scholar, horseman, he,
And all he did done perfectly
As though he had but that one trade alone.

XI

Some burn damp faggots, others may consume
The entire combustible world in one small room
As though dried straw, and if we turn about
The bare chimney is gone black out
Because the work had finished in that flare.
Soldier, scholar, horseman, he,
As 'twere all life's epitome.
What made us dream that he could comb grey hair?

XII

I had thought, seeing how bitter is that wind
That shakes the shutter, to have brought to mind   90
All those that manhood tried, or childhood loved
Or boyish intellect approved,
With some appropriate commentary on each;
Until imagination brought
A fitter welcome; but a thought
Of that late death took all my heart for speech.

145

An Irish Airman foresees his Death

I know that I shall meet my fate
Somewhere among the clouds above;
Those that I fight I do not hate,
Those that I guard I do not love;
My country is Kiltartan Cross,
My countrymen Kiltartan's poor,
No likely end could bring them loss
Or leave them happier than before.
Nor law, nor duty bade me fight,
Nor public men, nor cheering crowds,   10
A lonely impulse of delight
Drove to this tumult in the clouds;

I balanced all, brought all to mind,
The years to come seemed waste of breath,
A waste of breath the years behind
In balance with this life, this death.

146

Men improve with the Years

I am worn out with dreams;
A weather-worn, marble triton
Among the streams;
And all day long I look
Upon this lady's beauty
As though I had found in a book
A pictured beauty,
Pleased to have filled the eyes
Or the discerning ears,
Delighted to be but wise,
For men improve with the years;
And yet, and yet,
Is this my dream, or the truth?
O would that we had met
When I had my burning youth!
But I grow old among dreams,
A weather-worn, marble triton
Among the streams.

10

147

The Collar-bone of a Hare

Would I could cast a sail on the water
Where many a king has gone
And many a king's daughter,
And alight at the comely trees and the lawn,
The playing upon pipes and the dancing,

And learn that the best thing is
To change my loves while dancing
And pay but a kiss for a kiss.

I would find by the edge of that water
The collar-bone of a hare 10
Worn thin by the lapping of water,
And pierce it through with a gimlet and stare
At the old bitter world where they marry in churches,
And laugh over the untroubled water
At all who marry in churches,
Through the white thin bone of a hare.

148

Under the Round Tower

'Although I'd lie lapped up in linen
A deal I'd sweat and little earn
If I should live as live the neighbours,'
Cried the beggar, Billy Byrne;
'Stretch bones till the daylight come
On great-grandfather's battered tomb.'

Upon a grey old battered tombstone
In Glendalough beside the stream,
Where the O'Byrnes and Byrnes are buried,
He stretched his bones and fell in a dream 10
Of sun and moon that a good hour
Bellowed and pranced in the round tower;

Of golden king and silver lady,
Bellowing up and bellowing round,
Till toes mastered a sweet measure,
Mouth mastered a sweet sound,
Prancing round and prancing up
Until they pranced upon the top.

That golden king and that wild lady
Sang till stars began to fade, 20

Hands gripped in hands, toes close together,
Hair spread on the wind they made;
That lady and that golden king
Could like a brace of blackbirds sing.

'It's certain that my luck is broken,'
That rambling jailbird Billy said;
'Before nightfall I'll pick a pocket
And snug it in a feather-bed.
I cannot find the peace of home
On great-grandfather's battered tomb.'

30

149

Solomon to Sheba

Sang Solomon to Sheba,
And kissed her dusky face,
'All day long from mid-day
We have talked in the one place,
All day long from shadowless noon
We have gone round and round
In the narrow theme of love
Like an old horse in a pound.'

To Solomon sang Sheba,
Planted on his knees,
'If you had broached a matter
That might the learned please,
You had before the sun had thrown
Our shadows on the ground
Discovered that my thoughts, not it,
Are but a narrow pound.'

10

Said Solomon to Sheba,
And kissed her Arab eyes,
'There's not a man or woman
Born under the skies
Dare match in learning with us two,

20

And all day long we have found
There's not a thing but love can make
The world a narrow pound.'

150

The Living Beauty

I bade, because the wick and oil are spent
And frozen are the channels of the blood,
My discontented heart to draw content
From beauty that is cast out of a mould
In bronze, or that in dazzling marble appears,
Appears, but when we have gone is gone again,
Being more indifferent to our solitude
Than 'twere an apparition. O heart, we are old;
The living beauty is for younger men:
We cannot pay its tribute of wild tears.　　　10

151

A Song

I thought no more was needed
Youth to prolong
Than dumb-bell and foil
To keep the body young.
O who could have foretold
That the heart grows old?

Though I have many words,
What woman's satisfied,
I am no longer faint
Because at her side?　　　10
O who could have foretold
That the heart grows old?

I have not lost desire
But the heart that I had;
I thought 'twould burn my body
Laid on the death-bed,
*For who could have foretold
That the heart grows old?*

152

To a Young Beauty

Dear fellow-artist, why so free
With every sort of company,
With every Jack and Jill?
Choose your companions from the best;
Who draws a bucket with the rest
Soon topples down the hill.

You may, that mirror for a school,
Be passionate, not bountiful
As common beauties may,
Who were not born to keep in trim
With old Ezekiel's cherubim
But those of Beauvarlet.

I know what wages beauty gives,
How hard a life her servant lives,
Yet praise the winters gone:
There is not a fool can call me friend,
And I may dine at journey's end
With Landor and with Donne.

153

To a Young Girl

My dear, my dear, I know
More than another
What makes your heart beat so;

10

Not even your own mother
Can know it as I know,
Who broke my heart for her
When the wild thought,
That she denies
And has forgot,
Set all her blood astir   10
And glittered in her eyes.

154

The Scholars

Bald heads forgetful of their sins,
Old, learned, respectable bald heads
Edit and annotate the lines
That young men, tossing on their beds,
Rhymed out in love's despair
To flatter beauty's ignorant ear.

All shuffle there; all cough in ink;
All wear the carpet with their shoes;
All think what other people think;
All know the man their neighbour knows.   10
Lord, what would they say
Did their Catullus walk that way?

155

Tom O'Roughley

'Though logic-choppers rule the town,
And every man and maid and boy
Has marked a distant object down,
An aimless joy is a pure joy,'
Or so did Tom O'Roughley say
That saw the surges running by,
'And wisdom is a butterfly
And not a gloomy bird of prey.

'If little planned is little sinned
But little need the grave distress.
What's dying but a second wind?
How but in zig-zag wantonness
Could trumpeter Michael be so brave?'
Or something of that sort he said,
'And if my dearest friend were dead
I'd dance a measure on his grave.'

156

Shepherd and Goatherd

Shepherd. That cry's from the first cuckoo of the year.
  I wished before it ceased.

Goatherd.   Nor bird nor beast
  Could make me wish for anything this day,
  Being old, but that the old alone might die,
  And that would be against God's Providence.
  Let the young wish. But what has brought you here?
  Never until this moment have we met
  Where my goats browse on the scarce grass or leap
  From stone to stone.

Shepherd.   I am looking for strayed sheep;
  Something has troubled me and in my trouble
  I let them stray. I thought of rhyme alone,
  For rhyme can beat a measure out of trouble
  And make the daylight sweet once more; but when
  I had driven every rhyme into its place
  The sheep had gone from theirs.

Goatherd.   I know right well
  What turned so good a shepherd from his charge.

Shepherd. He that was best in every country sport
  And every country craft, and of us all
  Most courteous to slow age and hasty youth,
  Is dead.

Goatherd. The boy that brings my griddle-cake   20
  Brought the bare news.

Shepherd.   He had thrown the crook away
  And died in the great war beyond the sea.

Goatherd. He had often played his pipes among my hills,
  And when he played it was their loneliness,
  The exultation of their stone, that cried
  Under his fingers.

Shepherd.   I had it from his mother,
  And his own flock was browsing at the door.

Goatherd. How does she bear her grief? There is not a shepherd
  But grows more gentle when he speaks her name,
  Remembering kindness done, and how can I,   30
  That found when I had neither goat nor grazing
  New welcome and old wisdom at her fire
  Till winter blasts were gone, but speak of her
  Even before his children and his wife.

Shepherd. She goes about her house erect and calm
  Between the pantry and the linen-chest,
  Or else at meadow or at grazing overlooks
  Her labouring men, as though her darling lived,
  But for her grandson now; there is no change
  But such as I have seen upon her face   40
  Watching our shepherd sports at harvest-time
  When her son's turn was over.

Goatherd.   Sing your song.
  I too have rhymed my reveries, but youth
  Is hot to show whatever it has found,
  And till that's done can neither work nor wait.
  Old goatherds and old goats, if in all else
  Youth can excel them in accomplishment,
  Are learned in waiting.

Shepherd.   You cannot but have seen
  That he alone had gathered up no gear,
  Set carpenters to work on no wide table,   50
  On no long bench nor lofty milking shed

As others will, when first they take possession,
But left the house as in his father's time
As though he knew himself, as it were, a cuckoo,
No settled man. And now that he is gone
There's nothing of him left but half a score
Of sorrowful, austere, sweet, lofty pipe tunes.

Goatherd. You have put the thought in rhyme.

Shepherd.   I worked all day,
    And when 'twas done so little had I done
60 That maybe 'I am sorry' in plain prose
    Had sounded better to your mountain fancy.

                                           [*He sings.*]

    'Like the speckled bird that steers
    Thousands of leagues oversea,
    And runs or a while half-flies
    On his yellow legs through our meadows,
    He stayed for a while; and we
    Had scarcely accustomed our ears
    To his speech at the break of day,
    Had scarcely accustomed our eyes
70 To his shape at the rinsing pool
    Among the evening shadows,
    When he vanished from ears and eyes.
    I might have wished on the day
    He came, but man is a fool.'

Goatherd. You sing as always of the natural life,
    And I that made like music in my youth
    Hearing it now have sighed for that young man
    And certain lost companions of my own.

Shepherd. They say that on your barren mountain ridge
80 You have measured out the road that the soul treads
    When it has vanished from our natural eyes;
    That you have talked with apparitions.

Goatherd.   Indeed
    My daily thoughts since the first stupor of youth
    Have found the path my goats' feet cannot find.

Shepherd. Sing, for it may be that your thoughts have plucked
    Some medicable herb to make our grief
    Less bitter.

Goatherd.   They have brought me from that ridge
    Seed-pods and flowers that are not all wild poppy.

[Sings.]

    'He grows younger every second
    That were all his birthdays reckoned   90
    Much too solemn seemed;
    Because of what he had dreamed,
    Or the ambitions that he served,
    Much too solemn and reserved.
    Jaunting, journeying
    To his own dayspring,
    He unpacks the loaded pern
    Of all 'twas pain or joy to learn,
    Of all that he had made.
    The outrageous war shall fade;   100
    At some old winding whitethorn root
    He'll practise on the shepherd's flute,
    Or on the close-cropped grass
    Court his shepherd lass,
    Or put his heart into some game
    Till daytime, playtime seem the same;
    Knowledge he shall unwind
    Through victories of the mind,
    Till, clambering at the cradle-side,
    He dreams himself his mother's pride,   110
    All knowledge lost in trance
    Of sweeter ignorance.'

Shepherd. When I have shut these ewes and this old ram
    Into the fold, we'll to the woods and there
    Cut out our rhymes on strips of new-torn bark
    But put no name and leave them at her door.
    To know the mountain and the valley have grieved
    May be a quiet thought to wife and mother,
    And children when they spring up shoulder-high.

157

Lines written in Dejection

When have I last looked on
The round green eyes and the long wavering bodies
Of the dark leopards of the moon?
All the wild witches, those most noble ladies,
For all their broom-sticks and their tears,
Their angry tears, are gone.
The holy centaurs of the hills are vanished;
I have nothing but the embittered sun;
Banished heroic mother moon and vanished,
And now that I have come to fifty years
I must endure the timid sun.

158

The Dawn

I would be ignorant as the dawn
That has looked down
On that old queen measuring a town
With the pin of a brooch,
Or on the withered men that saw
From their pedantic Babylon
The careless planets in their courses,
The stars fade out where the moon comes,
And took their tablets and did sums;
I would be ignorant as the dawn
That merely stood, rocking the glittering coach
Above the cloudy shoulders of the horses;
I would be—for no knowledge is worth a straw—
Ignorant and wanton as the dawn.

159

On Woman

May God be praised for woman
That gives up all her mind,
A man may find in no man
A friendship of her kind
That covers all he has brought
As with her flesh and bone,
Nor quarrels with a thought
Because it is not her own.

Though pedantry denies,
It's plain the Bible means   10
That Solomon grew wise
While talking with his queens,
Yet never could, although
They say he counted grass,
Count all the praises due
When Sheba was his lass,
When she the iron wrought, or
When from the smithy fire
It shuddered in the water:
Harshness of their desire   20
That made them stretch and yawn,
Pleasure that comes with sleep,
Shudder that made them one.
What else He give or keep
God grant me—no, not here,
For I am not so bold
To hope a thing so dear
Now I am growing old,
But when, if the tale's true,
The Pestle of the moon   30
That pounds up all anew
Brings me to birth again—
To find what once I had
And know what once I have known,

Until I am driven mad,
Sleep driven from my bed,
By tenderness and care,
Pity, an aching head,
Gnashing of teeth, despair;
And all because of some one
Perverse creature of chance,
And live like Solomon
That Sheba led a dance.

40

160

The Fisherman

Although I can see him still,
The freckled man who goes
To a grey place on a hill
In grey Connemara clothes
At dawn to cast his flies,
It's long since I began
To call up to the eyes
This wise and simple man.
All day I'd looked in the face
What I had hoped 'twould be
To write for my own race
And the reality;
The living men that I hate,
The dead man that I loved,
The craven man in his seat,
The insolent unreproved,
And no knave brought to book
Who has won a drunken cheer,
The witty man and his joke
Aimed at the commonest ear,
The clever man who cries
The catch-cries of the clown,
The beating down of the wise
And great Art beaten down.

10

20

Maybe a twelvemonth since
Suddenly I began,
In scorn of this audience,
Imagining a man,
And his sun-freckled face,
And grey Connemara cloth,   30
Climbing up to a place
Where stone is dark under froth,
And the down-turn of his wrist
When the flies drop in the stream;
A man who does not exist,
A man who is but a dream;
And cried, 'Before I am old
I shall have written him one
Poem maybe as cold
And passionate as the dawn.'   40

161

The Hawk

'Call down the hawk from the air;
Let him be hooded or caged
Till the yellow eye has grown mild,
For larder and spit are bare,
The old cook enraged,
The scullion gone wild.'

'I will not be clapped in a hood,
Nor a cage, nor alight upon wrist,
Now I have learnt to be proud
Hovering over the wood   10
In the broken mist
Or tumbling cloud.'

'What tumbling cloud did you cleave,
Yellow-eyed hawk of the mind,
Last evening? that I, who had sat

Dumbfounded before a knave,
Should give to my friend
A pretence of wit.'

162

Memory

One had a lovely face,
And two or three had charm,
But charm and face were in vain
Because the mountain grass
Cannot but keep the form
Where the mountain hare has lain.

163

Her Praise

She is foremost of those that I would hear praised.
I have gone about the house, gone up and down
As a man does who has published a new book,
Or a young girl dressed out in her new gown,
And though I have turned the talk by hook or crook
Until her praise should be the uppermost theme,
A woman spoke of some new tale she had read,
A man confusedly in a half dream
As though some other name ran in his head.
She is foremost of those that I would hear praised.
I will talk no more of books or the long war
But walk by the dry thorn until I have found
Some beggar sheltering from the wind, and there
Manage the talk until her name come round.
If there be rags enough he will know her name
And be well pleased remembering it, for in the old days,
Though she had young men's praise and old men's blame,
Among the poor both old and young gave her praise.

164

The People

'What have I earned for all that work,' I said,
'For all that I have done at my own charge?
The daily spite of this unmannerly town,
Where who has served the most is most defamed,
The reputation of his lifetime lost
Between the night and morning. I might have lived,
And you know well how great the longing has been,
Where every day my footfall should have lit
In the green shadow of Ferrara wall;
Or climbed among the images of the past—   10
The unperturbed and courtly images—
Evening and morning, the steep street of Urbino
To where the duchess and her people talked
The stately midnight through until they stood
In their great window looking at the dawn;
I might have had no friend that could not mix
Courtesy and passion into one like those
That saw the wicks grow yellow in the dawn;
I might have used the one substantial right
My trade allows: chosen my company,   20
And chosen what scenery had pleased me best.'
Thereon my phoenix answered in reproof,
'The drunkards, pilferers of public funds,
All the dishonest crowd I had driven away,
When my luck changed and they dared meet my face,
Crawled from obscurity, and set upon me
Those I had served and some that I had fed;
Yet never have I, now nor any time,
Complained of the people.'

                              All I could reply
Was: 'You, that have not lived in thought but deed,   30
Can have the purity of a natural force,
But I, whose virtues are the definitions

Of the analytic mind, can neither close
The eye of the mind nor keep my tongue from speech.'
And yet, because my heart leaped at her words,
I was abashed, and now they come to mind
After nine years, I sink my head abashed.

165

His Phoenix

There is a queen in China, or maybe it's in Spain,
And birthdays and holidays such praises can be heard
Of her unblemished lineaments, a whiteness with no stain,
That she might be that sprightly girl trodden by a bird;
And there's a score of duchesses, surpassing womankind,
Or who have found a painter to make them so for pay
And smooth out stain and blemish with the elegance of his mind:
I knew a phoenix in my youth, so let them have their day.

The young men every night applaud their Gaby's laughing eye,
And Ruth St. Denis had more charm although she had poor luck;
From nineteen hundred nine or ten, Pavlova's had the cry,
And there's a player in the States who gathers up her cloak
And flings herself out of the room when Juliet would be bride
With all a woman's passion, a child's imperious way,
And there are—but no matter if there are scores beside:
I knew a phoenix in my youth, so let them have their day.

There's Margaret and Marjorie and Dorothy and Nan,
A Daphne and a Mary who live in privacy;
One's had her fill of lovers, another's had but one,
Another boasts, 'I pick and choose and have but two or three.'
If head and limb have beauty and the instep's high and light
They can spread out what sail they please for all I have to say,
Be but the breakers of men's hearts or engines of delight:
I knew a phoenix in my youth, so let them have their day.

There'll be that crowd, that barbarous crowd, through all the
    centuries,
And who can say but some young belle may walk and talk men wild

Who is my beauty's equal, though that my heart denies,
But not the exact likeness, the simplicity of a child,
And that proud look as though she had gazed into the burning sun,
And all the shapely body no tittle gone astray. 30
I mourn for that most lonely thing; and yet God's will be done:
I knew a phoenix in my youth, so let them have their day.

166

A Thought from Propertius

She might, so noble from head
To great shapely knees
The long flowing line,
Have walked to the altar
Through the holy images
At Pallas Athena's side,
Or been fit spoil for a centaur
Drunk with the unmixed wine.

167

Broken Dreams

There is grey in your hair.
Young men no longer suddenly catch their breath
When you are passing;
But maybe some old gaffer mutters a blessing
Because it was your prayer
Recovered him upon the bed of death.
For your sole sake—that all heart's ache have known,
And given to others all heart's ache,
From meagre girlhood's putting on
Burdensome beauty—for your sole sake 10
Heaven has put away the stroke of her doom,
So great her portion in that peace you make
By merely walking in a room.

Your beauty can but leave among us
Vague memories, nothing but memories.
A young man when the old men are done talking
Will say to an old man, 'Tell me of that lady
The poet stubborn with his passion sang us
When age might well have chilled his blood.'

20   Vague memories, nothing but memories,
But in the grave all, all, shall be renewed.
The certainty that I shall see that lady
Leaning or standing or walking
In the first loveliness of womanhood,
And with the fervour of my youthful eyes,
Has set me muttering like a fool.

You are more beautiful than any one,
And yet your body had a flaw:
Your small hands were not beautiful,
30   And I am afraid that you will run
And paddle to the wrist
In that mysterious, always brimming lake
Where those that have obeyed the holy law
Paddle and are perfect. Leave unchanged
The hands that I have kissed,
For old sake's sake.

The last stroke of midnight dies.
All day in the one chair
From dream to dream and rhyme to rhyme I have ranged
40   In rambling talk with an image of air:
Vague memories, nothing but memories.

168

A Deep-sworn Vow

Others because you did not keep
That deep-sworn vow have been friends of mine;
Yet always when I look death in the face,

When I clamber to the heights of sleep,
Or when I grow excited with wine,
Suddenly I meet your face.

169

Presences

This night has been so strange that it seemed
As if the hair stood up on my head.
From going-down of the sun I have dreamed
That women laughing, or timid or wild,
In rustle of lace or silken stuff,
Climbed up my creaking stair. They had read
All I had rhymed of that monstrous thing
Returned and yet unrequited love.
They stood in the door and stood between
My great wood lectern and the fire   10
Till I could hear their hearts beating:
One is a harlot, and one a child
That never looked upon man with desire,
And one, it may be, a queen.

170

The Balloon of the Mind

Hands, do what you're bid:
Bring the balloon of the mind
That bellies and drags in the wind
Into its narrow shed.

171

To a Squirrel at Kyle-na-no

Come play with me;
Why should you run
Through the shaking tree
As though I'd a gun
To strike you dead?
When all I would do
Is to scratch your head
And let you go.

172

On being asked for a War Poem

I think it better that in times like these
A poet's mouth be silent, for in truth
We have no gift to set a statesman right;
He has had enough of meddling who can please
A young girl in the indolence of her youth,
Or an old man upon a winter's night.

173

In Memory of Alfred Pollexfen

Five-and-twenty years have gone
Since old William Pollexfen
Laid his strong bones down in death
By his wife Elizabeth
In the grey stone tomb he made.
And after twenty years they laid
In that tomb by him and her
His son George, the astrologer;
And Masons drove from miles away

To scatter the Acacia spray   10
Upon a melancholy man
Who had ended where his breath began.
Many a son and daughter lies
Far from the customary skies,
The Mall and Eades's grammar school,
In London or in Liverpool;
But where is laid the sailor John
That so many lands had known,
Quiet lands or unquiet seas
Where the Indians trade or Japanese?   20
He never found his rest ashore,
Moping for one voyage more.
Where have they laid the sailor John?
And yesterday the youngest son,
A humorous, unambitious man,
Was buried near the astrologer,
Yesterday in the tenth year
Since he who had been contented long,
A nobody in a great throng,
Decided he must journey home,   30
Now that his fiftieth year had come,
And 'Mr. Alfred' be again
Upon the lips of common men
Who carried in their memory
His childhood and his family.
At all these death-beds women heard
A visionary white sea-bird
Lamenting that a man should die;
And with that cry I have raised my cry.

Upon a Dying Lady

174

I. Her Courtesy

With the old kindness, the old distinguished grace,
She lies, her lovely piteous head amid dull red hair
Propped upon pillows, rouge on the pallor of her face.
She would not have us sad because she is lying there,
And when she meets our gaze her eyes are laughter-lit,
Her speech a wicked tale that we may vie with her,
Matching our broken-hearted wit against her wit,
Thinking of saints and of Petronius Arbiter.

175

II. Certain Artists bring her Dolls and Drawings

Bring where our Beauty lies
A new modelled doll, or drawing,
With a friend's or an enemy's
Features, or maybe showing
Her features when a tress
Of dull red hair was flowing
Over some silken dress
Cut in the Turkish fashion,
Or, it may be, like a boy's.
We have given the world our passion,
We have naught for death but toys.

176

III. She turns the Dolls' Faces to the Wall

Because to-day is some religious festival
They had a priest say Mass, and even the Japanese,
Heel up and weight on toe, must face the wall
—Pedant in passion, learned in old courtesies,
Vehement and witty she had seemed—; the Venetian lady
Who had seemed to glide to some intrigue in her red shoes,
Her domino, her panniered skirt copied from Longhi;
The meditative critic; all are on their toes,
Even our Beauty with her Turkish trousers on.
Because the priest must have like every dog his day   10
Or keep us all awake with baying at the moon,
We and our dolls being but the world were best away.

177

IV. The End of Day

She is playing like a child
And penance is the play,
Fantastical and wild
Because the end of day
Shows her that some one soon
Will come from the house, and say—
Though play is but half done—
'Come in and leave the play.'

178

v. Her Race

She has not grown uncivil
As narrow natures would
And called the pleasures evil
Happier days thought good;
She knows herself a woman,
No red and white of a face,
Or rank, raised from a common
Unreckonable race;
And how should her heart fail her
Or sickness break her will
With her dead brother's valour
For an example still?

10

179

vi. Her Courage

When her soul flies to the predestined dancing-place
(I have no speech but symbol, the pagan speech I made
Amid the dreams of youth) let her come face to face,
Amid that first astonishment, with Grania's shade,
All but the terrors of the woodland flight forgot
That made her Diarmuid dear, and some old cardinal
Pacing with half-closed eyelids in a sunny spot
Who had murmured of Giorgione at his latest breath—
Aye, and Achilles, Timor, Babar, Barhaim, all
Who have lived in joy and laughed into the face of Death.

10

180

VII. Her Friends
bring her a Christmas Tree

Pardon, great enemy,
Without an angry thought
We've carried in our tree,
And here and there have bought
Till all the boughs are gay,
And she may look from the bed
On pretty things that may
Please a fantastic head.
Give her a little grace,
What if a laughing eye　　　　　　　　　　10
Have looked into your face?
It is about to die.

181

Ego Dominus Tuus

Hic. On the grey sand beside the shallow stream
　　Under your old wind-beaten tower, where still
　　A lamp burns on beside the open book
　　That Michael Robartes left, you walk in the moon
　　And though you have passed the best of life still trace,
　　Enthralled by the unconquerable delusion,
　　Magical shapes.

Ille.　　　　　　　By the help of an image
　　I call to my own opposite, summon all
　　That I have handled least, least looked upon.

Hic. And I would find myself and not an image.　　　　10

Ille. That is our modern hope and by its light
　　We have lit upon the gentle, sensitive mind

And lost the old nonchalance of the hand;
Whether we have chosen chisel, pen or brush,
We are but critics, or but half create,
Timid, entangled, empty and abashed,
Lacking the countenance of our friends.

Hic.   And yet
The chief imagination of Christendom,
Dante Alighieri, so utterly found himself
20   That he has made that hollow face of his
More plain to the mind's eye than any face
But that of Christ.

Ille.   And did he find himself
Or was the hunger that had made it hollow
A hunger for the apple on the bough
Most out of reach? and is that spectral image
The man that Lapo and that Guido knew?
I think he fashioned from his opposite
An image that might have been a stony face
Staring upon a Bedouin's horse-hair roof
30   From doored and windowed cliff, or half upturned
Among the coarse grass and the camel-dung.
He set his chisel to the hardest stone.
Being mocked by Guido for his lecherous life,
Derided and deriding, driven out
To climb that stair and eat that bitter bread,
He found the unpersuadable justice, he found
The most exalted lady loved by a man.

Hic. Yet surely there are men who have made their art
Out of no tragic war, lovers of life,
40   Impulsive men that look for happiness
And sing when they have found it.

Ille.   No, not sing,
For those that love the world serve it in action,
Grow rich, popular and full of influence,
And should they paint or write, still it is action:
The struggle of the fly in marmalade.

The rhetorician would deceive his neighbours,
The sentimentalist himself; while art
Is but a vision of reality.
What portion in the world can the artist have
Who has awakened from the common dream   50
But dissipation and despair?

Hic.   And yet
    No one denies to Keats love of the world;
    Remember his deliberate happiness.

Ille. His art is happy, but who knows his mind?
    I see a schoolboy when I think of him,
    With face and nose pressed to a sweet-shop window,
    For certainly he sank into his grave
    His senses and his heart unsatisfied,
    And made—being poor, ailing and ignorant,
    Shut out from all the luxury of the world,   60
    The coarse-bred son of a livery-stable keeper—
    Luxuriant song.

Hic.   Why should you leave the lamp
    Burning alone beside an open book,
    And trace these characters upon the sands?
    A style is found by sedentary toil
    And by the imitation of great masters.

Ille. Because I seek an image, not a book.
    Those men that in their writings are most wise
    Own nothing but their blind, stupefied hearts.
    I call to the mysterious one who yet   70
    Shall walk the wet sands by the edge of the stream
    And look most like me, being indeed my double,
    And prove of all imaginable things
    The most unlike, being my anti-self,
    And standing by these characters disclose
    All that I seek; and whisper it as though
    He were afraid the birds, who cry aloud
    Their momentary cries before it is dawn,
    Would carry it away to blasphemous men.

182

A Prayer on going into my House

God grant a blessing on this tower and cottage
And on my heirs, if all remain unspoiled,
No table or chair or stool not simple enough
For shepherd lads in Galilee; and grant
That I myself for portions of the year
May handle nothing and set eyes on nothing
But what the great and passionate have used
Throughout so many varying centuries
We take it for the norm; yet should I dream
Sinbad the sailor's brought a painted chest,
Or image, from beyond the Loadstone Mountain,
That dream is a norm; and should some limb of the devil
Destroy the view by cutting down an ash
That shades the road, or setting up a cottage
Planned in a government office, shorten his life,
Manacle his soul upon the Red Sea bottom.

183

The Phases of the Moon

An old man cocked his ear upon a bridge;
He and his friend, their faces to the South,
Had trod the uneven road. Their boots were soiled,
Their Connemara cloth worn out of shape;
They had kept a steady pace as though their beds,
Despite a dwindling and late risen moon,
Were distant still. An old man cocked his ear.

Aherne. What made that sound?

Robartes.   A rat or water-hen
    Splashed, or an otter slid into the stream.
    We are on the bridge; that shadow is the tower,

And the light proves that he is reading still.
He has found, after the manner of his kind,
Mere images; chosen this place to live in
Because, it may be, of the candle-light
From the far tower where Milton's Platonist
Sat late, or Shelley's visionary prince:
The lonely light that Samuel Palmer engraved,
An image of mysterious wisdom won by toil;
And now he seeks in book or manuscript
What he shall never find.

Aherne.   Why should not you   20
  Who know it all ring at his door, and speak
  Just truth enough to show that his whole life
  Will scarcely find for him a broken crust
  Of all those truths that are your daily bread;
  And when you have spoken take the roads again?

Robartes. He wrote of me in that extravagant style
  He had learned from Pater, and to round his tale
  Said I was dead; and dead I choose to be.

Aherne. Sing me the changes of the moon once more;
  True song, though speech: 'mine author sung it me'.   30

Robartes. Twenty-and-eight the phases of the moon,
  The full and the moon's dark and all the crescents,
  Twenty-and-eight, and yet but six-and-twenty
  The cradles that a man must needs be rocked in;
  For there's no human life at the full or the dark.
  From the first crescent to the half, the dream
  But summons to adventure, and the man
  Is always happy like a bird or a beast;
  But while the moon is rounding towards the full
  He follows whatever whim's most difficult   40
  Among whims not impossible, and though scarred,
  As with the cat-o'-nine-tails of the mind,
  His body moulded from within his body
  Grows comelier. Eleven pass, and then
  Athena takes Achilles by the hair,

Hector is in the dust, Nietzsche is born,
Because the hero's crescent is the twelfth.
And yet, twice born, twice buried, grow he must,
Before the full moon, helpless as a worm.
50   The thirteenth moon but sets the soul at war
In its own being, and when that war's begun
There is no muscle in the arm; and after,
Under the frenzy of the fourteenth moon,
The soul begins to tremble into stillness,
To die into the labyrinth of itself!

Aherne. Sing out the song; sing to the end, and sing
The strange reward of all that discipline.

Robartes. All thought becomes an image and the soul
Becomes a body: that body and that soul
60   Too perfect at the full to lie in a cradle,
Too lonely for the traffic of the world:
Body and soul cast out and cast away
Beyond the visible world.

Aherne.   All dreams of the soul
End in a beautiful man's or woman's body.

Robartes. Have you not always known it?

Aherne.   The song will have it
That those that we have loved got their long fingers
From death, and wounds, or on Sinai's top,
Or from some bloody whip in their own hands.
They ran from cradle to cradle till at last
70   Their beauty dropped out of the loneliness
Of body and soul.

Robartes.   The lover's heart knows that.

Aherne. It must be that the terror in their eyes
Is memory or foreknowledge of the hour
When all is fed with light and heaven is bare.

Robartes. When the moon's full those creatures of the full
Are met on the waste hills by country men

Who shudder and hurry by: body and soul
Estranged amid the strangeness of themselves,
Caught up in contemplation, the mind's eye
Fixed upon images that once were thought, 80
For perfected, completed, and immovable
Images can break the solitude
Of lovely, satisfied, indifferent eyes.

And thereupon with aged, high-pitched voice
Aherne laughed, thinking of the man within,
His sleepless candle and laborious pen.

Robartes. And after that the crumbling of the moon:
    The soul remembering its loneliness
    Shudders in many cradles; all is changed.
    It would be the world's servant, and as it serves, 90
    Choosing whatever task's most difficult
    Among tasks not impossible, it takes
    Upon the body and upon the soul
    The coarseness of the drudge.

Aherne.   Before the full
    It sought itself and afterwards the world.

Robartes. Because you are forgotten, half out of life,
    And never wrote a book, your thought is clear.
    Reformer, merchant, statesman, learned man,
    Dutiful husband, honest wife by turn,
    Cradle upon cradle, and all in flight and all 100
    Deformed, because there is no deformity
    But saves us from a dream.

Aherne.   And what of those
    That the last servile crescent has set free?

Robartes. Because all dark, like those that are all light,
    They are cast beyond the verge, and in a cloud,
    Crying to one another like the bats;
    But having no desire they cannot tell
    What's good or bad, or what it is to triumph
    At the perfection of one's own obedience;

110 And yet they speak what's blown into the mind;
Deformed beyond deformity, unformed,
Insipid as the dough before it is baked,
They change their bodies at a word.

Aherne.   And then?

Robartes. When all the dough has been so kneaded up
That it can take what form cook Nature fancies,
The first thin crescent is wheeled round once more.

Aherne. But the escape; the song's not finished yet.

Robartes. Hunchback and Saint and Fool are the last crescents.
The burning bow that once could shoot an arrow
120 Out of the up and down, the wagon-wheel
Of beauty's cruelty and wisdom's chatter—
Out of that raving tide—is drawn betwixt
Deformity of body and of mind.

Aherne. Were not our beds far off I'd ring the bell,
Stand under the rough roof-timbers of the hall
Beside the castle door, where all is stark
Austerity, a place set out for wisdom
That he will never find; I'd play a part;
He would never know me after all these years
130 But take me for some drunken country man;
I'd stand and mutter there until he caught
'Hunchback and Saint and Fool', and that they came
Under the three last crescents of the moon,
And then I'd stagger out. He'd crack his wits
Day after day, yet never find the meaning.

*And then he laughed to think that what seemed hard
Should be so simple—a bat rose from the hazels
And circled round him with its squeaky cry,
The light in the tower window was put out.*

184

The Cat and the Moon

The cat went here and there
And the moon spun round like a top,
And the nearest kin of the moon,
The creeping cat, looked up.
Black Minnaloushe stared at the moon,
For, wander and wail as he would,
The pure cold light in the sky
Troubled his animal blood.
Minnaloushe runs in the grass
Lifting his delicate feet.   10
Do you dance, Minnaloushe, do you dance?
When two close kindred meet,
What better than call a dance?
Maybe the moon may learn,
Tired of that courtly fashion,
A new dance turn.
Minnaloushe creeps through the grass
From moonlit place to place,
The sacred moon overhead
Has taken a new phase.   20
Does Minnaloushe know that his pupils
Will pass from change to change,
And that from round to crescent,
From crescent to round they range?
Minnaloushe creeps through the grass
Alone, important and wise,
And lifts to the changing moon
His changing eyes.

185

The Saint and the Hunchback

Hunchback. Stand up and lift your hand and bless
    A man that finds great bitterness
    In thinking of his lost renown.
    A Roman Caesar is held down
    Under this hump.

Saint.   God tries each man
    According to a different plan.
    I shall not cease to bless because
    I lay about me with the taws
    That night and morning I may thrash
    Greek Alexander from my flesh,
    Augustus Caesar, and after these
    That great rogue Alcibiades.

Hunchback. To all that in your flesh have stood
    And blessed, I give my gratitude,
    Honoured by all in their degrees,
    But most to Alcibiades.

186

Two Songs of a Fool

I

A speckled cat and a tame hare
Eat at my hearthstone
And sleep there;
And both look up to me alone
For learning and defence
As I look up to Providence.

I start out of my sleep to think
Some day I may forget
Their food and drink;

Or, the house door left unshut,   10
The hare may run till it's found
The horn's sweet note and the tooth of the hound.

I bear a burden that might well try
Men that do all by rule,
And what can I
That am a wandering-witted fool
But pray to God that He ease
My great responsibilities?

II

I slept on my three-legged stool by the fire,
The speckled cat slept on my knee;
We never thought to enquire
Where the brown hare might be,
And whether the door were shut.
Who knows how she drank the wind
Stretched up on two legs from the mat,
Before she had settled her mind
To drum with her heel and to leap?
Had I but awakened from sleep   10
And called her name, she had heard,
It may be, and had not stirred,
That now, it may be, has found
The horn's sweet note and the tooth of the hound.

187

Another Song of a Fool

This great purple butterfly,
In the prison of my hands,
Has a learning in his eye
Not a poor fool understands.

Once he lived a schoolmaster
With a stark, denying look;
A string of scholars went in fear
Of his great birch and his great book.

Like the clangour of a bell,
Sweet and harsh, harsh and sweet,
That is how he learnt so well
To take the roses for his meat.

188

The Double Vision of Michael Robartes

I

On the grey rock of Cashel the mind's eye
Has called up the cold spirits that are born
When the old moon is vanished from the sky
And the new still hides her horn.

Under blank eyes and fingers never still
The particular is pounded till it is man.
When had I my own will?
O not since life began.

Constrained, arraigned, baffled, bent and unbent
By these wire-jointed jaws and limbs of wood,
Themselves obedient,
Knowing not evil and good;

Obedient to some hidden magical breath.
They do not even feel, so abstract are they,
So dead beyond our death,
Triumph that we obey.

II

On the grey rock of Cashel I suddenly saw
A Sphinx with woman breast and lion paw,
A Buddha, hand at rest,
Hand lifted up that blest;   20

And right between these two a girl at play
That, it may be, had danced her life away,
For now being dead it seemed
That she of dancing dreamed.

Although I saw it all in the mind's eye
There can be nothing solider till I die;
I saw by the moon's light
Now at its fifteenth night.

One lashed her tail; her eyes lit by the moon
Gazed upon all things known, all things unknown,   30
In triumph of intellect
With motionless head erect.

That other's moonlit eyeballs never moved,
Being fixed on all things loved, all things unloved,
Yet little peace he had,
For those that love are sad.

O little did they care who danced between,
And little she by whom her dance was seen
So she had outdanced thought.
Body perfection brought,   40

For what but eye and ear silence the mind
With the minute particulars of mankind?
Mind moved yet seemed to stop
As 'twere a spinning-top.

In contemplation had those three so wrought
Upon a moment, and so stretched it out
That they, time overthrown,
Were dead yet flesh and bone.

III

I knew that I had seen, had seen at last
50 That girl my unremembering nights hold fast
Or else my dreams that fly
If I should rub an eye,

And yet in flying fling into my meat
A crazy juice that makes the pulses beat
As though I had been undone
By Homer's Paragon

Who never gave the burning town a thought;
To such a pitch of folly I am brought,
Being caught between the pull
60 Of the dark moon and the full,

The commonness of thought and images
That have the frenzy of our western seas.
Thereon I made my moan,
And after kissed a stone,

And after that arranged it in a song
Seeing that I, ignorant for so long,
Had been rewarded thus
In Cormac's ruined house.

Michael Robartes
and the Dancer

1921

Michael Robartes and the Dancer

He. Opinion is not worth a rush;
   In this altar-piece the knight,
   Who grips his long spear so to push
   That dragon through the fading light,
   Loved the lady; and it's plain
   The half-dead dragon was her thought,
   That every morning rose again
   And dug its claws and shrieked and fought.
   Could the impossible come to pass
   She would have time to turn her eyes,   10
   Her lover thought, upon the glass
   And on the instant would grow wise.

She. You mean they argued.

He.   Put it so;
   But bear in mind your lover's wage
   Is what your looking-glass can show,
   And that he will turn green with rage
   At all that is not pictured there.

She. May I not put myself to college?

He. Go pluck Athena by the hair;
   For what mere book can grant a knowledge   20
   With an impassioned gravity
   Appropriate to that beating breast,
   That vigorous thigh, that dreaming eye?
   And may the devil take the rest.

She. And must no beautiful woman be
   Learned like a man?

He.   Paul Veronese
          And all his sacred company
          Imagined bodies all their days
          By the lagoon you love so much,
30   For proud, soft, ceremonious proof
          That all must come to sight and touch;
          While Michael Angelo's Sistine roof,
          His 'Morning' and his 'Night' disclose
          How sinew that has been pulled tight,
          Or it may be loosened in repose,
          Can rule by supernatural right
          Yet be but sinew.

She.   I have heard said
          There is great danger in the body.

He. Did God in portioning wine and bread
40   Give man His thought or His mere body?

She. My wretched dragon is perplexed.

He. I have principles to prove me right.
          It follows from this Latin text
          That blest souls are not composite,
          And that all beautiful women may
          Live in uncomposite blessedness,
          And lead us to the like—if they
          Will banish every thought, unless
          The lineaments that please their view
50   When the long looking-glass is full,
          Even from the foot-sole think it too.

She. They say such different things at school.

190

Solomon and the Witch

And thus declared that Arab lady:
'Last night, where under the wild moon
On grassy mattress I had laid me,
Within my arms great Solomon,
I suddenly cried out in a strange tongue
Not his, not mine.'
                            Who understood
Whatever has been said, sighed, sung,
Howled, miau-d, barked, brayed, belled, yelled,
     cried, crowed,
Thereon replied: 'A cockerel
Crew from a blossoming apple bough   10
Three hundred years before the Fall,
And never crew again till now,
And would not now but that he thought,
Chance being at one with Choice at last,
All that the brigand apple brought
And this foul world were dead at last.
He that crowed out eternity
Thought to have crowed it in again.
For though love has a spider's eye
To find out some appropriate pain—   20
Aye, though all passion's in the glance—
For every nerve, and tests a lover
With cruelties of Choice and Chance;
And when at last that murder's over
Maybe the bride-bed brings despair,
For each an imagined image brings
And finds a real image there;
Yet the world ends when these two things,
Though several, are a single light,
When oil and wick are burned in one;   30
Therefore a blessed moon last night
Gave Sheba to her Solomon.'

'Yet the world stays.'
                  'If that be so,
Your cockerel found us in the wrong
Although he thought it worth a crow.
Maybe an image is too strong
Or maybe is not strong enough.'

'The night has fallen; not a sound
In the forbidden sacred grove
Unless a petal hit the ground,
Nor any human sight within it
But the crushed grass where we have lain;
And the moon is wilder every minute.
O! Solomon! let us try again.'

191

An Image from a Past Life

He. Never until this night have I been stirred.
The elaborate star-light throws a reflection
On the dark stream,
Till all the eddies gleam;
And thereupon there comes that scream
From terrified, invisible beast or bird:
Image of poignant recollection.

She. An image of my heart that is smitten through
Out of all likelihood, or reason,
And when at last,
Youth's bitterness being past,
I had thought that all my days were cast
Amid most lovely places; smitten as though
It had not learned its lesson.

He. Why have you laid your hands upon my eyes?
What can have suddenly alarmed you
Whereon 'twere best
My eyes should never rest?

What is there but the slowly fading west,
The river imaging the flashing skies,   20
All that to this moment charmed you?

She. A sweetheart from another life floats there
As though she had been forced to linger
From vague distress
Or arrogant loveliness,
Merely to loosen out a tress
Among the starry eddies of her hair
Upon the paleness of a finger.

He. But why should you grow suddenly afraid
And start—I at your shoulder—   30
Imagining
That any night could bring
An image up, or anything
Even to eyes that beauty had driven mad,
But images to make me fonder?

She. Now she has thrown her arms above her head;
Whether she threw them up to flout me,
Or but to find,
Now that no fingers bind,
That her hair streams upon the wind,   40
I do not know, that know I am afraid
Of the hovering thing night brought me.

192

Under Saturn

Do not because this day I have grown saturnine
Imagine that lost love, inseparable from my thought
Because I have no other youth, can make me pine;
For how should I forget the wisdom that you brought,
The comfort that you made? Although my wits have gone
On a fantastic ride, my horse's flanks are spurred
By childish memories of an old cross Pollexfen,

And of a Middleton, whose name you never heard,
And of a red-haired Yeats whose looks, although he died
Before my time, seem like a vivid memory.
You heard that labouring man who had served my people.
    He said
Upon the open road, near to the Sligo quay—
No, no, not said, but cried it out—'You have come again,
And surely after twenty years it was time to come.'
I am thinking of a child's vow sworn in vain
Never to leave that valley his fathers called their home.

November 1919

193

Easter, 1916

I have met them at close of day
Coming with vivid faces
From counter or desk among grey
Eighteenth-century houses.
I have passed with a nod of the head
Or polite meaningless words,
Or have lingered awhile and said
Polite meaningless words,
And thought before I had done
Of a mocking tale or a gibe
To please a companion
Around the fire at the club,
Being certain that they and I
But lived where motley is worn:
All changed, changed utterly:
A terrible beauty is born.

That woman's days were spent
In ignorant good-will,
Her nights in argument
Until her voice grew shrill.
What voice more sweet than hers

When, young and beautiful,
She rode to harriers?
This man had kept a school
And rode our wingèd horse;
This other his helper and friend
Was coming into his force;
He might have won fame in the end,
So sensitive his nature seemed,
So daring and sweet his thought.   30

This other man I had dreamed
A drunken, vainglorious lout.
He had done most bitter wrong
To some who are near my heart,
Yet I number him in the song;
He, too, has resigned his part
In the casual comedy;
He, too, has been changed in his turn,
Transformed utterly:
A terrible beauty is born.   40

Hearts with one purpose alone
Through summer and winter seem
Enchanted to a stone
To trouble the living stream.
The horse that comes from the road,
The rider, the birds that range
From cloud to tumbling cloud,
Minute by minute they change;
A shadow of cloud on the stream
Changes minute by minute;   50
A horse-hoof slides on the brim,
And a horse plashes within it;
The long-legged moor-hens dive,
And hens to moor-cocks call;
Minute by minute they live:
The stone's in the midst of all.

Too long a sacrifice
Can make a stone of the heart.
O when may it suffice?
60   That is Heaven's part, our part
To murmur name upon name,
As a mother names her child
When sleep at last has come
On limbs that had run wild.
What is it but nightfall?
No, no, not night but death;
Was it needless death after all?

For England may keep faith
For all that is done and said.
70   We know their dream; enough
To know they dreamed and are dead;
And what if excess of love
Bewildered them till they died?
I write it out in a verse—
MacDonagh and MacBride
And Connolly and Pearse
Now and in time to be,
Wherever green is worn,
Are changed, changed utterly:
80   A terrible beauty is born.

September 25, 1916

194

Sixteen Dead Men

O but we talked at large before
The sixteen men were shot,
But who can talk of give and take,
What should be and what not
While those dead men are loitering there
To stir the boiling pot?

You say that we should still the land
Till Germany's overcome;
But who is there to argue that
Now Pearse is deaf and dumb? 10
And is their logic to outweigh
MacDonagh's bony thumb?

How could you dream they'd listen
That have an ear alone
For those new comrades they have found,
Lord Edward and Wolfe Tone,
Or meddle with our give and take
That converse bone to bone?

195

The Rose Tree

'O words are lightly spoken,'
Said Pearse to Connolly,
'Maybe a breath of politic words
Has withered our Rose Tree;
Or maybe but a wind that blows
Across the bitter sea.'

'It needs to be but watered,'
James Connolly replied,
'To make the green come out again
And spread on every side, 10
And shake the blossom from the bud
To be the garden's pride.'

'But where can we draw water,'
Said Pearse to Connolly,
'When all the wells are parched away?
O plain as plain can be
There's nothing but our own red blood
Can make a right Rose Tree.'

196

On a Political Prisoner

She that but little patience knew,
From childhood on, had now so much
A grey gull lost its fear and flew
Down to her cell and there alit,
And there endured her fingers' touch
And from her fingers ate its bit.

Did she in touching that lone wing
Recall the years before her mind
Became a bitter, an abstract thing,
Her thought some popular enmity:
Blind and leader of the blind
Drinking the foul ditch where they lie?

When long ago I saw her ride
Under Ben Bulben to the meet,
The beauty of her country-side
With all youth's lonely wildness stirred,
She seemed to have grown clean and sweet
Like any rock-bred, sea-borne bird:

Sea-borne, or balanced on the air
When first it sprang out of the nest
Upon some lofty rock to stare
Upon the cloudy canopy,
While under its storm-beaten breast
Cried out the hollows of the sea.

197

The Leaders of the Crowd

They must to keep their certainty accuse
All that are different of a base intent;
Pull down established honour; hawk for news
Whatever their loose phantasy invent
And murmur it with bated breath, as though

The abounding gutter had been Helicon
Or calumny a song. How can they know
Truth flourishes where the student's lamp has shone,
And there alone, that have no solitude?
So the crowd come they care not what may come.   10
They have loud music, hope every day renewed
And heartier loves; that lamp is from the tomb.

198

Towards Break of Day

Was it the double of my dream
The woman that by me lay
Dreamed, or did we halve a dream
Under the first cold gleam of day?

I thought: 'There is a waterfall
Upon Ben Bulben side
That all my childhood counted dear;
Were I to travel far and wide
I could not find a thing so dear.'
My memories had magnified   10
So many times childish delight.

I would have touched it like a child
But knew my finger could but have touched
Cold stone and water. I grew wild
Even accusing Heaven because
It had set down among its laws:
Nothing that we love over-much
Is ponderable to our touch.

I dreamed towards break of day,
The cold blown spray in my nostril.   20
But she that beside me lay
Had watched in bitterer sleep
The marvellous stag of Arthur,
That lofty white stag, leap
From mountain steep to steep.

199

Demon and Beast

For certain minutes at the least
That crafty demon and that loud beast
That plague me day and night
Ran out of my sight;
Though I had long perned in the gyre,
Between my hatred and desire,
I saw my freedom won
And all laugh in the sun.

The glittering eyes in a death's head
Of old Luke Wadding's portrait said
Welcome, and the Ormondes all
Nodded upon the wall,
And even Strafford smiled as though
It made him happier to know
I understood his plan.
Now that the loud beast ran
There was no portrait in the Gallery
But beckoned to sweet company,
For all men's thoughts grew clear
Being dear as mine are dear.

But soon a tear-drop started up,
For aimless joy had made me stop
Beside the little lake
To watch a white gull take
A bit of bread thrown up into the air;
Now gyring down and perning there
He splashed where an absurd
Portly green-pated bird
Shook off the water from his back;
Being no more demoniac
A stupid happy creature
Could rouse my whole nature.

Yet I am certain as can be
That every natural victory
Belongs to beast or demon,
That never yet had freeman
Right mastery of natural things,
And that mere growing old, that brings
Chilled blood, this sweetness brought;
Yet have no dearer thought   40
Than that I may find out a way
To make it linger half a day.

O what a sweetness strayed
Through barren Thebaid,
Or by the Mareotic sea
When that exultant Anthony
And twice a thousand more
Starved upon the shore
And withered to a bag of bones!
What had the Caesars but their thrones?   50

200

The Second Coming

Turning and turning in the widening gyre
The falcon cannot hear the falconer;
Things fall apart; the centre cannot hold;
Mere anarchy is loosed upon the world,
The blood-dimmed tide is loosed, and everywhere
The ceremony of innocence is drowned;
The best lack all conviction, while the worst
Are full of passionate intensity.

Surely some revelation is at hand;
Surely the Second Coming is at hand.   10
The Second Coming! Hardly are those words out
When a vast image out of *Spiritus Mundi*
Troubles my sight: somewhere in sands of the desert
A shape with lion body and the head of a man,
A gaze blank and pitiless as the sun,

Is moving its slow thighs, while all about it
Reel shadows of the indignant desert birds.
The darkness drops again; but now I know
That twenty centuries of stony sleep
20　　Were vexed to nightmare by a rocking cradle,
And what rough beast, its hour come round at last,
Slouches towards Bethlehem to be born?

2 0 1

A Prayer for my Daughter

Once more the storm is howling, and half hid
Under this cradle-hood and coverlid
My child sleeps on. There is no obstacle
But Gregory's wood and one bare hill
Whereby the haystack- and roof-levelling wind,
Bred on the Atlantic, can be stayed;
And for an hour I have walked and prayed
Because of the great gloom that is in my mind.

I have walked and prayed for this young child an hour
10　　And heard the sea-wind scream upon the tower,
And under the arches of the bridge, and scream
In the elms above the flooded stream;
Imagining in excited reverie
That the future years had come,
Dancing to a frenzied drum,
Out of the murderous innocence of the sea.

May she be granted beauty and yet not
Beauty to make a stranger's eye distraught,
Or hers before a looking-glass, for such,
20　　Being made beautiful overmuch,
Consider beauty a sufficient end,
Lose natural kindness and maybe
The heart-revealing intimacy
That chooses right, and never find a friend.

Helen being chosen found life flat and dull
And later had much trouble from a fool,
While that great Queen, that rose out of the spray,
Being fatherless could have her way
Yet chose a bandy-leggèd smith for man.
It's certain that fine women eat   30
A crazy salad with their meat
Whereby the Horn of Plenty is undone.

In courtesy I'd have her chiefly learned;
Hearts are not had as a gift but hearts are earned
By those that are not entirely beautiful;
Yet many, that have played the fool
For beauty's very self, has charm made wise,
And many a poor man that has roved,
Loved and thought himself beloved,
From a glad kindness cannot take his eyes.   40

May she become a flourishing hidden tree
That all her thoughts may like the linnet be,
And have no business but dispensing round
Their magnanimities of sound,
Nor but in merriment begin a chase,
Nor but in merriment a quarrel.
O may she live like some green laurel
Rooted in one dear perpetual place.

My mind, because the minds that I have loved,
The sort of beauty that I have approved,   50
Prosper but little, has dried up of late,
Yet knows that to be choked with hate
May well be of all evil chances chief.
If there's no hatred in a mind
Assault and battery of the wind
Can never tear the linnet from the leaf.

An intellectual hatred is the worst,
So let her think opinions are accursed.
Have I not seen the loveliest woman born
Out of the mouth of Plenty's horn,
Because of her opinionated mind
Barter that horn and every good
By quiet natures understood
For an old bellows full of angry wind?

Considering that, all hatred driven hence,
The soul recovers radical innocence
And learns at last that it is self-delighting,
Self-appeasing, self-affrighting,
And that its own sweet will is Heaven's will;
She can, though every face should scowl
And every windy quarter howl
Or every bellows burst, be happy still.

And may her bridegroom bring her to a house
Where all's accustomed, ceremonious;
For arrogance and hatred are the wares
Peddled in the thoroughfares.
How but in custom and in ceremony
Are innocence and beauty born?
Ceremony's a name for the rich horn,
And custom for the spreading laurel tree.

June 1919

202

A Meditation in Time of War

For one throb of the artery,
While on that old grey stone I sat
Under the old wind-broken tree,
I knew that One is animate,
Mankind inanimate phantasy.

203

To be carved on a Stone at Thoor Ballylee

I, the poet William Yeats,
With old mill boards and sea-green slates,
And smithy work from the Gort forge,
Restored this tower for my wife George;
And may these characters remain
When all is ruin once again.

The Tower

1928

Sailing to Byzantium

I

That is no country for old men. The young
In one another's arms, birds in the trees,
—Those dying generations—at their song,
The salmon-falls, the mackerel-crowded seas,
Fish, flesh, or fowl, commend all summer long
Whatever is begotten, born, and dies.
Caught in that sensual music all neglect
Monuments of unageing intellect.

II

An aged man is but a paltry thing,
A tattered coat upon a stick, unless   10
Soul clap its hands and sing, and louder sing
For every tatter in its mortal dress,
Nor is there singing school but studying
Monuments of its own magnificence;
And therefore I have sailed the seas and come
To the holy city of Byzantium.

III

O sages standing in God's holy fire
As in the gold mosaic of a wall,
Come from the holy fire, perne in a gyre,
And be the singing-masters of my soul.   20
Consume my heart away; sick with desire
And fastened to a dying animal
It knows not what it is; and gather me
Into the artifice of eternity.

IV

Once out of nature I shall never take
My bodily form from any natural thing,
But such a form as Grecian goldsmiths make
Of hammered gold and gold enamelling
To keep a drowsy Emperor awake;
Or set upon a golden bough to sing
To lords and ladies of Byzantium
Of what is past, or passing, or to come.

1927

205

The Tower

I

What shall I do with this absurdity—
O heart, O troubled heart—this caricature,
Decrepit age that has been tied to me
As to a dog's tail?
                              Never had I more
Excited, passionate, fantastical
Imagination, nor an ear and eye
That more expected the impossible—
No, not in boyhood when with rod and fly,
Or the humbler worm, I climbed Ben Bulben's back
And had the livelong summer day to spend.
It seems that I must bid the Muse go pack,
Choose Plato and Plotinus for a friend
Until imagination, ear and eye,
Can be content with argument and deal
In abstract things; or be derided by
A sort of battered kettle at the heel.

II

I pace upon the battlements and stare
On the foundations of a house, or where
Tree, like a sooty finger, starts from the earth;
And send imagination forth   20
Under the day's declining beam, and call
Images and memories
From ruin or from ancient trees,
For I would ask a question of them all.

Beyond that ridge lived Mrs. French, and once
When every silver candlestick or sconce
Lit up the dark mahogany and the wine,
A serving-man, that could divine
That most respected lady's every wish,
Ran and with the garden shears   30
Clipped an insolent farmer's ears
And brought them in a little covered dish.

Some few remembered still when I was young
A peasant girl commended by a song,
Who'd lived somewhere upon that rocky place,
And praised the colour of her face,
And had the greater joy in praising her,
Remembering that, if walked she there,
Farmers jostled at the fair
So great a glory did the song confer.   40

And certain men, being maddened by those rhymes,
Or else by toasting her a score of times,
Rose from the table and declared it right
To test their fancy by their sight;
But they mistook the brightness of the moon
For the prosaic light of day—
Music had driven their wits astray—
And one was drowned in the great bog of Cloone.

Strange, but the man who made the song was blind;
Yet, now I have considered it, I find   50
That nothing strange; the tragedy began

With Homer that was a blind man,
And Helen has all living hearts betrayed.
O may the moon and sunlight seem
One inextricable beam,
For if I triumph I must make men mad.

And I myself created Hanrahan
And drove him drunk or sober through the dawn
From somewhere in the neighbouring cottages.
Caught by an old man's juggleries
He stumbled, tumbled, fumbled to and fro
And had but broken knees for hire
And horrible splendour of desire;
I thought it all out twenty years ago:

Good fellows shuffled cards in an old bawn;
And when that ancient ruffian's turn was on
He so bewitched the cards under his thumb
That all but the one card became
A pack of hounds and not a pack of cards,
And that he changed into a hare.
Hanrahan rose in frenzy there
And followed up those baying creatures towards—

O towards I have forgotten what—enough!
I must recall a man that neither love
Nor music nor an enemy's clipped ear
Could, he was so harried, cheer;
A figure that has grown so fabulous
There's not a neighbour left to say
When he finished his dog's day:
An ancient bankrupt master of this house.

Before that ruin came, for centuries,
Rough men-at-arms, cross-gartered to the knees
Or shod in iron, climbed the narrow stairs,
And certain men-at-arms there were
Whose images, in the Great Memory stored,
Come with loud cry and panting breast
To break upon a sleeper's rest
While their great wooden dice beat on the board.

As I would question all, come all who can;
Come old, necessitous, half-mounted man;   90
And bring beauty's blind rambling celebrant;
The red man the juggler sent
Through God-forsaken meadows; Mrs. French,
Gifted with so fine an ear;
The man drowned in a bog's mire,
When mocking muses chose the country wench.

Did all old men and women, rich and poor,
Who trod upon these rocks or passed this door,
Whether in public or in secret rage
As I do now against old age?   100
But I have found an answer in those eyes
That are impatient to be gone;
Go therefore; but leave Hanrahan,
For I need all his mighty memories.

Old lecher with a love on every wind,
Bring up out of that deep considering mind
All that you have discovered in the grave,
For it is certain that you have
Reckoned up every unforeknown, unseeing
Plunge, lured by a softening eye,   110
Or by a touch or a sigh,
Into the labyrinth of another's being;

Does the imagination dwell the most
Upon a woman won or woman lost?
If on the lost, admit you turned aside
From a great labyrinth out of pride,
Cowardice, some silly over-subtle thought
Or anything called conscience once;
And that if memory recur, the sun's
Under eclipse and the day blotted out.   120

                        III

    It is time that I wrote my will;
    I choose upstanding men
    That climb the streams until

The fountain leap, and at dawn
Drop their cast at the side
Of dripping stone; I declare
They shall inherit my pride,
The pride of people that were
Bound neither to Cause nor to State,
Neither to slaves that were spat on,
Nor to the tyrants that spat,
The people of Burke and of Grattan
That gave, though free to refuse—
Pride, like that of the morn,
When the headlong light is loose,
Or that of the fabulous horn,
Or that of the sudden shower
When all streams are dry,
Or that of the hour
When the swan must fix his eye
Upon a fading gleam,
Float out upon a long
Last reach of glittering stream
And there sing his last song.
And I declare my faith:
I mock Plotinus' thought
And cry in Plato's teeth,
Death and life were not
Till man made up the whole,
Made lock, stock and barrel
Out of his bitter soul,
Aye, sun and moon and star, all,
And further add to that
That, being dead, we rise,
Dream and so create
Translunar Paradise.

I have prepared my peace
With learned Italian things
And the proud stones of Greece,
Poet's imaginings
And memories of love,

Memories of the words of women,
All those things whereof
Man makes a superhuman
Mirror-resembling dream.

As at the loophole there
The daws chatter and scream,
And drop twigs layer upon layer.
When they have mounted up,
The mother bird will rest   170
On their hollow top,
And so warm her wild nest.

I leave both faith and pride
To young upstanding men
Climbing the mountain side,
That under bursting dawn
They may drop a fly;
Being of that metal made
Till it was broken by
This sedentary trade.   180

Now shall I make my soul,
Compelling it to study
In a learned school
Till the wreck of body,
Slow decay of blood,
Testy delirium
Or dull decrepitude,
Or what worse evil come—
The death of friends, or death
Of every brilliant eye   190
That made a catch in the breath—
Seem but the clouds of the sky
When the horizon fades;
Or a bird's sleepy cry
Among the deepening shades.

                        1926

Meditations in Time of Civil War

206

I. *Ancestral Houses*

Surely among a rich man's flowering lawns,
Amid the rustle of his planted hills,
Life overflows without ambitious pains;
And rains down life until the basin spills,
And mounts more dizzy high the more it rains
As though to choose whatever shape it wills
And never stoop to a mechanical
Or servile shape, at others' beck and call.

Mere dreams, mere dreams! Yet Homer had not sung
Had he not found it certain beyond dreams
That out of life's own self-delight had sprung
The abounding glittering jet; though now it seems
As if some marvellous empty sea-shell flung
Out of the obscure dark of the rich streams,
And not a fountain, were the symbol which
Shadows the inherited glory of the rich.

Some violent bitter man, some powerful man
Called architect and artist in, that they,
Bitter and violent men, might rear in stone
The sweetness that all longed for night and day,
The gentleness none there had ever known;
But when the master's buried mice can play,
And maybe the great-grandson of that house,
For all its bronze and marble, 's but a mouse.

O what if gardens where the peacock strays
With delicate feet upon old terraces,
Or else all Juno from an urn displays
Before the indifferent garden deities;
O what if levelled lawns and gravelled ways
Where slippered Contemplation finds his ease

And Childhood a delight for every sense,
But take our greatness with our violence?

What if the glory of escutcheoned doors,
And buildings that a haughtier age designed,
The pacing to and fro on polished floors
Amid great chambers and long galleries, lined
With famous portraits of our ancestors;
What if those things the greatest of mankind
Consider most to magnify, or to bless,
But take our greatness with our bitterness? 40

207

II. My House

An ancient bridge, and a more ancient tower,
A farmhouse that is sheltered by its wall,
An acre of stony ground,
Where the symbolic rose can break in flower,
Old ragged elms, old thorns innumerable,
The sound of the rain or sound
Of every wind that blows;
The stilted water-hen
Crossing stream again
Scared by the splashing of a dozen cows; 10

A winding stair, a chamber arched with stone,
A grey stone fireplace with an open hearth,
A candle and written page.
Il Penseroso's Platonist toiled on
In some like chamber, shadowing forth
How the daemonic rage
Imagined everything.
Benighted travellers
From markets and from fairs
Have seen his midnight candle glimmering. 20

Two men have founded here. A man-at-arms
Gathered a score of horse and spent his days

In this tumultuous spot,
Where through long wars and sudden night alarms
His dwindling score and he seemed castaways
Forgetting and forgot;
And I, that after me
My bodily heirs may find,
To exalt a lonely mind,
30   Befitting emblems of adversity.

208

III. My Table

Two heavy trestles, and a board
Where Sato's gift, a changeless sword,
By pen and paper lies,
That it may moralise
My days out of their aimlessness.
A bit of an embroidered dress
Covers its wooden sheath.
Chaucer had not drawn breath
When it was forged. In Sato's house,
10   Curved like new moon, moon-luminous,
It lay five hundred years.
Yet if no change appears
No moon; only an aching heart
Conceives a changeless work of art.
Our learned men have urged
That when and where 'twas forged
A marvellous accomplishment,
In painting or in pottery, went
From father unto son
20   And through the centuries ran
And seemed unchanging like the sword.
Soul's beauty being most adored,
Men and their business took
The soul's unchanging look;
For the most rich inheritor,

Knowing that none could pass Heaven's door
That loved inferior art,
Had such an aching heart
That he, although a country's talk
For silken clothes and stately walk, 30
Had waking wits; it seemed
Juno's peacock screamed.

209

IV. My Descendants

Having inherited a vigorous mind
From my old fathers, I must nourish dreams
And leave a woman and a man behind
As vigorous of mind, and yet it seems
Life scarce can cast a fragrance on the wind,
Scarce spread a glory to the morning beams,
But the torn petals strew the garden plot;
And there's but common greenness after that.

And what if my descendants lose the flower
Through natural declension of the soul, 10
Through too much business with the passing hour,
Through too much play, or marriage with a fool?
May this laborious stair and this stark tower
Become a roofless ruin that the owl
May build in the cracked masonry and cry
Her desolation to the desolate sky.

The Primum Mobile that fashioned us
Has made the very owls in circles move;
And I, that count myself most prosperous,
Seeing that love and friendship are enough, 20
For an old neighbour's friendship chose the house
And decked and altered it for a girl's love,
And know whatever flourish and decline
These stones remain their monument and mine.

210

v. The Road at My Door

An affable Irregular,
A heavily-built Falstaffian man,
Comes cracking jokes of civil war
As though to die by gunshot were
The finest play under the sun.

A brown Lieutenant and his men,
Half dressed in national uniform,
Stand at my door, and I complain
Of the foul weather, hail and rain,
A pear tree broken by the storm.

I count those feathered balls of soot
The moor-hen guides upon the stream,
To silence the envy in my thought;
And turn towards my chamber, caught
In the cold snows of a dream.

211

vi. The Stare's Nest by My Window

The bees build in the crevices
Of loosening masonry, and there
The mother birds bring grubs and flies.
My wall is loosening; honey-bees,
Come build in the empty house of the stare.

We are closed in, and the key is turned
On our uncertainty; somewhere
A man is killed, or a house burned,
Yet no clear fact to be discerned:
Come build in the empty house of the stare.

A barricade of stone or of wood;
Some fourteen days of civil war;

Last night they trundled down the road
That dead young soldier in his blood:
Come build in the empty house of the stare.

We had fed the heart on fantasies,
The heart's grown brutal from the fare;
More substance in our enmities
Than in our love; O honey-bees,
Come build in the empty house of the stare.   20

212

VII. I see Phantoms of Hatred and of the Heart's Fullness and of the Coming Emptiness

I climb to the tower-top and lean upon broken stone,
A mist that is like blown snow is sweeping over all,
Valley, river, and elms, under the light of a moon
That seems unlike itself, that seems unchangeable,
A glittering sword out of the east. A puff of wind
And those white glimmering fragments of the mist sweep by.
Frenzies bewilder, reveries perturb the mind;
Monstrous familiar images swim to the mind's eye.

'Vengeance upon the murderers,' the cry goes up,
'Vengeance for Jacques Molay.' In cloud-pale rags, or in lace,   10
The rage-driven, rage-tormented, and rage-hungry troop,
Trooper belabouring trooper, biting at arm or at face,
Plunges towards nothing, arms and fingers spreading wide
For the embrace of nothing; and I, my wits astray
Because of all that senseless tumult, all but cried
For vengeance on the murderers of Jacques Molay.

Their legs long, delicate and slender, aquamarine their eyes,
Magical unicorns bear ladies on their backs.
The ladies close their musing eyes. No prophecies,
Remembered out of Babylonian almanacs,   20
Have closed the ladies' eyes, their minds are but a pool
Where even longing drowns under its own excess;

Nothing but stillness can remain when hearts are full
Of their own sweetness, bodies of their loveliness.

The cloud-pale unicorns, the eyes of aquamarine,
The quivering half-closed eyelids, the rags of cloud or of lace,
Or eyes that rage has brightened, arms it has made lean,
Give place to an indifferent multitude, give place
To brazen hawks. Nor self-delighting reverie,
Nor hate of what's to come, nor pity for what's gone,
Nothing but grip of claw, and the eye's complacency,
The innumerable clanging wings that have put out the moon.

I turn away and shut the door, and on the stair
Wonder how many times I could have proved my worth
In something that all others understand or share;
But O! ambitious heart, had such a proof drawn forth
A company of friends, a conscience set at ease,
It had but made us pine the more. The abstract joy,
The half-read wisdom of daemonic images,
Suffice the ageing man as once the growing boy.

1923

213

Nineteen Hundred and Nineteen

I

Many ingenious lovely things are gone
That seemed sheer miracle to the multitude,
Protected from the circle of the moon
That pitches common things about. There stood
Amid the ornamental bronze and stone
An ancient image made of olive wood—
And gone are Phidias' famous ivories
And all the golden grasshoppers and bees.

We too had many pretty toys when young;
A law indifferent to blame or praise,
To bribe or threat; habits that made old wrong

Melt down, as it were wax in the sun's rays;
Public opinion ripening for so long
We thought it would outlive all future days.
O what fine thought we had because we thought
That the worst rogues and rascals had died out.

All teeth were drawn, all ancient tricks unlearned,
And a great army but a showy thing;
What matter that no cannon had been turned
Into a ploughshare? Parliament and king   20
Thought that unless a little powder burned
The trumpeters might burst with trumpeting
And yet it lack all glory; and perchance
The guardsmen's drowsy chargers would not prance.

Now days are dragon-ridden, the nightmare
Rides upon sleep: a drunken soldiery
Can leave the mother, murdered at her door,
To crawl in her own blood, and go scot-free;
The night can sweat with terror as before
We pieced our thoughts into philosophy,   30
And planned to bring the world under a rule,
Who are but weasels fighting in a hole.

He who can read the signs nor sink unmanned
Into the half-deceit of some intoxicant
From shallow wits; who knows no work can stand,
Whether health, wealth or peace of mind were spent
On master-work of intellect or hand,
No honour leave its mighty monument,
Has but one comfort left: all triumph would
But break upon his ghostly solitude.   40

But is there any comfort to be found?
Man is in love and loves what vanishes,
What more is there to say? That country round
None dared admit, if such a thought were his,
Incendiary or bigot could be found
To burn that stump on the Acropolis,
Or break in bits the famous ivories
Or traffic in the grasshoppers or bees.

II

When Loie Fuller's Chinese dancers enwound
50 A shining web, a floating ribbon of cloth,
It seemed that a dragon of air
Had fallen among dancers, had whirled them round
Or hurried them off on its own furious path;
So the Platonic Year
Whirls out new right and wrong,
Whirls in the old instead;
All men are dancers and their tread
Goes to the barbarous clangour of a gong.

III

Some moralist or mythological poet
60 Compares the solitary soul to a swan;
I am satisfied with that,
Satisfied if a troubled mirror show it,
Before that brief gleam of its life be gone,
An image of its state;
The wings half spread for flight,
The breast thrust out in pride
Whether to play, or to ride
Those winds that clamour of approaching night.

A man in his own secret meditation
70 Is lost amid the labyrinth that he has made
In art or politics;
Some Platonist affirms that in the station
Where we should cast off body and trade
The ancient habit sticks,
And that if our works could
But vanish with our breath
That were a lucky death,
For triumph can but mar our solitude.

The swan has leaped into the desolate heaven:
80 That image can bring wildness, bring a rage
To end all things, to end

What my laborious life imagined, even
The half-imagined, the half-written page;
O but we dreamed to mend
Whatever mischief seemed
To afflict mankind, but now
That winds of winter blow
Learn that we were crack-pated when we dreamed.

IV

We, who seven years ago
Talked of honour and of truth,   90
Shriek with pleasure if we show
The weasel's twist, the weasel's tooth.

V

Come let us mock at the great
That had such burdens on the mind
And toiled so hard and late
To leave some monument behind,
Nor thought of the levelling wind.

Come let us mock at the wise;
With all those calendars whereon
They fixed old aching eyes,   100
They never saw how seasons run,
And now but gape at the sun.

Come let us mock at the good
That fancied goodness might be gay,
And sick of solitude
Might proclaim a holiday:
Wind shrieked—and where are they?

Mock mockers after that
That would not lift a hand maybe
To help good, wise or great   110
To bar that foul storm out, for we
Traffic in mockery.

VI

Violence upon the roads: violence of horses;
Some few have handsome riders, are garlanded
On delicate sensitive ear or tossing mane,
But wearied running round and round in their courses
All break and vanish, and evil gathers head:
Herodias' daughters have returned again,
A sudden blast of dusty wind and after
120   Thunder of feet, tumult of images,
Their purpose in the labyrinth of the wind;
And should some crazy hand dare touch a daughter
All turn with amorous cries, or angry cries,
According to the wind, for all are blind.
But now wind drops, dust settles; thereupon
There lurches past, his great eyes without thought
Under the shadow of stupid straw-pale locks,
That insolent fiend Robert Artisson
To whom the love-lorn Lady Kyteler brought
130   Bronzed peacock feathers, red combs of her cocks.

1919

2 1 4

The Wheel

Through winter-time we call on spring,
And through the spring on summer call,
And when abounding hedges ring
Declare that winter's best of all;
And after that there's nothing good
Because the spring-time has not come—
Nor know that what disturbs our blood
Is but its longing for the tomb.

215

Youth and Age

Much did I rage when young,
Being by the world oppressed,
But now with flattering tongue
It speeds the parting guest.

1924

216

The New Faces

If you, that have grown old, were the first dead,
Neither catalpa tree nor scented lime
Should hear my living feet, nor would I tread
Where we wrought that shall break the teeth of Time.
Let the new faces play what tricks they will
In the old rooms; night can outbalance day,
Our shadows rove the garden gravel still,
The living seem more shadowy than they.

217

A Prayer for my Son

Bid a strong ghost stand at the head
That my Michael may sleep sound,
Nor cry, nor turn in the bed
Till his morning meal come round;
And may departing twilight keep
All dread afar till morning's back,
That his mother may not lack
Her fill of sleep.

Bid the ghost have sword in fist:
Some there are, for I avow

10

Such devilish things exist,
Who have planned his murder, for they know
Of some most haughty deed or thought
That waits upon his future days,
And would through hatred of the bays
Bring that to nought.

Though You can fashion everything
From nothing every day, and teach
The morning stars to sing,
You have lacked articulate speech
To tell Your simplest want, and known,
Wailing upon a woman's knee,
All of that worst ignominy
Of flesh and bone;

And when through all the town there ran
The servants of Your enemy,
A woman and a man,
Unless the Holy Writings lie,
Hurried through the smooth and rough
And through the fertile and waste,
Protecting, till the danger past,
With human love.

218

Two Songs from a Play

I

I saw a staring virgin stand
Where holy Dionysus died,
And tear the heart out of his side,
And lay the heart upon her hand
And bear that beating heart away;
And then did all the Muses sing
Of Magnus Annus at the spring,
As though God's death were but a play.

'Another Troy must rise and set,
Another lineage feed the crow,   10
Another Argo's painted prow
Drive to a flashier bauble yet.
The Roman Empire stood appalled:
It dropped the reins of peace and war
When that fierce virgin and her Star
Out of the fabulous darkness called.

II

In pity for man's darkening thought
He walked that room and issued thence
In Galilean turbulence;
The Babylonian starlight brought
A fabulous, formless darkness in;
Odour of blood when Christ was slain
Made all Platonic tolerance vain
And vain all Doric discipline.

Everything that man esteems
Endures a moment or a day.   10
Love's pleasure drives his love away,
The painter's brush consumes his dreams;
The herald's cry, the soldier's tread
Exhaust his glory and his might:
Whatever flames upon the night
Man's own resinous heart has fed.

2 1 9

Fragments

I

Locke sank into a swoon;
The Garden died;
God took the spinning-jenny
Out of his side.

II

Where got I that truth?
Out of a medium's mouth,
Out of nothing it came,
Out of the forest loam,
Out of dark night where lay
10   The crowns of Nineveh.

220

Leda and the Swan

A sudden blow: the great wings beating still
Above the staggering girl, her thighs caressed
By the dark webs, her nape caught in his bill,
He holds her helpless breast upon his breast.

How can those terrified vague fingers push
The feathered glory from her loosening thighs?
And how can body, laid in that white rush,
But feel the strange heart beating where it lies?

A shudder in the loins engenders there
10   The broken wall, the burning roof and tower
And Agamemnon dead.
                            Being so caught up,
So mastered by the brute blood of the air,
Did she put on his knowledge with his power
Before the indifferent beak could let her drop?

1923

221

On a Picture of
a Black Centaur by Edmund Dulac

Your hooves have stamped at the black margin of the wood,
Even where horrible green parrots call and swing.
My works are all stamped down into the sultry mud.
I knew that horse-play, knew it for a murderous thing.
What wholesome sun has ripened is wholesome food to eat,
And that alone; yet I, being driven half insane
Because of some green wing, gathered old mummy wheat
In the mad abstract dark and ground it grain by grain
And after baked it slowly in an oven; but now
I bring full-flavoured wine out of a barrel found   10
Where seven Ephesian topers slept and never knew
When Alexander's empire passed, they slept so sound.
Stretch out your limbs and sleep a long Saturnian sleep;
I have loved you better than my soul for all my words,
And there is none so fit to keep a watch and keep
Unwearied eyes upon those horrible green birds.

222

Among School Children

I

I walk through the long schoolroom questioning;
A kind old nun in a white hood replies;
The children learn to cipher and to sing,
To study reading-books and history,
To cut and sew, be neat in everything
In the best modern way—the children's eyes
In momentary wonder stare upon
A sixty-year-old smiling public man.

II

I dream of a Ledaean body, bent
Above a sinking fire, a tale that she
Told of a harsh reproof, or trivial event
That changed some childish day to tragedy—
Told, and it seemed that our two natures blent
Into a sphere from youthful sympathy,
Or else, to alter Plato's parable,
Into the yolk and white of the one shell.

III

And thinking of that fit of grief or rage
I look upon one child or t'other there
And wonder if she stood so at that age—
For even daughters of the swan can share
Something of every paddler's heritage—
And had that colour upon cheek or hair,
And thereupon my heart is driven wild:
She stands before me as a living child.

IV

Her present image floats into the mind—
Did Quattrocento finger fashion it
Hollow of cheek as though it drank the wind
And took a mess of shadows for its meat?
And I though never of Ledaean kind
Had pretty plumage once—enough of that,
Better to smile on all that smile, and show
There is a comfortable kind of old scarecrow.

V

What youthful mother, a shape upon her lap
Honey of generation had betrayed,
And that must sleep, shriek, struggle to escape
As recollection or the drug decide,

Would think her son, did she but see that shape
With sixty or more winters on its head,
A compensation for the pang of his birth,
Or the uncertainty of his setting forth?   40

VI

Plato thought nature but a spume that plays
Upon a ghostly paradigm of things;
Solider Aristotle played the taws
Upon the bottom of a king of kings;
World-famous golden-thighed Pythagoras
Fingered upon a fiddle-stick or strings
What a star sang and careless Muses heard:
Old clothes upon old sticks to scare a bird.

VII

Both nuns and mothers worship images,
But those the candles light are not as those   50
That animate a mother's reveries,
But keep a marble or a bronze repose.
And yet they too break hearts—O Presences
That passion, piety or affection knows,
And that all heavenly glory symbolise—
O self-born mockers of man's enterprise;

VIII

Labour is blossoming or dancing where
The body is not bruised to pleasure soul,
Nor beauty born out of its own despair,
Nor blear-eyed wisdom out of midnight oil.   60
O chestnut tree, great rooted blossomer,
Are you the leaf, the blossom or the bole?
O body swayed to music, O brightening glance,
How can we know the dancer from the dance?

223

Colonus' Praise
(From 'Oedipus at Colonus')

Chorus. Come praise Colonus' horses, and come praise
The wine-dark of the wood's intricacies,
The nightingale that deafens daylight there,
If daylight ever visit where,
Unvisited by tempest or by sun,
Immortal ladies tread the ground
Dizzy with harmonious sound,
Semele's lad a gay companion.

And yonder in the gymnasts' garden thrives
10   The self-sown, self-begotten shape that gives
Athenian intellect its mastery,
Even the grey-leaved olive-tree
Miracle-bred out of the living stone;
Nor accident of peace nor war
Shall wither that old marvel, for
The great grey-eyed Athena stares thereon.

Who comes into this country, and has come
Where golden crocus and narcissus bloom,
Where the Great Mother, mourning for her daughter
20   And beauty-drunken by the water
Glittering among grey-leaved olive-trees,
Has plucked a flower and sung her loss;
Who finds abounding Cephisus
Has found the loveliest spectacle there is.

Because this country has a pious mind
And so remembers that when all mankind
But trod the road, or splashed about the shore,
Poseidon gave it bit and oar,
Every Colonus lad or lass discourses
30   Of that oar and of that bit;
Summer and winter, day and night,
Of horses and horses of the sea, white horses.

224

Wisdom

The true faith discovered was
When painted panel, statuary,
Glass-mosaic, window-glass,
Amended what was told awry
By some peasant gospeller;
Swept the sawdust from the floor
Of that working-carpenter.
Miracle had its playtime where
In damask clothed and on a seat
Chryselephantine, cedar-boarded,   10
His majestic Mother sat
Stitching at a purple hoarded
That He might be nobly breeched
In starry towers of Babylon
Noah's freshet never reached.
King Abundance got Him on
Innocence; and Wisdom He.
That cognomen sounded best
Considering what wild infancy
Drove horror from His Mother's breast.   20

225

The Fool by the Roadside

When all works that have
From cradle run to grave
From grave to cradle run instead;
When thoughts that a fool
Has wound upon a spool
Are but loose thread, are but loose thread;

When cradle and spool are past
And I mere shade at last
Coagulate of stuff

10   Transparent like the wind,
      I think that I may find
      A faithful love, a faithful love.

226

Owen Aherne and his Dancers

I

A strange thing surely that my Heart, when love had come unsought
Upon the Norman upland or in that poplar shade,
Should find no burden but itself and yet should be worn out.
It could not bear that burden and therefore it went mad.

The south wind brought it longing, and the east wind despair,
The west wind made it pitiful, and the north wind afraid.
It feared to give its love a hurt with all the tempest there;
It feared the hurt that she could give and therefore it went mad.

I can exchange opinion with any neighbouring mind,
10   I have as healthy flesh and blood as any rhymer's had,
But O! my Heart could bear no more when the upland caught the
      wind;
I ran, I ran, from my love's side because my Heart went mad.

II

The Heart behind its rib laughed out. 'You have called me mad,'
      it said.
'Because I made you turn away and run from that young child;
How could she mate with fifty years that was so wildly bred?
Let the cage bird and the cage bird mate and the wild bird mate in
      the wild.'

'You but imagine lies all day, O murderer,' I replied.
'And all those lies have but one end, poor wretches to betray;
I did not find in any cage the woman at my side.
20   O but her heart would break to learn my thoughts are far away.'

'Speak all your mind,' my Heart sang out, 'speak all your mind;
   who cares,
Now that your tongue cannot persuade the child till she mistake
Her childish gratitude for love and match your fifty years?
O let her choose a young man now and all for his wild sake.'

A Man Young and Old

227

1. First Love

Though nurtured like the sailing moon
In beauty's murderous brood,
She walked awhile and blushed awhile
And on my pathway stood
Until I thought her body bore
A heart of flesh and blood.

But since I laid a hand thereon
And found a heart of stone
I have attempted many things
And not a thing is done,   10
For every hand is lunatic
That travels on the moon.

She smiled and that transfigured me
And left me but a lout,
Maundering here, and maundering there,
Emptier of thought
Than the heavenly circuit of its stars
When the moon sails out.

228

II. Human Dignity

Like the moon her kindness is,
If kindness I may call
What has no comprehension in't,
But is the same for all
As though my sorrow were a scene
Upon a painted wall.

So like a bit of stone I lie
Under a broken tree.
I could recover if I shrieked
My heart's agony
To passing bird, but I am dumb
From human dignity.

229

III. The Mermaid

A mermaid found a swimming lad,
Picked him for her own,
Pressed her body to his body,
Laughed; and plunging down
Forgot in cruel happiness
That even lovers drown.

230

IV. The Death of the Hare

I have pointed out the yelling pack,
The hare leap to the wood,
And when I pass a compliment
Rejoice as lover should

At the drooping of an eye,
At the mantling of the blood.

Then suddenly my heart is wrung
By her distracted air
And I remember wildness lost
And after, swept from there,   10
Am set down standing in the wood
At the death of the hare.

231

V. The Empty Cup

A crazy man that found a cup,
When all but dead of thirst,
Hardly dared to wet his mouth
Imagining, moon-accursed,
That another mouthful
And his beating heart would burst.
October last I found it too
But found it dry as bone,
And for that reason am I crazed
And my sleep is gone.   10

232

VI. His Memories

We should be hidden from their eyes,
Being but holy shows
And bodies broken like a thorn
Whereon the bleak north blows,
To think of buried Hector
And that none living knows.

The women take so little stock
In what I do or say

They'd sooner leave their cosseting
To hear a jackass bray;
My arms are like the twisted thorn
And yet there beauty lay;

The first of all the tribe lay there
And did such pleasure take—
She who had brought great Hector down
And put all Troy to wreck—
That she cried into this ear,
'Strike me if I shriek.'

233

VII. The Friends of his Youth

Laughter not time destroyed my voice
And put that crack in it,
And when the moon's pot-bellied
I get a laughing fit,
For that old Madge comes down the lane,
A stone upon her breast,
And a cloak wrapped about the stone,
And she can get no rest
With singing hush and hush-a-bye;
She that has been wild
And barren as a breaking wave
Thinks that the stone's a child.

And Peter that had great affairs
And was a pushing man
Shrieks, 'I am King of the Peacocks,'
And perches on a stone;
And then I laugh till tears run down
And the heart thumps at my side,
Remembering that her shriek was love
And that he shrieks from pride.

234

VIII. Summer and Spring

We sat under an old thorn-tree
And talked away the night,
Told all that had been said or done
Since first we saw the light,
And when we talked of growing up
Knew that we'd halved a soul
And fell the one in t'other's arms
That we might make it whole;
Then Peter had a murdering look,
For it seemed that he and she   10
Had spoken of their childish days
Under that very tree.
O what a bursting out there was,
And what a blossoming,
When we had all the summer-time
And she had all the spring!

235

IX. The Secrets of the Old

I have old women's secrets now
That had those of the young;
Madge tells me what I dared not think
When my blood was strong,
And what had drowned a lover once
Sounds like an old song.

Though Margery is stricken dumb
If thrown in Madge's way,
We three make up a solitude;
For none alive to-day   10
Can know the stories that we know
Or say the things we say:

How such a man pleased women most
Of all that are gone,
How such a pair loved many years
And such a pair but one,
Stories of the bed of straw
Or the bed of down.

236

X. His Wildness

O bid me mount and sail up there
Amid the cloudy wrack,
For Peg and Meg and Paris' love
That had so straight a back,
Are gone away, and some that stay
Have changed their silk for sack.

Were I but there and none to hear
I'd have a peacock cry,
For that is natural to a man
That lives in memory,
Being all alone I'd nurse a stone
And sing it lullaby.

10

237

XI. From 'Oedipus at Colonus'

Endure what life God gives and ask no longer span;
Cease to remember the delights of youth, travel-wearied aged man;
Delight becomes death-longing if all longing else be vain.

Even from that delight memory treasures so,
Death, despair, division of families, all entanglements of mankind
      grow,
As that old wandering beggar and these God-hated children know.

In the long echoing street the laughing dancers throng,
The bride is carried to the bridegroom's chamber through torchlight
　　and tumultuous song;
I celebrate the silent kiss that ends short life or long.

Never to have lived is best, ancient writers say;　　　　10
Never to have drawn the breath of life, never to have looked into
　　the eye of day;
The second best's a gay goodnight and quickly turn away.

238

The Three Monuments

They hold their public meetings where
Our most renownèd patriots stand,
One among the birds of the air,
A stumpier on either hand;
And all the popular statesmen say
That purity built up the State
And after kept it from decay;
Admonish us to cling to that
And let all base ambition be,
For intellect would make us proud　　　　10
And pride bring in impurity:
The three old rascals laugh aloud.

239

All Souls' Night

Epilogue to 'A Vision'

Midnight has come and the great Christ Church bell
And many a lesser bell sound through the room;
And it is All Souls' Night.
And two long glasses brimmed with muscatel
Bubble upon the table. A ghost may come;
For it is a ghost's right,

His element is so fine
Being sharpened by his death,
To drink from the wine-breath
While our gross palates drink from the whole wine.

I need some mind that, if the cannon sound
From every quarter of the world, can stay
Wound in mind's pondering,
As mummies in the mummy-cloth are wound;
Because I have a marvellous thing to say,
A certain marvellous thing
None but the living mock,
Though not for sober ear;
It may be all that hear
Should laugh and weep an hour upon the clock.

Horton's the first I call. He loved strange thought
And knew that sweet extremity of pride
That's called platonic love,
And that to such a pitch of passion wrought
Nothing could bring him, when his lady died,
Anodyne for his love.
Words were but wasted breath;
One dear hope had he:
The inclemency
Of that or the next winter would be death.

Two thoughts were so mixed up I could not tell
Whether of her or God he thought the most,
But think that his mind's eye,
When upward turned, on one sole image fell;
And that a slight companionable ghost,
Wild with divinity,
Had so lit up the whole
Immense miraculous house
The Bible promised us,
It seemed a gold-fish swimming in a bowl.

On Florence Emery I call the next,
Who finding the first wrinkles on a face
Admired and beautiful,

And by foreknowledge of the future vexed;
Diminished beauty, multiplied commonplace;
Preferred to teach a school
Away from neighbour or friend,
Among dark skins, and there
Permit foul years to wear
Hidden from eyesight to the unnoticed end.   50

Before that end much had she ravelled out
From a discourse in figurative speech
By some learned Indian
On the soul's journey. How it is whirled about
Wherever the orbit of the moon can reach,
Until it plunge into the sun;
And there, free and yet fast,
Being both Chance and Choice,
Forget its broken toys
And sink into its own delight at last.   60

I call MacGregor Mathers from his grave,
For in my first hard spring-time we were friends,
Although of late estranged.
I thought him half a lunatic, half knave,
And told him so, but friendship never ends;
And what if mind seem changed,
And it seem changed with the mind,
When thoughts rise up unbid
On generous things that he did
And I grow half contented to be blind!   70

He had much industry at setting out,
Much boisterous courage, before loneliness
Had driven him crazed;
For meditations upon unknown thought
Make human intercourse grow less and less;
They are neither paid nor praised.
But he'd object to the host,
The glass because my glass;
A ghost-lover he was
And may have grown more arrogant being a ghost.   80

But names are nothing. What matter who it be,
So that his elements have grown so fine
The fume of muscatel
Can give his sharpened palate ecstasy
No living man can drink from the whole wine.
I have mummy truths to tell
Whereat the living mock,
Though not for sober ear,
For maybe all that hear
90   Should laugh and weep an hour upon the clock.

Such thought—such thought have I that hold it tight
Till meditation master all its parts,
Nothing can stay my glance
Until that glance run in the world's despite
To where the damned have howled away their hearts,
And where the blessed dance;
Such thought, that in it bound
I need no other thing,
Wound in mind's wandering
100   As mummies in the mummy-cloth are wound.

Oxford, Autumn 1920

The Winding Stair
and Other Poems

1933

In Memory of
Eva Gore-Booth
and Con Markiewicz

The light of evening, Lissadell,
Great windows open to the south,
Two girls in silk kimonos, both
Beautiful, one a gazelle.
But a raving autumn shears
Blossom from the summer's wreath;
The older is condemned to death,
Pardoned, drags out lonely years
Conspiring among the ignorant.
I know not what the younger dreams—   10
Some vague Utopia—and she seems,
When withered old and skeleton-gaunt,
An image of such politics.
Many a time I think to seek
One or the other out and speak
Of that old Georgian mansion, mix
Pictures of the mind, recall
That table and the talk of youth,
Two girls in silk kimonos, both
Beautiful, one a gazelle.   20

Dear shadows, now you know it all,
All the folly of a fight
With a common wrong or right.
The innocent and the beautiful
Have no enemy but time;
Arise and bid me strike a match
And strike another till time catch;

Should the conflagration climb,
Run till all the sages know.
30   We the great gazebo built,
They convicted us of guilt;
Bid me strike a match and blow.

October 1927

2 4 1

Death

Nor dread nor hope attend
A dying animal;
A man awaits his end
Dreading and hoping all;
Many times he died,
Many times rose again.
A great man in his pride
Confronting murderous men
Casts derision upon
10   Supersession of breath;
He knows death to the bone—
Man has created death.

2 4 2

A Dialogue of Self and Soul

I

My Soul. I summon to the winding ancient stair;
    Set all your mind upon the steep ascent,
    Upon the broken, crumbling battlement,
    Upon the breathless starlit air,
    Upon the star that marks the hidden pole;
    Fix every wandering thought upon
    That quarter where all thought is done:
    Who can distinguish darkness from the soul?

My Self. The consecrated blade upon my knees
    Is Sato's ancient blade, still as it was,   10
    Still razor-keen, still like a looking-glass
    Unspotted by the centuries;
    That flowering, silken, old embroidery, torn
    From some court-lady's dress and round
    The wooden scabbard bound and wound,
    Can, tattered, still protect, faded adorn.

My Soul. Why should the imagination of a man
    Long past his prime remember things that are
    Emblematical of love and war?
    Think of ancestral night that can,   20
    If but imagination scorn the earth
    And intellect its wandering
    To this and that and t'other thing,
    Deliver from the crime of death and birth.

My Self. Montashigi, third of his family, fashioned it
    Five hundred years ago, about it lie
    Flowers from I know not what embroidery—
    Heart's purple—and all these I set
    For emblems of the day against the tower
    Emblematical of the night,   30
    And claim as by a soldier's right
    A charter to commit the crime once more.

My Soul. Such fullness in that quarter overflows
    And falls into the basin of the mind
    That man is stricken deaf and dumb and blind,
    For intellect no longer knows
    Is from the *Ought,* or *Knower* from the *Known*—
    That is to say, ascends to Heaven;
    Only the dead can be forgiven;
    But when I think of that my tongue's a stone.   40

II

My Self. A living man is blind and drinks his drop.
   What matter if the ditches are impure?
   What matter if I live it all once more?
   Endure that toil of growing up;
   The ignominy of boyhood; the distress
   Of boyhood changing into man;
   The unfinished man and his pain
   Brought face to face with his own clumsiness;

   The finished man among his enemies?—
50   How in the name of Heaven can he escape
   That defiling and disfigured shape
   The mirror of malicious eyes
   Casts upon his eyes until at last
   He thinks that shape must be his shape?
   And what's the good of an escape
   If honour find him in the wintry blast?

   I am content to live it all again
   And yet again, if it be life to pitch
   Into the frog-spawn of a blind man's ditch,
60   A blind man battering blind men;
   Or into that most fecund ditch of all,
   The folly that man does
   Or must suffer, if he woos
   A proud woman not kindred of his soul.

   I am content to follow to its source
   Every event in action or in thought;
   Measure the lot; forgive myself the lot!
   When such as I cast out remorse
   So great a sweetness flows into the breast
70   We must laugh and we must sing,
   We are blest by everything,
   Everything we look upon is blest.

243

Blood and the Moon

I

Blessed be this place,
More blessed still this tower;
A bloody, arrogant power
Rose out of the race
Uttering, mastering it,
Rose like these walls from these
Storm-beaten cottages—
In mockery I have set
A powerful emblem up,
And sing it rhyme upon rhyme   10
In mockery of a time
Half dead at the top.

II

Alexandria's was a beacon tower, and Babylon's
An image of the moving heavens, a log-book of the sun's journey
    and the moon's;
And Shelley had his towers, thought's crowned powers he called
    them once.

I declare this tower is my symbol; I declare
This winding, gyring, spiring treadmill of a stair is my ancestral
    stair;
That Goldsmith and the Dean, Berkeley and Burke have travelled
    there.

Swift beating on his breast in sibylline frenzy blind
Because the heart in his blood-sodden breast had dragged him
    down into mankind,   20
Goldsmith deliberately sipping at the honey-pot of his mind,

And haughtier-headed Burke that proved the State a tree,
That this unconquerable labyrinth of the birds, century after century,
Cast but dead leaves to mathematical equality;

And God-appointed Berkeley that proved all things a dream,
That this pragmatical, preposterous pig of a world, its farrow that
    so solid seem,
Must vanish on the instant if the mind but change its theme;

Saeva Indignatio and the labourer's hire,
The strength that gives our blood and state magnanimity of its
    own desire;
30   Everything that is not God consumed with intellectual fire.

                            III

        The purity of the unclouded moon
        Has flung its arrowy shaft upon the floor.
        Seven centuries have passed and it is pure;
        The blood of innocence has left no stain.
        There, on blood-saturated ground, have stood
        Soldier, assassin, executioner,
        Whether for daily pittance or in blind fear
        Or out of abstract hatred, and shed blood,
        But could not cast a single jet thereon.
40   Odour of blood on the ancestral stair!
        And we that have shed none must gather there
        And clamour in drunken frenzy for the moon.

                            IV

        Upon the dusty, glittering windows cling,
        And seem to cling upon the moonlit skies,
        Tortoiseshell butterflies, peacock butterflies.
        A couple of night-moths are on the wing.
        Is every modern nation like the tower,
        Half dead at the top? No matter what I said,
        For wisdom is the property of the dead,
50   A something incompatible with life; and power,
        Like everything that has the stain of blood,
        A property of the living; but no stain
        Can come upon the visage of the moon
        When it has looked in glory from a cloud.

244

Oil and Blood

In tombs of gold and lapis lazuli
Bodies of holy men and women exude
Miraculous oil, odour of violet.

But under heavy loads of trampled clay
Lie bodies of the vampires full of blood;
Their shrouds are bloody and their lips are wet.

245

Veronica's Napkin

The Heavenly Circuit; Berenice's Hair;
Tent-pole of Eden; the tent's drapery;
Symbolical glory of the earth and air!
The Father and His angelic hierarchy
That made the magnitude and glory there
Stood in the circuit of a needle's eye.

Some found a different pole, and where it stood
A pattern on a napkin dipped in blood.

246

Symbols

A storm-beaten old watch-tower,
A blind hermit rings the hour.

All-destroying sword-blade still
Carried by the wandering fool.

Gold-sewn silk on the sword-blade,
Beauty and fool together laid.

247

Spilt Milk

We that have done and thought,
That have thought and done,
Must ramble, and thin out
Like milk spilt on a stone.

248

The Nineteenth Century and After

Though the great song return no more
There's keen delight in what we have:
The rattle of pebbles on the shore
Under the receding wave.

249

Statistics

'Those Platonists are a curse,' he said,
'God's fire upon the wane,
A diagram hung there instead,
More women born than men.'

250

Three Movements

Shakespearean fish swam the sea, far away from land;
Romantic fish swam in nets coming to the hand;
What are all those fish that lie gasping on the strand?

251

The Seven Sages

The First. My great-grandfather spoke to Edmund Burke
   In Grattan's house.

The Second.   My great-grandfather shared
   A pot-house bench with Oliver Goldsmith once.

The Third. My great-grandfather's father talked of music,
   Drank tar-water with the Bishop of Cloyne.

The Fourth. But mine saw Stella once.

The Fifth.   Whence came our thought?

The Sixth. From four great minds that hated Whiggery.

The Fifth. Burke was a Whig.

The Sixth.   Whether they knew or not,
   Goldsmith and Burke, Swift and the Bishop of Cloyne
   All hated Whiggery; but what is Whiggery?   10
   A levelling, rancorous, rational sort of mind
   That never looked out of the eye of a saint
   Or out of drunkard's eye.

The Seventh.   All's Whiggery now,
   But we old men are massed against the world.

The First. American colonies, Ireland, France and India
   Harried, and Burke's great melody against it.

The Second. Oliver Goldsmith sang what he had seen,
   Roads full of beggars, cattle in the fields,
   But never saw the trefoil stained with blood,
   The avenging leaf those fields raised up against it.   20

The Fourth. The tomb of Swift wears it away.

The Third.   A voice
   Soft as the rustle of a reed from Cloyne
   That gathers volume; now a thunder-clap.

The Sixth. What schooling had these four?

The Seventh.   They walked the roads
    Mimicking what they heard, as children mimic;
    They understood that wisdom comes of beggary.

252

The Crazed Moon

Crazed through much child-bearing
The moon is staggering in the sky;
Moon-struck by the despairing
Glances of her wandering eye
We grope, and grope in vain,
For children born of her pain.

Children dazed or dead!
When she in all her virginal pride
First trod on the mountain's head
What stir ran through the countryside
Where every foot obeyed her glance!
What manhood led the dance!

Fly-catchers of the moon,
Our hands are blenched, our fingers seem
But slender needles of bone;
Blenched by that malicious dream
They are spread wide that each
May rend what comes in reach.

253

Coole Park, 1929

I meditate upon a swallow's flight,
Upon an aged woman and her house,
A sycamore and lime tree lost in night
Although that western cloud is luminous,

Great works constructed there in nature's spite
For scholars and for poets after us,
Thoughts long knitted into a single thought,
A dance-like glory that those walls begot.

There Hyde before he had beaten into prose
That noble blade the Muses buckled on,   10
There one that ruffled in a manly pose
For all his timid heart, there that slow man,
That meditative man, John Synge, and those
Impetuous men, Shawe-Taylor and Hugh Lane,
Found pride established in humility,
A scene well set and excellent company.

They came like swallows and like swallows went,
And yet a woman's powerful character
Could keep a swallow to its first intent;
And half a dozen in formation there,   20
That seemed to whirl upon a compass-point,
Found certainty upon the dreaming air,
The intellectual sweetness of those lines
That cut through time or cross it withershins.

Here, traveller, scholar, poet, take your stand
When all those rooms and passages are gone,
When nettles wave upon a shapeless mound
And saplings root among the broken stone,
And dedicate—eyes bent upon the ground,
Back turned upon the brightness of the sun   30
And all the sensuality of the shade—
A moment's memory to that laurelled head.

254

Coole and Ballylee, 1931

Under my window-ledge the waters race,
Otters below and moor-hens on the top,
Run for a mile undimmed in Heaven's face
Then darkening through 'dark' Raftery's 'cellar' drop,

Run underground, rise in a rocky place
In Coole demesne, and there to finish up
Spread to a lake and drop into a hole.
What's water but the generated soul?

Upon the border of that lake's a wood
Now all dry sticks under a wintry sun,
And in a copse of beeches there I stood,
For Nature's pulled her tragic buskin on
And all the rant's a mirror of my mood:
At sudden thunder of the mounting swan
I turned about and looked where branches break
The glittering reaches of the flooded lake.

Another emblem there! That stormy white
But seems a concentration of the sky;
And, like the soul, it sails into the sight
And in the morning's gone, no man knows why;
And is so lovely that it sets to right
What knowledge or its lack had set awry,
So arrogantly pure, a child might think
It can be murdered with a spot of ink.

Sound of a stick upon the floor, a sound
From somebody that toils from chair to chair;
Beloved books that famous hands have bound,
Old marble heads, old pictures everywhere;
Great rooms where travelled men and children found
Content or joy; a last inheritor
Where none has reigned that lacked a name and fame
Or out of folly into folly came.

A spot whereon the founders lived and died
Seemed once more dear than life; ancestral trees
Or gardens rich in memory glorified
Marriages, alliances and families,
And every bride's ambition satisfied.
Where fashion or mere fantasy decrees
Man shifts about—all that great glory spent—
Like some poor Arab tribesman and his tent.

We were the last romantics—chose for theme
Traditional sanctity and loveliness;
Whatever's written in what poets name
The book of the people; whatever most can bless
The mind of man or elevate a rhyme;
But all is changed, that high horse riderless,
Though mounted in that saddle Homer rode
Where the swan drifts upon a darkening flood.

255

For Anne Gregory

'Never shall a young man,
Thrown into despair
By those great honey-coloured
Ramparts at your ear,
Love you for yourself alone
And not your yellow hair.'

'But I can get a hair-dye
And set such colour there,
Brown, or black, or carrot,
That young men in despair   10
May love me for myself alone
And not my yellow hair.'

'I heard an old religious man
But yesternight declare
That he had found a text to prove
That only God, my dear,
Could love you for yourself alone
And not your yellow hair.'

256

Swift's Epitaph

Swift has sailed into his rest;
Savage indignation there
Cannot lacerate his breast.
Imitate him if you dare,
World-besotted traveller; he
Served human liberty.

257

At Algeciras—a Meditation upon Death

The heron-billed pale cattle-birds
That feed on some foul parasite
Of the Moroccan flocks and herds
Cross the narrow Straits to light
In the rich midnight of the garden trees
Till the dawn break upon those mingled seas.

Often at evening when a boy
Would I carry to a friend—
Hoping more substantial joy
Did an older mind commend—
Not such as are in Newton's metaphor,
But actual shells of Rosses' level shore.

Greater glory in the sun,
An evening chill upon the air,
Bid imagination run
Much on the Great Questioner;
What He can question, what if questioned I
Can with a fitting confidence reply.

November 1928

258

The Choice

The intellect of man is forced to choose
Perfection of the life, or of the work,
And if it take the second must refuse
A heavenly mansion, raging in the dark.
When all that story's finished, what's the news?
In luck or out the toil has left its mark:
That old perplexity an empty purse,
Or the day's vanity, the night's remorse.

259

Mohini Chatterjee

I asked if I should pray,
But the Brahmin said,
'Pray for nothing, say
Every night in bed,
"I have been a king,
I have been a slave,
Nor is there anything,
Fool, rascal, knave,
That I have not been,
And yet upon my breast   10
A myriad heads have lain." '

That he might set at rest
A boy's turbulent days
Mohini Chatterjee
Spoke these, or words like these.
I add in commentary,
'Old lovers yet may have
All that time denied—
Grave is heaped on grave
That they be satisfied—   20
Over the blackened earth

The old troops parade,
Birth is heaped on birth
That such cannonade
May thunder time away,
Birth-hour and death-hour meet,
Or, as great sages say,
Men dance on deathless feet.'

1928

260

Byzantium

The unpurged images of day recede;
The Emperor's drunken soldiery are abed;
Night resonance recedes, night-walkers' song
After great cathedral gong;
A starlit or a moonlit dome disdains
All that man is,
All mere complexities,
The fury and the mire of human veins.

Before me floats an image, man or shade,
Shade more than man, more image than a shade;
For Hades' bobbin bound in mummy-cloth
May unwind the winding path;
A mouth that has no moisture and no breath
Breathless mouths may summon;
I hail the superhuman;
I call it death-in-life and life-in-death.

Miracle, bird or golden handiwork,
More miracle than bird or handiwork,
Planted on the starlit golden bough,
Can like the cocks of Hades crow,
Or, by the moon embittered, scorn aloud
In glory of changeless metal
Common bird or petal
And all complexities of mire or blood.

At midnight on the Emperor's pavement flit
Flames that no faggot feeds, nor steel has lit,
Nor storm disturbs, flames begotten of flame,
Where blood-begotten spirits come
And all complexities of fury leave,
Dying into a dance,   30
An agony of trance,
An agony of flame that cannot singe a sleeve.

Astraddle on the dolphin's mire and blood,
Spirit after spirit! The smithies break the flood,
The golden smithies of the Emperor!
Marbles of the dancing floor
Break bitter furies of complexity,
Those images that yet
Fresh images beget,
That dolphin-torn, that gong-tormented sea.   40

1930

261

The Mother of God

The three-fold terror of love; a fallen flare
Through the hollow of an ear;
Wings beating about the room;
The terror of all terrors that I bore
The Heavens in my womb.

Had I not found content among the shows
Every common woman knows,
Chimney corner, garden walk,
Or rocky cistern where we tread the clothes
And gather all the talk?   10

What is this flesh I purchased with my pains,
This fallen star my milk sustains,
This love that makes my heart's blood stop
Or strikes a sudden chill into my bones
And bids my hair stand up?

262

Vacillation

I

Between extremities
Man runs his course;
A brand, or flaming breath,
Comes to destroy
All those antinomies
Of day and night;
The body calls it death,
The heart remorse.
But if these be right
What is joy?

II

A tree there is that from its topmost bough
Is half all glittering flame and half all green
Abounding foliage moistened with the dew;
And half is half and yet is all the scene;
And half and half consume what they renew,
And he that Attis' image hangs between
That staring fury and the blind lush leaf
May know not what he knows, but knows not grief.

III

Get all the gold and silver that you can,
Satisfy ambition, or animate
The trivial days and ram them with the sun,
And yet upon these maxims meditate:
All women dote upon an idle man
Although their children need a rich estate;
No man has ever lived that had enough
Of children's gratitude or woman's love.

No longer in Lethean foliage caught
Begin the preparation for your death
And from the fortieth winter by that thought
Test every work of intellect or faith   30
And everything that your own hands have wrought,
And call those works extravagance of breath
That are not suited for such men as come
Proud, open-eyed and laughing to the tomb.

IV

My fiftieth year had come and gone,
I sat, a solitary man,
In a crowded London shop,
An open book and empty cup
On the marble table-top.

While on the shop and street I gazed   40
My body of a sudden blazed;
And twenty minutes more or less
It seemed, so great my happiness,
That I was blessèd and could bless.

V

Although the summer sunlight gild
Cloudy leafage of the sky,
Or wintry moonlight sink the field
In storm-scattered intricacy,
I cannot look thereon,
Responsibility so weighs me down.   50

Things said or done long years ago,
Or things I did not do or say
But thought that I might say or do,
Weigh me down, and not a day
But something is recalled,
My conscience or my vanity appalled.

VI

A rivery field spread out below,
An odour of the new-mown hay
In his nostrils, the great lord of Chou
Cried, casting off the mountain snow,
'Let all things pass away.'

Wheels by milk-white asses drawn
Where Babylon or Nineveh
Rose; some conqueror drew rein
And cried to battle-weary men,
'Let all things pass away.'

From man's blood-sodden heart are sprung
Those branches of the night and day
Where the gaudy moon is hung.
What's the meaning of all song?
'Let all things pass away.'

VII

The Soul. Seek out reality, leave things that seem.
The Heart. What, be a singer born and lack a theme?
The Soul. Isaiah's coal, what more can man desire?
The Heart. Struck dumb in the simplicity of fire!
The Soul. Look on that fire, salvation walks within.
The Heart. What theme had Homer but original sin?

VIII

Must we part, Von Hügel, though much alike, for we
Accept the miracles of the saints and honour sanctity?
The body of Saint Teresa lies undecayed in tomb,
Bathed in miraculous oil, sweet odours from it come,
Healing from its lettered slab. Those self-same hands perchance
Eternalised the body of a modern saint that once
Had scooped out Pharaoh's mummy. I—though heart might find
    relief
Did I become a Christian man and choose for my belief

What seems most welcome in the tomb—play a predestined part.
Homer is my example and his unchristened heart.
The lion and the honeycomb, what has Scripture said?
So get you gone, Von Hügel, though with blessings on your head.

1932

263

Quarrel in Old Age

Where had her sweetness gone?
What fanatics invent
In this blind bitter town,
Fantasy or incident
Not worth thinking of,
Put her in a rage.
I had forgiven enough
That had forgiven old age.

All lives that has lived;
So much is certain;   10
Old sages were not deceived:
Somewhere beyond the curtain
Of distorting days
Lives that lonely thing
That shone before these eyes
Targeted, trod like Spring.

264

The Results of Thought

Acquaintance; companion;
One dear brilliant woman;
The best-endowed, the elect,
All by their youth undone,
All, all, by that inhuman
Bitter glory wrecked.

But I have straightened out
Ruin, wreck and wrack;
I toiled long years and at length
10   Came to so deep a thought
I can summon back
All their wholesome strength.

What images are these
That turn dull-eyed away,
Or shift Time's filthy load,
Straighten aged knees,
Hesitate or stay?
What heads shake or nod?

August 1931

265

Gratitude to the Unknown Instructors

What they undertook to do
They brought to pass;
All things hang like a drop of dew
Upon a blade of grass.

266

Remorse for Intemperate Speech

I ranted to the knave and fool,
But outgrew that school,
Would transform the part,
Fit audience found, but cannot rule
My fanatic[1] heart.

---

[1] I pronounce 'fanatic' in what is, I suppose, the older and more Irish way, so that the last line of each stanza contains but two beats.

I sought my betters: though in each
Fine manners, liberal speech,
Turn hatred into sport,
Nothing said or done can reach
My fanatic heart.   10

Out of Ireland have we come.
Great hatred, little room,
Maimed us at the start.
I carry from my mother's womb
A fanatic heart.

August 28, 1931

267

Stream and Sun at Glendalough

Through intricate motions ran
Stream and gliding sun
And all my heart seemed gay:
Some stupid thing that I had done
Made my attention stray.

Repentance keeps my heart impure;
But what am I that dare
Fancy that I can
Better conduct myself or have more
Sense than a common man?   10

What motion of the sun or stream
Or eyelid shot the gleam
That pierced my body through?
What made me live like these that seem
Self-born, born anew?

June 1932

Words for Music Perhaps

268

1. Crazy Jane and the Bishop

Bring me to the blasted oak
That I, midnight upon the stroke,
(All find safety in the tomb.)
May call down curses on his head
Because of my dear Jack that's dead.
Coxcomb was the least he said:
The solid man and the coxcomb.

Nor was he Bishop when his ban
Banished Jack the Journeyman,
(All find safety in the tomb.)
Nor so much as parish priest,
Yet he, an old book in his fist,
Cried that we lived like beast and beast:
The solid man and the coxcomb.

The Bishop has a skin, God knows,
Wrinkled like the foot of a goose,
(All find safety in the tomb.)
Nor can he hide in holy black
The heron's hunch upon his back,
But a birch-tree stood my Jack:
The solid man and the coxcomb.

Jack had my virginity,
And bids me to the oak, for he
(All find safety in the tomb.)
Wanders out into the night
And there is shelter under it,
But should that other come, I spit:
The solid man and the coxcomb.

269

II. Crazy Jane Reproved

I care not what the sailors say:
All those dreadful thunder-stones,
All that storm that blots the day
Can but show that Heaven yawns;
Great Europa played the fool
That changed a lover for a bull.
Fol de rol, fol de rol.

To round that shell's elaborate whorl,
Adorning every secret track
With the delicate mother-of-pearl,   10
Made the joints of Heaven crack:
So never hang your heart upon
A roaring, ranting journeyman.
Fol de rol, fol de rol.

270

III. Crazy Jane on the Day of Judgment

'Love is all
Unsatisfied
That cannot take the whole
Body and soul';
And that is what Jane said.

'Take the sour
If you take me,
I can scoff and lour
And scold for an hour.'
'That's certainly the case,' said he.   10

'Naked I lay
The grass my bed;
Naked and hidden away,
That black day';
And that is what Jane said.

'What can be shown?
What true love be?
All could be known or shown
If Time were but gone.'
20   *'That's certainly the case,' said he.*

271

IV. Crazy Jane and Jack the Journeyman

I know, although when looks meet
I tremble to the bone,
The more I leave the door unlatched
The sooner love is gone,
For love is but a skein unwound
Between the dark and dawn.

A lonely ghost the ghost is
That to God shall come;
I—love's skein upon the ground,
10   My body in the tomb—
Shall leap into the light lost
In my mother's womb.

But were I left to lie alone
In an empty bed,
The skein so bound us ghost to ghost
When he turned his head
Passing on the road that night,
Mine would walk being dead.

272

V. Crazy Jane on God

That lover of a night
Came when he would,
Went in the dawning light
Whether I would or no;
Men come, men go:
All things remain in God.

Banners choke the sky;
Men-at-arms tread;
Armoured horses neigh
Where the great battle was   10
In the narrow pass:
All things remain in God.

Before their eyes a house
That from childhood stood
Uninhabited, ruinous,
Suddenly lit up
From door to top:
All things remain in God.

I had wild Jack for a lover;
Though like a road   20
That men pass over
My body makes no moan
But sings on:
All things remain in God.

273

VI. Crazy Jane Talks with the Bishop

I met the Bishop on the road
And much said he and I.
'Those breasts are flat and fallen now
Those veins must soon be dry;

Live in a heavenly mansion,
Not in some foul sty.'

'Fair and foul are near of kin,
And fair needs foul,' I cried.
'My friends are gone, but that's a truth
Nor grave nor bed denied,
Learned in bodily lowliness
And in the heart's pride.

'A woman can be proud and stiff
When on love intent;
But Love has pitched his mansion in
The place of excrement;
For nothing can be sole or whole
That has not been rent.'

274

VII. Crazy Jane Grown Old Looks at the Dancers

I found that ivory image there
Dancing with her chosen youth,
But when he wound her coal-black hair
As though to strangle her, no scream
Or bodily movement did I dare,
Eyes under eyelids did so gleam:
Love is like the lion's tooth.

When she, and though some said she played
I said that she had danced heart's truth,
Drew a knife to strike him dead,
I could but leave him to his fate;
For, no matter what is said,
They had all that had their hate:
Love is like the lion's tooth.

Did he die or did she die?
Seemed to die or died they both?

God be with the times when I
Cared not a thraneen for what chanced
So that I had the limbs to try
Such a dance as there was danced—   20
Love is like the lion's tooth.

275

VIII. Girl's Song

I went out alone
To sing a song or two,
My fancy on a man,
And you know who.

Another came in sight
That on a stick relied
To hold himself upright:
I sat and cried.

And that was all my song—
When everything is told,   10
Saw I an old man young
Or young man old?

276

IX. Young Man's Song

'She will change,' I cried,
'Into a withered crone.'
The heart in my side,
That so still had lain,
In noble rage replied
And beat upon the bone:

'Uplift those eyes and throw
Those glances unafraid:
She would as bravely show
Did all the fabric fade;   10

No withered crone I saw
Before the world was made.'

Abashed by that report,
For the heart cannot lie,
I knelt in the dirt.
And all shall bend the knee
To my offended heart
Until it pardon me.

277

X. Her Anxiety

Earth in beauty dressed
Awaits returning spring.
All true love must die,
Alter at the best
Into some lesser thing.
Prove that I lie.

Such body lovers have,
Such exacting breath,
That they touch or sigh.
Every touch they give,
Love is nearer death.
Prove that I lie.

278

XI. His Confidence

Undying love to buy
I wrote upon
The corners of this eye
All wrongs done.
What payment were enough
For undying love?

10

I broke my heart in two
So hard I struck.
What matter? for I know
That out of rock,   10
Out of a desolate source,
Love leaps upon its course.

279

XII. Love's Loneliness

Old fathers, great-grandfathers,
Rise as kindred should.
If ever lover's loneliness
Came where you stood,
Pray that Heaven protect us
That protect your blood.

The mountain throws a shadow,
Thin is the moon's horn;
What did we remember
Under the ragged thorn?   10
Dread has followed longing,
And our hearts are torn.

280

XIII. Her Dream

I dreamed as in my bed I lay,
All night's fathomless wisdom come,
That I had shorn my locks away
And laid them on Love's lettered tomb:
But something bore them out of sight
In a great tumult of the air,
And after nailed upon the night
Berenice's burning hair.

XIV. His Bargain

Who talks of Plato's spindle;
What set it whirling round?
Eternity may dwindle,
Time is unwound,
Dan and Jerry Lout
Change their loves about.

However they may take it,
Before the thread began
I made, and may not break it
When the last thread has run,
A bargain with that hair
And all the windings there.

XV. Three Things

'O cruel Death, give three things back,'
Sang a bone upon the shore;
'A child found all a child can lack,
Whether of pleasure or of rest,
Upon the abundance of my breast':
A bone wave-whitened and dried in the wind.

'Three dear things that women know,'
Sang a bone upon the shore;
'A man if I but held him so
When my body was alive
Found all the pleasure that life gave':
A bone wave-whitened and dried in the wind.

'The third thing that I think of yet,'
Sang a bone upon the shore,
'Is that morning when I met

Face to face my rightful man
And did after stretch and yawn':
A bone wave-whitened and dried in the wind.

283

XVI. Lullaby

Beloved, may your sleep be sound
That have found it where you fed.
What were all the world's alarms
To mighty Paris when he found
Sleep upon a golden bed
That first dawn in Helen's arms?

Sleep, beloved, such a sleep
As did that wild Tristram know
When, the potion's work being done,
Roe could run or doe could leap
Under oak and beechen bough,
Roe could leap or doe could run;

Such a sleep and sound as fell
Upon Eurotas' grassy bank
When the holy bird, that there
Accomplished his predestined will,
From the limbs of Leda sank
But not from her protecting care.

284

XVII. After Long Silence

Speech after long silence; it is right,
All other lovers being estranged or dead,
Unfriendly lamplight hid under its shade,
The curtains drawn upon unfriendly night,
That we descant and yet again descant

Upon the supreme theme of Art and Song:
Bodily decrepitude is wisdom; young
We loved each other and were ignorant.

285

XVIII. Mad as the Mist and Snow

Bolt and bar the shutter,
For the foul winds blow:
Our minds are at their best this night,
And I seem to know
That everything outside us is
Mad as the mist and snow.

Horace there by Homer stands,
Plato stands below,
And here is Tully's open page.
How many years ago
Were you and I unlettered lads
Mad as the mist and snow?

You ask what makes me sigh, old friend,
What makes me shudder so?
I shudder and I sigh to think
That even Cicero
And many-minded Homer were
Mad as the mist and snow.

286

XIX. Those Dancing Days are Gone

Come, let me sing into your ear;
Those dancing days are gone,
All that silk and satin gear;
Crouch upon a stone,

Wrapping that foul body up
In as foul a rag:
I carry the sun in a golden cup,
The moon in a silver bag.

Curse as you may I sing it through;
What matter if the knave   10
That the most could pleasure you,
The children that he gave,
Are somewhere sleeping like a top
Under a marble flag?
I carry the sun in a golden cup,
The moon in a silver bag.

I thought it out this very day,
Noon upon the clock,
A man may put pretence away
Who leans upon a stick,
May sing, and sing until he drop,   20
Whether to maid or hag:
I carry the sun in a golden cup,
The moon in a silver bag.

287

xx. 'I am of Ireland'

'I am of Ireland,
And the Holy Land of Ireland,
And time runs on,' cried she.
'Come out of charity,
Come dance with me in Ireland.'

One man, one man alone
In that outlandish gear,
One solitary man
Of all that rambled there
Had turned his stately head.   10
'That is a long way off,

And time runs on,' he said,
'And the night grows rough.'

'I am of Ireland,
And the Holy Land of Ireland,
And time runs on,' cried she.
'Come out of charity
And dance with me in Ireland.'

'The fiddlers are all thumbs,
Or the fiddle-string accursed,
The drums and the kettledrums
And the trumpets all are burst,
And the trombone,' cried he,
'The trumpet and trombone,'
And cocked a malicious eye,
'But time runs on, runs on.'

'I am of Ireland,
And the Holy Land of Ireland,
And time runs on,' cried she.
'Come out of charity
And dance with me in Ireland.'

20

30

288

XXI. The Dancer at Cruachan[1] and Cro-Patrick

I, proclaiming that there is
Among birds or beasts or men,
One that is perfect or at peace,
Danced on Cruachan's windy plain,
Upon Cro-Patrick sang aloud;
All that could run or leap or swim
Whether in wood, water or cloud,
Acclaiming, proclaiming, declaiming Him.

[1]Pronounced in modern Gaelic as if spelt 'Crockan.'

289

XXII. Tom the Lunatic

Sang old Tom the lunatic
That sleeps under the canopy;
'What change has put my thoughts astray
And eyes that had so keen a sight?
What has turned to smoking wick
Nature's pure unchanging light?

'Huddon and Duddon and Daniel O'Leary,
Holy Joe, the beggar-man,
Wenching, drinking, still remain
Or sing a penance on the road;   10
Something made these eyeballs weary
That blinked and saw them in a shroud.

'Whatever stands in field or flood,
Bird, beast, fish or man,
Mare or stallion, cock or hen,
Stands in God's unchanging eye
In all the vigour of its blood;
In that faith I live or die.'

290

XXIII. Tom at Cruachan

On Cruachan's plain slept he
That must sing in a rhyme
What most could shake his soul:
'The stallion Eternity
Mounted the mare of Time,
'Gat the foal of the world.'

291

XXIV. Old Tom again

Things out of perfection sail
And all their swelling canvas wear,
Nor shall the self-begotten fail
Though fantastic men suppose
Building-yard and stormy shore,
Winding-sheet and swaddling-clothes.

292

XXV. The Delphic Oracle
upon Plotinus

Behold that great Plotinus swim
Buffeted by such seas;
Bland Rhadamanthus beckons him,
But the Golden Race looks dim,
Salt blood blocks his eyes.

Scattered on the level grass
Or winding through the grove
Plato there and Minos pass,
There stately Pythagoras
And all the choir of Love.

August 19, 1931

A Woman Young and Old

293

I. Father and Child

She hears me strike the board and say
That she is under ban
Of all good men and women,
Being mentioned with a man
That has the worst of all bad names;
And thereupon replies
That his hair is beautiful,
Cold as the March wind his eyes.

294

II. Before the World was Made

If I make the lashes dark
And the eyes more bright
And the lips more scarlet,
Or ask if all be right
From mirror after mirror,
No vanity's displayed:
I'm looking for the face I had
Before the world was made.

What if I look upon a man
As though on my beloved,
And my blood be cold the while
And my heart unmoved?
Why should he think me cruel
Or that he is betrayed?
I'd have him love the thing that was
Before the world was made.

10

295

III. *A First Confession*

I admit the briar
Entangled in my hair
Did not injure me;
My blenching and trembling
Nothing but dissembling,
Nothing but coquetry.

I long for truth, and yet
I cannot stay from that
My better self disowns,
For a man's attention
Brings such satisfaction
To the craving in my bones.

Brightness that I pull back
From the Zodiac,
Why those questioning eyes
That are fixed upon me?
What can they do but shun me
If empty night replies?

296

IV. *Her Triumph*

I did the dragon's will until you came
Because I had fancied love a casual
Improvisation, or a settled game
That followed if I let the kerchief fall:
Those deeds were best that gave the minute wings
And heavenly music if they gave it wit;
And then you stood among the dragon-rings.
I mocked, being crazy, but you mastered it
And broke the chain and set my ankles free,

Saint George or else a pagan Perseus;　　10
And now we stare astonished at the sea,
And a miraculous strange bird shrieks at us.

297

V. Consolation

O but there is wisdom
In what the sages said;
But stretch that body for a while
And lay down that head
Till I have told the sages
Where man is comforted.

How could passion run so deep
Had I never thought
That the crime of being born
Blackens all our lot?　　10
But where the crime's committed
The crime can be forgot.

298

VI. Chosen

The lot of love is chosen. I learnt that much
Struggling for an image on the track
Of the whirling Zodiac.
Scarce did he my body touch,
Scarce sank he from the west
Or found a subterranean rest
On the maternal midnight of my breast
Before I had marked him on his northern way,
And seemed to stand although in bed I lay.

I struggled with the horror of daybreak,　　10
I chose it for my lot! If questioned on

My utmost pleasure with a man
By some new-married bride, I take
That stillness for a theme
Where his heart my heart did seem
And both adrift on the miraculous stream
Where—wrote a learned astrologer—
The Zodiac is changed into a sphere.

299

VII. Parting

He. Dear, I must be gone
    While night shuts the eyes
    Of the household spies;
    That song announces dawn.

She. No, night's bird and love's
    Bids all true lovers rest,
    While his loud song reproves
    The murderous stealth of day.

He. Daylight already flies
    From mountain crest to crest.

She. That light is from the moon.

He. That bird . . .

She. Let him sing on,
    I offer to love's play
    My dark declivities.

10

300

VIII. Her Vision in the Wood

Dry timber under that rich foliage,
At wine-dark midnight in the sacred wood,
Too old for a man's love I stood in rage
Imagining men. Imagining that I could
A greater with a lesser pang assuage
Or but to find if withered vein ran blood,
I tore my body that its wine might cover
Whatever could recall the lip of lover.

And after that I held my fingers up,
Stared at the wine-dark nail, or dark that ran   10
Down every withered finger from the top;
But the dark changed to red, and torches shone,
And deafening music shook the leaves; a troop
Shouldered a litter with a wounded man,
Or smote upon the string and to the sound
Sang of the beast that gave the fatal wound.

All stately women moving to a song
With loosened hair or foreheads grief-distraught,
It seemed a Quattrocento painter's throng,
A thoughtless image of Mantegna's thought—   20
Why should they think that are for ever young?
Till suddenly in grief's contagion caught,
I stared upon his blood-bedabbled breast
And sang my malediction with the rest.

That thing all blood and mire, that beast-torn wreck,
Half turned and fixed a glazing eye on mine,
And, though love's bitter-sweet had all come back,
Those bodies from a picture or a coin
Nor saw my body fall nor heard it shriek,
Nor knew, drunken with singing as with wine,   30
That they had brought no fabulous symbol there
But my heart's victim and its torturer.

301

IX. A Last Confession

What lively lad most pleasured me
Of all that with me lay?
I answer that I gave my soul
And loved in misery,
But had great pleasure with a lad
That I loved bodily.

Flinging from his arms I laughed
To think his passion such
He fancied that I gave a soul
Did but our bodies touch,
And laughed upon his breast to think
Beast gave beast as much.

I gave what other women gave
That stepped out of their clothes,
But when this soul, its body off,
Naked to naked goes,
He it has found shall find therein
What none other knows,

And give his own and take his own
And rule in his own right;
And though it loved in misery
Close and cling so tight,
There's not a bird of day that dare
Extinguish that delight.

302

X. Meeting

Hidden by old age awhile
In masker's cloak and hood,
Each hating what the other loved,
Face to face we stood:
'That I have met with such,' said he,
'Bodes me little good.'

'Let others boast their fill,' said I,
'But never dare to boast
That such as I had such a man
For lover in the past;
Say that of living men I hate
Such a man the most.'

10

'A loony'd boast of such a love,'
He in his rage declared:
But such as he for such as me—
Could we both discard
This beggarly habiliment—
Had found a sweeter word.

303

XI. From the 'Antigone'

Overcome—O bitter sweetness,
Inhabitant of the soft cheek of a girl—
The rich man and his affairs,
The fat flocks and the fields' fatness,
Mariners, rough harvesters;
Overcome Gods upon Parnassus;

Overcome the Empyrean; hurl
Heaven and Earth out of their places,
That in the same calamity
10 Brother and brother, friend and friend,
Family and family,
City and city may contend,
By that great glory driven wild.

Pray I will and sing I must,
And yet I weep—Oedipus' child
Descends into the loveless dust.

[Parnell's Funeral and Other Poems

1935]

304

Parnell's Funeral

I

Under the Great Comedian's tomb the crowd.
A bundle of tempestuous cloud is blown
About the sky; where that is clear of cloud
Brightness remains; a brighter star shoots down;
What shudders run through all that animal blood?
What is this sacrifice? Can someone there
Recall the Cretan barb that pierced a star?

Rich foliage that the starlight glittered through,
A frenzied crowd, and where the branches sprang
A beautiful seated boy; a sacred bow;   10
A woman, and an arrow on a string;
A pierced boy, image of a star laid low.
That woman, the Great Mother imaging,
Cut out his heart. Some master of design
Stamped boy and tree upon Sicilian coin.

An age is the reversal of an age:
When strangers murdered Emmet, Fitzgerald, Tone,
We lived like men that watch a painted stage.
What matter for the scene, the scene once gone:
It had not touched our lives. But popular rage,
Hysterica passio dragged this quarry down.   20
None shared our guilt; nor did we play a part
Upon a painted stage when we devoured his heart.

Come, fix upon me that accusing eye.
I thirst for accusation. All that was sung,
All that was said in Ireland is a lie
Bred out of the contagion of the throng,
Saving the rhyme rats hear before they die.

Leave nothing but the nothings that belong
30 To this bare soul, let all men judge that can
Whether it be an animal or a man.

II

The rest I pass, one sentence I unsay.
Had de Valera eaten Parnell's heart
No loose-lipped demagogue had won the day,
No civil rancour torn the land apart.

Had Cosgrave eaten Parnell's heart, the land's
Imagination had been satisfied,
Or lacking that, government in such hands,
O'Higgins its sole statesman had not died.

Had even O'Duffy—but I name no more—
10 Their school a crowd, his master solitude;
Through Jonathan Swift's dark grove he passed, and there
Plucked bitter wisdom that enriched his blood.

305

Alternative Song for the Severed Head in 'The King of the Great Clock Tower'

Saddle and ride, I heard a man say,
Out of Ben Bulben and Knocknarea,
What says the Clock in the Great Clock Tower?
All those tragic characters ride
But turn from Rosses' crawling tide,
The meet's upon the mountain side.
A slow low note and an iron bell.

What brought them there so far from their home,
Cuchulain that fought night long with the foam,
10 *What says the Clock in the Great Clock Tower?*
Niamh that rode on it; lad and lass
That sat so still and played at the chess?

What but heroic wantonness?
A slow low note and an iron bell.

Aleel, his Countess; Hanrahan
That seemed but a wild wenching man;
What says the Clock in the Great Clock Tower?
And all alone comes riding there
The King that could make his people stare,
Because he had feathers instead of hair.   20
A slow low note and an iron bell.

Tune by Arthur Duff.

306

Two Songs Rewritten for the Tune's Sake

I

My Paistin Finn is my sole desire,
And I am shrunken to skin and bone,
For all my heart has had for its hire
Is what I can whistle alone and alone.
Oro, oro!
To-morrow night I will break down the door.

What is the good of a man and he
Alone and alone, with a speckled shin?
I would that I drank with my love on my knee,
Between two barrels at the inn.   10
Oro, oro!
To-morrow night I will break down the door.

Alone and alone nine nights I lay
Between two bushes under the rain;
I thought to have whistled her down that way,
I whistled and whistled and whistled in vain.
Oro, oro!
To-morrow night I will break down the door.

From The Pot of Broth
Tune: Paistin Finn

II

I would that I were an old beggar
Rolling a blind pearl eye,
For he cannot see my lady
Go gallivanting by;

A dreary, dreepy beggar
Without a friend on the earth
But a thieving rascally cur—
O a beggar blind from his birth;

Or anything else but a rhymer
Without a thing in his head
But rhymes for a beautiful lady,
He rhyming alone in his bed.

From The Player Queen

307

A Prayer for Old Age

God guard me from those thoughts men think
In the mind alone;
He that sings a lasting song
Thinks in a marrow-bone;

From all that makes a wise old man
That can be praised of all;
O what am I that I should not seem
For the song's sake a fool?

I pray—for fashion's word is out
And prayer comes round again—
That I may seem, though I die old,
A foolish, passionate man.

308

Church and State

Here is fresh matter, poet,
Matter for old age meet;
Might of the Church and the State,
Their mobs put under their feet.
O but heart's wine shall run pure,
Mind's bread grow sweet.

That were a cowardly song,
Wander in dreams no more;
What if the Church and the State
Are the mob that howls at the door!   10
Wine shall run thick to the end,
Bread taste sour.

August 1934

Supernatural Songs

309

1. Ribh at the Tomb of Baile and Aillinn

Because you have found me in the pitch-dark night
With open book you ask me what I do.
Mark and digest my tale, carry it afar
To those that never saw this tonsured head
Nor heard this voice that ninety years have cracked.
Of Baile and Aillinn you need not speak,
All know their tale, all know what leaf and twig,
What juncture of the apple and the yew,
Surmount their bones; but speak what none have heard.

The miracle that gave them such a death   10
Transfigured to pure substance what had once

Been bone and sinew; when such bodies join
There is no touching here, nor touching there,
Nor straining joy, but whole is joined to whole;
For the intercourse of angels is a light
Where for its moment both seem lost, consumed.

Here in the pitch-dark atmosphere above
The trembling of the apple and the yew,
20   Here on the anniversary of their death,
The anniversary of their first embrace,
Those lovers, purified by tragedy,
Hurry into each other's arms; these eyes,
By water, herb and solitary prayer
Made aquiline, are open to that light.
Though somewhat broken by the leaves, that light
Lies in a circle on the grass; therein
I turn the pages of my holy book.

310

II. Ribh denounces Patrick

An abstract Greek absurdity has crazed the man,
A Trinity that is wholly masculine. Man, woman, child (daughter
    or son),
That's how all natural or supernatural stories run.

Natural and supernatural with the self-same ring are wed.
As man, as beast, as an ephemeral fly begets, Godhead begets
    Godhead,
For things below are copies, the Great Smaragdine Tablet said.

Yet all must copy copies, all increase their kind;
When the conflagration of their passion sinks, damped by the
    body or the mind,
That juggling nature mounts, her coil in their embraces twined.

10   The mirror-scalèd serpent is multiplicity,
But all that run in couples, on earth, in flood or air, share God
    that is but three,
And could beget or bear themselves could they but love as He.

311

III. Ribh in Ecstasy

What matter that you understood no word!
Doubtless I spoke or sang what I had heard
In broken sentences. My soul had found
All happiness in its own cause or ground.
Godhead on Godhead in sexual spasm begot
Godhead. Some shadow fell. My soul forgot
Those amorous cries that out of quiet come
And must the common round of day resume.

312

IV. There

There all the barrel-hoops are knit,
There all the serpent-tails are bit,
There all the gyres converge in one,
There all the planets drop in the Sun.

313

V. Ribh considers Christian Love insufficient

Why should I seek for love or study it?
It is of God and passes human wit;
I study hatred with great diligence,
For that's a passion in my own control,
A sort of besom that can clear the soul
Of everything that is not mind or sense.

Why do I hate man, woman or event?
That is a light my jealous soul has sent.
From terror and deception freed it can

10 Discover impurities, can show at last
How soul may walk when all such things are past,
How soul could walk before such things began.

Then my delivered soul herself shall learn
A darker knowledge and in hatred turn
From every thought of God mankind has had.
Thought is a garment and the soul's a bride
That cannot in that trash and tinsel hide:
Hatred of God may bring the soul to God.

At stroke of midnight soul cannot endure
20 A bodily or mental furniture.
What can she take until her Master give!
Where can she look until He make the show!
What can she know until He bid her know!
How can she live till in her blood He live!

3 1 4

VI. He and She

As the moon sidles up
Must she sidle up,
As trips the scared moon
Away must she trip:
'His light had struck me blind
Dared I stop'.

She sings as the moon sings:
'I am I, am I;
The greater grows my light
10 The further that I fly'.
All creation shivers
With that sweet cry.

315

VII. *What Magic Drum?*

He holds him from desire, all but stops his breathing lest
Primordial Motherhood forsake his limbs, the child no longer rest,
Drinking joy as it were milk upon his breast.

Through light-obliterating garden foliage what magic drum?
Down limb and breast or down that glimmering belly move his
    mouth and sinewy tongue.
What from the forest came? What beast has licked its young?

316

VIII. *Whence had they Come?*

Eternity is passion, girl or boy
Cry at the onset of their sexual joy
'For ever and for ever'; then awake
Ignorant what Dramatis Personæ spake;
A passion-driven exultant man sings out
Sentences that he has never thought;
The Flagellant lashes those submissive loins
Ignorant what that dramatist enjoins,
What master made the lash. Whence had they come,
The hand and lash that beat down frigid Rome?   10
What sacred drama through her body heaved
When world-transforming Charlemagne was conceived?

3 1 7

IX. The Four Ages of Man

He with body waged a fight,
But body won; it walks upright.

Then he struggled with the heart;
Innocence and peace depart.

Then he struggled with the mind;
His proud heart he left behind.

Now his wars on God begin;
At stroke of midnight God shall win.

3 1 8

X. Conjunctions

If Jupiter and Saturn meet,
What a crop of mummy wheat!

The sword's a cross; thereon He died:
On breast of Mars the goddess sighed.

3 1 9

XI. A Needle's Eye

All the stream that's roaring by
Came out of a needle's eye;
Things unborn, things that are gone,
From needle's eye still goad it on.

320

XII. Meru

Civilisation is hooped together, brought
Under a rule, under the semblance of peace
By manifold illusion; but man's life is thought,
And he, despite his terror, cannot cease
Ravening through century after century,
Ravening, raging, and uprooting that he may come
Into the desolation of reality:
Egypt and Greece good-bye, and good-bye, Rome!
Hermits upon Mount Meru or Everest,
Caverned in night under the drifted snow,   10
Or where that snow and winter's dreadful blast
Beat down upon their naked bodies, know
That day brings round the night, that before dawn
His glory and his monuments are gone.

New Poems

1938

321

The Gyres

The gyres! the gyres! Old Rocky Face look forth;
Things thought too long can be no longer thought
For beauty dies of beauty, worth of worth,
And ancient lineaments are blotted out.
Irrational streams of blood are staining earth;
Empedocles has thrown all things about;
Hector is dead and there's a light in Troy;
We that look on but laugh in tragic joy.

What matter though numb nightmare ride on top
And blood and mire the sensitive body stain?
What matter? Heave no sigh, let no tear drop,
A greater, a more gracious time has gone;
For painted forms or boxes of make-up
In ancient tombs I sighed, but not again;
What matter? Out of Cavern comes a voice
And all it knows is that one word 'Rejoice.'

Conduct and work grow coarse, and coarse the soul,
What matter! Those that Rocky Face holds dear,
Lovers of horses and of women, shall
From marble of a broken sepulchre
Or dark betwixt the polecat and the owl,
Or any rich, dark nothing disinter
The workman, noble and saint, and all things run
On that unfashionable gyre again.

322

Lapis Lazuli

(*For Harry Clifton*)

I have heard that hysterical women say
They are sick of the palette and fiddle-bow,
Of poets that are always gay,
For everybody knows or else should know
That if nothing drastic is done
Aeroplane and Zeppelin will come out,
Pitch like King Billy bomb-balls in
Until the town lie beaten flat.

All perform their tragic play,
There struts Hamlet, there is Lear,
That's Ophelia, that Cordelia;
Yet they, should the last scene be there,
The great stage curtain about to drop,
If worthy their prominent part in the play,
Do not break up their lines to weep.
They know that Hamlet and Lear are gay;
Gaiety transfiguring all that dread.
All men have aimed at, found and lost;
Black out; Heaven blazing into the head:
Tragedy wrought to its uttermost.
Though Hamlet rambles and Lear rages,
And all the drop scenes drop at once
Upon a hundred thousand stages,
It cannot grow by an inch or an ounce.

On their own feet they came, or on shipboard,
Camel-back, horse-back, ass-back, mule-back,
Old civilisations put to the sword.
Then they and their wisdom went to rack:
No handiwork of Callimachus
Who handled marble as if it were bronze,   30
Made draperies that seemed to rise
When sea-wind swept the corner, stands;
His long lamp chimney shaped like the stem
Of a slender palm, stood but a day;
All things fall and are built again
And those that build them again are gay.

Two Chinamen, behind them a third,
Are carved in Lapis Lazuli,
Over them flies a long-legged bird
A symbol of longevity;   40
The third, doubtless a serving-man,
Carries a musical instrument.

Every discolouration of the stone,
Every accidental crack or dent
Seems a water-course or an avalanche,
Or lofty slope where it still snows
Though doubtless plum or cherry-branch
Sweetens the little half-way house
Those Chinamen climb towards, and I
Delight to imagine them seated there;   50
There, on the mountain and the sky,
On all the tragic scene they stare.
One asks for mournful melodies;
Accomplished fingers begin to play.
Their eyes mid many wrinkles, their eyes,
Their ancient, glittering eyes, are gay.

323

Imitated from the Japanese

A most astonishing thing
Seventy years have I lived;

(Hurrah for the flowers of Spring
For Spring is here again.)

Seventy years have I lived
No ragged beggar man,
Seventy years have I lived,
Seventy years man and boy,
And never have I danced for joy.

324

Sweet Dancer

The girl goes dancing there
On the leaf-sown, new-mown, smooth
Grass plot of the garden;
Escaped from bitter youth,
Escaped out of her crowd,
Or out of her black cloud.
Ah dancer, ah sweet dancer!

If strange men come from the house
To lead her away do not say
That she is happy being crazy;
Lead them gently astray;
Let her finish her dance,
Let her finish her dance.
Ah dancer, ah sweet dancer!

10

325

The Three Bushes

An incident from the 'Historia mei Temporis'
of the Abbé Michel de Bourdeille.

Said lady once to lover,
'None can rely upon
A love that lacks its proper food;
And if your love were gone
How could you sing those songs of love?
I should be blamed, young man.'
      O my dear, O my dear.

'Have no lit candles in your room,'
That lovely lady said,
'That I at midnight by the clock   10
May creep into your bed,
For if I saw myself creep in
I think I should drop dead.'
      O my dear, O my dear.

'I love a man in secret,
Dear chambermaid,' said she,
'I know that I must drop down dead
If he stop loving me,
Yet what could I but drop down dead
If I lost my chastity?'   20
      O my dear, O my dear.

'So you must lie beside him
And let him think me there,
And maybe we are all the same
Where no candles are,
And maybe we are all the same
That strip the body bare.'
      O my dear, O my dear.

But no dogs barked and midnights chimed,
And through the chime she'd say,
'That was a lucky thought of mine,   30

My lover looked so gay;'
But heaved a sigh if the chambermaid
Looked half asleep all day.
            O my dear, O my dear.

'No, not another song,' said he,
'Because my lady came
A year ago for the first time
At midnight to my room,
And I must lie between the sheets
When the clock begins to chime.'
            O my dear, O my dear.

'A laughing, crying, sacred song,
A leching song,' they said.
Did ever men hear such a song?
No, but that day they did.
Did ever man ride such a race?
No, not until he rode.
            O my dear, O my dear.

But when his horse had put its hoof
Into a rabbit hole
He dropped upon his head and died.
His lady saw it all
And dropped and died thereon, for she
Loved him with her soul.
            O my dear, O my dear.

The chambermaid lived long, and took
Their graves into her charge,
And there two bushes planted
That when they had grown large
Seemed sprung from but a single root
So did their roses merge.
            O my dear, O my dear.

When she was old and dying,
The priest came where she was;
She made a full confession.
Long looked he in her face,

And O, he was a good man
And understood her case.
   O my dear, O my dear.   70

He bade them take and bury her
Beside her lady's man,
And set a rose-tree on her grave.
And now none living can
When they have plucked a rose there
Know where its roots began.
   O my dear, O my dear.

326

The Lady's First Song

I turn round
Like a dumb beast in a show,
Neither know what I am
Nor where I go,
My language beaten
Into one name;
I am in love
And that is my shame.
What hurts the soul
My soul adores,   10
No better than a beast
Upon all fours.

327

The Lady's Second Song

What sort of man is coming
To lie between your feet?
What matter we are but women.
Wash; make your body sweet;

I have cupboards of dried fragrance
I can strew the sheet.
   The Lord have mercy upon us.

He shall love my soul as though
Body were not at all,
He shall love your body
Untroubled by the soul,
Love cram love's two divisions
Yet keep his substance whole.
   The Lord have mercy upon us.

Soul must learn a love that is
Proper to my breast,
Limbs a love in common
With every noble beast.
If soul may look and body touch
Which is the more blest?
   The Lord have mercy upon us.

328

The Lady's Third Song

When you and my true lover meet
And he plays tunes between your feet,
Speak no evil of the soul,
Nor think that body is the whole
For I that am his daylight lady
Know worse evil of the body;
But in honour split his love
Till either neither have enough,
That I may hear if we should kiss
A contrapuntal serpent hiss,
You, should hand explore a thigh,
All the labouring heavens sigh.

329

The Lover's Song

Bird sighs for the air,
Thought for I know not where,
For the womb the seed sighs.
Now sinks the same rest
On mind, on nest,
On straining thighs.

330

The Chambermaid's First Song

How came this ranger
Now sunk in rest,
Stranger with stranger,
On my cold breast.
What's left to sigh for,
Strange night has come;
God's love has hidden him
Out of all harm,
Pleasure has made him
Weak as a worm.   10

331

The Chambermaid's Second Song

From pleasure of the bed,
Dull as a worm,
His rod and its butting head
Limp as a worm,
His spirit that has fled
Blind as a worm.

332
An Acre of Grass

Picture and book remain,
An acre of green grass
For air and exercise,
Now strength of body goes;
Midnight an old house
Where nothing stirs but a mouse.

My temptation is quiet.
Here at life's end
Neither loose imagination,
Nor the mill of the mind
Consuming its rag and bone,
Can make the truth known.

Grant me an old man's frenzy.
Myself must I remake
Till I am Timon and Lear
Or that William Blake
Who beat upon the wall
Till truth obeyed his call;

A mind Michael Angelo knew
That can pierce the clouds
Or inspired by frenzy
Shake the dead in their shrouds;
Forgotten else by mankind
An old man's eagle mind.

333
What Then?

His chosen comrades thought at school
He must grow a famous man;
He thought the same and lived by rule,

All his twenties crammed with toil;
'What then?' sang Plato's ghost, 'what then?'

Everything he wrote was read,
After certain years he won
Sufficient money for his need,
Friends that have been friends indeed;
'What then?' sang Plato's ghost, 'what then?'   10

All his happier dreams came true—
A small old house, wife, daughter, son,
Grounds where plum and cabbage grew,
Poets and Wits about him drew;
'What then?' sang Plato's ghost, 'what then?'

'The work is done,' grown old he thought,
'According to my boyish plan;
Let the fools rage, I swerved in nought,
Something to perfection brought;'
But louder sang that ghost 'What then?'   20

334

Beautiful Lofty Things

Beautiful lofty things; O'Leary's noble head;
My father upon the Abbey stage, before him a raging crowd.
'This Land of Saints,' and then as the applause died out,
'Of plaster Saints;' his beautiful mischievous head thrown back.
Standish O'Grady supporting himself between the tables
Speaking to a drunken audience high nonsensical words;
Augusta Gregory seated at her great ormolu table
Her eightieth winter approaching; 'Yesterday he threatened my life,
I told him that nightly from six to seven I sat at this table
The blinds drawn up;' Maud Gonne at Howth station waiting a
    train,   10
Pallas Athena in that straight back and arrogant head:
All the Olympians; a thing never known again.

335

A Crazed Girl

That crazed girl improvising her music,
Her poetry, dancing upon the shore,
Her soul in division from itself
Climbing, falling she knew not where,
Hiding amid the cargo of a steamship
Her knee-cap broken, that girl I declare
A beautiful lofty thing, or a thing
Heroically lost, heroically found.

No matter what disaster occurred
She stood in desperate music wound
Wound, wound, and she made in her triumph
Where the bales and the baskets lay
No common intelligible sound
But sang, 'O sea-starved hungry sea.'

336

To Dorothy Wellesley

Stretch towards the moonless midnight of the trees
As though that hand could reach to where they stand,
And they but famous old upholsteries
Delightful to the touch; tighten that hand
As though to draw them closer yet.
                                        Rammed full
Of that most sensuous silence of the night
(For since the horizon's bought strange dogs are still)
Climb to your chamber full of books and wait,
No books upon the knee and no one there
But a great dane that cannot bay the moon
And now lies sunk in sleep.
                                        What climbs the stair?
Nothing that common women ponder on
If you are worth my hope! Neither Content

Nor satisfied Conscience, but that great family
Some ancient famous authors misrepresent,
The Proud Furies each with her torch on high.

337

The Curse of Cromwell

You ask what I have found and far and wide I go,
Nothing but Cromwell's house and Cromwell's murderous crew,
The lovers and the dancers are beaten into the clay,
And the tall men and the swordsmen and the horsemen where are
 they?
And there is an old beggar wandering in his pride
His fathers served their fathers before Christ was crucified.
   O what of that, O what of that
   What is there left to say?

All neighbourly content and easy talk are gone,
But there's no good complaining, for money's rant is on, 10
He that's mounting up must on his neighbour mount
And we and all the Muses are things of no account.
They have schooling of their own but I pass their schooling by,
What can they know that we know that know the time to die?
   O what of that, O what of that
   What is there left to say?

But there's another knowledge that my heart destroys
As the fox in the old fable destroyed the Spartan boy's
Because it proves that things both can and cannot be;
That the swordsmen and the ladies can still keep company; 20
Can pay the poet for a verse and hear the fiddle sound,
That I am still their servant though all are underground.
   O what of that, O what of that
   What is there left to say?

I came on a great house in the middle of the night
Its open lighted doorway and its windows all alight,
And all my friends were there and made me welcome too;
But I woke in an old ruin that the winds howled through;

And when I pay attention I must out and walk
30   Among the dogs and horses that understand my talk.
            O what of that, O what of that
            What is there left to say?

338

Roger Casement

(After reading 'The Forged Casement Diaries' by Dr. Maloney)

I say that Roger Casement
Did what he had to do,
He died upon the gallows
But that is nothing new.

Afraid they might be beaten
Before the bench of Time
They turned a trick by forgery
And blackened his good name.

A perjurer stood ready
10   To prove their forgery true;
They gave it out to all the world
And that is something new;

For Spring-Rice had to whisper it
Being their Ambassador,
And then the speakers got it
And writers by the score.

Come Tom and Dick, come all the troop
That cried it far and wide,
Come from the forger and his desk,
20   Desert the perjurer's side;

Come speak your bit in public
That some amends be made
To this most gallant gentleman
That is in quick-lime laid.

339

The Ghost of Roger Casement

O what has made that sudden noise?
What on the threshold stands?
It never crossed the sea because
John Bull and the sea are friends;
But this is not the old sea
Nor this the old seashore.
What gave that roar of mockery,
That roar in the sea's roar?

The ghost of Roger Casement
Is beating on the door.   10

John Bull has stood for Parliament,
A dog must have his day,
The country thinks no end of him
For he knows how to say
At a beanfeast or a banquet,
That all must hang their trust
Upon the British Empire,
Upon the Church of Christ.

The ghost of Roger Casement
Is beating on the door.   20

John Bull has gone to India
And all must pay him heed
For histories are there to prove
That none of another breed
Has had a like inheritance,
Or sucked such milk as he,
And there's no luck about a house
If it lack honesty.

The ghost of Roger Casement
Is beating on the door.   30

I poked about a village church
And found his family tomb

And copied out what I could read
In that religious gloom;
Found many a famous man there;
But fame and virtue rot.
Draw round beloved and bitter men,
Draw round and raise a shout;

The ghost of Roger Casement
40   *Is beating on the door.*

340

The O'Rahilly

Sing of the O'Rahilly
Do not deny his right;
Sing a 'the' before his name;
Allow that he, despite
All those learned historians,
Established it for good;
He wrote out that word himself,
He christened himself with blood.
                    How goes the weather?

10   Sing of the O'Rahilly
That had such little sense,
He told Pearse and Connolly
He'd gone to great expense
Keeping all the Kerry men
Out of that crazy fight;
That he might be there himself
Had travelled half the night.
                    How goes the weather?

'Am I such a craven that
20   I should not get the word
But for what some travelling man
Had heard I had not heard?'
Then on Pearse and Connolly
He fixed a bitter look,

'Because I helped to wind the clock
I come to hear it strike.'
   How goes the weather?

What remains to sing about
But of the death he met
Stretched under a doorway   30
Somewhere off Henry Street;
They that found him found upon
The door above his head
'Here died the O'Rahilly
R.I.P.' writ in blood.
   How goes the weather?

341

Come Gather Round Me Parnellites

Come gather round me Parnellites
And praise our chosen man,
Stand upright on your legs awhile,
Stand upright while you can,
For soon we lie where he is laid
And he is underground;
Come fill up all those glasses
And pass the bottle round.

And here's a cogent reason
And I have many more,   10
He fought the might of England
And saved the Irish poor,
Whatever good a farmer's got
He brought it all to pass;
And here's another reason,
That Parnell loved a lass.

And here's a final reason,
He was of such a kind
Every man that sings a song
Keeps Parnell in his mind   20

For Parnell was a proud man,
No prouder trod the ground,
And a proud man's a lovely man
So pass the bottle round.

The Bishops and the Party
That tragic story made,
A husband that had sold his wife
And after that betrayed;
But stories that live longest
30   Are sung above the glass,
And Parnell loved his country
And Parnell loved his lass.

342

The Wild Old Wicked Man

'Because I am mad about women
I am mad about the hills,'
Said that wild old wicked man
Who travels where God wills,
'Not to die on the straw at home,
Those hands to close these eyes,
That is all I ask, my dear,
From the old man in the skies.'
               Day-break and a candle end.

10   'Kind are all your words, my dear,
Do not the rest withhold,
Who can know the year, my dear,
When an old man's blood grows cold.
I have what no young man can have
Because he loves too much.
Words I have that can pierce the heart,
But what can he do but touch?'
               Day-break and a candle end.

Then said she to that wild old man
His stout stick under his hand,   20
'Love to give or to withhold
Is not at my command.
I gave it all to an older man
That old man in the skies.
Hands that are busy with His beads
Can never close those eyes.'
> *Day-break and a candle end.*

'Go your ways, O go your ways
I choose another mark,
Girls down on the seashore   30
Who understand the dark;
Bawdy talk for the fishermen
A dance for the fisher lads;
When dark hangs upon the water
They turn down their beds.'
> *Day-break and a candle end.*

'A young man in the dark am I
But a wild old man in the light
That can make a cat laugh, or
Can touch by mother wit   40
Things hid in their marrow bones
From time long passed away,
Hid from all those warty lads
That by their bodies lay.'
> *Day-break and a candle end.*

'All men live in suffering
I know as few can know,
Whether they take the upper road
Or stay content on the low,
Rower bent in his row-boat   50
Or weaver bent at his loom,
Horseman erect upon horseback
Or child hid in the womb.'
> *Day-break and a candle end.*

'That some stream of lightning
From the old man in the skies
Can burn out that suffering
No right taught man denies.
But a coarse old man am I,
I choose the second-best,
I forget it all awhile
Upon a woman's breast.'

Day-break and a candle end.

343

The Great Day

Hurrah for revolution and more cannon shot;
A beggar upon horseback lashes a beggar upon foot;
Hurrah for revolution and cannon come again,
The beggars have changed places but the lash goes on.

344

Parnell

Parnell came down the road, he said to a cheering man;
'Ireland shall get her freedom and you still break stone.'

345

What Was Lost

I sing what was lost and dread what was won,
I walk in a battle fought over again,
My king a lost king, and lost soldiers my men;
Feet to the Rising and Setting may run
They always beat on the same small stone.

346

The Spur

You think it horrible that lust and rage
Should dance attendance upon my old age;
They were not such a plague when I was young;
What else have I to spur me into song?

347

A Drunken Man's Praise of Sobriety

Come swish around my pretty punk
And keep me dancing still
That I may stay a sober man
Although I drink my fill.
Sobriety is a jewel
That I do much adore;
And therefore keep me dancing
Though drunkards lie and snore.
O mind your feet, O mind your feet,
Keep dancing like a wave,   10
And under every dancer
A dead man in his grave.
No ups and downs, my Pretty,
A mermaid, not a punk;
A drunkard is a dead man
And all dead men are drunk.

348

The Pilgrim

I fasted for some forty days on bread and buttermilk
For passing round the bottle with girls in rags or silk,
In country shawl or Paris cloak, had put my wits astray,
And what's the good of women for all that they can say
Is fol de rol de rolly O.

Round Lough Derg's holy island I went upon the stones,
I prayed at all the Stations upon my marrow bones,
And there I found an old man and though I prayed all day
And that old man beside me, nothing would he say
10   But fol de rol de rolly O.

All know that all the dead in the world about that place are stuck
And that should mother seek her son she'd have but little luck
Because the fires of Purgatory have ate their shapes away;
I swear to God I questioned them and all they had to say
Was fol de rol de rolly O.

A great black ragged bird appeared when I was in the boat;
Some twenty feet from tip to tip had it stretched rightly out,
With flopping and with flapping it made a great display
But I never stopped to question, what could the boatman say
20   But fol de rol de rolly O.

Now I am in the public house and lean upon the wall,
So come in rags or come in silk, in cloak or country shawl,
And come with learned lovers or with what men you may
For I can put the whole lot down, and all I have to say
Is fol de rol de rolly O.

349

Colonel Martin

I

The Colonel went out sailing,
He spoke with Turk and Jew
With Christian and with Infidel
For all tongues he knew.
'O what's a wifeless man?' said he
And he came sailing home.
He rose the latch and went upstairs
And found an empty room.
The Colonel went out sailing.

II

'I kept her much in the country   10
And she was much alone,
And though she may be there,' he said,
'She may be in the town,
She may be all alone there
For who can say,' he said,
'I think that I shall find her
In a young man's bed.'
The Colonel went out sailing.

III

The Colonel met a pedlar,
Agreed their clothes to swop,
And bought the grandest jewelry   20
In a Galway shop,
Instead of thread and needle
Put jewelry in the pack,
Bound a thong about his hand,
Hitched it on his back.
The Colonel went out sailing.

IV

The Colonel knocked on the rich man's door,
'I am sorry,' said the maid
'My mistress cannot see these things
But she is still abed,
And never have I looked upon
Jewelry so grand.'
'Take all to your mistress,'
And he laid them on her hand.
The Colonel went out sailing.

V

And he went in and she went on
And both climbed up the stair,
And O he was a clever man
For he his slippers wore,
And when they came to the top stair
He ran on ahead,
His wife he found and the rich man
In the comfort of a bed.
The Colonel went out sailing.

VI

The Judge at the Assize Court
When he heard that story told
Awarded him for damages
Three kegs of gold.
The Colonel said to Tom his man
'Harness an ass and cart,
Carry the gold about the town,
Throw it in every part.'
The Colonel went out sailing.

VII

And there at all street corners
A man with a pistol stood,
And the rich man had paid them well
To shoot the Colonel dead;
But they threw down their pistols
And all men heard them swear   60
That they could never shoot a man
Did all that for the poor.
The Colonel went out sailing.

VIII

'And did you keep no gold, Tom?
You had three kegs,' said he.
'I never thought of that, Sir;'
'Then want before you die.'
And want he did; for my own grand-dad,
Saw the story's end,
And Tom make out a living   70
From the sea-weed on the strand.
The Colonel went out sailing.

350

A Model for the Laureate

On thrones from China to Peru
All sorts of kings have sat
That men and women of all sorts
Proclaimed both good and great;
And what's the odds if such as these
For reason of the State
Should keep their lovers waiting,
    Keep their lovers waiting.

Some boast of beggar-kings and kings
Of rascals black and white
That rule because a strong right arm
Puts all men in a fright,
And drunk or sober live at ease
Where none gainsay their right,
And keep their lovers waiting,
    Keep their lovers waiting.

The Muse is mute when public men
Applaud a modern throne:
Those cheers that can be bought or sold
That office fools have run,
That waxen seal, that signature.
For things like these what decent man
Would keep his lover waiting?
    Keep his lover waiting?

351

The Old Stone Cross

A statesman is an easy man,
He tells his lies by rote;
A journalist makes up his lies
And takes you by the throat;
So stay at home and drink your beer
And let the neighbours vote,
    Said the man in the golden breastplate
    Under the old stone Cross.

Because this age and the next age
Engender in the ditch,
No man can know a happy man
From any passing wretch,
If Folly link with Elegance
No man knows which is which,
    Said the man in the golden breastplate
    Under the old stone Cross.

But actors lacking music
Do most excite my spleen,
They say it is more human
To shuffle, grunt and groan,   20
Not knowing what unearthly stuff
Rounds a mighty scene.
    Said the man in the golden breastplate
    Under the old stone Cross.

352

The Spirit Medium

Poetry, music, I have loved, and yet
Because of those new dead
That come into my soul and escape
Confusion of the bed,
Or those begotten or unbegotten
Perning in a band,
I bend my body to the spade
Or grope with a dirty hand.

Or those begotten or unbegotten.
For I would not recall   10
Some that being unbegotten
Are not individual,
But copy some one action
Moulding it of dust or sand
I bend my body to the spade
Or grope with a dirty hand.

An old ghost's thoughts are lightning
To follow is to die;
Poetry and music I have banished,
But the stupidity   20
Of root, shoot, blossom or clay
Makes no demand.
I bend my body to the spade
Or grope with a dirty hand.

353

Those Images

What if I bade you leave
The cavern of the mind?
There's better exercise
In the sunlight and wind.

I never bade you go
To Moscow or to Rome,
Renounce that drudgery,
Call the Muses home.

Seek those images
That constitute the wild,
The lion and the virgin,
The harlot and the child.

Find in middle air
An eagle on the wing,
Recognise the five
That make the Muses sing.

354

The Municipal Gallery
Re-visited

I

Around me the images of thirty years;
An ambush; pilgrims at the water-side;
Casement upon trial, half hidden by the bars,
Guarded; Griffith staring in hysterical pride;
Kevin O'Higgins' countenance that wears
A gentle questioning look that cannot hide
A soul incapable of remorse or rest;
A revolutionary soldier kneeling to be blessed.

II

An Abbot or Archbishop with an upraised hand
Blessing the Tricolour. 'This is not' I say   10
'The dead Ireland of my youth, but an Ireland
The poets have imagined, terrible and gay.'
Before a woman's portrait suddenly I stand;
Beautiful and gentle in her Venetian way.
I met her all but fifty years ago
For twenty minutes in some studio.

III

Heart smitten with emotion I sink down
My heart recovering with covered eyes;
Wherever I had looked I had looked upon
My permanent or impermanent images;   20
Augusta Gregory's son; her sister's son,
Hugh Lane, 'onlie begetter' of all these;
Hazel Lavery living and dying, that tale
As though some ballad singer had sung it all.

IV

Mancini's portrait of Augusta Gregory,
'Greatest since Rembrandt,' according to John Synge;
A great ebullient portrait certainly;
But where is the brush that could show anything
Of all that pride and that humility,
And I am in despair that time may bring   30
Approved patterns of women or of men
But not that selfsame excellence again.

V

My mediaeval knees lack health until they bend,
But in that woman, in that household where
Honour had lived so long, all lacking found.
Childless I thought 'my children may find here
Deep-rooted things,' but never foresaw its end,
And now that end has come I have not wept;
No fox can foul the lair the badger swept.

VI

40   (An image out of Spenser and the common tongue.)
John Synge, I and Augusta Gregory, thought
All that we did, all that we said or sang
Must come from contact with the soil, from that
Contact everything Antaeus-like grew strong.
We three alone in modern times had brought
Everything down to that sole test again,
Dream of the noble and the beggarman.

VII

And here's John Synge himself, that rooted man
'Forgetting human words,' a grave deep face.
50   You that would judge me do not judge alone
This book or that, come to this hallowed place
Where my friends' portraits hang and look thereon;
Ireland's history in their lineaments trace;
Think where man's glory most begins and ends
And say my glory was I had such friends.

355

Are You Content

I call on those that call me son,
Grandson, or great-grandson,
On uncles, aunts, great-uncles or great-aunts
To judge what I have done.
Have I, that put it into words,
Spoilt what old loins have sent?
Eyes spiritualised by death can judge,
I cannot, but I am not content.

He that in Sligo at Drumcliff
Set up the old stone Cross,   10
That red-headed rector in County Down
A good man on a horse,
Sandymount Corbets, that notable man
Old William Pollexfen,
The smuggler Middleton, Butlers far back,
Half legendary men.

Infirm and aged I might stay
In some good company,
I who have always hated work,
Smiling at the sea,   20
Or demonstrate in my own life
What Robert Browning meant
By an old hunter talking with Gods;
But I am not content.

[Last Poems
1938–1939]

356

Under Ben Bulben

I

Swear by what the Sages spoke
Round the Mareotic Lake
That the Witch of Atlas knew,
Spoke and set the cocks a-crow.

Swear by those horsemen, by those women,
Complexion and form prove superhuman,
That pale, long visaged company
That airs an immortality
Completeness of their passions won;
Now they ride the wintry dawn   10
Where Ben Bulben sets the scene.

Here's the gist of what they mean.

II

Many times man lives and dies
Between his two eternities,
That of race and that of soul,
And ancient Ireland knew it all.
Whether man dies in his bed
Or the rifle knocks him dead,
A brief parting from those dear
Is the worst man has to fear.   20
Though grave-diggers' toil is long,
Sharp their spades, their muscle strong,
They but thrust their buried men
Back in the human mind again.

III

You that Mitchel's prayer have heard
'Send war in our time, O Lord!'
Know that when all words are said
And a man is fighting mad,
Something drops from eyes long blind
30   He completes his partial mind,
For an instant stands at ease,
Laughs aloud, his heart at peace,
Even the wisest man grows tense
With some sort of violence
Before he can accomplish fate
Know his work or choose his mate.

IV

Poet and sculptor do the work
Nor let the modish painter shirk
What his great forefathers did,
40   Bring the soul of man to God,
Make him fill the cradles right.

Measurement began our might:
Forms a stark Egyptian thought,
Forms that gentler Phidias wrought.

Michael Angelo left a proof
On the Sistine Chapel roof,
Where but half-awakened Adam
Can disturb globe-trotting Madam
Till her bowels are in heat,
50   Proof that there's a purpose set
Before the secret working mind:
Profane perfection of mankind.

Quattrocento put in paint,
On backgrounds for a God or Saint,
Gardens where a soul's at ease;
Where everything that meets the eye
Flowers and grass and cloudless sky

Resemble forms that are, or seem
When sleepers wake and yet still dream,
And when it's vanished still declare,   60
With only bed and bedstead there,
That Heavens had opened.

                      Gyres run on;
When that greater dream had gone
Calvert and Wilson, Blake and Claude
Prepared a rest for the people of God,
Palmer's phrase, but after that
Confusion fell upon our thought.

            V

Irish poets learn your trade
Sing whatever is well made,
Scorn the sort now growing up   70
All out of shape from toe to top,
Their unremembering hearts and heads
Base-born products of base beds.
Sing the peasantry, and then
Hard-riding country gentlemen,
The holiness of monks, and after
Porter-drinkers' randy laughter;
Sing the lords and ladies gay
That were beaten into the clay
Through seven heroic centuries;   80
Cast your mind on other days
That we in coming days may be
Still the indomitable Irishry.

            VI

Under bare Ben Bulben's head
In Drumcliff churchyard Yeats is laid,
An ancestor was rector there
Long years ago; a church stands near,
By the road an ancient Cross.

No marble, no conventional phrase,
90   On limestone quarried near the spot
By his command these words are cut:

> Cast a cold eye
> On life, on death.
> Horseman, pass by!

357

Three Songs to the One Burden

I

The Roaring Tinker if you like,
But Mannion is my name,
And I beat up the common sort
And think it is no shame.
The common breeds the common,
A lout begets a lout,
So when I take on half a score
I knock their heads about.

From mountain to mountain ride the fierce horsemen.

10   All Mannions come from Manannan,
Though rich on every shore
He never lay behind four walls
He had such character,
Nor ever made an iron red
Nor soldered pot or pan;
His roaring and his ranting
Best please a wandering man.

From mountain to mountain ride the fierce horsemen.

Could Crazy Jane put off old age
20   And ranting time renew,
Could that old god rise up again
We'd drink a can or two,
And out and lay our leadership

On country and on town,
Throw likely couples into bed
And knock the others down.

From mountain to mountain ride the fierce horsemen.

II

My name is Henry Middleton
I have a small demesne,
A small forgotten house that's set
On a storm-bitten green,
I scrub its floors and make my bed,
I cook and change my plate,
The Post and Garden-boy alone
Have keys to my old gate.

From mountain to mountain ride the fierce horsemen.

Though I have locked my gate on them   10
I pity all the young,
I know what devil's trade they learn
From those they live among,
Their drink, their pitch and toss by day,
Their robbery by night;
The wisdom of the people's gone,
How can the young go straight?

From mountain to mountain ride the fierce horsemen.

When every Sunday afternoon
On the Green Lands I walk   20
And wear a coat in fashion,
Memories of the talk
Of hen wives and of queer old men
Brace me and make me strong;
There's not a pilot on the perch
Knows I have lived so long.

From mountain to mountain ride the fierce horsemen.

III

Come gather round me players all:
Come praise Nineteen-Sixteen,
Those from the pit and gallery
Or from the painted scene
That fought in the Post Office
Or round the City Hall,
Praise every man that came again,
Praise every man that fell.

From mountain to mountain ride the fierce horsemen.

10 Who was the first man shot that day?
The player Connolly,
Close to the City Hall he died;
Carriage and voice had he;
He lacked those years that go with skill
But later might have been
A famous, brilliant figure
Before the painted scene.

From mountain to mountain ride the fierce horsemen.

Some had no thought of victory
20 But had gone out to die
That Ireland's mind be greater,
Her heart mount up on high,
And no man knows what's yet to come
But Patrick Pearse has said
In every generation
Must Ireland's blood be shed.

From mountain to mountain ride the fierce horsemen.

358

The Black Tower

Say that the men of the old black tower
Though they but feed as the goatherd feeds
Their money spent, their wine gone sour,
Lack nothing that a soldier needs,
That all are oath-bound men
Those banners come not in.

There in the tomb stand the dead upright
But winds come up from the shore
They shake when the winds roar
Old bones upon the mountain shake.   10

Those banners come to bribe or threaten
Or whisper that a man's a fool
Who when his own right king's forgotten
Cares what king sets up his rule.
If he died long ago
Why do you dread us so?

There in the tomb drops the faint moonlight
But wind comes up from the shore
They shake when the winds roar
Old bones upon the mountain shake.   20

The tower's old cook that must climb and clamber
Catching small birds in the dew of the morn
When we hale men lie stretched in slumber
Swears that he hears the king's great horn.
But he's a lying hound;
Stand we on guard oath-bound.

There in the tomb the dark grows blacker
But wind comes up from the shore
They shake when the winds roar
Old bones upon the mountain shake.   30

359

Cuchulain Comforted

A man that had six mortal wounds, a man
Violent and famous, strode among the dead;
Eyes stared out of the branches and were gone.

Then certain Shrouds that muttered head to head
Came and were gone. He leant upon a tree
As though to meditate on wounds and blood.

A Shroud that seemed to have authority
Among those bird-like things came, and let fall
A bundle of linen. Shrouds by two and three

10   Came creeping up because the man was still.
And thereupon that linen-carrier said
'Your life can grow much sweeter if you will

'Obey our ancient rule and make a shroud;
Mainly because of what we only know
The rattle of those arms makes us afraid.

'We thread the needles' eyes and all we do
All must together do.' That done, the man
Took up the nearest and began to sew.

'Now we shall sing and sing the best we can
20   But first you must be told our character:
Convicted cowards all by kindred slain

'Or driven from home and left to die in fear.'
They sang but had nor human notes nor words,
Though all was done in common as before,

They had changed their throats and had the throats
    of birds.

360

Three Marching Songs

I

Remember all those renowned generations,
They left their bodies to fatten the wolves,
They left their homesteads to fatten the foxes,
Fled to far countries, or sheltered themselves
In cavern, crevice or hole,
Defending Ireland's soul.

Be still, be still, what can be said?
My father sang that song,
But time amends old wrong,
All that is finished, let it fade.   10

Remember all those renowned generations,
Remember all that have sunk in their blood,
Remember all that have died on the scaffold,
Remember all that have fled, that have stood,
Stood, took death like a tune
On an old tambourine.

Be still, be still, what can be said?
My father sang that song,
But time amends old wrong,
All that is finished, let it fade.   20

Fail and that history turns into rubbish,
All that great past to a trouble of fools;
Those that come after shall mock at O'Donnell
Mock at the memory of both O'Neills,
Mock Emmet, mock Parnell,
All the renown that fell.

Be still, be still, what can be said?
My father sang that song,
But time amends old wrong,
All that is finished, let it fade.   30

II

The soldier takes pride in saluting his Captain,
The devotee proffers a knee to his Lord,
Some back a mare thrown from a thoroughbred,
Troy backed its Helen, Troy died and adored;
Great nations blossom above;
A slave bows down to a slave.

What marches through the mountain pass?
No, no, my son, not yet;
That is an airy[1] spot
And no man knows what treads the grass.

We know what rascal might has defiled
The lofty innocent that it has slain,
We were not born in the peasant's cot
Where man forgives if the belly gain.
More dread the life that we live,
How can the mind forgive?

What marches through the mountain pass?
No, no, my son, not yet;
That is an airy spot
And no man knows what treads the grass.

What if there's nothing up there at the top?
Where are the captains that govern mankind?
What tears down a tree that has nothing within it?
A blast of wind, O a marching wind,
March wind, and any old tune,
March march and how does it run.

What marches through the mountain pass?
No, no, my son, not yet;
That is an airy spot
And no man knows what treads the grass.

[1]'Airy' may be an old pronunciation of 'eerie'. I often heard it in Galway & Sligo.

III

Grandfather sang it under the gallows:
'Hear, gentlemen, ladies, and all mankind:
Money is good and a girl might be better,
But good strong blows are delights to the mind.'
There, standing on the cart,
He sang it from his heart.

Robbers had taken his old tambourine,
But he took down the moon
And rattled out a tune;
Robbers had taken his old tambourine.   10

'A girl I had, but she followed another,
Money I had, and it went in the night,
Strong drink I had, and it brought me to sorrow,
But a good strong cause and blows are delight.'
All there caught up the tune:
'On, on, my darling man.'

Robbers had taken his old tambourine,
But he took down the moon
And rattled out a tune;
Robbers had taken his old tambourine.   20

'Money is good and a girl might be better,
No matter what happens and who takes the fall,
But a good strong cause'—the rope gave a jerk there,
No more sang he, for his throat was too small;
But he kicked before he died,
He did it out of pride.

Robbers had taken his old tambourine,
But he took down the moon
And rattled out a tune;
Robbers had taken his old tambourine.   30

3 6 1

In Tara's Halls

A man I praise that once in Tara's Halls
Said to the woman on his knees, 'Lie still,
My hundredth year is at an end. I think
That something is about to happen, I think
That the adventure of old age begins.
To many women I have said "lie still"
And given everything that a woman needs
A roof, good clothes, passion, love perhaps
But never asked for love, should I ask that
10   I shall be old indeed.'
                         Thereon the king
Went to the sacred house and stood between
The golden plough and harrow and spoke aloud
That all attendants and the casual crowd might hear:
'God I have loved, but should I ask return
Of God or women the time were come to die.'

He bade, his hundred and first year at end,
Diggers and carpenters make grave and coffin,
Saw that the grave was deep, the coffin sound,
Summoned the generations of his house
20   Lay in the coffin, stopped his breath and died.

3 6 2

The Statues

Pythagoras planned it. Why did the people stare?
His numbers, though they moved or seemed to move
In marble or in bronze, lacked character.
But boys and girls, pale from the imagined love
Of solitary beds, knew what they were,
That passion could bring character enough,
And pressed at midnight in some public place
Live lips upon a plummet-measured face.

No! Greater than Pythagoras, for the men
That with a mallet or a chisel modelled these   10
Calculations that look but casual flesh, put down
All Asiatic vague immensities,
And not the banks of oars that swam upon
The many-headed foam at Salamis.
Europe put off that foam when Phidias
Gave women dreams and dreams their looking glass.

One image crossed the many-headed, sat
Under the tropic shade, grew round and slow,
No Hamlet thin from eating flies, a fat
Dreamer of the Middle-Ages. Empty eye-balls knew   20
That knowledge increases unreality, that
Mirror on mirror mirrored is all the show.
When gong and conch declare the hour to bless,
Grimalkin crawls to Buddha's emptiness.

When Pearse summoned Cuchulain to his side
What stalked through the Post Office? What intellect,
What calculation, number, measurement, replied?
We Irish, born into that ancient sect
But thrown upon this filthy modern tide
And by its formless, spawning, fury wrecked   30
Climb to our proper dark, that we may trace
The lineaments of a plummet-measured face.

363

News for the Delphic Oracle

I

There all the golden codgers lay,
There the silver dew,
And the great water sighed for love
And the wind sighed too.
Man-picker Niamh leant and sighed
By Oisin on the grass;
There sighed amid his choir of love

Tall Pythagoras.
Plotinus came and looked about,
The salt flakes on his breast,
And having stretched and yawned awhile
Lay sighing like the rest.

II

Straddling each a dolphin's back
And steadied by a fin
Those Innocents re-live their death,
Their wounds open again.
The ecstatic waters laugh because
Their cries are sweet and strange,
Through their ancestral patterns dance,
And the brute dolphins plunge
Until in some cliff-sheltered bay
Where wades the choir of love
Proffering its sacred laurel crowns,
They pitch their burdens off.

III

Slim adolescence that a nymph has stripped,
Peleus on Thetis stares,
Her limbs are delicate as an eyelid,
Love has blinded him with tears;
But Thetis' belly listens.
Down the mountain walls
From where Pan's cavern is
Intolerable music falls.
Foul goat-head, brutal arm appear,
Belly, shoulder, bum,
Flash fishlike; nymphs and satyrs
Copulate in the foam.

364

Long-legged Fly

That civilisation may not sink
Its great battle lost,
Quiet the dog, tether the pony
To a distant post.
Our master Caesar is in the tent
Where the maps are spread,
His eyes fixed upon nothing,
A hand under his head.

Like a long-legged fly upon the stream
His mind moves upon silence.   10

That the topless towers be burnt
And men recall that face,
Move most gently if move you must
In this lonely place.
She thinks, part woman, three parts a child,
That nobody looks; her feet
Practise a tinker shuffle
Picked up on the street.

Like a long-legged fly upon the stream
Her mind moves upon silence.   20

That girls at puberty may find
The first Adam in their thought,
Shut the door of the Pope's chapel,
Keep those children out.
There on that scaffolding reclines
Michael Angelo.
With no more sound than the mice make
His hand moves to and fro.

Like a long-legged fly upon the stream
His mind moves upon silence.   30

365

A Bronze Head

Here at right of the entrance this bronze head,
Human, super-human, a bird's round eye,
Everything else withered and mummy-dead.
What great tomb-haunter sweeps the distant sky;
(Something may linger there though all else die;)
And finds there nothing to make its terror less
Hysterica-passio of its own emptiness?

No dark tomb-haunter once; her form all full
As though with magnanimity of light
Yet a most gentle woman; who can tell
Which of her forms has shown her substance right,
Or may be substance can be composite,
Profound McTaggart thought so, and in a breath
A mouthful hold the extreme of life and death.

But even at the starting-post, all sleek and new,
I saw the wildness in her and I thought
A vision of terror that it must live through
Had shattered her soul. Propinquity had brought
Imagination to that pitch where it casts out
All that is not itself. I had grown wild
And wandered murmuring everywhere 'my child, my child.'

Or else I thought her supernatural,
As though a sterner eye looked through her eye
On this foul world in its decline and fall;
On gangling stocks grown great, great stocks run dry,
Ancestral pearls all pitched into a sty,
Heroic reverie mocked by clown and knave,
And wondered what was left for massacre to save.

366

A Stick of Incense

Whence did all that fury come,
From empty tomb or Virgin womb?
Saint Joseph thought the world would melt
But liked the way his finger smelt.

367

Hound Voice

Because we love bare hills and stunted trees
And were the last to choose the settled ground,
Its boredom of the desk or of the spade, because
So many years companioned by a hound,
Our voices carry; and though slumber bound,
Some few half wake and half renew their choice,
Give tongue, proclaim their hidden name—'hound voice.'

The women that I picked spoke sweet and low
And yet gave tongue. 'Hound voices' were they all.
We picked each other from afar and knew   10
What hour of terror comes to test the soul,
And in that terror's name obeyed the call,
And understood, what none have understood,
Those images that waken in the blood.

Some day we shall get up before the dawn
And find our ancient hounds before the door,
And wide awake know that the hunt is on;
Stumbling upon the blood-dark track once more,
That stumbling to the kill beside the shore;
Then cleaning out and bandaging of wounds,   20
And chants of victory amid the encircling hounds.

368

John Kinsella's Lament for Mrs. Mary Moore

I

A bloody and a sudden end,
  Gunshot or a noose,
For death who takes what man would keep,
  Leaves what man would lose.
He might have had my sister
  My cousins by the score,
But nothing satisfied the fool
  But my dear Mary Moore,
None other knows what pleasures man
  At table or in bed.
What shall I do for pretty girls
  Now my old bawd is dead?

II

Though swift to strike a bargain
  Like an old Jew man,
Her bargain struck we laughed and talked
  And emptied many a can;
And O! but she had stories
  Though not for the priest's ear,
To keep the soul of man alive
  Banish age and care,
And being old she put a skin
  On everything she said.
What shall I do for pretty girls
  Now my old bawd is dead?

III

The priests have got a book that says
  But for Adam's sin
Eden's Garden would be there
  And I there within.

No expectation fails there
  No pleasing habit ends,
No man grows old, no girl grows cold,
  But friends walk by friends;
Who quarrels over half pennies
  That plucks the trees for bread?
What shall I do for pretty girls
  Now my old bawd is dead?

30

3 6 9

High Talk

Processions that lack high stilts have nothing that catches the eye.
What if my great-granddad had a pair that were twenty foot high,
And mine were but fifteen foot, no modern stalks upon higher,
Some rogue of the world stole them to patch up a fence or a fire.

Because piebald ponies, led bears, caged lions, make but poor
  shows,
Because children demand Daddy-long-legs upon his timber toes,
Because women in the upper stories demand a face at the pane
That patching old heels they may shriek, I take to chisel and
  plane.

Malachi Stilt-Jack am I, whatever I learned has run wild,
From collar to collar, from stilt to stilt, from father to child.

10

All metaphor, Malachi, stilts and all. A barnacle goose
Far up in the stretches of night; night splits and the dawn breaks
  loose;
I, through the terrible novelty of light, stalk on, stalk on;
Those great sea-horses bare their teeth and laugh at the dawn.

370

The Apparitions

Because there is safety in derision
I talked about an apparition,
I took no trouble to convince,
Or seem plausible to a man of sense,
Distrustful of that popular eye
Whether it be bold or sly.
Fifteen apparitions have I seen;
The worst a coat upon a coat-hanger.

I have found nothing half so good
As my long-planned half solitude,
Where I can sit up half the night
With some friend that has the wit
Not to allow his looks to tell
When I am unintelligible.
Fifteen apparitions have I seen;
The worst a coat upon a coat-hanger.

When a man grows old his joy
Grows more deep day after day,
His empty heart is full at length
But he has need of all that strength
Because of the increasing Night
That opens her mystery and fright.
Fifteen apparitions have I seen;
The worst a coat upon a coat-hanger.

371

A Nativity

What woman hugs her infant there?
Another star has shot an ear.

What made the drapery glisten so?
Not a man but Delacroix.

What made the ceiling waterproof?
Landor's tarpaulin on the roof.

What brushes fly and moth aside?
Irving and his plume of pride.

What hurries out the knave and dolt?
Talma and his thunderbolt.   10

Why is the woman terror-struck?
Can there be mercy in that look?

372

Man and the Echo

Man. In a cleft that's christened Alt
    Under broken stone I halt
    At the bottom of a pit
    That broad noon has never lit,
    And shout a secret to the stone.
    All that I have said and done,
    Now that I am old and ill,
    Turns into a question till
    I lie awake night after night
    And never get the answers right.   10
    Did that play of mine send out
    Certain men the English shot?
    Did words of mine put too great strain
    On that woman's reeling brain?
    Could my spoken words have checked
    That whereby a house lay wrecked?
    And all seems evil until I
    Sleepless would lie down and die.

Echo. Lie down and die.

Man.   That were to shirk

20   The spiritual intellect's great work
And shirk it in vain. There is no release
In a bodkin or disease,
Nor can there be a work so great
As that which cleans man's dirty slate.
While man can still his body keep
Wine or love drug him to sleep,
Waking he thanks the Lord that he
Has body and its stupidity,
But body gone he sleeps no more

30   And till his intellect grows sure
That all's arranged in one clear view
Pursues the thoughts that I pursue,
Then stands in judgment on his soul,
And, all work done, dismisses all
Out of intellect and sight
And sinks at last into the night.

Echo. Into the night.

Man.   O rocky voice
Shall we in that great night rejoice?
What do we know but that we face

40   One another in this place?
But hush, for I have lost the theme
Its joy or night seem but a dream;
Up there some hawk or owl has struck
Dropping out of sky or rock,
A stricken rabbit is crying out
And its cry distracts my thought.

373

The Circus Animals' Desertion

I

I sought a theme and sought for it in vain,
I sought it daily for six weeks or so.
Maybe at last being but a broken man
I must be satisfied with my heart, although
Winter and summer till old age began
My circus animals were all on show,
Those stilted boys, that burnished chariot,
Lion and woman and the Lord knows what.

II

What can I but enumerate old themes,
First that sea-rider Oisin led by the nose   10
Through three enchanted islands, allegorical dreams,
Vain gaiety, vain battle, vain repose,
Themes of the embittered heart, or so it seems,
That might adorn old songs or courtly shows;
But what cared I that set him on to ride,
I, starved for the bosom of his fairy bride.

And then a counter-truth filled out its play,
'The Countess Cathleen' was the name I gave it,
She, pity-crazed, had given her soul away
But masterful Heaven had intervened to save it.   20
I thought my dear must her own soul destroy
So did fanaticism and hate enslave it,
And this brought forth a dream and soon enough
This dream itself had all my thought and love.

And when the Fool and Blind Man stole the bread
Cuchulain fought the ungovernable sea;
Heart mysteries there, and yet when all is said
It was the dream itself enchanted me:

Character isolated by a deed
30   To engross the present and dominate memory.
Players and painted stage took all my love
And not those things that they were emblems of.

III

Those masterful images because complete
Grew in pure mind but out of what began?
A mound of refuse or the sweepings of a street,
Old kettles, old bottles, and a broken can,
Old iron, old bones, old rags, that raving slut
Who keeps the till. Now that my ladder's gone
I must lie down where all the ladders start
40   In the foul rag and bone shop of the heart.

374

Politics

'In our time the destiny of man
presents its meanings in political terms.'
THOMAS MANN

How can I, that girl standing there,
My attention fix
On Roman or on Russian
Or on Spanish politics,
Yet here's a travelled man that knows
What he talks about,
And there's a politician
That has both read and thought,
And maybe what they say is true
10   Of war and war's alarms,
But O that I were young again
And held her in my arms.

NARRATIVE
AND DRAMATIC

The Wanderings of Oisin

1889

*'Give me the world if Thou wilt, but grant me
an asylum for my affections.'*

TULKA

TO

EDWIN J. ELLIS

The Wanderings of Oisin

BOOK I

S. Patrick. You who are bent, and bald, and blind,
   With a heavy heart and a wandering mind,
   Have known three centuries, poets sing,
   Of dalliance with a demon thing.

Oisin. Sad to remember, sick with years,
   The swift innumerable spears,
   The horsemen with their floating hair,
   And bowls of barley, honey, and wine,
   Those merry couples dancing in tune,
   And the white body that lay by mine;   10
   But the tale, though words be lighter than air,
   Must live to be old like the wandering moon.

   Caoilte, and Conan, and Finn were there,
   When we followed a deer with our baying hounds,
   With Bran, Sceolan, and Lomair,
   And passing the Firbolgs' burial-mounds,
   Came to the cairn-heaped grassy hill
   Where passionate Maeve is stony-still;
   And found on the dove-grey edge of the sea
   A pearl-pale, high-born lady, who rode   20
   On a horse with bridle of findrinny;
   And like a sunset were her lips,
   A stormy sunset on doomed ships;
   A citron colour gloomed in her hair,
   But down to her feet white vesture flowed,
   And with the glimmering crimson glowed
   Of many a figured embroidery;
   And it was bound with a pearl-pale shell

That wavered like the summer streams,
30   As her soft bosom rose and fell.

S. Patrick. You are still wrecked among heathen dreams.

Oisin. 'Why do you wind no horn?' she said.
         'And every hero droop his head?
         The hornless deer is not more sad
         That many a peaceful moment had,
         More sleek than any granary mouse,
         In his own leafy forest house
         Among the waving fields of fern:
         The hunting of heroes should be glad.'

40   'O pleasant woman,' answered Finn,
         'We think on Oscar's pencilled urn,
         And on the heroes lying slain
         On Gabhra's raven-covered plain;
         But where are your noble kith and kin,
         And from what country do you ride?'

         'My father and my mother are
         Aengus and Edain, my own name
         Niamh, and my country far
         Beyond the tumbling of this tide.'

50   'What dream came with you that you came
         Through bitter tide on foam-wet feet?
         Did your companion wander away
         From where the birds of Aengus wing?'

         Thereon did she look haughty and sweet:
         'I have not yet, war-weary king,
         Been spoken of with any man;
         Yet now I choose, for these four feet
         Ran through the foam and ran to this
         That I might have your son to kiss.'

60   'Were there no better than my son
         That you through all that foam should run?'

         'I loved no man, though kings besought,
         Until the Danaan poets brought

Rhyme that rhymed upon Oisin's name,
And now I am dizzy with the thought
Of all that wisdom and the fame
Of battles broken by his hands,
Of stories builded by his words
That are like coloured Asian birds
At evening in their rainless lands.'   70

O Patrick, by your brazen bell,
There was no limb of mine but fell
Into a desperate gulph of love!
'You only will I wed,' I cried,
'And I will make a thousand songs,
And set your name all names above,
And captives bound with leathern thongs
Shall kneel and praise you, one by one,
At evening in my western dun.'

'O Oisin, mount by me and ride   80
To shores by the wash of the tremulous tide,
Where men have heaped no burial-mounds,
And the days pass by like a wayward tune,
Where broken faith has never been known,
And the blushes of first love never have flown;
And there I will give you a hundred hounds;
No mightier creatures bay at the moon;
And a hundred robes of murmuring silk,
And a hundred calves and a hundred sheep
Whose long wool whiter than sea-froth flows,   90
And a hundred spears and a hundred bows,
And oil and wine and honey and milk,
And always never-anxious sleep;
While a hundred youths, mighty of limb,
But knowing nor tumult nor hate nor strife,
And a hundred ladies, merry as birds,
Who when they dance to a fitful measure
Have a speed like the speed of the salmon herds,
Shall follow your horn and obey your whim,
And you shall know the Danaan leisure;   100
And Niamh be with you for a wife.'

Then she sighed gently, 'It grows late.
Music and love and sleep await,
Where I would be when the white moon climbs,
The red sun falls and the world grows dim.'

And then I mounted and she bound me
With her triumphing arms around me,
And whispering to herself enwound me;
But when the horse had felt my weight,
He shook himself and neighed three times:
Caoilte, Conan, and Finn came near,
And wept, and raised their lamenting hands,
And bid me stay, with many a tear;
But we rode out from the human lands.

In what far kingdom do you go,
Ah, Fenians, with the shield and bow?
Or are you phantoms white as snow,
Whose lips had life's most prosperous glow?
O you, with whom in sloping valleys,
Or down the dewy forest alleys,
I chased at morn the flying deer,
With whom I hurled the hurrying spear,
And heard the foemen's bucklers rattle,
And broke the heaving ranks of battle!
And Bran, Sceolan, and Lomair,
Where are you with your long rough hair?
You go not where the red deer feeds,
Nor tear the foemen from their steeds.

S. Patrick. Boast not, nor mourn with drooping head
    Companions long accurst and dead,
    And hounds for centuries dust and air.

Oisin. We galloped over the glossy sea:
    I know not if days passed or hours,
    And Niamh sang continually
    Danaan songs, and their dewy showers
    Of pensive laughter, unhuman sound,
    Lulled weariness, and softly round

110

120

130

My human sorrow her white arms wound.
We galloped; now a hornless deer
Passed by us, chased by a phantom hound   140
All pearly white, save one red ear;
And now a lady rode like the wind
With an apple of gold in her tossing hand;
And a beautiful young man followed behind
With quenchless gaze and fluttering hair.

'Were these two born in the Danaan land,
Or have they breathed the mortal air?'

'Vex them no longer,' Niamh said,
And sighing bowed her gentle head,
And sighing laid the pearly tip   150
Of one long finger on my lip.

But now the moon like a white rose shone
In the pale west, and the sun's rim sank,
And clouds arrayed their rank on rank
About his fading crimson ball:
The floor of Almhuin's hosting hall
Was not more level than the sea,
As, full of loving fantasy,
And with low murmurs, we rode on,
Where many a trumpet-twisted shell   160
That in immortal silence sleeps
Dreaming of her own melting hues,
Her golds, her ambers, and her blues,
Pierced with soft light the shallowing deeps.
But now a wandering land breeze came
And a far sound of feathery quires;
It seemed to blow from the dying flame,
They seemed to sing in the smouldering fires.
The horse towards the music raced,
Neighing along the lifeless waste;   170
Like sooty fingers, many a tree
Rose ever out of the warm sea;
And they were trembling ceaselessly,
As though they all were beating time,

Upon the centre of the sun,
To that low laughing woodland rhyme.
And, now our wandering hours were done,
We cantered to the shore, and knew
The reason of the trembling trees:
180   Round every branch the song-birds flew,
Or clung thereon like swarming bees;
While round the shore a million stood
Like drops of frozen rainbow light,
And pondered in a soft vain mood
Upon their shadows in the tide,
And told the purple deeps their pride,
And murmured snatches of delight;
And on the shores were many boats
With bending sterns and bending bows,
190   And carven figures on their prows
Of bitterns, and fish-eating stoats,
And swans with their exultant throats:
And where the wood and waters meet
We tied the horse in a leafy clump,
And Niamh blew three merry notes
Out of a little silver trump;
And then an answering whispering flew
Over the bare and woody land,
A whisper of impetuous feet,
200   And ever nearer, nearer grew;
And from the woods rushed out a band
Of men and ladies, hand in hand,
And singing, singing all together;
Their brows were white as fragrant milk,
Their cloaks made out of yellow silk,
And trimmed with many a crimson feather;
And when they saw the cloak I wore
Was dim with mire of a mortal shore,
They fingered it and gazed on me
210   And laughed like murmurs of the sea;
But Niamh with a swift distress
Bid them away and hold their peace;
And when they heard her voice they ran

And knelt there, every girl and man,
And kissed, as they would never cease,
Her pearl-pale hand and the hem of her dress.
She bade them bring us to the hall
Where Aengus dreams, from sun to sun,
A Druid dream of the end of days
When the stars are to wane and the world be done.   220

They led us by long and shadowy ways
Where drops of dew in myriads fall,
And tangled creepers every hour
Blossom in some new crimson flower,
And once a sudden laughter sprang
From all their lips, and once they sang
Together, while the dark woods rang,
And made in all their distant parts,
With boom of bees in honey-marts,
A rumour of delighted hearts.   230
And once a lady by my side
Gave me a harp, and bid me sing,
And touch the laughing silver string;
But when I sang of human joy
A sorrow wrapped each merry face,
And, Patrick! by your beard, they wept,
Until one came, a tearful boy;
'A sadder creature never stept
Than this strange human bard,' he cried;
And caught the silver harp away,   240
And, weeping over the white strings, hurled
It down in a leaf-hid, hollow place
That kept dim waters from the sky;
And each one said, with a long, long sigh,
'O saddest harp in all the world,
Sleep there till the moon and the stars die!'

And now, still sad, we came to where
A beautiful young man dreamed within
A house of wattles, clay, and skin;
One hand upheld his beardless chin,   250
And one a sceptre flashing out

Wild flames of red and gold and blue,
Like to a merry wandering rout
Of dancers leaping in the air;
And men and ladies knelt them there
And showed their eyes with teardrops dim,
And with low murmurs prayed to him,
And kissed the sceptre with red lips,
And touched it with their finger-tips.

260 He held that flashing sceptre up.
'Joy drowns the twilight in the dew,
And fills with stars night's purple cup,
And wakes the sluggard seeds of corn,
And stirs the young kid's budding horn,
And makes the infant ferns unwrap,
And for the peewit paints his cap,
And rolls along the unwieldy sun,
And makes the little planets run:
And if joy were not on the earth,
270 There were an end of change and birth,
And Earth and Heaven and Hell would die,
And in some gloomy barrow lie
Folded like a frozen fly;
Then mock at Death and Time with glances
And wavering arms and wandering dances.

'Men's hearts of old were drops of flame
That from the saffron morning came,
Or drops of silver joy that fell
Out of the moon's pale twisted shell;
280 But now hearts cry that hearts are slaves,
And toss and turn in narrow caves;
But here there is nor law nor rule,
Nor have hands held a weary tool;
And here there is nor Change nor Death,
But only kind and merry breath,
For joy is God and God is joy.'
With one long glance for girl and boy
And the pale blossom of the moon,
He fell into a Druid swoon.

And in a wild and sudden dance 290
We mocked at Time and Fate and Chance
And swept out of the wattled hall
And came to where the dewdrops fall
Among the foamdrops of the sea,
And there we hushed the revelry;
And, gathering on our brows a frown,
Bent all our swaying bodies down,
And to the waves that glimmer by
That sloping green De Danaan sod
Sang, 'God is joy and joy is God, 300
And things that have grown sad are wicked,
And things that fear the dawn of the morrow
Or the grey wandering osprey Sorrow.'

We danced to where in the winding thicket
The damask roses, bloom on bloom,
Like crimson meteors hang in the gloom,
And bending over them softly said,
Bending over them in the dance,
With a swift and friendly glance
From dewy eyes: 'Upon the dead 310
Fall the leaves of other roses,
On the dead dim earth encloses:
But never, never on our graves,
Heaped beside the glimmering waves,
Shall fall the leaves of damask roses.
For neither Death nor Change comes near us,
And all listless hours fear us,
And we fear no dawning morrow,
Nor the grey wandering osprey Sorrow.'

The dance wound through the windless woods; 320
The ever-summered solitudes;
Until the tossing arms grew still
Upon the woody central hill;
And, gathered in a panting band,
We flung on high each waving hand,
And sang unto the starry broods.
In our raised eyes there flashed a glow

Of milky brightness to and fro
As thus our song arose: 'You stars,
330   Across your wandering ruby cars
Shake the loose reins: you slaves of God,
He rules you with an iron rod,
He holds you with an iron bond,
Each one woven to the other,
Each one woven to his brother
Like bubbles in a frozen pond;
But we in a lonely land abide
Unchainable as the dim tide,
With hearts that know nor law nor rule,
340   And hands that hold no wearisome tool,
Folded in love that fears no morrow,
Nor the grey wandering osprey Sorrow.'

O Patrick! for a hundred years
I chased upon that woody shore
The deer, the badger, and the boar.
O Patrick! for a hundred years
At evening on the glimmering sands,
Beside the piled-up hunting spears,
These now outworn and withered hands
350   Wrestled among the island bands.
O Patrick! for a hundred years
We went a-fishing in long boats
With bending sterns and bending bows,
And carven figures on their prows
Of bitterns and fish-eating stoats.
O Patrick! for a hundred years
The gentle Niamh was my wife;
But now two things devour my life;
The things that most of all I hate:
Fasting and prayers.

    S. Patrick.   Tell on.

360   *Oisin.*   Yes, yes,
    For these were ancient Oisin's fate

Loosed long ago from Heaven's gate,
For his last days to lie in wait.

When one day by the tide I stood,
I found in that forgetfulness
Of dreamy foam a staff of wood
From some dead warrior's broken lance:
I turned it in my hands; the stains
Of war were on it, and I wept,
Remembering how the Fenians stept   370
Along the blood-bedabbled plains,
Equal to good or grievous chance:
Thereon young Niamh softly came
And caught my hands, but spake no word
Save only many times my name,
In murmurs, like a frighted bird.
We passed by woods, and lawns of clover,
And found the horse and bridled him,
For we knew well the old was over.
I heard one say, 'His eyes grow dim   380
With all the ancient sorrow of men';
And wrapped in dreams rode out again
With hoofs of the pale findrinny
Over the glimmering purple sea.
Under the golden evening light,
The Immortals moved among the fountains
By rivers and the woods' old night;
Some danced like shadows on the mountains,
Some wandered ever hand in hand;
Or sat in dreams on the pale strand,   390
Each forehead like an obscure star
Bent down above each hookèd knee,
And sang, and with a dreamy gaze
Watched where the sun in a saffron blaze
Was slumbering half in the sea-ways;
And, as they sang, the painted birds
Kept time with their bright wings and feet;
Like drops of honey came their words,
But fainter than a young lamb's bleat.

400   'An old man stirs the fire to a blaze,
        In the house of a child, of a friend, of a brother.
        He has over-lingered his welcome; the days,
        Grown desolate, whisper and sigh to each other;
        He hears the storm in the chimney above,
        And bends to the fire and shakes with the cold,
        While his heart still dreams of battle and love,
        And the cry of the hounds on the hills of old.

        'But we are apart in the grassy places,
        Where care cannot trouble the least of our days,
410   Or the softness of youth be gone from our faces,
        Or love's first tenderness die in our gaze.
        The hare grows old as she plays in the sun
        And gazes around her with eyes of brightness;
        Before the swift things that she dreamed of were done
        She limps along in an aged whiteness;
        A storm of birds in the Asian trees
        Like tulips in the air a-winging,
        And the gentle waves of the summer seas,
        That raise their heads and wander singing,
420   Must murmur at last, "Unjust, unjust";
        And "My speed is a weariness," falters the mouse,
        And the kingfisher turns to a ball of dust,
        And the roof falls in of his tunnelled house.
        But the love-dew dims our eyes till the day
        When God shall come from the sea with a sigh
        And bid the stars drop down from the sky,
        And the moon like a pale rose wither away.'

BOOK II

Now, man of croziers, shadows called our names
And then away, away, like whirling flames;
And now fled by, mist-covered, without sound,
The youth and lady and the deer and hound;
'Gaze no more on the phantoms,' Niamh said,
And kissed my eyes, and, swaying her bright head
And her bright body, sang of faery and man
Before God was or my old line began;
Wars shadowy, vast, exultant; faeries of old
Who wedded men with rings of Druid gold;   10
And how those lovers never turn their eyes
Upon the life that fades and flickers and dies,
Yet love and kiss on dim shores far away
Rolled round with music of the sighing spray:
Yet sang no more as when, like a brown bee
That has drunk full, she crossed the misty sea
With me in her white arms a hundred years
Before this day; for now the fall of tears
Troubled her song.
         I do not know if days
Or hours passed by, yet hold the morning rays   20
Shone many times among the glimmering flowers
Woven into her hair, before dark towers
Rose in the darkness, and the white surf gleamed
About them; and the horse of Faery screamed
And shivered, knowing the Isle of Many Fears,
Nor ceased until white Niamh stroked his ears
And named him by sweet names.
         A foaming tide
Whitened afar with surge, fan-formed and wide,
Burst from a great door marred by many a blow
From mace and sword and pole-axe, long ago   30
When gods and giants warred. We rode between
The seaweed-covered pillars; and the green
And surging phosphorus alone gave light
On our dark pathway, till a countless flight

Of moonlit steps glimmered; and left and right
Dark statues glimmered over the pale tide
Upon dark thrones. Between the lids of one
The imaged meteors had flashed and run
And had disported in the stilly jet,
40 And the fixed stars had dawned and shone and set,
Since God made Time and Death and Sleep: the other
Stretched his long arm to where, a misty smother,
The stream churned, churned, and churned—his lips apart,
As though he told his never-slumbering heart
Of every foamdrop on its misty way.
Tying the horse to his vast foot that lay
Half in the unvesselled sea, we climbed the stair
And climbed so long, I thought the last steps were
Hung from the morning star; when these mild words
50 Fanned the delighted air like wings of birds:
'My brothers spring out of their beds at morn,
A-murmur like young partridge: with loud horn
They chase the noontide deer;
And when the dew-drowned stars hang in the air
Look to long fishing-lines, or point and pare
An ashen hunting spear.
O sigh, O fluttering sigh, be kind to me;
Flutter along the froth lips of the sea,
And shores the froth lips wet:
60 And stay a little while, and bid them weep:
Ah, touch their blue-veined eyelids if they sleep,
And shake their coverlet.
When you have told how I weep endlessly,
Flutter along the froth lips of the sea
And home to me again,
And in the shadow of my hair lie hid,
And tell me that you found a man unbid,
The saddest of all men.'

A lady with soft eyes like funeral tapers,
70 And face that seemed wrought out of moonlit vapours,
And a sad mouth, that fear made tremulous
As any ruddy moth, looked down on us;
And she with a wave-rusted chain was tied

To two old eagles, full of ancient pride,
That with dim eyeballs stood on either side.
Few feathers were on their dishevelled wings,
For their dim minds were with the ancient things.

'I bring deliverance,' pearl-pale Niamh said.

'Neither the living, nor the unlabouring dead,
Nor the high gods who never lived, may fight　　　　　　　80
My enemy and hope; demons for fright
Jabber and scream about him in the night;
For he is strong and crafty as the seas
That sprang under the Seven Hazel Trees,
And I must needs endure and hate and weep,
Until the gods and demons drop asleep,
Hearing Aed touch the mournful strings of gold.'

'Is he so dreadful?'
　　　　　　　'Be not over-bold,
But fly while still you may.'
　　　　　　　　　　And thereon I:
'This demon shall be battered till he die,　　　　　　90
And his loose bulk be thrown in the loud tide.'

'Flee from him,' pearl-pale Niamh weeping cried,
'For all men flee the demons'; but moved not
My angry king-remembering soul one jot.
There was no mightier soul of Heber's line;
Now it is old and mouse-like. For a sign
I burst the chain: still earless, nerveless, blind,
Wrapped in the things of the unhuman mind,
In some dim memory or ancient mood,
Still earless, nerveless, blind, the eagles stood.　　　　100

And then we climbed the stair to a high door;
A hundred horsemen on the basalt floor
Beneath had paced content: we held our way
And stood within: clothed in a misty ray
I saw a foam-white seagull drift and float
Under the roof, and with a straining throat
Shouted, and hailed him: he hung there a star,
For no man's cry shall ever mount so far;

Not even your God could have thrown down that hall;
Stabling His unloosed lightnings in their stall,
He had sat down and sighed with cumbered heart,
As though His hour were come.

                      We sought the part
That was most distant from the door; green slime
Made the way slippery, and time on time
Showed prints of sea-born scales, while down through it
The captive's journeys to and fro were writ
Like a small river, and where feet touched came
A momentary gleam of phosphorus flame.
Under the deepest shadows of the hall
That woman found a ring hung on the wall,
And in the ring a torch, and with its flare
Making a world about her in the air,
Passed under the dim doorway, out of sight,
And came again, holding a second light
Burning between her fingers, and in mine
Laid it and sighed: I held a sword whose shine
No centuries could dim, and a word ran
Thereon in Ogham letters, 'Manannan';
That sea-god's name, who in a deep content
Sprang dripping, and, with captive demons sent
Out of the sevenfold seas, built the dark hall
Rooted in foam and clouds, and cried to all
The mightier masters of a mightier race;
And at his cry there came no milk-pale face
Under a crown of thorns and dark with blood,
But only exultant faces.

                      Niamh stood
With bowed head, trembling when the white blade shone,
But she whose hours of tenderness were gone
Had neither hope nor fear. I bade them hide
Under the shadows till the tumults died
Of the loud-crashing and earth-shaking fight,
Lest they should look upon some dreadful sight;
And thrust the torch between the slimy flags.
A dome made out of endless carven jags,

Where shadowy face flowed into shadowy face,
Looked down on me; and in the self-same place
I waited hour by hour, and the high dome,
Windowless, pillarless, multitudinous home
Of faces, waited; and the leisured gaze
Was loaded with the memory of days   150
Buried and mighty. When through the great door
The dawn came in, and glimmered on the floor
With a pale light, I journeyed round the hall
And found a door deep sunken in the wall,
The least of doors; beyond on a dim plain
A little runnel made a bubbling strain,
And on the runnel's stony and bare edge
A dusky demon dry as a withered sedge
Swayed, crooning to himself an unknown tongue:
In a sad revelry he sang and swung   160
Bacchant and mournful, passing to and fro
His hand along the runnel's side, as though
The flowers still grew there: far on the sea's waste
Shaking and waving, vapour vapour chased,
While high frail cloudlets, fed with a green light,
Like drifts of leaves, immovable and bright,
Hung in the passionate dawn. He slowly turned:
A demon's leisure: eyes, first white, now burned
Like wings of kingfishers; and he arose
Barking. We trampled up and down with blows   170
Of sword and brazen battle-axe, while day
Gave to high noon and noon to night gave way;
And when he knew the sword of Manannan
Amid the shades of night, he changed and ran
Through many shapes; I lunged at the smooth throat
Of a great eel; it changed, and I but smote
A fir-tree roaring in its leafless top;
And thereupon I drew the livid chop
Of a drowned dripping body to my breast;
Horror from horror grew; but when the west   180
Had surged up in a plumy fire, I drave
Through heart and spine; and cast him in the wave
Lest Niamh shudder.

> Full of hope and dread
> Those two came carrying wine and meat and bread,
> And healed my wounds with unguents out of flowers
> That feed white moths by some De Danaan shrine;
> Then in that hall, lit by the dim sea-shine,
> We lay on skins of otters, and drank wine,
> Brewed by the sea-gods, from huge cups that lay

190
> Upon the lips of sea-gods in their day;
> And then on heaped-up skins of otters slept.
> And when the sun once more in saffron stept,
> Rolling his flagrant wheel out of the deep,
> We sang the loves and angers without sleep,
> And all the exultant labours of the strong.
> But now the lying clerics murder song
> With barren words and flatteries of the weak.
> In what land do the powerless turn the beak
> Of ravening Sorrow, or the hand of Wrath?

200
> For all your croziers, they have left the path
> And wander in the storms and clinging snows,
> Hopeless for ever: ancient Oisin knows,
> For he is weak and poor and blind, and lies
> On the anvil of the world.

> *S. Patrick.*   Be still: the skies
> Are choked with thunder, lightning, and fierce wind,
> For God has heard, and speaks His angry mind;
> Go cast your body on the stones and pray,
> For He has wrought midnight and dawn and day.

> *Oisin.* Saint, do you weep? I hear amid the thunder

210
> The Fenian horses; armour torn asunder;
> Laughter and cries. The armies clash and shock,
> And now the daylight-darkening ravens flock.
> Cease, cease, O mournful, laughing Fenian horn!

> We feasted for three days. On the fourth morn
> I found, dropping sea-foam on the wide stair,
> And hung with slime, and whispering in his hair,
> That demon dull and unsubduable;
> And once more to a day-long battle fell,

And at the sundown threw him in the surge,
To lie until the fourth morn saw emerge   220
His new-healed shape; and for a hundred years
So warred, so feasted, with nor dreams nor fears,
Nor languor nor fatigue: an endless feast,
An endless war.

        The hundred years had ceased;
I stood upon the stair: the surges bore
A beech-bough to me, and my heart grew sore,
Remembering how I had stood by white-haired Finn
Under a beech at Almhuin and heard the thin
Outcry of bats.

        And then young Niamh came
Holding that horse, and sadly called my name;   230
I mounted, and we passed over the lone
And drifting greyness, while this monotone,
Surly and distant, mixed inseparably
Into the clangour of the wind and sea.

'I hear my soul drop down into decay,
And Manannan's dark tower, stone after stone,
Gather sea-slime and fall the seaward way,
And the moon goad the waters night and day,
That all be overthrown.

'But till the moon has taken all, I wage   240
War on the mightiest men under the skies,
And they have fallen or fled, age after age.
Light is man's love, and lighter is man's rage;
His purpose drifts and dies.'

And then lost Niamh murmured, 'Love, we go
To the Island of Forgetfulness, for lo!
The Islands of Dancing and of Victories
Are empty of all power.'

        'And which of these
Is the Island of Content?'

        'None know,' she said;
And on my bosom laid her weeping head.   250

BOOK III

Fled foam underneath us, and round us, a wandering and milky smoke,
High as the saddle-girth, covering away from our glances the tide;
And those that fled, and that followed, from the foam-pale distance broke;
The immortal desire of Immortals we saw in their faces, and sighed.

I mused on the chase with the Fenians, and Bran, Sceolan, Lomair,
And never a song sang Niamh, and over my finger-tips
Came now the sliding of tears and sweeping of mist-cold hair,
And now the warmth of sighs, and after the quiver of lips.

Were we days long or hours long in riding, when, rolled in a grisly peace,
An isle lay level before us, with dripping hazel and oak?
And we stood on a sea's edge we saw not; for whiter than new-washed fleece
Fled foam underneath us, and round us, a wandering and milky smoke.

And we rode on the plains of the sea's edge; the sea's edge barren and grey,
Grey sand on the green of the grasses and over the dripping trees,
Dripping and doubling landward, as though they would hasten away,
Like an army of old men longing for rest from the moan of the seas.

But the trees grew taller and closer, immense in their wrinkling bark;
Dropping; a murmurous dropping; old silence and that one sound;
For no live creatures lived there, no weasels moved in the dark:
Long sighs arose in our spirits, beneath us bubbled the ground.

And the ears of the horse went sinking away in the hollow night,
For, as drift from a sailor slow drowning the gleams of the
    world and the sun,
Ceased on our hands and our faces, on hazel and oak leaf, the
    light,
And the stars were blotted above us, and the whole of the
    world was one.

Till the horse gave a whinny; for, cumbrous with stems of the
    hazel and oak,
A valley flowed down from his hoofs, and there in the long
    grass lay,
Under the starlight and shadow, a monstrous slumbering folk,
Their naked and gleaming bodies poured out and heaped in the
    way.

And by them were arrow and war-axe, arrow and shield and
    blade;
And dew-blanched horns, in whose hollow a child of three
    years old
Could sleep on a couch of rushes, and all inwrought and inlaid,
And more comely than man can make them with bronze and
    silver and gold.

And each of the huge white creatures was huger than fourscore
    men;
The tops of their ears were feathered, their hands were the
    claws of birds,
And, shaking the plumes of the grasses and the leaves of the
    mural glen,
The breathing came from those bodies, long warless, grown
    whiter than curds.

The wood was so spacious above them, that He who has stars
    for His flocks
Could fondle the leaves with His fingers, nor go from His
    dew-cumbered skies;
So long were they sleeping, the owls had builded their nests in
    their locks,
Filling the fibrous dimness with long generations of eyes.

30

40

And over the limbs and the valley the slow owls wandered and
    came,
Now in a place of star-fire, and now in a shadow-place wide;
And the chief of the huge white creatures, his knees in the soft
    star-flame,
Lay loose in a place of shadow: we drew the reins by his side.

Golden the nails of his bird-claws, flung loosely along the dim
    ground;
In one was a branch soft-shining with bells more many than
    sighs
In midst of an old man's bosom; owls ruffling and pacing
    around
Sidled their bodies against him, filling the shade with their eyes.

And my gaze was thronged with the sleepers; no, not since the
    world began,
50   In realms where the handsome were many, nor in glamours by
    demons flung,
Have faces alive with such beauty been known to the salt eye of
    man,
Yet weary with passions that faded when the sevenfold seas
    were young.

And I gazed on the bell-branch, sleep's forebear, far sung by the
    Sennachies.
I saw how those slumberers, grown weary, their camping in
    grasses deep,
Of wars with the wide world and pacing the shores of the
    wandering seas,
Laid hands on the bell-branch and swayed it, and fed of
    unhuman sleep.

Snatching the horn of Niamh, I blew a long lingering note.
Came sound from those monstrous sleepers, a sound like the
    stirring of flies.
He, shaking the fold of his lips, and heaving the pillar of his
    throat,
60   Watched me with mournful wonder out of the wells of his eyes.

I cried, 'Come out of the shadow, king of the nails of gold!
And tell of your goodly household and the goodly works of
    your hands,
That we may muse in the starlight and talk of the battles of
    old;
Your questioner, Oisin, is worthy, he comes from the Fenian
    lands.'

Half open his eyes were, and held me, dull with the smoke of
    their dreams;
His lips moved slowly in answer, no answer out of them came;
Then he swayed in his fingers the bell-branch, slow dropping a
    sound in faint streams
Softer than snow-flakes in April and piercing the marrow like
    flame.

Wrapt in the wave of that music, with weariness more than of
    earth,
The moil of my centuries filled me; and gone like a sea-covered
    stone   70
Were the memories of the whole of my sorrow and the
    memories of the whole of my mirth,
And a softness came from the starlight and filled me full to the
    bone.

In the roots of the grasses, the sorrels, I laid my body as low;
And the pearl-pale Niamh lay by me, her brow on the midst of
    my breast;
And the horse was gone in the distance, and years after years
    'gan flow;
Square leaves of the ivy moved over us, binding us down to our
    rest.

And, man of the many white croziers, a century there I forgot
How the fetlocks drip blood in the battle, when the fallen on
    fallen lie rolled;
How the falconer follows the falcon in the weeds of the heron's
    plot,
And the name of the demon whose hammer made Conchubar's
    sword-blade of old.   80

And, man of the many white croziers, a century there I forgot
That the spear-shaft is made out of ashwood, the shield out of
   osier and hide;
How the hammers spring on the anvil, on the spearhead's
   burning spot;
How the slow, blue-eyed oxen of Finn low sadly at evening tide.

But in dreams, mild man of the croziers, driving the dust with
   their throngs,
Moved round me, of seamen or landsmen, all who are winter
   tales;
Came by me the kings of the Red Branch, with roaring of
   laughter and songs,
Or moved as they moved once, love-making or piercing the
   tempest with sails.

Came Blanid, Mac Nessa, tall Fergus who feastward of old
   time slunk,
Cook Barach, the traitor; and warward, the spittle on his beard
90   never dry,
Dark Balor, as old as a forest, car-borne, his mighty head sunk
Helpless, men lifting the lids of his weary and death-making
   eye.

And by me, in soft red raiment, the Fenians moved in loud
   streams,
And Grania, walking and smiling, sewed with her needle of
   bone.
So lived I and lived not, so wrought I and wrought not, with
   creatures of dreams,
In a long iron sleep, as a fish in the water goes dumb as a
   stone.

At times our slumber was lightened. When the sun was on
   silver or gold;
When brushed with the wings of the owls, in the dimness they
   love going by;
When a glow-worm was green on a grass-leaf, lured from his
   lair in the mould;
Half wakening, we lifted our eyelids, and gazed on the grass
100   with a sigh.

So watched I when, man of the croziers, at the heel of a century
    fell,
Weak, in the midst of the meadow, from his miles in the midst
    of the air,
A starling like them that forgathered 'neath a moon waking
    white as a shell
When the Fenians made foray at morning with Bran, Sceolan,
    Lomair.

I awoke: the strange horse without summons out of the
    distance ran,
Thrusting his nose to my shoulder; he knew in his bosom deep
That once more moved in my bosom the ancient sadness of man,
And that I would leave the Immortals, their dimness, their dews
    dropping sleep.

O, had you seen beautiful Niamh grow white as the waters are
    white,
Lord of the croziers, you even had lifted your hands and wept: 110
But, the bird in my fingers, I mounted, remembering alone that
    delight
Of twilight and slumber were gone, and that hoofs impatiently
    stept.

I cried, 'O Niamh! O white one! if only a twelve-houred day,
I must gaze on the beard of Finn, and move where the old men
    and young
In the Fenians' dwellings of wattle lean on the chessboards and
    play,
Ah, sweet to me now were even bald Conan's slanderous tongue!

'Like me were some galley forsaken far off in Meridian isle,
Remembering its long-oared companions, sails turning to
    threadbare rags;
No more to crawl on the seas with long oars mile after mile,
But to be amid shooting of flies and flowering of rushes and flags.'   120

Their motionless eyeballs of spirits grown mild with mysterious
    thought,
Watched her those seamless faces from the valley's glimmering
    girth;

As she murmured, 'O wandering Oisin, the strength of the
bell-branch is naught,
For there moves alive in your fingers the fluttering sadness of
earth.

'Then go through the lands in the saddle and see what the
mortals do,
And softly come to your Niamh over the tops of the tide;
But weep for your Niamh, O Oisin, weep; for if only your shoe
Brush lightly as haymouse earth's pebbles, you will come no
more to my side.

'O flaming lion of the world, O when will you turn to your
rest?'
130   I saw from a distant saddle; from the earth she made her moan:
'I would die like a small withered leaf in the autumn, for breast
unto breast
We shall mingle no more, nor our gazes empty their sweetness
lone

'In the isles of the farthest seas where only the spirits come.
Were the winds less soft than the breath of a pigeon who sleeps
on her nest,
Nor lost in the star-fires and odours the sound of the sea's
vague drum?
O flaming lion of the world, O when will you turn to your
rest?'

The wailing grew distant; I rode by the woods of the wrinkling
bark,
Where ever is murmurous dropping, old silence and that one
sound;
For no live creatures live there, no weasels move in the dark;
140   In a reverie forgetful of all things, over the bubbling ground.

And I rode by the plains of the sea's edge, where all is barren
and grey,
Grey sand on the green of the grasses and over the dripping
trees,
Dripping and doubling landward, as though they would hasten
away,

Like an army of old men longing for rest from the moan of the
    seas.

And the winds made the sands on the sea's edge turning and
    turning go,
As my mind made the names of the Fenians. Far from the hazel
    and oak,
I rode away on the surges, where, high as the saddle-bow,
Fled foam underneath me, and round me, a wandering and
    milky smoke.

Long fled the foam-flakes around me, the winds fled out of the
    vast,
Snatching the bird in secret; nor knew I, embosomed apart,   150
When they froze the cloth on my body like armour riveted
    fast,
For Remembrance, lifting her leanness, keened in the gates of
    my heart.

Till, fattening the winds of the morning, an odour of new-mown
    hay
Came, and my forehead fell low, and my tears like berries fell
    down;
Later a sound came, half lost in the sound of a shore far away,
From the great grass-barnacle calling, and later the shore-weeds
    brown.

If I were as I once was, the strong hoofs crushing the sand and
    the shells,
Coming out of the sea as the dawn comes, a chaunt of love on
    my lips,
Not coughing, my head on my knees, and praying, and wroth
    with the bells,
I would leave no saint's head on his body from Rachlin to Bera
    of ships.   160

Making way from the kindling surges, I rode on a bridle-path
Much wondering to see upon all hands, of wattles and
    woodwork made,
Your bell-mounted churches, and guardless the sacred cairn and
    the rath,

And a small and a feeble populace stooping with mattock and
  spade,

Or weeding or ploughing with faces a-shining with much-toil
  wet;
While in this place and that place, with bodies unglorious, their
  chieftains stood,
Awaiting in patience the straw-death, croziered one, caught in
  your net:
Went the laughter of scorn from my mouth like the roaring of
  wind in a wood.

And because I went by them so huge and so speedy with eyes so
  bright,
Came after the hard gaze of youth, or an old man lifted his
  head:
And I rode and I rode, and I cried out, 'The Fenians hunt
  wolves in the night,
So sleep thee by daytime.' A voice cried, 'The Fenians a long
  time are dead.'

A whitebeard stood hushed on the pathway, the flesh of his face
  as dried grass,
And in folds round his eyes and his mouth, he sad as a child
  without milk;
And the dreams of the islands were gone, and I knew how men
  sorrow and pass,
And their hound, and their horse, and their love, and their eyes
  that glimmer like silk.

And wrapping my face in my hair, I murmured, 'In old age they
  ceased';
And my tears were larger than berries, and I murmured, 'Where
  white clouds lie spread
On Crevroe or broad Knockfefin, with many of old they feast
On the floors of the gods.' He cried, 'No, the gods a long time
  are dead.'

And lonely and longing for Niamh, I shivered and turned me
  about,
The heart in me longing to leap like a grasshopper into her
  heart;

I turned and rode to the westward, and followed the sea's old
　　shout
Till I saw where Maeve lies sleeping till starlight and midnight
　　part.

And there at the foot of the mountain, two carried a sack full
　　of sand,
They bore it with staggering and sweating, but fell with their
　　burden at length.
Leaning down from the gem-studded saddle, I flung it five yards
　　with my hand,
With a sob for men waxing so weakly, a sob for the Fenians'
　　old strength.

The rest you have heard of, O croziered man; how, when
　　divided the girth,
I fell on the path, and the horse went away like a summer fly;　190
And my years three hundred fell on me, and I rose, and walked
　　on the earth,
A creeping old man, full of sleep, with the spittle on his beard
　　never dry.

How the men of the sand-sack showed me a church with its
　　belfry in air;
Sorry place, where for swing of the war-axe in my dim eyes the
　　crozier gleams;
What place have Caoilte and Conan, and Bran, Sceolan,
　　Lomair?
Speak, you too are old with your memories, an old man
　　surrounded with dreams.

S. Patrick. Where the flesh of the footsole clingeth on the burning
　　stones is their place;
Where the demons whip them with wires on the burning stones
　　of wide Hell,
Watching the blessèd ones move far off, and the smile on God's
　　face,
Between them a gateway of brass, and the howl of the angels
　　who fell.
　　　　　　　　　　　　　　　　　　　　　　　　　　　200

Oisin. Put the staff in my hands; for I go to the Fenians, O cleric,
　　to chaunt

The war-songs that roused them of old; they will rise, making
 clouds with their breath,
Innumerable, singing, exultant; the clay underneath them shall
 pant,
And demons be broken in pieces, and trampled beneath them in
 death.

And demons afraid in their darkness; deep horror of eyes and
 of wings,
Afraid, their ears on the earth laid, shall listen and rise up and
 weep;
Hearing the shaking of shields and the quiver of stretched
 bowstrings,
Hearing Hell loud with a murmur, as shouting and mocking we
 sweep.

We will tear out the flaming stones, and batter the gateway of
 brass
And enter, and none sayeth 'No' when there enters the strongly
 armed guest;
Make clean as a broom cleans, and march on as oxen move
 over young grass;
Then feast, making converse of wars, and of old wounds, and
 turn to our rest.

S. Patrick. On the flaming stones, without refuge, the limbs of the
 Fenians are tost;
None war on the masters of Hell, who could break up the
 world in their rage;
But kneel and wear out the flags and pray for your soul that is
 lost
Through the demon love of its youth and its godless and
 passionate age.

Oisin. Ah me! to be shaken with coughing and broken with old
 age and pain,
Without laughter, a show unto children, alone with
 remembrance and fear;
All emptied of purple hours as a beggar's cloak in the rain,
As a hay-cock out on the flood, or a wolf sucked under a
 weir.

It were sad to gaze on the blessèd and no man I loved of old
    there;
I throw down the chain of small stones! when life in my body
    has ceased,
I will go to Caoilte, and Conan, and Bran, Sceolan, Lomair,
And dwell in the house of the Fenians, be they in flames or at
    feast.

The Old Age
of Queen Maeve

1903

376

The Old Age of Queen Maeve

A certain poet in outlandish clothes
Gathered a crowd in some Byzantine lane,
Talked of his country and its people, sang
To some stringed instrument none there had seen,
A wall behind his back, over his head
A latticed window. His glance went up at times
As though one listened there, and his voice sank
Or let its meaning mix into the strings.

Maeve the great queen was pacing to and fro,
Between the walls covered with beaten bronze,
In her high house at Cruachan[1]; the long hearth,   10
Flickering with ash and hazel, but half showed
Where the tired horse-boys lay upon the rushes,
Or on the benches underneath the walls,
In comfortable sleep; all living slept
But that great queen, who more than half the night
Had paced from door to fire and fire to door.
Though now in her old age, in her young age
She had been beautiful in that old way
That's all but gone; for the proud heart is gone,   20
And the fool heart of the counting-house fears all
But soft beauty and indolent desire.
She could have called over the rim of the world
Whatever woman's lover had hit her fancy,
And yet had been great-bodied and great-limbed,
Fashioned to be the mother of strong children;

[1] Pronounced in modern Gaelic as if spelt 'Crockan.'

And she'd had lucky eyes and a high heart,
And wisdom that caught fire like the dried flax,
At need, and made her beautiful and fierce,
Sudden and laughing.
30   O unquiet heart,
Why do you praise another, praising her,
As if there were no tale but your own tale
Worth knitting to a measure of sweet sound?
Have I not bid you tell of that great queen
Who has been buried some two thousand years?

When night was at its deepest, a wild goose
Cried from the porter's lodge, and with long clamour
Shook the ale-horns and shields upon their hooks;
But the horse-boys slept on, as though some power
40   Had filled the house with Druid heaviness;
And wondering who of the many-changing Sidhe
Had come as in the old times to counsel her,
Maeve walked, yet with slow footfall, being old,
To that small chamber by the outer gate.
The porter slept, although he sat upright
With still and stony limbs and open eyes.
Maeve waited, and when that ear-piercing noise
Broke from his parted lips and broke again,
She laid a hand on either of his shoulders,
50   And shook him wide awake, and bid him say
Who of the wandering many-changing ones
Had troubled his sleep. But all he had to say
Was that, the air being heavy and the dogs
More still than they had been for a good month,
He had fallen asleep, and, though he had dreamed nothing,
He could remember when he had had fine dreams.
It was before the time of the great war
Over the White-Horned Bull and the Brown Bull.

She turned away; he turned again to sleep
60   That no god troubled now, and, wondering
What matters were afoot among the Sidhe,
Maeve walked through that great hall, and with a sigh

Lifted the curtain of her sleeping-room,
Remembering that she too had seemed divine
To many thousand eyes, and to her own
One that the generations had long waited
That work too difficult for mortal hands
Might be accomplished. Bunching the curtain up
She saw her husband Ailell sleeping there,
And thought of days when he'd had a straight body,　　70
And of that famous Fergus, Nessa's husband,
Who had been the lover of her middle life.

Suddenly Ailell spoke out of his sleep,
And not with his own voice or a man's voice,
But with the burning, live, unshaken voice
Of those that, it may be, can never age.
He said, 'High Queen of Cruachan and Magh Ai,
A king of the Great Plain would speak with you.'
And with glad voice Maeve answered him, 'What king
Of the far-wandering shadows has come to me,　　80
As in the old days when they would come and go
About my threshold to counsel and to help?'
The parted lips replied, 'I seek your help,
For I am Aengus, and I am crossed in love.'
'How may a mortal whose life gutters out
Help them that wander with hand clasping hand,
Their haughty images that cannot wither,
For all their beauty's like a hollow dream,
Mirrored in streams that neither hail nor rain
Nor the cold North has troubled?'
　　　　　　　　　　　　　He replied,　　90
'I am from those rivers and I bid you call
The children of the Maines out of sleep,
And set them digging under Bual's hill.
We shadows, while they uproot his earthy house,
Will overthrow his shadows and carry off
Caer, his blue-eyed daughter that I love.
I helped your fathers when they built these walls,
And I would have your help in my great need,
Queen of high Cruachan.'

'I obey your will
100   With speedy feet and a most thankful heart:
For you have been, O Aengus of the birds,
Our giver of good counsel and good luck.'
And with a groan, as if the mortal breath
Could but awaken sadly upon lips
That happier breath had moved, her husband turned
Face downward, tossing in a troubled sleep;
But Maeve, and not with a slow feeble foot,
Came to the threshold of the painted house
Where her grandchildren slept, and cried aloud,
110   Until the pillared dark began to stir
With shouting and the clang of unhooked arms.
She told them of the many-changing ones;
And all that night, and all through the next day
To middle night, they dug into the hill.
At middle night great cats with silver claws,
Bodies of shadow and blind eyes like pearls,
Came up out of the hole, and red-eared hounds
With long white bodies came out of the air
Suddenly, and ran at them and harried them.

120   The Maines' children dropped their spades, and stood
With quaking joints and terror-stricken faces,
Till Maeve called out, 'These are but common men.
The Maines' children have not dropped their spades
Because Earth, crazy for its broken power,
Casts up a show and the winds answer it
With holy shadows.' Her high heart was glad,
And when the uproar ran along the grass
She followed with light footfall in the midst,
Till it died out where an old thorn-tree stood.

130   Friend of these many years, you too had stood
With equal courage in that whirling rout;
For you, although you've not her wandering heart,
Have all that greatness, and not hers alone,
For there is no high story about queens
In any ancient book but tells of you;

And when I've heard how they grew old and died,
Or fell into unhappiness, I've said,
'She will grow old and die, and she has wept!'
And when I'd write it out anew, the words,
Half crazy with the thought, She too has wept!   140
Outrun the measure.
                I'd tell of that great queen
Who stood amid a silence by the thorn
Until two lovers came out of the air
With bodies made out of soft fire. The one,
About whose face birds wagged their fiery wings,
Said, 'Aengus and his sweetheart give their thanks
To Maeve and to Maeve's household, owing all
In owing them the bride-bed that gives peace.'
Then Maeve: 'O Aengus, Master of all lovers,
A thousand years ago you held high talk   150
With the first kings of many-pillared Cruachan.
O when will you grow weary?'
                They had vanished;
But out of the dark air over her head there came
A murmur of soft words and meeting lips.

Baile and Aillinn

1903

Baile and Aillinn

ARGUMENT. *Baile and Aillinn were lovers, but Aengus, the Master of Love, wishing them to be happy in his own land among the dead, told to each a story of the other's death, so that their hearts were broken and they died.*

I hardly hear the curlew cry,
Nor the grey rush when the wind is high,
Before my thoughts begin to run
On the heir of Ulad, Buan's son,
Baile, who had the honey mouth;
And that mild woman of the south,
Aillinn, who was King Lugaid's heir.
Their love was never drowned in care
Of this or that thing, nor grew cold
Because their bodies had grown old.   10
Being forbid to marry on earth,
They blossomed to immortal mirth.

About the time when Christ was born,
When the long wars for the White Horn
And the Brown Bull had not yet come,
Young Baile Honey-Mouth, whom some
Called rather Baile Little-Land,
Rode out of Emain with a band
Of harpers and young men; and they
Imagined, as they struck the way   20
To many-pastured Muirthemne,
That all things fell out happily,

And there, for all that fools had said,
Baile and Aillinn would be wed.

They found an old man running there:
He had ragged long grass-coloured hair;
He had knees that stuck out of his hose;
He had puddle-water in his shoes;
He had half a cloak to keep him dry,
30   Although he had a squirrel's eye.

O wandering birds and rushy beds,
You put such folly in our heads
With all this crying in the wind;
No common love is to our mind,
And our poor Kate or Nan is less
Than any whose unhappiness
Awoke the harp-strings long ago.
Yet they that know all things but know
That all this life can give us is
40   *A child's laughter, a woman's kiss.*
Who was it put so great a scorn
In the grey reeds that night and morn
Are trodden and broken by the herds,
And in the light bodies of birds
The north wind tumbles to and fro
And pinches among hail and snow?

That runner said: 'I am from the south;
I run to Baile Honey-Mouth,
To tell him how the girl Aillinn
50   Rode from the country of her kin,
And old and young men rode with her:
For all that country had been astir
If anybody half as fair
Had chosen a husband anywhere
But where it could see her every day.
When they had ridden a little way
An old man caught the horse's head
With: "You must home again, and wed

With somebody in your own land."
A young man cried and kissed her hand,   60
"O lady, wed with one of us";
And when no face grew piteous
For any gentle thing she spake,
She fell and died of the heart-break.'

Because a lover's heart's worn out,
Being tumbled and blown about
By its own blind imagining,
And will believe that anything
That is bad enough to be true, is true,
Baile's heart was broken in two;   70
And he, being laid upon green boughs,
Was carried to the goodly house
Where the Hound of Ulad sat before
The brazen pillars of his door,
His face bowed low to weep the end
Of the harper's daughter and her friend.
For although years had passed away
He always wept them on that day,
For on that day they had been betrayed;
And now that Honey-Mouth is laid   80
Under a cairn of sleepy stone
Before his eyes, he has tears for none,
Although he is carrying stone, but two
For whom the cairn's but heaped anew.

We hold, because our memory is
So full of that thing and of this,
That out of sight is out of mind.
But the grey rush under the wind
And the grey bird with crooked bill
Have such long memories that they still   90
Remember Deirdre and her man;
And when we walk with Kate or Nan
About the windy water-side,
Our hearts can hear the voices chide.
How could we be so soon content,

Who know the way that Naoise went?
And they have news of Deirdre's eyes,
Who being lovely was so wise—
Ah! wise, my heart knows well how wise.

100 Now had that old gaunt crafty one,
Gathering his cloak about him, run
Where Aillinn rode with waiting-maids,
Who amid leafy lights and shades
Dreamed of the hands that would unlace
Their bodices in some dim place
When they had come to the marriage-bed;
And harpers, pacing with high head
As though their music were enough
To make the savage heart of love
110 Grow gentle without sorrowing,
Imagining and pondering
Heaven knows what calamity;

'Another's hurried off,' cried he,
'From heat and cold and wind and wave;
They have heaped the stones above his grave
In Muirthemne, and over it
In changeless Ogham letters writ—
Baile, that was of Rury's seed.
But the gods long ago decreed
120 No waiting-maid should ever spread
Baile and Aillinn's marriage-bed,
For they should clip and clip again
Where wild bees hive on the Great Plain.
Therefore it is but little news
That put this hurry in my shoes.'

Then seeing that he scarce had spoke
Before her love-worn heart had broke,
He ran and laughed until he came
To that high hill the herdsmen name
130 The Hill Seat of Leighin, because
Some god or king had made the laws

That held the land together there,
In old times among the clouds of the air.

That old man climbed; the day grew dim;
Two swans came flying up to him,
Linked by a gold chain each to each,
And with low murmuring laughing speech
Alighted on the windy grass.
They knew him: his changed body was
Tall, proud and ruddy, and light wings   140
Were hovering over the harp-strings
That Edain, Midhir's wife, had wove
In the hid place, being crazed by love.

What shall I call them? fish that swim,
Scale rubbing scale where light is dim
By a broad water-lily leaf;
Or mice in the one wheaten sheaf
Forgotten at the threshing-place;
Or birds lost in the one clear space
Of morning light in a dim sky;   150
Or, it may be, the eyelids of one eye,
Or the door-pillars of one house,
Or two sweet blossoming apple-boughs
That have one shadow on the ground;
Or the two strings that made one sound
Where that wise harper's finger ran.
For this young girl and this young man
Have happiness without an end,
Because they have made so good a friend.

They know all wonders, for they pass   160
The towery gates of Gorias,
And Findrias and Falias,
And long-forgotten Murias,
Among the giant kings whose hoard,
Cauldron and spear and stone and sword,
Was robbed before earth gave the wheat;
Wandering from broken street to street

They come where some huge watcher is,
And tremble with their love and kiss.

170 They know undying things, for they
Wander where earth withers away,
Though nothing troubles the great streams
But light from the pale stars, and gleams
From the holy orchards, where there is none
But fruit that is of precious stone,
Or apples of the sun and moon.

What were our praise to them? They eat
Quiet's wild heart, like daily meat;
Who when night thickens are afloat
180 On dappled skins in a glass boat,
Far out under a windless sky;
While over them birds of Aengus fly,
And over the tiller and the prow,
And waving white wings to and fro
Awaken wanderings of light air
To stir their coverlet and their hair.

And poets found, old writers say,
A yew tree where his body lay;
But a wild apple hid the grass
190 With its sweet blossom where hers was;
And being in good heart, because
A better time had come again
After the deaths of many men,
And that long fighting at the ford,
They wrote on tablets of thin board,
Made of the apple and the yew,
All the love stories that they knew.

Let rush and bird cry out their fill
Of the harper's daughter if they will,
Beloved, I am not afraid of her. 200
She is not wiser nor lovelier,
And you are more high of heart than she,
For all her wanderings over-sea;
But I'd have bird and rush forget
Those other two; for never yet
Has lover lived, but longed to wive
Like them that are no more alive.

The
Shadowy Waters

1906

378

I walked among the seven woods of Coole,
Shan-walla, where a willow-bordered pond
Gathers the wild duck from the winter dawn;
Shady Kyle-dortha; sunnier Kyle-na-no,
Where many hundred squirrels are as happy
As though they had been hidden by green boughs
Where old age cannot find them; Pairc-na-lee,
Where hazel and ash and privet blind the paths;
Dim Pairc-na-carraig, where the wild bees fling
Their sudden fragrances on the green air;   10
Dim Pairc-na-tarav, where enchanted eyes
Have seen immortal, mild, proud shadows walk;
Dim Inchy wood, that hides badger and fox
And marten-cat, and borders that old wood
Wise Biddy Early called the wicked wood:
Seven odours, seven murmurs, seven woods.
I had not eyes like those enchanted eyes,
Yet dreamed that beings happier than men
Moved round me in the shadows, and at night
My dreams were cloven by voices and by fires;   20
And the images I have woven in this story
Of Forgael and Dectora and the empty waters
Moved round me in the voices and the fires,
And more I may not write of, for they that cleave
The waters of sleep can make a chattering tongue
Heavy like stone, their wisdom being half silence.
How shall I name you, immortal, mild, proud shadows?
I only know that all we know comes from you,
And that you come from Eden on flying feet.
Is Eden far away, or do you hide   30
From human thought, as hares and mice and coneys
That run before the reaping-hook and lie
In the last ridge of the barley? Do our woods

And winds and ponds cover more quiet woods,
More shining winds, more star-glimmering ponds?
Is Eden out of time and out of space?
And do you gather about us when pale light
Shining on water and fallen among leaves,
And winds blowing from flowers, and whirr of feathers
40   *And the green quiet, have uplifted the heart?*

I have made this poem for you, that men may read it
Before they read of Forgael and Dectora,
As men in the old times, before the harps began,
Poured out wine for the high invisible ones.

September 1900

379

The Harp of Aengus

Edain came out of Midhir's hill, and lay
Beside young Aengus in his tower of glass,
Where time is drowned in odour-laden winds
And Druid moons, and murmuring of boughs,
And sleepy boughs, and boughs where apples made
Of opal and ruby and pale chrysolite
Awake unsleeping fires; and wove seven strings,
Sweet with all music, out of his long hair,
Because her hands had been made wild by love.
When Midhir's wife had changed her to a fly,   10
He made a harp with Druid apple-wood
That she among her winds might know he wept;
And from that hour he has watched over none
But faithful lovers.

PERSONS IN THE POEM

FORGAEL

AIBRIC

SAILORS

DECTORA

380

The Shadowy Waters

A DRAMATIC POEM

The deck of an ancient ship. At the right of the stage is the mast, with a large square sail hiding a great deal of the sky and sea on that side. The tiller is at the left of the stage; it is a long oar coming through an opening in the bulwark. The deck rises in a series of steps behind the tiller, and the stern of the ship curves overhead. When the play opens there are four persons upon the deck. Aibric stands by the tiller. Forgael sleeps upon the raised portion of the deck towards the front of the stage. Two Sailors are standing near to the mast, on which a harp is hanging.

First Sailor. Has he not led us into these waste seas
    For long enough?

Second Sailor.   Aye, long and long enough.

First Sailor. We have not come upon a shore or ship
    These dozen weeks.

Second Sailor.   And I had thought to make
    A good round sum upon this cruise, and turn—
    For I am getting on in life—to something
    That has less ups and downs than robbery.

First Sailor. I am so tired of being a bachelor
    I could give all my heart to that Red Moll
    That had but the one eye.

Second Sailor.   Can no bewitchment
    Transform these rascal billows into women
    That I may drown myself?   10

First Sailor.   Better steer home,
    Whether he will or no; and better still
    To take him while he sleeps and carry him
    And drop him from the gunnel.

Second Sailor.   I dare not do it.

Were't not that there is magic in his harp,
I would be of your mind; but when he plays it
Strange creatures flutter up before one's eyes,
Or cry about one's ears.

First Sailor.   Nothing to fear.

20 *Second Sailor.* Do you remember when we sank that galley
At the full moon?

First Sailor.   He played all through the night.

Second Sailor. Until the moon had set; and when I looked
Where the dead drifted, I could see a bird
Like a grey gull upon the breast of each.
While I was looking they rose hurriedly,
And after circling with strange cries awhile
Flew westward; and many a time since then
I've heard a rustling overhead in the wind.

First Sailor. I saw them on that night as well as you.
30   But when I had eaten and drunk myself asleep
My courage came again.

Second Sailor.   But that's not all.
The other night, while he was playing it,
A beautiful young man and girl came up
In a white breaking wave; they had the look
Of those that are alive for ever and ever.

First Sailor. I saw them, too, one night. Forgael was playing,
And they were listening there beyond the sail.
He could not see them, but I held out my hands
To grasp the woman.

Second Sailor.   You have dared to touch her?

40 *First Sailor.* O she was but a shadow, and slipped from me.

Second Sailor. But were you not afraid?

First Sailor.   Why should I fear?

Second Sailor. 'Twas Aengus and Edain, the wandering lovers,
To whom all lovers pray.

First Sailor.   But what of that?
 A shadow does not carry sword or spear.

Second Sailor. My mother told me that there is not one
 Of the Ever-living half so dangerous
 As that wild Aengus. Long before her day
 He carried Edain off from a king's house,
 And hid her among fruits of jewel-stone
 And in a tower of glass, and from that day   50
 Has hated every man that's not in love,
 And has been dangerous to him.

First Sailor.   I have heard
 He does not hate seafarers as he hates
 Peaceable men that shut the wind away,
 And keep to the one weary marriage-bed.

Second Sailor. I think that he has Forgael in his net,
 And drags him through the sea.

First Sailor.   Well, net or none,
 I'd drown him while we have the chance to do it.

Second Sailor. It's certain I'd sleep easier o' nights
 If he were dead; but who will be our captain,   60
 Judge of the stars, and find a course for us?

First Sailor. I've thought of that. We must have Aibric with us,
 For he can judge the stars as well as Forgael.
           [Going towards Aibric.]
 Become our captain, Aibric. I am resolved
 To make an end of Forgael while he sleeps.
 There's not a man but will be glad of it
 When it is over, nor one to grumble at us.

Aibric. You have taken pay and made your bargain for it.

First Sailor. What good is there in this hard way of living,
 Unless we drain more flagons in a year   70
 And kiss more lips than lasting peaceable men
 In their long lives? Will you be of our troop
 And take the captain's share of everything
 And bring us into populous seas again?

Aibric. Be of your troop! Aibric be one of you
 And Forgael in the other scale! kill Forgael,
 And he my master from my childhood up!
 If you will draw that sword out of its scabbard
 I'll give my answer.

First Sailor.   You have awakened him.
              [To Second Sailor.]
80   We'd better go, for we have lost this chance.
                [They go out.]

Forgael. Have the birds passed us? I could hear your voice,
 But there were others.

Aibric.   I have seen nothing pass.

Forgael. You're certain of it? I never wake from sleep
 But that I am afraid they may have passed,
 For they're my only pilots. If I lost them
 Straying too far into the north or south,
 I'd never come upon the happiness
 That has been promised me. I have not seen them
 These many days; and yet there must be many
90 Dying at every moment in the world,
 And flying towards their peace.

Aibric.   Put by these thoughts,
 And listen to me for a while. The sailors
 Are plotting for your death.

Forgael.   Have I not given
 More riches than they ever hoped to find?
 And now they will not follow, while I seek
 The only riches that have hit my fancy.

Aibric. What riches can you find in this waste sea
 Where no ship sails, where nothing that's alive
 Has ever come but those man-headed birds,
 Knowing it for the world's end?

100 *Forgael.*   Where the world ends
 The mind is made unchanging, for it finds
 Miracle, ecstasy, the impossible hope,

The flagstone under all, the fire of fires,
The roots of the world.

Aibric.   Shadows before now
  Have driven travellers mad for their own sport.

Forgael. Do you, too, doubt me? Have you joined their plot?

Aibric. No, no, do not say that. You know right well
  That I will never lift a hand against you.

Forgael. Why should you be more faithful than the rest,
  Being as doubtful?

Aibric.   I have called you master   110
  Too many years to lift a hand against you.

Forgael. Maybe it is but natural to doubt me.
  You've never known, I'd lay a wager on it,
  A melancholy that a cup of wine,
  A lucky battle, or a woman's kiss
  Could not amend.

Aibric.   I have good spirits enough.

Forgael. If you will give me all your mind awhile—
  All, all, the very bottom of the bowl—
  I'll show you that I am made differently,
  That nothing can amend it but these waters,   120
  Where I am rid of life—the events of the world—
  What do you call it?—that old promise-breaker,
  The cozening fortune-teller that comes whispering,
  'You will have all you have wished for when you have earned
  Land for your children or money in a pot.'
  And when we have it we are no happier,
  Because of that old draught under the door,
  Or creaky shoes. And at the end of all
  How are we better off than Seaghan the fool,
  That never did a hand's turn? Aibric! Aibric!   130
  We have fallen in the dreams the Ever-living
  Breathe on the burnished mirror of the world
  And then smooth out with ivory hands and sigh,
  And find their laughter sweeter to the taste

For that brief sighing.

Aibric.   If you had loved some woman—

Forgael. You say that also? You have heard the voices,
For that is what they say—all, all the shadows—
Aengus and Edain, those passionate wanderers,
And all the others; but it must be love
140   As they have known it. Now the secret's out;
For it is love that I am seeking for,
But of a beautiful, unheard-of kind
That is not in the world.

Aibric.   And yet the world
Has beautiful women to please every man.

Forgael. But he that gets their love after the fashion
Loves in brief longing and deceiving hope
And bodily tenderness, and finds that even
The bed of love, that in the imagination
Had seemed to be the giver of all peace,
150   Is no more than a wine-cup in the tasting,
And as soon finished.

Aibric.   All that ever loved
Have loved that way—there is no other way.

Forgael. Yet never have two lovers kissed but they
Believed there was some other near at hand,
And almost wept because they could not find it.

Aibric. When they have twenty years; in middle life
They take a kiss for what a kiss is worth,
And let the dream go by.

Forgael.   It's not a dream,
But the reality that makes our passion
160   As a lamp shadow—no—no lamp, the sun.
What the world's million lips are thirsting for
Must be substantial somewhere.

Aibric.   I have heard the Druids
Mutter such things as they awake from trance.
It may be that the Ever-living know it—

No mortal can.

Forgael.   Yes; if they give us help.

Aibric. They are besotting you as they besot
The crazy herdsman that will tell his fellows
That he has been all night upon the hills,
Riding to hurley, or in the battle-host
With the Ever-living.

Forgael.   What if he speak the truth,   170
And for a dozen hours have been a part
Of that more powerful life?

Aibric.   His wife knows better.
Has she not seen him lying like a log,
Or fumbling in a dream about the house?
And if she hear him mutter of wild riders,
She knows that it was but the cart-horse coughing
That set him to the fancy.

Forgael.   All would be well
Could we but give us wholly to the dreams,
And get into their world that to the sense
Is shadow, and not linger wretchedly   180
Among substantial things; for it is dreams
That lift us to the flowing, changing world
That the heart longs for. What is love itself,
Even though it be the lightest of light love,
But dreams that hurry from beyond the world
To make low laughter more than meat and drink,
Though it but set us sighing? Fellow-wanderer,
Could we but mix ourselves into a dream,
Not in its image on the mirror!

Aibric.   While
We're in the body that's impossible.   190

Forgael. And yet I cannot think they're leading me
To death; for they that promised to me love
As those that can outlive the moon have known it,
Had the world's total life gathered up, it seemed,
Into their shining limbs—I've had great teachers.

Aengus and Edain ran up out of the wave—
You'd never doubt that it was life they promised
Had you looked on them face to face as I did,
With so red lips, and running on such feet,
200 And having such wide-open, shining eyes.

Aibric. It's certain they are leading you to death.
None but the dead, or those that never lived,
Can know that ecstasy. Forgael! Forgael!
They have made you follow the man-headed birds,
And you have told me that their journey lies
Towards the country of the dead.

Forgael. What matter
If I am going to my death?—for there,
Or somewhere, I shall find the love they have promised.
That much is certain. I shall find a woman,
210 One of the Ever-living, as I think—
One of the Laughing People—and she and I
Shall light upon a place in the world's core,
Where passion grows to be a changeless thing,
Like charmèd apples made of chrysoprase,
Or chrysoberyl, or beryl, or chrysolite;
And there, in juggleries of sight and sense,
Become one movement, energy, delight,
Until the overburthened moon is dead.

[*A number of Sailors enter hurriedly.*]

First Sailor. Look there! there in the mist! a ship of spice!
And we are almost on her!

220 *Second Sailor.* We had not known
But for the ambergris and sandalwood.

First Sailor. No; but opoponax and cinnamon.

Forgael [*taking the tiller from Aibric*]. The Ever-living have kept
my bargain for me,
And paid you on the nail.

Aibric. Take up that rope
To make her fast while we are plundering her.

First Sailor. There is a king and queen upon her deck,
  And where there is one woman there'll be others.

Aibric. Speak lower, or they'll hear.

First Sailor.   They cannot hear;
  They are too busy with each other. Look!
  He has stooped down and kissed her on the lips.   230

Second Sailor. When she finds out we have better men aboard
  She may not be too sorry in the end.

First Sailor. She will be like a wild cat; for these queens
  Care more about the kegs of silver and gold
  And the high fame that come to them in marriage,
  Than a strong body and a ready hand.

Second Sailor. There's nobody is natural but a robber,
  And that is why the world totters about
  Upon its bandy legs.

Aibric.   Run at them now,
  And overpower the crew while yet asleep!   240
                              [*The Sailors go out.*]
[*Voices and the clashing of swords are heard from the other ship,
  which cannot be seen because of the sail.*]

A Voice. Armed men have come upon us! O I am slain!

Another Voice. Wake all below!

Another Voice.   Why have you broken our sleep?

First Voice. Armed men have come upon us! O I am slain!

Forgael [*who has remained at the tiller*]. There! there they come!
    Gull, gannet, or diver,
  But with a man's head, or a fair woman's,
  They hover over the masthead awhile
  To wait their friends; but when their friends have come
  They'll fly upon that secret way of theirs.
  One—and one—a couple—five together;
  And I will hear them talking in a minute.   250
  Yes, voices! but I do not catch the words.

Now I can hear. There's one of them that says,
'How light we are, now we are changed to birds!'
Another answers, 'Maybe we shall find
Our heart's desire now that we are so light.'
And then one asks another how he died,
And says, 'A sword-blade pierced me in my sleep.'
And now they all wheel suddenly and fly
To the other side, and higher in the air.
260   And now a laggard with a woman's head
Comes crying, 'I have run upon the sword.
I have fled to my beloved in the air,
In the waste of the high air, that we may wander
Among the windy meadows of the dawn.'
But why are they still waiting? why are they
Circling and circling over the masthead?
What power that is more mighty than desire
To hurry to their hidden happiness
Withholds them now? Have the Ever-living Ones
270   A meaning in that circling overhead?
But what's the meaning? [*He cries out.*] Why do you linger there?
Why linger? Run to your desire,
Are you not happy wingèd bodies now?

                                 [*His voice sinks again.*]
Being too busy in the air and the high air,
They cannot hear my voice; but what's the meaning?
         [*The Sailors have returned. Dectora is with them.*]

Forgael [*turning and seeing her*]. Why are you standing with your
    eyes upon me?
You are not the world's core. O no, no, no!
That cannot be the meaning of the birds.
You are not its core. My teeth are in the world,
But have not bitten yet.

280   *Dectora.*   I am a queen,
And ask for satisfaction upon these
Who have slain my husband and laid hands upon me.
       [*Breaking loose from the Sailors who are holding her.*]
Let go my hands!

Forgael.   Why do you cast a shadow?
  Where do you come from? Who brought you to this place?
  They would not send me one that casts a shadow.

Dectora. Would that the storm that overthrew my ships,
  And drowned the treasures of nine conquered nations,
  And blew me hither to my lasting sorrow,
  Had drowned me also. But, being yet alive,
  I ask a fitting punishment for all   290
  That raised their hands against him.

Forgael.   There are some
  That weigh and measure all in these waste seas—
  They that have all the wisdom that's in life,
  And all that prophesying images
  Made of dim gold rave out in secret tombs;
  They have it that the plans of kings and queens
  Are dust on the moth's wing; that nothing matters
  But laughter and tears—laughter, laughter, and tears;
  That every man should carry his own soul
  Upon his shoulders.

Dectora.   You've nothing but wild words,   300
  And I would know if you will give me vengeance.

Forgael. When she finds out I will not let her go—
  When she knows that.

Dectora.   What is it that you are muttering—
  That you'll not let me go? I am a queen.

Forgael. Although you are more beautiful than any,
  I almost long that it were possible;
  But if I were to put you on that ship,
  With sailors that were sworn to do your will,
  And you had spread a sail for home, a wind
  Would rise of a sudden, or a wave so huge,   310
  It had washed among the stars and put them out,
  And beat the bulwark of your ship on mine,
  Until you stood before me on the deck—
  As now.

Dectora.   Does wandering in these desolate seas
And listening to the cry of wind and wave
Bring madness?

Forgael.   Queen, I am not mad.

Dectora.   Yet say
That unimaginable storms of wind and wave
Would rise against me.

Forgael.   No, I am not mad—
If it be not that hearing messages
320   From lasting watchers, that outlive the moon,
At the most quiet midnight is to be stricken.

Dectora. And did those watchers bid you take me captive?

Forgael. Both you and I are taken in the net.
It was their hands that plucked the winds awake
And blew you hither; and their mouths have promised
I shall have love in their immortal fashion;
And for this end they gave me my old harp
That is more mighty than the sun and moon,
Or than the shivering casting-net of the stars,
330   That none might take you from me.

Dectora [*first trembling back from the mast where the harp is and
        then laughing*].   For a moment
Your raving of a message and a harp
More mighty than the stars half troubled me,
But all that's raving. Who is there can compel
The daughter and the granddaughter of kings
To be his bedfellow?

Forgael.   Until your lips
Have called me their beloved, I'll not kiss them.

Dectora. My husband and my king died at my feet,
And yet you talk of love.

Forgael.   The movement of time
Is shaken in these seas, and what one does
340   One moment has no might upon the moment

That follows after.

Dectora.   I understand you now.
   You have a Druid craft of wicked sound
   Wrung from the cold women of the sea—
   A magic that can call a demon up,
   Until my body give you kiss for kiss.

Forgael. Your soul shall give the kiss.

Dectora.   I am not afraid,
   While there's a rope to run into a noose
   Or wave to drown. But I have done with words,
   And I would have you look into my face
   And know that it is fearless.

Forgael.   Do what you will,   350
   For neither I nor you can break a mesh
   Of the great golden net that is about us.

Dectora. There's nothing in the world that's worth a fear.
      [*She passes Forgael and stands for a moment looking into his
       face.*]
   I have good reason for that thought.
            [*She runs suddenly on to the raised part of the poop.*]
                              And now
   I can put fear away as a queen should.
      [*She mounts on to the bulwark and turns towards Forgael.*]
   Fool, fool! Although you have looked into my face
   You do not see my purpose. I shall have gone
   Before a hand can touch me.

Forgael [*folding his arms*].   My hands are still;
   The Ever-living hold us. Do what you will,
   You cannot leap out of the golden net.   360

First Sailor. No need to drown, for, if you will pardon us
   And measure out a course and bring us home,
   We'll put this man to death.

Dectora.   I promise it.

First Sailor. There is none to take his side.

Aibric.   I am on his side.
    I'll strike a blow for him to give him time
    To cast his dreams away.
        [*Aibric goes in front of Forgael with drawn sword. Forgael*
            takes the harp.]

First Sailor.   No other'll do it.
        [*The Sailors throw Aibric on one side. He falls and lies upon*
        the deck. They lift their swords to strike Forgael, who is
        about to play the harp. The stage begins to darken. The
        Sailors hesitate in fear.]

Second Sailor. He has put a sudden darkness over the moon.

Dectora. Nine swords with handles of rhinoceros horn
    To him that strikes him first!

First Sailor.   I will strike him first.
            [*He goes close up to Forgael with his sword lifted.*]
370   [*Shrinking back.*] He has caught the crescent moon out of the sky,
        And carries it between us.

Second Sailor.   Holy fire
    To burn us to the marrow if we strike.

Dectora. I'll give a golden galley full of fruit,
    That has the heady flavour of new wine,
    To him that wounds him to the death.

First Sailor.   I'll do it.
    For all his spells will vanish when he dies,
    Having their life in him.

Second Sailor.   Though it be the moon
    That he is holding up between us there,
    I will strike at him.

The Others.   And I! And I! And I!
                        [*Forgael plays the harp.*]

380   *First Sailor* [*falling into a dream suddenly*]. But you were saying
        there is somebody
        Upon that other ship we are to wake.

You did not know what brought him to his end,
But it was sudden.

Second Sailor.   You are in the right;
I had forgotten that we must go wake him.

Dectora. He has flung a Druid spell upon the air,
And set you dreaming.

Second Sailor.   How can we have a wake
When we have neither brown nor yellow ale?

First Sailor. I saw a flagon of brown ale aboard her.

Third Sailor. How can we raise the keen that do not know
What name to call him by?

First Sailor.   Come to his ship.   390
His name will come into our thoughts in a minute.
I know that he died a thousand years ago,
And has not yet been waked.

Second Sailor [*beginning to keen*]. Ohone! O! O! O!
The yew-bough has been broken into two,
And all the birds are scattered.

All the Sailors.   O! O! O! O!
                            [*They go out keening.*]

Dectora. Protect me now, gods that my people swear by.
      [*Aibric has risen from the deck where he had fallen. He has
          begun looking for his sword as if in a dream.*]

Aibric. Where is my sword that fell out of my hand
When I first heard the news? Ah, there it is!
      [*He goes dreamily towards the sword, but Dectora runs at it
          and takes it up before he can reach it.*]

Aibric [*sleepily*]. Queen, give it me.

Dectora.   No, I have need of it.

Aibric. Why do you need a sword? But you may keep it.   400
Now that he's dead I have no need of it,
For everything is gone.

A Sailor [*calling from the other ship*]. Come hither, Aibric,
   And tell me who it is that we are waking.

Aibric [*half to Dectora, half to himself*]. What name had that dead
      king? Arthur of Britain?
   No, no—not Arthur. I remember now.
   It was golden-armed Iollan, and he died
   Broken-hearted, having lost his queen
   Through wicked spells. That is not all the tale,
   For he was killed. O! O! O! O! O! O!
410   For golden-armed Iollan has been killed.
                                    [*He goes out.*]
      [*While he has been speaking, and through part of what follows
         one hears the wailing of the Sailors from the other ship.
         Dectora stands with the sword lifted in front of Forgael.*]

Dectora. I will end all your magic on the instant.
      [*Her voice becomes dreamy, and she lowers the sword slowly,
         and finally lets it fall. She spreads out her hair. She takes
         off her crown and lays it upon the deck.*]
   This sword is to lie beside him in the grave.
   It was in all his battles. I will spread my hair,
   And wring my hands, and wail him bitterly,
   For I have heard that he was proud and laughing,
   Blue-eyed, and a quick runner on bare feet,
   And that he died a thousand years ago.
   O! O! O! O!
                              [*Forgael changes the tune.*]
               But no, that is not it.
   I knew him well, and while I heard him laughing
420   They killed him at my feet. O! O! O! O!
   For golden-armed Iollan that I loved.
   But what is it that made me say I loved him?
   It was that harper put it in my thoughts,
   But it is true. Why did they run upon him,
   And beat the golden helmet with their swords?

Forgael. Do you not know me, lady? I am he
   That you are weeping for.

Dectora.   No, for he is dead.

O! O! O! O! for golden-armed Iollan.

Forgael. It was so given out, but I will prove
   That the grave-diggers in a dreamy frenzy 430
   Have buried nothing but my golden arms.
   Listen to that low-laughing string of the moon
   And you will recollect my face and voice,
   For you have listened to me playing it
   These thousand years.
     [*He starts up, listening to the birds. The harp slips from his
       hands, and remains leaning against the bulwarks behind
       him.*]
                     What are the birds at there?
   Why are they all a-flutter of a sudden?
   What are you calling out above the mast?
   If railing and reproach and mockery
   Because I have awakened her to love
   By magic strings, I'll make this answer to it: 440
   Being driven on by voices and by dreams
   That were clear messages from the Ever-living,
   I have done right. What could I but obey?
   And yet you make a clamour of reproach.

Dectora [*laughing*]. Why, it's a wonder out of reckoning
   That I should keen him from the full of the moon
   To the horn, and he be hale and hearty.

Forgael. How have I wronged her now that she is merry?
   But no, no, no! your cry is not against me.
   You know the counsels of the Ever-living, 450
   And all that tossing of your wings is joy,
   And all that murmuring's but a marriage-song;
   But if it be reproach, I answer this:
   There is not one among you that made love
   By any other means. You call it passion,
   Consideration, generosity;
   But it was all deceit, and flattery
   To win a woman in her own despite,
   For love is war, and there is hatred in it;
   And if you say that she came willingly— 460

Dectora. Why do you turn away and hide your face,
   That I would look upon for ever?

Forgael.   My grief!

Dectora. Have I not loved you for a thousand years?

Forgael. I never have been golden-armed Iollan.

Dectora. I do not understand. I know your face
   Better than my own hands.

Forgael.   I have deceived you
   Out of all reckoning.

Dectora.   Is it not true
   That you were born a thousand years ago,
   In islands where the children of Aengus wind
470   In happy dances under a windy moon,
   And that you'll bring me there?

Forgael.   I have deceived you;
   I have deceived you utterly.

Dectora.   How can that be?
   Is it that though your eyes are full of love
   Some other woman has a claim on you,
   And I've but half?

Forgael.   O no!

Dectora.   And if there is,
   If there be half a hundred more, what matter?
   I'll never give another thought to it;
   No, no, nor half a thought; but do not speak.
   Women are hard and proud and stubborn-hearted,
480   Their heads being turned with praise and flattery;
   And that is why their lovers are afraid
   To tell them a plain story.

Forgael.   That's not the story;
   But I have done so great a wrong against you,
   There is no measure that it would not burst.
   I will confess it all.

Dectora.   What do I care,
   Now that my body has begun to dream,
   And you have grown to be a burning sod
   In the imagination and intellect?
   If something that's most fabulous were true—
   If you had taken me by magic spells,   490
   And killed a lover or husband at my feet—
   I would not let you speak, for I would know
   That it was yesterday and not to-day
   I loved him; I would cover up my ears,
   As I am doing now. [*A pause.*] Why do you weep?

Forgael. I weep because I've nothing for your eyes
   But desolate waters and a battered ship.

Dectora. O why do you not lift your eyes to mine?

Forgael. I weep—I weep because bare night's above,
   And not a roof of ivory and gold.   500

Dectora. I would grow jealous of the ivory roof,
   And strike the golden pillars with my hands.
   I would that there was nothing in the world
   But my beloved—that night and day had perished,
   And all that is and all that is to be,
   All that is not the meeting of our lips.

Forgael. You turn away. Why do you turn away?
   Am I to fear the waves, or is the moon
   My enemy?

Dectora.   I looked upon the moon,
   Longing to knead and pull it into shape   510
   That I might lay it on your head as a crown.
   But now it is your thoughts that wander away,
   For you are looking at the sea. Do you not know
   How great a wrong it is to let one's thought
   Wander a moment when one is in love?
      [*He has moved away. She follows him. He is looking out over
         the sea, shading his eyes.*]
   Why are you looking at the sea?

Forgael.   Look there!

Dectora. What is there but a troop of ash-grey birds
    That fly into the west?

Forgael.   But listen, listen!

Dectora. What is there but the crying of the birds?

520 *Forgael.* If you'll but listen closely to that crying
    You'll hear them calling out to one another
    With human voices.

Dectora.   O, I can hear them now.
    What are they? Unto what country do they fly?

Forgael. To unimaginable happiness.
    They have been circling over our heads in the air,
    But now that they have taken to the road
    We have to follow, for they are our pilots;
    And though they're but the colour of grey ash,
    They're crying out, could you but hear their words,
530   'There is a country at the end of the world
    Where no child's born but to outlive the moon.'
        [*The Sailors come in with Aibric. They are in great excitement.*]

First Sailor. The hold is full of treasure.

Second Sailor.   Full to the hatches.

First Sailor. Treasure on treasure.

Third Sailor.   Boxes of precious spice.

First Sailor. Ivory images with amethyst eyes.

Third Sailor. Dragons with eyes of ruby.

First Sailor.   The whole ship
    Flashes as if it were a net of herrings.

Third Sailor. Let's home; I'd give some rubies to a woman.

Second Sailor. There's somebody I'd give the amethyst eyes to.

Aibric [*silencing them with a gesture*]. We would return to our
    own country, Forgael,

For we have found a treasure that's so great   540
Imagination cannot reckon it.
And having lit upon this woman there,
What more have you to look for on the seas?

Forgael. I cannot—I am going on to the end.
    As for this woman, I think she is coming with me.

Aibric. The Ever-living have made you mad; but no,
    It was this woman in her woman's vengeance
    That drove you to it, and I fool enough
    To fancy that she'd bring you home again.
    'Twas you that egged him to it, for you know   550
    That he is being driven to his death.

Dectora. That is not true, for he has promised me
    An unimaginable happiness.

Aibric. And if that happiness be more than dreams,
    More than the froth, the feather, the dust-whirl,
    The crazy nothing that I think it is,
    It shall be in the country of the dead,
    If there be such a country.

Dectora.   No, not there,
    But in some island where the life of the world
    Leaps upward, as if all the streams o' the world   560
    Had run into one fountain.

Aibric.   Speak to him.
    He knows that he is taking you to death;
    Speak—he will not deny it.

Dectora.   Is that true?

Forgael. I do not know for certain, but I know
    That I have the best of pilots.

Aibric.   Shadows, illusions,
    That the Shape-changers, the Ever-laughing Ones,
    The Immortal Mockers have cast into his mind,
    Or called before his eyes.

Dectora.   O carry me
   To some sure country, some familiar place.
570   Have we not everything that life can give
   In having one another?

Forgael.   How could I rest
   If I refused the messengers and pilots
   With all those sights and all that crying out?

Dectora. But I will cover up your eyes and ears,
   That you may never hear the cry of the birds,
   Or look upon them.

Forgael.   Were they but lowlier
   I'd do your will, but they are too high—too high.

Dectora. Being too high, their heady prophecies
   But harry us with hopes that come to nothing,
580   Because we are not proud, imperishable,
   Alone and winged.

Forgael.   Our love shall be like theirs
   When we have put their changeless image on.

Dectora. I am a woman, I die at every breath.

Aibric. Let the birds scatter, for the tree is broken,
   And there's no help in words. [*To the Sailors.*] To the other ship,
   And I will follow you and cut the rope
   When I have said farewell to this man here,
   For neither I nor any living man
   Will look upon his face again.
                         [*The Sailors go out.*]

Forgael [*to Dectora*].   Go with him,
590   For he will shelter you and bring you home.

Aibric [*taking Forgael's hand*]. I'll do it for his sake.

Dectora.   No. Take this sword
   And cut the rope, for I go on with Forgael.

Aibric [*half falling into the keen*]. The yew-bough has been broken
    into two,
    And all the birds are scattered—O! O! O!
    Farewell! farewell!
                                         [*He goes out.*]

Dectora.   The sword is in the rope—
    The rope's in two—it falls into the sea,
    It whirls into the foam. O ancient worm,
    Dragon that loved the world and held us to it,
    You are broken, you are broken. The world drifts away,
    And I am left alone with my beloved,   600
    Who cannot put me from his sight for ever.
    We are alone for ever, and I laugh,
    Forgael, because you cannot put me from you.
    The mist has covered the heavens, and you and I
    Shall be alone for ever. We two—this crown—
    I half remember. It has been in my dreams.
    Bend lower, O king, that I may crown you with it.
    O flower of the branch, O bird among the leaves,
    O silver fish that my two hands have taken
    Out of the running stream, O morning star,   610
    Trembling in the blue heavens like a white fawn
    Upon the misty border of the wood,
    Bend lower, that I may cover you with my hair,
    For we will gaze upon this world no longer.

Forgael [*gathering Dectora's hair about him*]. Beloved, having
    dragged the net about us,
    And knitted mesh to mesh, we grow immortal;
    And that old harp awakens of itself
    To cry aloud to the grey birds, and dreams,
    That have had dreams for father, live in us.

The Two Kings

1914

The Two Kings

King Eochaid came at sundown to a wood
Westward of Tara. Hurrying to his queen
He had outridden his war-wasted men
That with empounded cattle trod the mire,
And where beech trees had mixed a pale green light
With the ground-ivy's blue, he saw a stag
Whiter than curds, its eyes the tint of the sea.
Because it stood upon his path and seemed
More hands in height than any stag in the world
He sat with tightened rein and loosened mouth   10
Upon his trembling horse, then drove the spur;
But the stag stooped and ran at him, and passed,
Rending the horse's flank. King Eochaid reeled,
Then drew his sword to hold its levelled point
Against the stag. When horn and steel were met
The horn resounded as though it had been silver,
A sweet, miraculous, terrifying sound.
Horn locked in sword, they tugged and struggled there
As though a stag and unicorn were met
Among the African Mountains of the Moon,   20
Until at last the double horns, drawn backward,
Butted below the single and so pierced
The entrails of the horse. Dropping his sword
King Eochaid seized the horns in his strong hands
And stared into the sea-green eye, and so
Hither and thither to and fro they trod
Till all the place was beaten into mire.
The strong thigh and the agile thigh were met,
The hands that gathered up the might of the world,

30   And hoof and horn that had sucked in their speed
     Amid the elaborate wilderness of the air.
     Through bush they plunged and over ivied root,
     And where the stone struck fire, while in the leaves
     A squirrel whinnied and a bird screamed out;
     But when at last he forced those sinewy flanks
     Against a beech-bole, he threw down the beast
     And knelt above it with drawn knife. On the instant
     It vanished like a shadow, and a cry
     So mournful that it seemed the cry of one
40   Who had lost some unimaginable treasure
     Wandered between the blue and the green leaf
     And climbed into the air, crumbling away,
     Till all had seemed a shadow or a vision
     But for the trodden mire, the pool of blood,
     The disembowelled horse.
                         King Eochaid ran
     Toward peopled Tara, nor stood to draw his breath
     Until he came before the painted wall,
     The posts of polished yew, circled with bronze,
     Of the great door; but though the hanging lamps
50   Showed their faint light through the unshuttered windows,
     Nor door, nor mouth, nor slipper made a noise,
     Nor on the ancient beaten paths, that wound
     From well-side or from plough-land, was there noise;
     Nor had there been the noise of living thing
     Before him or behind, but that far off
     On the horizon edge bellowed the herds.
     Knowing that silence brings no good to kings,
     And mocks returning victory, he passed
     Between the pillars with a beating heart
60   And saw where in the midst of the great hall
     Pale-faced, alone upon a bench, Edain
     Sat upright with a sword before her feet.
     Her hands on either side had gripped the bench,
     Her eyes were cold and steady, her lips tight.
     Some passion had made her stone. Hearing a foot
     She started and then knew whose foot it was;
     But when he thought to take her in his arms

She motioned him afar, and rose and spoke:
'I have sent among the fields or to the woods
The fighting-men and servants of this house,   70
For I would have your judgment upon one
Who is self-accused. If she be innocent
She would not look in any known man's face
Till judgment has been given, and if guilty,
Would never look again on known man's face.'
And at these words he paled, as she had paled,
Knowing that he should find upon her lips
The meaning of that monstrous day.

                          Then she:
'You brought me where your brother Ardan sat
Always in his one seat, and bid me care him   80
Through that strange illness that had fixed him there,
And should he die to heap his burial-mound
And carve his name in Ogham.' Eochaid said,
'He lives?' 'He lives and is a healthy man.'
'While I have him and you it matters little
What man you have lost, what evil you have found.'
'I bid them make his bed under this roof
And carried him his food with my own hands,
And so the weeks passed by. But when I said,
"What is this trouble?" he would answer nothing,   90
Though always at my words his trouble grew;
And I but asked the more, till he cried out,
Weary of many questions: "There are things
That make the heart akin to the dumb stone."
Then I replied, "Although you hide a secret,
Hopeless and dear, or terrible to think on,
Speak it, that I may send through the wide world
For medicine." Thereon he cried aloud,
"Day after day you question me, and I,
Because there is such a storm amid my thoughts   100
I shall be carried in the gust, command,
Forbid, beseech and waste my breath." Then I:
"Although the thing that you have hid were evil,
The speaking of it could be no great wrong,
And evil must it be, if done 'twere worse

Than mound and stone that keep all virtue in,
And loosen on us dreams that waste our life,
Shadows and shows that can but turn the brain."
But finding him still silent I stooped down
And whispering that none but he should hear,
Said, "If a woman has put this on you,
My men, whether it please her or displease,
And though they have to cross the Loughlan waters
And take her in the middle of armed men,
Shall make her look upon her handiwork,
That she may quench the rick she has fired; and though
She may have worn silk clothes, or worn a crown,
She'll not be proud, knowing within her heart
That our sufficient portion of the world
Is that we give, although it be brief giving,
Happiness to children and to men."
Then he, driven by his thought beyond his thought,
And speaking what he would not though he would,
Sighed, "You, even you yourself, could work the cure!"
And at those words I rose and I went out
And for nine days he had food from other hands,
And for nine days my mind went whirling round
The one disastrous zodiac, muttering
That the immedicable mound's beyond
Our questioning, beyond our pity even.
But when nine days had gone I stood again
Before his chair and bending down my head
I bade him go when all his household slept
To an old empty woodman's house that's hidden
Westward of Tara, among the hazel-trees—
For hope would give his limbs the power—and await
A friend that could, he had told her, work his cure
And would be no harsh friend.
                              When night had deepened,
I groped my way from beech to hazel wood,
Found that old house, a sputtering torch within,
And stretched out sleeping on a pile of skins
Ardan, and though I called to him and tried
To shake him out of sleep, I could not rouse him.

I waited till the night was on the turn,
Then fearing that some labourer, on his way
To plough or pasture-land, might see me there,
Went out.
        Among the ivy-covered rocks,
As on the blue light of a sword, a man
Who had unnatural majesty, and eyes
Like the eyes of some great kite scouring the woods,   150
Stood on my path. Trembling from head to foot
I gazed at him like grouse upon a kite;
But with a voice that had unnatural music,
"A weary wooing and a long," he said,
"Speaking of love through other lips and looking
Under the eyelids of another, for it was my craft
That put a passion in the sleeper there,
And when I had got my will and drawn you here,
Where I may speak to you alone, my craft
Sucked up the passion out of him again   160
And left mere sleep. He'll wake when the sun wakes,
Push out his vigorous limbs and rub his eyes,
And wonder what has ailed him these twelve months."
I cowered back upon the wall in terror,
But that sweet-sounding voice ran on: "Woman,
I was your husband when you rode the air,
Danced in the whirling foam and in the dust,
In days you have not kept in memory,
Being betrayed into a cradle, and I come
That I may claim you as my wife again."   170
I was no longer terrified—his voice
Had half awakened some old memory—
Yet answered him, "I am King Eochaid's wife
And with him have found every happiness
Women can find." With a most masterful voice,
That made the body seem as it were a string
Under a bow, he cried, "What happiness
Can lovers have that know their happiness
Must end at the dumb stone? But where we build
Our sudden palaces in the still air   180
Pleasure itself can bring no weariness,

Nor can time waste the cheek, nor is there foot
That has grown weary of the wandering dance,
Nor an unlaughing mouth, but mine that mourns,
Among those mouths that sing their sweethearts' praise,
Your empty bed." "How should I love," I answered,
"Were it not that when the dawn has lit my bed
And shown my husband sleeping there, I have sighed,
'Your strength and nobleness will pass away.'
190   Or how should love be worth its pains were it not
That when he has fallen asleep within my arms,
Being wearied out, I love in man the child?
What can they know of love that do not know
She builds her nest upon a narrow ledge
Above a windy precipice?" Then he:
"Seeing that when you come to the deathbed
You must return, whether you would or no,
This human life blotted from memory,
Why must I live some thirty, forty years,
200   Alone with all this useless happiness?"
Thereon he seized me in his arms, but I
Thrust him away with both my hands and cried,
"Never will I believe there is any change
Can blot out of my memory this life
Sweetened by death, but if I could believe,
That were a double hunger in my lips
For what is doubly brief."
                                And now the shape
My hands were pressed to vanished suddenly.
I staggered, but a beech tree stayed my fall,
210   And clinging to it I could hear the cocks
Crow upon Tara.'
                        King Eochaid bowed his head
And thanked her for her kindness to his brother,
For that she promised, and for that refused.
Thereon the bellowing of the empounded herds
Rose round the walls, and through the bronze-ringed door
Jostled and shouted those war-wasted men,
And in the midst King Eochaid's brother stood,
And bade all welcome, being ignorant.

The Gift of
Harun Al-Rashid

1923

The Gift of Harun Al-Rashid

Kusta ben Luka is my name, I write
To Abd Al-Rabban; fellow-roysterer once,
Now the good Caliph's learned Treasurer,
And for no ear but his.
                    Carry this letter
Through the great gallery of the Treasure House
Where banners of the Caliphs hang, night-coloured
But brilliant as the night's embroidery,
And wait war's music; pass the little gallery;
Pass books of learning from Byzantium
Written in gold upon a purple stain,   10
And pause at last, I was about to say,
At the great book of Sappho's song; but no,
For should you leave my letter there, a boy's
Love-lorn, indifferent hands might come upon it
And let it fall unnoticed to the floor.
Pause at the Treatise of Parmenides
And hide it there, for Caliphs to world's end
Must keep that perfect, as they keep her song,
So great its fame.
                    When fitting time has passed
The parchment will disclose to some learned man   20
A mystery that else had found no chronicler
But the wild Bedouin. Though I approve
Those wanderers that welcomed in their tents
What great Harun Al-Rashid, occupied
With Persian embassy or Grecian war,
Must needs neglect, I cannot hide the truth
That wandering in a desert, featureless

As air under a wing, can give birds' wit.
In after time they will speak much of me
And speak but fantasy. Recall the year
When our beloved Caliph put to death
His Vizir Jaffer for an unknown reason:
'If but the shirt upon my body knew it
I'd tear it off and throw it in the fire.'
That speech was all that the town knew, but he
Seemed for a while to have grown young again;
Seemed so on purpose, muttered Jaffer's friends,
That none might know that he was conscience-struck—
But that's a traitor's thought. Enough for me
That in the early summer of the year
The mightiest of the princes of the world
Came to the least considered of his courtiers;
Sat down upon the fountain's marble edge,
One hand amid the goldfish in the pool;
And thereupon a colloquy took place
That I commend to all the chroniclers
To show how violent great hearts can lose
Their bitterness and find the honeycomb.
'I have brought a slender bride into the house;
You know the saying, "Change the bride with spring,"
And she and I, being sunk in happiness,
Cannot endure to think you tread these paths,
When evening stirs the jasmine bough, and yet
Are brideless.'

                    'I am falling into years.'

'But such as you and I do not seem old
Like men who live by habit. Every day
I ride with falcon to the river's edge
Or carry the ringed mail upon my back,
Or court a woman; neither enemy,
Game-bird, nor woman does the same thing twice;
And so a hunter carries in the eye
A mimicry of youth. Can poet's thought
That springs from body and in body falls

Like this pure jet, now lost amid blue sky,
Now bathing lily leaf and fish's scale,
Be mimicry?'
                    'What matter if our souls
Are nearer to the surface of the body
Than souls that start no game and turn no rhyme!
The soul's own youth and not the body's youth
Shows through our lineaments. My candle's bright,   70
My lantern is too loyal not to show
That it was made in your great father's reign.'

'And yet the jasmine season warms our blood.'

'Great prince, forgive the freedom of my speech:
You think that love has seasons, and you think
That if the spring bear off what the spring gave
The heart need suffer no defeat; but I
Who have accepted the Byzantine faith,
That seems unnatural to Arabian minds,
Think when I choose a bride I choose for ever;   80
And if her eye should not grow bright for mine
Or brighten only for some younger eye,
My heart could never turn from daily ruin,
Nor find a remedy.'
                    'But what if I
Have lit upon a woman who so shares
Your thirst for those old crabbed mysteries,
So strains to look beyond our life, an eye
That never knew that strain would scarce seem bright,
And yet herself can seem youth's very fountain,
Being all brimmed with life?'
                    'Were it but true   90
I would have found the best that life can give,
Companionship in those mysterious things
That make a man's soul or a woman's soul
Itself and not some other soul.'
                    'That love
Must needs be in this life and in what follows
Unchanging and at peace, and it is right

Every philosopher should praise that love.
But I being none can praise its opposite.
It makes my passion stronger but to think
100   Like passion stirs the peacock and his mate,
The wild stag and the doe; that mouth to mouth
Is a man's mockery of the changeless soul.'

And thereupon his bounty gave what now
Can shake more blossom from autumnal chill
Than all my bursting springtime knew. A girl
Perched in some window of her mother's house
Had watched my daily passage to and fro;
Had heard impossible history of my past;
Imagined some impossible history
110   Lived at my side; thought time's disfiguring touch
Gave but more reason for a woman's care.
Yet was it love of me, or was it love
Of the stark mystery that has dazed my sight,
Perplexed her fantasy and planned her care?
Or did the torchlight of that mystery
Pick out my features in such light and shade
Two contemplating passions chose one theme
Through sheer bewilderment? She had not paced
The garden paths, nor counted up the rooms,
120   Before she had spread a book upon her knees
And asked about the pictures or the text;
And often those first days I saw her stare
On old dry writing in a learned tongue,
On old dry faggots that could never please
The extravagance of spring; or move a hand
As if that writing or the figured page
Were some dear cheek.
                              Upon a moonless night
I sat where I could watch her sleeping form,
And wrote by candle-light; but her form moved,
130   And fearing that my light disturbed her sleep
I rose that I might screen it with a cloth.
I heard her voice, 'Turn that I may expound
What's bowed your shoulder and made pale your cheek';

And saw her sitting upright on the bed;
Or was it she that spoke or some great Djinn?
I say that a Djinn spoke. A live-long hour
She seemed the learned man and I the child;
Truths without father came, truths that no book
Of all the uncounted books that I have read,
Nor thought out of her mind or mine begot,   140
Self-born, high-born, and solitary truths,
Those terrible implacable straight lines
Drawn through the wandering vegetative dream,
Even those truths that when my bones are dust
Must drive the Arabian host.

                    The voice grew still,
And she lay down upon her bed and slept,
But woke at the first gleam of day, rose up
And swept the house and sang about her work
In childish ignorance of all that passed.
A dozen nights of natural sleep, and then   150
When the full moon swam to its greatest height
She rose, and with her eyes shut fast in sleep
Walked through the house. Unnoticed and unfelt
I wrapped her in a hooded cloak, and she,
Half running, dropped at the first ridge of the desert
And there marked out those emblems on the sand
That day by day I study and marvel at,
With her white finger. I led her home asleep
And once again she rose and swept the house
In childish ignorance of all that passed.   160
Even to-day, after some seven years
When maybe thrice in every moon her mouth
Murmured the wisdom of the desert Djinns,
She keeps that ignorance, nor has she now
That first unnatural interest in my books.
It seems enough that I am there; and yet,
Old fellow-student, whose most patient ear
Heard all the anxiety of my passionate youth,
It seems I must buy knowledge with my peace.
What if she lose her ignorance and so   170
Dream that I love her only for the voice,

That every gift and every word of praise
Is but a payment for that midnight voice
That is to age what milk is to a child?
Were she to lose her love, because she had lost
Her confidence in mine, or even lose
Its first simplicity, love, voice and all,
All my fine feathers would be plucked away
And I left shivering. The voice has drawn
180   A quality of wisdom from her love's
Particular quality. The signs and shapes;
All those abstractions that you fancied were
From the great Treatise of Parmenides;
All, all those gyres and cubes and midnight things
Are but a new expression of her body
Drunk with the bitter sweetness of her youth.
And now my utmost mystery is out.
A woman's beauty is a storm-tossed banner;
Under it wisdom stands, and I alone—
190   Of all Arabia's lovers I alone—
Nor dazzled by the embroidery, nor lost
In the confusion of its night-dark folds,
Can hear the armed man speak.

PART TWO

ADDITIONAL POEMS

A 1

The Island of Statues

AN ARCADIAN FAERY TALE—IN TWO ACTS

DRAMATIS PERSONÆ

Naschina, *Shepherdess*
Colin, *Shepherd*
Thernot, *Shepherd*
Almintor, *a Hunter*
Antonio, *his Page*
Enchantress of the Island
And a company of the Sleepers of the Isle.

ACT I

SCENE I

Before the cottage of Naschina. It is morning; and away in the depth of the heaven the moon is fading.

[*Enter Thernot with a lute.*]

Thernot. Maiden, come forth: the woods keep watch for thee;
　Within the drowsy blossom hangs the bee;
　'Tis morn: thy sheep are wandering down the vale—
　'Tis morn: like old men's eyes the stars are pale,
　And thro' the odorous air love-dreams are winging—
　'Tis morn, and from the dew-drench'd wood I've sped
　To welcome thee, Naschina, with sweet singing.
　　　　　[*Sitting on a tree-stem, he begins to tune his lute.*]

[*Enter Colin, abstractedly.*]

Colin. Come forth: the morn is fair; as from the pyre
　Of sad Queen Dido shone the lapping fire

10   Unto the wanderers' ships, or as day fills
        The brazen sky, so blaze the daffodils;
        As Argive Clytemnestra saw out-burn
        The flagrant signal of her lord's return,
        Afar, clear-shining on the herald hills,
        In vale and dell so blaze the daffodils;
        As when upon her cloud-o'er-muffled steep
        Œnone saw the fires of Troia leap,
        And laugh'd, so, so along the bubbling rills
        In lemon-tinted lines, so blaze the daffodils.
20   Come forth, come forth, my music flows for thee,
        A quenchless grieving of love melody.

                                        [*Raises his lute.*]

Thernot [*Sings*]. Now her sheep all browsing meet
                        By the singing waters' edge,
                    Tread and tread their cloven feet
                        On the ruddy river sedge,
                    For the dawn the foliage fingereth,
                        And the waves are leaping white,
                    She alone, my lady, lingereth
                        While the world is roll'd in light.

30   *Colin.* Shepherd, to mar the morning hast thou come?
            Hear me, and, shepherd, hearing me, grow dumb.

        [*Sings*]   Where is the owl that lately flew
                                Flickering under the white moonshine?
                            She sleeps with owlets two and two,
                                Sleepily close her round bright eyne;
                            O'er her nest the lights are blending:
                                Come thou, come, and to this string—
                            Though my love-sick heart is rending,
                                Not a sad note will I sing.

40   *Thernot.* I am not dumb: I'd sooner silent wait
            Within the fold to hear the creaking gate—

        [*Sings*]   The wood and the valley and sea
                                Awaken, awaken to new-born lustre;
                            A new day's troop of wasp and bee

Hang on the side of the round grape-cluster;
Blenching on high the dull stars sicken
Morn-bewildered, and the cup
Of the tarn where young waves quicken
Hurls their swooning lustre up.

Colin. I'll silence this dull singer— 50

[Sings]   Oh, more dark thy gleaming hair is
Than the peeping pansy's face,
And thine eyes more bright than faery's,
Dancing in some moony place,
And thy neck's a poisèd lily;
See, I tell thy beauties o'er,
As within a cellar chilly
Some old miser tells his store;
And thy memory I keep,
Till all else is empty chaff, 60
Till I laugh when others weep,
Weeping when all others laugh.

Thernot. I'll quench his singing with loud song—

[Sings wildly]   Come forth, for in a thousand bowers
Blossoms open dewy lips;
Over the lake the water-flowers
Drift and float like silver ships;
Ever ringing, ringing, ringing,
With unfaltering persistence,
Hundred-throated morn is singing, 70
Joy and love are one existence.

Colin [Sings].   Lone, and wanting thee, I weep;
Love and sorrow, one existence,
Sadness, soul of joy most deep,
Is the burthen and persistence
Of the songs that never sleep.
Love from heaven came of yore
As a token and a sign,
Singing o'er and o'er and o'er
Of his death and change malign. 80

Thernot. With fiery song I'll drown yon puny voice.

[*Leaping to his feet.*]

[*Sings*]   Passeth the moon with her sickle of light,
                  Slowly, slowly fadeth she,
                  Weary of reaping the barren night
                  And the desolate shuddering sea.

Colin [*Sings*].   Loud for thee the morning crieth,
    And my soul in waiting dieth,
    Ever dieth, dieth, dieth.

Thernot [*Sings*]. Far the morning vapours shatter,
90   As the leaves in autumn scatter.

Colin [*Sings*].   In the heart of the dawn the rivers are singing,
           Over them crimson vapours winging.

Thernot [*Sings*].   All the world is ringing, ringing;
           All the world is singing, singing.

Colin [*Sings*].   Lift my soul from rayless night—

Thernot [*Sings*].   Stricken all the night is past—

Colin [*Sings*].   Music of my soul and light—

Thernot [*Sings*].   Back the shadows creep aghast—

[*They approach one another, while singing, with angry gestures.*]

[*Enter Naschina.*]

Naschina. Oh, cease your singing! wild and shrill and loud,
100   On my poor brain your busy tumults crowd.

Colin. I fain had been the first of singing things
    To welcome thee, when o'er the owlet's wings
    And troubled eyes came morning's first-born glow;
    But yonder thing, yon idle noise, yon crow,
    Yon shepherd—

Thernot.   Came your spirit to beguile
    With singing sweet as e'er round lake-lulled isle
    Sing summer waves. But yonder shepherd vile,
    All clamour-clothed—

Colin.   Was't clamour when *I* sung,
  Whom men have named Arcadia's sweetest tongue.
                              [*A horn sounds.*]
  A horn! some troop of robbers winding goes   110
  Along the wood with subtle tread and bended bows.
                              [*An arrow passes above.*]
  Fly!

Thernot. Fly!
                              [*Colin and Thernot go.*]

Naschina.   So these brave shepherds both are gone;
  Courageous miracles!

      [*Enter Almintor and Antonio, talking together.*]

Almintor.   The sunlight shone
  Upon his wings. Thro' yonder green abyss
  I sent an arrow.

Antonio.   And I saw you miss;
  And far away the heron sails, I wis.

Almintor. Nay, nay, I miss'd him not; his days
  Of flight are done.
                      [*Seeing Naschina, and bowing low.*]

              Most fair of all who graze
  Their sheep in Arcady, Naschina, hail!
  Naschina, hail!   120

Antonio [*Mimicking him*]. Most fair of all who graze
  Their sheep in Arcady, Naschina, hail!
  Naschina, hail!

Almintor.   I'd drive thy woolly sheep,
  If so I might, along a dewy vale,
  Where all night long the heavens weep and weep,
  Dreaming in their soft odour-laden sleep;
  Where all night long the lonely moon, the white
  Sad Lady of the deep, pours down her light;
  And 'mong the stunted ash-trees' drooping rings,
      All flame-like gushing from the hollow stones,

130   By day and night a lonely fountain sings,
                 And there to its own heart for ever moans.

Naschina. I'd be alone.

Almintor.   We two, by that pale fount,
          Unmindful of its woes, would twine a wreath
                 As fair as any that on Ida's mount
          Long ere an arrow whizzed or sword left sheath
          The shepherd Paris for Œnone made,
          Singing of arms and battles some old stave,
          As lies dark water in a murmurous glade,
          Dreaming the live-long summer in the shade,
140   Dreaming of flashing flight and of the plumèd wave.

Antonio. Naschina, wherefore are your eyes so bright
          With tears?

Naschina.   I weary of ye. There is none
          Of all on whom Arcadian suns have shone
          Sustains his soul in courage or in might.
          Poor race of leafy Arcady, your love
          To prove what can ye do? What things above
          Sheep-guiding, or the bringing some strange bird,
          Or some small beast most wonderfully furr'd,
          Or sad sea-shells where little echoes sit?
150   Such quests as these, I trow, need little wit.

Antonio. And the great grey lynx's skin!

Naschina.   In sooth, methinks
          That I myself could shoot a great grey lynx.
                                        [*Naschina turns to go.*]

Almintor. Oh stay, Naschina, stay!

Naschina. Here, where men know the gracious woodland joys,
          Joy's brother, Fear, dwells ever in each breast—
          Joy's brother, Fear, lurks in each leafy way.
          I weary of your songs and hunter's toys.
          To prove his love a knight with lance in rest
          Will circle round the world upon a quest,
160   Until afar appear the gleaming dragon-scales:

From morn the twain until the evening pales
Will struggle. Or he'll seek enchanter old,
Who sits in lonely splendour, mail'd in gold,
And they will war, 'mid wondrous elfin-sights:
Such may I love. The shuddering forest lights
Of green Arcadia do not hide, I trow,
Such men, such hearts. But, uncouth hunter, thou
Know'st naught of this.

[*She goes.*]

Antonio. And, uncouth hunter, now—

Almintor. Ay, boy.

Antonio. Let's see if that same heron's dead.
[*The boy runs out, followed slowly by Almintor.*]

SCENE II

Sundown.—A remote forest valley.

[*Enter Almintor, followed by Antonio.*]

Antonio. And whither, uncouth hunter? Why so fast?
So! 'mid the willow-glade you pause at last.

Almintor. Here is the place, the cliff-encircled wood;
Here grow that shy, retiring sisterhood,
The pale anemones. We've sought all day,
And found.

Antonio. 'Tis well!—another mile of way
I could not go.

[*They sit down.*]

Almintor. Let's talk, and let's be sad,
Here in the shade.

Antonio. Why? Why?

Almintor. For what is glad?
For, look you, sad's the murmur of the bees,
Yon wind goes sadly, and the grass and trees
Reply like moaning of imprisoned elf:

10

The whole world's sadly talking to itself.
The waves in yonder lake where points my hand
Beat out their lives lamenting o'er the sand;
The birds that nestle in the leaves are sad,
Poor sad wood-rhapsodists.

Antonio.   Not so: they're glad.

Almintor. All rhapsody hath sorrow for its soul.

Antonio. Yon eager lark, that fills with song the whole
  Of this wide vale, embosomed in the air,
20 Is sorrow in his song, or any care?
  Doth not yon bird, yon quivering bird, rejoice?

Almintor. I hear the whole sky's sorrow in one voice.

Antonio. Nay, nay, Almintor, yonder song is glad.

Almintor. 'Tis beautiful, and therefore it is sad.

Antonio. Have done this phrasing, and say why, in sooth,
  Almintor, thou hast grown so full of ruth,
  And wherefore have we come?

Almintor.   A song to hear.

Antonio. But whence, and when?

Almintor.   Over the willows sere
  Out of the air.

Antonio.   And when?

Almintor.   When the sun goes down
30 Over the crown of the willows brown.
  Oh, boy, I'm bound on a most fearful quest;
  For so she willed—thou heard'st? Upon the breast
  Of yonder lake, from whose green banks alway
  The poplars gaze across the waters grey,
  And nod to one another, lies a green,
  Small island, where the full soft sheen
  Of evening and glad silence dwelleth aye,
  For there the great Enchantress lives.

Antonio.   And there
  Groweth the goblin flower of joy, her care,
  By many sought, and 'tis a forest tale,   40
  How they who seek are ever doomed to fail.
  Some say that all who touch the island lone
  Are changed for ever into moon-white stone.

Almintor. That flower I seek.

Antonio.   Thou never wilt return.

Almintor. I'll bring that flower to her, and so may earn
  Her love: to her who wears that bloom comes truth,
  And elvish wisdom, and long years of youth
  Beyond a mortal's years. I wait the song
  That calls.

Antonio.   O evil starred!

Almintor.   It comes along
  The wind at evening when the sun goes down   50
  Over the crown of the willows brown.
  See, yonder sinks the sun, yonder a shade
  Goes flickering in reverberated light.
  There! There! Dost thou not see?

Antonio.   I see the night,
  Deep-eyed, slow-footing down the empty glade.

A Voice [*Sings*]. From the shadowy hollow
        Arise thou and follow!

Almintor. Sad faery tones.

Antonio.   'Tis thus they ever seem,
  As some dead maiden's singing in a dream.

Voice.   When the tree was o'er-appled   60
        For mother Eve's winning
        I was at her sinning.
      O'er the grass light-endappled
        I wandered and trod,
        O'er the green Eden-sod;

And I sang round the tree
As I sing now to thee:
   Arise from the hollow,
   And follow, and follow!

70
Away in the green paradise,
   As I wandered unseen,
   (How glad was her mien!),
I saw her as you now arise;
   Before her I trod
   O'er the green Eden-sod,
And I sang round the tree,
As I sing now to thee:
   From the shadowy hollow
   Come follow! Come follow!

                     [*Almintor goes.*]

[*The Voice sings, dying away.*]
80
And I sang round the tree,
As I sing now to thee:
   From the green shaded hollow
   Arise, worm, and follow!

Antonio. I, too, will follow for this evil-starred one's sake
   Unto the dolorous border of the fairy lake.

                         [*Goes.*]

SCENE III

The Birth of Night.—The Island.—Far into the distance reach shadowy ways, burdened with the faery flowers. Knee-deep amongst them stand the immovable figures of those who have failed in their quest.

First Voice. See! oh, see! the dew-drowned bunches
   Of the monk's-hood how they shake,
   Nodding by the flickering lake,
There where yonder squirrel crunches
   Acorns green, with eyes awake.

Second Voice. I followed him from my green lair,
   But wide awake his two eyes were.

First Voice. Oh, learnèd is each monk's-hood's mind,
    And full of wisdom is each bloom,
    As, clothed in ceremonial gloom,   10
  They hear the story of the wind,
    That dieth slow with sunsick doom.

Second Voice. The south breeze now in dying fears
  Tells all his sinning in their ears.

First Voice. He says 'twas he, and 'twas no other,
    Blew my crimson cap away
    O'er the lake this very day.
  Hark! he's dead—my drowsy brother,
    And has not heard *Absolvo te.*

                             [*A pause.*]

First Voice. Peace, peace, the earth's a-quake. I hear   20
  Some barbarous, un-faery thing draw near.

               [*Enter Almintor.*]

Almintor. The evening gleams are green and gold and red
  Along the lake. The crane has homeward fled.
  And flowers around in clustering thousands are,
  Each shining clear as some unbaffled star;
  The skies more dim, though burning like a shield,
  Above these men whose mouths were sealed
  Long years ago, and unto stone congealed.
  And, oh! the wonder of the thing! each came
  When low the sun sank down in clotted flame   30
  Beyond the lake, whose smallest wave was burdened
  With rolling fire, beyond the high trees turbaned
  With clinging mist, each star-fought wanderer came
  As I, to choose beneath day's dying flame;
  And they are all now stone, as I shall be,
  Unless some pitying god shall succour me
  In this my choice.

             [*Stoops over a flower, then pauses.*]

        Some god might help; if so
  Mayhap 'twere better that aside I throw
  All choice, and give to chance for guiding chance

40   Some cast of die, or let some arrow glance
      For guiding of the gods. The sacred bloom
      To seek not hopeless have I crossed the gloom,
      With that song leading where harmonic woods
      Nourish the panthers in dim solitudes;
      Vast greenness, where eternal Rumour dwells,
      And hath her home by many-folded dells.
      I passed by many caves of dripping stone,
      And heard each unseen Echo on her throne,
      Lone regent of the woods, deep muttering,
50   And then new murmurs came new uttering
      In song, from goblin waters swaying white,
      Mocking with patient laughter all the night
      Of those vast woods; and then I saw the boat,
      Living, wide wingèd, on the waters float.
      Strange draperies did all the sides adorn,
      And the waves bowed before it like mown corn,
      The wingèd wonder of all Faery Land.
      It bore me softly where the shallow sand
      Binds, as within a girdle or a ring,
60   The lake-embosomed isle. Nay, this my quest
      Shall not so hopeless prove: some god may rest
      Upon the wind, and guide mine arrow's course.
          From yonder pinnacle above the lake
      I'll send mine arrow, now my one resource;
          The nighest blossom where it falls I'll take.

                    [*Goes out, fitting an arrow to his bow.*]

      A Voice. Fickle the guiding his arrow shall find!
          Some goblin, my servant, on wings that are fleet,
              That nestles alone in the whistling wind,
          Go pilot the course of his arrow's deceit!

                    [*The arrow falls. Re-enter Almintor.*]

70   *Almintor.* 'Tis here the arrow fell: the breezes laughed
          Around the feathery tip. Unto the shaft
          This blossom is most near. Statue! Oh, thou
          Whose beard a moonlight river is, whose brow

Is stone: old sleeper! this same afternoon
O'er much I've talked: I shall be silent soon,
If wrong my choice, as silent as thou art.
Oh! gracious Pan, take now thy servant's part.
He was our ancient god. If I speak low,
And not too clear, how will the new god know
But that I called on him?   80

[*Pulls the flower, and becomes stone. From among the flowers
a sound as of a multitude of horns.*]

A Voice.   Sleeping lord of archery,
                   No more a-roving shalt thou see
                   The panther with her yellow hide,
                   Of the forests all the pride,
                   Or her ever burning eyes,
                   When she in a cavern lies,
                   Watching o'er her awful young,
                   Where their sinewy might is strung
                   In the never-lifting dark.
                   No! Thou standest still and stark,   90
                   That of old wert moving ever,
                   But a mother panther never
                   O'er her young so eagerly
                   Did her lonely watching take
                   As I my watching lest you wake,
                   Sleeping lord of archery.

ACT II

SCENE I

The wood in the early evening.

[*Enter Antonio and Naschina.*]

Naschina. I, as a shepherd dressed, will seek and seek
     Until I find him. What a weary week,
     My pretty child, since he has gone, oh say
     Once more how on that miserable day
     He passed across the lake.

Antonio.   When we two came
 From the wood's ways, then, like a silver flame,
 We saw the dolorous lake; and then thy name
 He carved on trees, and with a sun-dry weed
 He wrote it on the sands (the owls may read
10 And ponder it if they will); then near at hand
 The boat's prow grated on the shallow sand,
 And loudly twice the living wings flapt wide,
 And, leaping to their feet, far Echoes cried,
 Each other answering. Then between each wing
 He sat, and then I heard the white lake sing,
 Curving beneath the prow; as some wild drake
 Half lit, so flapt the wings across the lake—
 Alas! I make you sadder, shepherdess.

Naschina. Nay, grief in feeding on old grief grows less.

20 *Antonio.* Grief needs much feeding then. Of him I swear
 We've talked and talked, and not a whit more rare
 Your weeping fits!

Naschina.   Look you, so very strait
 The barred woodpecker's mansion is and deep,
 No other bird may enter in.

Antonio.   Well?

Naschina.   Late—
 Aye, very lately, sorrow came to weep
 Within mine heart; and naught but sorrow now
 Can enter there.

Antonio.   See! See! above yon brow
 Of hill two shepherds come.

Naschina.   Farewell! I'll don
 My shepherd garments, and return anon.

            [*Goes.*]

    [*Enter Colin and Thernot.*]

30 *Thernot.* Two men who love one maid have ample cause

Of war. Of yore, two shepherds, where we pause,
Fought once for self-same reason on the hem
Of the wide woods.

Colin.   And the deep earth gathered them.

Thernot. We must get swords.

Colin.   Is't the only way? Oh, see,
   Yon is the hunter's, Sir Almintor's, page;
   Let him between us judge, for he can gauge
   And measure out the ways of chivalry.

Thernot. Sir Page, Almintor's friend, and therefore learned
   In all such things, pray let thine ears be turned,
   And hear, and judge.

Antonio.   My popinjay, what now?   40

Colin. This thing we ask: must we two fight?—Judge thou.
   Each came one morn, with welcoming of song,
   Unto her door; for this, where nod the long
   And shoreward waves, we nigh have fought; waves bring
   The brown weed burden, so the sword brings fear
   To us.

Thernot. Oh wise art thou in such a thing,
   Being Almintor's page. Now judge you here.
   We love Naschina both.

Antonio.   Whom loves *she* best?

Colin. She cares no whit for either, but has blest
   Almintor with her love.

         [*Enter Naschina, disguised as a shepherd boy.*]

Colin.   Who art thou?—speak,   50
   As the sea's furrows on a sea-tost shell,
   Sad histories are lettered on thy cheek.

Antonio. It is the shepherd Guarimond, who loveth well
   In the deep centres of the secret woods.
   Old miser hoards of grief to tell and tell:

Young Guarimond he tells them o'er and o'er,
To see them drowned by those vast solitudes,
With their unhuman sorrows.

Naschina.   Cease! no more!
Thou hast an over-nimble tongue.

Colin.   Thy grief,
What is it, friend?

60 *Antonio.*   He lost i' the woods the chief
And only sheep he loved of all the troop.

Colin. More grief is mine. No man shall ever stoop
Beneath the weight of greater grief than I;
I like you, and, in sooth I know not why.
Now, judge, must shepherd Thernot there and I
For this thing fight—we love one maid?

Naschina.   Her name?

Colin. Naschina.

Naschina.   Oh, I know her well—a lame,
Dull-witted thing, with face red squirrel-brown.

Antonio. A long, brown grasshopper of maids!

Naschina.   Peace, sir!

70 *Colin.* 'Tis clear that you have seen her not. The crown
Is not more fair and joyous than she is
Of beams a-flicker on yon lonely fir,
Nor faeries in the honey-heart of June astir.
By bosky June I swear, and by the bee, her minister.

Naschina. There is no way but that ye fight I wis,
If *her* ye love.

Thernot.   Aye, Colin, we must fight.

Colin. Aye, fight we must.
                    [*Antonio and Naschina turn to go.*]

Naschina.   Tell me, Antonio, might
They get them swords, and both or either fall?

Antonio. No, no; when that shall be, then men may call
   Down to their feet the stars that shine alone,   80

   Each one at gaze for aye upon his whirling throne.

                                                           [They go.]

SCENE II

*A remote part of the forest.—Through black and twisted trees the
lake is shining under the red evening sky.*

   [Enter Naschina, as a shepherd-boy, and Antonio.]

Antonio. Behold, how like a swarm of fiery bees
   The light is dancing o'er the knotted trees,
   In busy flakes; re-shining from the lake,
   Through this night-vested place the red beams break.

Naschina. From the deep earth unto the lurid sky
   All things are quiet in the eve's wide eye.

Antonio. The air is still above, and still each leaf,
   But loud the grasshopper that sits beneath.

Naschina. And, boy, saw you, when through the forest we
   Two came, his name and mine on many a tree   10
   Carved; here, beyond the lake's slow-muffled tread,
   In sand his name and mine I've also read.

Antonio. Yonder's the isle in search whereof we came;
   The white waves wrap it in a sheet of flame,
   And yonder huddling blackness draweth nigh—
   The faery ship that swims athwart the sky.

Naschina. Antonio, if I return no more,
   Then bid them raise my statue on the shore;
   Here where the round waves come, here let them build,
   Here, facing to the lake, and no name gild;   20
   A white, dumb thing of tears, here let it stand,
   Between the lonely forest and the sand.

Antonio. The boat draws near and near. You heed me not!

Naschina. And when the summer's deep, then to this spot
   The Arcadians bring, and bid the stone be raised
   As I am standing now—as though I gazed,
   One hand brow-shading, far across the night,
   And one arm pointing thus, in marble white.
   And once a-year let the Arcadians come,
30   And 'neath it sit, and of the woven sum
   Of human sorrow let them moralize;
   And let them tell sad histories, till their eyes
   All swim with tears.

Antonio.   The faery boat's at hand;
   You must be gone; the rolling grains of sand
   Are 'neath its prow, and crushing shells.

Naschina [*turning to go*]. And let the tale be mournful each one tells.
         [*Antonio and Naschina go out.*]

[*Re-enter Antonio.*]

Antonio. I would have gone also; but far away
   The faery thing flew with her o'er the gray
   Slow waters, and the boat and maiden sink
40   Away from me where mists of evening drink
   To ease their world-old thirst along the brink
   Of sword-blue waves of calm; while o'er head blink
   The mobs of stars in gold and green and blue,
   Piercing the quivering waters through and through,
   The ageless sentinels who hold their watch
   O'er grief. The world drinks sorrow from the beams
   And penetration of their eyes.
         [*Starting forward.*]
         Where yonder blotch
   Of lilac o'er the pulsing water gleams,
   Once more those shepherds come. Mayhap some mirth
50   I'll have. Oh, absent one, 'tis not for dearth
   Of grief. And if they say, 'Antonio laughed,'
   Say then,—'A popinjay before grief's shaft
   Pierced through, chattering from habit in the sun,
   Till his last wretchedness was o'er and done.'

A Voice from among the trees. Antonio!

[*Enter Colin and Thernot.*]

Thernot.   We have resolved to fight.

Antonio. To yonder isle, where never sail was furled,
From whose green banks no living thing may rove,
And see again the happy woodland light,
Naschina's gone, drawn by a thirst of love,
And that was strange; but *this* is many a world   60
More wonderful!

Thernot.   And we have swords.

Antonio.   O night
Of wonders! eve of prodigies!

Colin.   Draw! draw!

Antonio [*aside*]. He'll snap his sword.

Thernot.   Raised is the lion's paw.

[*Colin and Thernot fight.*]

Antonio. Cease! Thernot's wounded, cease! They will not heed.
Fierce thrust! A tardy blossom had the seed,
But heavy fruit. How swift the argument
Of those steel tongues! Crash, swords! Well thrust! Well bent
Aside!—

[*A far-off multitudinous sound of horns.*]

          The wild horns told Almintor's end,
And of Naschina's now they tell—rend! rend!
Oh, heart! Her dirge! With rushing arms the waves   70
Cast on the sound, on, on. This night of graves,
The spinning stars—the toiling sea—whirl round
My sinking brain!—Cease!—Cease! Heard ye yon sound?
The dirge of her ye love. Cease!—Cease!

[*An echo in a cliff in the heart of the forest sends mournfully
back the blast of the horns. Antonio rushes away, and the
scene closes on Colin and Thernot still fighting.*]

SCENE III

The Island. Flowers of manifold colour are knee-deep before a gate
of brass, above which, in a citron-tinctured sky, glimmer a few stars.
At intervals come mournful blasts from the horns among the flowers.

> *First Voice.* What do you weave so fair and bright?

> *Second Voice.* The cloak I weave of Sorrow.
>   Oh, lovely to see in all men's sight
> Shall be the cloak of Sorrow,
>   In all men's sight.

> *Third Voice.* What do you build with sails for flight?

> *Fourth Voice.* A boat I build for Sorrow.
>   Oh, swift on the seas all day and night
> Saileth the rover Sorrow,
>   All day and night.

> *Fifth Voice.* What do you weave with wool so white?

> *Sixth Voice.* The sandals these of Sorrow.
>   Soundless shall be the footfall light,
> In each man's ears, of Sorrow,
>   Sudden and light.

[*Naschina, disguised as a shepherd-boy, enters with the Enchantress,*
  the beautiful familiar of the Isle.]

Naschina. What are the voices that in flowery ways
    Have clothed their tongues with song of songless days?

Enchantress. They are the flowers' guardian sprites;
        With streaming hair as wandering lights
        They passed a-tiptoe everywhere,
        And never heard of grief or care
        Until this morn. The sky with wrack
        Was banded as an adder's back,
        And they were sitting round a pool.
        At their feet the waves in rings
        Gently shook their moth-like wings;
        For there came an air-breath cool
        From the ever-moving pinions

Of the happy flower minions.
But a sudden melancholy   30
Filled them as they sat together;
Now their songs are mournful wholly
As they go with drooping feather.

Naschina.   O Lady, thou whose vestiture of green
Is rolled as verdant smoke! O thou whose face
Is worn as though with fire! O goblin queen,
Lead me, I pray thee, to the statued place!

Enchantress. Fair youth, along a wandering way
I've led thee here, and as a wheel
We turned around the place alway,   40
Lest on thine heart the stony seal
As on those other hearts were laid.
Behold the brazen-gated glade!

[*She partially opens the brazen gates. The statues are seen within.
Some are bending, with their hands among the flowers; others
are holding withered flowers.*]

Naschina. Oh, let me pass! The spells from off the heart
Of my sad hunter-friend will all depart
If on his lips the enchanted flower be laid.
Oh, let me pass!
                    [*Leaning with an arm upon each gate.*]

Enchantress.   That flower none
Who seek may find, save only one,
A shepherdess long years foretold;
And even she shall never hold   50
The flower, save some thing be found
To die for her in air or ground.
And none there is; if such there were,
E'en then, before her shepherd hair
Had felt the island breeze, my lore
Had driven her forth, for evermore
To wander by the bubbling shore,
Laughter-lipped, but for her brain
A guerdon of deep-rooted pain,

60   And in her eyes a lightless stare;
For, if severed from the root
The enchanted flower were;
From my wizard island lair,
And the happy wingèd day,
I, as music that grows mute
On a girl's forgotten lute,
Pass away—

Naschina. Your eyes are all aflash. She is not here.

Enchantress. I'd kill her if she were. Nay, do not fear!
70   With you I am all gentleness; in truth,
There's little I'd refuse thee, dearest youth.

Naschina. It is my whim! bid some attendant sprite
Of thine cry over wold and water white,
That one shall die, unless one die for her.
'Tis but to see if anything will stir
For such a call. Let the wild word be cried
As though she whom you fear had crossed the wide
Swift lake.

Enchantress. A very little thing that is
And shall be done, if you will deign to kiss
My lips, fair youth.

80   *Naschina.*   It shall be as you ask.

Enchantress. Forth! forth! O spirits, ye have heard your task!

Voices. We are gone!

Enchantress [*sitting down by Naschina*]. Fair shepherd, as we
wandered hither,
My words were all: 'Here no loves wane and wither,
Where dream-fed passion is and peace encloses,
Where revel of foxglove is and revel of roses.'
My words were all: 'O whither, whither, whither
Wilt roam away from this rich island rest?'
I bid thee stay, renouncing thy mad quest,
90   But thou wouldst not, for then thou wert unblest

And stony-hearted; now thou hast grown kind,
And thou wilt stay. All thought of what they find
In the far world will vanish from thy mind,
Till thou rememberest only how the sea
Has fenced us round for all eternity.
But why art thou so silent? Didst thou hear
I laughed?

Naschina.   And why is that a thing so dear?

Enchantress. From thee I snatched it; e'en the fay that trips
    At morn, and with her feet each cobweb rends,
    Laughs not. It dwells alone on mortal lips: 100
    Thou'lt teach me laughing, and I'll teach thee peace
    Here where laburnum hangs her golden fleece;
    For peace and laughter have been seldom friends.
    But, for a boy, how long thine hair has grown!
    Long citron coils that hang around thee, blown
    In shadowy dimness. To be fair as thee
    I'd give my fairy fleetness, though I be
    Far fleeter than the million-footed sea.

A Voice.   By wood antique, by wave and waste,
    Where cypress is and oozy pine,   110
      Did I on quivering pinions haste,
    And all was quiet round me spread,
    As quiet as the clay-cold dead.
    I cried the thing you bade me cry.
      An owl, who in an alder tree
    Had hooted for an hundred years,
      Upraised his voice, and hooted me.
    E'en though his wings were plumeless stumps,
      And all his veins had near run dry,
    Forth from the hollow alder trunk   120
      He hooted as I wandered by.
    And so with wolf, and boar, and steer.
      And one alone of all would hark,
    A man who by a dead man stood.
      A starlit rapier, half blood-dark,
    Was broken in his quivering hand.

As blossoms, when the winds of March
Hold festival across the land,
He shrank before my voice, and stood
130   Low bowed and dumb upon the sand.
A foolish word thou gavest me!
        For each within himself hath all
The world within his folded heart—
        His temple and his banquet hall;
And who will throw his mansion down
        Thus for another's bugle call!

Enchantress. But why this whim of thine? A strange unrest,
        Alien as cuckoo in a robin's nest,
        Is in thy face, and lips together pressed;
140   And why so silent? I would have thee speak.
        Soon wilt thou smile, for here the winds are weak
        As moths with broken wings, and as we sit
        The heavens all star throbbing are alit.

Naschina. But art thou happy?

Enchantress.   Let me gaze on thee,
        At arm's length thus; till dumb eternity
        Has rolled away the stars and dried the sea
        I could gaze, gaze upon thine eyes of grey;
        Gaze on till ragged Time himself decay.
        Ah! you are weeping; here should all grief cease.

Naschina. But art thou happy?

150   *Enchantress.*   Youth, I am at peace.

Naschina. But art thou happy?

Enchantress.   Those grey eyes of thine,
        Have they ne'er seen the eyes of lynx or kine,
        Or aught remote; or hast thou never heard
        'Mid babbling leaves a wandering song-rapt bird
        Going the forest through, with flutings weak;
        Or hast thou never seen, with visage meek,
        A hoary hunter leaning on his bow,
        To watch thee pass? Yet deeper than men know
        These are at peace.

A Voice.   Sad lady, cease!   160
   I rose, I rose
     From the dim wood's foundation—
   I rose, I rose
     Where in white exultation
   The long lily blows,
   And the wan wave that lingers
     From flood-time encloses
   With infantine fingers
     The roots of the roses.
   Now here I come winging;   170
     I there had been keeping
     A mouse from his sleeping,
   With shouting and singing.

Enchantress. How sped thy quest? This prelude we'll not hear it.
  I' faith thou ever wast a wordy spirit!

The Voice. A wriggling thing on the white lake moved,
     As the canker-worm on a milk-white rose;
   And down I came as a falcon swoops
     When his sinewy wings together close.
   I 'lit by the thing, 'twas a shepherd-boy,   180
     Who, swimming, sought the island lone;
   Within his clenchèd teeth a sword.
     I heard the dreadful monotone
   The water-serpent sings his heart
   Before a death. O'er wave and bank
     I cried the words you bid me cry.
   The shepherd raised his arms and sank,
     His rueful spirit fluttered by.

Naschina [*aside*]. I must bestir myself. Both dead for me!
  Both dead!—No time for thinking.

[*Aloud*]   I am she,   190
  That shepherdess: arise, and bring to me,
  In silence, that famed flower of wizardry,
  For I am mightier now by far than thee,
  And faded now is all thy wondrous art.
          [*The Enchantress points to a cleft in a rock.*]

I see within a cloven rock dispart
A scarlet bloom. Why raisest thou, pale one,
O famous dying minion of the sun,
Thy flickering hand? What mean the lights that rise
As light of triumph in thy goblin eyes—
In thy wan face?

200   *Enchantress.*   Hear, daughter of the days.
Behold the loving loveless flower of lone ways,
Well-nigh immortal in this charmèd clime;
Thou shalt outlive thine amorous happy time,
And dead as are the lovers of old rhyme
Shall be the hunter-lover of thy youth.
Yet evermore, through all thy days of ruth,
Shall grow thy beauty and thy dreamless truth;
As a hurt leopard fills with ceaseless moan
And aimless wanderings the woodlands lone,
210   Thy soul shall be, though pitiless and bright
It is, yet shall it fail thee day and night
Beneath the burden of the infinite,
In those far years, O daughter of the days.
And when thou hast these things for ages felt,
The red squirrel shall rear her young where thou hast dwelt—
Ah, woe is me! I go from sun and shade,
And the joy of the streams where long-limbed herons wade;
And never any more the wide-eyed bands
Of the pied panther-kittens from my hands
220   Shall feed. I shall not in the evenings hear
Again the woodland laughter, and the clear
Wild cries, grown sweet with lulls and lingerings long.
I fade, and shall not see the mornings wake,
A-fluttering the painted populace of lake
And sedgy stream, and in each babbling brake
And hollow lulling the young winds with song.
I dream!—I cannot die!—not die! No! no!
I hurl away these all unfaery fears.
Have I not seen a thousand seasons ebb and flow
230   The tide of stars? Have I not seen a thousand years
The summers fling their scents? Ah, subtile and slow,
The warmth of life is chilling, and the shadows grow

More dark beneath the poplars, where yon owl
Lies torn and rotting. The fierce kestrel birds
Slew thee, poor sibyl: comrades thou and I;
For ah, our lives were but two starry words
Shouted a moment 'tween the earth and sky.
Oh, death is horrible! and foul, foul, foul!

Naschina. I know not of the things thou speakest. What
    Of him on yonder brazen-gated spot, 240
    By thee spell-bound?

Enchantress.   Thou shalt know more:
    Meeting long hence the phantom herdsman, king
    Of the dread woods; along their russet floor
    His sleuth-hounds follow every fairy thing.
                [Turns to go. Naschina tries to prevent her.]
    Before I am too weak, oh let me fly,
    Fierce mortal, and crouched low beside the lake
    In a far stillness of the island die.
                             [Goes.]

Naschina [following]. Will he have happiness? Great sobs her
    being shake.

Voices [Sing]. A man has the fields of heaven,
        But soulless a fairy dies, 250
            As a leaf that is old, and withered, and cold,
            When the wintry vapours rise.

    Soon shall our wings be stilled,
        And our laughter over and done:
    So let us dance where the yellow lance
        Of the barley shoots in the sun.

    So let us dance on the fringèd waves,
        And shout at the wisest owls
    In their downy caps, and startle the naps
        Of the dreaming water-fowls, 260

    And fight for the black sloe-berries,
        For soulless a fairy dies,
        As a leaf that is old, and withered, and cold,
        When the wintry vapours rise.

[*Re-enter Naschina.*]

Naschina. I plucked her backwards by her dress of green.
 To question her—oh no, I did not fear,
 Because St. Joseph's image hangeth here
 Upon my necklace. But the goblin queen
 Faded and vanished: nothing now is seen,
270 Saving a green frog dead upon the grass.
 As figures moving mirrored in a glass,
 The singing shepherds, too, have passed away.
 O Arcady, O Arcady, this day
 A deal of evil and of change hath crossed
 Thy peace. Ah, now I'll wake these sleepers, lost
 And woe-begone. For them no evil day!
       [*Throws open the brazen gates.*]
 [*To Almintor*] O wake! wake! wake! for soft as a bee sips
 The fairy flower lies upon thy lips.

Almintor. I slept, 'twas sultry, and scarce circling shook
280 The falling hawthorn bloom. By mere and brook
 The otters dreaming lay. Naschina!

Naschina.   Ay!
 Behold the hapless sleepers standing by.
 I will dissolve away the faeries' guile;
 So be thou still, dear heart, a little while!
 [*To the Second Sleeper*] Old warrior, wake! for soft as a bee sips
 The fairy blossom lies upon thy lips.

Sleeper. Have I slept long?

Naschina.   Long years.

The Sleeper.   With hungry heart
 Doth still the Wanderer rove? With all his ships
 I saw him from sad Dido's shores depart,
290 Enamoured of the waves' impetuous lips.

Naschina. Those twain are dust. Wake! Light as a bee sips
 The fairy blossom lies upon thy lips;
 Seafarer, wake!

Third Sleeper.   Was my sleep long?

Naschina.   Long years.

Third Sleeper.
    A rover I who come from where men's ears
    Love storm and stained with mist the new moons flare.
    Doth still the man whom each stern rover fears—
    The austere Arthur—rule from Uther's chair?

Naschina. He is long dead.
                  Wake! soft as a bee sips
    The goblin flower lieth on thy lips.

Fourth Sleeper. Was my sleep long, O youth?

Naschina.   Long, long and deep.   300

The Sleeper. As here I came I saw god Pan. He played
    An oaten pipe unto a listening faun,
    Whose insolent eyes unused to tears would weep.
    Doth he still dwell within the woody shade,
    And rule the shadows of the eve and dawn?

Naschina. Nay, he is gone. Wake! wake! as a bee sips
    The fairy blossom broods upon thy lips.
    Sleeper, awake!

Fifth Sleeper.   How long my sleep?

Naschina.   Unnumbered
    The years of goblin sleep.

The Sleeper.   Ah! while I slumbered,
    How have the years in Troia flown away?   310
    Are still the Achaians' tented chiefs at bay?
    Where rise the walls majestical above,
    There dwells a little fair-haired maid I love.

The Sleepers all together. She is long ages dust.

The Sleeper.   Ah, woe is me!

First Sleeper. Youth, here will we abide, and be thou king
    Of this lake-nurtured isle!

Naschina.   Let thy king be
   Yon archer, he who hath the halcyon's wing
   As flaming minstrel-word upon his crest.

All the Sleepers. Clear-browed Arcadian, thou shalt be our king!

320 *Naschina.* O, my Almintor, noble was thy quest;
   Yea, noble and most knightly hath it been.

All the Sleepers. Clear-browed Arcadian, thou shalt be our king!

Almintor. Until we die within the charmèd ring
   Of these star-shuddering skies, you are the queen.

   [*The rising moon casts the shadows of Almintor and the Sleepers
   far across the grass. Close by Almintor's side, Naschina is
   standing, shadowless.*]

A 2

Love and Death

Behold the flashing waters,
   A cloven, dancing jet,
That from the milk-white marble
   For ever foam and fret;
Far off in drowsy valleys
   Where the meadow-saffrons blow,
The feet of summer dabble
   In their coiling calm and slow.
The banks are worn for ever
   By a people sadly gay: 10
A Titan, with loud laughter,
   Made them of fire and clay.
Go ask the springing flowers,
   And the flowing air above,
What are the twin-born waters,
   And they'll answer Death and Love.

With wreaths of withered flowers
   Two lonely spirits wait,
With wreaths of withered flowers,
   'Fore paradise's gate. 20
They may not pass the portal,
   Poor earth-enkindled pair,
Though sad is many a spirit
   To pass and leave them there
Still staring at their flowers,
   That dull and faded are.
If one should rise beside thee,
   The other is not far.
Go ask the youngest angel,
   She will say with bated breath, 30
By the door of Mary's garden
   Are the spirits Love and Death.

A 3

The Seeker

A DRAMATIC POEM — IN TWO SCENES

SCENE I

A woodland valley at evening. Around a wood fire sit three Shepherds.

First Shepherd. Heavy with wool the sheep are gathered in,
    And through the mansion of the spirit rove
    My dreams round thoughts of plenty, as in gloom
    Of desert-caves the red-eyed panthers rove
    And rove unceasing round their dreadful brood.

Second Shepherd. O brother, lay thy flute upon thy lips;
    It is the voice of all our hearts that laugh.

    [*The first Shepherd puts the flute to his lips; there comes from it
    a piercing cry. He drops it.*]

First Shepherd. It is possessed.

Second Shepherd.   A prophesying voice.

Third Shepherd. Nay, give it me, and I will sound a measure;
10   And unto it we'll dance upon the sward.

    [*Puts it to his lips. A voice out of the flute still more mournful.*]

First Shepherd. An omen!

Second Shepherd.   An omen!

Third Shepherd. A creeping horror is all over me.

    [*Enter an Old Knight. They cast themselves down before him.*]

Knight. Are all things well with you and with your sheep?

Second Shepherd. Yes, all is very well.

First Shepherd.   Whence comest thou?

Knight. Shepherds, I came this morning to your land
    From threescore years of dream-led wandering

Where spice-isles nestle on the star-trod seas,
And where the polar winds and waters wrestle
In endless dark, and by the weedy marge
Of Asian rivers, rolling on in light.   20
But now my wandering shall be done, I know.
A voice came calling me to this your land,
Where lies the long-lost forest of the sprite,
The sullen wood. But many woods I see
Where to themselves innumerable birds
Make moan and cry.

First Shepherd.   Within yon sunless valley,
   Between the hornèd hills—

Knight.   Shepherds, farewell!
   And peace be with you, peace and wealth of days.

Second Shepherd. Seek not that wood, for there the goblin snakes
   Go up and down, and raise their heads and sing   30
   With little voices songs of fearful things.

Third Shepherd. No shepherd foot has ever dared its depths.

First Shepherd. The very squirrel dies that enters there.

Knight. Shepherds, farewell!   [*Goes.*]

Second Shepherd.   He soon will be—

First Shepherd.   Ashes
   Before the wind.

Third Shepherd.   Saw you his eyes a-glitter?
   His body shake?

Second Shepherd.   Ay, quivering as yon smoke
   That from the fire is ever pouring up
   Among the boughs, blue as the halcyon's wing,
   Star-envious.

Third Shepherd. He was a spirit, brother.

Second Shepherd. The blessèd God was good to send us such,   40
   To make us glad with wonder as we sat
   Weary of watching round the fire at night.

SCENE II

*A ruined palace in the forest. Away in the depth of the shadow of
the pillars a motionless Figure.*

[*Enter the Old Knight.*]

Knight. Behold, I bend before thee to the ground
  Until my beard is in the twisted leaves
  That with their fiery ruin fill the hall,
  As words of thine through fourscore years have filled
  My echoing heart. Now raise thy voice and speak!
  Even from boyhood, in my father's house,
  That was beside the waterfall, thy words
  Abode, as banded adders in my breast.
  Thou knowest this, and how from 'mid the dance
10 Thou called'st me forth.

                    And how thou madest me
  A coward in the field; and all men cried:
  'The spirits stole his heart and gave instead
  A peering hare's;' and yet I murmured not,
  Knowing that thou hadst singled me with word
  Of love from out a dreamless race for strife,
  Through miseries unhuman ever on
  To joys unhuman, and to thee—Speak! Speak!
    [*He draws nearer to the Figure. A pause.*]
  Behold, I bend before thee to the ground;
  Thou wilt not speak, and I with age am near
20 To Death. His darkness and his chill I feel.
  Were all my wandering days of no avail,
  Untouched of human joy or human love?
  Then let me see thy face before I die.
  Behold, I bend before thee to the ground!
  Behold, I bend! Around my beard in drifts
  Lie strewn the yellow leaves—the clotted leaves.
    [*He gathers up the leaves and presses them to his breast.*]
  I'm dying! Oh, forgive me if I touch
  Thy garments' hem, thou visionary one!
    [*He goes close to the Figure. A sudden light bursts over it.*]
  A bearded witch, her sluggish head low bent

On her broad breast! Beneath her withered brows 30
Shine dull unmoving eyes. What thing art thou?

Figure. I know not what I am.

Knight.   I sought thee not.

Figure. Lover, the voice that summoned thee was mine.

Knight. For all I gave the voice, for all my youth,
    For all my joy—ah, woe!
    [*The Figure raises a mirror, in which the face and the form of the
    Knight are shadowed. He falls.*]

Figure [*bending over him and speaking in his ear*].
    What, lover, die before our lips have met?

Knight. Again, the voice! the voice!   [*Dies.*]

A4

Life

The child pursuing lizards in the grass,
    The sage, who deep in central nature delves,
The preacher watching for the evil hour to pass,
    All these are souls that fly from their dread selves.

———

The squirrel yonder, hushed and wise,
    Forswears his wandering 'mong the pine,
And wherefore, then, should thy grey eyes
    Wander away from mine?

The talking winds have found their home,
    Eve-soothed in some far leafy rest, 10
And wherefore should thy bright brow roam
    Madonna from my breast?

A little while and—red eve dies—
    Our love shall be of yesterday,
Ah, let us kiss each other's eyes,
    And laugh our love away.

———

'I laughed upon the lips of Sophocles,
   I go as soft as folly; I am Fate.'
This heard I where among the apple trees,
   Wild indolence and music have no date.

20

A 5

The Two Titans

A POLITICAL POEM

The vision of a rock where lightnings whirl'd
   Bruising the darkness with their crackling light;
The waves, enormous wanderers of the world,
   Beat on it with their hammers day and night.
Two figures crouching on the black rock, bound
   To one another with a coiling chain;
A grey-haired youth, whose cheeks had never found,
   Or long ere this had lost their ruddy stain;
A sibyl, with fierce face as of a hound

10   That dreams. She moveth, feeling in her brain
The lightnings pulse—behold her, aye behold—
   Ignoble joy, and more ignoble pain
Cramm'd all her youth; and hates have bought and sold
   Her spirit. As she moves, the foam-globes burst
Over her spotted flesh and flying hair
   And her gigantic limbs. The weary thirst
Unquenchable still glows in her dull stare,
   As round her, slow on feet that have no blood,
The phantoms of her faded pleasures walk;

20   And trailing crimson vans, a mumbling brood,
Ghosts of her vanished glories, muse and stalk
   About the sea. Before her lies that youth,
Worn with long struggles; and the waves have sung
   Their passion and their restlessness and ruth
Through his sad soul for ever old and young,
   Till their fierce miseries within his eyes
Have lit lone tapers.
                  Now the night was cast,

Making all one o'er rock and sea and skies;
And when once more the lightning Genii passed,
   Strewing upon the rocks their steel-blue hair, 30
I saw him stagger with the clanking chain,
   Trailing and shining 'neath the flickering glare.
With little cries of joy he kissed the rain
   In creviced rocks, and laughed to the old sea,
And, nodding to and fro, sang songs of love,
   And flowers and little children. Suddenly
Dropt down the velvet darkness from above,
   Hiding away the ocean's yelping flocks.
When flash on flash once more the lightning came,
   The youth had flung his arms around the rocks, 40
And in the sibyl's eyes a languid flame
   Was moving. Bleeding now, his grasp unlocks,
And he is dragged again before her feet.
   Why not? He is her own; and crouching nigh
Bending her face o'er his, she watches meet
   And part his foaming mouth with eager eye—

To place a kiss of fire on the dim brow
   Of Failure, and to crown her crownless head,
That all men evermore may humbly bow
   Down to the mother of the foiled and dead. 50
For this did the Eternal Darkness bring
   Thither thy dust, and knead it with a cry,
Gathered on her own lips, Oh youth, and fling
   Failure for glory down on thee, and mould
Thy withered foe, and with the purple wing
   Of ocean fan thee into life, and fold
For ever round thy waking and thy sleep
The darkness of the whirlwind shattered deep.

A 6

On Mr. Nettleship's
Picture at the
Royal Hibernian Academy

Yonder the sickle of the moon sails on,
But here the Lioness licks her soft cub
Tender and fearless on her funeral pyre;
Above, saliva dripping from his jaws,
The Lion, the world's great solitary, bends
Lowly the head of his magnificence
And roars, mad with the touch of the unknown,
Not as he shakes the forest; but a cry
Low, long and musical. A dew-drop hung
Bright on a grass blade's under side, might hear,
Nor tremble to its fall. The fire sweeps round
Re-shining in his eyes. So ever moves
The flaming circle of the outer Law,
Nor heeds the old, dim protest and the cry
The orb of the most inner living heart
Gives forth. He, the Eternal, works His will.

A7

Mosada

Mosada, *a Moorish lady*
Ebremar, *a monk*
Cola, *a lame boy*
Monks and Inquisitors

SCENE I

*A little Moorish room in the village of Azubia. In the centre of the
room a chafing-dish.*

[*Mosada alone.*]

Mosada. Three times the roses have grown less and less,
   And thrice the peaches flushed upon the walls,
   And thrice the corn around the sickles flamed,
   Since 'mong my people, tented on the hills,
   Where they all summer feed their wandering flocks,
   He stood a messenger. In April's prime
   (Swallows were flashing their white breasts above
   Or perching on the tents, a-weary still
   From waste seas cross'd, yet ever garrulous)
   Along the velvet vale I saw him come—   10
   Feet of dark Gomez, where now wander ye?
   In autumn, when far down the mountain slopes
   The heavy clusters of the grapes were full,
   I saw him sigh and turn and pass away;
   For I and all my people were accurst
   Of his sad God; and down among the grass
   Hiding my face, I cried long, bitterly.
   'Twas evening, and the cricket nation sang
   Around my head and danced among the grass;
   And all was dimness, till a dying leaf   20
   Slid circling down and softly touched my lips
   With dew, as though 'twere sealing them for death.
   Yet somewhere in the footsore world we meet,
   We two, before we die; for Azolar,

The star-taught Moor, said thus it was decreed
By those wan stars that sit in company
Above the Alpujarras on their thrones:
That when the stars of our nativity
Draw star to star, as on that eve he passed
30   Down the long valleys from my people's tents,
We meet—we two. [*She opens the casement. A sound
         of laughter floats in.*] How merry all these are
Among the fruit! But there, lame Cola crouches
Away from all the others. Now the sun
Sinks, shining on the little crucifix
Hung on his doublet—dear and mournful child,
Seër of visions! Now eve falls asleep,
The hour of incantation comes a-tiptoe,
And Cola, seeing, knows the sign and rises.
Thus do I burn these precious herbs, whose smoke
40   Pours up and floats in fragrance round my head
In coil on coil of azure.

                    [*Enter Cola.*]
                    All is ready.

Cola. I will not share your sin.

Mosada.   This is no sin.
No sin to see in coil on coil of azure
Pictured, where wander the beloved feet
Whose footfall I have longed for, three sad summers.
Why these new fears?

Cola.   The great monk Ebremar,
The dark still man, has come and says 'tis sin.

Mosada. They say the wish itself is half the sin;
Then has this one been sinned full many times.
50   Yet 'tis no sin; my father taught it me.
He was a man most learned and most mild,
Who, dreaming to a wondrous age, lived on,
Tending the roses round his lattice door.
For years his days had dawned and faded thus
Among the plants; the flowery silence fell

Deep in his soul, like rain upon a soil
Worn by the solstice fierce, and made it pure.
Would he teach any sin?

Cola.   Gaze in the cloud
   Yourself.

Mosada.   None but the innocent can see.

Cola. They say I am all ugliness; lame-footed   60
   I am; one shoulder turned awry—why then
   Should I be good? But you are beautiful.

Mosada. I cannot see.

Cola.   The beetles, and the bats,
   And spiders are my friends; I'm theirs, and they are
   Not good; but you are like the butterflies.

Mosada. I cannot see! I cannot see! but you
   Shall see a thing to talk on when you're old,
   Under a lemon tree beside your door;
   And all the elders sitting in the sun
   Will wondering listen, and this tale shall ease   70
   For long the burthen of their talking griefs.

Cola. Upon my knees I pray you, let it sleep,
   The vision.

Mosada.   You are pale and weeping. Child,
   Be not afraid, you'll see no fearful thing.
   Thus, thus I beckon from her viewless fields—
   Thus beckon to our aid a Phantom fair
   And calm, robed all in raiment moony white.
   She was a great enchantress once of yore,
   Whose dwelling was a tree-wrapt island, lulled
   Far out upon the water world and ringed   80
   With wonderful white sands, where never yet
   Were furled the wings of ships. There in a dell,
   A lily-blanchèd place, she sat and sang,
   And in her singing wove around her head
   White lilies, and her song flew forth afar
   Along the sea; and many a man grew hushed

In his own house or 'mong the merchants grey,
Hearing the far-off singing guile, and groaned,
And manned an argosy and sailing died.
90   In the far isle she sang herself asleep,
But now I wave her hither to my side.

Cola. Stay, stay, or I will hold your white arms down.
Ah me! I cannot reach them—here and there
Darting you wave them, darting in the vapour.
Heard you? Your lute hung in the window sounded!
I feel a finger drawn across my cheek!

Mosada. The phantoms come; they come, they come, they come!
I wave them hither, my breast heaves with joy.
Ah! now I'm Eastern-hearted once again,
100   And, while they gather round my beckoning arms,
I'll sing the songs the dusky lovers sing,
Wandering in sultry palaces of Ind,
A lotus in their hands—   [*The door is flung open.*]

[*Enter the Officers of the Inquisition.*]

First Inquisitor.   Young Moorish girl
Taken in magic, in the Church's name
I here arrest thee.

Mosada.   It was Allah's will.
Touch not this boy, for he is innocent.

Cola. Forgive! for I have told them everything.
They said I'd burn in hell unless I told.
                    [*She turns away—he clings to her dress.*]
Forgive me!

Mosada.   It was Allah's will.

Second Inquisitor.   The cords.

110   *Mosada.* No need to bind my hands. Where are ye, sirs?
For ye are hid with vapour.

Second Inquisitor.   Round the stake
The vapour is much thicker.

Cola.   God! the stake!

Ye said that ye would fright her from her sin—
No more; take me instead of her, great sirs.
She was my only friend; I'm lame, you know—
One shoulder twisted, and the children cry
Names after me.

First Inquisitor.   Lady—

Mosada.   I come.

Cola [following].   Forgive,
    Forgive, or I will die.

Mosada [stooping and kissing him]. 'Twas Allah's will.

SCENE II

A room in the building of the Inquisition of Granada, lighted by a stained window, picturing St. James of Spain.

[*Monks and Inquisitors.*]

First Monk. Will you not hear my last new song?

First Inquisitor.   Hush, hush!
    So she must burn, you say?

Second Inquisitor.   She must in truth.

First Inquisitor. Will he not spare her life? How would one matter
    When there are many?

Second Monk.   Ebremar will stamp
    This heathen horde away. You need not hope;
    And know you not she kissed that pious child
    With poisonous lips, and he is pining since?

First Monk. You're full of wordiness. Come, hear my song.

Second Monk. In truth, an evil race. Why strive for her,
    A little Moorish girl?

Second Inquisitor.   Small worth.

First Monk.   My song—   10

First Inquisitor. I had a sister like her once, my friend.

[*Touching the first Monk on the shoulder.*]

Where is our brother Peter? When you're nigh,
He is not far. I'd have him speak for her.
I saw his jovial mood bring once a smile
To sainted Ebremar's sad eyes. I think
He loves our brother Peter in his heart.
If Peter would but ask her life—who knows?

First Monk. He digs his cabbages. He brings to mind
    That song I've made. 'Tis of an Irish tale.
20   A saint of Munster, when much fasting, saw
    This vision of Peter and the burning gate.

[*Sings*]   I saw a stranger tap and wait
                Beside the door of Peter's gate,
                The stranger shouted, 'Open wide
                Thy sacred door;' but Peter cried,
                'No, thy home is deepest hell,
                Deeper than the deepest well.'
                Then the stranger softly crew—
                'Cock-a-doodle-doodle-do!'
30   Answered Peter: 'Enter in,
                Friend; but 'twere a deadly sin
                Ever more to speak a word
                Of any unblessed earthly bird.'

First Inquisitor. Be still; I hear the step of Ebremar.
    Yonder he comes; bright-eyed, and hollow-cheeked
    From fasting—see, the red light slanting down
    From the great painted window wraps his brow,
    As with an aureole.

          [*Ebremar enters. They all bow to him.*]

First Inquisitor.   My suit to you—

Ebremar. I will not hear; the Moorish girl must die.
40   I will burn heresy from this mad earth,
    And—

First Inquisitor. Mercy is the manna of the world.

Ebremar. The wage of sin is death.

Second Monk.   No use. No use.

First Inquisitor. My lord, if it must be, I pray descend
    Yourself into the dungeon 'neath our feet
    And importune with weighty words this Moor,
    That she forswear her heresies and save
    Her soul from seas of endless flame in hell.

Ebremar. I speak alone with servants of the Cross
    And dying men—and yet—But no, farewell.

Second Monk. No use.

Ebremar. Away! [*They go.*] Hear, thou enduring God,   50
    Who giveth to the golden-crested wren
    Her hanging mansion. Give to me, I pray,
    The burthen of Thy truth. Reach down Thy hands
    And fill me with Thy rage, that I may bruise
    The heathen. Yea, and shake the sullen kings
    Upon their thrones. The lives of men shall flow
    As quiet as the little rivulets
    Beneath the sheltering shadow of Thy Church;
    And Thou shalt bend, enduring God, the knees
    Of the great warriors whose names have sung   60
    The world to its fierce infancy again.

SCENE III

The dungeon of the Inquisition. The morning of the auto-da-fé dawns dimly through a barred window. A few faint stars are shining. Swallows are circling in the dimness without.

[*Mosada, alone.*]

Mosada. Oh, swallows, swallows, swallows, will ye fly
    This eve, to-morrow, or to-morrow night
    Above the farm-house by the little lake
    That rustles in the reeds with patient pushes,
    Soft as the whispering of a lost footstep
    Circling the brain? My brothers now pass down
    Along the cornfield, where the poppies grow,
    To their farm work; how silent all will be!

But no, in this warm weather, 'mong the hills,
10 Will move the faint far thunder-sound, as though
The world were dreaming in its summer sleep;
That will be later, day is dawning.
Hassan is with them too—he was so small,
A weak, thin child, when last I saw him there.
He will be taller now—'twas long ago.

The men are busy in the glimmering square.
I hear the murmur as they raise the beams
To build the circling seats, where high in air
Soon will the churchmen nod above the crowd.
20 I'm not of that pale company whose feet
Ere long shall falter through the noisy square,
And not come thence; for here in this small ring—
Hearken, ye swallows!—I have hoarded up
A poison drop. A toy, a fancy once,
A fashion with us Moorish maids, begot
Of dreaming and of watching by the door
The shadows pass; but now, I love my ring,
For it alone of all the world will do
My bidding. [*Sucks poison from the ring.*] Now 'tis done, and I
    am glad
30 And free—'twill thieve away with sleepy mood
My thoughts, and yonder brightening patch of sky
With three bars crossed, and these four walls my world,
And yon few stars grown dim, like eyes of lovers
The noisy world divides. How soon a deed
So small makes one grow weak and tottering!
Where shall I lay me down? That question is
A weighty question, for it is the last.
Not there, for there a spider weaves her web.
Nay here, I'll lay me down where I can watch
40 The burghers of the night fade one by one.
An apple-blossom circles in the gloom,
Floating from yon barred window. Small new-comer,
Thou'rt welcome. Lie there close against my fingers.
I wonder which is whitest, they or thou.
'Tis thou, for they've grown blue around the nails.

My blossom, I am dying, and the stars
Are dying too. They were full seven stars;
Two only now they are, two side by side.

Oh, Allah! it was thus they shone that night
When my lost lover left these arms. My Gomez   50
We meet at last, the ministering stars
Of our nativity hang side by side,
And throb within the circles of green dawn.
Too late, too late, for I am near to death.
I try to lift mine arms—they fall again.
This death is heavy in my veins like sleep.
I cannot even crawl along the stones
A little nearer those bright stars. Tell me,
Is it your message, stars, that when death comes
My soul shall touch with his, and the two flames   60
Be one? I think all's finished now and sealed.

[After a pause enter Ebremar.]

Ebremar. Young Moorish girl, thy final hour is here;
    Cast off thy heresies, and save thy soul
    From the undying worm. She sleeps—[*Starting.*] Mosada—
    Oh, God!—awake! thou shalt not die. She sleeps,
    Her head cast backward in her unloosed hair.
    Look up, look up, thy Gomez is by thee.
    A fearful paleness creeps across her breast
    And out-spread arms. [*Casting himself down by her.*] Be not so
        pale, dear love.
    Oh, can my kisses bring a flush no more   70
    Upon thy face? How heavily thy head
    Hangs on my breast! Listen, we shall be safe.
    We'll fly from this before the morning star.
    Dear heart, there is a secret way that leads
    Its paven length towards the river's marge
    Where lies a shallop in the yellow reeds.
    Awake, awake, and we will sail afar,
    Far, far along the fleet white river's face—
    Alone with our own whispers and replies—
    Alone among the murmurs of the dawn.   80

Once in thy nation none shall know that I
Was Ebremar, whose thoughts were fixed on God,
And heaven, and holiness.

Mosada.   Let's talk and grieve,
For that's the sweetest music for sad souls.
Day's dead, all flame-bewildered, and the hills
In list'ning silence gazing on our grief.
I never knew an eve so marvellous still.

Ebremar. Her dreams are talking with old years. Awake,
Grieve not, for Gomez kneels beside thee—

Mosada.   Gomez,
90   'Tis late, wait one more day; below the hills
The foot-worn way is long, and it grows dark.
It is the darkest eve I ever knew.

Ebremar. I kneel by thee—no parting now—look up.
She smiles—is happy with her wandering griefs.

Mosada. So you must go; kiss me before you go.
Oh, would the busy minutes might fold up
Their thieving wings that we might never part.
I never knew a night so honey-sweet.

Ebremar. There is no leave-taking. I go no more.
100   Safe on the breast of Gomez lies thy head,
Unhappy one.

Mosada.   Go not, go not, go not;
For night comes fast. Look down on me, my love,
And see how thick the dew lies on my face.
I never knew a night so dew-bedrowned.

Ebremar. Oh, hush the wandering music of thy mind.
Look on me once. Why sink your eyelids thus?
Why do you hang so heavy in my arms?
Love, will you die when we have met? One look
Give to thy Gomez.

Mosada.   Gomez—he has gone
110   From here, along the shadowy way that winds

Companioning the river's pilgrim torch.
I'll see him longer if I stand out here
Upon the mountain's brow. [*She tries to stand and totters.*
  Ebremar supports her, and she stands as if pointing down into a
  valley.]   Yonder he treads
The path o'er-muffled with the leaves—dead leaves,
Like happy thoughts grown sad in evil days.
He fades among the mists; how fast they come,
And pour upon the world! Ah! well-a-day!
Poor love and sorrow, with their arms thrown round
Each other's necks, and whispering as they go,
Still wander through the world. He's gone, he's gone.   120
I'm weary—weary, and 'tis very cold.
I'll draw my cloak around me; it is cold.
I never knew a night so bitter cold.   [*Dies.*]

                [*Enter Monks and Inquisitors.*]

First Inquisitor. My lord, you called?

Ebremar.   Not I. This maid is dead.

First Monk. From poison; for you cannot trust these Moors.
  You're pale, my lord.

First Inquisitor [*aside*]. His lips are quivering;
The flame that shone within his eyes but now
Has flickered and gone out.

Ebremar.   I am not well.
'Twill pass. I'll see the other prisoners now,
And importune their souls to penitence,   130
So they escape from hell. But, pardon me,
Your hood is threadbare—see that it be changed
Before we take our seats above the crowd.
                            [*They go out.*]

A 8

Remembrance

Remembering thee, I search out these faint flowers
   Of rhyme; remembering thee, this crescent night,
    While o'er the buds, and o'er the grass-blades, bright
And clinging with the dew of odorous showers,
With purple sandals sweep the grave-eyed hours—
   Remembering thee, I muse, while fades in flight
    The honey-hearted leisure of the light,
And hanging o'er the hush of willow bowers,

Of ceaseless loneliness and high regret
   Sings the young wistful spirit of a star
     Enfolden in the shadows of the East,
     And silence holding revelry and feast;
   Just now my soul rose up and touched it, far
In space, made equal with a sigh, we met.

A 9

A Dawn-Song

From the waves the sun hath reeled,
   Proudly in his saffron walking;
Sleep in some far other field
   Goes his poppies now a-hawking;
From the hills of earth have pealed
   Murmurs of her children talking—
My companions, two and two,
Gathering mushrooms in the dew.

Wake, *ma cushla*, sleepy-headed;
   Trembles as a bell of glass
All heaven's floor, with vapours bedded—
   And along the mountains pass,
With their mushrooms lightly threaded
   On their swaying blades of grass,

Lads and lasses, two and two,
Gathering mushrooms in the dew.

Wake! the heron, rising, hath
   Showered away the keen dew drops;
Weasel warms him on the path,
   Half asleep the old cow crops,   20
In the fairy-haunted rath,
   Dewy-tongued, the daisy tops—
We will wander, I and you,
Gathering mushrooms in the dew.

For your feet the morning prayeth:
   We will find her favourite lair,
Straying as the heron strayeth,
   As the moorfowl and the hare,
While the morning star decayeth
   In the bosom of the air—   30
Gayest wanderers, I and you,
Gathering mushrooms in the dew.

A10

The Fairy Pedant

Scene:—A circle of Druidic stones.

First Fairy. Afar from our lawn and our levée,
   O sister of sorrowful gaze!
Where the roses in scarlet are heavy
   And dream of the end of their days,
You move in another dominion
   And hang o'er the historied stone:
Unpruned is your beautiful pinion
   Who wander and whisper alone.

All. Come away while the moon's in the woodland,
   We'll dance and then feast in a dairy.   10
Though youngest of all in our good band,
   You are wasting away, little fairy.

Second Fairy. Ah! cruel ones, leave me alone now
    While I murmur a little and ponder
The history here in the stone now;
    Then away and away will I wander,
And measure the minds of the flowers,
    And gaze on the meadow-mice wary,
And number their days and their hours—

All. You are wasting away, little fairy.

Second Fairy. O shining ones, lightly with song pass,
    Ah! leave me, I pray you and beg.
My mother drew forth from the long grass
    A piece of a nightingale's egg,
And cradled me here where are sung,
    Of birds even, longings for aery
Wild wisdoms of spirit and tongue.

All. You are wasting away, little fairy.

First Fairy [*turning away*]. Though tenderest roses
        were round you,
    The soul of the pitiless place
With pitiless magic has bound you—
    Ah! woe for the loss of your face,
And loss of your laugh and its lightness—
    Ah! woe for your wings and your head—
Ah! woe for your eyes and their brightness—
    Ah! woe for your slippers of red.

All. Come away while the moon's in the woodland,
    We'll dance and then feast in a dairy.
Though youngest of all in our good band,
    She is wasting away, little fairy.

A11

Song of Spanish Insurgents

Oh! would on the hills of the falcons we tended our flocks
   The rams and the ewes and the young lambs that follow
      them bleating—
Away and away 'mong the dewberries over the rocks,
   With the sun on their wool and the width of their wide
      foreheads beating.
Oh, would that we were with our flocks on the face of the
    mountain
   A-counting the falcons above us, on wide wings a-hover,
   As they watch for the trembling field-mice, who steal from
      the clover
To drink of the dew of the spray-dabbled rim of the fountain.
   We have girded our swords, we have girded our swords for
    our flocks,
   For the quiet and stillness and peace of the dew-covered
    rocks.   10

Rejoicing we gather, rejoicing from tending the vine
   And startling with laughter the heart of the dream-ridden
      day:
Wine-stainèd and shouting we trampled the press of the wine.
   In our hearts is the ache and hunger of the battle; away
   In the vineyards are brooding the merle and the throstle
    and jay.

We have girded our swords that the land may have silence
    and peace
   And we may have stillness for days of a measureless toil
   On the fiery plains of the valley where labourless coil
The rivers whose labourless voices will never more cease;
   But will laugh by our graves as they laugh where our
      forefathers are,   20
   With a laughter as light as the pulse and the beat of a star.

A 1 2

[How beautiful thy colors are, oh marvellous morn of May]

How beautiful thy colors are, oh marvellous morn of May,
   The black-birds pour their copious lays; would Leigha were here,
The cuckoos sing unceasingly; how welcome day by day
   The gay and noble seasons; the summer swallows shear
The streams beside the branchy wood, the horses seek the pool,
   The heather spreads her long loose hair; the frail marsh-cottons
      grow,
The far bewildered planets pour on all an influence cool,
   And seas are lulled in quietness, and lavish blossoms blow.

A 1 3

How Ferencz Renyi Kept Silent

HUNGARY, 1848

We, too, have seen our bravest and our best
In prisons thrown, and mossy ruin rest
Where homes once whitened vale and mountain crest;
Therefore, O nation of the bleeding breast,
Libations, from the Hungary of the West.

Before his tent the General sips his wine,
Waves off the flies, and warms him in the shine.
The Austrian Haynau he, in many lands
Famous, a man of rules, a victor. Stands
Before him one well guarded, with bound hands;
Schoolmaster he, a dreamer, fiddler, first
In every dance, by children sought. 'Accurst,
Thy name is?'
                'Renyi.'
                    'Of?'
                         'This village.'
                              'Good!'

10

Hiding the rebels worm in yonder wood
Or yonder mountains. Where? Thou shalt be free—
Silence! Thou shalt be dead!'

                    Now suddenly
The spirit of young Renyi has grown old.
He turns where, hung like drops of dripping gold,
Flashing and flickering with ever-undulant wing
About a sun-flushed dove-cot, cooing, cling   20
Innumerable pigeons. Not on these
He muses. He a brown farm-house sees,
Where shadow of cherry, and shadow of apple trees,
Enclose a quiet place of beds box-bordered, bees,
Hives, currant bushes. There his kin are. High
Above, the woods where with the soft mild eye
Of her he loved fixed on him full of light,
Often he had bent down some bough all bright
With berries. Placid as a homeward bee,
Glad, simple—nay, he sought not mystery,   30
Nor, gazing forth where life's sad sickles reap,
Searched the unsearchable—why good men weep;
Why those who do good often be not good,
Why they who will the highest sometimes brood,
Clogged in a marsh where the slow marsh clay clings,
Abolished by a mire of little things,
Untuned by their own striving.
                      If one such
Were here, he would turn death into a crutch;
But this one—this one.
                 Now his head drops low,
Drops on his bosom, sombre, moist and slow.   40
'Choose!' Restless Haynau's fingers tapping go.
This sullen peasant spoils the good sunshine,
This sullen peasant spoils the good red wine.
He whispers to a soldier, who goes out—
A neighbouring cricket lifts his shrilly shout
Reiterant. A bird goes by the tent,
A lizard crawls—the two men gaze intent,
As though they'd vowed to measure all its ways.

Returns that soldier in the evening rays
50 Half hid. He brings the peasant's only kin,
Two women, withered one and small and thin,
Bent low with toil and hoariest years. The other
Of middle age.

            'His sister here and mother.'
The soldier thus, and Haynau—'Peasant, speak
If these be precious.'

            'I am old and weak,'
That ancient mother cries, 'speak not, my son.
I'm weak, and by the hands shall hold each one
Of my dead children soon, whate'er betide,
For I am old and weak.'

            And at her side
60 The sister: 'Sell thy country, and the shame
Of traitor evermore is on our name.'
Haynau, the man of system, lifts his hand
Serene. They're led away, and where a band
Of soldiers ranked is on a grassy spot,
A score of yards off under a willow, shot.

'Now hath he kith or kin, or any friend?'
A soldier answers: 'By the camp's far end
I saw a girl afraid to be too near,
Afraid to be too far.' 'Ay, bring her here!'

70 Time goes. The flakèd fire of evening crawls
Along the tents, the fields, the village walls.
The hare hath laid asleep her frolic wits,
And every flower above its shadow sits.
'On this embroidered cloud,' the sun hath said,
'A little will I lay my weary head,
Among the gold, the amber, and the red.'
A careful field-mouse finds a fallen crumb;
Now steps draw close, he hides beneath a drum.
That maiden bring they. When the tall red deer
80 In trouble is, the doe will linger near.
A peasant pale and pretty, her eyes for fear,
Like small brown moths, a-tremble.

                                'Renyi say
Where worm the rebels, or my bullets lay
The young one with the others.'

                             Renyi's pale
But speechless, and the maiden with long wail
Flings her before him. 'Save thyself and me.
Speak, Ferencz, speak. We love each other. See,
I am so young. Dost thou no longer know,
Beloved, how two little years ago
I came the first time to thy village school?   90
Thou hast forgotten. On the oaken stool
I sat me down beside thee, and I knew
So little. As the months passed by we grew
To love each other. In my prayer-book still
The violets are that on the wooded hill
We gathered. Ferencz, nay, I must not die:
I am to be your wife. A village high
And lost and far in yonder hills I know;
There far away from all we two will go,
And be so happy.'

                    To his hands she clings,   100
With cries and murmurs. Suddenly he flings
Away her clinging hands, and turns. She throws
Her arms around his feet. The signal goes
From Haynau's lifted fingers—two draw nigh
And seize her, and thus floats her quivering cry:
'Assassin, assassin! thou who let'st me die,
I curse thee—curse thee!'

                    Renyi silent stands,
And she is dragged to where the willow bands
With quiet shade its ever dewy-plot.
Noise! and a flash, a momentary blot.   110
So ends a brain—a world!

                    The smoke goes up,
Creeping along the heavens' purple cup,
Higher and higher gold with evening light;

It seems to fondle, with a finger bright
And soft, one glimmering star.

                        Renyi has cast
His bonds away, sore struggling.

                        Now at last
Haynau, thine hour has come, thy followers far
Under the willow.

                  Nay, to yonder star,
Yon bauble of the heavens, he lifts his hands,
And over tillage fields and pasture lands
And where the hill rises and the vale dips
He rushes rolling a mad laugh out of his lips.

A14

She Who Dwelt among the Sycamores

A FANCY

A little boy outside the sycamore wood
   Saw on the wood's edge gleam an ash-grey feather;
   A kid, held by one soft white ear for tether,
Trotted beside him in a playful mood.
A little boy inside the sycamore wood
   Followed a ringdove's ash-grey gleam of feather.
   Noon wrapt the trees in veils of violet weather,
And on tiptoe the winds a-whispering stood.
Deep in the woodland paused they, all their feet
   Lapped in the lemon daffodils; a bee
In the long grass—their eyes droop low—a seat
   Of moss, a maiden weaving. Singeth she:
'I am lone Lady Quietness, my sweet,
   And on this loom I weave thy destiny.'

A 1 5

The Fairy Doctor

The fairy doctor comes our way
  Over the sorrel-covered wold—
Now sadly, now unearthly gay,
  A little withered man, and old.

He knows by signs of secret wit
  The man whose hour of death draws nigh,
And who will moan in the under pit,
  And who foregather in the sky.

He sees the fairy hosting move
  By heath or hollow or rushy mere,   10
And then his heart flows full of love,
  And full his eyes of fairy cheer.

Cures he hath for cow or goat
  With fairy-smitten udders dry—
Cures for calves with 'plaining throat,
  That sickening near their mothers lie;

And many a herb and many a spell
  For hurts and ails and lover's moan—
For all save him who pining fell,
  Glamoured by fairies for their own.   20

Now be courteous, now be kind,
  Lest he may some glamour fold
Closely round us, body and mind—
  The little withered man, and old.

A 16

The Protestants' Leap (Lug-na-Gal, Sligo)

The Cromwellian Speaks

Malformed our guide as from a failing tribe
    Harried and starved as suits earth's crazy rust,
Tiller of sordid cliffs, the strong man's jibe,
    All over grey from sitting in the dust.

On his pale eyes and forehead moist with hair,
    Hanging like red iron drippings down a rock,
Fell from his pinewood torch a smoky flare.
    Fifty and twain by many a mountainous block.

Clotted in clay and on the hill's edge laid,
10   With horses breathing heavily, we wound
Skyward along a path turf cutters made,
    Sound from four hundred hoofs, from us no sound.

Rolled over us the clouds in grisly smoke,
    When moonless, starless, stood we on the height,
Gazing, and vaguely through the darkness broke,
    From a low dusky pool, a pallid light.

Above, the bats went shrilling to and fro,
    The bubbles from the eels arose, and slipped
Poolward dull frogs luxurious, in the slow
20   Water his flame the grey guide, whispering, dipped.

He had one shoulder low, one shoulder high,
    And he was lame, we might have known him then,
No minor minion, Belial, Molock, aye,
    Or Satan murmuring in his favourite den

To the grey slime. Thus he 'Along the brown
    Mould follow me, nor hold ye silence deep,
The rebels where I lead ye, laid them down,
    Weary, and they are very fast asleep.'

Awhile the heavens touching dew bright mould,
    Round us, who in our saddles spurring bent,
Lay level as, neath God's imminent finger rolled,   30
    Our fifty hearts brimmed over with content.

Then down a dripping way we spurred together,
    The grey guide rose a form of flying mist,
As over mountain laurel, over heather,
    The grey guide leading ever on more swift

Went we, and loosed the sword in the long sheath,
    For near the idolators we surely came.
The flashing of the flint fires underneath
    Our hoofs made an interminable flame.   40

The ground sloped ever steeper and more steep,
    More headlong we, our raiment in the wind
Beyond our shoulders 'gan to roar and leap,
    And bellowed all the blue bare world behind.

       *   *   *   *

Senseless, for many moments, I lay still,
    Then I arose, on knees and fingers propped;
My weary horse had fallen, with a will
    He the spare dew bright grasses near me cropped.

I thrust one foot forth, and found emptiness—
    It swung over an abyss before my gaze;
Blackness, a thousand feet down, more or less,   50
    And a waste water's few, far tranquil rays,

As from a lidless eye, and here and there
    A sound of torrents in the invisible woods,
Else silence. Once a meteor's fickle flare,
    That slanted, slipping from the starry broods,

Showed the mild mountains, mournful in their shrouds;
    Showed the dim river, like a wandering spark;
Showed where the ash wood on the pine wood crowds;
    Showed a far eagle brooding on the dark.   60

A17

Love Song
From the Gaelic

My love, we will go, we will go, I and you,
And away in the woods we will scatter the dew;
And the salmon behold, and the ousel too,
My love, I and you, we will hear, we will hear,
The calling afar of the doe and the deer,
And the bird in the branches will cry for us clear,
And the cuckoo unseen in his festival mood;
And death, oh my fair one, will never come near
In the bosom afar of the fragrant wood.

A18

The Phantom Ship

Flames the shuttle of the lightning across the driving sleet,
Ay, and shakes in sea-green waverings along the fishers' street;
Gone the stars and gone the white moon, gone and puffed away
    and dead.
Never storm arose so swiftly; scarce the children were in bed,
Scarce the old and wizen houses had their doors and windows
    shut.
Ah! it dwelt within the twilight as the worm within the nut.
'Waken, waken, sleepy fishers; no hour is this for sleep,'
Cries a voice at roaring midnight beside the moonless deep.
Half dizzy with the lightning there runs a gathering band—
10 'Watcher, wherefore have ye called us?' Eyes go after his lean hand,
And the fisher men and women from the dripping harbour wall
See the darkness slow disgorging a vessel blind with squall.
'Bring the ropes now! Stand ye by now! See, she rounds the
    harbour clear.
God! they're mad to fly such canvas!' Ah! what bell-notes do they
    hear?

Say what ringer rings at midnight; for, in the belfry high,
Slow the chapel bell is tolling as though the dead passed by.
Round she comes in stays before them; cease the winds, and on
    their poles
Cease the sails their flapping uproar, and the hull no longer rolls.
Now a scream from all those fishers, for there on deck there be
All the drowned that ever were drowned from that village by the
    sea;   20
And the ghastly ghost-flames glimmer all along the taffrail rails
On the drowned men's hands and faces, on the spars and on the
    sails.
Hush'd the fishers, till a mother calls by name her drownèd son;
Then each wife and maid and mother calls by name some
    drownèd one.
Stands each grey and silent phantom on the same regardless spot—
Joys and fears in their grey faces that the live earth knoweth not;
Down the vapours fall and hide them from the children of a day,
And the winds come down and blow them with the vapours far
    away.
Hang the mist-threads for a little while like cobwebs in the air;
Then the stars grow out of heaven with their countenances fair. 30

'Pray for the souls in purgatory,' the pale priest trembling cries.
            *   *   *   *   *
Prayed those forgotten fishers, till in the eastern skies
Came olive fires of morning and on the darkness fed,
By the slow heaving ocean—mumbling mother of the dead.

A19

A Legend

A drowned city is supposed to lie under the waters of Lough Gill.

> The Maker of the stars and worlds
>   Sat underneath the market cross,
> And the old men were walking, walking,
>   And little boys played pitch and toss.

'The props,' said He, 'of stars and worlds
    Are prayers of patient men and good.'
The boys, the women, and old men,
    Listening, upon their shadows stood.

A grey professor passing cried,
    'How few the mind's intemperance rule!
What shallow thoughts about deep things!
    The world grows old and plays the fool.'

The mayor came, leaning his deaf ear—
    There was some talking of the poor—
And to himself cried, 'Communist!'
    And hurried to the guard-house door.

The bishop came with open book,
    Whispering along the sunny path;
There was some talking of man's god,
    His god of stupor and of wrath.

The bishop murmured, 'Atheist!
    How sinfully the wicked scoff!'
And sent the old men on their way,
    And drove the boys and women off.

The place was empty now of people.
    A cock came by upon his toes;
An old horse looked across a fence,
    And on the rail he rubbed his nose.

The Maker of the stars and worlds
    To His own house did him betake,
And on that city dropped a tear,
    And now that city is a lake.

A20

Time and
the Witch Vivien

A marble-flagged, pillared room. Magical instruments in one corner. A fountain in the centre.

Vivien [*looking down into the fountain*].
    Where moves there any beautiful as I,
    Save, with the little golden greedy carp,
    Gold unto gold, a gleam in its long hair,
    My image yonder?   [*Spreading her hand over the water.*]
               Ah, my beautiful,
    What roseate fingers!   [*Turning away.*]
            No; nor is there one
    Of equal power in spells and secret rites.
    The proudest or most coy of spirit things,
    Hide where he will, in wave or wrinkled moon,
    Obeys.
          Some fierce magician flies or walks
    Beyond the gateway—by the sentries now—   10
    Close and more close—I feel him in my heart—
    Some great one. No; I hear the wavering steps
    Without there of a little, light old man;
    I dreamt some great one.
    [*Catching sight of her image, and spreading her hand over the
        water.*]
                 Ah, my beautiful,
    What roseate fingers!

[*Enter Time as an old pedlar, with a scythe, an hour-glass, and a
    black bag.*]
             [*Laughing.*] So then it is you.
    The wrinkled squanderer of human wealth.
    Come here. Be seated now; I'd buy of you.
    Come, father.

Time.   Lady, I nor rest nor sit.

Vivien. Well then, to business; what is in your bag?

Time [*putting the bag and hour-glass on the table and resting on
    his scythe*].
20 Grey hairs and crutches, crutches and grey hairs,
    Mansions of memories and mellow thoughts
    Where dwell the minds of old men having peace,
    And—

Vivien.   No; I'll none of these, old Father Wrinkles.

Time. Some day you'll buy them, maybe.

Vivien.   Never!

Time [*laughing*].   Never?

Vivien. Why do you laugh?

Time.   I laugh the last always.

        [*She lays the hour-glass on one side. Time rights it again.*]

Vivien. I do not need your scythe. May that bring peace
    To those your 'mellow' wares have wearied out.
    I'd buy your glass.

Time.   My glass I will not sell.
    Without my glass I'd be a sorry clown.

30 *Vivien.* Yet whiter beard have you than Merlin had.

Time. No taste have I for slumber 'neath an oak.

Vivien. When were you born?

Time.   Before your grandam Eve.

Vivien. Oh, I am weary of that foolish tale.
    They say you are a gambler and a player
    At chances and at moments with mankind.
    I'll play you for your old hour-glass.
                              You see
    I keep such things about me; they are food
    For antiquarian meditation.   [*Brings dice.*]

Time.   Ay,
    We throw three times.

Vivien. Three-six.

40

Time. Four-six.

Vivien. Five-six. Ha, Time!

Time. Double sixes!

Vivien. I lose! They're loaded dice. Time always plays
With loaded dice. Another chance! Come, father;
Come to the chess, for young girls' wits are better
Than old men's any day, as Merlin found.
                    [*Places the chess-board on her knees.*]
The passing of those little grains is snow
Upon my soul, old Time.
                              [*She lays the hour-glass on its side.*]

Time.   No; thus it stands.
                              [*Rights it again.*]
For other stakes we play. You lost the glass.

50

Vivien. Then give me triumph in my many plots.
Time. Defeat is death.
Vivien.   Should my plots fail I'd die.
                              [*They play.*]
Thus play we first with pawns, poor things and weak;
And then the great ones come, and last the king.
So men in life and I in magic play;
First dreams, and goblins, and the lesser sprites,
And now with Father Time I'm face to face.
                              [*They play.*]
I trap you.

Time.   Check.

Vivien.   I did miscalculate,
Being dull to-day, or you had lost the game.
Chance, and not skill, has favoured you, old father!
                                                      60
                              [*She plays.*]

Time. Check.

Vivien.   Ah! how bright your eyes. How swift your moves.
How still it is! I hear the carp go splash,

And now and then a bubble rise. I hear
A bird walk on the doorstep.   [*She plays.*]

Time.   Check once more.

Vivien. I must be careful now. I have such plots—
     Such war plots, peace plots, love plots—every side;
     I cannot go into the bloodless land
     Among the whimpering ghosts.

Time.   Mate thus.

Vivien.   Already?
                                              [*She dies.*]
     Chance hath a skill!

A 2 1

[Full moody is my love and sad]

Full moody is my love and sad,
     His moods bow low his sombre crest,
I hold him dearer than the glad,
     And he shall slumber on my breast.

My love hath many an evil mood,
     Ill words for all things soft and fair,
I hold him dearer than the good,
     My fingers feel his amber hair.

No tender wisdom floods the eyes
     That watch me with their suppliant light—
I hold him dearer than the wise,
     And for him make me wise and bright.

A22

Kanva on Himself

Now wherefore hast thou tears innumerous?
  Hast thou not known all sorrow and delight
Wandering of yore in forests rumorous,
  Beneath the flaming eyeballs of the night,

And as a slave been wakeful in the halls
  Of Rajas and Mahrajas beyond number?
Hast thou not ruled among the gilded walls?
  Hast thou not known a Raja's dreamless slumber?

Hast thou not sat of yore upon the knees
  Of myriads of beloveds, and on thine
Have not a myriad swayed below strange trees   10
  In other lives? Hast thou not quaffed old wine

By tables that were fallen into dust
  Ere yonder palm commenced his thousand years?
Is not thy body but the garnered rust
  Of ancient passions and of ancient fears?

Then wherefore fear the usury of Time,
  Or Death that cometh with the next life-key?
Nay, rise and flatter her with golden rhyme,
  For as things were so shall things ever be.   20

A23

A Lover's Quarrel among the Fairies

A moonlit moor. Fairies leading a child.

Male Fairies. Do not fear us, earthly maid!
    We will lead you hand in hand
  By the willows in the glade,
    By the gorse on the high land,

By the pasture where the lambs
    Shall awake with lonely bleat,
Shivering closer to their dams
    From the rustling of our feet.

You will with the banshee chat,
    And will find her good at heart,
Sitting on a warm smooth mat
    In the green hill's inmost part.

We will bring a crown of gold,
    Bending humbly every knee,
Now thy great white doll to hold—
    Oh, so happy would we be!

Ah! it is so very big,
    And we are so very small!
So we dance a fairy jig
    To the fiddle's rise and fall.

Yonder see the fairy girls
    All their jealousy display,
Lift their chins and toss their curls,
    Lift their chins and turn away.

See you, brother, Cranberry Fruit—
    Ho! ho! ho! the merry blade!—
Hugs and pets and pats a newt,
    Teasing every wilful maid.

Girl Fairies. Lead they one with foolish care,
    Deafening us with idle sound—
One whose breathing shakes the air,
    One whose footfall shakes the ground.

Come you, Coltsfoot, Mousetail, come!
    Come I know where, far away,
Owls there be whom age makes numb;
    Come and tease them till the day.

Puffed like puff-balls on a tree,
   Scoff they at the modern earth—
Ah! how large mice used to be
   In their days of youthful mirth!   40

Come, beside a sandy lake,
   Feed a fire with stems of grass;
Roasting berries steam and shake—
   Talking hours swiftly pass!

Long before the morning fire
   Wake the larks upon the green.
Yonder foolish ones will tire
   Of their tall, new-fangled queen.

They will lead her home again
   To the orchard-circled farm;   50
At the house of weary men
   Raise the door-pin with alarm,

And come kneeling on one knee,
   While we shake our heads and scold
This their wanton treachery,
   And our slaves be as of old.

A24

The Priest and the Fairy

Unto the heart of the woodland straying,
Where the shaking leaf with the beam was playing,

Musingly wandered the village priest.
As the summer voice of the daytime ceased,

He came to the home of the forest people
From where the old ivy crawls round the old steeple,

And under a shady oak-tree sat,
Where the moss was spread like his own doormat.

The tangled thoughts of the finished day
10   Fled from his brow where the hair was grey;

And as the time to darkness plodded,
He thought wise things as his grey head nodded.

How 'the only good is musing mild,
And evil still is action's child.

'With action all the world is vexed,'
He'd find for this some holy text.

                    *   *   *   *

He'd slept among the singing trees,
Among the murmurs of the bees,

A full hour long, when rose a feather
20   Out of a neighbouring bunch of heather;

And then a pointed face was seen
Beneath a pointed cap of green;

And straight before the sleeping priest
There stood a man, of men the least—

Three spans high as he rose to his feet,
And his hair was as yellow as waving wheat.

Now, what has a fairy to do with a priest
Who is six feet high in his socks at least?

He drew from his cap a feather grey,
30   On the nose of the sleeper he made it play;

The sleeper awoke with a sudden start,
With open mouth and beating heart.

He had dreamed the cow had got within
His garden ringed with jessamine,

And many a purple gillyflower eaten,
And under her hoofs the marigolds beaten.

Then 'gan to speak that goblin rare,
Brushing back his yellow hair:

'Man of wisdom, from thy sleeping
40   I have roused thee; for the weeping

'Of our great queen is ever heard
Among the haunts of bee and bird.

'We buried late in a hazel dell
A fairy whom we loved full well;

'The swiftest he to dance or fly,
And his hair was as dark as a plover's eye.

'Man of wisdom, dost thou know
Whither the souls of fairies go?'

The priest looked neither to right nor left,
Nigh of his wits by fear bereft.   50

'Ave Marie,' muttered he
Over the beads of his rosary.

The fairies' herald spake once more:
'Say and thrice anigh thy door

'Every summer wilt thou see
Wild bees' honey laid for thee.'

The father dropt his rosary—
'They are lost, they are lost, each one,' cried he.

And then his heart grew well-nigh dead
Because of the thing his tongue had said.   60

As a wreath of smoke in wind-blown flight
The fairy vanished from his sight,

And came to where his brethren stood,
Away in the heart of the antique wood;

And when they heard that tale of his
They grew so very still, I wis

Were you a fairy you'd have heard
The breathing of the smallest bird,

The beating of a leveret's heart;
And then the fay queen sobbed apart,   70

And all the sad fay chivalry
Lifted their voices bitterly.

                *   *   *   *

A woodman on his homeward way
Heard the voice of their dismay,

And said, 'Yon bittern cries, in truth,
As though his days were full of ruth.

'If I were free to do as little
80   As dance upon the spear-grass brittle,

'Or seek where sweetest water bubbles,
Remote from all the hard earth troubles,

'And cut no wood the whole day long,
I'd glad folks' hearts with blither song.'

A 25

Street Dancers

Singing in this London street,
To the rhythm of their feet,
By a window's feeble light
Are two ragged children bright—
Larger sparrows of the town,
Nested among vapours brown.
Far away the starry mirth
10   Overhangs the wooded earth.

If these merry ones should know,
Dancing by the window glow,
Starry laughter, woodland leisure,
Would they foot so fleet a measure?
                Ah no!

Maybe now in some far lane,
Dancing on the moon's broad stain,
Watched of placid poplar-trees
Children sing in twos and threes.
20   Hush! hush! hush! On every lip
Lies a chilly finger tip,
As there floats from fields afar
Clamour of the lone nightjar.

If these merry ones should know,
Dancing by the window glow,
Other people's mirth and pleasure,
Would they foot so fleet a measure?
      Ah no!

Maybe in some isle of isles,
In the South Sea's azure miles,
Dance the savage children small,
Singing to their light footfall.
Hush! hush! hush! they pause and point   30
Where a shell the seas anoint,
Dropping liquid rainbow light,
Rolls along the sea sands white.

If these merry ones should know,
Dancing by the window glow,
Other people's mirth and pleasure,
Would they foot so fleet a measure?
      Ah no!

Maybe now a Bedouin's brood,   40
Laughing goes in wildest mood,
Past the spears and palm-stems dry,
Past the camel's dreaming eye.
Hush! hush! hush! they pause them where
Bows the Bedouin's whitening hair—
Peace of youth and peace of age,
Thoughtless joy and sorrow sage.

If these merry ones should know,
Dancing by the window glow,
Other people's mirth and pleasure,   50
Would they foot so fleet a measure?
      Ah no!

Others know the healing earth,
Others know the starry mirth;
They will wrap them in the shroud,
Sorrow-worn, yet placid-browed.
London streets have heritage,

Blinder sorrows, harder wage—
Sordid sorrows of the mart,
60   Sorrows eating brain and heart.

If these merry ones should know,
Dancing by the window glow,
Of the healing earth May-treasure,
Would they foot so fleet a measure?
                    Ah no!

A26

Quatrains and Aphorisms

I

The child who chases lizards in the grass,
The sage who deep in central nature delves,
The preacher watching for the ill hour to pass—
All these are souls who fly from their dread selves.

II

Two spirit-things a man hath for his friends—
Sorrow, that gives for guerdon liberty,
And joy, the touching of whose finger lends
To lightest of all light things sanctity.

III

10   Long thou for nothing, neither sad nor gay;
Long thou for nothing, neither night nor day;
Not even 'I long to see thy longing over,'
To the ever-longing and mournful spirit say.

IV

The ghosts went by me with their lips apart
From death's late languor as these lines I read
On Brahma's gateway, 'They within have fed
The soul upon the ashes of the heart.'

V

This heard I where, amid the apple trees,
Wild indolence and music have no date,
'I laughed upon the lips of Sophocles,
I go as soft as folly; I am Fate.'   20

VI

Around, the twitter of the lips of dust
A tossing laugh between their red abides;
With patient beauty yonder Attic bust
In the deep alcove's dimness smiles and hides.

VII

The heart of noon folds silence and folds sleep,
For noon and midnight from each other borrow,
And Joy, in growing deeper and more deep,
Walks in the vesture of her sister Sorrow.

A 27

In Church

She prays for father, mother dear,
    To Him with thunder shod,
She prays for every falling tear
    In the holy church of God.

For all good men now fallen ill,
    For merry men that weep,
For holiest teachers of His will,
    And common men that sleep.

The sunlight flickering on the pews,
  The sunlight in the air,
The flies that dance in threes, in twos,
  They seem to join her prayer—

Her prayer for father, mother dear,
  To Him with thunder shod,
A prayer for every falling tear
  In the holy church of God.

A28

A Summer Evening

The living woods forego their care,
  Their dread of autumn's mortal wing,
And shake their birds upon the air,
  And like a silver trumpet ring.

The giddy bee's complacent croon,
  Where long grey grasses bow and bend,
In all its honey-thickened tune
  Has no word of the sulphurous end.

The sunflowers weave a golden clime,
  As though their season had no date,
Nod to the iron shoes of Time,
  And play with his immortal hate.

And, maiden, be thou mirthful too,
  Lay down the burden of thy race,
For God is walking in the dew,
  An evening presence fills the place.

The hollow woodlands feel Him there,
  And dread no more foul autumn's wing,
And shake their birds upon the air,
  And like a silver trumpet ring.

A29

In the Firelight

Come and dream of kings and kingdoms,
    Cooking chestnuts on the bars—
Round us the white roads are endless,
    Mournful under mournful stars.

Whisper lest we too may sadden,
    Round us herds of shadows steal—
Care not if beyond the shadows
    Flieth Fortune's furious wheel.

Kingdoms rising, kingdoms falling,
    Bowing nations, plumèd wars—   10
Weigh them in an hour of dreaming,
    Cooking chestnuts on the bars.

A30

Mourn—And Then Onward!

Ye on the broad high mountains of old Eri,
    Mourn all the night and day,
The man is gone who guided ye, unweary,
    Through the long bitter way.

Ye by the waves that close in our sad nation,
    Be full of sudden fears,
The man is gone who from his lonely station
    Has moulded the hard years.

Mourn ye on grass-green plains of Eri fated,
    For closed in darkness now   10
Is he who laboured on, derided, hated,
    And made the tyrant bow.

Mourn—and then onward, there is no returning
    He guides ye from the tomb;
His memory now is a tall pillar, burning
    Before us in the gloom!

A 3 1

When you are Sad

When you are sad,
    The mother of the stars weeps too,
And all her starlight is with sorrow mad,
    And tears of fire fall gently in the dew.

When you are sad,
    The mother of the wind mourns too,
And her old wind that no mirth ever had,
    Wanders and wails before my heart most true.

When you are sad,
    The mother of the wave sighs too,
And her dim wave bids man be no more glad,
    And then the whole world's trouble weeps with you.

10

A 3 2

Where My Books Go

All the words that I gather,
    And all the words that I write,
Must spread out their wings untiring,
    And never rest in their flight,
Till they come where your sad, sad heart is,
    And sing to you in the night,
Beyond where the waters are moving,
    Storm darkened or starry bright.

London, January 1892

A 3 3

The Ballad of Earl Paul

'Shield breaker, break a shield to-day,
    And John will pardon thee,
And thou canst dwell in thine own home,
    On the cliff by the sea,

'And half forget this bed of straw
    And this hard flag of stone,
For a knight, come from Normandy,
    Has twelve knights overthrown;

'And all down from Northumberland
    To the green Isle of Wight   10
Men cry "Bring Paul, Shield breaker,
    To throw the Norman knight." '

Thus spake the Town Jailor
    To the Earl of Kinsale,
And flung down clashing on the floor
    A coat of gilded mail.

Earl Paul stood on the bed of straw,
    And answered unto him:
'Go bring me my old armour
    That the red rust makes dim.'   20

When Paul rode from the town
    He blinked and blinked his eyes
Like a grey owl men harry out
    Unto the white skies.

'Shield breaker, great shield breaker,'
    Was cried in street and lane
When hundreds stood about to see
    The Captive from Kinsale.

Earl Paul came where the king sat,
    With many a lovely face   30

30

And plumed heads about him,
    Before a sanded place;

And stood in his dim armour,
    And looked on no one there
Though the glad cry, 'Shield-breaker,'
    Leaped up into the air.

With shield and armour wrought with gold,
    A hurting beam of light,
Amid a cloud of banners,
    Stood there the Norman knight.

40

Singing a love rhyme to himself,
    And smiling from sweet thought,
For he had overthrown twelve knights
    And made their glory naught.

The dim spear met the bright spear,
    And made the bright spear bend,
For God gives power to the sad
    Till day and night time end.

The dim spear breaks the bright shield
    And pierced the mirthful breast,
For God gives power to the sad
    Till all things are at rest.

50

The people cried 'Shield-breaker!'
    And John rose up and stood,
Saying, 'Earl Paul is pardoned
    For his great hardihood.

'I bid him ask what gift he will,
    Then go to his own land,
Or stay with me beside the Thames,
    Sitting on my right hand.'

60

'I ask that I and all my race,'
    The Earl of Kinsale said,
'May stand before thy race and thee
    And keep a covered head.'

Then turned he from the king's court,
   With a clang of his dim mail,
And came and dwelt in his own house,
   On the cliff of Kinsale.

Sligo, April 4th.

A 34

The Danaan Quicken Tree

Beloved, hear my bitter tale!—
   Now making busy with the oar,
Now flinging loose the slanting sail,
   I hurried from the woody shore,
And plucked small fruits on Innisfree.
   (Ah, mournful Danaan quicken tree!)

A murmuring faery multitude,
   When flying to the heart of light
From playing hurley in the wood
   With creatures of our heavy night,
A berry threw for me—or thee.
   (Ah, mournful Danaan quicken tree!)

And thereon grew a tender root,
   And thereon grew a tender stem,
And thereon grew the ruddy fruit
   That are a poison to all men
And meat to the Aslauga Sidhe.
   (Ah, mournful Danaan quicken tree!)

If when the battle is half won,
   I fling away my sword, blood dim,
Or leave some service all undone,
   Beloved, blame the Danaan whim,
And blame the snare they set for me.
   (Ah, mournful Danaan quicken tree!)

Cast out all hope, cast out all fear,
    And taste with me the faeries' meat,
For while I blamed them I could hear
    Dark Joan call the berries sweet,
Where Niamh heads the revelry.
30   (Ah, mournful Danaan quicken tree!)

A35

Wisdom and Dreams

I pray that I ever be weaving
    An intellectual tune,
But weaving it out of threads
    From the distaff of the moon.

Wisdom and dreams are one,
    For dreams are the flowers ablow,
And Wisdom the fruit of the garden:
    God planted him long ago.

A36

[The wind blows out of the gates of the day]

The wind blows out of the gates of the day,
The wind blows on the lonely heart,
And the lonely heart is withered away.
While the faeries dance in a place apart,
Shaking their milk-white feet in a ring,
Tossing their milk-white arms in the air;
For they hear the wind laugh and murmur and sing
Of a land where even the old are fair,
And even the wise are merry of tongue;
10 But I heard a reed of Coolaney say,
    'When the wind has laughed and murmured and sung
And the lonely heart is withered away!'

A37

[The poet, Owen Hanrahan, under a bush of may]

The poet, Owen Hanrahan, under a bush of may
Calls down a curse on his own head because it withers grey;
Then on the speckled eagle cock of Ballygawley Hill
Because it is the oldest thing that knows of cark and ill;
And on the yew that has been green from the times out of mind
By the Steep Place of the Strangers and the Gap of the Wind;
And on the great grey pike that broods in Castle Dargan Lake
Having in his long body a many a hook and ache;
Then curses he old Paddy Bruen of the Well of Bride
Because no hair is on his head and drowsiness inside.   10
Then Paddy's neighbour, Peter Hart, and Michael Gill, his friend,
Because their wandering histories are never at an end.
And then old Shemus Cullinan, shepherd of the Green Lands
Because he holds two crutches between his crooked hands;
Then calls a curse from the dark North upon old Paddy Doe,
Who plans to lay his withering head upon a breast of snow,
Who plans to wreck a singing voice and break a merry heart;
He bids a curse hang over him till breath and body part,
But he calls down a blessing on the blossom of the may
Because it comes in beauty, and in beauty blows away.   20

A38

[Impetuous heart be still, be still]

Impetuous heart be still, be still,
Your sorrowful love can never be told,
Cover it up with a lonely tune.
He who could bend all things to His will
Has covered the door of the infinite fold
With the pale stars and the wandering moon.

A39

[Lift up the white knee]

Lift up the white knee;
Hear what they sing,
Those young dancers
That in a ring
Raved but now
Of the hearts that broke
Long, long ago
For their sake.

'But the dance changes,
Lift up the gown,
All that sorrow
Is trodden down.'

10

A40

[Out of sight is out of mind]

Out of sight is out of mind:
Long have man and woman-kind,
Heavy of will and light of mood,
Taken away our wheaten food,
Taken away our Altar stone;
Hail and rain and thunder alone,
And red hearts we turn to grey,
Are true till Time gutter away.

A41

A Song of the Rosy-Cross

He who measures gain and loss,
   When he gave to thee the Rose,
Gave to me alone the Cross;

Where the blood-red blossom blows
In a wood of dew and moss,
   There thy wandering pathway goes,
Mine where waters brood and toss;
   Yet one joy have I, hid close,
He who measures gain and loss,
   When he gave to thee the Rose,   10
Gave to me alone the Cross.

A 4 2

[Seven paters seven times]

Seven paters seven times,
Send Mary by her Son,
Send Bridget by her mantle,
Send God by His strength,
Between us and the faery host,
Between us and the demons of the air.

A 4 3

The Glove and the Cloak

I saw her glitter and gleam,
   And stood in my sorrow apart,
And said: 'She has fooled me enough',
   And thought that she had no heart.

I stood with her cloak on my arm,
   And said: 'I will see her no more',
When something folded and small
   Fell at my feet on the floor,—

The little old glove of a child:
   I felt a sudden tear start,   10
And murmured: 'O long grey cloak,
   Keep hidden and covered her heart!'

A44

The Blood Bond

from the play 'Grania,' by George Moore and W. B. Yeats

Finn. This sod has bound us
    Like brother to brother,
    Like son to father.
    Let him who breaks it
    Be driven from the threshold
    Of God-kind and man-kind.

Diarmuid. Let the sea bear witness,
    Let the wind bear witness,
    Let the earth bear witness,
10   Let the fire bear witness,
    Let the dew bear witness,
    Let the stars bear witness!

Finn. Six that are deathless,
    Six holy creatures,
    Have witnessed the binding.

A45

Spinning Song

There are seven that pull the thread.
One lives under the waves,
And one where the winds are wove,
And one in the old gray house
Where the dew is made before dawn;
One lives in the house of the sun,
And one in the house of the moon,
And one lives under the boughs
Of the golden apple tree;
10 And one spinner is lost.
Holiest, holiest seven,
Put all your power on the thread
I have spun in the house this night!

A46

[I will go cry with the woman]

I will go cry with the woman,
For yellow-haired Donough is dead,
With a hempen rope for a neckcloth,
And a white cloth on his head.
I am come to cry with you, woman,
My hair is unwound and unbound;
I remember him ploughing his field,
Turning up the red side of the ground,
And building his barn on the hill
With the good mortared stone;   10
O! we'd have pulled down the gallows
Had it happened in Enniscrone!

A47

[Do not make a great keening]

Do not make a great keening
When the graves have been dug to-morrow.
Do not call the white-scarfed riders
To the burying that shall be to-morrow.

Do not spread food to call strangers
To the wakes that shall be to-morrow;
Do not give money for prayers
For the dead that shall die to-morrow. . . .

A48

[They shall be remembered for ever]

They shall be remembered for ever,
They shall be alive for ever,
They shall be speaking for ever,
The people shall hear them for ever.

A49

[O Biddy Donahoe]

O Biddy Donahoe,
I'll tell you what you'll do;
You'll take the name of Patterson,
And I'll be Donahoe!

A50

[The spouse of Naoise, Erin's woe]

The spouse of Naoise, Erin's woe,
Helen and Venus long ago,
Their charms would fade, their fame would flee,
Beside mo gradh, mo stor, mo chree,
    My Sibby, O!

Her eyes are gray like morning dew,
Her curling hair falls to her shoe,
The swan is blacker than—my nail,
Beside my queen, my Granuaile,
10   My Sibby, O!

The King of France would give his throne
To share her pillow (what's the rhyme at all?)
So would I myself. . . .
The Spanish fleet is on the sea
To carry away mo gradh, mo stor!
    My Sibby, O!

A51

[There's broth in the pot for you, old man]

There's broth in the pot for you, old man,
There's broth in the pot for you, old man,
    There's cabbage for me

And broth for you,
And beef for Jack the journeyman.

I wish you were dead, my gay old man,
I wish you were dead, my gay old man,
  I wish you were dead
  And a stone at your head,
So as I'd marry poor Jack the journeyman.   10

A 52

[There's nobody'll call out for him]

Brian. There's nobody'll call out for him,
 But smiths will turn their anvils,
 The millers turn their wheels,
 The farmers turn their churns,
 The witches turn their thumbs,
 Till he be broken and splintered into pieces.

Mayor. He might, if he'd a mind to it,
 Be digging out our tongues,
 Or dragging out our hair,
 Or bleaching us like calves,   10
 Or weaning us like lambs,
 But for the kindness and the softness that is in him.

First Cripple. The curse of the poor be upon him,
 The curse of the widows upon him,
 The curse of the children upon him,
 The curse of the bishops upon him,
 Until he be as rotten as an old mushroom!

Second Cripple. The curse of wrinkles be upon him!
 Wrinkles where his eyes are,
 Wrinkles where his nose is,   20
 Wrinkles where his mouth is,
 And a little old devil looking out of every wrinkle!

Brian. And nobody will sing for him,
 And nobody will hunt for him,

And nobody will fish for him,
And nobody will pray for him,
But ever and always curse him and abuse him.

A 53

[The four rivers that run there]

The four rivers that run there,
Through well-mown level ground,
Have come out of a blessed well
That is all bound and wound
By the great roots of an apple
And all the fowls of the air
Have gathered in the wide branches
And keep singing there.

A 54

['Why is it,' Queen Edain said]

First Musician. 'Why is it,' Queen Edain said,
    'If I do but climb the stair
    To the tower overhead,
    When the winds are calling there,
    Or the gannets calling out
    In waste places of the sky,
    There's so much to think about
    That I cry, that I cry?'

Second Musician. But her goodman answered her:
    'Love would be a thing of naught
    Had not all his limbs a stir
    Born out of immoderate thought;
    Were he anything by half,
    Were his measure running dry.
    Lovers, if they may not laugh,
    Have to cry, have to cry.'

10

The Three Musicians [*together*]
  But is Edain worth a song
  Now the hunt begins anew?
  Praise the beautiful and strong;
  Praise the redness of the yew;   20
  Praise the blossoming apple-stem.
  But our silence had been wise.
  What is all our praise to them
  That have one another's eyes?

A 55

[Come ride and ride to the garden]

Come ride and ride to the garden,
Come ride and ride with a will:
For the flower comes with the fruit there
Beyond a hill and a hill.

Refrain

Come ride and ride to the garden,
Come ride like the March wind;
There's barley there, and water there,
And stabling to your mind.

The Archangels stand in a row there
And all the garden bless,   10
The Archangel Axel, Victor the angel
Work at the cider press.

Refrain

Come ride and ride to the garden, &c.

O scent of the broken apples!
O shuffling of holy shoes!
Beyond a hill and a hill there
In the land that no one knows.

Refrain

Come ride and ride to the garden, &c.

A 5 6

[May this fire have driven out]

May this fire have driven out
The Shape-Changers that can put
Ruin on a great king's house
Until all be ruinous.
Names whereby a man has known
The threshold and the hearthstone,
Gather on the wind and drive
The women none can kiss and thrive,
For they are but whirling wind,
Out of memory and mind.
They would make a prince decay
With light images of clay
Planted in the running wave;
Or, for many shapes they have,
They would change them into hounds
Until he had died of his wounds,
Though the change were but a whim;
Or they'd hurl a spell at him,
That he follow with desire
Bodies that can never tire
Or grow kind, for they anoint
All their bodies, joint by joint,
With a miracle-working juice
That is made out of the grease
Of the ungoverned unicorn.
But the man is thrice forlorn,
Emptied, ruined, wracked, and lost,
That they follow, for at most
They will give him kiss for kiss
While they murmur, 'After this
Hatred may be sweet to the taste.'
Those wild hands that have embraced
All his body can but shove
At the burning wheel of love
Till the side of hate comes up.

10

20

30

Therefore in this ancient cup
May the sword-blades drink their fill
Of the home-brew there, until
They will have for masters none
But the threshold and hearthstone.   40

A 5 7

[Cuchulain has killed kings]

Cuchulain has killed kings,
Kings and sons of kings,
Dragons out of the water,
And witches out of the air,
Banachas and Bonachas and people of the woods.

Witches that steal the milk,
Fomor that steal the children,
Hags that have heads like hares,
Hares that have claws like witches,
All riding a-cock-horse   10
Out of the very bottom of the bitter black North.

He has killed kings,
Kings and the sons of kings,
Dragons out of the water,
And witches out of the air,
Banachas and Bonachas and people of the woods.

A 5 8

[Love is an immoderate thing]

Love is an immoderate thing
And can never be content
Till it dip an ageing wing
Where some laughing element
Leaps and Time's old lanthorn dims.
What's the merit in love-play,

In the tumult of the limbs
That dies out before 'tis day,
Heart on heart, or mouth on mouth,
All that mingling of our breath,
When love-longing is but drouth
For the things come after death?

10

A 59

[They are gone, they are gone.
The proud may lie by the proud]

First Musician. They are gone, they are gone. The proud may lie
by the proud.

Second Musician. Though we were bidden to sing, cry nothing
loud.

First Musician. They are gone, they are gone.

Second Musician.   Whispering were enough.

First Musician. Into the secret wilderness of their love.

Second Musician. A high, grey cairn. What more is to be said?

First Musician. Eagles have gone into their cloudy bed.

A 60

[I put under the power of my prayer]

I put under the power of my prayer
All that will give me help.
Rafael keep him Wednesday,
Sachiel feed him Thursday,
Hamiel provide him Friday,
Cassiel increase him Saturday.

A61

[O come all ye airy bachelors]

'O come all ye airy bachelors,
　A warning take by me,
A sergeant caught me fowling,
　And he fired his gun so free.

His comrades came to his relief,
　And I was soon trepanned,
And bound up like a woodcock
　That had fallen into their hands.

The judge said transportation,
　The ship was on the strand;
They have yoked me to the traces
　For to plough Van Diemen's Land!'

10

A62

[O, Johnny Gibbons,
my five hundred healths to you]

'O, Johnny Gibbons, my five hundred healths to you!
It's long you are away from us over the sea!'

'O, Johnny Gibbons, it's you were the prop to us.
You to have left us, we are foals astray!'

'Our hope and our darling, our heart dies with you,
You to have failed us, we are foals astray!'

A63

[O, the lion shall lose his strength]

'O, the lion shall lose his strength,
  And the bracket-thistle pine,
And the harp shall sound sweet, sweet at length,
  Between the eight and nine!'

A64

[Three that are watching my time to run]

Three that are watching my time to run,
The worm, the Devil, and my son,
To see a loop around their neck,
It's that would make my heart to lep!

A65

[My man is the best]

[*Laegaire's wife sings.*] My man is the best.
  What other has fought
  The cat-headed men
  That mew in the sea
  And carried away
  Their long-hidden gold?
  They struck with their claws
  And bit with their teeth,
  But Laegaire my husband
  Put all to the sword.

[*Conall's wife sings.*] My husband has fought
  With strong men in armour.
  Had he a quarrel
  With cats, it is certain
  He'd war with none

But the stout and heavy
With good claws on them.
What glory in warring
With hollow shadows
That helplessly mew?   20

[*Emer sings.*] My man is the best.
And Conall's wife
And the wife of Laegaire
Know that they lie
When they praise their own
Out of envy of me.
My man is the best,
First for his own sake,
Being the bravest
And handsomest man   30
And the most beloved
By the women of Ireland
That envy me,
And then for his wife's sake
Because I'm the youngest
And handsomest queen.

A66

[The friends that have it I do wrong]

The friends that have it I do wrong
When ever I remake a song,
Should know what issue is at stake:
It is myself that I remake.

A67

[I was going the road one day]

I was going the road one day
(O the brown and the yellow beer),
And I met with a man that was no right man
(O my dear, O my dear).

'Give me your wife,' said he
(O the brown and the yellow beer),
'Till the sun goes down and an hour of the clock'
(O my dear, O my dear).

'Good-bye, good-bye, my husband
(O the brown and the yellow beer),
For a year and a day by the clock of the sun'
(O my dear, O my dear).

'I know of a girl' said I
(O the brown and the yellow beer),
'Who can shorten the time by the clock and the sun'
(O my dear, O my dear).

'And one's as good as another
(O the brown and the yellow beer),
So get you away with your no right man'
(O my dear, O my dear).

A68

[Accursed who brings to light of day]

Accursed who brings to light of day
The writings I have cast away!
But blessed he that stirs them not
And lets the kind worm take the lot!

A69

[Nothing that he has done]

Nothing that he has done;
His mind that is fire,
His body that is sun,
Have set my head higher
Than all the world's wives.
Himself on the wind
Is the gift that he gives,
Therefore women-kind,
When their eyes have met mine,
Grow cold and grow hot,   10
Troubled as with wine
By a secret thought,
Preyed upon, fed upon
By jealousy and desire,
For I am moon to that sun,
I am steel to that fire.

A70

[Laegaire is best]

Laegaire is best;
Between water and hill,
He fought in the West
With cat-heads, until
At the break of day
All fell by his sword,
And he carried away
Their hidden hoard.

A 7 1

[Who stole your wits away]

Who stole your wits away
And where are they gone?

Who dragged your wits away
Where no one knows?
Or have they run off
On their own pair of shoes?

I'll find your wits again.
Come, for I saw them roll
To where old badger mumbles
In the black hole.

No, but an angel stole them
The night that you were born,
And now they are but a rag
On the moon's horn.

A 7 2

[I hear the wind a-blow]

I hear the wind a-blow,
I hear the grass a-grow,
And all that I know, I know.

A 7 3

[Were I but crazy for love's sake]

Were I but crazy for love's sake
I know who'd measure out his length,
I know the heads that I should break,
For crazy men have double strength.

I know—all's out to leave or take,
Who mocks at music mocks at love;
Were I but crazy for love's sake,
No need to pick and choose. Enough!
I know the heads that I should break.

A74

[The man that I praise]

'The man that I praise,'
Cries out the empty well,
'Lives all his days
Where a hand on the bell
Can call the milch cows
To the comfortable door of his house.
Who but an idiot would praise
Dry stones in a well?'

'The man that I praise,'
Cries out the leafless tree,   10
'Has married and stays
By an old hearth, and he
On naught has set store
But children and dogs on the floor.
Who but an idiot would praise
A withered tree?'

A75

[I call to the eye of the mind]

I call to the eye of the mind
A well long choked up and dry
And boughs long stripped by the wind,
And I call to the mind's eye
Pallor of an ivory face,

Its lofty dissolute air,
A man climbing up to a place
The salt sea wind has swept bare.

What were his life soon done!
Would he lose by that or win?
A mother that saw her son
Doubled over a speckled shin,
Cross-grained with ninety years,
Would cry, 'How little worth
Were all my hopes and fears
And the hard pain of his birth!'

A76

[The boughs of the hazel shake]

First Musician. The boughs of the hazel shake,
   The sun goes down in the west.

Second Musician. The heart would be always awake,
   The heart would turn to its rest.

Both Musicians. 'Why should I sleep?' the heart cries,
   'For the wind, the salt wind, the sea wind,
   Is beating a cloud through the skies;
   I would wander always like the wind.'

'O wind, O salt wind, O sea wind!'
Cries the heart, 'it is time to sleep;
Why wander and nothing to find?
Better grow old and sleep.'

A77

[O God, protect me]

O God, protect me
From a horrible deathless body
Sliding through the veins of a sudden.

A78

[He has lost what may not be found]

He has lost what may not be found
Till men heap his burial-mound
And all the history ends.
He might have lived at his ease,
An old dog's head on his knees,
Among his children and friends.

A79

[Come to me, human faces]

Come to me, human faces,
Familiar memories;
I have found hateful eyes
Among the desolate places,
Unfaltering, unmoistened eyes.

Folly alone I cherish,
I choose it for my share;
Being but a mouthful of air,
I am content to perish;
I am but a mouthful of sweet air.   10

O lamentable shadows,
Obscurity of strife!
I choose a pleasant life
Among indolent meadows;
Wisdom must live a bitter life.

A80

[Why does my heart beat so]

Why does my heart beat so?
Did not a shadow pass?
It passed but a moment ago.
Who can have trod in the grass?
What rogue is night-wandering?
Have not old writers said
That dizzy dreams can spring
From the dry bones of the dead?
And many a night it seems
That all the valley fills
With those fantastic dreams.
They overflow the hills,
So passionate is a shade,
Like wine that fills to the top
A grey-green cup of jade,
Or maybe an agate cup.

A81

[Why should the heart take fright]

Why should the heart take fright?
What sets it beating so?
The bitter sweetness of the night
Has made it but a lonely thing.
Red bird of March, begin to crow!
Up with the neck and clap the wing,
Red cock, and crow!

My head is in a cloud;
I'd let the whole world go;
My rascal heart is proud
Remembering and remembering.
Red bird of March, begin to crow!

Up with the neck and clap the wing,
Red cock, and crow!

The dreaming bones cry out
Because the night winds blow
And heaven's a cloudy blot.
Calamity can have its fling.
Red bird of March, begin to crow!
Up with the neck and clap the wing,   20
Red cock, and crow!

A 8 2

[At the grey round of the hill]

I

At the grey round of the hill
Music of a lost kingdom
Runs, runs and is suddenly still.
The winds out of Clare-Galway
Carry it: suddenly it is still.

I have heard in the night air
A wandering airy music;
And moidered in that snare
A man is lost of a sudden,
In that sweet wandering snare.   10

What finger first began
Music of a lost kingdom?
They dream that laughed in the sun.
Dry bones that dream are bitter,
They dream and darken our sun.

Those crazy fingers play
A wandering airy music;
Our luck is withered away,
And wheat in the wheat-ear withered,
And the wind blows it away.   20

II

My heart ran wild when it heard
The curlew cry before dawn
And the eddying cat-headed bird;
But now the night is gone.
I have heard from far below
The strong March birds a-crow.
Stretch neck and clap the wing,
Red cocks, and crow!

A 8 3

[A woman's beauty is like a white]

A woman's beauty is like a white
Frail bird, like a white sea-bird alone
At daybreak after stormy night
Between two furrows upon the ploughed land:
A sudden storm, and it was thrown
Between dark furrows upon the ploughed land.
How many centuries spent
The sedentary soul
In toils of measurement
Beyond eagle or mole,
Beyond hearing or seeing,
Or Archimedes' guess,
To raise into being
That loveliness?

A strange, unserviceable thing,
A fragile, exquisite, pale shell,
That the vast troubled waters bring
To the loud sands before day has broken.
The storm arose and suddenly fell
Amid the dark before day had broken.
What death? what discipline?
What bonds no man could unbind,
Being imagined within

The labyrinth of the mind,
What pursuing or fleeing,
What wounds, what bloody press,
Dragged into being
This loveliness?

A84
[White shell, white wing]

White shell, white wing!
I will not choose for my friend
A frail, unserviceable thing
That drifts and dreams, and but knows
That waters are without end
And that wind blows.

A85
[Why does your heart beat thus]

Why does your heart beat thus?
Plain to be understood,
I have met in a man's house
A statue of solitude,
Moving there and walking;
Its strange heart beating fast
For all our talking.
O still that heart at last.

O bitter reward
Of many a tragic tomb!
And we though astonished are dumb
Or give but a sigh and a word,
A passing word.

Although the door be shut
And all seem well enough,
Although wide world hold not

10

A man but will give you his love
The moment he has looked at you,
He that has loved the best
May turn from a statue
His too human breast.

O bitter reward
Of many a tragic tomb!
And we though astonished are dumb
Or give but a sigh and a word,
A passing word.

What makes your heart so beat?
What man is at your side?
When beauty is complete
Your own thought will have died
And danger not be diminished;
Dimmed at three-quarter light,
When moon's round is finished
The stars are out of sight.

O bitter reward
Of many a tragic tomb!
And we though astonished are dumb
Or give but a sigh and a word,
A passing word.

A86

Reprisals

To Major Robert Gregory, airman

Considering that before you died
You had brought down some nineteen planes,
I think that you were satisfied,
And life at last seemed worth the pains.
'I have had more happiness in one year
Than in all other years' you said;
And battle joy may be so dear
A memory even to the dead
It chases common thought away.

Yet rise from your Italian tomb,   10
Flit to Kiltartan cross and stay
Till certain second thoughts have come
Upon the cause you served, that we
Imagined such a fine affair:
Half-drunk or whole mad soldiery
Are murdering your tenants there;
Men that revere your father yet
Are shot at on the open plain;
Where can new-married women sit
To suckle children now? Armed men   20
May murder them in passing by
Nor parliament, nor law take heed;—
Then stop your ears with dust and lie
Among the other cheated dead.

November 23rd 1920

A87

[Motionless under the moon-beam]

First Musician. Motionless under the moon-beam,
   Up to his feathers in the stream;
   Although fish leap, the white heron
   Shivers in a dumbfounded dream.

Second Musician. God has not died for the white heron.

Third Musician. Although half famished he'll not dare
   Dip or do anything but stare
   Upon the glittering image of a heron,
   That now is lost and now is there.

Second Musician. God has not died for the white heron.   10

First Musician. But that the full is shortly gone
   And after that is crescent moon,
   It's certain that the moon-crazed heron
   Would be but fishes' diet soon.

Second Musician. God has not died for the white heron.

A88

[O, but the mockers' cry]

O, but the mockers' cry
Makes my heart afraid,
As though a flute of bone
Taken from a heron's thigh,
A heron crazed by the moon,
Were cleverly, softly played.

A89

[Take but His love away]

Take but His love away,
Their love becomes a feather
Of eagle, swan or gull,
Or a drowned heron's feather
Tossed hither and thither
Upon the bitter spray
And the moon at the full.

A90

[Lonely the sea-bird lies at her rest]

First Musician. Lonely the sea-bird lies at her rest,
    Blown like a dawn-blenched parcel of spray
    Upon the wind, or follows her prey
    Under a great wave's hollowing crest.

Second Musician. God has not appeared to the birds.

Third Musician. The ger-eagle has chosen his part
    In blue deep of the upper air
    Where one-eyed day can meet his stare;
    He is content with his savage heart.

Second Musician. God has not appeared to the birds.   10

First Musician. But where have last year's cygnets gone?
   The lake is empty; why do they fling
   White wing out beside white wing?
   What can a swan need but a swan?

Second Musician. God has not appeared to the birds.

A91

The Hero, the Girl, and the Fool

The Girl. I rage at my own image in the glass
   That's so unlike myself that when you praise it
   It is as though you praised another, or even
   Mocked me with praise of my mere opposite;
   And when I wake towards morn I dread myself,
   For the heart cries that what deception wins
   Cruelty must keep; therefore be warned and go
   If you have seen that image and not the woman.

The Hero. I have raged at my own strength because you
      have loved it.

The Girl. If you are no more strength than I am beauty   10
   I had better find a convent and turn nun;
   A nun at least has all men's reverence
   And needs no cruelty.

The Hero.   I have heard one say
   That men have reverence for their holiness
   And not themselves.

The Girl.   Say on and say
   That only God has loved us for ourselves,
   But what care I that long for a man's love?

The Fool by the Roadside. When all works that have
   From cradle run to grave
   From grave to cradle run instead;   20
   When thoughts that a fool

Has wound upon a spool
Are but loose thread, are but loose thread;
When cradle and spool are past
And I mere shade at last
Coagulate of stuff
Transparent like the wind,
I think that I may find
A faithful love, a faithful love.

A 9 2

[Shall I fancy beast or fowl]

Decima. Shall I fancy beast or fowl?
   Queen Pasiphae chose a bull,
   While a passion for a swan
   Made Queen Leda stretch and yawn,
   Wherefore spin ye, whirl ye, dance ye,
   Till Queen Decima's found her fancy.

Chorus
Wherefore spin ye, whirl ye, dance ye,
Till Queen Decima's found her fancy.

Decima. Spring and straddle, stride and strut,
   Shall I choose a bird or brute?
   Name the feather or the fur
   For my single comforter?

Chorus
Wherefore spin ye, whirl ye, dance ye,
Till Queen Decima's found her fancy.

Decima. None has found, that found out love,
   Single bird or brute enough;
   Any bird or brute may rest
   An empty head upon my breast.

Chorus
Wherefore spin ye, whirl ye, dance ye,
Till Queen Decima's found her fancy.

A 9 3

[Upon the round blue eye I rail]

Upon the round blue eye I rail,
Damnation on the milk-white horn.

A 9 4

Song of the Drunkard

The drunkard with the painted eyes
Discovered thought is misery,
Now, with drum and rattle, he
Bids a drunken God arise.

A 9 5

[What message comes to famous Thebes from the Golden House]

Chorus

What message comes to famous Thebes from the Golden House?
What message of disaster from that sweet-throated Zeus?
What monstrous thing our fathers saw do the seasons bring?
Or what that no man ever saw, what new monstrous thing?
Trembling in every limb I raise my loud importunate cry,
And in a sacred terror wait the Delian God's reply.

Apollo chase the God of Death that leads no shouting men,
Bears no rattling shield and yet consumes this form with pain.
Famine takes what the plague spares, and all the crops are lost;
No new life fills the empty place—ghost flits after ghost   10
To that God-trodden western shore, as flit benighted birds.
Sorrow speaks to sorrow, but no comfort finds in words.

Hurry him from the land of Thebes with a fair wind behind
Out on to that formless deep where not a man can find

Hold for an anchor-fluke, for all is world-enfolding sea;
Master of the thunder-cloud, set the lightning free,
And add the thunder-stone to that and fling them on his head,
For death is all the fashion now, till even Death be dead.

We call against the pallid face of this God-hated God
20 The springing heel of Artemis in the hunting sandal shod,
The tousle-headed Maenads, blown torch and drunken sound,
The stately Lysian king himself with golden fillet crowned,
And in his hands the golden bow and the stretched golden string,
And Bacchus' wine-ensanguined face that all the Maenads sing.

A96

[The Delphian rock has spoken out, now must a wicked mind]

The Delphian rock has spoken out, now must a wicked mind,
Planner of things I dare not speak and of this bloody wrack,
Pray for feet that are as fast as the four hoofs of the wind:
Cloudy Parnassus and the Fates thunder at his back.

That sacred crossing-place of lines upon Parnassus' head,
Lines that have run through North and South, and run through
     West and East,
That navel of the world bids all men search the mountain wood,
The solitary cavern, till they have found that infamous beast.

A97

[For this one thing above all I would be praised as a man]

For this one thing above all I would be praised as a man,
That in my words and my deeds I have kept those laws in mind
Olympian Zeus, and that high clear Empyrean,

Fashioned, and not some man or people of mankind,
Even those sacred laws nor age nor sleep can blind.

A man becomes a tyrant out of insolence,
He climbs and climbs, until all people call him great,
He seems upon the summit, and God flings him thence;
Yet an ambitious man may lift up a whole State,
And in his death be blessed, in his life fortunate.   10

And all men honour such; but should a man forget
The holy images, the Delphian Sibyl's trance,
And the world's navel-stone, and not be punished for it
And seem most fortunate, or even blessed perchance,
Why should we honour the Gods, or join the sacred dance?

A98

[Oedipus' nurse, mountain of many a hidden glen]

Oedipus' nurse, mountain of many a hidden glen,
Be honoured among men;
A famous man, deep-thoughted, and his body strong;
Be honoured in dance and song.

Who met in the hidden glen? Who let his fancy run
Upon nymph of Helicon?
Lord Pan or Lord Apollo or the mountain Lord
By the Bacchantes adored?

A99

[What can the shadow-like generations of man attain]

What can the shadow-like generations of man attain
But build up a dazzling mockery of delight that under their touch
    dissolves again?
Oedipus seemed blessed, but there is no man blessed amongst men.

Oedipus overcame the woman-breasted Fate;
He seemed like a strong tower against Death and first among the
    fortunate;
He sat upon the ancient throne of Thebes, and all men called him
    great.

But, looking for a marriage-bed, he found the bed of his birth,
Tilled the field his father had tilled, cast seed into the same
    abounding earth;
Entered through the door that had sent him wailing forth.

10   Begetter and begot as one! How could that be hid?
What darkness cover up that marriage-bed? Time watches, he is
    eagle-eyed.
And all the works of man are known and every soul is tried.

Would you had never come to Thebes, nor to this house,
Nor riddled with the woman-breasted Fate, beaten off Death and
    succoured us,
That I had never raised this song, heartbroken Oedipus!

A100

[Make way for Oedipus. All people said]

Make way for Oedipus. All people said,
'That is a fortunate man';
And now what storms are beating on his head!
Call no man fortunate that is not dead.
The dead are free from pain.

A101

[Huddon, Duddon, and Daniel O'Leary]

Huddon, Duddon, and Daniel O'Leary[1]
Delighted me as a child;
But where that roaring, ranting crew
Danced, laughed, loved, fought through
Their brief lives I never knew.

Huddon, Duddon, and Daniel O'Leary
Delighted me as a child.
I put three persons in their place
That despair and keep the pace
And love wench Wisdom's cruel face.   10

Huddon, Duddon, and Daniel O'Leary
Delighted me as a child.
Hard-living men and men of thought
Burn their bodies up for nought,
I mock at all so burning out.

[1]As a child I pronounced the word as though it rhymed to 'dairy'.

A102

[Astrea's holy child]

Astrea's holy child!
A rattle in the wood
Where a Titan strode!
His rattle drew the child
Into that solitude.
Barrum, barrum, barrum.

We wandering women,
Wives for all that come,
Tried to draw him home;
And every wandering woman   10
Beat upon a drum.
Barrum, barrum, barrum.

But the murderous Titans
Where the woods grow dim
Stood and waited him.
The great hands of those Titans
Tore limb from limb.
Barrum, barrum, barrum.

On virgin Astrea
That can succour all
Wandering women call;
Call out to Astrea
That the moon stood at the full.
Barrum, barrum, barrum.

20

A103

[Move upon Newton's town]

Move upon Newton's town,
The town of Hobbes and of Locke,
Pine, spruce, come down
Cliff, ravine, rock:
What can disturb the corn?
What makes it shudder and bend?
The rose brings her thorn,
The Absolute walks behind.

A104

[Should H. G. Wells afflict you]

Should H. G. Wells afflict you
Put whitewash in a pail;
Paint: 'Science—opium of the suburbs'
On some waste wall.

A105

Three Songs to the Same Tune

I

Grandfather sang it under the gallows:
'Hear, gentlemen, ladies, and all mankind:
Money is good and a girl might be better,
But good strong blows are delights to the mind.'
There, standing on the cart,
He sang it from his heart.

Those fanatics all that we do would undo;
Down the fanatic, down the clown;
Down, down, hammer them down,
Down to the tune of O'Donnell Abu.   10

'A girl I had, but she followed another,
Money I had, and it went in the night,
Strong drink I had, and it brought me to sorrow,
But a good strong cause and blows are delight.'
All there caught up the tune:
'On, on, my darling man'.

Those fanatics all that we do would undo;
Down the fanatic, down the clown;
Down, down, hammer them down,
Down to the tune of O'Donnell Abu.   20

'Money is good and a girl might be better,
No matter what happens and who takes the fall,
But a good strong cause'—the rope gave a jerk there,
No more sang he, for his throat was too small;
But he kicked before he died,
He did it out of pride.

Those fanatics all that we do would undo;
Down the fanatic, down the clown;
Down, down, hammer them down,
Down to the tune of O'Donnell Abu.   30

II

Justify all those renowned generations;
They left their bodies to fatten the wolves,
They left their homesteads to fatten the foxes,
Fled to far countries, or sheltered themselves
In cavern, crevice, hole,
Defending Ireland's soul.

'Drown all the dogs,' said the fierce young woman,
'They killed my goose and a cat.
Drown, drown in the water-butt,
10   *Drown all the dogs,' said the fierce young woman.*

Justify all those renowned generations,
Justify all that have sunk in their blood,
Justify all that have died on the scaffold,
Justify all that have fled, that have stood,
Stood or have marched the night long
Singing, singing a song.

'Drown all the dogs,' said the fierce young woman,
'They killed my goose and a cat.
Drown, drown in the water-butt,
20   *Drown all the dogs,' said the fierce young woman.*

Fail, and that history turns into rubbish,
All that great past to a trouble of fools;
Those that come after shall mock at O'Donnell,
Mock at the memory of both O'Neills,
Mock Emmet, mock Parnell:
All the renown that fell.

'Drown all the dogs,' said the fierce young woman,
'They killed my goose and a cat.
Drown, drown in the water-butt,
30   *Drown all the dogs,' said the fierce young woman.*

III

The soldier takes pride in saluting his Captain,
The devotee proffers a knee to his Lord,
Some back a mare thrown from a thoroughbred,
Troy backed its Helen, Troy died and adored;
Great nations blossom above;
A slave bows down to a slave.

'Who'd care to dig 'em,' said the old, old man,
'Those six feet marked in chalk?
Much I talk, more I walk;
Time I were buried,' said the old, old man.   10

When nations are empty up there at the top,
When order has weakened or faction is strong,
Time for us all to pick out a good tune,
Take to the roads and go marching along.
March, march—how does it run?—
O any old words to a tune.

'Who'd care to dig 'em,' said the old, old man,
'Those six feet marked in chalk?
Much I talk, more I walk;
Time I were buried,' said the old, old man.   20

Soldiers take pride in saluting their Captain,
Where are the Captains that govern mankind?
What happens a tree that has nothing within it?
O marching wind, O a blast of the wind,
Marching, marching along.
March, march, lift up the song:

'Who'd care to dig 'em,' said the old, old man,
'Those six feet marked in chalk?
Much I talk, more I walk;
Time I were buried,' said the old, old man.   30

A106

[Let images of basalt, black, immovable]

Let images of basalt, black, immovable,
Chiselled in Egypt, or ovoids of bright steel
Hammered and polished by Brancusi's hand,
Represent spirits. If spirits seem to stand
Before the bodily eyes, speak into the bodily ears,
They are not present but their messengers.
Of double nature these, one nature is
Compounded of accidental phantasies.
We question; it but answers what we would
Or as phantasy directs—because they have drunk
10   the blood.

A107

[They dance all day that dance in Tir-nan-oge]

Second Attendant. They dance all day that dance in Tir-nan-oge.

First Attendant. There every lover is a happy rogue;
And should he speak, it is the speech of birds.
No thought has he, and therefore has no words,
No thought because no clock, no clock because
If I consider deeply, lad and lass,
Nerve touching nerve upon that happy ground,
Are bobbins where all time is bound and wound.

Second Attendant. O never may that dismal thread run loose;

10   *First Attendant.* For there the hound that Oisin saw pursues
The hornless deer that runs in such a fright;
And there the woman clasps an apple tight
For all the clamour of a famished man.
They run in foam, and there in foam they ran,
Nor can they stop to take a breath that still
Hear in the foam the beating of a bell.

A108

[O what may come]

O what may come
Into my womb?

He longs to kill
My body, until
That sudden shudder
And limbs lie still.

O, what may come
Into my womb,
What caterpillar
My beauty consume? 10

A109

[O, but I saw a solemn sight]

First Attendant. O, but I saw a solemn sight;
  Said the rambling, shambling travelling-man;
  Castle Dargan's ruin all lit,
  Lovely ladies dancing in it.

Second Attendant. What though they danced! Those days
    are gone,
  Said the wicked, crooked, hawthorn tree;
  Lovely lady or gallant man
  Are blown cold dust or a bit of bone.

First Attendant. O, what is life but a mouthful of air?
  Said the rambling, shambling travelling-man; 10
  Yet all the lovely things that were
  Live, for I saw them dancing there.

Second Attendant. Nobody knows what may befall,
  Said the wicked, crooked, hawthorn tree.
  I have stood so long by a gap in the wall
  Maybe I shall not die at all.

A110

[To Garret or Cellar a wheel I send]

To Garret or Cellar a wheel I send,
But every butterfly to a friend.

A111

[The bravest from the gods but ask]

The bravest from the gods but ask:
A house, a sword, a ship, a mask.

A112

[Decline of day]

Decline of day,
A leaf drifts down;
O dark leaf clay
On Nineveh's crown!

A113

[Would I were there when they turn and Theban robbers face]

Would I were there when they turn and Theban robbers face,
Amid the brazen roar of shields, Colonus in chase;
Whether by the Pythian strand, or further away to the west
Where immortal spirits reveal the life of the blessed
To the living man that has sworn to let none living know;
Or it may be north and west amid Oea's desolate snow.
No matter how steep the climb Colonus follows the track,
No matter how loose the rein Theseus rides at their back;
And the captives turn in the saddle, turn their heads at his call.

Swords upon brazen shields and brazen helmets fall.   10
Creon is captured or slain, many are captured or slain.
Terrible the men of Colonus, terrible Theseus' men.
O glitter of bridle and bit; O lads in company
To the son of Rhea that rides upon the horses of the sea
Vowed, and to the Goddess Pallas Athena vowed!
O that I had seen it all mounted upon a cloud!
O that I had run thither, a bird upon the wind!
I have but imagined it all, seen it in the eye of the mind,
And cannot know what happened for all the words I say,
And therefore to God's daughter Pallas Athena pray   20
To bring the lads and the horses and the luckless ladies home,
And when that prayer is finished that a double blessing come
From the running ground of the deer, from the mountain land to
    this,
Pray to the brother and sister, Apollo and Artemis.

A114

[What is this portent?
What does it shadow forth?]

What is this portent? What does it shadow forth?
Have Heaven and Earth in dreadful marriage lain?
What shall the allotted season bring to birth?
This blind old ragged, rambling beggar-man
Calls curses upon cities, upon the great,
And scatters at his pleasure rich estate.

Thunder has stirred the hair upon my head.
What horror comes to birth? What shall be found,
That travail finished, on the lowly bed?
Never in vain the dreadful thunder sounds,   10
Nor can the living lightning flash in vain;
Heaven has borne a child and shrieks from pain.

Once more that dreadful sound! God pity us
When all is finished on the bed of earth,
Nor hold us all unclean for Oedipus.

Whatever fate maternal sky bring forth,
Pity Colonus, nor lay us under ban
Because of Oedipus the beggar-man.

Come, King of Athens, father of the land—
Whether at Poseidon's altars and the still
Unfinished sacrifice, or close at hand—
A blind old beggar-man proclaims God's will,
Proclaims a blessing on the land and us;
Come, King of Athens, come, King Theseus.

20

A115

[I call upon Persephone,
queen of the dead]

I call upon Persephone, queen of the dead,
And upon Hades, king of night, I call;
Chain all the Furies up that he may tread
The perilous pathway to the Stygian hall
And rest among his mighty peers at last,
For the entanglements of God are past.

Nor may the hundred-headed dog give tongue
Until the daughter of Earth and Tartarus
That even bloodless shades call Death has sung
The travel-broken shade of Oedipus
Through triumph of completed destiny
Into eternal sleep, if such there be.

10

A116

[He had famished in a wilderness]

He had famished in a wilderness,
Braved lions for my sake,
And all men lie that say that I

Bade that swordsman take
His head from off his body
And set it on a stake.

He swore to sing my beauty
Though death itself forbade.
They lie that say, in mockery
Of all that lovers said,   10
Or in mere woman's cruelty
I bade them fetch his head.

O what innkeeper's daughter
Shared the Byzantine crown?
Girls that have governed cities,
Or burned great cities down,
Have bedded with their fancy-man
Whether a king or clown;

Gave their bodies, emptied purses
For praise of clown or king,   20
Gave all the love that women know!
O they had their fling,
But never stood before a stake
And heard the dead lips sing.

A117

[Every loutish lad in love]

Every loutish lad in love
Thinks his wisdom great enough,
What cares love for this and that?
To make all his parish stare,
As though Pythagoras wandered there.
Crown of gold or dung of swine.

Should old Pythagoras fall in love
Little may he boast thereof.
What cares love for this and that?

10

Days go by in foolishness.
O how great their sweetness is!
Crown of gold or dung of swine.

Open wide those gleaming eyes,
That can make the loutish wise.
What cares love for this and that?
Make a leader of the schools
Thank the Lord, all men are fools.
Crown of gold or dung of swine.

A118

[Child and darling, hear my song]

Child and darling, hear my song,
Never cry I did you wrong;
Cry that wrong came not from me
But my virgin cruelty.

Great my love before you came,
Greater when I loved in shame,
Greatest when there broke from me
Storm of virgin cruelty.

A119

[I sing a song of Jack and Jill]

I sing a song of Jack and Jill.
Jill had murdered Jack;
The moon shone brightly;
Ran up the hill, and round the hill,
Round the hill and back.
A full moon in March.

Jack had a hollow heart, for Jill
Had hung his heart on high;
The moon shone brightly;
Had hung his heart beyond the hill. 10
A twinkle in the sky.
A full moon in March.

A120

[Why must those holy,
haughty feet descend]

Second Attendant. Why must those holy, haughty feet descend
  From emblematic niches, and what hand
  Ran that delicate raddle through their white?
  My heart is broken, yet must understand.
  What do they seek for? Why must they descend?

First Attendant. For desecration and the lover's night.

Second Attendant. I cannot face that emblem of the moon
  Nor eyelids that the unmixed heavens dart,
  Nor stand upon my feet, so great a fright
  Descends upon my savage, sunlit heart. 10
  What can she lack whose emblem is the moon?

First Attendant. But desecration and the lover's night.

Second Attendant. Delight my heart with sound; speak yet again.
  But look and look with understanding eyes
  Upon the pitchers that they carry; tight
  Therein all time's completed treasure is:
  What do they lack? O cry it out again.

First Attendant. Their desecration and the lover's night.

A121

[Clip and lip and long for more]

Clip and lip and long for more,
Mortal men our abstracts are;
What of the hands on the Great Clock face?
All those living wretches crave
Prerogatives of the dead that have
Sprung heroic from the grave.
A moment more and it tolls midnight.

Crossed fingers there in pleasure can
Exceed the nuptial bed of man;
What of the hands on the Great Clock face?
A nuptial bed exceed all that
Boys at puberty have thought,
Or sybils in a frenzy sought.
A moment more and it tolls midnight.

What's prophesied? What marvel is
Where the dead and living kiss?
What of the hands on the Great Clock face?
Sacred Virgil never sang
All the marvel there begun,
But there's a stone upon my tongue.
A moment more and it tolls midnight.

A122

Dedication

First I greet McCartan, revolutionary leader.
He, disguised as a sailor before the mast,
Travelled to and fro across the Atlantic,
He, though but a landsman, went to the mast-head;
Then Farrell, steel king, master of men,
Among his children, grandchildren and great-grandchildren;
Then that old Abbey actor, Dudley Digges,

Now a notable man on stage and on screen;
Then those others that are but names or names
At the bottom of a letter, fifty men.   10

A 1 2 3

[This they nailed upon a post]

'This they nailed upon a post
On the night my leg was lost,'
Said the old, old herne that had but one leg.

'He that a herne's egg dare steal
Shall be changed into a fool,'
Said the old, old herne that had but one leg.

'And to end his fool breath
At a fool's hand meet his death,'
Said the old, old herne that had but one leg.

A 1 2 4

[When I take a beast to my joyful breast]

When I take a beast to my joyful breast,
Though beak and claw I must endure,
Sang the bride of the Herne, and the Great Herne's bride,
No lesser life, man, bird or beast,
Can make unblessed what a beast made blessed,
Can make impure what a beast made pure.

Where is he gone, where is that other,
He that shall take my maidenhead?
Sang the bride of the Herne, and the Great Herne's bride,
Out of the moon came my pale brother,   10
The blue-black midnight is my mother.
Who will turn down the sheets of the bed?

When beak and claw their work begin
Shall horror stir in the roots of my hair,
Sang the bride of the Herne, and the Great Herne's bride,
And who lie there in the cold dawn
When all that terror has come and gone?
Shall I be the woman lying there?

A125

[When beak and claw their work began]

When beak and claw their work began
What horror stirred in the roots of my hair?
Sang the bride of the Herne, and the Great Herne's bride.
But who lay there in the cold dawn,
When all that terror had come and gone?
Was I the woman lying there?

A126

[Why should not Old Men be Mad?]

Why should not old men be mad?
Some have known a likely lad
That had a sound fly fisher's wrist
Turn to a drunken journalist;
A girl that knew all Dante once
Live to bear children to a dunce;
A Helen of social welfare dream
Climb on a wagonette to scream.
Some think it matter of course that chance
Should starve good men and bad advance,
That if their neighbours figured plain,
As though upon a lighted screen,
No single story would they find
Of an unbroken happy mind,
A finish worthy of the start.

10

Young men know nothing of this sort
Observant old men know it well;
And when they know what old books tell
And that no better can be had
Know why an old man should be mad. 20

A127

[Crazy Jane on the Mountain]

I am tired of cursing the Bishop
(Said Crazy Jane)
Nine books or nine hats
Would not make him a man.
I have found something worse
To meditate on.
A King had some beautiful cousins
But where are they gone?
Battered to death in a cellar
And he stuck to his throne. 10
Last night I lay on the mountain
(Said Crazy Jane)
There in a two horsed carriage
That on two wheels ran
Great bladdered Emer sat,
Her violent man
Cuchulain, sat at her side,
Thereupon,
Propped upon my two knees,
I kissed a stone; 20
I lay stretched out in the dirt
And I cried tears down.

A128

[Avalon]

I lived among great houses,
Riches drove out rank,
Base drove out the better blood,
And mind and body shrank.
No Oscar ruled the table,
But I'd a troop of friends
That knowing better talk had gone
Talked of odds and ends.
Some knew what ailed the world
But never said a thing
So I have picked a better trade
And night and morning sing:
Tall dames go walking in grass green Avalon.

Am I a great Lord Chancellor
That slept upon the Sack?
Commanding officer that tore
The khaki from his back?
Or am I de Valera,
Or the King of Greece,
Or the man that made the motors?
Ach, call me what you please!
Here's a Montenegrin lute
And its old sole string
Makes me sweet music
And I delight to sing:
Tall dames go walking in grass green Avalon.

With boys and girls about him,
With any sort of clothes,
With a hat out of fashion,
With old patched shoes,
With a ragged bandit cloak,
With an eye like a hawk,
With a stiff straight back,
With a strutting turkey walk,

With a bag full of pennies,
With a monkey on a chain,
With a great cock's feather,
With an old foul tune.
Tall dames go walking in grass green Avalon.

A129

[The harlot sang to the beggarman]

The harlot sang to the beggarman.
I meet them face to face
Conall, Cuchulain, Usna's boys,
All that most ancient race;
Maeve had three in an hour they say;
I adore those clever eyes
Those muscular bodies but can get
No grip upon their thighs.
I meet those long pale faces
Hear their great horses, then   10
Recall what centuries have passed
Since they were living men.
That there are still some living
That do my limbs unclothe
But that the flesh my flesh has gripped
I both adore and loathe.

Are those things that men adore and loathe
Their sole reality?
What stood in the Post Office
With Pearse and Connolly?   20
What comes out of the mountain
Where men first shed their blood?
Who thought Cuchulain till it seemed
He stood where they had stood.

No body like his body
Has modern woman borne,
But an old man looking back on life
Imagines it in scorn.
A statue's there to mark the place
30   By Oliver Sheppard done.
So ends the tale that the harlot
Sang to the beggarman.

APPENDIXES

APPENDIX A

Yeats's Notes in The Collected Poems, 1933

The Spelling of Gaelic Names

In this edition of my poems I have adopted Lady Gregory's spelling of
Gaelic names, with, I think, two exceptions. The 'd' of 'Edain' ran too well
in my verse for me to adopt her perhaps more correct 'Etain,' and for some
reason unknown to me I have always preferred 'Aengus' to her 'Angus.' In
her *Gods and Fighting Men* and *Cuchulain of Muirthemne* she went as
close to the Gaelic spelling as she could without making the names unpro-
nounceable to the average reader.[1] —1933.

Crossways. The Rose   *(pages 3, 25)*

Many of the poems in *Crossways,* certainly those upon Indian subjects or
upon shepherds and fauns, must have been written before I was twenty, for
from the moment when I began *The Wanderings of Oisin,* which I did at
that age, I believe, my subject-matter became Irish. Every time I have
reprinted them I have considered the leaving out of most, and then remem-
bered an old school friend who has some of them by heart, for no better
reason, as I think, than that they remind him of his own youth.[2] The little
Indian dramatic scene was meant to be the first scene of a play about a man
loved by two women, who had the one soul between them, the one woman
waking when the other slept, and knowing but daylight as the other only
night. It came into my head when I saw a man at Rosses Point carrying two
salmon. 'One man with two souls,' I said, and added, 'O no, two people
with one soul.'[3] I am now once more in *A Vision* busy with that thought,
the antitheses of day and of night and of moon and of sun.[4] *The Rose* was
part of my second book, *The Countess Cathleen and Various Legends and
Lyrics,* 1892,[5] and I notice upon reading these poems for the first time for
several years that the quality symbolized as The Rose differs from the Intel-
lectual Beauty of Shelley and of Spenser in that I have imagined it as suf-
fering with man and not as something pursued and seen from afar.[6] It must
have been a thought of my generation, for I remember the mystical painter
Horton, whose work had little of his personal charm and real strangeness,
writing me these words, 'I met your beloved in Russell Square, and she was
weeping,' by which he meant that he had seen a vision of my neglected
soul.[7]—1925.

The Hosting of the Sidhe   *(page 51)*

The gods of ancient Ireland, the Tuatha de Danaan, or the Tribes of the goddess Danu, or the Sidhe, from Aes Sidhe, or Sluagh Sidhe, the people of the Faery Hills, as these words are usually explained, still ride the country as of old. Sidhe is also Gaelic for wind, and certainly the Sidhe have much to do with the wind.[8] They journey in whirling wind, the winds that were called the dance of the daughters of Herodias in the Middle Ages, Herodias doubtless taking the place of some old goddess.[9] When old country people see the leaves whirling on the road they bless themselves, because they believe the Sidhe to be passing by. Knocknarea is in Sligo, and the country people say that Maeve, still a great queen of the western Sidhe, is buried in the cairn of stones upon it.[10] I have written of Clooth-na-Bare in *The Celtic Twilight*. She 'went all over the world, seeking a lake deep enough to drown her faery life, of which she had grown weary, leaping from hill to hill, and setting up a cairn of stones wherever her feet lighted, until, at last, she found the deepest water in the world in little Lough Ia, on the top of the bird mountain, in Sligo.' I forget, now, where I heard this story, but it may have been from a priest at Collooney. Clooth-na-Bare is evidently a corruption of Cailleac Bare, the old woman of Bare, who, under the names Bare, and Berah, and Beri, and Verah, and Dera, and Dhira, appears in the legends of many places.[11]—1899–1906.

The Host of the Air   *(page 52)*

This poem is founded on an old Gaelic ballad that was sung and translated for me by a woman at Ballisodare in County Sligo; but in the ballad the husband found the keeners keening his wife when he got to his house.[12]—1899.

He mourns for the Change that has come upon Him and his Beloved and longs for the End of the World   *(page 57)*

My deer and hound are properly related to the deer and hound that flicker in and out of the various tellings of the Arthurian legends, leading different knights upon adventures, and to the hounds and to the hornless deer at the beginning of, I think, all tellings of Oisin's journey to the country of the young. The hound is certainly related to the Hounds of Annwoyn or of Hades, who are white, and have red ears, and were heard, and are, perhaps, still heard by Welsh peasants, following some flying thing in the night winds;[13] and is probably related to the hounds that Irish country people believe will awake and seize the souls of the dead if you lament them too loudly or too soon. An old woman told a friend and myself that she saw what she thought were white birds, flying over an enchanted place, but found, when she got near, that they had dogs' heads; and I do not doubt that my hound and these dog-headed birds are of the same family. I got my hound and deer out of a last-century Gaelic poem about Oisin's journey to the country of the young. After the hunting of the hornless deer, that leads him to the seashore, and while he is riding over the sea with Niamh, he sees amid the waters—I have not the Gaelic poem by me, and describe it from memory—a young man following a girl who has a golden apple, and afterwards a hound with one red ear following a deer with no horns.[14] This hound and this deer seem plain images of the desire of the man 'which is for the woman,' and 'the desire of the woman which is for the desire of the man,' and of all desires that are as these. I have read them in this way in *The Wanderings of Oisin,* and have made my lover sigh because he has seen in their faces 'the immortal desire of Immortals.'[15]

The man in my poem who has a hazel wand may have been Aengus, Master of Love;[16] and I have made the boar without bristles come out of the West, because the place of sunset was in Ireland, as in other countries, a place of symbolic darkness and death.—1899.

The Cap and Bells   *(page 61)*

I dreamed this story exactly as I have written it, and dreamed another long dream after it, trying to make out its meaning, and whether I was to write it in prose or verse. The first dream was more a vision than a dream, for it was beautiful and coherent, and gave me the sense of illumination and exaltation that one gets from visions, while the second dream was confused and meaningless. The poem has always meant a great deal to me, though, as is the way with symbolic poems, it has not always meant quite the same thing. Blake would have said, 'The authors are in eternity,' and I am quite sure they can only be questioned in dreams.[17]—1899.

The Valley of the Black Pig   *(page 62)*

All over Ireland there are prophecies of the coming rout of the enemies of Ireland, in a certain Valley of the Black Pig, and these prophecies are, no doubt, now, as they were in the Fenian days, a political force.[18] I have heard of one man who would not give any money to the Land League,[19] because the Battle could not be until the close of the century; but, as a rule, periods of trouble bring prophecies of its near coming. A few years before my time, an old man who lived at Lissadell, in Sligo, used to fall down in a fit and rave out descriptions of the Battle; and a man in Sligo has told me that it will be so great a battle that the horses shall go up to their fetlocks in blood, and that their girths, when it is over, will rot from their bellies for lack of a hand to unbuckle them.[20] If one reads Rhys' *Celtic Heathendom* by the light of Frazer's *Golden Bough,* and puts together what one finds there about the boar that killed Diarmuid, and other old Celtic boars and sows, one sees that the battle is mythological, and that the Pig it is named from must be a type of cold and winter doing battle with the summer, or of death battling with life.[21]—1899–1906.

The Secret Rose   *(page 66)*

I find that I have unintentionally changed the old story of Conchubar's death. He did not see the Crucifixion in a vision but was told of it. He had

been struck by a ball made out of the dried brains of an enemy and hurled
out of a sling; and this ball had been left in his head, and his head had been
mended, the *Book of Leinster* says, with thread of gold because his hair
was like gold.[22] Keeting, a writer of the time of Elizabeth, says: 'In that state
did he remain seven years, until the Friday on which Christ was crucified,
according to some historians; and when he saw the unusual changes of the
creation and the eclipse of the sun and the moon at its full, he asked of
Bucrach, a Leinster Druid, who was along with him, what was it that
brought that unusual change upon the planets of Heaven and Earth. "Jesus
Christ, the Son of God," said the Druid, "who is now being crucified by the
Jews." "That is a pity," said Conchubar; "were I in his presence I would
kill those who were putting him to death." And with that he brought out
his sword, and rushed at a woody grove which was convenient to him, and
began to cut and fell it; and what he said was, that if he were among the
Jews, that was the usage he would give them, and from the excessiveness of
his fury which seized upon him, the ball started out of his head, and some
of the brain came after it, and in that way he died. The wood of Lan-
shraigh, in Feara Rois, is the name by which that shrubby wood is called.'[23]

I have imagined Cuchulain meeting Fand 'walking among flaming dew,'
because, I think, of something in Mr. Standish O'Grady's books.[24]

I have founded the man 'who drove the gods out of their liss,' or fort,
upon something I have read about Caoilte after the battle of Gabhra, when
almost all his companions were killed, driving the gods out of their liss,
either at Osraighe, now Ossory, or at Eas Ruaidh, now Asseroe, a waterfall
at Ballyshannon, where Ilbreac, one of the children of the goddess Danu,
had a liss. But maybe I only read it in Mr. Standish O'Grady, who has a fine
imagination, for I find no such story in Lady Gregory's book.[25]

I have founded 'the proud dreaming king' upon Fergus, the son of
Roigh, but when I wrote my poem here, and in the song in my early book,
'Who will drive with Fergus now?' I only knew him in Mr. Standish
O'Grady, and my imagination dealt more freely with what I did know than
I would approve of to-day.[26]

I have founded 'him who sold tillage, and house, and goods,' upon
something in 'The Red Pony,' a folk-tale in Mr. Larminie's *West Irish Folk
Tales*. A young man 'saw a light before him on the high-road. When he
came as far, there was an open box on the road, and a light coming up out
of it. He took up the box. There was a lock of hair in it. Presently he had
to go to become the servant of a king for his living. There were eleven boys.
When they were going out into the stable at ten o'clock, each of them took
a light but he. He took no candle at all with him. Each of them went into
his own stable. When he went into his stable he opened the box. He left it
in a hole in the wall. The light was great. It was twice as much as in the
other stables.' The king hears of it, and makes him show him the box. The
king says, 'You must go and bring me the woman to whom the hair
belongs.' In the end, the young man, and not the king, marries the
woman.[27]—1899–1906.

Responsibilities. Introductory Rhymes   *(page 101)*

'Free of the ten and four' is an error I cannot now correct, without more rewriting than I have a mind for. Some merchant in Villon, I forget the reference, was 'free of the ten and four.' Irish merchants exempted from certain duties by the Irish Parliament were, unless memory deceives me again—I cannot remember my authority—'free of the eight and six.'[28]—1914.

Poems beginning with that 'To a Wealthy Man' and ending with that 'To a Shade'   *(pages 106–09)*

In the thirty years or so during which I have been reading Irish newspapers, three public controversies have stirred my imagination. The first was the Parnell controversy. There were reasons to justify a man's joining either party, but there were none to justify, on one side or on the other, lying accusations forgetful of past service, a frenzy of detraction.[29] And another was the dispute over *The Playboy*. There may have been reasons for opposing as for supporting that violent, laughing thing, though I can see the one side only, but there cannot have been any for the lies, for the unscrupulous rhetoric spread against it in Ireland, and from Ireland to America.[30] The third prepared for the Corporation's refusal of a building for Sir Hugh Lane's famous collection of pictures. . . .

[Note.—I leave out two long paragraphs which have been published in earlier editions of these poems. There is no need now to defend Sir Hugh Lane's pictures against Dublin newspapers. The trustees of the London National Gallery, through his leaving a codicil to his will unwitnessed, have claimed the pictures for London, and propose to build a wing to the Tate Gallery to contain them. Some that were hostile are now contrite, and doing what they can, or letting others do unhindered what they can, to persuade Parliament to such action as may restore the collection to Ireland—Jan. 1917.][31]

These controversies, political, literary, and artistic, have showed that neither religion nor politics can of itself create minds with enough receptivity to become wise, or just and generous enough to make a nation. Other cities have been as stupid—Samuel Butler laughs at shocked Montreal for hiding the Discobolus in a lumber-room[32]—but Dublin is the capital of a nation, and an ancient race has nowhere else to look for an education. Goethe in *Wilhelm Meister* describes a saintly and naturally gracious woman, who, getting into a quarrel over some trumpery detail of religious observance, grows—she and all her little religious community—angry and vindictive.[33] In Ireland I am constantly reminded of that fable of the futility of all discipline that is not of the whole being. Religious Ireland—and the pious Protestants of my childhood were signal examples—thinks of divine things as a round of duties separated from life and not as an element that may be discovered in all circumstance and emotion, while political Ireland sees the good citizen but as a man who holds to certain opinions and not as a man of good will. Against all this we have but a few educated men and the remnants of an old traditional culture among the poor. Both were stronger forty years ago, before the rise of our new middle class which made its first public display during the nine years of the Parnellite split, showing how base at moments of excitement are minds without culture.— 1914.

Lady Gregory in her Life of Sir Hugh Lane assumes that the poem which begins 'Now all the truth is out' (p. 108) was addressed to him. It was not; it was addressed to herself.—1922.[34]

The Dolls (page 126)

The fable for this poem came into my head while I was giving some lectures in Dublin. I had noticed once again how all thought among us is frozen into 'something other than human life.'[35] After I had made the poem, I looked up one day into the blue of the sky, and suddenly imagined, as if lost in the blue of the sky, stiff figures in procession. I remembered that they were the habitual image suggested by blue sky, and looking for a second fable called them 'The Magi' (p. 125), complementary forms of those enraged dolls.—1914.

'unpacks the loaded pern' (page 145)

When I was a child at Sligo I could see above my grandfather's trees a little column of smoke from 'the pern mill,' and was told that 'pern' was another name for the spool, as I was accustomed to call it, on which thread was wound.[36] One could not see the chimney for the trees, and the smoke looked as if it came from the mountain, and one day a foreign sea-captain asked me if that was a burning mountain.—1919.

The Phases of the Moon (page 164)
The Double Vision of Michael Robartes (page 172)
Michael Robartes and the Dancer (page 177)

Years ago I wrote three stories in which occur the names of Michael Robartes and Owen Aherne. I now consider that I used the actual names of two friends, and that one of these friends, Michael Robartes, has but lately returned from Mesopotamia, where he has partly found and partly thought out much philosophy.[37] I consider that Aherne and Robartes, men to whose namesakes I had attributed a turbulent life or death, have quarrelled with me. They take their place in a phantasmagoria in which I endeavour to explain my philosophy of life and death. To some extent I wrote these poems as a text for exposition.—1922.

Sailing to Byzantium (Stanza IV, page 198)

I have read somewhere that in the Emperor's palace at Byzantium was a tree made of gold and silver, and artificial birds that sang.[38]

The Tower   *(page 198)*

The persons mentioned are associated by legend, story and tradition with the neighbourhood of Thoor Ballylee or Ballylee Castle, where the poem was written.[39] Mrs. French lived at Peterswell in the eighteenth century and was related to Sir Jonah Barrington, who described the incident of the ears and the trouble that came of it.[40] The peasant beauty and the blind poet are Mary Hynes and Raftery, and the incident of the man drowned in Cloone Bog is recorded in my *Celtic Twilight*.[41] Hanrahan's pursuit of the phantom hare and hounds is from my *Stories of Red Hanrahan*.[42] The ghosts have been seen at their game of dice in what is now my bedroom, and the old bankrupt man lived about a hundred years ago. According to one legend he could only leave the Castle upon a Sunday because of his creditors, and according to another he hid in the secret passage.

In the passage about the Swan in Part III I have unconsciously echoed one of the loveliest lyrics of our time—Mr. Sturge Moore's 'Dying Swan.' I often recited it during an American lecturing tour, which explains the theft.

THE DYING SWAN

> O silver-throated Swan
> Struck, struck! A golden dart
> Clean through thy breast has gone
> Home to thy heart.
> Thrill, thrill, O silver throat!
> O silver trumpet, pour
> Love for defiance back
> On him who smote!
> And brim, brim o'er
> With love; and ruby-dye thy track
> Down thy last living reach
> Of river, sail the golden light—
> Enter the sun's heart—even teach,
> O wondrous-gifted Pain, teach thou
> The god to love, let him learn how.[43]

When I wrote the lines about Plato and Plotinus I forgot that it is something in our own eyes that makes us see them as all transcendence. Has not Plotinus written: 'Let every soul recall, then, at the outset the truth that soul is the author of all living things, that it has breathed the life into them all, whatever is nourished by earth and sea, all the creatures of the air, the divine stars in the sky; it is the maker of the sun; itself formed and ordered this vast heaven and conducts all that rhythmic motion—and it is a principle distinct from all these to which it gives law and movement and life, and it must of necessity be more honourable than they, for they gather or dissolve as soul brings them life or abandons them, but soul, since it never can abandon itself, is of eternal being'?[44]—1928.

Meditations in Time of Civil War   *(page 204)*

These poems were written at Thoor Ballylee in 1922, during the civil war. Before they were finished the Republicans blew up our 'ancient bridge' one midnight. They forbade us to leave the house, but were otherwise polite, even saying at last 'Good-night, thank you,' as though we had given them the bridge.

The sixth poem is called 'The Stare's Nest by My Window.' In the west of Ireland we call a starling a stare, and during the civil war one built in a hole in the masonry by my bedroom window.

In the second stanza of the seventh poem occur the words, 'Vengeance on the murderers of Jacques Molay.' A cry for vengeance because of the murder of the Grand Master of the Templars seems to me fit symbol for those who labour from hatred, and so for sterility in various kinds. It is said to have been incorporated in the ritual of certain Masonic societies of the eighteenth century, and to have fed class-hatred.[45]

I suppose that I must have put hawks into the fourth stanza because I have a ring with a hawk and a butterfly upon it, to symbolize the straight road of logic, and so of mechanism, and the crooked road of intuition: 'For wisdom is a butterfly and not a gloomy bird of prey.'[46]—1928.

Nineteen Hundred and Nineteen   *(Sixth poem, page 214)*

The country people see at times certain apparitions whom they name now 'fallen angels,' now 'ancient inhabitants of the country,' and describe as riding at whiles 'with flowers upon the heads of the horses.'[47] I have assumed in the sixth poem that these horsemen, now that the times worsen, give way to worse. My last symbol, Robert Artisson, was an evil spirit much run after in Kilkenny at the start of the fourteenth century.[48] Are not those who travel in the whirling dust also in the Platonic Year?[49] See p. 212.

Two Songs from a Play   *(page 216)*

These songs are sung by the Musicians in my play 'The Resurrection.'[50]

Among School Children   *(Stanza V, page 220)*

I have taken the 'honey of generation' from Porphyry's essay on 'The Cave of the Nymphs,' but find no warrant in Porphyry for considering it the 'drug' that destroys the 'recollection' of pre-natal freedom. He blamed a cup of oblivion given in the zodiacal sign of Cancer.[51]

The Winding Stair and Other Poems   *(page 235)*

'I am of Ireland' (p. 271) is developed from three or four lines of an Irish four-teenth-century dance song somebody repeated to me a few years ago.[52] 'The sun in a golden cup' in the poem that precedes it, though not 'The moon in a silver bag,' is a quotation from somewhere in Mr. Ezra Pound's 'Cantos.'[53]

In this book and elsewhere, I have used towers, and one tower in particular, as symbols and have compared their winding stairs to the philosophical gyres, but it is hardly necessary to interpret what comes from the main track of thought and expression. Shelley uses towers constantly as symbols, and there are gyres in Swedenborg, and in Thomas Aquinas and certain classical authors.[54] Part of the symbolism of 'Blood and the Moon' (p. 241) was suggested by the fact that Thoor Ballylee has a waste room at the top and that butterflies come in through the loopholes and die against the window-panes. The 'learned astrologer' in 'Chosen' (p. 277) was Macrobius, and the particular passage was found for me by Dr. Sturm, that too little known poet and mystic. It is from Macrobius's comment upon 'Scipio's Dream' (Lib. I. Cap. XII. Sec. 5): '. . . when the sun is in Aquarius, we sacrifice to the Shades, for it is in the sign inimical to human life; and from thence, the meeting-place of Zodiac and Milky Way, the descending soul by its defluction is drawn out of the spherical, the sole divine form, into the cone.'[55] In 'The Mother of God' (p. 253) the words 'A fallen flare through the hollow of an ear' are, I am told, obscure. I had in my memory Byzantine mosaic pictures of the Annunciation, which show a line drawn from a star to the ear of the Virgin. She received the Word through the ear, a star fell, and a star was born.

When *The Winding Stair* was published separately by Macmillan & Co. it was introduced by the following dedication:

DEAR DULAC,[56]

I saw my *Hawk's Well* played by students of our Schools of Dancing and of Acting a couple of years ago in a little theatre called 'The Peacock,' which shares a roof with the Abbey Theatre. Watching Cuchulain in his lovely mask and costume, that ragged old masked man who seems hundreds of years old, that Guardian of the Well, with your great golden wings and dancing to your music, I had one of those moments of excitement that are the dramatist's reward and decided there and then to dedicate to you my next book of verse.[57]

'A Woman Young and Old' was written before the publication of *The Tower,* but left out for some reason I cannot recall. I think that I was roused to write 'Death' and 'Blood and the Moon' by the assassination of Kevin O'Higgins, the finest intellect in Irish public life, and, I think I may add, to some extent, my friend.[58] 'A Dialogue of Self and Soul' was written in the spring of 1928 during a long illness, indeed finished the day before a Cannes doctor told me to stop writing. Then in the spring of 1929 life returned as an impression of the uncontrollable energy and daring of the great creators; it seemed that but for journalism and criticism, all that evasion and explanation, the world would be torn in pieces. I wrote 'Mad as the Mist and Snow,' a mechanical little song, and after that almost all that group of poems called in memory of those exultant weeks 'Words for Music Perhaps.' Then ill again, I warmed myself back into life with 'Byzantium' and 'Veronica's Napkin,' looking for a theme that might befit my years. Since then I have added a few poems to 'Words for Music Perhaps,' but always keeping the mood and plan of the first poems.

1933

The Wanderings of Oisin   *(page 361)*

The poem is founded upon the Middle Irish dialogues of S. Patrick and
Oisin and a certain Gaelic poem of the last century.[59] The events it
describes, like the events in most of the poems in this volume, are supposed
to have taken place rather in the indefinite period, made up of many peri-
ods, described by the folktales, than in any particular century; it therefore,
like the later Fenian stories themselves, mixes much that is mediaeval with
much that is ancient. The Gaelic poems do not make Oisin go to more than
one island, but a story in *Silva Gadelica* describes 'four paradises,' an
island to the north, an island to the west, an island to the south, and
Adam's paradise in the east.[60]—1912.

The Shadowy Waters   *(page 411)*

I published in 1902 a version of *The Shadowy Waters*, which, as I had no
stage experience whatever, was unsuitable for stage representation, though
it had some little success when played during my absence in America in
1904, with very unrealistic scenery before a very small audience of culti-
vated people. On my return I rewrote the play in its present form, but
found it still too profuse in speech for stage representation. In 1906 I made
a stage version, which was played in Dublin in that year.[61] The present ver-
sion must be considered as a poem only.—1922.

Notes to Appendix A

1. Lady Gregory's books were published by John Murray (London) in 1902 and 1904. Had Yeats understood Old Irish orthography he would have been less unhappy with the spelling *Étaín,* since the *t* in that name is pronounced *d.* His 'Aengus' is preferable to Lady Gregory's 'Angus.' The latter is a purely modern anglicization, not an Irish spelling at all. 'Aengus' is the Middle Irish spelling of a name spelled 'Oengus' in Old Irish, and 'Aonghus' in Modern Irish, however Yeats alighted on it.

2. Presumably Charles Johnston (1867–1931), a schoolmate of Yeats at the High School in Dublin who shared his interest in the occult. See 'I Became an Author' (1938), in *Uncollected Prose by W. B. Yeats,* vol. 2, ed. John P. Frayne and Colton Johnson (New York: Columbia University Press, 1975), p. 507.

3. Yeats refers to 'Anashuya and Vijaya.' Rosses Point is a small village near Sligo.

4. London: T. Werner Laurie, 1925. (In fact published in January 1926.)

5. *The Countess Kathleen and Various Legends and Lyrics* (London: T. Fisher Unwin, 1892). The heading 'The Rose' was not used until *Poems* (London: T. Fisher Unwin, 1895).

6. Percy Bysshe Shelley (1792–1822) and Edmund Spenser (1552?–99), English poets. Yeats is probably thinking of Shelley's 'Hymn to Intellectual Beauty' and Spenser's 'Foure Hymnes.'

7. Yeats is apparently recalling a letter of 6 May 1896 from the mystical painter William Thomas Horton (1864–1919). Horton wrote of a 'vision' he had had of Yeats that morning: 'Yeats—naked and gaunt, with long black dishevelled hair falling partly over the face of a deathly whiteness, with eyes that flame yet have within them depths of unutterable sadness. He is wearily going on his way following many lights that dance in front and at side of him. Behind him follows with outstretched arms a lovely girl in long trailing white garments, weeping. Within Yeats, a knocking is heard & a Voice "My son, my son, open thou unto me & I will give thee Light." ' See George Mills Harper, *W. B. Yeats and W. T. Horton: The Record of an Occult Friendship* (London: Macmillan, 1980), p. 101. Russell Square is in London, not far from Yeats's residence at 18 Woburn Buildings.

8. *Tuatha Dé Danann,* 'the peoples of the goddess Dana or Danu [the nominative does not occur, so must be inferred],' was the name assigned to the Irish pagan gods by learned Christians to reduce their status by including them among earlier settlers of Ireland. Dana/Danu was the mother of the gods. Despite the euhemerization, the *Tuatha* were well known to be immortal beings—dwelling in islands and lakes, inside mountains, and especially inside the megalithic burial-tumuli that abound in Ireland. The word for a supernaturally inhabited mound is *síd* (Old Irish), *síodh, sí* (Modern Irish). *Aes Síde* (OI), *Aos Sídhe/Sí*

(Mod. I.) means 'mound folk.' *Slóg/Sluag Síde* (OI), *Sluagh/Slua Sídhe/Sí* (Mod. I.) means 'mound army.' Both terms denote the super-natural beings miscalled 'faeries.' Old Irish *side, sithe,* Mod. I. *sidhe, sí,* means a 'blast, puff, gust,' not 'wind' *per se.* The word is unrelated to the word for 'mound.'

9. Herodias is a witch-goddess in Germanic mythology. Yeats might have read about her in Jacob Grimm's *Teutonic Mythology,* trans. J. S. Stallybrass (London: G. Bell and Sons, 1883–88). Grimm explains that 'quite early in the Mid. Ages the christian mythus of *Herodias* got mixed up with our native heathen fables: those notions about dame *Holda* and the "furious host" and the nightly jaunts of sorceresses were grafted on it, the Jewish king's daughter had the part of a *heathen goddess* assigned her. . . , and her worship found numerous adherents. In the same circle moves *Diana,* the lunar deity of night, the wild huntress; Diana, Herodias, and Holda stand for one another, or side by side' (I, 285–86). Further, 'to this day' a whirlwind 'is accounted for in Lower Saxony (about Celle) by the dancing *Herodias* whirling about in the air' (I, 285, n. 1), and 'Hero-dias was dragged into the circle of night-women . . . because she *played* and *danced,* and since her death goes booming through the air as the "wind's bride" ' (III, 1057).

   The name Herodias comes from the story of John the Baptist, who denounced the marriage of Herod Antipas to Herodias, the divorced wife of his half-brother Herod Philip and daughter of his half-brother Aristobulus. During his birthday celebration, Herod Antipas is so impressed by the dancing of Herodias's daughter by Herod Philip that he swears to give her anything she asks; prompted by her mother, she asks for the head of John the Baptist, who is then killed (Matt. 14:1–12; Mark 6:17–29). In most of the accounts cited by Grimm, the daughter is also named Herodias; but Biblical tradition follows the Jewish historian Flavius Josephus in naming her Salome.

10. Medb (OI, pronounced 'Methv'), Medhbh, Maedhbh (Mod. I., pro-nounced 'Maiv') was, in the Ulster Cycle, queen of Connacht and instigator of the war in the epic *Táin Bó Cuailgne.*

11. *Cailleach Bhéarra* (OI *Caillech Bérri*), 'The Veiled Woman [or, Hag] of Beare [a region in County Cork],' is what the speaker of a very long ninth-century poem calls herself. She laments her transformation from youth and beauty to decrepitude (as perhaps a nun or anchoress). The poem has been read literally, as the reminiscences of an aged nun, and allegorically, as Christian Ireland sighing for her pagan past. The figure of the old woman entered the popular imagination and became fused with 'hag' folktales. She surfaces in Yeats's 'The Untir-ing Ones,' in *The Celtic Twilight: Men and Women, Dhouls and Faeries* (London: Lawrence and Bullen, 1893), pp. 109–14, which he here slightly misquotes. Lough Ia is correctly Lough Dagea (*Loch Dá Ghé,* 'Two-Goose Lake') on Slieve Daeane (*Sliabh Dá Éan,* 'Two-Bird Mountain') near Sligo. In a note added to 'The Untiring Ones' in *The Celtic Twilight* (London: A. H. Bullen, 1902), p. 134, Yeats muddled

the name by suggesting that 'perhaps Lough Ia is my mishearing, or the story-teller's mispronunciation of Lough Leath'—a name he got 'from a friend of mine' and said to mean 'the Grey Lake.' 'Grey Lake' would be *Loch Liath*, but, though Yeats says 'there are many Lough Leaths,' there are in fact none. Yeats doubtless took the name from Standish James O'Grady (1846–1928), whom he cites in earlier versions of this note (VP pp. 800–03): in *The Flight of the Eagle* (London: Lawrence and Bullen, 1897), pp. 255–57 and 296–97, O'Grady so names ('Lough Liath') the lake on Slieve Fuadh in County Armagh which is the traditional home of the *Cailleach Bhéarra*.

Yeats's priest-informant, if he existed, was apparently familiar with W. G. Wood-Martin's *History of Sligo, County and Town* (Dublin: Hodges Figgis, 1882–92), which tells the story of the drowning of 'a giantess named Veragh' (III, 354); and his *Pagan Ireland: An Archaeological Sketch* (London and New York: Longmans, Green, 1895), which explains that 'Prominent in Irish folklore are two celebrated "hags," Aine or Aynia, and *Bhéartha* (Vera), variously styled Vera, Verah, Berah, Berri, Dirra, and Dhirra. . . . the legends regarding Vera are widely prevalent' (p. 126).

12. Ballisodare is a village near Sligo, the principal town in County Sligo. The ballad is untraced.

13. In her edition of *The Mabinogion* (London: Bernard Quaritch, 1877), p. 363, Lady Charlotte Guest notes that 'Annwvyn, or Annwn, is frequently rendered "Hell," though, perhaps, "The Lower Regions" would more aptly express the meaning which the name conveys. The Dogs of Annwn are the subject of an ancient Welsh superstition, which was once universally believed in throughout the Principality, and which it would seem is not yet quite extinct. It is said that they are sometimes heard at night passing through the air overhead, as if in full cry in pursuit of some object.'

14. The poem, by the eighteenth-century poet Mícheál Coimín (Michael Comyn), is *Laoidh Oisín ar Thír na n-Óg*, ed. & trans. Bryan O'Looney, *Transactions of the Ossianic Society*, 4 (1859), as 'Lay of Oisin on the Land of Youth.' Yeats alludes to these stanzas (p. 249):

> We saw also, by our sides
> A hornless fawn leaping nimbly,
> And a red-eared white dog,
> Urging it boldly in the chase.

> We beheld also, without fiction,
> A young maid on a brown steed,
> A golden apple in her right hand,
> And she going on the top of the waves.

> We saw after her
> A young rider on a white steed,
> Under a purple, crimson mantle of satin,
> And a gold-headed sword in his hand.

15. Yeats is recalling a statement from the *Table Talk* of the English poet
    Samuel Taylor Coleridge (1772–1834), which he would have read in
    *Table Talk of Samuel Taylor Coleridge and The Rime of the Ancient
    Mariner, Christabel, & c.,* intro. Henry Morley, 3rd ed. (London:
    George Routledge and Sons, n.d.), p. 65: 'The man's desire is for the
    woman; but the woman's desire is rarely other than for the desire of
    the man' (23 July 1827). The other quotation is from 'The Wander-
    ings of Oisin' (III.4).

16. Aengus is a god frequently associated with love and lovers in Irish
    mythological stories.

17. Describing his *Milton* in a letter to Thomas Butts on 6 July 1803, the
    English poet William Blake (1757–1827) explained that 'I may
    praise it, since I dare not pretend to be any other than the secretary;
    the authors are in Eternity.' Yeats found the letter in Alexander
    Gilchrist, *Life of William Blake,* 2nd ed. (London: Macmillan,
    1880), I, 187. The letter is cited in *The Works of William Blake,* ed.
    Edwin John Ellis and W. B. Yeats (London: Bernard Quaritch, 1893),
    I, vii, and elsewhere.

18. In a note to his edition of 'The Chase of the Enchanted Pigs of
    Aenghus an Bhrogha,' *Fenian Poems, Second Series, Transactions of
    the Ossianic Society,* 6 (1861), 143, John O'Daly refers to 'the cele-
    brated valley of the Black Pig in Ulster, concerning which there are
    so many curious old legends current among the peasantry.' By 'the
    Fenian days' Yeats may possibly mean the days of Finn and Oisin,
    'Fenians' being a usual nineteenth-century rendering of *Fianna*
    (Finn's war-bands) much used by Yeats himself. More probably,
    Yeats refers to the Fenian Brotherhood, which, taking its name from
    Finn's forces, was founded in 1858 by James Stephens (1824–1901)
    to promote armed rebellion against English rule; the movement
    petered out after the unsuccessful Fenian Rising of 1867.

19. The Land League was formed in 1879 by Michael Davitt
    (1846–1906) to protect tenants from eviction and to win 'the land of
    Ireland for the people of Ireland.' It was suppressed by the govern-
    ment in 1881.

20. Lissadell is a barony near Sligo. Lissadell House was the home of
    Yeats's friends Constance (1868–1927) and Eva (1870–1926) Gore-
    Booth.

21. In *Lectures on the Origin and Growth of Religion as Illustrated by
    Celtic Heathendom,* 2nd ed. (London: Williams and Norgate, 1892),
    pp. 506–17, John Rhys discusses the boar which killed the Irish
    mythological hero Diarmuid as well as 'other mythic swine' (p. 511).
    In *The Golden Bough: A Study in Comparative Religion* (London
    and New York: Macmillan, 1890), II, 26–31, James G. Frazer notes
    that in various cultures the pig is an embodiment of the 'corn-spirit':
    'the corn-spirit is conceived as embodied in an animal; this divine
    animal is slain, and its flesh and blood are partaken of by the har-
    vesters. Thus . . . the pig is eaten sacramentally by ploughmen in
    spring' (p. 31).

22. Conchubar is king of Ulster in both the Ulster, or Red Branch, Cycle, and in the Mythological Cycle of Old Irish tales, and in the epic *Táin Bó Cuailgne*. The *Book of Leinster* (so miscalled through error; it is properly the *Book of Noughaval*) is a large manuscript miscellany, compiled between 1151 and 1201, of which 187 leaves, or 374 pages, survive. Its contents are very various. Yeats could have found the *Book of Leinster* version of the Death of Conchubar in Eugene O'Curry's *Lectures on the Manuscript Materials of Ancient Irish History*, 2nd ed. (Dublin: Hinch and Traynor, 1878), pp. 637–43.

23. Geoffrey Keating (ca. 1570–ca. 1650) wrote his *History of Ireland* between 1620 and 1634. For his account of the death of Conchubar, see the Irish Texts Society edition of the *History of Ireland* (London: D. Nutt, 1902–14), II, 203.

24. Cuchulain is the central hero of the Old Irish Red Branch, or Ulster, Cycle of tales, and hero of the epic *Táin Bó Cuailgne*. In the story *Serglige Con Chulaind* ('Cuchulain's Wasting-Sickness'), Fand, wife of the god Manannán mac Lir, tempts Cuchulain to become her consort among the immortals. Yeats would have found the image of 'fiery dew' in Standish James O'Grady's *History of Ireland* (London: Sampson Low, Searle, Marston, & Rivington; Dublin: E. Ponsonby, 1878–80), II, 73, or his *History of Ireland: Critical and Philosophical*, I (London: Sampson Low; Dublin: E. Ponsonby, 1881), 107. Yeats mentions 'fiery dew' in 'The Wisdom the the King,' in *The Secret Rose* (London: Lawrence & Bullen, 1897), p. 21.

25. Caoilte mac Rónáin was a close companion of Fionn mac Cumhail, leader of the *Fianna* (a kind of standing army drawn from all parts of Ireland) and a central figure in the Fenian Cycle of Irish heroic tales. In his *History of Ireland: Critical and Philosophical*, Standish James O'Grady twice notes that after the defeat of the *Fianna* at the Battle of Gabhra in 297, 'Coelté invaded the haunted hill of Ass-a-roe, at Ballyshannon, expelled the weird inhabitants, and dwelt there ever after' (pp. 324–25); 'Coelté, after the destruction of the Fians, entered the host of the Tuatha De Danán, and lived immortal and invisible in the island. He stormed the enchanted fortress of the gods of the Erne at Assaroe, and entered himself into its possession, where he dwelt for many centuries' (p. 353). A more detailed account of the incident is provided by Eugene O'Curry in his commentary on 'The Fate of the Children of Tuireann,' *Atlantis*, 4 (1863), 213–33. In *On the Manners and Customs of the Ancient Irish* (London: Williams and Norgate; Dublin: W. B. Kelly; New York: Scribner, Welford, 1873), III, 366, O'Curry mentions '*Ilbhreac, a Tuath Dé Danann* at *Eas Ruaidh* (now the Falls of Ballyshannon, in the country Donegal),' which may explain Yeats's reference to Ilbhreac as 'one of the children of the goddess Danu'—Danu was the mother or maternal ancestor of all the gods.

26. Fergus mac Raoich is an important character in the Red Branch Cycle of stories; in the epic *Táin Bó Cuailgne* he is the lover of Maeve, queen of Connacht. He had been king of Ulster, but as a con-

dition for marrying him, Ness insisted he allow her son, Conchubar, to reign for a year in his stead. During the year Ness manipulated the nobles so that when the time was up they refused to allow Fergus to reclaim his position. Yeats slightly misquotes the first line of 'Who goes with Fergus?,' first published in *The Countess Kathleen and Various Legends and Lyrics.* One of Yeats's sources for Fergus was O'Grady's *History of Ireland,* esp. II, 249–50. But there were others, including Sir Samuel Ferguson's 'The Abdication of Fergus Mac Roy,' in *Lays of the Western Gael, and Other Poems* (London: Bell and Daldy, 1864), quoted by Yeats in an earlier version of this note (VP p. 813).

27. Summarized and misquoted from William Larminie, 'The Red Pony,' *West Irish Folk-Tales and Romances* (London: Elliot Stock, 1893), esp. pp. 212–13.

28. Yeats mistranslates l. 22 of 'Epître à ses amis' by the French poet François Villon (1431–?): 'nobles hommes, francs de quart et de dix,' 'noblemen, free of the quarter and the tenth' (referring to different kinds of taxes). As noted by Richard Eaton of the Custom-House Dublin in *A book of rates inwards and outwards with the neat-duties and drawbacks payable on importation and exportation of all sorts of merchandise,* 2nd ed. (Dublin, 1767), the earlier system, whereby wholesale merchants were not required to pay import duties until their merchandise had been sold to retailers, had been 'discontinued': 'at present every importer pays down his excise at importation; with this difference, that all merchants capable of such account [i.e., wholesalers under the former system] have an allowance or discount out of the excise, of 10 per cent on all wine and tobacco, and 6 per cent on all other goods, but retailers and consumptioners pay down their excise without any deduction as the law directs.' Benjamin Yeats (1750–95), Yeats's great-great-grandfather, is listed in Wilson's *Dublin Directory* from 1783 to 1794 as 'free of the six and ten per cent tax at the Custom-house, Dublin'.

29. Charles Stewart Parnell (1846–91) lost his leadership of the Irish party in the British Parliament late in 1890, after he was named co-respondent in a divorce suit filed by Captain William Henry O'Shea (1840–1905) against his wife, Katharine (1845–1921).

30. *The Playboy of the Western World* by John Millington Synge (1871–1909) opened at the Abbey Theatre on 26 January 1907. Beginning with the next performance (28 January), the play caused rioting in the theatre, some members of the audience judging it a slander upon the Irish people.

31. In 1907, Hugh Lane (1875–1915) founded the Dublin Municipal Gallery and offered an important collection of paintings as a gift, on the condition that a permanent building be erected. After the Dublin Corporation rejected a design by Edwin Lutyens (1869–1944) for a gallery over the Liffey, Lane withdrew his offer and bequeathed his collection to the National Gallery in London. On 3 February 1915, Lane wrote a codicil to his will restoring the paintings to Ireland. But

Lane was drowned on the *Lusitania* on 7 May 1915 with the codicil unwitnessed, and the English government refused to accept its authority. The controversy dragged on until two decades after Yeats's death. For the longer version of Yeats's note, see VP pp. 819–20.

32. In 'A Psalm of Montreal,' first published in *The Spectator* for 18 May 1878, Samuel Butler (1835–1902) comments on the discovery of a plaster cast of the Discobolus (a statue of a discus-thrower by the Greek sculptor Myron, ca. 480–445 B.C.) in a Montreal lumber-room.

33. Yeats apparently refers to the narrator of Book VI of *Wilhelm Meisters Lehrjahre* (1795–96) by Johann Wolfgang von Goethe (1749–1832). In Thomas Carlyle's translation (1824), the Book is called 'Confessions of a Fair Saint.'

34. In *Hugh Lane's Life and Achievement* (London: John Murray, 1921), p. 138, Lady Gregory introduces Yeats's poem with the statement 'And this is to Hugh, to "A Friend whose Work has come to Nothing." '

35. Yeats is recalling a passage from William Blake's *Public Address* (1809–10): "Princes appear to me to be Fools Houses of Commons & Houses of Lords appear to me to be fools they seem to me to be something Else besides Human Life."

36. Yeats refers to William Pollexfen (1811–92), his maternal grandfather.

37. Robartes and Aherne, characters in the stories 'Rosa Alchemica' (1896), 'The Tables of the Law' (1896), and 'The Adoration of the Magi' (1897), reappear in the first edition of *A Vision* (London: T. Werner Laurie, 1925).

38. The probable source is *The History of the Decline and Fall of the Roman Empire* (1776–88) by Edward Gibbon (1737–94), which Yeats would have read in the edition by J. B. Bury (London: Methuen, 1909–14), VI, 81. The Emperor was Theophilus, who ruled from 829 until his death in 842.

39. Early in 1917, Yeats purchased 'Ballylee Castle,' a tower constructed by the Normans in the 13th or 14th century, with two attached cottages. He restored the property and lived there for several summers, beginning in 1919. Yeats named the property Thoor Ballylee, 'Thoor' being his rendition of Irish *Túr,* tower.

40. The story of Mrs. French is found in the chapter on 'Irish Gentry and Their Retainers' in *Personal Sketches of His Own Times* (1827–32) by Sir Jonah Barrington (1760–1834). The event occurred in 1778. Yeats's source was *Recollections of Jonah Barrington,* intro. George Birmingham (Dublin: Talbot Press, [1918]), pp. 30–31.

41. Mary Hynes was a celebrated beauty who died in the early 1840s. The blind poet Anthony Raftery (1784–1835) wrote of her in 'Mary Hynes, or The Posy Bright,' in *Songs Ascribed to Raftery,* ed. Douglas Hyde (Dublin: Gill and Son, 1903), pp. 331–33. Yeats wrote of her in 'Dust Hath Closed Helen's Eye,' a story added to the

1902 edition of *The Celtic Twilight,* pp. 35–49; it includes a transla-
tion of Raftery's poem by Lady Gregory.

42. Hanrahan is an invented character. Yeats refers to 'Red Hanrahan,'
the opening tale in *Stories of Red Hanrahan* (Dundrum: Dun Emer
Press, 1904), pp. 1–15.

43. 'The Dying Swan' by Yeats's friend T. Sturge Moore (1870–1944).
Although first published in *The Sea is Kind* (London: Grant
Richards, 1914), p. 111, the text here follows the Collected Edition
of *The Poems* (London: Macmillan, 1932), II, 7, except for 'light. . /
Enter the sun's heart. .even. . . .'

44. Plato (ca. 429–347 B.C.), Greek philosopher; Plotinus (205–69/70),
Neoplatonic philosopher, probably born in Egypt. Yeats quotes from
Plotinus: The Divine Mind, Being the Treatises of the Fifth Ennead,
trans. Stephen MacKenna (London: The Medici Society, 1926), p. 2.
The dash should be a colon.

45. The Knights Templar were formed in 1118 as a monastic-military Order
to defend the Christian kingdom and to protect pilgrims visiting the
Holy Land; the Order was dissolved by Pope Clement V in 1312. Jacques
de Molay (1244–1314) was burned at the stake after repudiating his
recantation. Freemason societies, which began in the seventeenth cen-
tury, were often understood as anti-Catholic associations.

46. Yeats slightly misquotes ll. 7–8 of his 'Tom O'Roughley.'

47. Yeats discusses the alternative explanations in his note on 'The
Trooping Fairies' in *Fairy and Folk Tales of the Irish Peasantry* (Lon-
don: Walter Scott; New York: Thomas Whittaker; Toronto: W. J.
Gage, 1888), pp. 1–3. The detail of the flowers is included in his
essay on 'The Tribes of Danu' in *The New Review* (November
1897); see *Uncollected Prose by W. B. Yeats,* Vol. 2, p. 58.

48. Robert Artisson appears in *The Historie of Ireland* (1577) by
Raphael Holinshed (d. 1580?) as the incubus of Dame Alice Kyteler,
who was condemned as a witch on 2 July 1324. Holinshed explains
that 'she was charged to haue nightly conference with a spirit called
Robert Artisson, to whom she sacrificed in the high way ix red
cockes, & ix peacocks eies.'

49. As Yeats explained in his 1934 Introduction to *The Resurrection,*
'Ptolemy thought the precession of the equinoxes moved at the rate
of a degree every hundred years, and that somewhere about the time
of Christ and Caesar the equinoctial sun had returned to its original
place in the constellations, completing and recommencing the thirty-
six thousand years, or three hundred and sixty incarnations of a hun-
dred years apiece, of Plato's Man of Ur [Er]. Hitherto almost every
philosopher had some different measure for the Greatest Year, but
this Platonic Year, as it was called, soon displaced all others. . . .'
Explorations (London: Macmillan, 1962), p. 395.

50. The play was first published in *The Adelphi* for June 1927.

51. Porphyry (232/3–ca. 305) is a Neoplatonic philosopher. Yeats would
have known his *De Antro Nympharum* in the paraphrase translation
by Thomas Taylor (1758–1835), 'Concerning the Cave of the

Nymphs,' first published ca. 1788 and included in Taylor's *Select Works* (London, 1823). Porphyry notes that honey 'aptly represents the pleasure and delight of descending into the fascinating realms of generation.' Taylor also quotes from Macrobius (see n. 55 below) on the descent of the soul into matter: 'As soon, therefore, as the soul gravitates towards body, in this first production of herself, she begins to experience a material tumult, that is, matter flowing into her essence. And this is what Plato remarks in the Phaedo, that the soul is drawn into the body, staggering with recent intoxication; signifying by this the new drink of matter's impetuous flood, through which the soul becoming defiled and heavy, is drawn into a terrene situation. But the starry *cup,* placed between Cancer and Lion, is a symbol of this mystic truth, signifying that descending souls first experience intoxication in that part of the heavens, through the influx of matter.'

52. 'Icham of Irlaunde,' an anonymous lyric dating from 1300–1350 and included in St John D. Seymour, *Anglo-Irish Literature, 1200–1582* (Cambridge: University Press, 1929), p. 98. The friend was the Irish writer Frank O'Connor (1903–66).

53. The phrase is from Canto XXIII by Ezra Pound (1885–1972), which Yeats read in *A Draft of the Cantos 17–27* (London: John Rodker, 1928), p. 33.

54. Percy Bysshe Shelley (1792–1822), English poet; Emanuel Swedenborg (1688–1772), Swedish mystical philosopher; St. Thomas Aquinas (1225–74), Italian scholastic theologian.

55. Frank Pearce Sturm (1879–1942) was a medical doctor and a devoted student of Yeats's work. Having read *A Vision,* Sturm wrote to Yeats on 22 January 1926: 'Every book I pick up seems to speak with the voice of W. B. Giraldus, of cones & gyres. The other night it was Aquinas, tonight it is Macrobius, in his commentary on *Scipio's Dream,* where he says (Lib I Cap xii Sec 5) ". . . when the Sun is in Aquarius, we sacrifice to the Shades, for it is in the sign inimical to human life; and from thence, the meeting place of Zodiac & Milky Way, the descending soul by its defluxion is drawn out of the spherical, the sole divine form, into a cone." ' *Frank Pearce Sturm: His Life, Letters, and Collected Work,* ed. Richard Taylor (Urbana: University of Illinois Press, 1969), p. 92. Ambrosius Theodosius Macrobius is a fifth-century Neoplatonist, best known for his commentary on the *Somnium Scipionis* by Marcus Tullius Cicero (106–43 B.C.).

56. *The Winding Stair and Other Poems* (London & New York: Macmillan, 1933) was dedicated to Yeats's friend Edmund Dulac (1882–1953), who had designed many of the covers for Yeats's books as well as the ring mentioned by Yeats in his note on 'Meditations in Time of Civil War.'

57. Characters in *At the Hawk's Well,* first published in 1917. The Peacock theatre was used primarily for experimental plays.

58. Kevin O'Higgins (1892–1927), Minister for Justice and External Affairs in the Irish Free State, was assassinated on 10 July 1927.

59. The 'certain Gaelic poem' is that by Michael Comyn cited in note 14

above. Yeats would have come across dialogues between St. Patrick
and Oisin in a wide variety of sources.

60. Although it was not published until three years after *The Wanderings
of Oisin,* the story referred to is 'The Adventure of Cian's son Teigue'
in *Silva Gadelica* (London: Williams and Norgate, 1892), II, 391–92,
by the Irish scholar Standish Hayes O'Grady (1832–1915).

61. *The Shadowy Waters* was first published not in 1902 but in 1900
(*The North American Review,* May 1900). It was performed by the
Irish National Theatre Society at Molesworth Hall in Dublin on 14
January 1904. The revised version was first published in *Poems,
1899–1905* (London: A. H. Bullen; Dublin: Maunsel, 1906) and was
produced at the Abbey on 8 December 1906.

APPENDIX B

Music from New Poems, 1938

MUSIC FOR 'THE THREE BUSHES.'
By Edmund Dulac[1]

MUSIC FOR 'THE CURSE OF CROMWELL.'
Traditional Irish Air[2]

MUSIC FOR
'COME GATHER ROUND ME PARNELLITES.'
Traditional Irish Air[3]

MUSIC FOR 'THE PILGRIM.'
TRADITIONAL IRISH AIR[4]

MUSIC FOR 'COLONEL MARTIN.'
TRADITIONAL IRISH AIR[5]

Notes to Appendix B

1. Yeats's friend Edmund Dulac (1882–1953) had previously composed some music for the play *At the Hawk's Well*.

2. The body of the song is a version of *An Smachdaoin Crón,* variously translated as 'The Little Brown Mallet' or 'The Copper-coloured Stick of Tobacco.' Yeats might have found the song under the second title in A. P. Graves's *The Irish Song Book* (London: T. Fisher Unwin, 1894), pp. 59–61. The use of the final musical phrase as a chorus is not traditional.

3. The song is that provided by Richard Michael Levey (1811–99) for the lyric 'Limerick is Beautiful' in the play *The Colleen Bawn* by Dion Boucicault (1820–90). See, for instance, the *Emerald Isle Song Book* (Dublin: M. H. Gill, n.d.), p. 101. Levey's song is a 6/8 version of *Fáinne Geal an Lae,* usually translated as 'The Dawning of the Day.'

4. The song is a loose adaptation of *Bruach na Carraige Báine,* literally 'The Brink of the White Rock' but usually known as 'To Plough the Rocks of Bawn.' Yeats might have found versions of the song in James Clarence Mangan's *The Poets and Poetry of Munster,* 3rd ed. (Dublin and London: James Duffy, 1883), pp. 337 & 348. The addition to the chorus is not traditional.

5. This song has not yet been traced. When published in *A Broadside* (December 1937), it was ascribed to Art O'Murnaghan, a composer and stage-manager at the Gate Theatre. The source was changed to 'Traditional Irish Air' in *New Poems*. It has been suggested that the song is an adaptation of the tune which William Percy French (1854–1920) wrote in 1889 for his comic poem 'Slattery's Mounted Fut,' but there are only some similarities in rhythm to support such a claim. Cf. *The Best of Percy French* (London: E.M.I., 1980), p. 30.

EXPLANATORY NOTES

The purpose of these notes is to annotate all specific allusions in the poems. Annotation of other kinds, as well as interpretive commentary, has been avoided. Thus, for example, information on Yeats's sources is given only when Yeats called attention to them (whether in the poem or in a note), as with 'Imitated from the Japanese.' Cross-references to Yeats's other works or to passages in his correspondence are not offered, except in some rare instances where such references provide the most concise annotation. Unnamed individuals are normally not identified, except in poems explicitly presented as autobiographical statements, as with the work beginning 'Pardon, old fathers.'

This last omission perhaps requires comment, as many readers of Yeats are accustomed to approaching a particular poem 'knowing' that it is about a certain person—be it Maud Gonne, Olivia Shakespear, Margot Ruddock, or whomever. However, firm evidence for many of those identifications is lacking. Moreover, it is arguable that Yeats did not wish to narrow the meanings of those poems by presenting them as statements about specific autobiographical situations. A key instance is 'Upon a Dying Lady.' Although it is clear from Yeats's correspondence that the poem developed from the death of Mabel Beardsley (1871–1916), sister of the English artist Aubrey Beardsley (1872–98), Yeats did not entitle the work 'Upon a Dying Lady: To Mabel Beardsley,' nor did he include in any printing a note identifying the woman in the poem; nor did he identify her when reading from the poem in a B.B.C. broadcast on 10 April 1932. Indeed, as late as 1 June 1934, the writer Ernest Rhys (1859–1946)—who was more acquainted with Yeats's circle than most readers—thought it necessary to ask him, 'was the poem "On a Dying Lady" about Beardsley's sister?' (*Letters to W. B. Yeats*, ed. Richard J. Finneran, George Mills Harper, and William M. Murphy [London: Macmillan, 1977], II, 563). Yeats's reply has not yet been traced, but if it is ever located, I suspect we will discover that Yeats answered, in effect, that although the poem may have been 'about' Mabel Beardsley, he preferred to present it as a universal statement on death and dying, much as he told Hugh Lane that 'To a Wealthy Man . . .' was addressed to 'an imaginary person' (see note to 114.4).

These Explanatory Notes draw extensively on Yeats's own notes to his poems, either through quotation or through cross-reference to Appendix A. However, it should be noted that Yeats revised his notes almost as often as his poems, and it has not been possible to quote all the versions of a particular note. Thus readers interested in alternative texts of Yeats's notes (including those in Appendix A) should consult *The Variorum Edition of the Poems of W. B. Yeats,* ed. Peter Allt and Russell K. Alspach (New York: Macmillan, 1957; corrected third printing, 1966), cited as VP.

The spelling of Gaelic names has not been regularized in quotations, whether from Yeats or from other writers. Otherwise, a standard spelling is usually offered in the annotations themselves (e.g., 'Maeve,' as most familiar to Yeats's readers, rather than the Old Irish 'Medb' [Modern Irish 'Medhbh,' 'Maedhbh'] or the variants found in Yeats and others, 'Maev,' 'Maiv,' or 'Maive').

On some occasions information in the annotations has been repeated, especially when a cross-reference to another note would not be significantly shorter. Thus readers interested in tracing all of Yeats's references to a specific person or place will need to consult *A Concordance to the Poems of W. B. Yeats,* ed. Stephen Maxfield Parrish, programmed by James Allan Painter (Ithaca: Cornell University Press, 1963), which is keyed to VP.

Some of these notes will doubtless strike some readers as superfluous. However, it should be remembered that this edition will be distributed throughout the world. It thus did not seem possible to assume a 'common body of knowledge' which all readers of this volume would share. Indeed, even within the English-speaking world, such an assumption is now hazardous—and one would face the further difficulty of deciding what is included in the 'common body of knowledge' (e.g., Blake but not Landor? Plato but not Plotinus? Alexander but not Alcibiades?). Furthermore, the placement of these notes at the end of the volume is designed to ensure that readers not needing information on a particular allusion will not be burdened by any.

*

Although in one sense these notes are indebted to all of Yeats scholarship, I have drawn most heavily on three works: George Brandon Saul, *Prolegomena to the Study of Yeats's Poems* (Philadelphia: University of Pennsylvania Press, 1957); A. Norman Jeffares, *A Commentary on* The Collected Poems *of W. B. Yeats* (London: Macmillan, 1968)—a revised version, *A New Commentary on the Poems of W. B. Yeats* (London: Macmillan, 1984), incorporates most (but not all) of the additions and corrections from the first edition of *The Poems* (1983); and James P. McGarry, *Place Names in the Writings of William Butler Yeats,* ed. Edward Malins (Gerrards Cross: Colin Smythe, 1976). For readers interested in the kind of annotation and interpretation not offered in the following notes, the *New Commentary* is the most extensive guide available, though it is not free from errors and omissions, some of which are noted in *Review,* 7 (1985): 163–89.

*

Lyrical: a heading used for poems 1–303 in the *Collected Poems* (1933).

Crossways: title and date first appear in *Poems* (1895). The works were selected from *The Wanderings of Oisin and Other Poems* (1889) and *The Countess Kathleen and Various Legends and Lyrics* (1892). The epigraph is from 'Night the Ninth,' l. 653, of *Vala* (later titled *The Four Zoas*) by the English poet William Blake (1757–1827). In *The Works of William Blake,* ed. Edwin John Ellis and Yeats (London: Bernard Quaritch, 1893), III, 131, the line reads 'And all the Nations were threshed out, and the stars threshed from their husks.' A.E. is George W. Russell (1867–1935), an Irish writer and painter and a close friend of Yeats. See p. 599 for Yeats's note on *Crossways*.

1.1: Arcadia is a mountainous region of southern Greece, imaged in the pastoral tradition as an ideal realm of rustic contentment.

1.9: Chronos is the Greek word for 'time'; personified by Pindar as 'the father of all.' The similarity of Chronos with Kronos, one of the Titans, led to the latter's identification with Time in cosmogonic speculation.

1.12: in the Christian religion, the Rood is the cross on which Jesus Christ was crucified.

4: in Hindu mythology, Anasūyā ('uncomplaining') is a daughter of Daksha; there are various figures named Vijayā ('victorious'). Anasūyā is also a character in *Śakuntalā* (see note to 4.66–68). The 'Golden Age' is traditionally the earliest age of man, characterized by peace and happiness. It is not likely that Yeats intends a specific reference to the Golden Age of Hindu mythology, *kṛita-yuga*.

4.13: in Hindu mythology, *amrita* is the drink of the gods and the elixir of immortality.

4.14: Brahmā is a supreme god in Hinduism, associated with the creation of the universe.

4.26: described by Yeats as 'The Indian Cupid' (1889; VP p. 72) or 'The Indian Eros' (1895; VP p. 796), Kāma is a god of love in Hindu mythology.

4.66–68: Yeats refers to Kaśyapa, depicted in Hinduism as a great progenitor; his wives included the thirteen daughters of Daksha. Hemakūta ('Golden Peak') is a sacred mountain imagined as lying north of the Himalayas and often identified with the mountain Kailāsa. Yeats found these references in *Śakuntalā*, a Sanskrit drama by Kālidāsa (?350–600?), which he read in the translation by Monier Williams (available to him in several different editions).

9: in his 1887 note on the poem, Yeats explained that 'Goll or Gall lived in Ireland about the third century. The battle wherein he lost his reason furnished matter for a bardic chronicle still extant. O'Curry, in his "Manuscript Materials of Irish History," thus tells the tale: "Having entered the battle with extreme eagerness, his excitement soon increased to frenzy, and after having performed astounding deeds of valour he fled in a state of derangement from the scene of slaughter, and never stopped until he plunged into the wild seclusion of a deep glen far up the country. This glen has ever since been called Glen-na-Gealt, or the Glen of the Lunatics, and it is even to this day believed in the south that all the lunatics of Erin would resort to this spot if they were allowed to be free" ' (VP p. 857). Yeats's slight misquotation is from Eugene O'Curry, *Lectures on the Manuscript Materials of Ancient Irish History*, 2nd ed. (Dublin: Hinch and Traynor, 1878), p. 316. O'Curry makes Gall not a king but the fifteen-year-old son of the king of Ulster; he derived the episode from a version of 'The Battle of Ventry.' In the oldest version of that tale, composed in the fifteenth century, Gall does not flee in frenzy but dies heroically in the combat. The author of O'Curry's variant, dating from either the eighteenth or the nineteenth century, has lifted his addition from the tradition of *Suibhne Geilt* ('Mad Suibhne'), a king who fled in frenzy into the woods after the battle of Moira (Magh Rath) in 637, and to whom many extant poems are attributed, said to have been composed in his wild state. Thirty-one of these are gathered into a twelfth-century frame tale, *Buile Shuibhne* ('Suibhne's Frenzy').

Although in a later and shortened version of his note Yeats claimed that the Glen of Lunatics is 'near Cork' (VP p. 796), it is usually placed in the north, in County Antrim.

9.2–3: *Magh Itha* ('The Plain of Corn') in County Donegal, fancifully said to be named after Ith, one of the Milesians, early invaders of Ireland in the medieval *Book of Invasions*. *Emain Macha* ('The Twins of Macha [a horse-goddess]'), capital of heroic-age Ulster; prominent in the Red Branch Cycle of Old Irish sagas. Invar Amargin (*Inber Amergin*, 'Amergin's Estuary'), the mouth of the Avoca River in County Wicklow; named after a mythical poet who appears as Conchubar's druid in the Red Branch stories and was borrowed by the *Book of Invasions* and made a son of Míl, and druid of the Milesians.

9.9: an *ollamh* was the highest degree among the learned caste in the ancient Irish system of learning. As Eugene O'Curry explains, the study of an *ollamh* could include the materials 'of law, of history, and of philosophy properly so called, as well as of languages, of music, of druidism, and of poetry in all its departments, and the practice of recitation in prose and verse' (*Lectures*, p. 2, n. 2).

9.11: Yeats glossed 'Northern cold' by noting that 'The Fomoroh, the powers of death and darkness and cold and evil, came from the north' (1895; VP p. 796), explaining in another note that 'Fomoroh means from under the sea, and is the name of the gods of night and death and cold. The Fomoroh were misshapen and had now the heads of goats and bulls, and now but one leg, and one arm that came out of the middle of their breasts. They were the ancestors of the evil faeries and, according to one Gaelic writer, of all misshapen persons. The giants and the leprecauns are expressly mentioned as of the Fomoroh' (1895; VP p. 795). The Fomorians were demons or evil gods in pagan Irish mythology, converted by the euhemerizing *Book of Invasions* into a race of pirates preying on early settlers of Ireland. The translation of their name was doubtless provided to Yeats by Douglas Hyde, who later explained in *A Literary History of Ireland* (New York: Charles Scribner's Sons, 1899), p. 282, that 'the Fomorians . . . are usually described as African sea-robbers, but the etymology of whose name seems to point to a mythological origin "men from under sea." ' Yeats (or Hyde) also probably draws on a passage, *De senchas na torothor .i. na luprucan 7 na fomorach* ('On the lore of monsters, i.e., the pygmies and the fomorians') in the *Sex Aetatis Mundi* contained in *The Book of the Dun Cow*, a manuscript miscellany made about 1100, translated by Whitley Stokes in 'Mythological Notes,' *Revue Celtique*, 1 (1870–72), 257: 'Ham is the first person who was cursed after the deluge; and so that he is Cain's successor after the deluge; and so that of him were born *Luchrupáin* and *Fomoraig* and *Goborchinn* (horse-heads?) and every unshapely appearance moreover that is on human beings.'

9.55: As noted by Eugene O'Curry in *On the Manners and Customs of the Ancient Irish* (London: Williams and Norgate; New York: Scribner, Welford, 1873), 3:362–63, a tympan was 'a stringed instrument . . . played on with . . . a fiddlebow.'

9.62: Yeats glossed Orchil as 'A Fomoroh and a sorceress, if I remember rightly. I forget whatever I may have once known about her' (1899: VP p. 796). Yeats would have come across Orchil (first mentioned in the 1895 text of the poem) in Standish James O'Grady's *The Coming of Cuculain: A Romance of the Heroic Age* (London: Methuen, 1894), where she is called 'the queen of the infernal regions' (p. 62n) and 'a great sorceress who ruled the world under the earth' (p. 109n).

9.68: 'ulalu' *(aililiú)*, usually spelled 'ululu' (as in some of the early printings of the poem), is a cry or exclamation of wonder or mourning.

10: Yeats explained that 'The places mentioned are round about Sligo. Further Rosses is a very noted locality. There is here a little point of rocks where, if anyone falls asleep, there is a danger of their waking silly, the fairies having carried off their souls' (1888; VP p. 797).

10.2–3: more usually 'Slish [Irish *slis*–, 'sloped'] Wood,' on the south shore of Lough Gill, County Sligo. The island is Innisfree (see note to poem A34).

10.15: Rosses Point, a small seaside village near Sligo.

10.29: *Gleann an Chairte* ('Valley of the Monumental Stone'), a lake near Sligo.

12: Yeats claimed that 'This is an attempt to reconstruct an old song from three lines imperfectly remembered by an old peasant woman in the village of Ballysodare, Sligo, who often sings them to herself' (1889: VP p. 90). The work is close to the first two stanzas of a poem with the same title in the P. J. McCall Ballad Collection in the National Library of Ireland. Yeats glossed 'salley' as 'willow' (1895; VP p. 797).

13: Yeats claimed that 'This poem is founded upon some things a fisherman said to me when out fishing in Sligo Bay' (1895; VP p. 797).

14: in separate notes to the 1888 printing of the poem, Yeats explained that 'Coloony is a few miles south of the town of Sligo. Father O'Hart lived there in the last century, and was greatly beloved. These lines accurately record the tradition. No one who has held the stolen land has prospered. It has changed owners many times' (VP p. 93); and that

Father O'Rorke is the priest of the parishes of Ballysadare and Kilvarnet, and it is from his learnedly and faithfully and sympathetically written history of these parishes that I have taken the story of Father John, who had been priest of these parishes, dying in the year 1739. Coloony is a village in Kilvarnet.

Some sayings of Father John's have come down. Once when he was sorrowing greatly for the death of his brother, the people said to him, 'Why do you sorrow so for your brother when you forbid us to keen?' 'Nature,' he answered, 'forces me, but ye force nature.' His memory and influence survives, in the fact that to the present day there has been no keening in Coloony.

He was a friend of the celebrated poet and musician, Carolan. (VP p. 797)

Yeats refers to chapter IV, section 2 ('Right Rev. John Hart') of T. O'Rorke, *History, Antiquities, and Present State of the Parishes of Ballysadare and Kilvarnet, in the County of Sligo* (Dublin: James Duffy, 1878). Carolan lived from 1670 to 1738. In a revised version of this note published in 1892, Yeats further commented that 'The robbery of the lands of Father O'Hart was one of those incidents which occurred sometimes, though but rarely, during the time of the penal laws. Catholics, who were forbidden to own landed property, evaded the law by giving some honest Protestant nominal possession of their estates. There are instances on record in which poor men were nominal owners of unnumbered acres' (VP p. 798). The penal laws against Roman Catholics were enacted from 1695 to 1727.

14.3: Yeats glossed 'shoneen' as 'upstart' and explained that '*Shoneen* is the diminutive of shone (Ir. *Séon*). There are two Irish names for John— one is *Shone*, the other is *Shawn* (Ir. *Seághan*). Shone is the "grandest" of the two, and is applied to the gentry. Hence *Shoneen* means "a little gentry John," and is applied to upstarts and "big" farmers, who ape the rank of gentlemen' (1888; VP pp. 92, 797). Yeats's information is not quite accurate. 'Shawn' is *Seán* (French *Jean*; *Seághan* is archaic, French *Jehan*), a common Irish name. No Irishman is ever called *Séon*, which is English 'John,' and means John Bull. A *Seóinín* is one who apes *Englishmen*, not gentlemen.

14.6: Yeats glossed 'sleiveen' as 'mean fellow' and explained that '*Sleiveen*, not to be found in the dictionaries, is a comical Irish word (at least in Connaught) for a rogue. It probably comes from *sliabh*, a mountain, meaning primarily a mountaineer, and in a secondary sense, on the principle that mountaineers are worse than anybody else, a rogue. I am indebted to Mr. Douglas Hyde for these details [here and at 14.3], as for many others' (1888; VP pp. 92, 797–98). Douglas Hyde (1860–1949), a close friend of Yeats, was a Gaelic scholar and a folklorist. Nevertheless, 'sleiveen' in fact does occur in dictionaries. It is Irish *slíbhín*, 'a sly person, a schemer,' and derives from *slí*, 'a way, a course of action,' not from *sliabh*, 'a mountain.'

14.22–23: the reference is to professional keeners, hired to cry aloud and recite extempore verses in praise of the deceased.

14.27: Colloney, a village in County Sligo.

14.30: Knocknarea, a mountain in County Sligo.

14.31: Knocknashee, a round hill near Achrony, County Sligo.

14.35: Tireragh, a barony in County Sligo.

14.36: Ballinafad, a village in County Sligo.

14.37: Inishmurray, an island off the coast of County Sligo.

15: Yeats claimed that the poem was based on 'a sermon preached in the chapel at Howth if I remember rightly' (1907; VP p. 843). Howth is a fishing village on a promontory on the north side of Dublin Bay, several miles east of the centre of Dublin but inside the city limits; Yeats lived there from 1881 to 1883.

15.24: Kinsale, a seaport in County Cork.

15.32: a boreen (Irish *bóithrín*, 'little road, lane') is Hiberno-English for a narrow road or lane.

15.48: for 'keenin'' see note to 14.22–23.

16: Yeats explained that 'This ballad is founded on an incident—probably in its turn a transcript from Tipperary tradition—in Kickham's "Knocknagow" ' (1892; VP p. 798). Yeats refers to chapter 55 of *Knocknagow or the Homes of Tipperary* (1879) by Charles J. Kickham (1828–82).

16.7: apparently the horse, unnamed in *Knocknagow* and called 'Dermot' in many of the intermediate printings of the poem, is named after the Lollards, followers of the English ecclesiastical reformer John Wycliffe (ca. 1320–84).

16.10: Rody is the name of the huntsman in *Knocknagow.*

The Rose: title and date first used in *Poems* (1895) for works from *The Countess Cathleen and Various Legends and Lyrics* (1892) and one later poem. "Who goes with Fergus" added in the 1912 edition of *Poems;* "To Some I have Talked with by the Fire" in the 1933 *Collected Poems.* The epigraph is from Book X, chapter 27, of the *Confessions* of St. Augustine: 'Too late I loved Thee, O Thou Beauty of ancient days, yet ever new! too late I loved Thee!', in the translation by E. B. Pusey, the one used by Yeats's friend Arthur Symons in his edition of *The Confessions* (London and Newcastle-on-Tyne, [1898]), p. 271. The English scholar-poet and critic Lionel Johnson (1867–1902) was a friend of Yeats. For Yeats's note on *The Rose,* see p. 599.

17: for Rood, see note to 1.12. Yeats explained that 'The Rose is a favourite symbol with the Irish poets. It has given a name to more than one poem, both Gaelic and English, and is used, not merely in love poems, but in addresses to Ireland, as in De Vere's line, "The little black rose shall be red at last," and in Mangan's "Dark Rosaleen." I do not, of course, use it in this latter sense' (1892; VP pp. 798–99). *The Sisters, Inisfail, and Other Poems* (London: Longmans, Green and Roberts; Dublin: McGlashan and Gill, 1861), p. 293, by the Irish poet Aubrey De Vere (1788–1846), includes an untitled poem beginning 'The little black rose shall be red at last'. 'Dark Rosaleen' is one of the best known works by the Irish poet James Clarence Mangan (1803–49). See also Yeats's note to poem 64.

17.3: for Cuchulain, see note to poem 19.

17.4–5: for Fergus and the Druid, see note to poem 18.

17.23: *Éire* is the normal Irish word for 'Ireland'; in Old Irish it was *Ériu.* The etymology is uncertain, but the medieval *Book of Invasions* asserts it was the name of a queen of the *Tuatha Dé Danann,* euhemerized by that book into a race of earlier inhabitants of Ireland.

18: Yeats explained that Fergus was 'the poet of the Red Branch cycle. . . . He was once king of all Ireland, and, as the legend is shaped by Ferguson, gave up his throne that he might live at peace hunting in the woods' (1899; VP p. 795). The reference is to 'The Abdication of Fergus Mac Roy' by Sir Samuel Ferguson (1810–86). Ferguson's version of the legend is largely the product of his own imagination. In the stories of the Ulster, or Red Branch, Cycle, Fergus mac Roich was not a poet, and was never king of all Ireland. He was king of Ulster, and was tricked out of his throne by his wife, Ness, on behalf of her son Conchubar. In the epic *Táin Bó Cuailgne*, he is the lover of Maeve, queen of Connacht. Druids were ancient Celtic priests and medicine men. See also Yeats's note to 'The Secret Rose,' p. 601.

18.10: described by Yeats as 'King of all Ireland in the time of the Red Branch kings' (1895; VP p. 795), Conchubar was Fergus's step-son and successor. He is never described in the Cycle tales as king of any territory more extensive than Ulster.

19: Yeats explained that 'Cuchullin (pronounced Cuhoolin) was the great warrior of the Conorian cycle. My poem is founded on a West of Ireland legend given by Curtin in his "Myths and Folklore of Ireland." The bardic tradition is very different' (1892; VP p. 799). The correct pronunciation of Cuchulain is Koo-hullin; Yeats is pronouncing a long vowel as short and a short vowel as long. 'Conor' is an anglicization of a modern pronunciation of Conchubar. Yeats refers to the tale 'Cuculin' in *Myths and Folk-Lore of Ireland* (Boston: Little, Brown, 1890), pp. 304–26, esp. pp. 324–26, by the American folklorist Jeremiah Curtin (1838–1906).

19.2: Emer, the name of Cuchulain's wife, is apparently an error for Aoife, the Amazon on whom Cuchulain begot his son, Conlaech. Curtin calls the woman simply 'the Virago of Alba' (p. 324).

19.45: for Conchubar, see note to 18.10.

20.4: in Greek mythology, Troy is destroyed by the Greeks during the Trojan War, fought over the abduction of Helen by Paris.

20.5: Yeats explained that Usna was 'The father of Naisi, the lover, and Ardan and Anly, the friends of Deirdre. Deirdre's beautiful lament over their bodies has been finely translated by Sir Samuel Ferguson' (1895; VP p. 799). Naoise, accompanied by his brothers Ainnle and Ardan, elopes with Deirdre, whom Conchubar had selected to become his queen; eventually lured back to Ireland, the three brothers are killed by Conchubar's forces. Yeats refers to Ferguson's 'Deirdra's Lament for the Sons of Usnach,' included in his *Lays of the Western Gael, and Other Poems* (London: Bell and Daldy, 1864).

21.1: in Christian tradition, the archangel Michael is the conqueror of Satan.

23: Yeats explained that Grania was 'A beautiful woman, who fled with Dermot to escape from the love of aged Finn. She fled from place to place over Ireland, but at last Dermot was killed at Sligo upon the seaward point of Benbulben, and Finn won her love and brought her, leaning upon his neck, into the assembly of the Fenians, who burst into inextinguishable laughter' (1895; VP p. 795). *The Pursuit of Diarmaid and Gráinne* is the most fully developed story in the Fenian saga-cycle. The version Yeats follows is that of Standish Hayes O'Grady, *Transactions of the Ossianic Society*, 3 (1857), based on an eighteenth-century manuscript (by his testimony) that has not since been identified. Of the forty-one extant manuscripts of the tale, O'Grady's ending, with Grania returning to Finn, occurs in only one, Royal Irish Academy MS. 23L27, written 1737–38. Both the oldest and the second oldest manuscripts have Gráinne exhorting her children to wreak vengeance on Finn. A cromlech is a prehistoric stone structure consisting of a large flat stone resting on three or more horizontal stones. In many parts of Ireland cromlechs are known as 'beds' of Diarmuid and Grania, where they are supposed to have spent a night while in flight from Finn.

24: Innisfree (*Inis Fraoigh*, 'Heather Island') is a small island in Lough Gill, County Sligo.

25.7: possibly the planets known to the ancient Greeks (earlier versions of the line read 'The old planets seven') or the seven stars of the Pleiades, named after the daughters of Atlas and Pleione in Greek mythology.

27.7: Odysseus is the central figure in Homer's *Odyssey*, which tells of his adventures from the fall of Troy until his return to Ithaca ten years later.

27.8: Priam, king of Troy, was killed by Neoptolemus during the fall of Troy.

29: Yeats explained that 'The birds of fairyland are white as snow. The "Danaan Shore" is, of course, *Tier-nan-oge*, or fairyland' (1892; VP p. 799). As noted in one of Yeats's sources, P. W. Joyce's *Old Celtic Romances* (London: David Nutt, 1879), p. 310, 'The ancient Irish had a sort of dim, vague belief that there was a land where people were always youthful, suffered no disease, and lived for ever. This country they called by various names: *Tír na mbeo*, the land of the [ever-]living; *Tír na nÓg*, the land of the [ever-]youthful; *Moy-Mell*, the plain of pleasure, etc. It had its own inhabitants—fairies; but mortals were sometimes brought there; and while they lived in it, were gifted with the everlasting youth and beauty of the fairy people themselves, and partook of their pleasures.' For the *Tuatha Dé Danann*, see Yeats's note on p. 600.

29.3: presumably Venus, if a specific star is intended.

31: the poem was first a song in scene V of the 1892 text of Yeats's play *The Countess Kathleen*.

31.9: in the Christian religion, the Virgin Mary is the mother of Jesus Christ.

32: see note to poem 18.

33.1: Dromahair, a village in County Leitrim.

33.13: Yeats refers to 'the barony of Lisadell, in County Sligo' (1896; VP p. 161). Lissadell House was the home of Yeats's friends Constance (1868–1927) and Eva (1870–1926) Gore-Booth.

33.25: the Well of Scanavin is in County Sligo.

33.37: *Lug na nGall*, 'The Hollow of the Foreigners,' a townland in Glencar valley in County Sligo.

34: in 1924 Yeats commented that 'This poem, which I have just re-written, was first published in its original form in 1890 as a dedication to a book of selections from the Irish Novelists. Even in its re-written form it is a sheaf of wild oats' (VP p. 129). The volume was *Representative Irish Tales* (New York and London: G. P. Putnam's Sons [1891]).

34.1: for the bell-branch, see note to 375.III.53.

34.2: for Eire, see note to 17.23.

34.24: Munster is one of the four provinces of Ireland. Connemara is a district in County Galway.

35: Yeats described the first version of this poem as 'little more than a translation into verse of the very words of an old Wicklow peasant' (1895; VP p. 799). In 1908 he commented that the poem derives from 'words spoken by a man on the Two Rock Mountain to a friend of mine' (VP p. 844). Two Rock Mountain is near County Dublin; the friend is the Irish writer George W. Russell (1867–1935). Yeats wrote of the incident in the story 'A Visionary' in *The Celtic Twilight: Men and Women, Dhouls and Faeries* (London: Lawrence and Bullen, 1893), pp. 17–25.

36: Yeats explained that 'This ballad is founded on the Kerry version of an old folk tale' (1892; VP p. 800).

36.25: mavrone *(mo bhrón)*, 'my grief.'

38.1: for Danaan, see Yeats's note on p. 600.

39.4: Irish *rann*, a quatrain, verse, or stanza.

39.18: Thomas Davis (1814–45), Irish political leader and writer; James Clarence Mangan (1803–49), Irish poet; Sir Samuel Ferguson (1810–86), Irish poet and antiquary.

The Wind Among the Reeds: published as a separate volume in 1899; the order of the poems here first used in *Poems, Second Series* (1909). In 1908 Yeats noted that 'When I wrote these poems I had so meditated over the images that came to me in writing "Ballads and Lyrics" [poems 1–16, 34–36, 38, and 76], "The Rose" [poems 17–31, 33, 37, 39, and 49], and "The Wanderings of Oisin" [poem 375], and other images from Irish folklore, that they had become true symbols. I had sometimes when awake, but more often in sleep, moments of vision, a state very unlike dreaming, when these images took upon themselves what seemed an independent life and became a part of a mystic language, which seemed always as if it would bring me some strange revelation. Being troubled at what was thought a reckless obscurity, I tried to explain myself in lengthy notes, into which I put all the little learning I had, and more wilful phantasy than I now think admirable, though what is most mystical still seems to me the most true' (VP p. 800).

40: see Yeats's note, p. 600, which includes information on the Sidhe, Knocknarea, and Clooth-na-Bare. Earlier versions of the note (VP pp. 800–803) offer more details on Clooth-na-Bare as well as the following additional commentary on the Sidhe:

They are almost always said to wear no covering upon their heads, and to let their hair stream out; and the great among them, for they have great and simple, go much upon horseback. If any one becomes too much interested in them, and sees them over much, he loses all interest in ordinary things. I shall write a great deal elsewhere about such enchanted persons, and can give but an example or two now.

A woman near Gort, in Galway, says: 'There is a boy, now, of the Cloran's; but I wouldn't for the world let them think I spoke of him; it's two years since he came from America, and since that time he never went to Mass, or to church, or to fairs, or to market, or to stand on the cross roads, or to hurling, or to nothing. And if any one comes into the house, it's into the room he'll slip, not to see them; and as to work, he has the garden dug to bits, and the whole place smeared with cow dung; and such a crop as was never seen; and the alders all plaited till they look grand. One day he went as far as the chapel; but as soon as he got to the door he turned straight round again, as if he hadn't power to pass it. I wonder he wouldn't get the priest to read a Mass for him, or something; but the crop he has is grand, and you may know well he has some to help him.' One hears many stories of the kind; and a man whose son is believed to go out riding among them at night tells me that he is careless about everything, and lies in bed until it is late in the day. A doctor believes this boy to be mad. Those that are at times 'away,' as it is called, know all things, but are afraid to speak. A countryman at Kiltartan says, 'There was one of the Lydons—John—was away for seven years, lying in his bed, but brought away at nights, and he knew everything; and one, Kearney, up in the mountains, a cousin of his own, lost two hoggets, and came and told him, and he knew the very spot where they were, and told him, and he got them back again. But *they* were vexed at that, and took away the power, so that he never knew anything again, no more than another.' This wisdom is the wisdom of the fools of the Celtic stories, that was above all the wisdom of the wise. Lomna, the fool of Fiann, had so great wisdom that his head, cut from his body, was still able to sing and prophesy; and a writer in the 'Encyclopaedia Britannica' writes that Tristram, in the oldest form of the tale of Tristram and Iseult, drank wisdom, and madness the shadow of wisdom, and not love, out of the magic cup.

The great of the old times are among the Tribes of Danu, and are kings and queens among them. (1899; VP p. 801)

Yeats was in the midst of publishing a series of six articles on Irish folk-lore in various periodicals from November 1897 to April 1902. See *Uncollected Prose by W. B. Yeats,* II, ed. John P. Frayne and Colton Johnson (London: Macmillan, 1975), pp. 54–70, 74–87, 94–108, 167–83, 219–36, and 267–82. The anecdotes about Cloran and John Lydon were retold, with different names, in the *Fortnightly Review* for April 1902 (*Uncollected Prose,* II, 267–68). A 'hogget' is a yearling sheep. Yeats found the story of Lomna in John Rhys's *Lectures on the Origin and Growth of Religion as Illustrated by Celtic Heathendom,* 2nd ed. (London: Williams and Norgate, 1892), pp. 98–99. Rhys explains that 'the association of poetry, prophecy and idiocy with one another is so thoroughly Celtic as to need no remark . . .' (p. 99). No available edition of the *Encyclopaedia Britannica* suggests that the potion drunk by Tristan produced wisdom rather than love. Yeats may be thinking of a work cited in the entry on 'Romance' by H. R. Tedder and Michael Kerney in the 9th edition (XX [1886], 632–61), Edward Tyrrel Leith's *On the Legend of Tristan: Its Origin in Myth and Its Development in Romance* (Bombay: at The Education Society's Press, 1868). Leith notes that a French scholar 'compares the tale of the Love Potion to the Magical Brew of Science . . . which occurs in the old Welsh legend of Taliesin in the "Mabinogion" translated by Lady Charlotte Guest' (p. 10) and that 'the vase described by Taliesin . . . possesses the property of inspiring poetic genius; conferring wisdom; and laying bare the future, the mysteries of nature, and the riches of human knowledge' (p. 23n).

40.3: for Caoilte, see Yeats's note on 'The Secret Rose', p. 601. Also, in 1899 Yeats explained that 'Caolte was a companion of Fiann; and years after his death he appeared to a king in a forest, and was a flaming man, that he might lead him in the darkness. When the king asked him who he was, he said, "I am your candlestick." I do not remember where I have read this story, and I have, maybe, half forgotten it' (VP p. 801). Yeats's source was Standish James O'Grady's *History of Ireland: Critical and Philosophical,* Vol. I (London: Sampson Low; Dublin: E. Ponsonby, 1881), p. 354: 'The King of Ireland once lost his way in a dark forest, when suddenly a tall, slender warrior preceded him, bearing a torch. At parting, the King said, "What art thou?" "Thy candlestick," answered the warrior. Said the Monarch: "Methinks the two eyes of Coelté are in the candlestick." '

40.4: Yeats explained that 'Niam was a beautiful woman of the Tribes of Danu that led Oisin to the Country of the Young' (1899; VP p. 801). See poem 375.

44: for Yeats's note, see p. 600. *The Wind Among the Reeds* offered a much longer commentary:

Some writers distinguish between the Sluagh Gaoith, the host of the air, and Sluagh Sidhe, the host of the Sidhe, and describe the host of the air as of a peculiar malignancy. Dr. Joyce says, 'of all the different kinds of goblins . . . air demons were most dreaded by the people. The[y] lived among clouds, and mists, and rocks, and hated the human race with the utmost malignity.' A very old Arann charm, which contains the words 'Send God, by his strength, between us and the host of the Sidhe, between us and the host of the air,' seems also to distinguish among them. I am inclined, however, to think that the distinction came in with Christianity and its belief about the prince of the air, for the host of the Sidhe, as I have already explained, are closely associated with the wind.

They are said to steal brides just after their marriage, and sometimes in a blast of wind. A man in Galway says, 'At Aughanish there were two couples came to the shore to be married, and one of the newly married women was in the boat with the priest, and they going back to the island; and a sudden blast of wind came, and the priest said some blessed words that were able to save himself, but the girl was swept.'

This woman was drowned; but more often the persons who are taken 'get the touch,' as it is called, and fall into a half dream, and grow indifferent to all things, for their true life has gone out of the world, and is among the hills and the forts of the Sidhe. A faery doctor has told me that his wife 'got the touch' at her marriage because there was one of them that wanted her; and the way he knew for certain was, that when he took a pitchfork out of the rafters, and told her it was a broom, she said, 'It is a broom.' She was, the truth is, in the magical sleep, to which people have given a new name lately, that makes the imagination so passive that it can be moulded by any voice in any world into any shape. A mere likeness of some old woman, or even old animal, some one or some thing the Sidhe have no longer a use for, is believed to be left instead of the person who is 'away;' this some one or some thing can, it is thought, be driven away by threats, or by violence (though I have heard country women say that violence is wrong), which perhaps awakes the soul out of the magical sleep. The story in the poem is founded on an old Gaelic ballad that was sung and translated for me by a woman at Ballisodare in County Sligo; but in the ballad the husband found the keeners keening his wife when he got to his house. She was 'swept' at once; but the Sidhe are said to value those the most whom they but cast into a half dream, which may last for years, for they need the help of a living person in most of the things they do. There are many stories of people who seem to die and be buried—though the country people will tell you it is but some one or some thing put in their place that dies and is buried—and yet are brought back afterwards. These tales are perhaps memories of true awakenings out of the magical sleep, moulded by the imagination, under the influence of a mystical doctrine, which it understands too literally, into the shape of some well-known traditional tale. One does not hear them as one hears the others, from the persons who are 'away,' or from their wives or husbands; and one old man, who had often seen the Sidhe, began one of them with 'Maybe it is all vanity.'

Here is a tale that a friend of mine heard in the Burren hills, and it is a type of all:—

'There was a girl to be married, and she didn't like the man, and she cried when the day was coming, and said she wouldn't go along with him. And so the mother said, "Get into the bed, then, and I'll say that you're sick." And so she did. And when the man came the mother said to him, "You can't get her, she's sick in the bed." And he looked in and said, "That's not my wife that's in the bed, it's some old hag." And the mother began to cry and to roar. And he went out and got two hampers of turf, and made a fire, that they thought he was going to burn the house down. And when the fire was kindled, "Come out now," says he, "and we'll see who you are, when I'll put you on the fire." And when she heard that, she gave one leap, and was out of the house, and they saw, then, it was an old hag she was. Well, the man asked the advice of an old woman, and she bid him go to a faery-bush that was near, and he might get some word of her. So he went there at night, and saw all sorts of grand people, and they in carriages or riding on horses, and among them he could see the girl he came to look for. So he went again to the old woman, and she said, "If you can get the three bits of blackthorn out of her hair, you'll get her again." So that night he went again, and that time he only got hold of a bit of her hair. But the old woman told him that was no use, and that he was put back now, and it might be twelve nights before he'd get her. But on the fourth night he got the third bit of blackthorn, and he took her, and she came away with him. He never told the mother he had got her; but one day she saw her at a fair, and, says she, "That's my daughter; I know her by the smile and by the laugh of her," and she with a shawl about her head. So the husband said, "You're right there, and hard I worked to get her." She spoke often of the grand things she saw underground, and how she used to have wine to drink, and to drive out in a carriage wth four horses every night. And she used to be able to see her husband when he came to look for her, and she was greatly afraid he'd get a drop of the wine, for then he would have come underground and never left it again. And she was glad herself to come to earth again, and not to be left there.'

The old Gaelic literature is full of the appeals of the Tribes of the goddess Danu to mortals whom they would bring into their country; but the song of Midher to the beautiful Etain, the wife of the king who was called Echaid the ploughman, is the type of all.

'O beautiful woman, come with me to the marvellous land where one listens to a sweet music, where one has spring flowers in one's hair, where the body is like snow from head to foot, where no one is sad or silent, where teeth are white and eyebrows are black . . . cheeks red like foxglove in flower. . . . Ireland is beautiful, but not so beautiful as the Great Plain I call you to. The beer of Ireland is heady, but the beer of the Great Plain is much more heady. How marvellous is the country I am speaking of! Youth does not grow old there. Streams with warm flood flow there; sometimes mead, sometimes wine. Men are charming and without a blot there, and love is not forbidden there. O woman, when you come into my powerful country you will wear a crown of gold upon your head. I will give you the flesh of swine, and you will have beer and milk to drink, O beautiful woman. O beautiful woman, come with me!' (1899; VP pp. 803–05)

'Sluagh Gaoith' should be 'Sluagh Gaoithe.' Yeats slightly misquotes from P. W. Joyce's story 'Fergus O'Mara and the Demons,' included in *Good and Pleasant Reading* (Dublin: M. H. Gill and Son, 1892); Yeats reprinted the work in *Irish Fairy Tales* (London: T. Fisher Unwin, 1892). For the Aran charm, see poem A42. In Christianity, 'Prince of the Power of the Air' (Eph. 2.2) is a name for Satan. Yeats had explained the connection of the Sidhe with the wind in his note on poem 40 (see p. 600). The 'new name' for the 'magical sleep' is 'hypnosis,' which came into common usage in the 1880s. The friend is almost surely Lady Gregory; for Burren, see note to poem 48. Yeats had published the story of the two couples in 'The Prisoners of the Gods' (*Nineteenth Century*, Jan. 1898), and he later retold the story of the broom and the pitchfork in 'Irish Witch Doctors' (*Fortnightly Review*, Sept. 1900). See *Uncollected Prose by W. B. Yeats*, II, ed. John P. Frayne and Colton Johnson (London: Macmillan, 1975), pp. 80 and 228–29. For the legend of Midhir, Edain, and Eochaid, see poems 379 and 381. Though there were several versions of Midhir's song to Edain available to Yeats, his paraphrase seems closest to the text in Kuno Meyer and Alfred Nutt, *The Voyage of Bran* (London: David Nutt, 1895–97), I, 176. For Yeats's 1893 note on the poem, see VP p. 143.

44.4: a small lake in County Sligo.

46: in an 1899 note to this poem and to poem 61, Yeats explained that 'I use the wind as a symbol of vague desires and hopes, not merely because the Sidhe are in the wind, or because the wind bloweth as it listeth, but because wind and spirit and vague desire have been associated everywhere. A highland scholar tells me that his country people use the wind in their talk and in their proverbs as I use it in my poem' (VP p. 806).

46.1: for Danaan, see Yeats's note on 'The Hosting of the Sidhe,' p. 600.

46.3: usually 'gier-eagle,' a bird described in the Bible as unclean (Lev. 11.18 and Deut. 14.17); probably the Egyptian vulture.

46.12: for Mary, see note to 31.9.

47.5: for Fire, see note to 17.23.

48: in an 1899 note, Yeats explained that

> The Tribes of the Goddess Danu can take all shapes, and those that are in the waters take often the shape of fish. A woman of Burren, in Galway, says, 'There are more of them in the sea than on the land, and they sometimes try to come over the side of the boat in the form of fishes, for they can take their choice shape.' At other times they are beautiful women; and another Galway woman says, 'Surely those things are in the sea as well as on land. My father was out fishing one night off Tyrone. And something came beside the boat that had eyes shining like candles. And then a wave came in, and a storm rose all in a minute, and whatever was in the wave, the weight of it had like to sink the boat. And then they saw that it was a woman in the sea that had the shining eyes. So my father went to the priest, and he bid him always to take a drop of holy water and a pinch of salt out in the boat with him, and nothing could harm him.'
>
> The poem was suggested to me by a Greek folk song; but the folk belief of Greece is very like that of Ireland, and I certainly thought, when I wrote it, of Ireland, and of the spirits that are in Ireland. An old man who was cutting a quickset hedge near Gort, in Galway, said, only the other day, 'One time I was cutting timber over in Inchy, and about eight o'clock one morning, when I got there, I saw a girl picking nuts, with her hair hanging down over her shoulders; brown hair; and she had a good, clean face, and she was tall, with nothing on her head, and her dress no way gaudy, but simple. And when she felt me coming she gathered herself up, and was gone, as if the earth had swallowed her up. And I followed her, and looked for her, but I never could see her again from that day to this, never again.'
>
> The country Galway people use the word 'clean' in its old sense of fresh and comely. (VP p. 806)

For the *Tuatha Dé Danann,* see Yeats's note on 'The Hosting of the Sidhe,' p. 600. Burren (*boireann,* 'rock; rocky land') is the name of several places in all parts of Ireland, but the best known is The Burren in County Clare, immediately adjacent to the County Galway line. Yeats, as an inter-

mittent sojourner in County Galway, may have misunderstood the
nearby Burren of Clare to have been in Galway. Tyrone (*Tír Eoghain,*
'Eoghan's Land') is a large inland county in Northern Ireland, and con-
sequently has no offshore sea in which to fish. It does border, on the east,
on Lough Neagh, largest lake in Ireland and site of much supernatural
tradition. The informant, if basically Irish-speaking, may be confusing *Tír
Eoghain* with *Tír Conaill* (Conall's Land), the Irish name for County
Donegal, along the Atlantic Coast just west of Tyrone, or with *Inis
Eoghain* (Eoghan's Island)—the Inishowen peninsula in the north of
County Donegal. The Greek folk song is probably 'The Three Fishes,' in
New Folklore Researches. Greek Folk Poesy, trans. Lucy M. J. Garnett
(London: David Nutt, 1896), I, 69. For Inchy, see note to 378.13. Yeats
retold the anecdote of the wood-cutter in 'Enchanted Woods,' a story
added to the 1902 edition of *The Celtic Twilight* (London: A. H. Bullen).
Yeats described Aengus as 'The god of youth, beauty, and poetry. He
reigned in Tir-nan-Oge, the country of the young' (1895; VP p. 794).

48.1: for hazel, see note to poem 75.

49.2: Yeats explained that 'The "seed of the fire" is the Irish phrase for the
little fragment of burning turf and hot ashes which remains in the hearth
from the day before' (1894; VP p. 151).

52: for Yeats's note to this poem, see p. 600. See also VP pp. 153 and 807
for earlier versions of the note.

53: in 1899 Yeats explained that

November, the old beginning of winter, or of the victory of the Fomor, or
powers of death, and dismay, and cold, and darkness, is associated by the
Irish people with the horse-shaped Púcas, who are now mischievous spirits,
but were once Fomorian divinities. I think that they may have some connec-
tion with the horses of Mannannan, who reigned over the country of the
dead, where the Fomorian Tethra reigned also; and the horses of Mannan-
nan, though they could cross the land as easily as the sea, are constantly
associated with the waves. Some neo-platonist, I forget who, describes the
sea as a symbol of the drifting indefinite bitterness of life, and I believe there
is like symbolism intended in the many Irish voyages to the islands of
enchantment, or that there was, at any rate, in the mythology out of which
these stories have been shaped. I follow much Irish and other mythology,
and the magical tradition, in associating the North with night and sleep, and
the East, the place of sunrise, with hope, and the South, the place of the sun
when at its height, with passion and desire, and the West, the place of sun-
set, with fading and dreaming things. (VP p. 808)

For the Fomorians, see note to 9.11. Yeats wrote of 'The Pooka, *rectè
Púca,*' in *Fairy and Folk Tales of the Irish Peasantry* (London: Walter
Scott; New York: Thomas Whittaker; Toronto: W. J. Gage, 1888), p.
94, classifying it as one of the 'Solitary Fairies' and commenting that
'He has many shapes—is now a horse, now an ass, now a bull, now a
goat, now an eagle. Like all spirits, he is only half in the world of form.'
Tethra in euhemerizing stories is a king of the Fomorians; older mytho-
logical stories have him ruling *Tír na nÓg,* suggesting Yeats was correct

to identify him as a ruler of the dead. Manannán mac Lir, identified as belonging to the *Tuatha Dé Danann,* is god of the sea. If Yeats was thinking of a specific Neoplatonist, it might have been Thomas Taylor, who asked in *A Dissertation on the Eleusinian and Bacchic Mysteries* (Amsterdam [for London], 1790) 'is not the ocean a proper emblem of a material nature, whirling and stormy, and perpetually rolling without admitting any period of repose?' (p. 165).

59: see Yeats's note, p. 601.

60: see Yeats's note, p. 601. See also VP pp. 161 and 808–11 for earlier versions of the note.

60.5: for cromlech, see note to poem 23.

61: see note to poem 46.

61.13: for Niamh, see note to 40.4.

61.16: in Egyptian mythology, the Phoenix lives for 500 years, is consumed in fire by its own act, and rises in youthful freshness from its own ashes.

64: in an 1899 note to this poem and to poems 72 and 75, Yeats explained that

The Rose has been for many centuries a symbol of spiritual love and supreme beauty. The Count Goblet D'Alviella thinks that it was once a symbol of the sun,—itself a principal symbol of the divine nature, and the symbolic heart of things. The lotus was in some Eastern countries imagined blossoming upon the Tree of Life, as the Flower of Life, and is thus represented in Assyrian bas-reliefs. Because the Rose, the flower sacred to the Virgin Mary, and the flower that Apuleius' adventurer ate, when he was changed out of the ass's shape and received into the fellowship of Isis, is the western Flower of Life, I have imagined it growing upon the Tree of Life. I once stood beside a man in Ireland when he saw it growing there in a vision, that seemed to have rapt him out of his body. He saw the garden of Eden walled about, and the top of a high mountain, as in certain mediaeval diagrams, and after passing the Tree of Knowledge, on which grew fruit full of troubled faces, and through whose branches flowed, he was told, sap that was human souls, he came to a tall, dark tree, with little bitter fruits, and was shown a kind of stair or ladder going up through the tree, and told to go up; and near the top of the tree, a beautiful woman, like the Goddess of Life associated with the tree in Assyria, gave him a rose that seemed to have been growing upon the tree. One finds the Rose in the Irish poets, sometimes as a religious symbol, as in the phrase, 'the Rose of Friday,' meaning the Rose of austerity, in a Gaelic poem in Dr. Hyde's 'Religious Songs of Connacht;' and, I think, was a symbol of woman's beauty in the Gaelic song, 'Roseen Dubh;' and a symbol of Ireland in Mangan's adaptation of 'Roseen Dubh,' 'My Dark Rosaleen,' and in Mr. Aubrey de Vere's 'The Little Black Rose.' I do not know any evidence to prove whether this symbol came to Ireland with mediaeval Christianity, or whether it has come down from Celtic times. I have read somewhere that a stone engraved with a Celtic god, who holds up what looks like a rose in one hand, has been found somewhere in England; but I cannot find the reference, though I certainly made a note of it. If the Rose was really a symbol of Ireland among the Gaelic poets, and if

'Roseen Dubh' is really a political poem, as some think, one may feel pretty certain that the ancient Celts associated the Rose with Eire, or Fotla, or Banba—goddesses who gave their names to Ireland—or with some principal god or goddess, for such symbols are not suddenly adopted or invented, but come out of mythology.

I have made the Seven Lights, the constellation of the Bear, lament for the theft of the Rose, and I have made the Dragon, the constellation Draco, the guardian of the Rose, because these constellations move about the pole of the heavens, the ancient Tree of Life in many countries, and are often associated with the Tree of Life in mythology. It is this Tree of Life that I have put into the 'Song of Mongan' [an earlier title of poem 75] under its common Irish form of a hazel; and, because it sometimes has the stars for fruit, I have hung upon it 'the Crooked Plough' and the 'Pilot' star, as Gaelic-speaking Irishmen sometimes call the Bear and the North star. I have made it an axle-tree in 'Aedh hears the Cry of the Sedge' [an earlier title of poem 64], for this was another ancient way of representing it. (VP pp. 811–12)

In *The Migration of Symbols* (Westminster: Archibald Constable, 1894), p. 150, the Count Goblet D'Alviella notes that 'the Rosette—whether derived from the rose, the lotus, or any other flower—forms an essentially solar symbol.' Yeats refers to an incident in *The Golden Ass* by the Latin writer Lucius Apuleius (ca. 123–?). In the section of *The Religious Songs of Connacht* printed in the *New Ireland Review*, 6, No. 6 (Feb. 1897), 381, 384, Douglas Hyde prints a poem by the Gaelic writer Tadhg Gaedhealach Ó Súilliobháin (1715–95) which begins 'A Róis na h-aoine.' Explaining that he will not attempt a literal translation 'for I am not always sure of his meaning,' Hyde begins his English version 'Rose of the Universality.' *Aoine* is the normal Irish word for 'Friday,' but its literal meaning is 'fasting'; this explains Yeats's equation of Friday with austerity. Hyde's translation arises from taking *aoine* to be an abstract noun from *aon*, 'one,' but he is mistaken. For the other poems referring to the rose, see note to poem 17. 'Roseen Dubh' (*Róisín Dubh*, 'Dark Little Rose') is an anonymous seventeenth-century poem in which Ireland is allegorized as the Rose. The poem, however, is based on an earlier love-song, in which the rose was merely the beloved girl. The rose is not a traditional symbol of Ireland; the word (*ros* or *rós*) is rare in Old Irish, occurring only in specifically Christian contexts. In citing 'a stone engraved with a Celtic god,' Yeats is apparently misremembering John Rhys's *Lectures on the Origin and Growth of Religion as Illustrated by Celtic Heathendom,* 2nd ed. (London: Williams and Norgate, 1892). Describing a monument discovered at Chester, Rhys notes that it has 'a goblet on one side of the inscription and what appears to have been a rose on the other: the monument is unfortunately in a very bad state of preservation' (p. 65). However, Rhys also explains that the inscription is not Celtic: 'it should rather be regarded as a monument of the piety of a German in the army at Chester in the year 154' (p. 58). Éire (Ériu), Fotla, and Banba, by medieval times accepted as names for Ireland, are explained in the *Book of Invasions* as the names of three queens of the *Tuatha Dé Danann,* each of whom asked the invading Milesians to name the country after her. The names may have been originally regional: Banba is of British Celtic origin ('Plain of Peaks') and was a name for the region around Tara. An axle-tree is an imaginary line around which the heavens are supposed to revolve.

66.1: 'Cumhal the king' in the first printing of the poem; apparently not related to the pagan gleeman of that name in the story 'The Crucifixion of the Outcast' (included in *The Secret Rose,* 1897).

66.2: 'Dathi the Blessed' in the first printing of the poem; apparently not related to the fifth-century Irish king Nath Í mac Fiachrach, also mentioned in 'The Crucifixion of the Outcast.'

67: see Yeats's note, p. 601. See also VP pp. 812–14 for earlier versions of the note.

67.3: the Holy Sepulchre is the tomb of Christ in Jerusalem.

67.9: the Magi were a priestly caste of ancient Persia; in Christian tradition, the wise men who journey from the East to see the infant Christ are Magi.

67.15: Emer is the wife of Cuchulain.

67.16: a liss (*lios;* Old Irish *les*) was originally an enclosed space, a courtyard, but in popular usage denotes a (usually small) mound believed to be inhabited by supernatural beings.

69.3–5: the imagery suggests the crucifixion of Christ. Yeats presumably refers to the brook Kidron (the spelling in many of the early printings of the poem), which flows south between Jerusalem and the Mount of Olives. (The Kedron is the unnamed stream referred to in I Mac. 16.5–10.)

71.6: presumably the Virgin Mary, as earlier versions of the poem read 'Mary of the wounded heart.'

72: see Yeats's note to poem 64. See also VP p. 174 for Yeats's 1898 note on this poem.

75: see Yeats's note to poem 64. Also, in his 1898 note on this poem, Yeats commented that ' "The Country of the Young" is a name in the Celtic poetry for the country of the gods and of the happy dead. The hazel tree was the Irish tree of Life or of Knowledge, and in Ireland it was doubtless, as elsewhere, the tree of the heavens' (VP p. 177).

76: Dooney Rock is on the shore of Lough Gill in County Sligo.

76.3: Kilvarnet is a townland near the village of Ballinacarrow, County Sligo.

76.4: *Machaire Buí,* 'Yellow Plain' or 'Yellow Battlefield,' the townland of Magheraboy, on the southwest outskirts of Sligo.

76.8: Sligo, in northwestern Ireland, was the home of Yeats's maternal grandparents and the place where Yeats spent a considerable part of his childhood.

76.10: in Christian tradition, Saint Peter is depicted as the gate-keeper of Heaven.

In the Seven Woods: first published in 1903, including 'The Old Age of Queen Maeve' and 'Baile and Aillinn' (poems 376–77). Expanded by three poems in 1906 (poem A54 later eliminated) and two poems in 1908. In the 1903 edition, which included the play *On Baile's Strand,* Yeats noted that

> I made some of the poems walking among the Seven Woods, before the big wind of nineteen hundred and three blew down so many trees, & troubled the wild creatures, & changed the look of things; and I thought out there a good part of the play which follows. The first shape of it came to me in a dream, but it changed much in the making, foreshadowing, it may be, a change which will bring a less dream-burdened will into my verses. I never re-wrote anything so many times; for at first I could not make these wills that stream into mere life poetical. But now I hope to do easily much more of the kind, and that our new Irish players will find the buskin and the sock. (VP pp. 814–15)

77: the Seven Woods are part of Coole Park, the estate of Yeats's close friend Lady Gregory (1852–1932). See poem 378 for their names.

77.6: Tara, in County Meath, inaugural place of kings of the Uí Néill dynasty, who aspired to rule all Ireland and encouraged a literary cult of Tara as a primordial capital. The site is a megalithic cemetery, suggesting it always had sacral significance, but it is doubtful that it was ever actually inhabited.

77.14: *Páirc na Laoi,* 'the field of the calves,' one of the Seven Woods.

82.6: Slieve Aughty (*Sliabh Echtge,* 'Echtge's Mountain'), a range of mountains in County Galway and County Clare. Echtge is said to have been a woman of the *Tuatha Dé Danann,* hence a goddess.

82.12: for Danann, see Yeats's note to 'The Hosting of the Sidhe,' p. 600.

82.17–18: for the swans, see poem 377.

83.22: Adam, the first man in the Bible, was expelled from the Garden of Eden because of disobedience (Gen. 2.15–3.24).

84: Red Hanrahan, a character invented by Yeats and depicted in several early stories. For Knocknarea, Maeve, and Clooth-na-Bare (here presumably used as the name of a mountain), see Yeats's note to 'The Hosting of the Sidhe,' p. 600.

84.1: Cummen Strand is in County Sligo, on the road from Sligo to Strandhill.

84.5: a personification of Ireland, as in Yeats's play *Cathleen ni Houlihan* (1902).

84.14: for Rood, see note to 1.12.

86.1: in Arthurian legend, the Forest of Brocéliande in Brittany is the home of Merlin.

86.2–3: in Arthurian legend, Avalon is the island to which the mortally wounded Arthur is carried to be cured of his wounds. Lancelot lived on the Joyous Isle for several years with Elayne. As explained in Yeats's probable source, John Rhys's *Studies in the Arthurian Legend* (Oxford: Clarendon Press, 1891), p. 147, 'Some time after the birth of Elayne's son Galahad, she made her appearance at Arthur's court at a great festival, and her friend Dame Brysen practised her arts on Lancelot with such success, that Guinevere became so jealous of Elayne that she drove her away from the court, and that Lancelot became distraught. His madness lasted several years, until at last he chanced to come again to Corbyn, where he was recognized by Elayne and Dame Brysen. They had him bound and placed by the vessel of the Holy Grail, which restored him to his senses. Afterwards he instructed Elayne to ask her father, King Pelles, to assign them a place where they might live together. The king gave them "the Castel of Blyaunt" in "the Joyous Yle," described as enclosed in iron, with a fair water deep and large.'

86.4: Uladh, Ulster. For Naoise, see note to 20.5.

86.6: as P. W. Joyce explained in *Old Celtic Romances* (London: David Nutt, 1879), p. 309, 'The Gaelic tales abound in allusions to a beautiful country situated under the sea—an enchanted land sunk at some remote time, and still held under spell. In some romantic writings it is called *Tir-fa-Thonn,* the land beneath the waves.'

86.8: for Aengus, see note to poem 48. Given the reference in 'The Harp of Aengus' (poem 379) to 'Aengus in his tower of glass' (l.2), 'Land-of-the-Tower' may refer to Tory Island. Usually understood in Irish mythology as the site of the Tower of Conann, a king of the Fomorians, in the redaction by the Welsh writer Nennius (fl. 796) the island is associated with the Milesians and the tower is a tower of glass. See H. d'Arbois de Jubainville, *The Irish Mythological Cycle and Celtic Mythology* (1884), trans. Richard Irvine Best (Dublin: Hodges, Figgis; London: Simpkin, Marshall, 1903), p. 67.

86.9–10: an incident from the 'Adventures of the Children of the King of Norway,' which Yeats would have found in Douglas Hyde's edition and translation of *Giolla an Fhiugha or, The Lad of the Ferule [and] Eachtra Cloinne Righ na h-Ioruaidhe or, The Adventures of the Children of the King of Norway* (London: David Nutt for the Irish Texts Society, 1899), pp. 128–31.

86.11: Branwen, daughter of Llyr, is the title-character of the Second Branch of the Welsh *Mabinogi,* and wife of Matholwch, king of Ireland. One of her brothers is Manawyddan fab Lyr, probably to be identified with the Irish Manannán mac Lir. Guinevere is the wife of King Arthur.

86.12: for Niamh, see note to 40.4; for Fand, see Yeats's note to 'The Secret Rose,' p. 601. Liban (*Lí Ban,* 'Women's Beauty') is the sister of Fand, and wife of Labraid; confusion with her husband's name may have produced the spelling 'Laban.' In *Lectures on the Origin and Growth of Religion as Illustrated by Celtic Heathendom,* 2nd ed. (London: Williams and Norgate, 1892), p. 463, John Rhys notes that in some accounts 'Liban is a woman in charge of a magic well, which, when neglected by her, overwhelms her and changes her into an otter.'

86.13: another incident from the 'Adventures of the Children of the King of Norway' (pp. 118–21).

86.14: dun *(dún),* a fort.

86.18: the hunter's moon is the full moon following the harvest moon, which itself falls within a fortnight of the autumnal equinox on 22/23 September.

89: a psaltery is a stringed instrument originating in the Near East and used in Europe from the twelfth century to the late Middle Ages. Yeats had the musician Arnold Dolmetsch (1858–1940) construct a psaltery for use in his experiments in speaking verse to music.

89.14: the Three in One presumably refers to the Trinity in the Christian religion.

90.41, 45: in Christian tradition, the archangel Gabriel is usually depicted as sounding the trumpet which heralds the Last Judgment, and the archangel Michael is usually depicted as the warrior angel, the conqueror of Satan. However, in his 1910 essay on 'J. M. Synge and the Ireland of His Time,' *Essays and Introductions* (London: Macmillan, 1961), p. 316, Yeats refers to 'Saint Michael with the trumpet that calls the body to resurrection.' And in 'The Trembling of the Veil' (1922), *Autobiographies* (London: Macmillan, 1955), p. 269, Yeats notes that 'Gabriel is angel of the Moon in the Cabbala and might, I considered, command the waters at a pinch.'

The Green Helmet and Other Poems: first published by the Cuala Press in 1910. The 1912 Macmillan edition adds six poems, but four of these were later transferred to *Responsibilities*. Both the 1910 and 1912 volumes include the play *The Green Helmet*.

91: in a note to the first printing of the poem, Yeats explained that 'A few days ago I dreamed that I was steering a very gay and elaborate ship upon some narrow water with many people upon its banks, and that there was a figure upon a bed in the middle of the ship. The people were pointing to the figure and questioning, and in my dream I sang verses which faded as I awoke, all but this fragmentary thought, "We call it, it has such dignity of limb, by the sweet name of Death." I have made my poem out of my dream and the sentiment of my dream, and can almost say, as Blake did, "The Authors are in Eternity" ' (1908; VP p. 253). For the source of the Blake quotation, see Yeats's note to 'The Cap and Bells,' p. 601.

92: Homer is the most important poet in ancient Greek literature. The 'woman' is Helen, whose abduction by Paris led to the Trojan War.

94: see note to 20.4.

96: the first seven lines draw on *A King and no King* (acted 1611; printed 1619) by the English playwrights Francis Beaumont (1584–1616) and John Fletcher (1579–1625). Arbaces, king of Iberia, falls in love with his supposed sister, Panthea, who has grown to womanhood during his long absence. It is then learned that Arbaces is not the son of the former king but of the Lord Protector. Panthea is thus queen of Iberia, Arbaces is unrelated to her, and the lovers can be united.

97.2: for Homer, see note to poem 92.

99.4: the colt is presumably Pegasus, a winged horse in Greek mythology; connected with poetry through the account by Pausanias of his creation of the Fountain of Hippocrene, sacred to the Muses.

99.6: Olympus, the highest mountain on the Greek peninsula and the home of the gods in Greek mythology.

102: University College, Dublin, founded in 1854 as the Catholic University of Ireland; in 1908 it became one of the three Constituent Colleges of the National University of Ireland. The contrast is with Trinity College, Dublin, founded in 1591.

106: the Abbey Theatre in Dublin, an outgrowth of earlier theatrical enterprises, was founded by Yeats and others in 1904. The poem is based on 'Tyard, on me blasmoit, à mon commencement' by the French poet Pierre de Ronsard (1524–85), as in *Œuvres Complètes,* ed. Gustave Cohen ([Paris]: Librarie Gallimard, 1950), I, 116.

106.1: *An Craoibhín Aoibhinn* (usually translated 'the Pleasant Little Branch,' perhaps more correctly 'the Delightful Shrub'), the pen-name of Douglas Hyde.

106.11: a minor sea-god in Greek mythology, Proteus is noted for his power to take all manner of shapes.

108: the Galway races are held each summer.

Responsibilities: published by the Cuala Press in 1914, including 'The Two Kings' (poem 381) and the play *The Hour-Glass.* In *Responsibilities and Other Poems* (1916), the play is deleted but 'The man that I praise' (i.e., poem A74) added. The source of the first epigraph has not yet been traced: it may well have been written by Yeats, possibly with the assistance of Ezra Pound. The second epigraph is from the *Analects* of the Chinese sage Confucius (ca. 551–479? B.C.), Book VII, Chapter V: 'The Master said, "Extreme is my decay. For a long time I have not dreamed, as I was wont to do, that I saw the duke of Châu," ' in the translation by James Legge. Yeats (again, perhaps assisted by Pound) may have been using the edition of *Confucius et Mencius,* trans. M. G. Pauthier (Paris: Charpentier, Libraire-Éditeur, 1841), where the transliteration 'Khoung-fou-tseu' appears (p. iii). The 'duke of Châu' is Châu-kung (d. 1105 B.C.), Chinese author and statesman.

112: see Yeats's note, p. 603.

112.3: Benjamin Yeats (1750–95), Yeats's great-great-grandfather, a wholesale linen merchant.

112.5: John Yeats (1774–1846), Yeats's great-grandfather, rector of Drumcliff Church in County Sligo and friend of the Irish patriot Robert Emmet (1778–1803).

112.10: in 1773 Benjamin Yeats married Mary Butler (1751–1834), who was connected with the Irish Ormondes, the Butler family of great wealth and power that had settled in Ireland in the twelfth century. In 1835, William Butler Yeats (1806–62), Yeats's grandfather, married Jane Grace Corbet (1811–76), daughter of William Corbet (1757–1824) and Grace Armstrong Corbet (1774–1864). Both the Corbets and especially the Armstrongs had a long history of military service.

112.11–12: at the Battle of the Boyne in 1690, William III (1650–1702), who was Dutch, defeated James II (1633–1701).

112.13–14: William Middleton (ca. 1770–1832), Yeats's maternal great-grandfather, a ship-owner, merchant, and possibly smuggler. Yeats describes the incident in Biscay Bay, between Spain and France, in 'Reveries Over Childhood and Youth' (1916), *Autobiographies* (London: Macmillan, 1955), p. 36.

112.15: Wilham Pollexfen (1811–92), Yeats's maternal grandfather, a ship-owner and merchant.

112.20: Yeats was born on 13 June 1865; the poem first appeared in the Cuala Press *Responsibilities,* published on 25 May 1914.

113: the Grey Rock is *Craig Liath* in County Clare, the home in Irish fairy lore of Aoibheall. Before the Battle of Clontarf, fought against the Danes in 1014, Aoibheall offers her favourite, Dubhlaing O'Hartagan, two hundred years of pleasant life in her company if he would refrain from joining his friend Murchadh, son of King Brian Boru, in the battle. He refuses and is killed in the battle, along with Murchadh and Brian Boru. Yeats mentioned the story in early versions of his note on 'The Hosting of the Sidhe' (VP p. 802). It was available to him in numerous sources, including Nicholas O'Kearney's 'The Festivities at the House of Conan,' *Transactions of the Ossianic Society,* 2 (1855), 98–102. Aoibheall is usually depicted as a *leannán sidhe,* or fairy mistress, described by Yeats in *Fairy and Folk Tales of the Irish Peasantry* (London: Walter Scott; New York: Thomas Whittaker; Toronto: W. J. Gage, 1888), p. 81, as 'the Gaelic muse, for she gives inspiration to those she persecutes. The Gaelic poets die young, for she is restless, and will not let them remain long on earth—this malignant phantom.' Whether by changing 'Aoibheall' (spelled in various ways, such as Lady Gregory's 'Aoibhell') to 'Aoife' Yeats meant to substitute the mother of Cuchulain's son (see note to 19.2) for the fairy goddess is uncertain but improbable.

113.2: a chop-house in London, the meeting place of the Rhymers' Club, a group of poets who gathered together in the early 1890s.

113.10: Goibniu the Smith, of the *Tuatha Dé Danann,* described by H. d'Arbois de Jubainville in *The Irish Mythological Cycle and Celtic Mythology* (1884), trans. Richard Irvine Best (Dublin: Hodges, Figgis; London: Simpkin, Marshall, 1903) as 'a sort of kitchen god' (p. 174). He was renowned for his ale, which gave immortality to those who drank it.

113.15: *Sliabh na mBan* ('The Mountain of the Women'), a mountain in County Tipperary, headquarters of Bodb Derg, a king of the *Tuatha Dé Danann.*

113.62: Ernest Dowson (1867–1900) and Lionel Johnson (1867–1902), poets and members of the Rhymers' Club.

114: see Yeats's note, p. 603.

114.2–3: generic names for the people, especially the poor. *Paídín* (dim. of *Pádraig*), 'Paddy.'

114.4: quotation not yet traced. In sending this poem to Hugh Lane, Yeats explained that 'I have tried to meet the argument in Lady Ardilaun's letter to somebody' but also added 'The "correspondent" to whom the poem is addressed is of course an imaginary person' (*Letters,* ed. Allan Wade [London: Rupert Hart-Davis, 1954], p. 573). See also a letter to Lady Gregory of ca. 15 December 1912, in 'Some New Letters from W. B. Yeats to Lady Gregory,' ed. Donald T. Torchiana and Glenn O'Malley, *Review of English Studies,* 4, No. 3 (July 1963), 12: 'I have a poem in my head about Lane's Gallery and Lord Ardilaun but may not be able to write it. I will try. It is not tactless and does not name Lord Ardilaun and might help the fund.'

114.9: Ercole d'Este I (1431–1505), Duke of Ferrara, depicted in *The Book of the Courtier* (1528) by Baldassare Castiglione (1478–1529) as a patron of the arts.

114.12: Titus Maccius Plautus (ca. 254–184 B.C.), Roman playwright, much favoured by the Duke of Ferrara.

114.14: Guidobaldo di Montefeltro (1472–1508), Duke of Urbino, also highly praised in *The Book of the Courtier.*

114.20: Cosimo de Medici (1389–1464), first of the Medici family to rule Florence and a patron of the arts; exiled to Venice in 1433 but returned in triumph a year later.

114.23: Michelozzo de Bartolommeo (1396–1472), architect, accompanied Cosimo de Medici into exile and designed for him the Library in St. Mark's, Florence.

115: see Yeats's note, p. 603.

115.8: Irish patriot (1830–1907), banished from Ireland in 1874, returned in 1885, an important influence on the young Yeats.

115.17: the 'wild geese' are Irishmen who emigrated to the continent after the Treaty of Limerick (1691) and during the times of the Penal Laws (1695–1727).

115.20: Lord Edward Fitzgerald (1763–98), leader of the 1798 Rising.

115.21: Robert Emmett (1778–1803) was executed for his leadership of an abortive revolution. Wolfe Tone (1763–98) was involved in the 1798 Rising; he took his own life while under sentence of death.

116: see Yeats's note, p. 603, which identifies the friend as Lady Gregory.

117: see Yeats's note, p. 603. For Paudeen, see note to 114.2.

118: see Yeats's note, p. 603. The 'Shade' is Parnell.

118.9: discussing the opposition to Lane's proposed Gallery in a 1914 note, Yeats explained that

The first serious opposition began in the 'Irish Catholic,' the chief Dublin clerical paper, and Mr. William Murphy the organiser of the recent lock-out and Mr. Healy's financial supporter in his attack upon Parnell, a man of great influence, brought to its support a few days later his newspapers 'The Evening Herald' and 'The Irish Independent,' the most popular of Irish daily papers. He replied to my poem 'To a Wealthy Man' (I was thinking of a very different wealthy man) from what he described as 'Paudeen's point of view,' and 'Paudeen's point of view' it was. (VP pp. 819–20)

William Martin Murphy (1844–1919) supported Timothy Michael Healy (1855–1931) and organized a lock-out in opposition to the unionizing activities of James Larkin (1876–1947). In a letter published in the *Irish Times* for 18 January 1913, p. 5, Murphy suggested that 'If "Paudeen's pennies," so contemptuously poetised a few days ago in the Press by Mr. W. B. Yeats, are to be abstracted from "Paudeen's" pocket, at least give him an opportunity of saying whether he approves of the process or not.' 'To a Wealthy Man . . .' had been published in the *Irish Times* for 11 January 1913.

118.19: Parnell is buried in Glasnevin Cemetery, Dublin.

119: see note to 20.4.

120: see Yeats's note on poems 114–18, p. 603.

120.4: Don Juan, legendary hero of numerous literary and musical works, sentenced to hell for his libertine activities.

121.5: *líbín* is a term for the minnow *(Phoxinus phoxinus)*, and *lón* means 'provision, food, fare,' so *líbín-lón* could be intended as a calque on 'minnow-fare,' although the attempt violates Irish syntax and Irish grammar. Dinneen's *Irish-English Dictionary* offers *líbín leamhan* as meaning 'a minnow,' but this is attested nowhere else and it is difficult to know how Dinneen would analyze its literal sense ('moth minnow'?).

121.6: a small town in County Galway.

121.8: Guaire Aidne (d. 663), king of Connacht, celebrated for his generosity.

124.1: there are many places throughout Ireland called 'Windy Gap' *(Bearna na Gaoithe)*. The reference here may be to the one opposite Carraroe Church in County Sligo, although in one of the manuscripts of *The Speckled Bird* Yeats writes that 'There is among the hills to the south of Galway Bay, a valley called in Irish "Gleann-na-Gae" and in English "Windy Gap," which is a translation of the Irish name. . . .' See *The Speckled Bird: With Variant Versions,* ed. William H. O'Donnell (Toronto: McClelland and Stewart, [1977]), p. 141.

124.9: 'skelping' is a dialect word meaning 'striking,' 'slapping,' or 'beating.'

125.4: Cruachan, in County Roscommon, the ancient capital of Connacht.

125.8: the Maini are usually understood as the children of Maeve and Ailill, queen and king of Connacht in Irish mythology. As explained by John Rhys in *Lectures on the Origin and Growth of Religion as Illustrated by Celtic Heathendom,* 2nd ed. (London: Williams and Norgate, 1892), pp. 366–70, the Maini traditionally number either seven or eight.

125.25: a cave near Cruachan, fabled as the mouth of the underworld.

125.50: see note to 113.10.

125.58: 24 June, the feast of the nativity of St. John the Baptist and about the time of the summer solstice.

125.86: in the Christian religion, Easter is the annual celebration of the resurrection of Christ; the date varies between 22 March and 25 April.

125.98, 100: see note to 90.41.

126: *The Player Queen* was first produced in 1919 and first published in 1922.

129.5: a mountain near the County Dublin border.

130.4: According to the *Fama Fraternitatis* (1614) of Johann Valentin Andreae (1586–1654), Christian Rosenkreuz (1378–?) was the founder of the Fraternity of the Rosy Cross; many years after his death, his body was discovered undecayed in his tomb. Rosicrucian materials were used in the Order of the Golden Dawn, the occult society to which Yeats belonged for much of his life.

139: see Yeats's note on 'The Dolls,' p. 604. For the Magi, see note to 67.9.

139.7: Christ was crucified on Calvary, outside the wall of Jerusalem.

140: see Yeats's note, p. 604.

142.6: from the Epilogue to *Poetaster* (produced 1601; published 1602) by the English playwright Ben Jonson (1572–1637), also printed as 'An Ode to Himself' in *Underwoods* (1640): 'Leave me. There's something come into my thought / That must and shall be sung high and aloof, / Safe from the wolf's black jaw, and the dull ass's hoof.'

142.7: *Coill na gCnó,* 'The Wood of Nuts,' one of the Seven Woods of Coole.

The Wild Swans at Coole: first published by the Cuala Press in 1917, the volume including the play *At the Hawk's Well.* For the 1919 Macmillan edition, the play was deleted and seventeen additional poems included. In the later edition Yeats explained that

> This book is, in part, a reprint of *The Wild Swans at Coole,* printed a year ago on my sister's hand-press at Dundrum, Co. Dublin. I have not, however, reprinted a play which may be part of a book of new plays suggested by the dance plays of Japan, and I have added a number of new poems. Michael Robartes and John Aherne, whose names occur in one or other of these, are characters in some stories I wrote years ago, who have once again become a part of the phantasmagoria through which I can alone express my convictions about the world. I have the fancy that I read the name John Aherne among those of men prosecuted for making a disturbance at the first production of 'The Play Boy,' which may account for his animosity to myself. (VP p. 852)

> The Dun Emer, later Cuala, Press, was founded in 1903 by Elizabeth Corbet ('Lollie') Yeats (1868–1940). *At the Hawk's Well* and other plays influenced by the Japanese Nōh drama were published in *Four Plays for Dancers* (1921). For Robartes and Aherne, see Yeats's note, p. 604. The Dublin newspapers do not list a 'John Aherne' ('Owen Aherne' in the early stories) as among those prosecuted for the riots at the first performances of Synge's *The Playboy of the Western World* (see Yeats's note, p. 603). Coole Park was the estate of Lady Gregory in County Galway.

144: Robert Gregory (1881–1918) was Lady Gregory's only child. Yeats included the following note to the first printing of the poem: '(Major Robert Gregory, R.F.C. [Royal Flying Corps], M.C. [Military Cross], Legion of Honour, was killed in action on the Italian Front, January 23, 1918).' (VP p. 323)

144.1: see Yeats's note on 'The Tower,' p. 605.

144.17: see note to 113.62.

144.25: John Millington Synge (1871–1909), Irish playwright and friend of Yeats.

144.33: George Pollexfen (1839–1910), a maternal uncle of Yeats.

144.34: Mayo, a county in Ireland.

144.39: astrological terms for heavenly bodies that are separated by 180°, 90°, and 120°, respectively. Pollexfen was a student of astrology.

144.47: Sir Philip Sidney (1554–86), English writer, statesman, and soldier.

144.58: Castle Taylor, in County Galway, home of the Taylor family. Rox-
borough, in County Galway, the childhood home of Lady Gregory.

144.59: Esserkelly, near Ardrahan, County Galway.

144.60: Moneen, adjoining Esserkelly.

144.66: Clare, a county in Ireland.

145.5: the cross-roads in Kiltartan, a barony near Coole Park.

146.2: in Greek mythology, the Tritons are mermen.

148.4: presumably a descendant of Billy Byrne of Ballymanus, a Wicklow
hero in the 1798 Rising executed in July of that year.

148.8: Glendalough (*Gleann Da Loch,* 'The Valley of Two Lakes'), near
Laragh in County Wicklow; renowned for its round tower, it is the site
of a monastic centre founded by St. Kevin (d. 618).

148.9: the most famous member of the O'Byrnes of Wicklow was Fiach
MacHugh O'Byrne (ca. 1544–97), who fought against the English until
his execution by the forces of Sir William Russell.

149: several books of the Old Testament are traditionally ascribed to
Solomon (ca. 972–ca. 932 B.C.), king of the Hebrews. The visit of the
queen of Sheba (an area in Arabia) to Solomon is described in I Kings
10.1–13. Yeats may also draw on Arabic traditions about Solomon and
Sheba.

152.11: for the cherubim of the prophet Ezekiel (fl. 592 B.C.), see especially
Ezek. 10.1–22.

152.12: Jacques Firmin Beauvarlet (1731–97), French painter and
engraver.

152.18: Walter Savage Landor (1775–1864), John Donne (1571 or
1572–1631), English authors.

154.12: Gaius Valerius Catullus (84?–54? B.C.), Roman poet.

155: apparently Tom O'Roughley is an invented character. Roughley is a
promontory north of Sligo.

155.13: for Michael, see note to 90.41.

156.97: see Yeats's note, p. 604.

157.7: in Greek mythology, the Centaurs are usually depicted as having the
upper part of a human body and the four-legged body of a horse.

158.3–4: *Emain Macha* ('The Twins of Macha'), the capital of Ulster in
Irish mythology. Identified with a hill called Navan Fort two miles from
the centre of the town of Armagh (*Ard Macha,* 'Macha's Height'), it
may well be that the two hills—Armagh and Navan Fort—together con-
stituted 'The Twins of Macha.' Macha was a horse-goddess who bore
twins on the site, according to *Noinden Ulad* ('The Debility of the
Ulstermen'). The story of her measuring with the pin of a brooch is spu-
rious, based on a folk-etymology of *Emain* as *eó maín,* 'precious pin.'
Yeats found it in Standish James O'Grady's *History of Ireland: Critical
and Philosophical,* Vol. I (London: Sampson Low; Dublin: E. Ponsonby,
1881), 181: 'with the spear of her brooch she marked on the plain the
circuit of the city of Emain Macha.'

158.6: See note to 218.II.4.

158.10–12: in classical mythology, Helios, the sun-god, is often conceived
as driving a chariot across the sky each day, from east to west.

159.11–16: for Solomon and Sheba, see note to poem 149. Solomon was renowned for his wisdom.

159.30: the pestle is a traditional symbol of fertility and birth. It is associated, for example, with the Roman god Pilumnus and the Hindu goddess Soma (a deity of the moon).

160.4: Connemara, an area in County Galway.

163.11: the 'long war' is presumably World War I.

164.9–13: for Ferrara and Urbino, see notes to 114.9 and 114.14. The duchess is Elisabetta Gonzaga (1471–1526), Duchess of Urbino.

165.4: Leda. See poem 220.

165.9: Gaby Deslys (1884–1920), French actress and dancer.

165.10: Ruth St. Denis (1878–1968), American dancer.

165.11: Anna Matveyevna Pavlova (1885–1931), Russian ballerina.

165.12–13: probably Julia Marlowe (1866–1950), born in England but raised in America, well known for her roles in Shakespeare's plays, as in *Romeo and Juliet.*

166: Sextus Propertius (ca. 50–ca. 16 B.C.), Roman poet. The poem is loosely based on the second poem of Book II (ca. 26 B.C.).

166.6: in Greek mythology, the Olympian goddess of wisdom, patron of the arts of peace, ruler of storms, and a guardian of cities; usually understood as a virgin goddess.

166.7: for centaur, see note to 157.7.

171: see note to 142.7.

173: Alfred Pollexfen (1854–1916), the youngest of Yeats's maternal uncles.

173.2–4: William Pollexfen (1811–92) and Elizabeth Middleton Pollexfen (1819–92), Yeats's maternal grandparents. William died six weeks after the death of Elizabeth.

173.8–10: George Pollexfen (1839–1910) had been a member of the Freemasons, a secret fraternal order. Describing the funeral in a letter to Lady Gregory, Yeats noted that 'The Masons (there were 80 of them) had their own service and one by one threw acacia leaves into the grave with the traditional Masonic goodbye "Alas my brother so mote it be" ' (*Letters,* ed. Allan Wade [London: Rupert Hart-Davis, 1954], p. 553). Acacia is a woody shrub or tree of the mimosa family.

173.15: a street and school in Sligo.

173.17: John Pollexfen (1845–1900), who died and was buried in Liverpool.

173.24–31: Alfred Pollexfen returned to Sligo from Liverpool in 1910, to take the place of his brother George in the family firm of W. & G. T. Pollexfen and Company.

174.8: Petronius Arbiter (1st century A.D.), Roman writer.

176.7: Pietro Longhi (1702–62), Italian painter.

179.4–6: for Diarmuid and Grania, see note to poem 23.

179.8: Giorgione (ca. 1478–1510), Venetian painter.

179.9: Achilles, in Greek mythology the son of Peleus and Thetis, kills Hector in the Trojan War. Tamerlane, also Timur (ca. 1336–1405), Mongol conqueror. Babar, popular name of Zahir-ud-din-Mohammed

(1480–1530), founder of the Mogul empire of India. Barhaim is apparently an error for Bahram, who appears in stanza 17 of Edward FitzGerald's translation of the *Rubáiyát of Omar Khayyám* (London: Bernard Quaritch, 1859), p. 4, as a 'great Hunter.' In his notes, FitzGerald glosses 'Bahrám Gur—*Bahrám of the Wild Ass,* from his fame in hunting it—a Sassanian Sovereign, had also his Seven Castles (like the King of Bohemia!) each of a different Colour . . .' (p. 20). Bahram was king of Persia from 420–30. As Sir Percy Sykes explains in *A History of Persia* (London: Macmillan, 1930), I, 431, 'Persian legend represents him as placing the crown between two raging lions, and when . . . his cousin, who was the choice of the nobles, declined to make the attempt, Bahram, with the courage which was so conspicuous throughout his career, attempted to take possession of it and succeeded.'

181: The title is from the *Vita Nuova* (ca. 1292–93) of the Italian writer Dante Alighieri (1265–1321), which Yeats read in the translation by Dante Gabriel Rossetti (1818–82), first published in 1861. Dante recounts the vision of 'a lord of terrible aspect to such as should gaze upon him, but who seemed therewithal to rejoice inwardly that it was a marvel to see. Speaking he said many things, among the which I could understand but few; and of these, this: *Ego dominus tuus.*' Rossetti translates the phrase 'I am thy master' (*The New Life [La Vita Nuova] of Dante Alighieri,* trans. Dante Gabriel Rossetti [London: Ellis and Elvey, 1900], p. 28).

181.1: the speakers' names are Latin pronouns for 'this' and 'that.' Used in combination, *hic* usually refers to 'the latter' and *ille* to 'the former,' though the meanings are sometimes reversed.

181.4: for Michael Robartes, see Yeats's note, p. 604.

181.22: Jesus Christ, son of God in the Christian religion.

181.26: Guido Cavalcanti (ca. 1230–1300) and probably Lapo Gainni (ca. 1270–ca. 1330), poets and friends of Dante.

181.29: Bedouin, Arabic for 'tent dwellers,' nomad peoples of interior Arabia.

181.37: Beatrice, Dante's beloved, probably Beatrice Portinari (1266–90).

181.52: John Keats (1795–1821), English poet.

182: see note to poem 144.

182.4: Galilee, a region in Palestine associated with the life of Christ.

182.10–11: 'Sinbad the Sailor' is one of the tales in the *Arabian Nights' Entertainment,* a collection of Arabic stories translated into English in the nineteenth century, most notably by Sir Richard Burton in 1885–88. Sinbad's ship is wrecked against a loadstone mountain on his sixth voyage.

182.16: a long narrow sea between Africa and Arabia.

183: see Yeats's note, p. 604.

183.4: Connemara, an area in County Galway.

183.15: title character of 'Il Penseroso' (1632) by the English poet John Milton (1608–74).

183.16: title character of 'Prince Athanase' (1817) by the English poet Percy Bysshe Shelley (1792–1822).

183.17: 'The Lonely Tower,' an engraving used to illustrate 'Il Penseroso' in *The Shorter Poems of Milton* (London: Seeley, 1889) by the English artist Samuel Palmer (1805–81).

183.27: Walter Pater (1839–94), English writer and critic.

183.28: the death of Robartes is alluded to in 'The Adoration of the Magi' (1897).

183.45: for Athena, see note to 166.6; for Achilles, see note to 179.9. Yeats refers to the *Iliad*, I, 197 and XXII, 330.

183.46: Hector, eldest son of Priam and Hecuba, is killed by Achilles in the Trojan War. Friedrich Nietzsche (1844–1900), German philosopher.

183.67: Mt. Sinai, on the Sinai peninsula between the Mediterranean and the Red Sea; in the Bible, the place where Moses receives the Ten Commandments.

184.5: a cat belonging to Yeats's close friend Maud Gonne (1866–1953).

185.4: Caesar, a title given to the Roman emperor.

185.10: Alexander the Great (356–323 B.C.), king of Macedonia and conqueror of much of Asia.

185.11: Gaius Julius Caesar Octavianus (63 B.C.–A.D. 14), first Roman emperor.

185.12: Alcibiades (ca. 450–404 B.C.), Athenian statesman and general.

186.6: in the Christian religion, Providence is the foreknowing and beneficent care and government of God.

188: see Yeats's note, p. 604.

188.1: Rock of Cashel, County Tipperary, ancient site of the kings of Munster; noted for its ecclesiastical ruins, particularly the chapel constructed between 1127 and 1134 by Cormac Mac Carrthaig (d. 1138).

188.18: in Greek mythology, a sphinx has typically the body of a lion; wings; and the head and bust of a woman. Originally a monster, in later Greek art the sphinx becomes an enigmatic messenger of the gods.

188.19: Gautama Siddhartha, known as the Buddha, 'the enlightened one' (ca. 563–ca. 483 B.C.), Indian philosopher, founder of Buddhism.

188.56: Helen of Troy. See note to 20.4.

Michael Robartes and the Dancer: first published by the Cuala Press in 1921. In the Preface to that edition Yeats explained that

A few of these poems may be difficult to understand, perhaps more difficult than I know. Goethe has said that the poet needs all philosophy, but that he must keep it out of his work. After the first few poems I came into possession of Michael Robartes' exposition of the *Speculum Angelorum et Hominum* of Geraldus, and in the excitement of arranging and editing could no more keep out philosophy than could Goethe himself at certain periods of his life. I have tried to make understanding easy by a couple of notes, which are at any rate much shorter than those Dante wrote on certain of his odes in the *Convito*, but I may not have succeeded. It is hard for a writer, who has spent so much labour upon his style, to remember that thought, which seems to him natural and logical like that style, may be unintelligible to others. The first excitement over, and the thought changed into settled conviction, his interest in simple, that is to say normal emotion, is always I think increased; he is no longer looking for candlestick and matches but at the objects in the room.

I have given no account of Robartes himself, nor of his discovery of the explanation of Geraldus' diagrams and pictures in the traditional knowledge of a certain obscure Arab tribe, for I hope that my selection from the great mass of his letters and table talk, which I owe to his friend John Aherne, may be published before, or at any rate but soon after this little book, which, like all hand-printed books will take a long time for the setting up and printing off and for the drying of the pages. (VP p. 853)

The allusion to Goethe probably refers to some remarks in his *Conversations with Eckermann*, especially 'Schiller's *Wallenstein* is so great that there is nothing else like it of the same sort; yet you will find that even these two powerful helpers—history and philosophy—have injured parts of the work, and hinder a purely poetical success' (23 July 1827); and 'I have always kept myself free from philosophy' (4 February 1829). In the 'Introduction by Owen Aherne' to the first edition of *A Vision* (1925), Aherne tells of the discovery by Michael Robartes of the *Speculum Angelorum et Hominum* ('Mirror of Angels and Men'; incorrectly *Hominorum* in *A Vision*) by one Giraldus; the meaning of the diagrams in the book were explained to Robartes by a tribe of Judwalis ('diagrammatists,' an invented name). Dante's *Il Convito* was written ca. 1304–07. See also Yeats's note, p. 604.

189: see Yeats's note, p. 604.
189.19: for Athena, see note to 166.6.
189.26: Paolo Veronese (1528–88), Italian painter.
189.32–33: Michelangelo Buonarroti (1475–1564), Italian artist. He painted the ceiling of the Sistine Chapel in Rome in 1508–12. *Morning* (more usually *The Dawn*) and *Night* are statues in the Medici Chapel in Florence.
189.39–40: presumably an allusion to Christ's Last Supper (see Luke 22.14–20).
190: for Solomon and Sheba, see note to poem 149.
190.11: in Christian theology, the Fall of Man occurs when Adam and Eve partake of the forbidden fruit of knowledge of good and evil (traditionally imaged as an apple).
191: Yeats's 1921 note draws on the fictional correspondence between Michael Robartes and Owen Aherne:

Robartes writes to Aherne under the date May 12th, 1917. 'I found among the Judwalis much biographical detail, probably legendary, about Kustaben-Luki. He saw occasionally during sleep a woman's face and later on found in a Persian painting a face resembling, though not identical with the dream-face, which was he considered that of a woman loved in another life. Presently he met & loved a beautiful woman whose face also resembled, without being identical, that of his dream. Later on he made a long journey to purchase the painting which was, he said, the better likeness, and found on his return that his mistress had left him in a fit of jealousy.' In a dialogue and in letters, Robartes gives a classification and analysis of dreams which explain the survival of this story among the followers of Kusta-ben-Luki. They distinguished between the memory of concrete images and the abstract memory, and affirm that no concrete dream-image is ever from our memory. This is not only true they say of dreams, but of those visions seen between sleeping and waking. This doctrine at first found me incredulous, for I thought it contradicted by my experience and by all I have read, not however a very great amount, in books of psychology and of psychoanalysis. Did I not frequently dream of some friend, or relation, or that I was at school? I found, however, when I studied my dreams, as I was directed in a dialogue, that the image seen was never really that of friend, or relation, or my old school, though it might very closely resemble it. A substitution had taken place, often a very strange one, though I forgot this if I did not notice it at once on waking. The name of some friend, or the conceptions 'my father' and 'at school,' are a part of the abstract memory and therefore of the dream life, but the image of my father, or my friend, or my old school, being a part of the personal concrete memory appeared neither in sleep nor in visions between sleep and waking. I found sometimes that my father, or my friend, had been represented in sleep by a stool or a chair, and I concluded that it was the entire absence of my personal concrete memory that enabled me to accept such images without surprise. Was it not perhaps this very absence that constituted sleep? Would I perhaps awake if a single concrete image from my memory came before me? Even these images—stool, chair, etc. were never any particular stool, chair, etc. that I had known. Were these images, however, from the buried memory? had they floated up from the subconscious? had I seen them perhaps a long time ago and forgotten having done so? Even if that were so, the exclusion of the conscious memory was a new, perhaps important truth; but Robartes denied their source even in the subconscious. It seems a corroboration that though I often see between sleep and waking elaborate landscape, I have never seen one that seemed a possible representation of any place I have ever lived near from childhood up. Robartes traces these substitute images to different sources. Those that come in sleep are (1) from the state immediately preceding our birth; (2) from the *Spiritus Mundi*—that is to say, from a general storehouse of images which have ceased to be a property of any personality or spirit. Those that come between sleeping and waking are, he says, re-shaped by what he calls the 'automatic faculty' which can create pattern, balance, etc. from the impressions made upon the senses, not of ourselves, but of others bound to us by certain emotional links though perhaps entire strangers, and preserved in a kind of impersonal mirror, often simply called the 'record,' which takes much the same place in his system the lower strata of the astral light does among the disciples of Elephas Levi. This does not exhaust the contents of dreams for we have to account also for certain sentences, for certain ideas which are not concrete images and yet do not arise from our personal memory, but at the moment I have merely to account for certain images that affect passion or affection. Robartes writes to Aherne in a letter dated May 15th, 1917: 'No lover, no husband has ever met in dreams the true image of wife or mistress. She who has perhaps filled his whole life with joy or disquiet cannot enter there. Her image can fill every moment of his waking life but only its counterfeit comes to him in sleep; and he who classifies these counterfeits will find that just in so far as they become concrete, sensuous, they are distinct individuals; never types but individuals. They are the forms of those whom he has loved in some past earthly life, chosen from *Spiritus Mundi* by the subconscious will, and through them, for they are not always hollow shades, the dead at whiles outface a living rival.' They are the forms of Over Shadowers as they are called. All violent passion has to be expiated or atoned, by one in life, by one in the state between life and life, because, as the Judwalis believe, there is always deceit or cruelty; but it is only in sleep that we can see these forms of those who as spirits may influence all our waking thought. Souls that are once linked by emotion never cease till the last drop of that emotion is exhausted—call it desire, hate or what you will—to affect one another, remaining always as it were in contact. Those whose past passions are unatoned seldom love living man or woman but only those loved long ago, of whom the living man or woman is but a brief symbol forgotten when some phase of some atonement is finished; but because in general the form does not pass into the memory, it is the moral being of the dead that is symbolised. Under certain circumstances, which are precisely described, the form indirectly, and not necessarily from dreams, enters the living memory; the subconscious will, as in Kusta-ben-Luki in the story, selects among pictures, or other ideal representations, some form that resembles what was once the physical body of the Over Shadower, and this ideal form becomes to the living man an obsession, continually perplexing and frustrating natural instinct. It is therefore only after full atonement or expiation, perhaps after many lives, that a natural deep satisfying love becomes possible, and this love, in all subjective natures, must precede the Beatific Vision.

When I wrote An Image from a Past Life, I had merely begun my study of the various papers upon the subject, but I do not think I misstated Robartes' thought in permitting the woman and not the man to see the Over Shadower or Ideal Form, whichever it was. No mind's contents are necessarily shut off from another, and in moments of excitement images pass from one mind to another with extraordinary ease, perhaps most easily from that portion of the mind which for the time being is outside consciousness. I use the word 'pass' because it is familiar, not because I believe any movement in space to be necessary. The second mind sees what the first has already seen, that is all. (VP pp. 821–23)

For Judwalis, see note above to *Michael Robartes and the Dancer*. Ḳusṭā ben Lūḳā (d. ca. 912–13) was an Arabian doctor and translator. Éliphas Lévi Zahed was the pseudonym of Alphonse Louis Constant (1810?–75), a French occultist. Yeats wrote 'An Image from a Past Life' in 1919.

192.7–9: presumably William Pollexfen (1811–92), Yeats's maternal grandfather; William Middleton (1820–82), Yeats's maternal great-uncle; the Reverend William Butler Yeats (1806–62), Yeats's paternal grandfather.

192.12: Sligo, a town in northwestern Ireland, the home of Yeats's maternal grandparents; Yeats spent much of his childhood there.

193: on 24 April 1916, the day after Easter Sunday, an Irish Republic was proclaimed, and a force of approximately 700 Irish Volunteers occupied parts of Dublin. The rebellion was suppressed by the British forces, the final surrender occurring on 29 April 1916.

193.17: presumably Constance Gore-Booth (1868–1927), whom Yeats had known since the 1890s. In 1900 she married Count Casimir Joseph Dunin-Markiewicz (1874–1932).

193.24–25: presumably Patrick Pearse (1879–1916), Irish writer and founder of St. Enda's School in County Dublin; for the horse, see note to 99.4.

193.26: presumably Thomas MacDonagh (1878–1916), Irish writer.

193.31: presumably Major John MacBride (1865–1916), Irish revolutionary and the estranged husband of Maud Gonne.

193.68–69: Home Rule for Ireland had passed into law in September 1914 but had been simultaneously suspended for the duration of World War I, the English government promising to implement it thereafter.

193.76: James Connolly (1868–1916), military commander of the Irish forces during the rebellion.

194: fifteen of the leaders of the Easter Rebellion were executed by the English from 3–12 May 1916. To their number Yeats has apparently added Sir Roger Casement (1864–1916), executed on 3 August 1916 by the English for attempting to bring arms to Ireland from Germany.

194.10: see note to 193.24.

194.12: see note to 193.26.

194.16: Lord Edward Fitzgerald (1763–98) and Wolfe Tone (1763–98), two of the leaders of the 1798 Rising.

195.2: see note to 193.24 and to 193.76.

195.4: for the Rose as a symbol of Ireland, see note to poem 17.

196: presumably Countess Markiewicz (see note to 193.17).

196.14: a mountain north of the town of Sligo.

197.6: a mountain in Boeotia, in Greek mythology sacred to the Muses.

198.5: probably *Sruth-in-aghaidh-an-aird* ('the stream against the height'), which falls from the slope of Ben Bulben into Glencar Lake near Sligo.

198.23: the stag is a common image in Arthurian legend, a group of tales about a mythical early king of Britain (probably loosely based on a chieftain or general named Arthur of the 5th–6th centuries). Yeats referred to 'the white stag that flits in and out of the tales of Arthur' in *The Celtic Twilight* (London: A. H. Bullen, 1902), p. 109. Mrs. Yeats claimed (*New Commentary*, p. 198) that the source was the white stag in Malory's *Le Morte d'Arthur* which appears at the wedding feast of Arthur and Guinevere and is hunted and killed by Sir Gawain; but there is also a white stag hunted and killed by Arthur in 'Geraint the Son of Erbin' in *The Mabinogion*, trans. Lady Charlotte Guest (London: Bernard Quaritch, 1877), pp. 141–84.

199.5: 'to pern' is to move with a circular, spinning motion; cf. Yeats's note on 'unpacks the loaded pern,' p. 604. For gyre, see note to poem 200.

199.10: a portrait of Luke Wadding (1588–1657), an Irish Franciscan, by the Spanish painter José Ribera (1588–1652).

199.11: portraits of prominent members of the Butler family. Cf. note to 112.10.

199.13: Sir Thomas Wentworth, 1st Earl of Strafford (1593–1641) and Lord Deputy of Ireland from 1632/33–40.

199.17: the National Gallery in Dublin, the location of the above portraits.

199.23: presumably the lake in St. Stephen's Green in Dublin, near the National Gallery.

199.44: the territory of upper Egypt, belonging to the Egyptian Thebes.

199.45: Lake Mareotis, south of Alexandria.

199.46: St. Anthony of Egypt (251?–ca. 350), a founder of Christian monasticism, lived much of his life in the desert near Thebes.

199.50: Caesar was a title given to the Roman emperor, stemming from the cognomen of Gaius Julius Caesar (100–44 B.C.).

200: Yeats's 1921 note draws on the fictional correspondence between Michael Robartes and Owen Aherne:

> Robartes copied out and gave to Aherne several mathematical diagrams from the *Speculum,* squares and spheres, cones made up of revolving gyres intersecting each other at various angles, figures sometimes of great complexity. His explanation of these, obtained invariably from the followers of Kusta-ben-Luki, is founded upon a single fundamental thought. The mind, whether expressed in history or in the individual life, has a precise movement, which can be quickened or slackened but cannot be fundamentally altered, and this movement can be expressed by a mathematical form. A plant or an animal has an order of development peculiar to it, a bamboo will not develop evenly like a willow, nor a willow from joint to joint, and both have branches, that lessen and grow more light as they rise, and no characteristic of the soil can alter these things. A poor soil may indeed check or stop the movement and a rich prolong and quicken it. Mendel has shown that his sweet-peas bred long and short, white and pink varieties in certain mathematical proportions, suggesting a mathematical law governing the transmission of parental characteristics. To the Judwalis, as interpreted by Michael Robartes, all living mind has likewise a fundamental mathematical movement, however adapted in plant, or animal, or man to particular circumstance; and when you have found this movement and calculated its relations, you can foretell the entire future of that mind. A supreme religious act of their faith is to fix the attention on the mathematical form of this movement until the whole past and future of humanity, or of an individual man, shall be present to the intellect as if it were accomplished in a single moment. The intensity of the Beatific Vision when it comes depends upon the intensity of this realisation. It is possible in this way, seeing that death is itself marked upon the mathematical figure, which passes beyond it, to follow the soul into the highest heaven and the deepest hell. This doctrine is, they contend, not fatalistic because the mathematical figure is an expression of the mind's desire, and the more rapid the development of the figure the greater the freedom of the soul. The figure while the soul is in the body, or suffering from the consequences of that life, is frequently drawn as a double cone, the narrow end of each cone being in the centre of the broad end of the other.

It had its origin from a straight line which represents, now time, now emotion, now subjective life, and a plane at right angles to this line which represents, now space, now intellect, now objective life; while it is marked out by two gyres which represent the conflict, as it were, of plane and line, by two movements, which circle about a centre because a movement outward on the plane is checked by and in turn checks a movement onward upon the line; & the circling is always narrowing or spreading, because one movement or other is always the stronger. In other words, the human soul is always moving outward into the objective world or inward into itself; & this movement is double because the human soul would not be conscious were it not suspended between contraries, the greater the contrast the more intense the consciousness. The man, in whom the movement inward is stronger than the movement outward, the man who sees all reflected within himself, the subjective man, reaches the narrow end of a gyre at death, for death is always, they contend, even when it seems the result of accident, preceded by an intensification of the subjective life; and has a moment of revelation immediately after death, a revelation which they describe as his being carried into the presence of all his dead kindred, a moment whose objectivity is exactly equal to the subjectivity of death. The objective man on the other hand, whose gyre moves outward, receives at this moment the revelation, not of himself seen from within, for that is impossible to objective man, but of himself as if he were somebody else. This figure is true also of history, for the end of an age, which always receives the revelation of the character of the next age, is represented by the coming of one gyre to its place of greatest expansion and of the other to that of its greatest contraction. At the present moment the life gyre is sweeping outward, unlike that before the birth of Christ which was narrowing, and has almost reached its greatest expansion. The revelaion which approaches will however take its character from the contrary movement of the interior gyre. All our scientific, democratic, fact-accumulating, heterogeneous civilization belongs to the outward gyre and prepares not the continuance of itself but the revelation as in a lightning flash, though in a flash that will not strike only in one place, and will for a time be constantly repeated, of the civilization that must slowly take its place. This is too simple a statement, for much detail is possible. There are certain points of stress on outer and inner gyre, a division of each, now into ten, now into twenty-eight, stages or phases. However in the exposition of this detail so far as it affects the future, Robartes had little help from the Judwalis either because they cannot grasp events outside their experience, or because certain studies seem to them unlucky. ' "For a time the power" they have said to me,' (writes Robartes) ' "will be with us, who are as like one another as the grains of sand, but when the revelation comes it will not come to the poor but to the great and learned and establish again for two thousand years prince & vizier. Why should we resist? Have not our wise men marked it upon the sand, and it is because of these marks, made generation after generation by the old for the young, that we are named Judwalis." '

Their name means makers of measures, or as we would say, of diagrams.

(VP pp. 823–25)

For most of the allusions in this passage, see note to *Michael Robartes and the Dancer;* for Ḵusṭā ben Lūḵā, see note to poem 191. The Austrian scientist Gregor Johann Mendel (1822–84) formulated laws governing the inheritance of certain characteristics.

In Christian tradition, the Second Coming is the return of Christ at the apocalypse (Matt. 24, esp. 31–46).

200.12: see note to poem 191, where *Spiritus Mundi* is described as 'a general storehouse of images which have ceased to be a property of any personality or spirit.'

200.22: a town near Jerusalem, the birthplace of Christ in Christian tradition.

201: Anne Butler Yeats, born 26 February 1919.

201.4: the poem is set at Thoor Ballylee (see Yeats's note, p. 605), near the estate of Lady Gregory.

201.6: the Atlantic Ocean, to the west of Thoor Ballylee.

201.27: in Greek art, Aphrodite, goddess of love, beauty, and fertility, is often depicted being born out of the sea.

201.29: in Homer, Aphrodite is married to Hephaestus, god of fire and especially the smithy fire, usually depicted as lame.

201.32: in Greek mythology, the horns of Amalthea, the goat that nursed Zeus, flowed with nectar and ambrosia; one of them broke off and was filled with fruits and given to Zeus. The cornucopia thus became a symbol of plenty.

203: see Yeats's note on 'The Tower,' p. 605.

203.3: Gort is a village in Galway, near Thoor Ballylee.

203.4: Yeats had married Bertha Georgie Hyde-Lees (1892–1968) on 20 October 1917.

The Tower: first published in 1928, the collection including 'The Gift of Harun Al-Rashid' but not 'Fragments,' which was added in the *Collected Poems* (1933). In 1933 Yeats also changed the order of the poems and substituted 'The Fool by the Roadside' for 'The Hero, the Girl, and the Fool.'

204: the ancient city of Byzantium was rebuilt as Constantinople by the Roman emperor Constantine I (287?–337). Yeats discusses the city at some length in *A Vision.*

204.19: for 'perne in a gyre,' see note to 199.5.

204.27–29: see Yeats's note, p. 605.

205: see Yeats's note, p. 605, for the allusions not glossed below.

205.9: see note to 196.14.

205.11: in Greek mythology, the nine Muses are the patrons of arts and sciences.

205.48: Cloone Bog is in County Galway, near Gort.

205.52: by tradition, the epic poet Homer was blind.

205.53: see note to 20.4.

205.65: a bawn (*bán*) is a pasture or a yard (sometimes fortified).

205.85: Yeats discusses the 'Great Memory passing on from generation to generation,' essentially a repository of archetypal images, in the 'Anima Mundi' section of *Per Amica Silentia Lunae* (see *Later Essays*, ed. William H. O'Donnell [New York: Scribner, 1994], pp. 16–32).

205.132: Edmund Burke (1729–97), political writer; Henry Grattan (1746–1820), political leader.

205.156: presumably a Paradise beyond the moon and thus timeless.

205.181: although 'make my soul' is usually glossed as an Irish expression meaning 'prepare for death,' Yeats also used it in a wider sense, as in an 1891 letter to Katharine Tynan: 'We shall help good people to "make their souls" quite as much as any of your *Irish Monthly* writers' (*Letters,* p. 174).

206: the Irish Civil War was fought in 1922–23 between the Free State Government and the Republicans, the latter not accepting the terms of the Anglo-Irish Treaty, which had been signed in London on 6 December 1921 and accepted by the Irish parliament on 7 January 1922. For the allusions not glossed below, see Yeats's note, p. 606.

206.9: see note to poem 92.

206.27: in Roman mythology, Juno is queen of the gods and a protector of women.

207.1: the poem is set at Thoor Ballylee (see Yeats's note to 'The Tower,' p. 605).

207.14: see note to 183.15.

208.2: Junzo Sato presented Yeats with a ceremonial Japanese sword in March 1920.

208.8: the English poet Geoffrey Chaucer was born ca. 1340.

208.32: for Juno, see note to 206.27. As a symbol of immortality, the peacock was sacred to Juno. No source has yet been traced for Yeats's reference in *A Vision* (London: T. Werner Laurie, 1925), p. 180, to the peacock's scream symbolizing the end of a civilization.

209.3: Anne Yeats (b. 26 Feb. 1919) and Michael Butler Yeats (b. 22 August 1921).

209.17: in Ptolemaic astronomy, the Primum Mobile is the outermost concentric sphere, carrying the spheres of the fixed stars and the planets in its daily revolution.

209.21: presumably Lady Gregory (1852–1932).

209.22: presumably George Yeats (see note to 203.4).

210.1: the Irregulars were members of the Irish Republican Army.

210.2: Falstaff is a comic character in several plays by William Shakespeare.

210.6: members of the army of the Free State Government.

213: during the course of 1919, armed conflicts between the English-controlled government of Ireland and the Irish Republican Army became more frequent.

213.6: probably the olive-wood statue of Athena Polias in the Erechtheum, one of the central buildings (constructed 421–407 B.C.) on the Athenian Acropolis.

213.7: Phidias (ca. 490–ca. 432 B.C.), Athenian sculptor, best known for his chryselephantine statues of Athena and Zeus.

213.8: in the *History of the Peloponnesian War* (1.6) Thucydides mentions the Athenian fashion of 'fastening up their hair in a knot held by a golden grasshopper as a brooch.' The bees may derive from the chapter on 'The Heroic Age in Greek Art' in Walter Pater's *Greek Studies: A Series of Essays* (London and New York: Macmillan, 1895), which mentions 'the golden honeycomb of Daedalus' (p. 217). In early printings of this poem, both artefacts were ascribed to Phidias ('his golden grasshoppers and bees').

213.19–20: cf. Isaiah 2.4 'And they shall beat their swords into plowshares and their spears into pruninghooks; nation shall not lift up sword against nation, neither shall they learn war any more.'

213.46: see note to 213.6.

213.49: Loïe Fuller (1862–1928), American dancer best known for her serpentine dance. Her troupe of dancers were in fact Japanese, not Chinese.

213.54: see Yeats's note, p. 606.

213.59–60: if a specific allusion, probably to *Prometheus Unbound* (1820) by Percy Bysshe Shelley: 'My soul is like an enchanted boat / Which, like a sleeping swan, doth float / Upon the silver waves of thy sweet singing . . .' (II.v.72–74).

213.72: probably not intended as a specific allusion, though Yeats may be thinking of Thomas Taylor in *De Antro Nympharum* (see Yeats's note to 'Among School Children,' p. 606). Taylor explains that after departed souls have passed the Stygian river, 'they are entirely ignorant of their pristine life on earth. . . . However, by means of the blood, departed spirits recognize material forms, and recollect their pristine condition on the earth.'

213.118: see Yeats's note to 'The Hosting of the Sidhe,' p. 600.

213.128–29: see Yeats's note, p. 606.

217: Michael Butler Yeats, b. 22 August 1921.

217.17ff: 'You' is God, seen later in the stanza as Christ. In Christian tradition, Christ is taken to Egypt by the Virgin Mary and her husband Joseph to escape from the wrath of King Herod, who was afraid of the prophecy that Christ would supplant him (see Matt. 2.1–18).

218: see Yeats's note, p. 606.

218.I.1–8: this stanza recounts the death and, implicitly, the resurrection of Dionysus, the god of wine and fertility in Greek mythology. Though there are varied and sometimes conflicting legends, the essentials are the birth of Dionysus from the god Zeus and a mortal woman; the jealousy of Hera, Zeus' wife, leading to Dionysus being torn to pieces and devoured by the Titans; the saving of his heart by Athena, who carries it to Zeus; and Zeus' swallowing of the heart, leading to the rebirth of Dionysus, in common legend by Semele.

218.I.6–7: for the Muses, see note to 205.11; for Magnus Annus ('Great Year'), see note on Yeats's allusion to the Platonic Year, p. 606.

218.I.9–16: this stanza recounts the birth of Christ through reference to the *Fourth Eclogue* (40 B.C.) of the Roman poet Virgil (70–19 B.C.). At the end of the Golden Age, Astraea, daughter of Zeus and Themis and goddess of justice, withdraws from the earth and is transformed into the constellation Virgo. In a passage which Yeats quotes in *A Vision* (London: T. Werner Laurie, 1925), p. 152, Virgil prophesies the return of Astraea and the start of a new Golden Age. Beginning with the Council of Nicea in 325, the *Fourth Eclogue* was seen as a foretelling of the birth of Christ, Astraea being equated with the Virgin Mary and the star Spica (Alpha Virginis), the most prominent star in the constellation Virgo, with the Star of Bethlehem. Moreover, in *A Vision* Yeats explains that 'the vernal equinox at the birth of Christ' falls between the signs Pisces and Aries in the Zodiac and that the sun's 'transition from Pisces to Aries had for generations been associated with the ceremonial death and resurrection of Dionysus. Near that transition the women wailed him, and night showed the full moon separating from the constellation Virgo, with the star in the wheatsheaf, or in the child, for in the old maps she is represented carrying now one now the other' (p. 156). Thus the stanza implicitly parallels Virgin Mary/Christ not only with Virgo/Spica but also with Athena/Dionysus.

In the *Fourth Eclogue* Virgil also prophesies another Trojan War and another journey by Jason and the Argonauts on the ship *Argo* in search of the Golden Fleece.

218.I.16: in *Select Passages Illustrating Neo-Platonism* (London: Society for Promoting Christian Knowledge; New York and Toronto: Macmillan, 1923), E. R. Dodds explains that 'it was in Plato's city that Greek thought made its last stand against the Church which it envisaged as "a fabulous and formless darkness mastering the loveliness of the world" ' (p. 8). Dodds is loosely paraphrasing *The Lives of the Sophists* (ca. 396) by the Greek sophist Eunapius (ca. 347–ca. 420). Writing about Antoninus (d. ca. 390), son of Eustathius, Eunapius notes that 'he foretold to all his followers that after his death the temple would cease to be, and even the great and holy temples of Serapis would pass into formless darkness and be transformed, and that a fabulous and unseemly gloom would hold sway over the fairest things on earth. To all these prophecies time bore witness, and in the end his prediction gained the force of an oracle' (Philostratus and Eunapius, *The Lives of the Sophists,* trans. Wilmer Cave Wright [London: Heinemann; New York: G. P. Putnam's Sons, 1922], p. 417).

218.II.2: in *The Resurrection,* 'that room' is the site of Christ's Last Supper.

218.II.3: Galilee, a region in Palestine, was the chief scene of the ministry of Christ.

218.II.4: in the 1925 *A Vision,* Yeats refers to 'Babylonian mathematical starlight' (p. 181; cf. p. 217). Yeats associates the rise of astrology in

Babylon, an ancient city in Mesopotamia, with the development of exact science and a corresponding reduction in man's status in relation to the universe.

218.II.7–8: the classical world epitomized by the philosophy of Plato and the Doric style of architecture.

219.I.1: John Locke (1632–1704), English philosopher and founder of British empiricism.

219.I.2–4: a parody of the creation of Eve from one of Adam's ribs in the Garden of Eden (Gen. 2.18–23). The spinning-jenny, a device capable of spinning many threads at once, was invented ca. 1765 by James Hargreaves (d. 1778), an Englishman.

219.II.6: an ancient city, capital of the Assyrian Empire; fell in 612 B.C.

220: in a note to the first publication of the poem, Yeats explained that

> I wrote Leda and the Swan because the editor of a political review asked me for a poem. I thought, 'After the individualist, demagogic movement, founded by Hobbes and popularized by the Encyclopaedists and the French Revolution, we have a soil so exhausted that it cannot grow that crop again for centuries.' Then I thought, 'Nothing is now possible but some movement from above preceded by some violent annunciation.' My fancy began to play with Leda and the Swan for metaphor, and I began this poem; but as I wrote, bird and lady took such possession of the scene that all politics went out of it, and my friend tells me that his 'conservative readers would misunderstand the poem.' (1924; VP p. 828)

Yeats refers to George W. Russell (see note to *Crossways,* p. 624), who became editor of the *Irish Statesman* in 1923. Thomas Hobbes (1588–1679) was an English philosopher. The Encyclopaedists were the group of writers who produced the French *Encyclopédie* (1751–72; supplement 1776–77), a major factor in the development of the French Revolution of 1789–99.

In classical mythology, the god Zeus comes to the mortal Leda in the form of a swan. The result of the union varies in different accounts. In the second edition of *A Vision* (London: Macmillan, 1937), p. 51, Yeats adopts the version in which the offspring are Helen, Clytemnestra, and the Dioscuri (Castor and Polydeuces). However, in an unpublished typescript for the 1925 edition of *A Vision* (*A Critical Edition of Yeats's* A Vision [*1925*], ed. George Mills Harper and Walter Kelly Hood [London: Macmillan, 1978], notes, p. 65), Clytemnestra is not included in a list of the children, which suggests that Yeats was then following the common variant in which Clytemnestra is a daughter of Leda by her husband, Tyndareus. The abduction of Helen by Paris caused the Trojan War and the destruction of Troy. The Greek forces were commanded by Agamemnon, brother of Menelaus, Helen's first husband. On his return from the war, Agamemnon is murdered by Aegisthus, lover of his wife, Clytemnestra.

221: Edmund Dulac (1882–1953), artist and illustrator, friend of Yeats. For centaur, see note to 157.7.

221.7: describing a particular variety of wheat in *A Popular Account of the*

Ancient Egyptians (London: John Murray, 1854), II, 39, J. Gardner Wilkinson explains that 'this is the kind which has been lately grown in England, and which is *said* to have been raised from grains found in the tombs of Thebes.'

221.11–12: in Christian legend, seven martyrs were immured in a cave near the ancient city of Ephesus during the persecution of Decius (d. 251). Two centuries later they awoke and were taken before Theodosius II (401–50), their story confirming his wavering faith. Alexander the Great (356–323 B.C.) captured Ephesus in 334 B.C.; his empire quickly dissolved after his death.

221.13: in Roman mythology, the god Saturn (identified with the Greek Kronos) ruled the world in the Golden Age of peace and plenty.

222.9: see note to poem 220.

222.15–16: in Plato's *Symposium,* the Greek playwright Aristophanes (ca. 450–ca. 385 B.C.) argues that primal man was double, in a nearly spherical shape, until Zeus divided him in two, as a cooked egg divided by a hair. Love is seen as an attempt to regain the lost unity.

222.26: an artist of fifteenth-century Italy (the first printing of the poem refers to Leonardo da Vinci, 1452–1519).

222.34: see Yeats's note, p. 606.

222.41: Plato (ca. 429–347 B.C.), Greek philosopher.

222.43: Aristotle (384–322 B.C.), Greek philosopher, here described as tutor to Alexander the Great.

222.45: Pythagoras (ca. 582–ca. 507 B.C.), Greek philosopher, discoverer of the mathematical basis of musical intervals; the detail of his golden thigh is reported by Iamblichus in his Life of Pythagoras, which Yeats probably read in the 1818 translation by Thomas Taylor.

222.47: see note to 205.11.

223: a chorus from Yeats's translation of *Oedipus at Colonus* by the Greek playwright Sophocles (ca. 496–406 B.C.). The full text of Yeats's version was first published in the *Collected Plays* (1934).

223.1: Colonus, a district just north of Athens, connected with horses because of the worship there of the god Poseidon, who gave the gift of horses to man.

223.8: Dionysus (see note to 218.I.1–8).

223.9–16: the 'gymnasts' garden' is the Academy, a park and gymnasium on the outskirts of Athens, adjoining Colonus, and the site of the school founded by Plato (ca. 385 B.C.). The olive was the gift of the goddess Athena to mankind; an olive in the Academy is said to have sprung up next after the primal olive (near the west end of the Erechtheum on the Acropolis).

223.19: Demeter, a corn-goddess in Greek mythology; her daughter, Persephone, is carried off into the underworld by Hades.

223.23: a river flowing past the west side of Athens.

223.28: Poseidon taught men to row as well as to ride.

224.7: probably Joseph, husband of the Virgin Mary.

224.11: the Virgin Mary, mother of Christ.

224.13: Jesus Christ, son of God in the Christian religion.

224.14: for Babylon, see note to 218.II.4.

224.15: in Biblical tradition, the Flood covered the entire world; only Noah and the others on board the ark survived (Gen. 6.5–7.19).

224.16–17: an allegorical account of the incarnation of Christ by God through the Virgin Mary.

226: for Owen Aherne, see Yeats's note, p. 604.

226.2: Normandy, a region in France.

232.5: for Hector, see note to 183.46.

236.3: in Greek mythology, Paris, the son of Priam and Hecuba, abducts Helen to Troy.

237: see note to poem 223.

237.6: Oedipus and his daughters, Antigone and Ismene.

238: monuments on O'Connell Street in Dublin to the English hero Horatio Nelson (1758–1805) and the Irish political leaders Daniel O'Connell (1775–1847) and Charles Stewart Parnell (1846–91). Nelson's Pillar, between the others, was the tallest of the three.

239: in the Roman Catholic church, All Souls' Day (usually 2 November) is the feast on which the church on earth prays for the souls of all the faithful departed still suffering in Purgatory. Yeats includes the poem at the end of both the 1925 and 1937 versions of *A Vision*.

239.1: Christ Church, one of the colleges of Oxford University.

239.21: William Thomas Horton (1864–1919), mystical painter and illustrator.

239.25: Amy Audrey Locke (1881–1916), Horton's beloved.

239.41: Florence Farr Emery (1869–1917), English actress.

239.46 ff.: Emery left England in 1912 to teach at a school in India.

239.53: probably Sir Ponnambalam Ramanathan (1851–1930), who founded the College where Emery taught.

239.61: MacGregor Mathers (1854–1918), occultist and one of the founders of the Order of the Golden Dawn. Yeats met him perhaps as early as 1887 but certainly no later than 1890; they became estranged after a quarrel over Order matters in 1900.

The Winding Stair and Other Poems: first published in 1933. See Yeats's note, p. 606.

240: Eva Gore-Booth (1870–1926), poet, and Constance Gore-Booth Markiewicz (1868–1927), revolutionary. Countess Markiewicz was sentenced to death for her part in the 1916 Easter Rising, but the sentence was later commuted to penal servitude for life; she was released in the general amnesty of June 1917 and remained active in Irish politics and labour affairs. Yeats had known the sisters since 1894.

240.1: Lissadell (*Lios a' Daill,* 'The Courtyard of the Blind Man'), the Gore-Booth family home in County Sligo.

240.11: Utopia, an ideal state.

240.16: the Georgian style of architecture dates from 1714–1820. Lissadell was constructed in 1832.

241: see Yeats's note, p. 606.

242.10: see note to 208.2.

242.25: Bishū Osafuné Motoshigé, or Motoshigé of the later generation, flourished in the Era of Ōei (1394–1428).

243: see Yeats's note, p. 606.

243.13: the lighthouse (constructed ca. 280 B.C.) on Pharos at Alexandria was one of the Seven Wonders of the World. For Babylon, see note to 218.II.4.

243.15: Percy Bysshe Shelley refers to 'Thought's crowned powers' in *Prometheus Unbound* (IV.103), published in 1820.

243.18: Oliver Goldsmith (1728–74), writer; Jonathan Swift (1667–1745), writer and Dean of St. Patrick's Cathedral in Dublin from 1713; George Berkeley (1685–1753), philosopher; Edmund Burke (1729–97), political writer and orator. All were born in Ireland.

243.28: a phrase from the epitaph on Swift's tomb in St. Patrick's Cathedral, Dublin; translated by Yeats as 'savage indignation' (poem 256).

245: see Yeats's note, p. 606. In Christian legend, the Veronica is a veil or handkerchief which a woman gave Christ to wipe his face as he was on the way to Calvary; when he returned it, the cloth retained the imprint of his face.

245.1: 'The Heavenly Circuit' is the title of one of the sections (II.2) of the *Enneads* of the Neoplatonic philosopher Plotinus (205–69/70); God is placed at the centre of the universe, with all things circling around him. See *Plotinus: Psychic and Physical Treatises; Comprising the Second and Third Enneads,* trans. Stephen MacKenna (London: the Medici Society, 1921), pp. 154–59. According to legend, the hair of Berenice II (ca. 273–221 B.C.), offered for the safe return from war of her husband Ptolemy III (ca. 284–221 B.C.), king of Egypt, became a constellation, *Coma Berenices.* In *The Blind Beggar of Alexandria* (1598), the English playwright George Chapman (1559–1634) refers to 'Berenice's ever-burning hair'.

245.2: the 'Tent-pole of Eden' may be what Yeats calls in his note to poem 64 'the pole of the heavens'.

245.7: the Cross on which Christ was crucified.

249.1: followers of the Greek philosopher Plato (ca. 429–347 B.C.).

250.1: William Shakespeare (1564–1616), English playwright.

250.2: the Romantic movement began in the late eighteenth century and continued into the nineteenth.

251: see note to 243.18 for Burke, Goldsmith, Berkeley ('the Bishop of Cloyne'), and Swift.

251.2: Henry Grattan (1746–1820), Irish patriot and orator.

251.5: Berkeley believed in the medicinal properties of tar-water.

251.6: Swift's name for Esther Johnson (d. 1728), the recipient of the letters in his *Journal to Stella* (published 1766–68).

251.7: the Whig Party in English politics derived from the liberal aristocrats who supported the Protestant William III against the Catholic James II; it was opposed by the Tories, conservative country gentlemen and merchants.

253: Coole Park is the estate of Lady Gregory in County Galway.

253.9: Douglas Hyde (1860–1949), Irish scholar and translator.

253.10: for the Muses, see note to 205.11.

253.11: the 'one' is Yeats (*Autobiographies* [London: Macmillan, 1955], p. 457).

253.13: John Millington Synge (1871–1909), Irish playwright.

253.14: John Shawe-Taylor (1866–1911), active in the land reform movement; Hugh Lane (1875–1915), art collector and critic. Both were nephews of Lady Gregory.

254: for Coole, see note on poem 253; for Thoor Ballylee, see Yeats's note, p. 605.

254.1–7: Yeats mistakenly suggests that the river which runs past Thoor Ballylee flows into Coole Lake. The Irish poet Raftery (1784–1835) was blind (thus 'dark'). In 'Mary Hynes, or the Posy Bright,' in *Songs Ascribed to Raftery*, ed. Douglas Hyde (Dublin: Gill and Son, 1903), p. 331, Raftery writes 'The cellar is strong in Ballylee,' which Hyde glosses as follows: 'Said to allude to a great deep pool in the river, near which the house was.' Mary Hynes lived at Ballylee. See also Yeats's note to 'The Tower,' p. 605.

254.47: see note to poem 92.

255: Anne Gregory (b. 1911), a grandchild of Lady Gregory.

256: except for the first line and 'world-besotted,' a close translation of the Latin epitaph on the tomb of Jonathan Swift in St. Patrick's Cathedral, Dublin.

257: Algeciras is a city in southern Spain, opposite Gibraltar.

257.3–4: Morocco is on the African side of the Strait of Gibraltar.

257.11: the English scientist Sir Isaac Newton (1642–1727) once commented that 'I do not know how I may appear to the world; but to myself I seem to have been only like a boy, playing on the seashore, and diverting myself, in now and then finding another pebble or prettier shell than ordinary, while the great ocean of truth lay all undiscovered before me.' David Brewster, *Memoirs of the Life, Writings, and Discoveries of Sir Isaac Newton* (Edinburgh: T. Constable, 1855), II, 407.

257.12: see note to 10.15.

257.16: presumably God.

259: Yeats met Mohini Chatterjee (1858–1936), an Indian Brāhmin, or sage, in Dublin in 1885 or 1886.

260: see note to poem 204.

260.4: presumably Hagia Sophia, also known as Santa Sophia, a church constructed in Byzantium in 532–37 by the emperor Justinian I (483–565).

260.11: in Greek mythology, Hades, a son of Kronos, is lord of the lower world, the abode of the dead. The 'bobbin' may be analogous to 'Plato's spindle' (see note to 281.1).

260.25: in *The Age of Justinian and Theodora: A History of the Sixth Century A.D.*, 2nd ed. (London: G. Bell and Sons, 1912), I, 69, William Gordon Holmes describes 'the Forum of Constantinople, which presents itself as an extension of the Mese [the main street of the city]. This open space, the most signal ornament of Constantinople, is called prescriptively the Forum; and sometimes, from its finished marble floor, "The Pavement." '

260.33: as Mrs. Arthur Strong explains in *Apotheosis and After Life: Three Lectures on Certain Phases of Art and Religion in the Roman Empire* (London: Constable, 1915), p. 215, dolphins 'form a mystic escort of the dead to the Islands of the Blest.'

261: see Yeats's note, p. 606.

262.11ff.: *The Mabinogi*, a collection of Welsh romances, describes a 'tall tree by the side of the river, one half of which was in flames from the root to the top, and the other half was green and in full leaf.' Yeats owned the 1877 edition of a translation of *The Mabinogi* by Lady Charlotte Guest (London: Bernard Quaritch) and marked the quoted passage (p. 109). He also cited the passage in his essay on 'The Celtic Element in Literature' (1903). See *Essays and Introductions* (London: Macmillan, 1961), p. 176.

262.16ff.: in Greek mythology, Attis is a vegetation god; to prevent his marriage to another, Cybele, an earth-goddess, causes him to castrate himself. After his death he is transformed into a pine tree. As James G. Frazer explains in *The Golden Bough: A Study in Comparative Religion* (London and New York: Macmillan, 1890), during his festival (22–27 March) 'the effigy of a young man was attached to the middle' of a ceremonial pine tree as 'a representation of his coming to life again in tree-form' (I, 297–99). The high priest of Cybele, called Attis, was traditionally a eunuch.

262.27: in classical mythology, Lethe is a river in Hades; drinking its waters causes forgetfulness of the past.

262.35: Yeats's 'fiftieth year' would have been the period when he was 49 years old, i.e., 13 June 1914–12 June 1915.

262.59: presumably Châu-kung (d. 1105 B.C.), Chinese author and statesman, known as the 'Duke of Chou'; cf. the second epigraph to *Responsibilities*.

262.63: for Babylon, see note to 218.II.4; for Nineveh, see note to 219.II.6.

262.74: in the Bible, the prophet Isaiah is purified by an angel who touches a live coal to his lips (Isa. 6.6–7).

262.77: for Homer, see note to poem 92; for original sin, see note to 83.22.

262.78: Baron Friedrich von Hügel (1852–1925), Catholic religious philosopher, author of *The Mystical Element of Religion as Studied in St. Catherine of Genoa and Her Friends* (1908).

262.80: Saint Teresa of Avila (1515–82), Spanish Carmelite nun and one of the principal saints of the Catholic Church. In *The Life of Saint Teresa* (London: Herbert & Daniel, [1911]), p. 606, Alice Lady Lovat explains that 'the wood of the coffin was filled with earth and water, but the body of the saint was intact, her flesh white and soft, as flexible as when she was buried, and still emitted the same delicious and penetrating smell. Moreover, her limbs exuded a miraculous oil which bore a similar perfume, and embalmed the air and everything with which it came into contact.'

262.84: after death, the Pharaohs, ancient kings of Egypt, were mummified.

262.88: in the Bible, Samson kills a lion and later extracts honey from its carcass; from this experience he forms a riddle, 'Out of the eater came what is eaten, and out of the strong came what is sweet.' Samson later tells his wife the answer and thereby discovers her infidelity (Judg. 14.5–20).

267: see note to 148.8.

Words for Music Perhaps: many of the poems in *The Winding Stair and Other Poems* had been included in *Words for Music Perhaps and Other Poems* (Dublin: Cuala Press, 1932). See Yeats's note, p. 606.

268–74: Crazy Jane is a fictitious character, based in part on 'Cracked Mary,' a woman who lived near Gort in County Galway. Yeats doubtless was familiar with the ballad 'Crazy Jane' by Matthew Gregory Lewis (1775–1818), as in his *Poems* (London: Hatchard, 1812), pp. 24–25.

268.5: Yeats first used 'Jack the Journeyman' as a name in a lyric in the play *The Pot of Broth* (1903). Yeats would have found the name in Lady Gregory's play *The Losing Game* (1902), and he may have also known an Anglo-Irish street ballad entitled 'The Roving Journeyman,' as in ' "Roving Journeyman"—"The Boys of Malabaun" ' (Manchester: Bebbington, n.d.).

269.5: in Greek mythology, Europa, daughter of Agenor, king of Tyre, is carried off by the god Zeus, who comes to her in the form of a bull.

270: in Christianity, the Day of Judgment is the apocalypse, when the good and evil are judged and sent to either heaven or hell.

274.18: Irish *tráithnín*, a blade of grass.

280.8: see note to 245.1.

281.1: in Book X of Plato's *Republic*, Glaucon tells the story of the experiences of Er in the other world, including his vision of the 'spindle of Necessity': 'Now when the spirits which were in the meadow had tarried seven days, on the eighth they were obliged to continue on their journey, and on the fourth day after he said that they came to a place where they could see a line of light, like a column let down from above, extending right through the whole heaven and through the earth, in colour resembling the rainbow, only brighter and purer; another day's journey brought them to the place, and there, in the midst of the light, they saw reaching from heaven the ends by which it is fastened: for this light is the belt of heaven, and holds together the circle of the universe, like the undergirders of a trireme. From these ends is extended the spindle of Necessity, on which all the revolutions turn.' *The Dialogues of Plato,* trans. B. Jowett, 2nd ed. (Oxford: Clarendon Press, 1875), III, 513–14.

281.5: fictitious names.

283.4–6: see note to 20.4.

283.8: in the medieval romance of Tristan and Isolde, Tristan is sent to Ireland to bring Isolde to Cornwall to be the bride of King Mark. A potion which they unknowingly drink makes their love irresistible.

283.13–18: see note to poem 220. The 'holy bird' is Zeus. Sparta is located on the west bank of the Eurotas river.

285: see Yeats's note, p. 606.

285.7: Horace (65–8 B.C.), Roman writer; for Homer, see note to poem 92.

285.8: Plato (ca. 429–347 B.C.), Greek philosopher.

285.8, 16: Marcus Tullius Cicero (106–43 B.C.), Roman orator.

286: see Yeats's note, p. 606.

287: see Yeats's note, p. 606.

288: for Cruachan, see note to 125.4. Croagh Patrick (*Cruach Phadraig,* 'Patrick's Heap'), a mountain in County Mayo, is a centre for Christian pilgrimage, associated with the life of St. Patrick.

289: Tom the Lunatic is apparently a fictitious character. Yeats draws on 'Tom o' Bedlam,' a term applied to inmates of Bedlam Hospital, a London insane asylum, who were released periodically to beg for money to pay their keep. Cf. Shakespeare's *King Lear,* III.iv.131ff.

289.7: characters in 'Donald and his Neighbours,' in *The Royal Hibernian Tales* (Dublin: C. M. Warren, n.d.). Yeats included the story in his *Fairy and Folk Tales of the Irish Peasantry* (London: Walter Scott; New York: Thomas Whittaker; Toronto: W. J. Gage, 1888), pp. 299–303.

289.8: probably not a specific reference; 'Holy Joe' colloquially identifies someone excessively and ostentatiously pious.

290: for Cruachan, see note to 125.4.

292: the Delphic Oracle is the supreme oracle in Greek mythology; Plotinus (205–69/70) is a Neoplatonic philosopher. In the *Life of Plotinus,* the philosopher Porphyry has Amelius consult the Oracle to learn the fate of Plotinus' soul after his death. See *Plotinus: The Ethical Treatises, Being the Treatises of the First Ennead with Porphyry's Life of Plotinus...,* trans. Stephen MacKenna (London: the Medici Society, 1917), pp. 22–23.

292.3: a son of Zeus and Europa in Greek mythology, Rhadamanthus is a ruler and judge of Elysium, to which certain favoured heroes are translated by the gods and are exempt from death.

292.4: the immortals.

292.8: Plato (ca. 429–347 B.C.), Greek philosopher; Minos is another son of Zeus and Europa and a judge in Elysium.

292.9: Pythagoras (ca. 582–ca. 507 B.C.), Greek philosopher.

A Woman Young and Old: see Yeats's note, p. 606.

295: in a note on this poem and poems 298–99 in *The Winding Stair* (New York: Fountain Press, 1929), Yeats explained that 'I have symbolized a woman's love as the struggle of the darkness to keep the sun from rising from its earthly bed. In the last stanza of The Choice [later 'Chosen,' poem 298] I change the symbol to that of the souls of man and woman ascending through the Zodiac. In some Neoplatonist or Hermatist— whose name I forget—the whorl changes into a sphere at one of the points where the Milky Way crosses the Zodiac' (VP p. 830). Yeats dates the note 'Rapallo/March, 1928.' See also Yeats's note, p. 606.

296.10: the killing of a dragon has a prominent place in the legends surrounding both St. George (d. 303), patron saint of England, and the Greek mythological hero Perseus, the son of Zeus and Danaë.

298: see Yeats's note, p. 606, which identifies the 'learned astrologer,' and also the note to poem 295.

299: see note to poem 295.

300.19: for Quattrocento, see note to 222.26.

300.20: Andrea Mantegna (1431–1506), Italian painter.

303: a chorus from Sophocles' *Antigone.*

303.6: in Greek mythology, the mountain Parnassus is sacred to Apollo, Dionysus, and the Muses.

303.7: the Empyrean is the highest heaven, in ancient cosmology a sphere of fire.

303.10: Antigone's brothers, Eteocles and Polynices, die at each other's hands.

303.15: Oedipus is Antigone's father. At the end of the play, Antigone commits suicide after being entombed in a vault by Creon.

[*Parnell's Funeral and Other Poems*]: this section includes the poems from *A Full Moon in March* (London: Macmillan, 1935), except for 'Three Songs to the Same Tune' (poem A105), later revised as 'Three Marching Songs' (poem 360). The heading 'Parnell's Funeral and Other Poems' appears on the page preceding the poems in the volume.

304: in *The King of the Great Clock Tower: Commentaries and Poems* (Dublin: Cuala Press, 1934; New York: Macmillan, 1935), Yeats offered a 'Commentary on "A Parnellite at Parnell's Funeral" ' (the title in those editions of Part I of 'Parnell's Funeral'; Part II was placed at the end of the 'Commentary'). Given below is the 1935 text, followed by annotations:

I

When lecturing in America I spoke of Four Bells, four deep tragic notes, equally divided in time, so symbolising the war that ended in the Flight of the Earls; the Battle of the Boyne; the coming of French influence among our peasants; the beginning of our own age; events that closed the sixteenth, seventeenth, eighteenth and nineteenth centuries. My historical knowledge, such as it is, begins with the Second Bell.

II

When Huguenot artists designed the tapestries for the Irish House of Lords, depicting the Battle of the Boyne and the siege of Derry, they celebrated the defeat of their old enemy Louis XIV, and the establishment of a Protestant Ascendency which was to impose upon Catholic Ireland an oppression copied in all details from that imposed upon the French Protestants. Did my own great-great-grandmother, the Huguenot Marie Voisin feel a vindictive triumph, or did she remember that her friend Archbishop King had been a loyal servant of James II and had, unless greatly slandered, accepted his present master after much vacillation, and that despite episcopal vehemence, his clergy were suspected of a desire to restore a Catholic family to the English throne. The Irish House of Lords, however, when it ordered the Huguenot tapestries, probably accepted the weaver's argument that the Battle of the Boyne was to Ireland what the defeat of the Armada had been to England. Armed with this new power, they were to modernise the social structure, with great cruelty but effectively, and to establish our political nationality by quarrelling with En-

gland over the wool trade, a protestant monopoly. At the base of the social
structure, but hardly within it, the peasantry dreamed on in their medieval
sleep; the Gaelic poets sang of the banished Catholic aristocracy; 'My fathers
served their fathers before Christ was crucified' sang one of the most famous.
Ireland had found new masters, and was to discover for the first time in its
history that it possessed a cold, logical intellect. That intellect announced its
independence when Berkeley, then an undergraduate of Trinity College,
wrote in his *Commonplace Book,* after a description of the philosophy of
Hobbes, Newton and Locke, the fashionable English philosophy of his day,
'We Irish do not think so.' An emotion of pride and confidence at that time
ran through what there was of an intellectual minority. The friends who gave
Berkeley his first audience, were to found 'The Dublin' now 'The Royal
Dublin Society,' perhaps to establish that scientific agriculture described and
praised by Arthur Young. The historical dialectic trampled upon their minds
in that brutal Ireland, product of two generations of civil war, described by
Swift in a well-known sermon; they were the trodden grapes and became wine.
When Berkeley landed in America, he found himself in a nation running the
same course, though Ireland was too close to England to keep its independence
through the Napoleonic Wars. America, however, as his letters show, had nei-
ther the wealth nor the education of contemporary Ireland; no such violence
of contraries, as of black upon white, had stung it into life.

III

The influence of the French Revolution woke the peasantry from the
medieval sleep, gave them ideas of social justice and equality, but prepared
for a century disastrous to the national intellect. Instead of the Protestant
Ascendency with its sense of responsibility, we had the Garrison, a political
party of Protestant and Catholic landowners, merchants and officials. They
loved the soil of Ireland; the returned Colonial Governor crossed the Chan-
nel to see the May flowers in his park; the merchant loved with an ardour, I
have not met elsewhere, some sea-board town where he had made his
money, or spent his youth, but they could give to a people they thought unfit
for self-government, nothing but a condescending affection. They preferred
frieze-coated humourists, dare-devils upon horseback, to ordinary men and
women; created in Ireland and elsewhere an audience that welcomed the vivid
imaginations of Lever, Lover, Somerville and Ross. These writers, especially
the first, have historical importance, so completely have they expressed a social
phase. Instead of the old half medieval peasantry came an agrarian political
party, that degraded literature with rhetoric and insincerity. Its novels,
poems, essays, histories showed Irish virtue struggling against English and
landlord crime; historical characters that we must admire or abhor accord-
ing to the side they took in politics. Certain songs by Davis, Carlton's *Valen-
tine McClutchy,* Kickham's *Knocknagow,* Mitchel's *History of Ireland,*
numberless forgotten books in prose and verse founded or fostered a distor-
tion we have not yet escaped. In the eighties of the last century came a third
school: three men too conscious of intellectual power to belong to party,
George Bernard Shaw, Oscar Wilde, George Moore, the most complete indi-
vidualists in the history of literature, abstract, isolated minds, without a

memory or a landscape. It is this very isolation, this defect, as it seems to me, which has given Bernard Shaw an equal welcome in all countries, the greatest fame in his own lifetime any writer has known. Without it, his wit would have waited for acceptance upon studious exposition and commendation.

IV

I heard the first note of the Fourth Bell forty years ago on a stormy October morning. I had gone to Kingstown Pier to meet the Mail Boat that arrived about 6 A.M. I was expecting a friend, but met what I thought much less of at the time, the body of Parnell. I did not go to the funeral, because, being in my sensitive and timid youth, I hated crowds, and what crowds implied, but my friend went. She told me that evening of the star that fell in broad daylight as Parnell's body was lowered into the grave—was it a collective hallucination or an actual event? Years after Standish O'Grady was to write:—

'I state a fact—it was witnessed by thousands. While his followers were committing Charles Parnell's remains to the earth, the sky was bright with strange lights and flames. Only a coincidence possibly, and yet persons not superstitious have maintained that there is some mysterious sympathy between the human soul and the elements, and that storm, and other elemental disturbances have too often succeeded or accompanied great battles to be regarded as only fortuitous. . . . Those flames recall to my memory what is told of similar phenomena, said to have been witnessed when tidings of the death of Saint Columba overran the north-west of Europe.'

I think of the symbolism of the star shot with an arrow, described in the appendix to my book *Autobiographies*. I ask if the fall of a star may not upon occasion, symbolise an accepted sacrifice.

Dublin had once been a well-mannered, smooth-spoken city. I knew an old woman who had met Davis constantly and never knew that he was in politics until she read his obituary in the newspaper. Then came agrarian passion; Unionists and Nationalists ceased to meet, but each lived behind his party wall an amiable life. This new dispute broke through all walls; there are old men and women I avoid because they have kept that day's bitter tongue. Upon the other hand, we began to value truth. According to my memory and the memory of others, free discussion appeared among us for the first time, bringing the passion for reality, the satiric genius that informs *Ulysses, The Playboy of the Western World, The Informer, The Puritan* and other books, and plays; the accumulated hatred of years was suddenly transferred from England to Ireland. James Joyce has no doubt described something remembered from his youth in that dinner table scene in *The Portrait of the Artist as a Young Man,* when after a violent quarrel about Parnell and the priests, the host sobs, his head upon the table, 'My dead King'.

We had passed through an initiation like that of the Tibetan ascetic, who staggers half dead from a trance, where he has seen himself eaten alive and has not yet learnt that the eater was himself.

V

As we discussed and argued, the national character changed, O'Connell, the great comedian, left the scene and the tragedian Parnell took his place. When we talked of his pride; of his apparent impassivity when his hands were full of blood because he had torn them with his nails, the proceeding epoch with its democratic bonhomie, seemed to grin through a horse collar. He was the symbol that made apparent, or made possible (are there not historical limbos where nothing is possible?) that epoch's contrary: contrary, not negation, not refutation; the spring vegetables may be over, they have not been refuted. I am Blake's disciple, not Hegel's: 'contraries are positive. A negation is not a contrary.' (VP pp. 832–35)

*   *   *

Yeats was on a lecture tour in America from October 1932 to January 1933. Some of the material in the 'Commentary' was included in one of his talks, Yeats explaining in the Preface to *The King of the Great Clock Tower* that 'in "At Parnell's Funeral" I rhymed passages from a lecture I had given in America' (VP p. 835). See 'Modern Ireland: An Address to American Audiences, 1932–1933,' ed. Curtis Bradford, in *Irish Renaissance: A Gathering of Essays, Memoirs, and Letters from The Massachusetts Review*, ed. Robin Skelton and David R. Clark (Dublin: Dolmen Press, 1965), pp. 13–25. The Flight of the Earls occurred in 1607, when many Irish nobles fled the country because of their opposition to the colonization policies of James I (1566–1625), king of England. At the Battle of the Boyne in 1690, the forces of William III (1650–1702), king of England, defeated those of James II (1633–1701), the former king, thereby establishing Protestant domination of Ireland. The French aided the Irish during the insurrection of 1798.

Most of the Huguenots, the Calvinist Protestants of France, left the country in 1685, when Louis XIV (1638–1715) revoked the Edict of Nantes (1595), which had guaranteed them religious freedom; many of those who settled in Ireland became active in the linen and weaving trades. The tapestries in the Irish House of Lords were manufactured by Robert Baillie of Dublin and were installed in 1733; the chief artist, Melcior Van der Hagen, the chief weaver, Jan Van Beaver, and many of the workers came from Flanders. Although Baillie contracted for six tapestries, he produced only the *Battle of the Boyne* and the *Defence of Londonderry*, the latter commemorating the unsuccessful fifteen-week siege of Londonderry by James II in 1689. Baillie's workshop was said to be in Parnell Street. Mary Voisin, the daughter of a Huguenot, Claude Voisin, who came to Ireland in 1634, was in fact Yeats's great-great-great-grandmother on his father's side; her marriage to Edmond Butler provided the Butler line in the Yeats family. William King (1650–1729) became Archbishop of Dublin in 1703; he supported the penal legislation against Roman Catholics. The Spanish Armada was defeated by the English in 1588. In 1699 the English parliament prohibited the export of woolen goods from Ireland to any country except England, from which Ireland was already effectively excluded by high duties; the duties were removed in 1739, but Ireland was still forbidden to trade with other countries until 1779–80. Yeats quotes from the 'Last Lines' of the Irish poet Egan O'Rahilly (1670–1726); he follows the translation of Frank O'Connor (1903–66) in *The Wild Bird's Nest: Poems from the Irish* (Dublin: Cuala Press, 1932), p. 23, except that

O'Connor has 'followed,' not 'served.' A literal translation of O'Rahilly's line is: 'The princes under whom my ancestor was before the death of Christ.' The philosophers and scientists mentioned are George Berkeley (1685–1753), Thomas Hobbes (1588–1679), Sir Isaac Newton (1642–1727), and John Locke (1632–1704). In *Berkeley's Commonplace Book*, ed. G. A. Johnston (London: Faber, 1930), p. 111, Berkeley comments on the ideas of Newton and then states 'There are men who say there are insensible extensions. There are others who say the wall is not white, the fire is not hot, &c. We Irishmen cannot attain to these truths.' Yeats found the reference in J. M. Hone and M. M. Rossi, *Bishop Berkeley: His Life, Writings, and Philosophy* (London: Faber, 1931), p. 28, to which he provided an Introduction. The Dublin Society was founded in 1731. Yeats refers to *A Tour in Ireland with General Observations on the Present State of that Kingdom* (London: for T. Cadell and J. Dodsley, 1780) by the English agriculturist Arthur Young (1741–1820). The sermon by Jonathan Swift (1667–1745) is probably 'A Sermon on the Wretched Condition of Ireland,' *The Works of the Rev. Dr. Jonathan Swift*, ed. Thomas Sheridan (London, 1784), XII, 122–37. Berkeley went to America in 1728; the Napoleonic Wars, waged by or against Napoleon I (1769–1821) of France, date from 1803–15.

The French Revolution dates from 1789–99. The 'Garrison' was not a political party *per se,* but an alliance of mutual interests. The Irish novelists cited are Charles Lever (1806–72); Samuel Lover (1797–1868); and Edith Somerville (1858–1949) and Violet Martin (1862–1915), who wrote under the name 'Somerville and Ross.' Yeats also refers to Thomas Davis (1814–45), a nationalist and poet; the novel *Valentine McClutchy* (1845) by William Carleton (1794–1869); the novel *Knocknagow* (1879) by Charles J. Kickham (1828–82); the *History of Ireland* (1868) by the nationalist John Mitchel (1815–75); the playwrights George Bernard Shaw (1856–1950) and Oscar Wilde (1854–1900); and the novelist George Moore (1852–1933).

The Irish politician Charles Stewart Parnell (1846–91) died in Brighton on 6 October 1891 and was buried in Glasnevin Cemetery in Dublin on 11 October 1891. Yeats had gone to meet his beloved, Maud Gonne (1866–1953). The quotation is from *The Story of Ireland* (London: Methuen, 1894), pp. 210–12, by Standish James O'Grady (1846–1928). In *Autobiographies* (London: Macmillan, 1926), Yeats included a new opening to Part VI of 'The Stirring of the Bones.' The addition, first published in *The Criterion* and *The Dial* for July 1923, describes a vision Yeats had seen of 'a galloping centaur, and a moment later a naked woman of incredible beauty, standing upon a pedestal and shooting an arrow at a star' (p. 458). In the 'Notes,' pp. 473–77, Yeats discusses the archetypal significance of the vision, drawing on information supplied to him by Vacher Burch, later lecturer at Liverpool Cathedral and the author of several studies of religion (the unnamed 'man learned in East Mediterranean Antiquities,' p. 473). Essentially, the vision is interpreted as analogous to 'the Mother-Goddess whose representative priestess shot the arrow at the child whose sacrificial death symbolized the death and resurrection of the Tree-spirit, or Apollo.' Burch told Yeats that 'she is pictured upon certain Cretan coins of the fifth century B.C. as a slightly draped, beautiful woman sitting in the heart of a branching tree' (p. 475) and cited George Francis Hill, *A Handbook of Greek and Roman Coins* (London: Macmillan, 1899), p. 163. Yeats refers to the novel *Ulysses* (1922) by James Joyce (1882–1941); the play *The Playboy of the Western World* (1907) by John Millington Synge (1871–1909); and the novels *The Informer* (1925) and *The Puritan* (1931) by Liam O'Flaherty (1896–1984). The scene in Joyce's *A Portrait of the Artist as a Young Man* (1916) occurs in Chapter I; the quoted remark is made not by the 'host' (Simon Dedalus) but by one of the guests, Mr. Casey.

Daniel O'Connell (1775–1847) was an important political leader in the first half of the nineteenth century. Parnell became the dominant figure in Irish politics in 1879 and remained so until November 1890, when his liaison with Mrs. Katharine O'Shea (1845–1921) became public knowledge and the majority of his party repudiated his leadership. Yeats quotes from Book II (title) of *Milton* (1804) by the English poet William Blake (1757–1827). Georg Wilhelm Friedrich Hegel (1770–1831) was a German philosopher.

304.I.1–15: see Yeats's 'Commentary' and accompanying annotation.

304.I.15: no such coin is included in G. F. Hill's *Coins of Ancient Sicily* (London: Archibald Constable, 1903). If Yeats looked into Hill's *A Handbook of Greek and Roman Coins,* he would have come across not only a coin showing 'the Cretan goddess seated in her tree' (p. 163; Plate 4.2) but also a Lycian coin on which 'a cultus-statue of the form of Artemis known as Eleuthera is represented in the branches of a tree which is attacked by two men with axes and defended by snakes which dart forth from its roots' (p. 170; Plate 14.4). Hill notes that 'it would be easy to multiply the instances of obscure and complex myths which figure on coins, especially in the rich series of the cities of the provinces in imperial times' (p. 170).

304.I.17: Robert Emmet (1778–1803), Lord Edward Fitzgerald (1763–98), and Wolfe Tone (1763–98), Irish nationalists. Emmet was executed; Fitzgerald died of his wounds; Tone took his own life on the morning of his execution.

304.I.20: hysteria, causing suffocation or choking. Cf. William Shakespeare's *King Lear* (produced 1606; published 1608): 'Hysterica passio, down, thou climbing sorrow' (II.iv.56).

304.I.28: in 'The Proceedings of the Great Bardic Institution,' ed. & trans. Professor [Owen] Connellan, *Transactions of the Ossianic Society,* 5 (1860), the poet Senchan causes ten mice to die by his satire. In a long note (pp. 76–77), Connellan refers to a paper presented to the Royal Irish Academy in 1853 by James H. Todd 'on the subject of the power once believed to be possessed by the Irish Bards of rhyming rats to death, or causing them to migrate by the power of rhyme.' Cf. William Shakespeare's *As You Like It* (produced ca. 1599; published 1623): 'I was never so berhymed since Pythagoras' time that I was an Irish rat, which I can hardly remember' (III.ii.175–77).

304.II.2: Eamon de Valera (1882–1975) became President of the Executive Council of the Irish Free State after the general election of February 1932 and maintained that position during Yeats's lifetime.

304.II.5: William Cosgrave (1880–1965), first President of the Executive Council of the Irish Free State (1922–32).

304.II.8: for O'Higgins, see Yeats's note, p. 606.

304.II.9: Eoin O'Duffy (1892–1944), first Commander of the Civic Guard; after his dismissal by de Valera early in 1933, he formed the 'Blueshirts' movement and eventually became President of the Fine Gael party, before suddenly resigning from politics (although not permanently) on 22 September 1934.

304.II.11: for Swift, see Yeats's 'Commentary.'

305: Yeats's play *The King of the Great Clock Tower* was first published in 1934 and first produced on 30 July 1934 at the Abbey Theatre, Dublin.

305.2: for Ben Bulben, see note to 196.14; for Knocknarea, see note to 14.30.

305.5: see note to 10.15.

305.9: see note to poem 19.

305.11: see note to 40.4.

305.11–12: see note to 20.5. In Yeats's play *Deirdre* (1907), Deirdre and Naoise play chess while awaiting their fate at the hands of Conchubar.

305.15: in Yeats's play *The Countess Kathleen* (later *Cathleen*), first published in 1892, the poet Aleel is in love with the Countess.

305.15–16: see Yeats's note to 'The Tower,' p. 605.

305.19–20: the main character in Yeats's story 'The Wisdom of the King,' included in *The Secret Rose* (London: Lawrence & Bullen, 1897), pp. 11–24.

305.credit: Arthur Duff composed the music for *The Pot of Broth*.

306.I: a song added to the 1922 version of Yeats's play *The Pot of Broth*, first published in 1903. *Páistín Fionn* ('Fair-haired little child,' i.e., 'Fair Maid') is a popular Irish folksong. The refrain was first included in *A Full Moon in March* (1935).

306.II: lines 1 and 6–12 were first published in Yeats's play *The Player Queen* (1922); ll. 2–5 were added in *A Full Moon in March* but never included in the play itself.

306.II.5: 'dreepy,' a dialectal word used in Ireland, means 'drooping, droopy, spiritless' (OED).

308.5–6, 11–12: the wine and bread presumably refer to the Christian Eucharist ceremony.

309–20: in *The King of the Great Clock Tower*, Yeats included a 'Commentary on Supernatural Songs.' Given below is the text from the 1935 edition:

An Irish poet during a country walk talked of the Church of Ireland, he had preferences for this or that preacher, Archbishop Gregg had pleased him by accepting certain recent Lambeth decrees; one could be a devout communi-

cant and accept all the counsels before the Great Schism that separated
Western from Eastern Christianity in the ninth century. In course of time the
Church of Ireland would feel itself more in sympathy with early Christian
Ireland than could a Church that admitted later developments of doctrine. I
said that for the moment I associated early Christian Ireland with India; Shri
Purohit Swami, protected during his pilgrimage to a remote Himalayan
shrine by a strange great dog that disappeared when danger was past, might
have been that blessed Cellach who sang upon his deathbed of bird and
beast; Bagwan Shri Hamsa's pilgrimage to Mount Kaílás, the legendary
Meru, and to lake Manas Sarowa, suggested pilgrimages to Croagh Patrick
and to Lough Derg. A famous philosopher believed that every civilisation
began, no matter what its geographical origin, with Asia, certain men of sci-
ence that all of us when still in the nursery were, if not African, exceedingly
Asiatic. Saint Patrick must have found in Ireland, for he was not its first mis-
sionary, men whose Christianity had come from Egypt, and retained char-
acteristics of those older faiths that have become so important to our
invention. Perhaps some man young enough for so great a task might dis-
cover there men and women he could honour—to adapt the words of
Goethe—by conferring their names upon his own thoughts; perhaps I myself
had made a beginning.

While this book was passing through the press I wrote the poems for that
old hermit Ribh. I did not explain the poems in *The King of the Great Clock
Tower,* nor will I explain these. I would consider Ribh, were it not for his
ideas about the Trinity, an orthodox man. (VP pp. 837–38)

The Irish poet was probably F. R. Higgins (1896–1941). John Allen
Fitzgerald Gregg (1873–1961) was Archbishop of Dublin from
1920–38. Lambeth Palace in London is the site of the decennial confer-
ences of the bishops of the Anglican Communion. Yeats presumably
refers to recent ecumenical developments: in 1925 the Church recog-
nized the validity of Anglican ordinations by certain Eastern Orthodox
Churches; the 1930 Lambeth Conference allowed Anglicans to receive
Holy Communion in other denominations when it was not possible for
them to attend an Anglican Church and passed a resolution on Church
Unity; and in 1932 intercommunion was established with certain Old
Catholic Churches on the continent. The schism between what became
the Roman Catholic Church and the Eastern Orthodox Church spanned
several centuries. By dating the break in the ninth century, Yeats is
emphasizing the objections of Photius (ca. 820–ca. 892), patriarch of
Constantinople, to the inclusion of *filioque* ('and the Son') in the
Nicene-Constantinopolitan Creed. Photius was excommunicated by the
Fourth Council of Constantinople (869–70). Yeats supplied the Intro-
duction to *An Indian Monk: His Life and Adventures* (London:
Macmillan, 1932) by Shri Purohit Swami (1882–1941), which includes
the story of 'the dog, my faithful God-sent companion' (p. 180). Cellach
Mac Aodh, St. Celsus, was Archbishop of Armagh from 1105 to 1129;
Yeats knew of him through the 'Life of S. Cellach of Killala,' in Standish
Hayes O'Grady's *Silva Gadelica* (London: Williams and Norgate,

1892), II, 50–69. Yeats wrote the Introduction to *The Holy Mountain: Being the Story of a Pilgrimage to Lake Mānas and of Initiation on Mount Kailās in Tibet,* trans. Shri Purohit Swāmi (London: Faber, 1934), by Bhagwān Shri Hamsa (1878–?). Mount Kailāsa in Tibet is the twin of Mount Meru, in Hindu mythology located in the centre of Paradise; Lake Mānasa (Mānasarovara), formed by the right palm of the goddess Satī, is at the southern foot of Mount Kailāsa. For Croagh Patrick, see note to poem 288; Lough Derg, on the borders of County Donegal and County Fermanagh in Ireland, is also associated with the life of St. Patrick. The 'famous philosopher' is probably Hegel, especially in his Introduction to *Philosophy of History,* trans. J. Sibree (New York: P. F. Collier, 1902): 'in Asia arose the light of the spirit, and therefore the history of the world' (p. 158); 'the history of the world travels from east to west, for Europe is absolutely the end of history, Asia the beginning' (p. 163). The identification of the 'certain men of science' is uncertain, but a possibility is the American scientist William King Gregory (1876–1970). Although not related to Lady Gregory, Gregory had the same publisher. In *Our Face from Fish to Man* (New York and London: G. P. Putnam's Sons, 1929), Gregory suggests that 'in the [African] negro pygmy . . . the nose has remained in a low stage of foetal development' (p. 164). Yeats might have come across his article on 'Did Man Originate in Central Asia?' in *Scientific Monthly,* 24 (May 1927), 385–401. In 'Il conte di Carmagnola. Tragedia di Alessandro Mazoni. Milano,' first published in *Über Kunst und Altertum,* 2, No. 3 (Sept. 1820), Goethe stated that 'for the poet no person is historical, it is his pleasure to create his moral world and for this purpose he renders to certain people in history the honour of lending their names to his creations.' Since Yeats referred to the remark in the 1904 *Samhain,* a likely source is a 1902 volume in the Weimar Edition of *Goethes Werke* (Series I, Vol. 41, Part I, p. 206). Yeats wrote *Supernatural Songs* in the summer of 1934; the Cuala Press *The King of the Great Clock Tower* was completed in the last week of October 1934. In the Christian religion, the Trinity consists of the Father, the Son, and the Holy Ghost.

In the Preface to *A Full Moon in March,* Yeats noted that 'The hermit Ribh in "Supernatural Songs" is an imaginary critic of St. Patrick. His Christianity, come perhaps from Egypt like much early Irish Christianity, echoes pre-Christian thought.' (1935; VP p. 857)

309: for Baile and Aillinn, see poem 377 and note.

310.6: one of the Hermetic works ascribed to Hermes Trismegistus ('Thoth the very great'), a name given to the Egyptian god of writing.

316.4: 'the characters in the play.'

316.7: not a specific allusion.

316.11–12: Charlemagne (742–814), son of Pepin the Short (ca. 715–68) and Bertha, daughter of Count Charibert of Laon, was crowned Emperor of the West by Pope Leo III in 800.

318: Yeats associated the astrological conjunction of the planets Jupiter and Saturn with an 'Antithetical or subjective' dispensation, that of the planets Mars and Venus ('the goddess'; she was unfaithful to her husband Vulcan with Mars) with a 'Christian or objective' dispensation. See *The Letters of W. B. Yeats,* ed. Allan Wade (London: Rupert Hart-Davis, 1954), p. 828.

318.2: for 'mummy wheat,' see note to 221.7.

318.3: 'He' is Christ.

320: see Yeats's 'Commentary on Supernatural Songs,' p. 678. In the Preface to *The King of the Great Clock Tower,* Yeats noted that 'a poem upon Mount Meru came spontaneously, but philosophy is a dangerous theme. . . .' (1934–35; VP p. 855)

320.9: Mount Everest, on the border of Tibet and Nepal in the Himalayas.

New Poems: published by the Cuala Press in May 1938.

321: for the gyres, see note to poem 200.

321.1: 'Old Rocky Face' is probably not intended as a specific allusion.

321.6: Empedocles (ca. 493–ca. 433 B.C.), Greek philosopher.

321.7: see note to 183.46.

322: on 4 July 1935, Yeats received a lapis lazuli carving, dating from the Ch'ien Lung period (1739–95), as a seventieth birthday present from Henry (Harry) Talbot de Vere Clifton (1908–71), who by then had published two volumes of poetry.

322.6: Zeppelins, rigid airships designed by Ferdinand Graf von Zeppelin (1838–1917), were used to bomb London in World War I, the war which also involved the first military use of airplanes.

322.7: a pun on William III at the Battle of the Boyne (see note to poem 304) and Kaiser Wilhelm (1859–1941), German emperor and king of Prussia during World War I. 'The Battle of the Boyne,' an anonymous ballad in *Irish Minstrelsy,* ed. H. Halliday Sparling (London: Walter Scott, 1888), p. 444, describes how 'King James he pitched his tents between/The lines for to retire;/But King William threw his bomb-balls in,/And set them all on fire.'

322.10–11: Hamlet and Ophelia are characters in William Shakespeare's *Hamlet* (produced ca. 1603; published 1603–04), Lear and Cordelia in his *King Lear* (produced 1606; published 1608).

322.29: the Greek sculptor Callimachus (fl. late fifth century B.C.) refined the employment of the running drill. For the Erechtheum in Athens he made a golden lamp with a long bronze chimney, shaped like a palm tree, that reached to the roof, described by Pausanias (fl. ca. 150) in his *Description of Greece* (I.26.6–7).

323: sending a version of this poem to Dorothy Wellesley in very late December 1936, Yeats explained that 'I made this poem out of a prose translation of a Japanese Hokku in praise of Spring' (*Letters on Poetry from W. B. Yeats to Dorothy Wellesley,* intro. Kathleen Raine [London: Oxford University Press, 1964], p. 116), a *hokku* being a Japanese poem of seventeen syllables, divided into three lines of five, seven, and five syllables. Yeats's apparent source was *An Anthology of Haiku Ancient and Modern,* trans. Asatarō Miyamori (Tokyo: Maruzen, 1932), in which the poems often are followed by a prose commentary by the editor.

Although many of the 973 poems in the anthology concern the spring, Yeats is probably drawing on 'My Longing After Departed Spring' by Gekkyo (1745–1824): 'My longing after the departed Spring/Is not the same every year.' Miyamori explains that 'the transition of the seasons is the same every year but the poet's sentiments toward them are different as he grows older. This verse seems to be a modification of the first two lines of a famous Chinese poem:—"Every year the flowers are the same;/Every year the men are not the same" ' (p. 487).

325: the source which Yeats cites is fictitious. The name is apparently based on Pierre de Bourdeilles (ca. 1527–1614), lord of the Abbey of Brantôme in France and prolific author; his works include *Vie des Hommes illustres et grands Capitaines français, Vie des Dames illustres, Vie des Dames galantes,* and *Memoires de Pierre Bourdeilles, seigneur de Brantosme.* Yeats may have chosen 'Bourdeille' because of the possible puns on *bourde* ('a fib or humbug') and *bordel* ('a brothel'); and he may have taken 'Michel' from Michel Bourdaille (d. 1694), a theologian and religious writer. The invented title means 'History of my Times.'

328.10: in the Biblical story of the Fall of Man, Satan takes the form of a serpent when he tempts Adam and Eve (Gen. 3.1–24).

332.15: Timon is a character in William Shakespeare's *Timon of Athens* (1623), based on a semilegendary Greek misanthrope (fl. after 450 B.C.); for Lear, see note to 322.10–11.

332.16: William Blake (1757–1827), English poet.

332.19: Michelangelo Buonarroti (1475–1564), Italian artist.

333.5: Plato (ca. 429–347 B.C.), Greek philosopher.

334.1: John O'Leary (1830–1907), Irish patriot.

334.2: Yeats's father, John Butler Yeats (1839–1922), defended John Millington Synge's *The Playboy of the Western World* during a public debate in the Abbey Theatre on 4 February 1907.

334.5: Standish James O'Grady (1846–1928), Irish historian and novelist, presumably at the dinner given by T. P. Gill of *The Daily Express* in honour of the Irish Literary Theatre on 11 May 1899.

334.7: Lady Gregory (1852–1932), Yeats's close friend and collaborator. Writing in her Journal on 11 April 1922 about a threat by one of her tenants to take over some land from Coole Park by violence if necessary, Lady Gregory notes that she referred him to her brother and 'showed how easy it would be to shoot me through the unshuttered window if he wanted to use violence.' See *Lady Gregory's Journals: Volume One: Books One to Twenty-Nine, 10 October 1916–24 February 1925,* ed. Daniel J. Murphy (Gerrards Cross: Colin Smythe, 1978), p. 337.

334.10: Maud Gonne (1866–1953), Yeats's beloved, presumably on 4 August 1891, the day after she had rejected Yeats's first proposal of marriage. See Yeats's *Memoirs,* ed. Denis Donoghue (London: Macmillan, 1972), p. 46. For Howth, see note to poem 15.

334.11: see note to 166.6.

334.12: in Greek mythology, the Olympians are the dynasty of gods headed by Zeus.

335.14: the quotation is adapted from a song which appears in the essay

'Almost I Tasted Ecstasy' in *The Lemon Tree* (London: J. M. Dent, 1937), p. 9, by the English poet and actress Margot Ruddock (1907–51). Having suffered a mental breakdown in Barcelona and broken her knee-cap in a fall from a window, Ruddock 'crept into the hold' (p. 8) of a ship and began to sing 'Sea-starved, hungry sea. . . .'

336: Dorothy Wellesley (1889–1956), English poet and friend of Yeats since 1935.

336.14–16: in Greek mythology, the Furies are the Erinyes, avenging spirits who punish wrongs, especially those done to kindred. Yeats apparently draws on Jane Ellen Harrison's *Prolegomena to the Study of Greek Religion*, 3rd ed. (Cambridge: University Press, 1922), which explains that although 'the Erinyes are primarily the vengeful souls of murdered men,' 'already in Homer they have passed out of this stage and are personified almost beyond recognition' (p. 215). Worse, with Heraclitus the 'Erinyes are cosmic beyond the imagination of Homer' and are 'in the widest sense ministers of Justice' (p. 217). Harrison concludes that 'there is nothing that so speedily blurs and effaces the real origins of things as this insistent Greek habit of impersonation' (p. 215). Likewise, in his discussion of the Erinyes in *The Cults of the Greek States*, V (Oxford: Clarendon Press, 1909), Lewis Richard Farnell shows how 'the genius of Aeschylus partly succeeded in imposing a fallacious view upon later literature' (p. 440). Yeats may have taken the detail of the torches from Harrison's description of the Semnae (pp. 248–50).

337: in 1649–50, Oliver Cromwell (1599–1658), later Lord Protector of England, led a punitive expedition into Ireland.

337.6: see Part II of Yeats's 'Commentary on "A Parnellite at Parnell's Funeral," ' p. 672, for the source of this line.

337.12: for the Muses, see note to 205.11.

337.18: a story included in the Life of the Athenian statesman Lycurgus (ca. 390–ca. 325/4 B.C.) in *vitae X oratorum (Lives of the ten orators)*, spuriously assigned to the Greek philosopher and biographer Plutarch (ca. 46–ca. 120): having hidden a stolen fox under his clothes, a Spartan boy allows it to gnaw him to death rather than be detected in his crime.

338: for Casement, see note to poem 194. During his trial and subsequent appeals, rumours were circulated about the existence of certain diaries by Casement depicting his homosexual activities. In *The Forged Casement Diaries* (Dublin and Cork: Talbot Press, 1936), the Irish-American physician and writer William J. Maloney (1881–1952) claimed that the diaries had been forged by the British and that Sir Cecil Arthur Spring-Rice (1859–1918), British Ambassador to America, and the English poet Alfred Noyes (1880–1958), then lecturing in America, had helped to circulate the rumours to turn American public opinion against Casement. Maloney quoted from an article by Noyes in the *Philadelphia Public Ledger* for 31 August 1916, in which he wrote of Casement that 'I cannot print his own written confessions about himself, for they are filthy beyond all description. But I have seen and read them and they touch the lowest depths that human degradation has ever touched. Page after page of his diary would be an insult to a pig's trough to let the foul record touch it' (p. 105). In the first version of this poem, printed in *The Irish Press* for 2 February 1937, line 17 read 'Come Alfred Noyes and all the troup.' Noyes responded in a letter headed 'Alfred Noyes Replies to W. B. Yeats,' published in *The Irish Press* for 12 February 1937, claiming that he had cited the diaries only very occasionally and only after Casement's execution, and that he had been shown a typed copy of them 'in circumstances which then seemed to preclude all doubt of . . . authenticity' (p. 8). Noyes suggested that a tribunal be established to examine the original diaries, consisting of Yeats and the historian George Peabody Gooch (1873–1968), editor of the *Contemporary Review*. Yeats responded with a new version of the poem—omitting Noyes' name—published in *The Irish Press* for 13 February 1937, at the end of a letter headed 'Mr. Noyes' "Noble Letter"/Mr. Yeats Revises Song':

The Editor, The Irish Press
    Dear Sir,—I accept Mr. Alfred Noyes' explanation and I thank him for his noble letter. I, too, think that the British Government should lay the diaries before some tribunal acceptable to Ireland and to England. He suggests that Dr. G. P. Gooch, a great expert in such matters, and I should 'be associated with such an inquiry.' I have neither legal training nor training in the examination of documents, nor have I the trust of the people. But I thank him for his courtesy in suggesting my name.
    I add a new version of my song. Mr. Noyes' name is left out but I repeat my accusation that a slander based on forged diaries was spread through the world and that, whatever the compulsion, 'Spring Rice had to whisper it.' He was an honourable, able man in the ordinary affairs of life; why then did he not ask whether the evidence had been submitted to the accused? The British Government would have been compelled to answer.

Art Critic's Fury.

    I was dining with the wife of a Belgian Cabinet Minister after the Casement's condemnation, perhaps after his execution; somebody connected with The Times was there; he said they had been asked to draw attention to the diaries. I said that it was infamous to blacken Casement's name with evidence that had neither been submitted to him nor examined at his trial. Presently Roger Fry, the famous art critic, came in, and the journalist repeated his statement, and Roger Fry commented with unmeasured fury. I do not remember whether The Times spoke of the diaries or not.
    Had Spring Rice been a free man he would have shared my indignation and that of Roger Fry. (VP p. 838)

The Times (London) did not mention the diaries—and then not explicitly—until the day after Casement's execution. In an editorial on 4 August 1916, *The Times* noted that 'we cannot help protesting against certain other attempts which have been made to use the Press for the purpose of raising issues which are utterly damaging to Casement's character, but have no connexion whatever with the charges on which he was tried. These issues should either have been raised in public and in a straightforward manner, or they should have been left severely alone. It would have been fortunate, indeed, for every one concerned, and the simplest act of justice, if he had been shot out of hand on the Kerry coast. But if there was ever any virtue in the pomp and circumstance of a great State Trial, it can only be weakened by inspired innuendoes which, whatever their substance, are now irrelevant, improper, and un-English' (p. 7). Roger Fry (1866–1934) was an English painter and art critic.

339: see note to poem 338.

339.4: John Bull is a popular name for the English nation personified.

339.21: the establishment of the British Empire in India is traditionally dated 1757; India did not achieve dominion status until 1947.

339.31: the Casements were established in County Antrim in the early eighteenth century.

340: The O'Rahilly (1875–1916), that is, the head of the O'Rahilly clan, was killed during the Easter Rebellion (see note to poem 193).

340.12: see notes to 193.24 and 193.76.

340.14: The O'Rahilly was from County Kerry.

340.31: The O'Rahilly was shot in Henry Street (alongside the General Post Office), scene of some of the heaviest fighting during the Easter Rebellion.

341: see Yeats's 'Commentary on "A Parnellite at Parnell's Funeral," ' p. 672, esp. part V and notes.

341.27: Captain William Henry O'Shea (1840–1905) and Katherine O'Shea (1845–1921). In 'Parnell,' in *Essays: 1931–1936* (Dublin: Cuala Press, 1937), Yeats claimed that *Parnell Vindicated: The Lifting of the Veil* (London: Constable, 1931) by the Irish nationalist and writer Henry Harrison (1867–1954) 'proved beyond controversy . . . that Captain O'Shea knew of their liaison from the first; that he sold his wife for money and for other substantial advantages; that for £20,000, could Parnell have raised that sum, he was ready to let the divorce proceedings go, not against Parnell, but him-self . . .' (p. 2).

344: see poem 304.

348.6: Lough Derg, a small lake on the borders of County Donegal and County Fermanagh, is known as 'St. Patrick's Purgatory,' as St. Patrick is alleged to have fasted there and received a vision of the next world. It is the site of the most important pilgrimage in Ireland.

348.7: a series of representations (usually fourteen) of the stages in Christ's passion and crucifixion.

348.13: in Catholic theology, Purgatory is the state after death in which the soul destined for heaven is purified of taint.

349: based on a story about Richard Martin (1754–1834), member of the Irish Parliament (1776–1800) and Colonel of the Galway Volunteers. Yeats knew the tale as early as 1910, when he cited it in a lecture as 'told him by a Galway shepherd' (*Evening Telegraph* [Dublin], 4 March 1910, p. 2).

349.1–3: in the version included by Lady Gregory in *The Kiltartan History*

Book (London: T. Fisher Unwin, 1926), pp. 80–83, the Colonel 'went travelling through England and France and Spain and Portugal' (p. 80).

349.43: the 'rich man' was John Petrie of Soho, a district in London.

349.46: presumably a circuit court in Galway, though in fact the case was decided by Lord Kenyon in the Guildhall in London in 1797.

349.49: Martin was awarded £10,000.

350: Poet Laureate is the title given to the poet who receives a stipend as an officer of the English Royal Household; he is expected to provide poems for official occasions such as coronations, weddings, and so on. The Poet Laureate at the time was John Masefield (1878–1967), who had composed 'A Prayer for the King's Reign' (*The Times* [London], 28 April 1937) to celebrate the accession of George VI (1895–1952). George became king when his brother Edward VIII (1894–1972) abdicated in order to marry Mrs. Wallis Simpson (1896–1986), who was divorced.

350.17: for the Muses, see note to 205.11.

351.7–8: if a specific allusion, possibly to Denadhach, whom Yeats mentions in the story 'Drumcliff and Rosses' in *The Celtic Twilight* (1893): 'At Drumcliff there is a very ancient graveyard. The *Annals of the Four Masters* have this verse about a soldier named Denadhach, who died in 871: "A pious soldier of the race of Conn lies under hazel crosses at Drumcliff." Not very long ago an old woman, turning to go into the churchyard at night to pray, saw standing before her a man in armour, who asked her where she was going. It was "the pious soldier of the race of Conn," says local wisdom, still keeping watch, with his ancient piety, over the graveyard' (*Mythologies* [London: Macmillan, 1959], pp. 92–93).

352.6: for 'perning,' see note to 199.5.

353.8: for the Muses, see note to 205.11.

354: the Municipal Gallery of Modern Art in Dublin. In a speech delivered at the Banquet of the Irish Academy of Letters on 17 August 1937 and printed in *A Speech and Two Poems* (Dublin: privately printed at the Sign of the Three Candles, 1937), Yeats announced a grant he had received from some American admirers and explained that

> . . . I have not yet got all their names, and, when I have, I may still have to wait a little time [to thank them]. I think, though I cannot be sure, that a good poem is forming in my head—a poem that I can send them. A poem about the Ireland that we have all served, and the movement of which I have been a part.
>
> For a long time I had not visited the Municipal Gallery. I went there a week ago and was restored to many friends. I sat down, after a few minutes, overwhelmed with emotion. There were pictures painted by men, now dead, who were once my intimate friends. There were the portraits of my fellow-workers; there was that portrait of Lady Gregory, by Mancini, which John Synge thought the greatest portrait since Rembrandt; there was John Synge himself; there, too, were portraits of our Statesmen; the events of the last thirty years in fine pictures: a peasant ambush, the trial of Roger Casement, a pilgrimage to Lough Derg, event after event: Ireland not as she is displayed

in guide book or history, but, Ireland seen because of the magnificent vitality of her painters, in the glory of her passions.

   For the moment I could think of nothing but that Ireland: that great pictured song. The next time I go, I shall stand once more in veneration before the work of the great Frenchmen. It is said that an Indian ascetic, when he has taken a certain initiation on a mountain in Tibet, is visited by all the Gods. In those rooms of the Municipal Gallery I saw Ireland in spiritual freedom, and the Corots, the Rodins, the Rousseaus were the visiting gods. (VP pp. 839–40)

The French artists mentioned are Jean Corot (1796–1875), Auguste Rodin (1840–1917), and Théodore Rousseau (1812–67). The mountain in Tibet is Mount Kailāsa (see Yeats's 'Commentary on Supernatural Songs,' p. 678). For the paintings mentioned in the second paragraph quoted, see the notes below. However, some of the identifications are uncertain, and the extent to which Yeats intended to accurately describe a specific painting is open to question (cf. ll. 8–10).

354.2: the first painting is probably *The Men of the West* by Seán Keating (b. 1889); the second is *St. Patrick's Purgatory* by Sir John Lavery (1856–1941).

354.3–4: *The Court of Criminal Appeal* by Lavery; for Casement, see notes to poems 194 and 338.

354.4: probably *Arthur Griffith* by Lavery; Griffith (1871–1922) was an Irish political leader.

354.5–7: *Kevin O'Higgins* by Lavery; for O'Higgins, see Yeats's note to *The Winding Stair and Other Poems,* p. 606.

354.8–10: *The Blessing of the Colours* by Lavery, though the stanzaic division and the punctuation suggest two pictures, not one.

354.13–16: perhaps *Lady Charles Beresford* by the English artist John Singer Sargent (1856–1925), an American artist who worked mainly in England. Lady Beresford (ca. 1853–1922) was the wife of Charles William de la Poer, Baron Beresford of Metemmeh and Curraghmore, County Waterford.

354.21: *Robert Gregory* by the English artist Charles Shannon (1863–1937); for Gregory, see note to poem 144.

354.21–22: probably *Sir Hugh Lane* by Sargent; for Lane, see Yeats's note on poems 114–18, p. 603.

354.22: the quotation is from the dedication in the first edition of William Shakespeare's *Sonnets* (1609): 'To the onlie begetter of these insuing sonnets Mr. W. H. all happinesse and that eternite promised by our everliving poet wisheth the well-wishing adventurer in setting forth.'

354.23: the 'living' Hazel Lavery (d. 1935) is probably Lavery's *Portrait of Lady Lavery,* though Yeats may also be thinking of his *Hazel Lavery* and *Lady Lavery;* the 'dying' portrait is Lavery's *The Unfinished Harmony.*

354.25: *Lady Gregory* by Antonio Mancini (1852–1930); for Gregory, see note to 334.7.

354.26: Rembrandt Harmensz van Rijn (1606–69), Dutch painter and etcher.

354.39–40: cf. ll. 216–17 of 'The Ruins of Time' by the English poet Edmund Spenser (1552?–99), included by Yeats in his *Poems of Spenser* (Edinburgh: T. C. & E. C. Jack, 1906), p. 72: 'He is now gone, the whiles the Foxe is crept/Into the hole, the which the badger swept.' Yeats printed ll. 183–224 of 'The Ruins of Time' under the title 'The Death of the Earl of Leicester.'

354.44: in Greek mythology, the giant Antaeus, son of Poseidon and Earth, grows stronger when in contact with the earth.

354.48–49: *John M. Synge* by Yeats's father, John Butler Yeats; for Synge, see Yeats's note on poems 114–18, p. 603. The quotation is apparently based on Synge's poem 'Prelude,' especially l. 7 ('did but half remember human words').

355.9–10: see note to 112.5.

355.11–13: see note to 112.10. Robert Corbet (?–1872), Yeats's great-uncle, lived at Sandymount Castle on the outskirts of Dublin with his mother, Grace Armstrong Corbet (1774–1861), and his aunt, Jane Armstrong Clendenin. Yeats was born at Sandymount.

355.14: see note to 112.15.

355.15: see note to 112.13–14; see note to 112.10.

355.22–23: in *Pauline* (1833), the English poet Robert Browning (1812–89) refers to '. . . an old hunter/Talking with gods . . .' (ll. 323–24).

[*Last Poems*]: the contents and order of this section follow a manuscript table of contents for an untitled volume (which was also to have included the plays *Purgatory* and *The Death of Cuchulain*). Yeats must have written the list in the last week or two of his life. It is not known whether Yeats had selected the title 'Last Poems.'

Eight of the poems were published in periodicals in Yeats's lifetime, and six others were so printed after his death. The remaining five poems were first published in *Last Poems and Two Plays* (Dublin: Cuala Press, 1939).

356: Ben Bulben is a mountain in County Sligo, north of the town of Sligo.

356.1–2: see note to 199.45. The area around Lake Mareotis is associated with the rise of Christian monasticism in the fourth century.

356.3: the titular character in 'The Witch of Atlas' (1824) by the English poet Percy Bysshe Shelley (1792–1822).

356.11: Ben Bulben is associated with some of the events in the Fenian cycle of Irish mythology, particularly the death of Diarmuid.

356.25–26: in his *Jail Journal* (1854), the Irish nationalist John Mitchel (1815–75) asked 'Give us war in our time, O Lord!' *Jail Journal* (Dublin: M. H. Gill and Son, n.d.), p. 358; entry for 19 November 1853.

356.43: the Neoplatonic philosopher Plotinus (205–69/70), said by Eunapius to have been born in Lyco or Lycopolis in Egypt. See *Plotinus: The Divine Mind, Being the Treatises of the Fifth Ennead*, trans. Stephen MacKenna (London: The Medici Society, 1926), p. 74: 'Still the arts are not to be slighted on the ground that they create by imitation of natural objects; for, to begin with, these natural objects are themselves imitations; then, we must recognise that they give no bare reproduction of the thing seen but go back to the Ideas from which Nature itself derives, and, furthermore, that much of their work is all their own; they are holders of beauty and add where nature is lacking. Thus Pheidias wrought the Zeus upon no model among things of sense but by apprehending what form Zeus must take if he chose to become manifest to sight' (V.8.1).

356.44: Phidias (ca. 490–ca. 432 B.C.), Greek sculptor.

356.45–47: see note to 189.32–33. The ceiling of the Sistine Chapel includes a depiction of Adam about to be touched into life by God.

356.53: see note to 222.26.

356.64: Edward Calvert (1799–1883), English artist; possibly George Wilson (1848–90) but probably Richard Wilson (1714–82), English artists; William Blake (1757–1827), English poet and engraver; Claude Lorrain (1600–82), French artist.

356.66: Samuel Palmer (1805–81), English artist. Describing Blake's illustrations to Thornton's *Virgil* and alluding to Hebrews 4.9, Palmer wrote that 'they are like all that wonderful artist's works the drawing aside of the fleshly curtain, and the glimpse which all the most holy, studious saints and sages have enjoyed, of that rest which remaineth to the people of God.' A. H. Palmer, *The Life and Letters of Samuel Palmer* (London: Seeley, 1892), pp. 15–16.

356.84–87: the Reverend John Yeats, 'Parson John' (1774–1846), was Rector of Drumcliff Church in County Sligo from 1811–46. Yeats was reinterred in Drumcliff on 17 September 1948, with the tombstone bearing the epitaph of ll. 92–94.

357: see poem A105 and notes.

357.I.10: in Irish mythology, Manannán mac Lir is a god associated with the sea and with the Land of the Young.

357.I.19: see poems 268–74.

357.II.1: Henry Middleton, a cousin of Yeats, lived alone in a supposedly haunted house called Elsinore at Rosses Point in County Sligo.

357.II.20: the Green Lands are the unfenced part of Rosses Point from Deadman's Point inland, in County Sligo.

357.III.2: see note to poem 193.

357.III.5–6: much of the fighting during the Easter Rebellion took place around the City Hall and especially the General Post Office.

357.III.11: the actor Seán Connolly had first appeared at the Abbey Theatre in 1913.

357.III.24–26: see note to 193.24. The idea of blood sacrifice is common in Pearse's writings. In 'Modern Ireland: An Address to American Audiences, 1932–1933,' ed. Curtis Bradford, in *Irish Renaissance: A Gathering of Essays, Memoirs, and Letters from The Massachusetts Review* (Dublin: Dolmen Press, 1965), p. 22, Yeats recalled 'Then one year when I was passing through Dublin on my way to London from Galway, where I spent my summers, someone said "There is going to be trouble—Pearse is going through Ireland preaching the blood sacrifice—he says blood must be shed in every generation." ' See, for example,

Pearse's *Political Writings and Speeches* (Dublin: Talbot Press, 1952), pp. 65–66, 76, 87, 205, 223, and 230. Yeats might even have been present for Pearse's speech at the Robert Emmet Commemoration in New York on 8 March 1914, in which Pearse noted that 'We are older than England and we are stronger than England. In every generation we have renewed the struggle, and so it shall be unto the end. When England thinks she has trampled out our blood in battle, some brave man rises and rallies us again; when England thinks she has purchased us with a bribe, some good man redeems us by a sacrifice' (p. 76).

358.7: in *A Social History of Ancient Ireland* (London: Longmans, Green, 1903), P. W. Joyce explains that 'occasionally the bodies of kings and chieftains were buried in a standing posture, arrayed in full battle costume, with the face turned towards the territories of their enemies' (I, 551). Eógan Bél, a king of Connacht killed at the Battle of Sligo in 543 or 547, is said to be so buried on Knocknarea, a mountain in County Sligo.

359: for Cuchulain, see note to poem 19.

359.7–9: probably not a specific allusion, but reminiscent of the Myth of Er in Book X of Plato's *Republic* (cf. note to 281.1), in which unborn souls have placed before them 'lots and samples of life': 'There he saw the soul which had once been Orpheus choosing the life of a swan out of enmity to the race of women, hating to be born of a woman because they had been his murderers; he saw also the soul of Thamyras choosing the life of a nightingale. . . .' *The Dialogues of Plato,* trans. B. Jowett, 2nd ed. (Oxford: Clarendon Press, 1875), III, 515, 517.

360.I.23: presumably Red Hugh O'Donnell (ca. 1571–1602), who fought against the English in the rebellion which ended with the Battle of Kinsale (1601–02).

360.I.24: presumably Hugh O'Neill (1550–1616), who led the Irish forces in the rebellion and whose departure from Ireland along with his followers in September 1607 became known as 'The Flight of the Earls'; and his nephew Owen Roe O'Neill (ca. 1590–1649), who commanded the Confederation of Kilkenny and defeated the Scots in the Battle of Benburb on 5 June 1646.

360.I.25: Robert Emmet (1778–1803), Irish patriot who led an abortive rebellion in 1803; for Parnell, see poem 304.

360.II.4: see note to 20.4.

361: for Tara, see note to 77.6.

362.2: the Greek philosopher Pythagoras (ca. 582–ca. 507 B.C.) developed a theory of numbers.

362.14ff.: the Greeks defeated the Persians at the Battle of Salamis in 480 B.C.

362.15: for Phidias, see note to 356.44.

362.17–18: writing to Ethel Mannin on 28 June 1938, Yeats suggested that 'In reading the third stanza remember the influence on modern sculpture and on the great seated Buddha of the sculptors who followed Alexander' (*Letters of W. B. Yeats,* ed. Allan Wade [London: Rupert Hart-Davis, 1954], p. 911; cf. Yeats's *A Vision* [London: Macmillan, 1937],

p. 271). That is, the conquest of northwest India by Alexander the Great in 326 B.C. resulted in a Greek influence on the traditional representations of Buddha.

362.19–20: in *The Trembling of the Veil* (1922), Yeats referred to 'a mind that has no need of the intellect to remain sane, though it give itself to every fantasy: the dreamer of the Middle Ages. It is "the fool of Faery . . . wide and wild as a hill", the resolute European image that yet half remembers Buddha's motionless meditation, and has no trait in common with the wavering, lean image of hungry speculation, that cannot but because of certain Hamlets of our stage fill the mind's eye. Shakespeare himself foreshadowed a symbolic change, that is, a change in the whole temperament of the world, for though he called his Hamlet "fat" and even "scant of breath", he thrust between his fingers agile rapier and dagger' (*Autobiographies* [London: Macmillan, 1955], pp. 141–42).

362.24: Grimalkin is a name for a cat, often with fiendish connotations, as in Shakespeare's *Macbeth* (I.i.9); for Buddha, see note to 188.19.

362.25–26: for Pearse, see note to 193.24; for Cuchulain, see note to poem 19. Yeats told Mannin that 'Cuchulain is in the last stanza because Pearse and some of his followers had a cult of him. The Government has put a statue of Cuchulain in the rebuilt post office to commemorate this' (*Letters*, p. 911; cf. note to A129.30). For the Post Office, see note to 357.III.5–6.

363: see poem 292 and notes. This poem depicts what Plotinus discovers in Elysium.

363.5–6: see note to 40.4.

363.8: see note to 362.2.

363.15: in the final text, 'Those Innocents' is presumably a reference to the immortals described in the first stanza, re-living their journey to Elysium. However, most commentators have preferred the reading of the penultimate typescript in the National Library of Ireland, 'The Holy Innocents,' an allusion to the children of Bethlehem killed by order of Herod the Great in an attempt to destroy the infant Christ (see Matt. 2.16–18). In 1930 Yeats was planning to publish a volume entitled *Byzantium,* to include the poem of that name. In a letter to T. Sturge Moore, who was to design the book cover, Yeats asked: 'Do you know Raphael's statue of the Dolphin carrying one of the Holy Innocents to Heaven?' See *W. B. Yeats and T. Sturge Moore: Their Correspondence, 1901–1937,* ed. Ursula Bridge (London: Routledge & Kegan Paul, 1953), p. 165. The original of the statue, designed by the Italian artist Raphael Santi (1483–1520) but executed by one of his followers, is in The Hermitage in Leningrad, but several copies exist.

363.20: for the dolphins, see note to 260.33.

363.26: in Greek mythology, Peleus, son of Aeacus and Endeis, captures and weds Thetis, one of the Nereids.

363.31: in Greek mythology, the god Pan, son of Hermes, is associated with fertility; he is often depicted as loving caverns and is traditionally half-goatish in shape.

363.35: in Greek mythology, nymphs are female nature spirits, satyrs masculine and bestial spirits of woods and hills.

364.5: see note to 185.11.

364.11ff.: given the allusion to *The Tragical History of Dr. Faustus* (performed 1588?; published 1604) by the English playwright Christopher Marlowe (1564–93)—'Was this the face that launched a thousand ships/And burnt the topless towers of Ilium?' (V.i.94–95)—this stanza presumably describes Helen of Troy (see note to 20.4).

364.21–26: see note to 356.45–47.

365.7: see note to 304.I.20.

365.13: in *The Nature of Existence* (Cambridge: University Press, 1921), the philosopher J. M. E. McTaggart (1866–1925) discusses the nature of 'compound substances,' attempting to demonstrate that 'all substances are compound' (p. 138; see also p. 142).

366.2: the Virgin Mary, mother of Christ in the Christian religion.

366.3: Saint Joseph, husband of the Virgin Mary.

368: fictitious characters.

368.21: Irish *craiceann a chur ar scéal*, 'to put a skin on a story,' means to put a finish or polish on it, to make it plausible.

368.26: see note to 83.22.

369.9: Malachi ('my messenger') is the supposed author of the last book of the Old Testament in the Bible; St. Malachy (1095–1148) is an Irish saint, known for his reforms; Malachi Mulligan is the name applied to Yeats's friend Oliver St. John Gogarty (1878–1957) by James Joyce (1882–1941) in *Ulysses* (1922).

371.1–2: the birth of Christ. See Yeats's note, p. 606.

371.4: Ferdinand-Victor-Eugène Delacroix (1798–1863), French painter.

371.6: Walter Savage Landor (1775–1864), English writer.

371.8: Sir Henry Irving (1838–1905), English actor, best known for his Shakespearean roles.

371.10: François Joseph Talma (1763–1826), French actor.

372.1: a glen on the side of Knocknarea, a mountain in County Sligo.

372.11: *Cathleen ni Houlihan,* first produced by the Irish National Dramatic Company in Dublin on 2 April 1902. In *Irish Literature and Drama in the English Language: A Short History* (London: Nelson, 1936), p. 158, the Irish writer Stephen Gwynn (1864–1950) noted that 'the effect of *Cathleen ni Houlihan* on me was that I went home asking myself if such plays should be produced unless one was prepared for people to go out to shoot and be shot.' See note to poem 194.

372.14: presumably Margot Ruddock (see note to 335.14).

372.16: probably Coole, the home of Lady Gregory. After her death in 1932, the house (owned by the Irish Forestry Department) fell into disrepair; it was sold to a contractor and demolished in 1942.

373.10–16: see poem 375.

373.18: *The Countess Cathleen,* first produced by the Irish Literary Theatre in Dublin on 8 May 1899, with Maud Gonne in the title role. The Countess sells her soul to the devil to ransom the souls of her starving people but is saved at the end.

373.25: *On Baile's Strand,* first produced by the Irish National Theatre Society in Dublin on 27 December 1904. At the end of the play, Cuchulain, having unknowingly killed his son, is fighting the waves while the Fool and the Blind Man go off to steal from the ovens.

374: Yeats found the quotation from the German writer Thomas Mann (1875–1955) in 'Public Speech and Private Speech in Poetry,' *Yale Review,* 27, No. 3 (March 1938), 545–46, by the American writer Archibald MacLeish (1892–1982). The essay included some comments on Yeats's own works.

Narrative and Dramatic: a heading used for poems 375–82 in the *Collected Poems* (1933).

375: first published in *The Wanderings of Oisin and Other Poems* (1889). The Czech painter Josef Tulka was born in 1846. In 1880–81 he painted eight lunettes in the National Theatre at Prague. Then, as noted by Jaromír Neumann in *Modern Czech Painting and the Classical Tradition* (Prague: Artia, [1960?]), p. 29, 'Tulka's pure heart, so full of promise, came to grief; an emotional tragedy more guessed at than known robbed Czech art of this great talent. It seems probable that he ended his days in an Italian monastery (Monte Cassino?) after first destroying in 1882 all the paintings in his studio, together with his musical compositions. He left no traces behind him.' No source for the words ascribed to Tulka has yet been found, and it is possible that they were invented by Yeats. Edwin J. Ellis (1848–1916) collaborated with Yeats on the 1893 three-volume edition of Blake. See Yeats's note, p. 608.

375.I.1: St. Patrick (ca. 385–ca. 461) was primarily responsible for introducing Christianity into Ireland.

375.I.5: described by Yeats as 'the poet of the Fenian cycle of legend' (1899; VP p. 796), Oisin is the son of Finn.

375.I.13: for Caoilte, see note to 40.3. Conán Maíl ('the bald' or 'cropheaded'), a Fenian warrior, is described by Yeats as 'The Thersites of the Fenian cycle' (1895; VP p. 795), Thersites in Greek mythology being an ugly, foul-tongued character. Fionn mac Cumhaill, the central figure in the Fenian cycle in Irish mythology, is described by Yeats as 'A very famous hero, and chief of the heroes of Ireland in his time' (1899; VP p. 795).

375.I.15: Bran and Sceolan are not only hounds but also cousins of Finn, his maternal aunt Uirne having been transformed into a dog while pregnant. See Nicholas O'Kearney's translation of 'The Festivities at the House of Conan,' *Transactions of the Ossianic Society,* 2 (1855), 160–65. Lomair was another of Finn's hounds.

375.I.16: in Irish mythology, the Firbolgs are a race of invaders. Yeats described them as 'An early race who warred vainly upon the Fomorians, or Fomoroh, before the coming of the Tuath de Danaan. Certain Firbolg kings, killed at Southern Moytura, are supposed to be buried at Ballisodare. It is by their graves that Usheen [Oisin] and his companions rode' (1895; VP p. 795). For the Fomorians, see note to 9.11; for the

Tuatha Dé Danann, see Yeats's note, P. 600. At the first battle of Moy-
tura, also known as the battle of Southern Moytura, the *Tuatha Dé
Danann* defeated the Firbolgs and killed their king, Eochaid mac Eirc.
Since, according to H. d'Arbois de Jubainville in *The Irish Mythological
Cycle and Celtic Mythology* (1884), trans. Richard Irvine Best (Dublin:
Hodges Figgis; London: Simpkin, Marshall, 1903), p. 93, 'Eochaid was
buried where he fell,' Yeats may be confusing the first battle of Moytura
with the second battle, also known as the battle of Northern Moytura,
which was fought near Sligo and in which the *Tuatha Dé Danann*
defeated the Fomorians. Ballisodare is a town in County Sligo.

375.I.18: for Maeve, see Yeats's note, p. 600. In 1895 Yeats explained that
Maeve was 'A famous queen of the Red Branch cycle. She is rumoured
to be buried under the cairn on Knocknarea. Ferguson speaks of "the
shell-heaped cairn of Maive high up on haunted Knocknarea," but in-
accurately, for the cairn is of stones' (VP p. 796). The Ulster, or Red
Branch, cycle is one of the major cycles in Irish mythology. In *Congal*
(London: G. Bell, 1872), the Irish poet Samuel Ferguson (1810–86)
refers to 'the shell-heaped Cairn of Maev / High up on haunted
Knocknarea' (III.218–19). Knocknarea is a mountain in County Sligo.

375.I.21: findrinny is *fiondruine,* from Old Irish *find-bruine,* literally
'white bronze'; apparently an amalgam of either copper or gold with sil-
ver. Yeats called it 'A kind of red bronze' in 1895 and 'A kind of white
bronze' in 1899 (VP p. 794). His confusion may echo that of Eugene
O'Curry, who in *On the Manners and Customs of the Ancient Irish*
(London: Williams and Norgate, 1873) usually calls it 'white bronze'
but near the end of his work admits that 'we are at a loss to know
whether it was a distinct metallic alloy, a kind of white bronze, or gold,
or silver, or some special type of carving and ornamentation of white
metal' (III, 167).

375.I.41–43: Oscar, son of Oisin, was killed at the battle of Gabhra (297),
described by Yeats as 'The great battle in which the power of the Fen-
ians was broken' (1895; VP p. 795).

375.I.47: Yeats called Aengus (the Middle Irish spelling of Old Irish *Oen-
gus,* Mod. Irish *Aonghus*) 'The god of youth, beauty, and poetry. He
reigned in Tir-nan-oge, the country of the young'; and Edain (OI *Étaín,*
Mod. I. *Éadaoin*) 'a famous legendary queen who went away and lived
among the Shee' (1895; VP p. 794). The imagined union of Aengus and
Edain was construed out of the fragments that until 1930 were all that
was known of *Tochmarc Étaíne* ('The Wooing of Étaín'). The full text,
since recovered, shows Aengus was foster-son to Midhir for whom he
obtained Edain as wife; Fuamnach, Midhir's previous wife, turned
Edain into a fly, who took refuge with Aengus; that was the extent of
their liaison. See poem 381.

375.I.48: Yeats explained that 'Niam was a beautiful woman of the Tribes
of Danu that led Oisin to the Country of the Young' (1899; VP p. 801).
Her name means 'lustre' or 'brilliance.'

375.I.53: see Yeats's note to poem 377.

375.I.63: for Danaan, see Yeats's note to 'The Hosting of the Sidhe,' p.

600. Also, in 1895 Yeats explained that 'Tuath De Danaan means the Race of the Gods of Dana. Dana was the mother of all the ancient gods of Ireland. They were the powers of light and life and warmth, and did battle with the Fomoroh, or powers of night and death and cold. Robbed of offerings and honour, they have gradually dwindled in the popular imagination until they have become the Faeries' (VP p. 796).

375.I.116: Yeats noted that the Fenians were 'The great military order of which Finn was chief' (1895; VP p. 795).

375.I.156: the Hill of Allen in County Kildare was the home of Finn and the headquarters of the Fianna.

375.I.219: for Druid, see note to poem 18.

375.I.383: for findrinny, see note to 375.I.21.

375.II.84: in 1895 Yeats commented that 'There was once a well overshadowed by seven sacred hazel trees, in the midst of Ireland. A certain lady plucked their fruit, and seven rivers arose out of the well and swept her away. In my poems this well is the source of all the waters of this world, which are therefore sevenfold' (VP p. 796). Yeats's source for this legend has not yet been traced. Cf. *Cormac's Glossary,* trans. John O'Donovan, ed. Whitley Stokes (Calcutta: Irish Archaeological and Celtic Society, 1868): 'The ancient Irish poets believed that there were fountains at the heads of the chief rivers of Ireland, over each of which grew nine hazels, that those hazels produced at certain times beautiful red nuts which fell on the surface of the water, that the salmon of the rivers came up and ate them, that the eating of them was the cause of the red spots on the salmon's belly, that whoever could catch and eat one of these salmon would be endued with the sublimest poetic intellect' (p. 35).

375.II.87: in 1895 Yeats glossed Aedh as 'A God of death. All who hear his harp playing die. He was one of the two gods who appeared to Cuhoollin before his death, according to the bardic tale' (VP p. 794). In a later version of the note, Yeats cites his source, Standish James O'Grady's *History of Ireland* (London: Sampson Low, Searle, Marston, & Rivington; Dublin: E. Ponsonby, 1878–80), II, 319. O'Grady explains that Aedh 'carries a harp of pure gold; and against the melody of that harp they say that not even the gods themselves are secure; and it is said, too, that he is the strongest of the gods, and in the end will slay them all. . . . And there is no singing so sweet as his, and no music like the music of his harp, suggesting things never seen or heard, beauty beyond all beauty, and nobleness to which the knighthood of earth may not be compared, and visions of love and bliss, and of worlds fair and good.'

375.II.95: Heber was one of the sons of Mile, leader of the Milesians, a race of invaders of Ireland in the pseudo-histories contrived by medieval scribes. In 1895 Yeats commented that Heber and his brother Heremon 'were the ancestors of the merely human inhabitants of Ireland' (VP p. 795).

375.II.128: the Ogham script, representing twenty letters of the alphabet by slashes and notches, survives chiefly in inscriptions in stone, which preserve the earliest recorded form of the Irish language, dating to as early as the third century; it continued in use, for inscriptions, virtually to modern times. For Manannán mac Lir, see note to 357.I.10. Also, in

1895 Yeats explained that 'Mananan, the sea-god, was a son of Lir, the infinite waters' (VP p. 796). Manannán's presumptive father, Lear (spelled so in the nominative case; the word means 'sea, ocean'), never occurs as a person. Manannán possessed two famous swords.

375.II.134–35: presumably Christ, son of God in the Christian religion.

375.III.53: Yeats explained that the bell-branch was 'A legendary branch whose shaking cast all men into a gentle sleep' (1895; VP p. 794). In the story 'Cormac's Adventures in the Land of Promise,' Cormac mac Airt gains the magical branch after granting an unknown warrior three requests—thereby losing his wife, son, and daughter; but the warrior turns out to be Manannán, and the family is reunited. A sennachie (Irish *seanchaí*) is a reciter of ancient lore.

375.III.80: the 'demon' was the smith Culann. Conchubar mac Nessa, king of Ulster, is a central figure in the Ulster, or Red Branch, cycle of Irish mythology. In 1895 Yeats explained that 'He was King of all Ireland in the time of the Red Branch kings' (VP p. 795), but in Old Irish literature Conchubar is never more than king of Ulster.

375.III.89: Yeats explained that Blanid (properly *Bláthnait*—Keating uses corrupt Early Modern forms of the Old Irish names) was 'The heroine of a beautiful and sad story told by Keating' (1895; VP p. 794), referring to the *History of Ireland* by Geoffrey Keating (ca. 1570–ca. 1650). Curaoi, the son of Daire (properly *Cú-Roí mac Dairi*), assists Cuchulain in the sack of Manainn. He claims as his prize Blanaid, the daughter of the lord of Manainn. Cuchulain refuses him, but Curaoi carries off Blanaid and defeats Cuchulain when he attempts to retrieve her. Later, Blanaid conspires with Cuchulain to murder Curaoi. Curaoi's harper, Feircheirtne (properly *Ferchertne*), avenges him by killing Blanaid, committing suicide in the process. See the Irish Texts Society of the *History of Ireland* (London: by D. Nutt, 1902–14), II, 224–26. Keating's source is *Aided Con Roí Mac Dári* ('The Death of Cú-Roí mac Dáire'); see edition and translation by R. I. Best in *Ériu*, 2 (1905), 20–35. For Fergus, see Yeats's note, p. 601. Also, in 1895 Yeats commented that Fergus 'was the poet of the Red Branch cycle. . . . He was once king of all Ireland, but gave up his throne that he might live at peace hunting in the woods' (VP p. 795).

375.III.90: Yeats explained that 'Barach enticed Fergus away to a feast, that the sons of Usna might be killed in his absence. Fergus had made an oath never to refuse a feast from him, and so was compelled to go, though all unwillingly' (1895; VP p. 794), referring to Fergus's role in the Deirdre legend (see note to 20.5).

375.III.91: Balor was a leader of the Fomorians; a glance from one of his eyes was deadly. Yeats noted that he was 'The Irish Chimera, the leader of the hosts of darkness at the great battle of good and evil, life and death, light and darkness, which was fought out on the strands of Moytura, near Sligo' (1895; VP p. 794), referring to the second battle of Moytura (see note to 375.I.16). In Greek mythology, the Chimera is a monster compounded of lion, goat, and serpent or dragon (lion in front, dragon behind, goat in the middle).

375.III.94: in 1895 Yeats explained that Grania was 'A beautiful woman, who fled with Dermot to escape from the love of aged Finn. She fled from place to place over Ireland, but at last Dermot was killed at Sligo upon the seaward point of Benbulben, and Finn won her love and brought her, leaning upon his neck, into the assembly of the Fenians, who burst into inextinguishable laughter' (VP p. 795). Yeats's source for this deformed version of the story is Standish Hayes O'Grady. See note to poem 23.

375.III.117: that is, an imaginary island in the centre of the earth.

375.III.160: Rathlin Island, off the coast of County Antrim. Beare or Bere Island, County Cork, said to be named after Béara, supposedly a Spanish princess, wife of Eoghan Mór ('the Great'), legendary king of Munster alleged to have wrested rule of the southern half of Ireland from Conn Cétchathach ('Hundred-Fighter,' popularly 'of the Hundred Battles').

375.III.163: a rath is an ancient Irish fort or dwelling.

375.III.167: a 'straw death' is 'a natural death in one's bed' (OED).

375.III.179: *Craobh Ruadh* ('Red Branch'), the building at Emain Macha (see note to 9.2–3) in which Conchubar and the heroes of the Red Branch lived. Or perhaps Creeveroe in County Antrim. Knockfefin has not been identified, but might be *Cnoc Femein* ('The Hill of Femen'), for *Síd Femen* ('The Mound of Femen'), headquarters of the supernatural people of Munster, near Slievenamon (*Sliabh na mBan Femen*, 'The Mountain of the Women of Femen').

375.III.184: Knocknarea (see note to 375.I.18).

375.III.198: in 1895 Yeats explained that 'In the older Irish books Hell is always cold, and this is probably because the Fomoroh, or evil powers, ruled over the north and the winter. Christianity adopted as far as possible the Pagan symbolism in Ireland as elsewhere, and Irish poets, when they became Christian, did not cease to speak of "the cold flagstone of Hell". The folktales, and Keating in his description of Hell, make use, however, of the ordinary fire symbolism' (VP pp. 795–96). The quotation has not yet been traced, though there are separate references in *Fenian Poems*, ed. John O'Daly, *Transactions of the Ossianic Society*, 4 (1859), to 'cold hell' (pp. 15, 119) and 'the flag-stones of pain' (p. 45). No description of Hell in Keating's *History of Ireland* has yet been traced, nor did pre-Christian Ireland apparently have any sense of a Hell, hot or cold.

375.III.222: presumably (though anachronistically) the 'chain of small stones' is a rosary.

376: first published in *The Fortnightly Review* (April 1903) and then included in *In the Seven Woods* (1903). Maeve (Medb), queen of Connacht, is a central figure in the Irish epic *Táin Bó Cuailgne*.

376.2: see note to poem 204. The first eight lines of this poem were not added until the 1933 *Collected Poems*.

376.11: Maeve's palace was at Cruachan in County Roscommon.

376.40: for Druid, see note to poem 18.

376.41: for the Sidhe, see Yeats's note, p. 600.

376.57–58: in the 'Pillow Talk' prelude added to *Táin Bó Cuailgne* in the eleventh century, Maeve, angered that her great white-horned bull had gone over to her husband's herds, invades Ulster to try to capture a great brown bull.

376.71: for Fergus, see note to poem 18. Ness was his wife.

376.77: Magh Ai is a large plain in County Roscommon, dominated by Cruachan.

376.78: Yeats's note to poem 377 refers to 'The Great Plain' of the Otherworld.

376.84: see note to 375.I.47.

376.92: see note to 125.8.

376.93: Ethal Anbual, from the Sidhe of Connacht, father of Caer.

376.101: see Yeats's note to poem 377 for the birds of Aengus.

377: first published in *The Monthly Review* (July 1902) and then included in *In the Seven Woods* (1903). In a note to the first printing, Yeats suggested that

> It is better, I think, to explain at once some of the allusions to my mythological people and things, instead of breaking up the reader's attention with a series of foot-notes. What the 'long wars for the White Horn and the Brown Bull' were, and who 'Deirdre the harper's daughter' was, and why Cuchullain was called 'the hound of Ulad,' I shall not explain. The reader will find all that he needs to know about them, and about the story of Baile and Aillinn itself, in Lady Gregory's 'Cuchullain of Muirthemne,' the most important book that has come out of Ireland in my time. 'The Great Plain' is the Land of the Dead and of the Happy; it is also called 'The Land of the Living Heart,' and many beautiful names besides. And Findrias and Falias and Gorias and Murias were the four mysterious cities whence the Tuatha De Danaan, the divine race, came to Ireland, cities of learning out of sight of the world, where they found their four talismans, the spear, the stone, the cauldron, and the sword. The birds that flutter over the head of Aengus are four birds that he made out of his kisses; and when Baile and Aillinn take the shape of swans linked with a golden chain, they take the shape that other enchanted lovers took before them in the old stories. Midhir was a king of the Sidhe, or people of faery, and Etain his wife, when driven away by a jealous woman, took refuge once upon a time with Aengus in a house of glass, and there I have imagined her weaving harp-strings out of Aengus' hair. I have brought the harp-strings into 'The Shadowy Waters,' where I interpret the myth in my own way. (VP p. 188)

For the 'long war,' see note to 375.57–58. For Deirdre, see note to 20.5; she was the daughter of Fedlimid, Conchubar's story-teller. Cuchulain's original name was Setanta. After he killed the ferocious hound of the smith Culann and offered to take its place, he was named 'the Hound of Culann,' or Cuchulain. Uladh is Ulster. A version of the Baile and Aillinn story is found in Lady Gregory's *Cuchulain of Muirthemne* (London: John Murray, 1902), pp. 305–06. For the *Tuatha Dé Danann,* see Yeats's note, p. 600. For Aengus, see note to 375.I.47. For the story of Midhir and Edain, see poem 379. Edain it is true took refuge with Aengus, but in the shape of a purple fly, inconvenient for weaving. The 'house of glass' was a kind of cage Aengus carried her around in: in *Lectures on the Ori-*

gin and Growth of Religion as Illustrated by Celtic Heathendom, 2nd ed. (London: Williams and Norgate, 1892), p. 145, John Rhys describes it as 'a glass *grianan* or sun-bower, where she fed on fragrance and the bloom of odoriferous flowers.' 'The Shadowy Waters,' poem 380.

377.5: Baile was the son of Buan, an Ulster goddess, and Mesgedra (properly Mes Gegra), king of Leinster.

377.7: Lugaid was the son of Cú-Roí mac Dairi, king of Munster; see note to 375.III.89.

377.16–17: in *Cuchulain of Muirthemne,* p. 305, Lady Gregory notes that Baile 'was of the race of Rudraige, and although he had but little land belonging to him, he was the heir of Ulster, and every one that saw him loved him, both man and woman, because he was so sweet-spoken; and they called him Baile of the Honey Mouth.' *Clanna Rudraige* ('descendants of Rudraige') is a term for the Ulster heroes other than Cuchulain, used in later Ulster tales, after genealogists had invented a pedigree for them, through Rudraige, from Ír, son of Míl.

377.18: see note to 9.2–3.

377.21: Cuchulain's homeland, a plain in County Louth.

377.117: see note to 375.II.128.

377.130: Dun Ailinne, a hill-fort in County Kildare, one of the seats of the kings of Leinster; Leighin *(Laighin)* is Leinster.

377.194: the battle between Cuchulain and Ferdiad in the *Táin Bó Cuailgne.*

378–80: see Yeats's note, p. 608. See also VP pp. 815–17 for earlier versions of the note. Lady Gregory (1852–1932), Yeats's close friend and collaborator on many of his plays.

378.1: the estate of Lady Gregory, near Gort, County Galway.

378.2: probably *Sean-bhalla,* 'old wall'; perhaps *Sean-bhealach,* 'old road.'

378.4: *Coill Dorcha,* 'Dark Wood'; *Coill na gCnó,* 'The Wood of the Nuts.'

378.7: *Páirc na Laoi,* 'The Field of the Calves.'

378.9: *Páirc na Carraige,* 'The Field of the Rock,' or *Páirc na gCarraig,* 'The Field of the Stones.'

378.11: *Páirc na dTarbh,* 'The Field of the Bulls.'

378.13: *[Coill na] n-Insín* 'The Wood of the Watermeadows.'

378.15: described by Yeats in *Dramatis Personae* (1935) as 'a famous Clare witch,' Biddy Early died ca. 1880. See *Autobiographies* (London: Macmillan, 1955), p. 401.

379: in a 1908 note, Yeats commented that

I took the Aengus and Edain of *The Shadowy Waters* from poor translations of the various Aengus stories, which, new translated by Lady Gregory, make up so much of what is most beautiful in both her books. They had, however, so completely become a part of my own thought that in 1897, when I was still working on an early version of *The Shadowy Waters,* I saw one night with my bodily eyes, as it seemed, two beautiful persons, who would, I believe, have answered to their names. The plot of the play itself has, however, no definite old story for its foundation, but was woven to a very great extent out of certain visionary experiences. (VP p. 817)

Yeats refers to Lady Gregory's *Cuchulain of Muirthemne* (London: John Murray, 1902) and *Gods and Fighting Men* (London: John Murray, 1904). For Aengus, see note to 375.I.47. Midhir, a king of the sidhe, brought a second wife, Edain, home to his first wife, Fuamnach, who transformed Edain into a purple fly, that was carried by a wind to Aengus's house, the tumulus of Newgrange in the Boyne Valley. Aengus contrived a crystal house to carry Edain about in, but Fuamnach, learning where Edain was hidden, conjured a second wind to blow the fly out of the house. After blowing about in the winds for 1,012 years, the fly is swallowed by a woman who becomes pregnant and bears a reincarnated Edain. See also note to poem 377.

379.4, 11: for Druid, see note to poem 18.

380.9: not a specific allusion.

380.129: not a specific allusion.

380.162: for the Druids, see note to poem 18.

380.169: the Irish game of hurling.

380.404: for Arthur, see note to 198.23.

380.406–08: in 'The Adventures of the Children of the King of Norway' (see note to 86.9), 'Golden-armed Iollan, son of the King of Almain,' attempts to win the love of 'the daughter of the King-Under-Wave'; he and his twelve foster-brothers are enchanted by a 'little man [with] a gentle-stringed harp' and behead each other (pp. 126–27).

381: first published in *Poetry* (Chicago) in October 1913 and then included in *Responsibilities* (1914, 1916). See note to poem 379 for the earlier events in the legend. The reborn Edain marries Eochaid Airem (Eochaid the Ploughman), king of Tara, but Midhir in a board-game with Eochaid wins the right to embrace Edain. Midhir and Edain, in the shape of birds, fly out through the smoke-hole of the king's house and return to the mounds. Eochaid digs up the mounds to regain her, but is duped into accepting her identical daughter as his wife, while Edain remains with Midhir.

381.1: in a note to the 1913 printings of the poem, Yeats explained that 'Eochaid is pronounced Yohee' (VP p. 120).

381.2: for Tara, see note to 77.6.

381.20: the Ruwenzori, a mountain range in central Africa.

381.83: see note to 375.II.128.

381.113: Loughlan *(Lochlann)* is Scandinavia.

382: first published in *English Life and The Illustrated Review* (January 1924) and then included in *The Tower* (1928), Yeats calling it 'Part of an unfinished set of poems, dialogues and stories between John Ahern and Michael Robartes, Kusta ben Luka, a philosopher of Bagdad, and his Bedouin followers' (VP p. 830). A more extensive commentary was included in *The Dial* (June 1924) and *The Cat and the Moon and Certain Poems* (1924). Given below is the text from *The Cat and the Moon*:

This poem is founded on the following passage in a letter of Owen Ahern's, which I am publishing in 'A Vision'.

'After the murder for an unknown reason of Jaffer, head of the family of the Barmecides, Harun-al-Rashid seemed as though a great weight had fallen from him, and in the rejoicing of the moment, a rejoicing that seemed to Jaffar's friends a disguise for his remorse, he brought a new bride into the house. Wishing to confer an equal happiness upon his friend, he chose a young bride for Kusta-ben-Luka. According to one tradition of the desert, she had, to the great surprise of her friends, fallen in love with the elderly philosopher, but according to another Harun bought her from a passing merchant. Kusta, a christian like the Caliph's own physician, had planned, one version of the story says, to end his days in a Monastery at Nisibis, while another story has it that he was deep in a violent love affair that he had arranged for himself. The only thing upon which there is general agreement is that he was warned by a dream to accept the gift of the Caliph, and that his wife a few days after the marriage began to talk in her sleep, and that she told him all those things which he had searched for vainly all his life in the great library of the Caliph and in the conversation of wise men. One curious detail has come down to us in Bedouin tradition. When awake she was a merry girl with no more interest in matters of the kind than other girls of her age, and Kusta, the apple of whose eye she had grown to be, fearing that it would make her think his love but self-interest, never told her that she talked to him in her sleep. Michael Robartes frequently heard Bedouins quoting this as proof of Kusta-ben-Luka's extraordinary wisdom . . . . even in the other world Kusta's bride is supposed to remain in ignorance of her share in founding the religion of the Judwalis, and for this reason young girls, who think themselves wise, are ordered by their fathers and mothers to wear little amulets on which her name has been written. All these contradictory stories seem to be a confused recollection of the contents of a little old book, lost many years ago with Kusta-ben-Luka's larger book, in the desert battle which I have already described. This little book was discovered according to tradition, by some Judwali scholar or saint, between the pages of a greek book which had once been in the Caliph's library. The story of the discovery may however be the invention of a much later age to justify some doctrine, or development of old doctrine, that it may have contained.'

In my poem I have greatly elaborated this bare narrative, but I do not think it too great a poetical licence to describe Kusta as hesitating between the poems of Sappho and the treatise of Parmenides as hiding places. Gibbon says the poems of Sappho were still extant in the twelfth century, and it does not seem impossible that a great philosophical work, of which we possess only fragments, may have found its way into an Arab library of the eighth century. Certainly there are passages of Parmenides, that for instance numbered one hundred and thirty by Burkitt, and still more in his immediate predecessors, which Kusta would have recognised as his own thought. This from Herakleitus for instance 'Mortals are Immortals and Immortals are Mortals, the one living the other's death and dying the other's life.' (VP pp. 828–29)

For Aherne and Robartes, see Yeats's note, p. 604. Hārūn al-Rashīd (766–809) was Caliph from 786 until his death. The Barāmika was an Iranian family of secretaries and viziers to the Abbasid caliphs. Yahyā was vizier from 786–803, when Hārūn al-Rashīd imprisoned him and one of his sons, executing his other son, Dja'far, who had been the Caliph's favourite. Ḳustā ben Lūḳā (d. ca. 912–13) was a doctor and a translator. Nisbis, in Syria, was the ancient residence of Armenian kings. For Bedouin, see note to 181.29. Yeats invented the tribe of Judwalis ('diagrammatists'). In *A Vision* (London: T. Werner Laurie, 1925), Michael Robartes explains that 'The Judwali had once possessed a learned book called "The Way of the Soul between the Sun and the Moon" and attributed to a certain Kusta ben Luka, Christian Philosopher at the Court of Harun Al-Raschid, and . . . this, and a smaller book describing the personal life of the philosopher, had been lost or destroyed in desert fighting . . .' (p. xix). Sappho (ca. 612 B.C.–?) was a Greek poet. In *The History of the Decline and Fall of the Roman Empire*, ed. J. B. Bury (London: Methuen, 1909–14), the historian Edward Gibbon (1737–94) notes that her works were still studied in the twelfth century (VII, 111). Parmenides (ca. 514 B.C.–?) and Heraclitus (ca. 535–ca. 475 B.C.) were Greek philosophers. Yeats refers to *Early Greek Philosophy* (London: A. & C. Black, 1892) by John Burnet. In his own copy he marked the passage from Parmenides, ll. 127–32 ('130' is the marginal line number): 'The narrower circles are filled with unmixed fire, and those surrounding them with night, and in the midst of these rushes their portion of fire. In the midst of these circles is the divinity that directs the course of all things; for she rules over all painful birth and all begetting, driving the female to the embrace of the male, and the male to that of the female. First of all the gods she contrived Eros' (p. 188; citations omitted). Yeats also marked the passage from Heraclitus (Fragment 67 in Burnet's numbering) in his copy of *Early Greek Philosophy*: 'Mortals are immortals and immortals are mortals, the one living the other's death and dying the other's life' (p. 138).

382.2: Abd Al-Rabban, called 'Faristah' in the first printing of the poem, has not yet been traced.

382.6: Yeats commented that 'The banners of the Abbasid Caliphs were black as an act of mourning for those who had fallen in battle at the establishment of the dynasty' (1924; VP pp. 461, 829). The Abbāsid Caliphs ruled from 750 to 1258.

382.135: a Djinn is a supernatural being, who can be either benevolent or malicious.

382.184: Yeats explained that ' "All those gyres and cubes and midnight things" refers to the geometrical forms which Robartes describes the Judwali Arabs as making upon the sand for the instruction of their young people, & which, according to tradition, were drawn or described in sleep by the wife of Kusta-ben-Luka' (1924; VP p. 830).

A1: first published as a whole in *The Dublin University Review,* April–July 1885. II.iii.1–15 and 249–64 had been published in *The Dublin University Review,* March 1885, as 'Voices' and 'Song of the Faeries.' All of II.iii included in *The Wanderings of Oisin and Other Poems* (1889) as 'Island of Statues / A Fragment.' Beginning in *Poems* (1895), II.iii.1–15 was included in 'Crossways' as 'The Cloak, the Boat, and the Shoes' (poem 3). For Arcadia, see note to 1.1.

A1.I.i.9: in Greek mythology, Dido, daughter of Belus, king of Tyre, leaves Tyre and founds Carthage after her husband is murdered by her brother. Yeats follows the account in Virgil's *Aeneid:* Dido falls in love with Aeneas, and when he follows a divine command and leaves her, she throws herself on a pyre and dies.

A1.I.i.12–13: in Greek mythology, Agamemnon, king of Argos, leads the Greek expedition to Troy to recover Helen; upon his return, he is killed by Aegisthus, the lover of his wife, Clytemnestra.

A1.I.i.16–17: in Greek mythology, Oenone is a nymph of Mt. Ida, from the summit of which the gods watch the battles on the plain of Troy. She was loved by Paris, who left her for Helen; when she learns that he has been wounded by Philoctetes with one of Heracles' arrows, she at first refuses to cure him. By the time she relents and goes to Troy, Paris has died, and she kills herself.

A1.I.i.134–36: see note to A1.I.i.16–17.

A1.I.ii.60 ff.: in the Bible, Eve is the wife of Adam, created from his side. They are expelled from the Garden of Eden after they taste the forbidden fruit (traditionally imaged as an apple).

A1.I.iii.19: *ego absolve te,* 'I absolve thee'; said by the priest in the Roman Catholic Church rite of penance, signifying and enacting the forgiveness of sins by God.

A1.I.iii.77: for Pan, see note to 363.31.

A1.II.iii: including this scene in *The Wanderings of Oisin and Other Poems* (1889), Yeats offered the following 'Summary of Previous Scenes':

Two shepherds meet at dawn before the door of the shepherdess Naschina and sing to her in rivalry. Their voices grow louder and louder as they try to sing each other down. At last she comes out, a little angry. An arrow flies across the scene. The two shepherds fly, being full of Arcadian timidity. Almintor, who is loved by Naschina, comes in, having shot the arrow at a heron. Naschina receives him angrily. 'No one in Arcadia is courageous,' she says. Others, to prove their love, go upon some far and dangerous quest. They but bring Arcadian gifts, small birds and beasts. She goes again angrily into her cottage. Almintor seeks the enchanted island, to find for her the mysterious flower, guarded there by the Enchantress and her spirits. He is led thither by a voice singing in a valley. The island is full of flowers and of people turned into stone. They chose the wrong flower. He also chooses wrong, and is turned into stone. Naschina resolves to seek him disguised as a shepherd. On her way she meets with the two shepherds of Scene I; they do not recognize her, but like to be near her. They tell her they love one maid; she answers, if that be so, they must clearly settle it by combat. She, not believing they will do so, passes on and comes to the edge of the lake in which is the enchanted island, and is carried over in a boat with wings. The shepherds also come to the edge of the lake. They fight fiercely, made courageous by love. One is killed. The scene quoted gives the adventures of Naschina on the island. (VP p. 665)

A1.II.iii.267: in the Christian religion, Joseph is the husband of the Virgin Mary.

A1.II.iii.288: Aeneas (see note to A1.I.i.9).

A1.II.iii.297: for Arthur, see note to 198.23. Arthur's father was Uther Pendragon.

A1.II.iii.311: the Achaeans are Achilles' men and Agamemnon's followers.

A2: published in *The Dublin University Review*, May 1885.

A2.11: in Greek mythology, the Titans are the older gods who preceded the Olympians.

A2.31: presumably the Virgin Mary, mother of Christ in the Christian religion.

A3: first published in *The Dublin University Review*, September 1885, and included in *The Wanderings of Oisin and Other Poems* (1889).

A4: first published in *The Dublin University Review*, February 1886; see note to poem A26.

A4.17: Sophocles (ca. 496–406 B.C.), Greek dramatist.

A5: published in *The Dublin University Review*, March 1886. For the title, see note to A2.11.

A5.29: Genii are nature spirits, especially spirits of fire or air.

A6: first published in *The Dublin University Review*, April 1886, and included in *The Wanderings of Oisin and Other Poems* (1889). The painting is *Refuge* by the English artist J. T. Nettleship (1841–1902), sketched and described in *Royal Hibernian Academy, 1886*, the Illustrated Art Supplement to *The Dublin University Review*, March 1886, as follows:

Refuge. 'In the midst of the fire, and they have no hurt.' J.T. Nettleship.—This is undoubtedly an impressive picture. On a rocky eminence, driven together into unexpected brotherhood by fear, we have a lion and lioness and their cub; beside the lioness, and with the air of one that feels itself in security, an antelope is crouched. The lioness has forgotten her fear in maternal solicitude, and with touching intentness is licking her cub. The cub meantime has scented out the antelope, and divines its natural prey. There is something in the attitude of the cub which lets us know that the antelope has only just reached this doubtful asylum. Beyond the lioness a lynx watches, with pricked ears, the flutterings of a bird. Over all dominates the central form of the king of beasts. He stands with tail outstretched and head laid low, the saliva drops from his mouth, and he is roaring—not as when he shakes the forest—but a low musical roar at once of defiance and despair. Beyond the rolling fire and smoke we see a glimpse of a serene sky, in which is just visible the crescent moon in its first quarter. (p. 24)

A7: first published in *The Dublin University Review*, June 1886, and included in *The Wanderings of Oisin and Other Poems* (1889).

A7.I.s.d.: 'village of Azubia' not yet traced. Yeats may be thinking of Zubia, a village near Granada, which he could have found preceded by 'Az,' Arabic for 'the' (thus Az-Zubia or A-Zubia).

A7.I.24: Azolar is presumably a fictitious character.

A7.I.27: mountains in Andalusia, a region in southern Spain with a strong Moorish influence.

A7.I.102: India.

A7.I.103: the Spanish Inquisition, the announced purpose of which was to detect converted Moors and Jews who were insincere, was established in 1478.

A7.I.105: Allah is the Supreme Being of the Mohammedans.

A7.II.s.d.: St. James the Greater (d. ca. 43), especially venerated in Spain.

A7.II.19–21: neither the tale nor the saint has yet been traced; in the two printings of the poem in 1886, Yeats referred to a 'Russian tale' and 'a saint of Russia.' Munster is a province of Ireland. In Christian tradition, St. Peter is depicted as the gate-keeper to Heaven.

A7.III.s.d.: an auto-da-fé is the ceremony accompanying the pronouncement of guilt by the Inquisition, followed by the execution by the secular authorities.

A8: published in *The Irish Monthly*, July 1886.

A9: published in *The Irish Fireside*, 5 February 1887.

A9.9: *mo chúisle*, 'my pulse,' a term of endearment.

A9.21: for rath, see note to 375.III.163.

A10: first published in *The Irish Monthly*, March 1887, and included in *The Wanderings of Oisin and Other Poems* (1889). For the Druids, see note to poem 18.

A11: published in *North & South*, 5 March 1887. There were numerous rebellions in nineteenth-century Spain; Yeats may refer to a short-lived insurrection of September 1886.

A12: Published in *The Gael*, 27 April 1887. The poem is Yeats's adaptation of a translation from the Irish which he found in *Fenian Poems*, ed. John O'Daly, *Transactions of the Ossianic Society*, 4 (1859), p. 303. O'Daly notes that the work 'was considered to be the first composition of Finn' (p. 304, n. 7).

A12.2: Yeats's 'would that Leigha were here,' based on O'Donovan's 'would that Laigaig were here,' assumes 'Leigha' to be a proper noun. Although the medieval Irish manuscript reads *Dia mbeith laigaig ann,* this is a textual error, emended by Kuno Meyer in *Four Old Irish Songs of Summer and Winter* (London: David Nutt, 1903) to *Dia mbeith lai gai gann* and translated 'If there be a slender shaft of day.' The Royal Irish Academy Dictionary lists *lai gai gann* as 'a slender shaft of day.' Cf. a letter from Yeats to Edith Shackelton Heald on 15 March [1938]: ' "If only Laegha were here," as the mediaeval Irish song to Spring says' (*Letters*, p. 907).

A13: first published in *The Pilot* (Boston), 6 August 1887, and included in *The Wanderings of Oisin and Other Poems* (1889). Ferencz Renyi is a legendary hero of the Hungarian Revolution; Yeats probably read of him in *The Pall Mall Gazette* for 17 September 1886. Although the rebellion against Austrian domination occurred in 1848–49, the date is imprecise, as Baron Julius Jacob von Haynau (1786–1853) did not become commander-in-chief of the Austrian forces until 30 May 1849.

A13.1: 'the Hungary of the West' is Ireland, on the analogy of Hungary/Austria, Ireland/England.

A14: first published in *The Irish Monthly*, September 1887, and included in *The Wanderings of Oisin and Other Poems* (1889).

A15: first published in *The Irish Fireside,* 10 September 1887, and included in *The Wanderings of Oisin and Other Poems* (1889).

A16: Published in *The Gael,* 19 November 1887. Yeats could have found what he describes as the 'authentic' version of the legend recounted in the poem in W. G. Wood-Martin's *History of Sligo, County and Town* (Dublin: Hodges, Figgis, 1882–92), III, 384–85: the event supposedly occurred in 1642 and involved troops of Sir Frederick Hamilton. Yeats retold the story in 'The Curse of the Fires and of the Shadows,' in *The Secret Rose* (London: Lawrence & Bullen, 1897), pp. 67–79.

In *The Gael* the poem was accompanied by the following note, almost surely by Yeats although ascribed to the editor:

Lug-na-Gal is a very grey cliff overlooking that Glen-car lake, where Dermot and Grania had once a cranoque (whereof the remnants were found some years back). Concerning this cliff are two legends, or rather two versions of a legend. This the protestant and ascendancy one. Certain papists, at their old massacreing habit again, did hurl at dead of night, by main force, upon the stones beneath, many mild martyrs who were protestants. This the authentic and peasant one! Certain Cromwellian protestants, at their old massacreing habit again, rode forth at dead of night, priest and rebel hunting, and being met, below the mountains, by a peasant who volunteered as guide, were led into space, all save one, over this precipice of Lug-na-Gal which, interpreted, means the Protestant's Leap. Beneath, in the debris, some years ago, were found old rusty sabres.

It was not so long since Spencer had written of the people—'Out of every corner of the woods and glyns they came creeping forth upon their hands, for their legs could not bear them; they looked like anatomies of death, they spake like ghosts crying out of their graves: They did eat the dead carrions, happy where they could find them; yea, and one another soon after: insomuch as the very carcases they spared not to scrape out of their graves.' And during the interval, England had not ceased this planting—as the 'Times' would have phrased it—the 'institutions of that more civilized country' instead of our 'slovenly barbarism.' Therefore I have made the guide one whose incorruptable heart moved in a body corrupted by generations of famine, suffering, fear, and foiled projects. One of those whose fruitless lives have saved Ireland at any rate from the modern worship of success.

For Lug-na-Gal ('The Hollow of the Foreigners') and Glen-car, see notes to 33.37 and 10.29. For Diarmuid and Grania, see note to poem 23; a crannog is a lake-dwelling. For Cromwell, see note to poem 337. The quotation is from *A View of the Present State of Ireland* (written 1596; pub. 1633) by the English writer Edmund Spenser (1552?–99), as in *Spenser's Prose Works,* ed. Rudolf Gottfried (Baltimore: Johns Hopkins University Press, 1949), p. 158. Yeats refers to *The Times* (London).

A16.23–24: in the Bible, Belial is a term to describe an evil or worthless person or thing, as in 2 Cor. 6.15, where Belial is the name of the Antichrist; Moloch is a Semitic deity whose worship involves the sacrifice of children; and Satan is the embodiment of evil.

A17: published in *Poems and Ballads of Young Ireland* (1888). Based on the translation of a Gaelic song included by Edward Walsh in his Introduction to *Irish Popular Songs*, 2nd ed. (Dublin: John O'Daly, 1883), p. 18.

A18: first published in *The Providence Sunday Journal*, 27 May 1888, and included in *The Wanderings of Oisin and Other Poems* (1889).

A19: first published in *The Vegetarian*, 22 December 1888, and included in *The Wanderings of Oisin and Other Poems* (1889). In the *History of Sligo, County and Town* (Dublin: Hodges, Figgis, 1882–92), I, 51, W. G. Wood-Martin explains that 'there is a tradition that the original town stood on a plain, now overspread by the waters of Lough Gill, and that the islets now studding the bosom of the lake are but the crests of verdant knolls which formerly adorned its green expanse. As proof, the remains of houses or buildings are said to be visible at the bottom of the lake on a sunshiny day.'

A20: published in *The Wanderings of Oisin and Other Poems* (1889). In Arthurian legend, the enchantress Vivien entraps the magician Merlin in an oak tree.

A20.32: for Eve, see note to A1.I.ii.60.

A21: first published in *The Wanderings of Oisin and Other Poems* (1889) and then included in the story 'Dhoya' in *John Sherman and Dhoya* (1891).

A22: published in *The Wanderings of Oisin and Other Poems* (1891). Yeats presumably refers to the sage Kaṇva who brings up the titular character in the Sanskrit drama *Śakuntalā* (see note to 4.66–68).

A22.6: a raja is an Indian king, prince, or chief, a maharaja a ruling chief of one of the principal states (thus superior to a raja).

A22.20: presumably an allusion to the final phrase of the lesser doxology: 'As it was in the beginning, is now, and ever shall be, world without end.'

A23: published in *The Wanderings of Oisin and Other Poems* (1889).

A24: published in *The Wanderings of Oisin and Other Poems* (1889).

A24.51: 'Hail, Mary,' the first words of a prayer to the Virgin Mary in the Christian religion.

A25: first published in *The Wanderings of Oisin and Other Poems* (1889) and then in *The Leisure Hour*, April 1890.

A25.28: the Pacific Ocean, particularly the southern section.

A25.40: for Bedouin, see note to 181.29.

A26: first published in this form in *The Wanderings of Oisin and Other Poems* (1889). Lines 21–24 and 5–8 had been printed as 'In a Drawing-Room' in *The Dublin University Review*, January 1886; lines 1–4 and 17–20 had been printed as lines 1–4 and 17–20 of 'Life' in *The Dublin University Review*, February 1886 (poem A4).

A26.15: for Brahma, see note to 4.14.

A26.19: for Sophocles, see note to A4.17.

A26.23: Attica, the part of Greece including Athens.

A27: published in *The Girl's Own Paper*, 8 June 1889.

A28: published in *The Girl's Own Paper*, 6 July 1889.

A29: published in *The Leisure Hour*, March 1891.

A30: published in *United Ireland*, 10 October 1891. An elegy for Charles Stewart Parnell (see poem 304), who died on 6 October 1891.

A30.1: for Eri, see note to 17.23.

A31: published in *The Countess Kathleen and Various Legends and Lyrics* (1892).

A32: published in *Irish Fairy Tales* (1892).

A33: published in *The Irish Weekly Independent,* 8 April 1893. The poem tells the legendary story of the opposition to King John of England (1167?–1216) by Sir John de Courcey (d. ca. 1217–19). The events narrated would have occurred ca. 1205–10. It is not known why Yeats uses the name 'Paul.'

A33.7: in 1204 King John was forced to surrender most of his lands in France, including those in Normandy.

A33.9: a county in northern England.

A33.10: an island off the coast of southern England.

A33.14: a seaport in County Cork in Ireland.

A33.59: the Thames, the principal river of England, flows past Windsor Castle, the main residence of English monarchs.

A34: published in *The Bookman,* May 1893, with the following note:

> It is said that an enchanted tree grew once on the little lake-island of Innisfree, and that its berries were, according to one legend, poisonous to mortals, and according to another, able to endow them with more than mortal powers. Both legends say that the berries were the food of the *Tuatha de Danaan,* or faeries. Quicken is the old Irish name for the mountain ash. The Dark Joan mentioned in the last verse is a famous faery who often goes about the roads disguised as a clutch of chickens. Niam is the famous and beautiful faery who carried Oisin into Faeryland. *Aslauga Shee* means faery host. (VP p. 742)

> In the *History of Sligo, County and Town* (Dublin: Hodges, Figgis, 1882–92), I, 63–64, W. G. Wood-Martin recounts the legend of the 'forbidden fruit' on the island of Innisfree in County Sligo. For the *Tuatha Dé Danann,* see Yeats's note, p. 600. In 'The Festivities at the House of Conan,' *Transactions of the Ossianic Society,* 2 (1855), 19, Nicholas O'Kearney explains that 'we had also our "Siubhan Dubh na Boinne" (Black Joanna of the Boyne), who, on Halloweve, would favor the house, that was usually kept tidy and clean, with a visit in the shape of a large black fowl of strange appearance, and by her presence bestow good luck upon the family during the ensuing year.' For Niamh, see 375.I.48, *An sluagh sidhe,* 'The host of the mound': the fairy-host.

A35: published in *The Bookman,* December 1892.

A36: a song from the play *The Land of Heart's Desire,* published in 1894 and included in all subsequent editions.

A36.10: a small village in County Sligo.

A37: a poem from the story 'The Curse of Hanrahan the Red,' published in 1894 and included in all subsequent editions. The characters' names are fictitious.

A37.3: more correctly Ballydawley *(Baile Ui Dálaigh),* the townland of O'Daly in County Sligo.

A37.6: for 'the Steep Place of the Strangers,' see note to 33.37. For the Gap of the Wind, see note to 124.1; here the one mentioned must be that in County Sligo.

A37.7: Castle Dargan, a ruin on the edge of Dargan Lake in County Sligo.

A37.9: *Tobar Bríde,* 'Brigit's Well,' a townland in County Sligo named after a holy well dedicated to St. Bridget.

A37.13: for the Green Lands, see note to 375.II.20.

A38: first published as 'The Lover to his Heart' in the special Christmas number of *The Social Review* (Dublin), 7 December 1894; added to the 1895 edition of *The Countess Cathleen* and included in all subsequent editions.

A39: a song from the play *The Countess Cathleen,* first printed in the 1895 edition and included in all subsequent editions.

A40: a poem from the story 'The Wisdom of the King,' published in 1895 and included in all subsequent editions.

A41: published in *The Bookman,* October 1895. The title refers to the central symbol of the Rosicrucian Order (see note to 130.4).

A42: a poem from the story 'The Adoration of the Magi,' first published in 1897 and included in all subsequent editions; a revision of a mistranslation of the first six lines of a Gaelic poem in Domhnall Ó Fotharta's *Siamsa an Gheimhridh* (Dublin, 1892), sent to Yeats by the poet and translator G. A. Greene (1853–1921) in a letter of 2 November 1896. The story also offers an inaccurate version of the Gaelic text itself.

A42.2: the Virgin Mary, mother of Christ in the Christian religion.

A42.3: St. Bridget (ca. 453–ca. 523) founded a monastery in Kildare and is a patron saint of Ireland.

A43: published in *Roma* (Rome, Italy), 1897.

A44: a song from the play *Diarmuid and Grania* by Yeats and George Moore, published in *A Broad Sheet,* January 1902. The play was performed on 21 October 1901 but was not published until 1951. For Finn and Diarmuid, see note to poem 23.

A45: a song from the play *Diarmuid and Grania* by Yeats and George Moore, published in *A Broad Sheet,* January 1902. The play was performed on 21 October 1901 but was not published until 1951; that text does not include poem A45.

A46: a song from the play *Cathleen ni Houlihan,* first published in 1902 and included in all subsequent editions.

A46.2: in a note in *The United Irishman* for 5 May 1902 (*Variorum Plays,* pp. 234–35), Yeats describes 'one yellow-haired Donough' as a martyr to the cause of Irish independence, presumably around the time of the 1798 Rising.

A46.12: a seaside village in County Sligo.

A47: a song from the play *Cathleen ni Houlihan,* first published in 1902 and included in all subsequent editions.

A47.3: James P. McGarry explains in *Place Names in the Writings of William Butler Yeats,* ed. Edward Malins (Gerrards Cross: Colin Smythe, 1976), p. 96, that 'it is the usual practice for young men in rural Ireland to wear white bands or scarves on one shoulder across the breast and tied under the other arm with a black ribbon, at funerals, usually those of young men, and tragic deaths.'

A48: a song from the play *Cathleen ni Houlihan*, first published in 1902 and included in all subsequent editions.

A49: a song from the play *Where There is Nothing*, first published in the 1902 editions but omitted from the 1903 printings.

A50: a song from the play *The Pot of Broth*, first published in 1903 and retained in subsequent editions through that of 1911.

A50.1: for Naoise, see note to 20.5; for Erin, see note to 17.23.

A50.2: for Helen, see note to 20.4; in Roman mythology, Venus is a goddess of love and beauty.

A50.4: *mo ghrádh,* 'my love'; *mo stór,* 'my treasure'; *mo chroí,* 'my heart.'

A50.9: Granuaile, Grania or Grace O'Malley (ca. 1530–ca. 1600), was a renowned pirate queen; in Jacobite poetry, her name was used as a personification of Ireland.

A51: a song from the play *The Pot of Broth*, first published in 1903 and retained in all subsequent editions.

A51.5: see note to 268.5.

A52: a song from the play *The King's Threshold*, first published in 1904 and retained in all subsequent editions.

A53: a song from the play *The King's Threshold*, first published in 1904 and retained in all subsequent editions.

A54: a song from the play *Deirdre*, first published as 'Queen Edaine' in *McClure's Magazine,* September 1905; as 'The Praise of Deirdre' in *The Shanachie,* Spring 1906; as 'The Entrance of Deirdre / A Lyric Chorus' in *Poems 1899–1905* (1906); as 'Chorus for a Play' in *The Poetical Works, Vol. I* (1906); and as 'Songs from Deirdre / I' in *Poems: Second Series* (1909). Included in the play in 1907 and retained in all subsequent editions. In *The Shanachie,* Yeats described the poem as 'A chorus from an unfinished play called "The House of Usnach." Deirdre is about to enter the house of the Red Branch. Three women, wandering musicians, sing these lines' (VP p. 771). In *Poems 1899–1905,* he explained that 'Two women are waiting the entrance of Deirdre into the House of the Red Branch. They hear her coming and begin to sing. She comes into the house at the end of the second verse, and the women seeing her standing by Naoise and shrinking back from the house, not understanding that she is afraid of what is to come, think that it is love that has made her linger thus' (VP pp. 771–72). In *The Poetical Works, Vol. I,* Yeats commented that 'It is sung at the entrance of Deirdre into the House of the Red Branch by certain wandering musicians. She comes to the threshold at the end of the second verse, and they, seeing her whispering to Naoise who is beside her, think that she is busy with her love, not knowing that she is hesitating in fear' (VP p. 772). For Edain, see poem 379.

A55: a song from the play *The Travelling Man* by Lady Gregory, first published in *The Shanachie,* Spring 1906. In *Seven Short Plays* (Dublin: Maunsel, 1909), p. 201, Lady Gregory noted that 'I owe the Rider's Song . . . to W. B. Yeats.'

A55.11: in *A Book of Saints and Wonders Put Down Here by Lady Gregory According to the Old Writings and the Memory of the People of Ire-*

land (Dundrum: Dun Emer Press, 1906), the angel Axal is associated with the life of St. Columcille (e.g., pp. 16–17) and the angel Victor with the life of St. Patrick (e.g., p. 53).

A56: a song from the play *On Baile's Strand*. First published as 'Against Witchcraft' in *The Shanachie*, Spring 1906; included in the play in 1906 and retained in all subsequent editions.

A57: a song from the play *On Baile's Strand*, first published in the 1906 edition and retained in all subsequent editions.

A57.1: for Cuchulain, see note to poem 19.

A57.5: in *A Social History of Ireland* (London: Longmans, Green, 1903), I, 269–70, P. W. Joyce explains that 'in many remote, lonely glens there dwelt certain fierce apparitions—females—called *Geniti-glinni,* "genii or sprites of the valley" . . . , and others called *Bocanachs* (male goblins), and *Bananachs* (females): often in company with *Demna aeir* or demons of the air. At any terrible battle-crisis, many or all of these . . . were heard shrieking and howling with delight, some in the midst of the carnage, some far off in their lonely haunts. Just before one of Cuculainn's fierce onslaughts, the "*Bocanachs* and the *Bananachs,* and the *Geniti-glinni,* and the demons of the air, responded to his shout of defiance: and the *nemon, i.e.,* the *badb,* confounded the army [of Maeve, Cuculain's enemy] so that the men dashed themselves against the points of each other's spears and weapons, and one hundred warriors dropped dead with terror." '

A57.7: for the Fomorians, see note to 9.11.

A58: a song from the play *Deirdre,* first published in 1907 and included in all subsequent editions. The poem was printed separately as 'Songs from Deirdre / II' in *Poems: Second Series* (1909).

A59: a song from the play *Deirdre,* first published in 1907 and included in all subsequent editions. The poem was printed separately as 'Songs from Deirdre / III' in *Poems: Second Series* (1909).

A60: a song from the play *The Unicorn from the Stars,* first published in 1908 and included in all subsequent editions.

A60.3–6: the names are taken from the 'Table of the Archangels, Angels, Metals, Days of the Week, and Colours attributed to each Planet' in *The Key of Solomon the King (Clavicula Salomonis),* ed. S. Liddell MacGregor Mathers (London: George Redway, 1888), p. 8. Raphael is the angel of Wednesday, Sachiel the angel of Thursday, Haniel the archangel of Friday, and Cassiel the angel of Saturday. Cf. St. Columcille's 'Farewell to Aran' in *A Book of Saints and Wonders Put Down Here by Lady Gregory According to the Old Writings and the Memory of the People of Ireland* (Dundrum: Dun Emer Press, 1906), pp. 22–24, where Raphael is associated with Tuesday and Sariel with Thursday; Haniel and Cassiel are not mentioned.

A61: a song from the play *The Unicorn from the Stars,* first published in 1908 and included in all subsequent editions.

A61.12: an island south of Australia, named after Anton van Diemen (1593–1645), a Dutch colonial official.

A62: a song from the play *The Unicorn from the Stars,* first published in

1908 and included in all subsequent editions. According to Douglas
Hyde in *Songs Ascribed to Raftery* (Dublin: Gill and Son, 1903), p. 197,
n. 2, Johnny Gibbons was 'a well-known outlaw,' living around the time
of the 1798 Rebellion.

A63: a song from the play *The Unicorn from the Stars,* first published in
1908 and included in all subsequent editions. The lion is a symbol of
England, the thistle of Scotland, the harp of Ireland.

A64: a song from the play *The Unicorn from the Stars,* first published in
1908 and included in all subsequent editions.

A65: a song from the play *The Golden Helmet,* published in 1908. The
poem is not retained in the revised version of the play, *The Green Hel-
met* (1910). The play involves a dispute between Conall Cearnach
('Conall the Triumphant' [his cognomen may really mean 'the
Horned']) and Laoghaire Buadhach ('Laoghaire the Victorious'), heroes
in the Ulster, or Red Branch, cycle of Irish heroic sagas. It is based on a
long tale called *Fled Bricrend* ('Bricriu's Feast'); the contest among the
wives is an episode of the tale that is usually called 'The Word-War of
the Women of Ulster.' The speakers of the three stanzas are Laegaire's
wife, Conall's wife, and Emer, Cuchulain's wife.

A66: published in Volume Two of the *Collected Works in Verse and Prose*
(1908).

A67: a song from the play *The Hour-Glass.* Lines 1–4 were first included in
the version of the play published in *The Unicorn from the Stars and
Other Plays* (1908). They were retained in the play in the text published
in Volume IV of the *Collected Works in Verse and Prose* (1908), and in
an Appendix Yeats offered the first three stanzas, explaining that 'One
sometimes has need of more lines of the little song, and I have put into
English rhyme three of the many verses of a Gaelic ballad' (VP p. 778).
Lines 1–4 were not retained in the play itself in any subsequent edition,
but Yeats included the three stanzas in the Notes to *Plays in Prose and
Verse* (1922), commenting that 'One sometimes has need of a few words
for the Pupils to sing at their first or second entrance, and I have put into
English rhyme three of the many verses of a Gaelic ballad' (VP p. 778).
Yeats added the last two stanzas in 1937 to the Notes for the unpub-
lished Scribner 'Dublin Edition.' Yeats's source was a translation of an
Irish folksong by Lady Gregory, published as 'The Noble Enchanter' in
the Christmas number of *The Irish Homestead* (December 1901).

A68: published in Volume VIII of *The Collected Works in Verse and Prose*
(1908).

A69: a song from the play *The Green Helmet,* first published in the Abbey
Theatre Programme for the production on 10 February 1910; included
in the published play later in 1910 and in all subsequent editions. The
poem is sung by Emer about Cuchulain (cf. poem A65).

A70: a song from the play *The Green Helmet,* first published in 1910
(although expanded from a song in *The Golden Helmet,* 1908) and
included in all subsequent editions. For Laegaire, see note to poem A65.

A71: a song from *The Hour-Glass,* first published in *The Mask,* April
1913, and included in all subsequent editions.

A72: a song from *The Hour Glass*, first published in *The Mask*, April 1913, and included in all subsequent editions.

A73: a song from the play *The Countess Cathleen*, first published in 1913 and included in all subsequent editions.

A74: a song from the play *At the Hawk's Well*. First published separately as 'The Well and the Tree' in *Responsibilities and Other Poems* (1916); included in the play in 1917 and in all subsequent editions.

A75: a song from the play *At the Hawk's Well*, first published in 1917 and included in all subsequent editions.

A76: a song from the play *At the Hawk's Well*, first published in 1917 and included in all subsequent editions.

A77: a song from the play *At the Hawk's Well*, first published in 1917 and included in all subsequent editions.

A78: a song from the play *At the Hawk's Well*, first published in 1917 and included in all subsequent editions.

A79: a song from the play *At the Hawk's Well*, first published in 1917 and included in all subsequent editions.

A80: a song from the play *The Dreaming of the Bones*, first published in 1919 and included in all subsequent editions. Published separately as 'Why does my Heart beat so?' in *Selected Poems* (1929).

A81: a song from the play *The Dreaming of the Bones*, first published in 1919 and included in all subsequent editions. Published separately as 'Why should the Heart take Fright?' in *Selected Poems* (1929).

A82: a song from the play *The Dreaming of the Bones*, first published in 1919 and included in all subsequent editions. Published separately as 'At the Grey Round of the Hill' in *Selected Poems* (1929).

A82.4: a townland in County Galway in Ireland.

A83: a song from the play *The Only Jealousy of Emer*, first published in 1919 and included in all subsequent editions. Published separately as 'A Woman's Beauty is like a White Frail Bird' in *Selected Poems* (1929).

A83.12: Archimedes (ca. 287–212 B.C.), Greek mathematician and inventor.

A84: a song from the play *The Only Jealousy of Emer*, first published in 1919 and included in all subsequent editions.

A85: a song from the play *The Only Jealousy of Emer*, first published in 1919 and included in all subsequent editions. Published separately as 'Why does your Heart beat thus?' in *Selected Poems* (1929).

A86: Apparently accepted for publication by *The Nation* (London) in late November or early December 1920, the poem was withdrawn at Lady Gregory's request and remained unpublished in Yeats's lifetime. A version of the poem, though not the final text, was first published in *Rann: An Ulster Quarterly of Poetry*, No. 2 (Autumn 1948). For Robert Gregory, see note to poem 144. 'Reprisals' refers to the actions of the English-controlled Irish government forces against the Irish Republican Army.

A86.11: see note to 145.5.

A87: a song from the play *Calvary*, first published in 1921 and included in all subsequent editions.

A88: a song from the play *Calvary*, first published in 1921 and included in all subsequent editions.

A89: a song from the play *Calvary*, first published in 1921 and included in all subsequent editions.

A89.1: 'His' refers to Christ in the play.

A90: a song from the play *Calvary*, first published in 1921 and included in all subsequent editions.

A91: first published in *Seven Poems and a Fragment* (1922); included in *The Tower* (1928). For the *Collected Poems*, Yeats printed only the last twelve lines, under the title 'The Fool by the Roadside' (poem 225); previously published in that form in *A Vision* (1925). *Poems* (1949) improperly reverts to the longer version.

A92: a song from the play *The Player Queen*, first published in 1922 and included in all subsequent editions. Decima is a character in the play.

A92.2: Pasiphaë, daughter of Helios and wife of Minos, king of Crete, mated with a bull and bore a creature half-man and half-bull, the Minotaur.

A92.3: for Leda, see poem 220.

A93: a song from the play *The Player Queen*, first published in 1922 and included in all subsequent editions. The poem's subject is a unicorn.

A94: a song from the play *The Resurrection*, included only in the version in *The Adelphi*, June 1927.

A95: a chorus from Yeats's translation of Sophocles' *King Oedipus*, first published in 1928 and included in all subsequent editions.

A95.1: Thebes is the chief city in Boeotia in ancient Greece. The 'Golden House' is the temple at Delphi, on Mt. Parnassus, site of the sacred oracle of Apollo. The temple also contained a treasury.

A95.2: as the father of Apollo, Zeus speaks through him.

A95.4: in Greek mythology, Parnassus is a mountain sacred to the gods; the Fates are three women who control man's destiny.

A95.6: Delos, a small island in the Aegean Sea, is the birthplace of Apollo.

A95.7: Ares, in Greek mythology a god of war, called by Sophocles 'the Destroyer.'

A95.11: the Atlantic Ocean.

A95.20: Artemis, in Greek mythology an earth goddess often depicted as a virgin huntress, was the sister of Apollo.

A95.21: see note to A102.7.

A95.22: correctly Lycian. Apollo was the chief deity in Lycia, a mountainous country in the south-west of Asia Minor.

A95.24: Bacchus is the Lydian name for Dionysus, god of wine and of fertility.

A96: a chorus from Yeats's translation of Sophocles' *King Oedipus*, first published in 1928 and included in all subsequent editions.

A96.1: see note to A95.1.

A96.7: in Greek mythology, the omphalos (a stone of navel shape) at Delphi was considered to be the centre of the earth.

A96.8: the 'beast' is the murderer of Laius (later discovered to be Oedipus).

A97: a chorus from Yeats's translation of Sophocles' *King Oedipus*, first published in 1928 and included in all subsequent editions.

A97.3: Zeus is the greatest of the Olympian gods; for the Empyrean, see note to 303.7.

A97.12: see note to A95.1.

A97.13: see note to A96.7.

A98: a chorus from Yeats's translation of Sophocles' *King Oedipus,* first published in 1928 and included in all subsequent editions.

A98.1: Mt. Cithaeron, where Oedipus was abandoned as an infant.

A98.6: the Helicon, a mountain in Boeotia, is sacred to Apollo and the Muses.

A98.7: for Pan, see note to 363.31; the 'mountain Lord' is Dionysus.

A98.8: the Bacchantes are the Maenads (see note to A102.7).

A99: a chorus from Yeats's translation of Sophocles' *King Oedipus,* first published in 1928 and included in all subsequent editions.

A99.4: the Sphinx, whose riddle Oedipus solved and thereby became king.

A99.6: for Thebes, see note to A95.1.

A100: a chorus from Yeats's translation of Sophocles' *King Oedipus,* first published in 1928 and included in all subsequent editions.

A101: first published in *Stories of Michael Robartes and His Friends* (1931) and then included in *A Vision* (1937). For 'Huddon, Duddon, and Daniel O'Leary,' see note to 289.7.

A101.8: in *A Vision,* the characters are named Peter Huddon, John Duddon, and Daniel O'Leary.

A102: a song from the play *The Resurrection,* first published in *Stories of Michael Robartes and His Friends* (1931) and included in all subsequent editions.

A102.1: for Astrea, see note to 218.1.9–16; in the context of *The Resurrection,* the child is Dionysus.

A102.3: for the Titans, see note to A2.11.

A102.7: the Maenads, women who are followers of Dionysus.

A103: first published in the 'Introduction to *Fighting the Waves*' in *The Dublin Magazine,* April–June 1932, and included in *Wheels and Butterflies* (1934).

A103.1: Sir Isaac Newton (1642–1727), English scientist.

A103.2: Thomas Hobbes (1588–1679) and John Locke (1632–1704), English philosophers.

A104: first published in the 'Introduction to *Fighting the Waves*' in *The Dublin Magazine,* April–June 1932, and included in *Wheels and Butterflies* (1934). H. G. Wells (1866–1946) is an English writer.

A104.3: in *Zur Kritik der Hegelschen Rechtsphilosophie* (1844; 'Towards a Critique of Hegel's Philosophy of Right'), the German political philosopher Karl Marx (1818–83) wrote that 'Die Religion . . . ist das Opium des Volkes' ('Religion . . . is the opium of the people').

A105: first published in *The Spectator,* 23 February 1934; last published in this form in full in *A Full Moon in March* (1935), though Part III was later included in *A Broadside,* December 1935. Yeats then revised the poem to 'Three Marching Songs' (poem 360), included in *Last Poems and Two Plays* (1939). *Poems* (1949) improperly retains the earlier work in the section 'From "A Full Moon in March." '

In *The Spectator,* Yeats offered the following note:

In politics I have but one passion, and one thought, rancour against all who, except under the most dire necessity, disturb public order, a conviction that public order cannot long persist without the rule of educated and able men. That order was everywhere their work, is still as much a part of their tradition as the *Iliad* or the Republic of Plato; their rule once gone, it lies an empty shell for the passing fool to kick in pieces. Some months ago that passion laid hold upon me with the violence which unfits the poet for all politics but his own. While the mood lasted, it seemed that our growing disorder, the fanaticism that inflamed it like some old bullet embedded in the flesh, was about to turn our noble history into an ignoble farce. For the first time in my life I wanted to write what some crowd in the street might understand and sing; I asked my friends for a tune; they recommended that old march, 'O'Donnell Abu.' I first got my chorus, 'Down the fanatic, down the clown,' then the rest of the first song. But I soon tired of its rhetorical vehemence, thought that others would tire of it unless I found myself some gay playing upon its theme, some half-serious exaggeration and defence of its rancorous chorus, and therefore I made the second version. Then I put into a simple song a commendation of the rule of the able and educated, man's old delight in submission; I wrote round the line 'The soldier takes pride in saluting his captain,' thinking the while of a Gaelic poet's lament for his lost masters: 'My fathers served their fathers before Christ was crucified.' I read my songs to friends, they talked to others, these others talked, and now companies march to the words 'Blueshirt Abu,' and a song that is all about shamrocks and harps or seems all about them, because its words have the particular variation upon the cadence of 'Yankee Doodle' Young Ireland reserved for that theme. I did not write that song; I could not if I tried. Here are my songs. Anybody may sing them, choosing 'clown' and 'fanatic' for himself, if they are singable—musicians say they are, but may flatter—and worth singing. (VP pp. 543–44)

The *Iliad* is one of the two major works of the Greek poet Homer, the *Republic* an important work of the Greek philosopher Plato. The words to '*Ó Domhnaill Abú!*' (understood as 'O'Donnell to Victory,' probably really 'O'Donnell Above!') were written by Michael Joseph McCann (1824?–1883), but the song became famous not with the tune McCann had intended but with one adapted from a melody by Joseph Haliday (1775–1846), the inventor of the bugle. For the 'Gaelic poet,' see Part II of Yeats's 'Commentary on "A Parnellite at Parnell's Funeral," ' p. 672. For the 'Blueshirts,' see note to 304.II.9. 'Yankee Doodle' is a folksong of uncertain origin. The Young Ireland movement was founded in 1842 and culminated in an abortive rebellion in August 1848.

Yeats also offered a 'Commentary on The Three Songs' in *Poetry* (Chicago), December 1934, and in both editions of *The King of the Great Clock Tower, Commentaries and Poems* (1934, 1935). Given below is the text of the 1935 edition:

For thirty years I have been a director of the Abbey Theatre. It is a famous theatre, known to students of dramatic literature all over the world, but company and building are small, it often turns many away from its cheaper seats. It holds some five hundred persons; that five hundred, or whatever moiety of it is there on any particular evening, is mainly boys and girls out of the shops and factories. They come again and again to a favourite play, all others are casual or uncertain, except some old adherents who have lasted out the thirty years, and a few students from the National University. If it were in Poland, in Sweden, in some Balkan State, it would have four or five times as many in company, in audience, draw into that audience those that were highly educated or highly placed, have behind it for moments of emergency ample Government support. It would be expected to send its best players now and again to foreign countries that it might raise the prestige of its nation as do the bronze replicas of the Roman wolf, a masterpiece of Etruscan art, the Italian Government has set up in America wherever Italian emigrants are numerous. When I was a foolish lad I hoped for something of the kind. When I founded the Irish Literary Society, the National Literary Society, barred from the Chair politicians and Lord Mayors that literature might live its own sincere life, I hoped for a literature Ireland would honour as Poland honours its literature. Synge, Lady Gregory, A.E. came first; then many novelists and dramatists; Moore and Shaw turned their thoughts to Ireland; nobody could have hoped for so much genius. But most of these writers are better known in other countries, even our novelists who describe in simple, vivid speech the circumstance and history of their country, find most of their readers among the Irish in America, and in England; more perhaps among Englishmen and Americans, without Irish blood, than in Ireland. Sometimes I receive a little propagandist paper issued by the Polish Government, written in French, and find there pictures of the noble eighteenth century palace where the Polish Academy of Letters meets. Our not less distinguished Academy meets in a room hired for five shillings a night. The explanation is that our upper class cares nothing for Ireland except as a place for sport, that the rest of the population is drowned in religious and political fanaticism. Poland is a Catholic nation and some ten years ago inflicted upon the national enemy an overwhelming, world-famous defeat, but its fanaticism, if it has any, thwarts neither science, nor art, nor letters. Sometimes as the representative of the Abbey Theatre I have called upon some member of Mr. Cosgrave's or Mr. de Valera's government to explain some fanatical attack—we are a State Theatre though our small subsidy has been lately reduced—once as a member of the Irish Academy to complain of the illegal suppression of a book, and upon each occasion I came away with the conviction that the Minister felt exactly as I felt but was helpless: the mob reigned. If that reign is not broken our public life will move from violence to violence, or from violence to apathy, our Parliament disgrace and debauch those that enter it; our men of letters live like outlaws in their own country. It will be broken when some government seeks unity of culture not less than economic unity, welding to the purpose museum, school, university, learned institution. A nation should be like an audience in some great theatre—'In the theatre,' said Victor Hugo, 'the mob becomes a people'—watching the sacred drama of its own history; every spectator finding self and neighbour there, finding all the world there as we find the sun in the bright spot under the burning glass. We know the world through abstractions, statistics, time tables, through images that refuse to compose themselves into a clear design. Such knowledge thins the blood. To know it in the concrete we must know it near at hand; religion itself during our first impressionable years in the dramatis personæ of our own narrow stage; I think of those centuries before the great schism had divided East and West accepted by Catholic and Protestant alike. Into the drama must enter all that have lived with precision and energy; Major Sirr, picture lover, children lover, hateful oppressor, should he strike some creative fancy, not less than Emmet and Fitzgerald; the Ascendency, considering its numbers as fruitful of will and intellect as any stock on earth, not less than those Wild Geese, those Catholic gentlemen who, in the words of Swift, carried into foreign service 'a valour' above 'that of all nations'.

If any Government or party undertake this work it will need force, marching men (the logic of fanaticism, whether in a woman or a mob is drawn from a premise protected by ignorance and therefore irrefutable); it will promise not this or that measure but a discipline, a way of life; that sacred drama must to all native eyes and ears become the greatest of the parables. There is no such government or party today; should either appear I offer it these trivial songs and what remains to me of life.

April 1934.

P.S. Because a friend belonging to a political party wherewith I had once some loose associations, told me that it had, or was about to have, or might be persuaded to have, some such aim as mine, I wrote these songs. Finding that it neither would nor could, I increased their fantasy, their extravagance, their obscurity, that no party might sing them.

(VP pp. 835-37)

The Abbey Theatre held its first performance on 27 December 1904; Yeats was then President of the Irish National Theatre Society and later became one of the three Directors of the National Theatre Society Limited. The National University is University College, Dublin. Yeats and others founded the Irish Literary Society in London and the National Literary Society in Dublin in 1892, though a preliminary meeting towards the founding of the former was held on 28 December 1891. The Irish writers mentioned are John Millington Synge (1871-1909), Lady Gregory (1852-1932), George W. Russell, 'A. E.' (1867-1935), George Moore (1852-1933), and George Bernard Shaw (1856-1950). Yeats refers to *Pologne Littéraire*, No. 87 (15 December 1933), which includes a long article on 'L'Académie Polonaise des Belles-Lettres' and photographs of its meeting-place, the Palais Potocki (p. 1). Yeats had been instrumental in starting an Irish Academy of Letters in 1932. The 1921 Treaty of Riga awarded Poland most of the territorial claims over which the Russo-Polish War (1920) had been fought. William Thomas Cosgrave (1880-1965) was President of the Executive Council of the Irish Free State until 1932, when he was succeeded by Eamon de Valera (1882-1975). The Abbey Theatre received a government subsidy of £850 for 1925-26; thereafter the subsidy was £1000, until it was reduced to £750 in 1933. Yeats found the quotation from the French writer Victor Hugo (1802–85) in *Victor Hugo's Intellectual Autobiography,* ed. L. O'Rourke (New York and London: Funk & Wagnalls, 1907), pp. 369–70. For the 'great schism,' see Yeats's 'Commentary on Supernatural Songs,' p. 678. Henry Charles Sirr (1764–1841) was town-major of Dublin; he took part in the capture of Lord Edward Fitzgerald (1763–98). Fitzgerald and Robert Emmet (1778–1803) were Irish patriots. For the Wild Geese, see note to 115.17. In a letter to Charles Wogan, dated [July–2 August 1732], which Yeats would have read in *The Works of the Rev. Dr. Jonathan Swift,* ed. Thomas Sheridan (London, 1784), XII, 452–53, Swift noted that 'although I have no great regard for your trade [a soldier], from the judgment I make of those who profess it in these kingdoms, yet I cannot but highly esteem those Gentlemen of *Ireland,* who, with all the disadvantages of being exiles and strangers, have been able to distinguish themselves by their valour and conduct in so many parts of Europe, I think, above all other nations; which ought to make the English ashamed of the reproaches they cast on the ignorance, the dulness, and the want of courage, in the Irish natives. . . .' The 'friend' was probably Captain Dermot MacManus.

A105.II.23–25: see note to 360.I.23–25.

A105.III.4: see note to 20.4.

A106: first published in the Introduction to *The Words Upon the Window-pane* (1934) and included in *Wheels and Butterflies* (1934).

A106.3: Constantin Brancusi (1876–1957), Rumanian sculptor.

A107: a song from the play *The King of the Great Clock Tower,* first published in *Life and Letters,* November 1934, and included in all subsequent editions.

A107.1: *Tír na nÓg,* 'the Land of the Young': the elysium of Irish mythology, home of the gods and of the dead.

A107.10 ff.: see 375.I.139–45 and also Yeats's note on 'He mourns . . .', p. 600.

A108: a song from the play *The King of the Great Clock Tower,* first published in *Life and Letters,* November 1934, and included in all subsequent editions.

A109: a song from the play *The King of the Great Clock Tower,* first published in *Life and Letters,* November 1934, and included in all subsequent editions. Published separately as 'The Wicked Hawthorn Tree' in *A Broadside,* February 1935.

A109.3: for Castle Dargan, see note to A37.7.

A110: published in *Wheels and Butterflies* (1934).

A111: published in *Wheels and Butterflies* (1934).

A112: published in the Introduction to *The Cat and the Moon* in *Wheels and Butterflies* (1934).

A112.4: for Nineveh, see note to 219.10.

A113: a chorus from Yeats's translation of Sophocles' *Oedipus at Colonus,* first published in *The Collected Plays* (1934) and included in all subsequent editions.

A113.1: for Thebes, see note to A95.1.

A113.2: that is, the warriors of Colonus.

A113.3: the Pythian strand is the shore of the bay of Eleusis just beyond the pass of Daphne, 'Pythian' because of a temple of Apollo in the pass; 'further away to the west' refers to the temple of Eleusis, sacred to the goddesses Demeter and Persephone.

A113.6: 'Oea' has not been convincingly identified, but it is probably a part of Mt. Aegaleos.

A113.8: Theseus, king of Athens, is a character in the play.

A113.14: Poseidon, god of the sea and of horses, was a son of Kronos and Rhea.

A113.15: for Athena, see note to 166.6.

A113.24: twins of Zeus and Leto.

A114: a chorus from Yeats's translation of Sophocles' *Oedipus at Colonus,* first published in *The Collected Plays* (1934) and included in all subsequent editions.

A114.4: Oedipus.

A114.19: for the king of Athens, see note to A113.8.

A114.20: see note to A113.14.

A115: a chorus from Yeats's translation of Sophocles' *Oedipus at Colonus,* first published in *The Collected Plays* (1934) and included in all subsequent editions.

A115.1–2: in Greek mythology, Persephone is the wife of Hades, god of the lower world.

A115.3: the Erinyes (see note to 336.13–14).

A115.4: the Styx is the major river in the lower world.

A115.7: Cerberus, the dog which guards the entrance to Hades.

A115.8: the children of Ge (Earth) and Tartarus are Typhoeus and Echinda. Echinda is a monster, half woman and half serpent; by Typhoeus she is the mother of Cerberus. In using 'daughter,' Yeats is following the translation in Paul Masqueray's edition, *Sophocle,* Tome II (Paris: Société d'édition 'Les Belles-Lettres,' 1924), p. 216, rather than that in R. C. Jebb's edition, *Sophocles: The Plays and Fragments,* Part II, 3rd ed. (1900; rpt. Cambridge: University Press, 1928), p. 243. Jebb offers 'son of Earth and Tartarus' and suggests that the allusion is to Thanatos, the god of death.

A116: a song from the play *A Full Moon in March,* first published separately as 'The Singing Head and the Lady' in *The Spectator,* 7 December 1934; included in the play in *A Full Moon in March* (1935) and all subsequent editions.

A116.13–14: Theopano (ca. 941–ca. 1013), the daughter of a tavern-keeper, married Romanus II (939–63), Emperor of Byzantium, in 956. She exercised considerable authority in the court.

A116.14: for Byzantium, see note to poem 204.

A117: a song from the play *A Full Moon in March,* first published in *Poetry* (Chicago), March 1935, and included in all subsequent editions.

A117.5: for Pythagoras, see note to 222.45.

A118: a song from the play *A Full Moon in March,* first published in *Poetry* (Chicago), March 1935, and included in all subsequent editions.

A119: a song from the play *A Full Moon in March,* first published in *Poetry* (Chicago), March 1935, and included in all subsequent editions. *Jack and Jill* is a well-known nursery rhyme; Yeats considerably alters the traditional plot, which does not involve murder.

A120: a song from the play *A Full Moon in March,* first published in *Poetry* (Chicago), March 1935, and included in all subsequent editions.

A121: a song from the play *The King of the Great Clock Tower,* first published in *A Full Moon in March* (1935) and included in all subsequent editions.

A121.18: Virgil (70–19 B.C.), Roman poet.

A122: published in *A Speech and Two Poems* (privately printed, Dublin: at the Sign of the Three Candles, 1937).

A122.1: Patrick McCartan (1878–1963), an Irish-American who organized an American 'Testimonial Committee for W. B. Yeats,' which presented Yeats with grants of £600 in June 1937 (announced at a banquet of the Irish Academy of Letters on 17 August 1937) and of £400 in June 1938.

A122.5: James A. Farrell (1863–1943), Chairman of the 'American Testimonial Committee for W. B. Yeats,' was President of the U.S. Steel Corporation, 1911–32.

A122.7: Dudley Digges (1879–1947) was a leading actor in the Irish theatre until he moved to America in 1904.

A123: a song from the play *The Herne's Egg,* first published in 1938 and included in all subsequent editions.

A124: a song from the play *The Herne's Egg,* first published in 1938 and included in all subsequent editions.

A125: a song from the play *The Herne's Egg,* first published in 1938 and included in all subsequent editions.

A126: published posthumously in *On the Boiler* ([1939]); improperly included in *Last Poems & Plays* (1940).

A126.5: Dante Alighieri (1265–1321), Italian writer.

A126.7: for Helen, see note to 20.4.

A127: published posthumously in *On the Boiler* ([1939]); improperly included in *Last Poems & Plays* (1940).

A127.1–2: see poem 268.

A127.7–10: George V (1865–1936), king of England; his cousins were Nicholas II (1868–1918), last tsar of Russia, and his family, murdered in July 1918.

A127.15–17: Emer is the wife of Cuchulain (see note to poem 19). In *On the Boiler* (Dublin: Cuala Press, [1939]), p. 24n, Yeats explains that 'In a fragment from some early version of "The Courting of Emer[,]" Emer is chosen for the strength and volume of her bladder. This strength and volume were certainly considered signs of vigour. A woman of divine origin was murdered by jealous rivals because she made the deepest hole in the snow with her urine.' No such reference to Emer has been traced in Irish mythology. Yeats found the other story in 'The Deaths of Lugaid and Derbforgaill,' trans. Carl Marstrander, *Ériu,* 5 (1911), 201–18. Derbforgill, 'daughter of the king of Norway,' married Lugaid of the Red Stripe. She was killed by some jealous women after winning a contest in which several women made pillars of snow and urinated on them: 'she goes on the pillar and it poured from her to the ground' (p. 215). Cuchulain had planned to marry Derbforgill before he married Emer, but had become blood-kin to her by sucking a wound she had incurred, to heal it; so he arranged her marriage to Lugaid. Maeve was also renowned for her bladder; on the retreat from Ulster at the end of the *Táin* she cut three ravines with her flow at a place still called, the text says, *Fual Medba* ('Maeve's Piss').

A128: published posthumously in *On the Boiler* ([1939]); improperly included in *Last Poems & Plays* (1940).

A128.5: presumably the writer Oscar Wilde (1854–1900), though possibly Oscar Tschirky (1866–1950), the maître d'hôtel at the Waldorf-Astoria in New York since its opening in 1893 ('Oscar of the Waldorf').

A128.13: for Avalon, see note to 86.2–3.

A128.14–15: in the English House of Lords, the Lord Chancellor sits upon a cloth-covered square bag of wool, symbolic of his office. It is uncertain whether Yeats intends here a specific allusion. If so, the best suggestion is that made by Donald T. Torchiana in *W. B. Yeats & Georgian Ireland* (Evanston: Northwestern University Press; London: Oxford University Press, 1966), p. 356: Frederick Edwin Smith (1872–1930), Earl of Birkenhead and Lord Chancellor from 1919 to 1922.

A128.16–17: again, if a specific allusion, probably (as Torchiana suggests, pp. 355–56) Sir Hubert de la Poer Gough (1870–1963). As commanding officer of the Third Cavalry Brigade based at the Curragh, he was the leader of the 'Curragh Mutiny' in March 1914, refusing to promise to fight against the Ulster Volunteers. He resigned and was dismissed from the army, although he was later reinstated.

A128.18: Eamon de Valera (1882–1975), who became President of the Executive Council of the Irish Free State in 1932.

A128.19: presumably George II (1890–1947), restored to the throne of Greece in November 1935.

A128.20: probably William Richard Morris (1887–1963), Lord Nuffield, Chairman of Morris Motors Ltd (1919–52), mentioned elsewhere in *On the Boiler*. The American Henry Ford (1863–1947), who pioneered the mass production of automobiles, has also been suggested.

A128.22: Montenegro is a region in Yugoslavia.

A129: a song from the play *The Death of Cuchulain*, published posthumously in *Last Poems and Two Plays* (1939) and included in all subsequent editions.

A129.3: for Conall and Cuchulain, see note to poem A65. The sons of Usna were Naoise, Ainnle, and Ardan (see note to 20.5).

A129.5: for Maeve, see Yeats's note to 'The Hosting of the Sidhe,' p. 600.

A129.19: see note to 357.III.5–6.

A129.20: see notes to 193.24 and 193.76.

A129.29: see note to 362.25–26.

A129.30: Oliver Sheppard (1865–1941), Irish sculptor. His *The Death of Cuchulain* was executed ca. 1911–12 and in 1935 placed in the General Post Office as a memorial to the 1916 Easter Rebellion.

TEXTUAL NOTES

Part A lists the copy-texts which have been used for each poem in this edition. Part B indicates all of the emendations to those copy-texts which have been made in this edition. The citations provide poem and line numbers, followed by the *unemended* reading of the copy-text. When the variant includes the lack of line-end punctuation in the copy-text, the first word of the following line is included in the citation; likewise, words before and/or after the emended word are provided when necessary for clarity. Part B also cites what authority, if any, exists for the emendations.

For a detailed discussion of the rationale behind the selection and emendation of the copy-texts, interested readers are referred to this writer's *Editing Yeats's Poems: A Reconsideration* (London: Macmillan; New York: St. Martin's Press, 1990).

Abbreviations used in the Textual Notes

AV(B)	*A Vision* (London: Macmillan, 1937)
B	*The Bookman* (London)
BL	British Library, Department of Manuscripts
CP	*The Collected Poems* (London: Macmillan, 1933)
CPl	*The Collected Plays* (London: Macmillan, 1934)
CPMBY	Copy of CP with corrections by Yeats, inscribed 'Michael Yeats from W. B. Yeats November 1933' (collection Michael B. Yeats)
CTS	Carbon typescript
CW	*The Collected Works in Verse and Prose* (Stratford-on-Avon: Shakespeare Head Press, 1908)
DUR	*Dublin University Review*
EdL	Corrected page proofs for *Poems* in the Edition de Luxe, date-stamps 22 July–4 October 1932 (NLI 30,262)
FMM	*A Full Moon in March* (London: Macmillan, 1935)
G	*The Gael* (Dublin)
GOP	*The Girl's Own Paper*
HRC	Humanities Research Centre, University of Texas at Austin
HRC-S	Materials submitted by Yeats to Charles Scribner's Sons in 1937 for their unpublished 'Dublin Edition' (HRC)
LH	*The Leisure Hour*
LM	*The London Mercury*
MS	Manuscript
Myth	Corrected page proofs for *Mythologies* in the Edition de Luxe, date-stamps 30 September–26 October 1931 (NLI 30,030)

NLI	National Library of Ireland
TS	Typescript
WB	*Wheels and Butterflies* (London: Macmillan, 1934)
WO	*The Wanderings of Oisin and Other Poems* (London: Kegan Paul, Trench & Co., 1889)
WOP	Corrected copy of WO signed 'Edward Garnett from W. B. Yeats Sept 26 1890' (Robert H. Taylor Collection, Princeton University Library)
WOPM	Corrected copy of WO inscribed by Yeats 'This copy is not to be lent as I have made corrections etc in it that I do not ~~wish~~ want to lose' (Pierpont Morgan Library). An asterisk after the abbreviation indicates that Yeats queried the projected revision.
WOR	Corrected copy of WO from the collection of Edwin J. Ellis, signed by Yeats with the notation 'corrections in this book made at my dictation' and dated 'May 7. 1889' (Reading University Library)
WS	*The Winding Stair and Other Poems* (London: Macmillan, 1933)

A. Copy-texts used for this edition

Poems	*Texts*
1–110	CP
111	Corrected copy of CP, HRC-S
112–82	CP
183	AV(B)
184–238	CP
239	AV(B)
240–303	BL Additional Manuscript 55878 [corrected page proofs for WS, date-stamps 27 July–2 August 1933]
304–05	FMM
306.I	*Poems* (London: Macmillan, 1949)
306.II–309	FMM
310	Corrected copy of FMM, HRC-S
311–20	FMM
321–55	*New Poems* (Dublin: Cuala Press, 1938); with corrections dictated by Yeats, inscribed 'George from WBY' (collection Michael B. Yeats)
356	TS, NLI 13,593 (52)
357	CTS, MS, NLI 13,593 (31)
358	TS, NLI 30,200
359	CTS, NLI 13,593 (50)
360	TS, NLI 13,593 (35)
361	TS, NLI 13,593 (32)
362	TS, Meisei University

363	CTS, NLI 13,593 (34)
364	TS, NLI 13,593 (36)
365	TS, HRC (before corrections)
366	CTS, HRC
367	LM (December 1938)
368	LM (December 1938)
369–71	LM (December 1938)
372–74	LM (January 1939)
375–82	CP
A1.I–II.ii	DUR (April–June 1885)
A1.II.iii	WO
A2	DUR (May 1885)
A3	WO
A4	DUR (February 1886)
A5	DUR (March 1886)
A6–7	WO
A8	*The Irish Monthly* (July 1886)
A9	*The Irish Fireside* (5 February 1887)
A10	WO
A11	*North & South* (5 March 1887)
A12	G (27 April 1887)
A13–15	WO
A16	G (19 November 1887)
A17	*Poems and Ballads of Young Ireland* (Dublin: M. H. Gill and Son, 1888); copy corrected by Yeats, inscribed 'Lady Gregory from W B Yeats Dec 5. 1910' (Emory University Library)
A18–20	WO
A21	CW, volume 7
A22–24	WO
A25	LH (April 1890)
A26	WO
A27	GOP (8 June 1889)
A28	GOP (6 July 1889)
A29	LH (March 1891)
A30	*United Ireland* (10 October 1891)
A31	*The Countess Kathleen and Various Legends and Lyrics* (London: T. Fisher Unwin, 1892)
A32	*Irish Fairy Tales* (London: T. Fisher Unwin, 1892)
A33	*Irish Weekly Independent,* 8 April 1893
A34	B (May 1893)
A35	B (December 1893)
A36	Corrected copy of CPl, HRC-S [the poem is also reprinted at the end of the play, with slight variants in punctuation]
A37	Myth
A38–39	CPl
A40	Myth
A41	B (October 1895)

A42	Myth
A43	*Roma* (Rome, Italy), 1897
A44–45	*A Broad Sheet* (January 1902)
A46–48	CPl
A49	*Where There Is Nothing* (privately printed, 1902) [American privately printed large paper edition]
A50	*The Pot of Broth* (London: A. H. Bullen, 1911)
A51–54	CPl
A55	Lady Gregory, *Seven Short Plays* (Dublin: Maunsel, 1909)
A56–64	CPl
A65	CW, volume 4
A66	CW, volume 2
A67	Corrected page of notes to *Plays in Prose and Verse* (1922), HRC-S
A68	CW, volume 8
A69–85	CPl
A86	TS, NLI 13,583
A87–90	CPl
A91	*The Tower* [revised edition] (London: Macmillan, 1929)
A92–93	CPl
A94	*The Adelphi* (June 1927)
A95–100	CPl
A101	AV(B)
A102	CPl
A103–04	WB
A105.I, II	FMM
A105.III	*A Broadside* (December 1935)
A106	WB
A107–09	FMM
A110–12	WB
A113–15	CPl
A116–21	FMM
A122	*A Speech and Two Poems* (privately printed, Dublin: at the Sign of the Three Candles, 1937)
A123–25	*The Herne's Egg* (London: Macmillan, 1938)
A126–28	NLI 30,485 [corrected page proofs for the first edition of *On the Boiler* (Dublin: Cuala Press, [1939])]
A129	TS, NLI 8772 (7)

B. Emendations to the copy-texts

Poem	Reading of copy-text	Authority for emendation
6.15–16	[no stanza division]	All earlier printings
77.4	Parc-na-lee	EdL
111.14	run.	Cf. l. 6

121.8, 19, 26, 54	Guare	CPMBY
167.36	sakes'	EdL [correction possibly not by Yeats]
239.subtitle	An Epilogue	CP
253.14	Shaw Taylor	Letter from Mrs. Yeats to Thomas Mark, 14 June 1939 (Macmillan, London); proper name
289.13	flood/Bird	WS
291.2	yellow canvas	WS (errata slip)
305.11	Niam	Yeats's spelling since CP
315.5	tongue,/What	No contemporary evidence
322.29	Calimachus	LM (March 1938); proper name
333.12	wife daughter	TS, NLI 13,593 (11); *The Erasmian* (Dublin), April 1937
334.11	Athene	Final page proofs for *New Poems* (NLI 30,008)
337.31–32	[not indented]	*A Broadside* (August 1937)
354.40	tongue)	No contemporary evidence
355.15	Butlers'	TS, NLI 13,593 (30)
356.title	Benbulben	Cf. ll. 11 and 84
356.2	Mariotic	Cf. 199.15; letter from Mrs. Yeats to Thomas Mark, 15 April 1939 (Macmillan, London)
356.4	set all the	Different TS, NLI 13,593 (52); TS, University College, Dublin
356.14	eternities/That	Different TS, NLI 13,593 (52)
356.15	soul/And	Different TS, NLI 13,593 (52)
356.20–21	[stanza break]	Different TS, NLI 13,593 (52)
356.45	Michaelangelo	Cf. 189.32 and 364.26
356.53	Quattro-cento	Cf. 222.26 and 300.19
356.85	Druncliff	Cf. 355.9
357.I.10	Maughan	Cf. l. 2
357.I.10	Mananaan	Cf. 375.II.128, 173, 236
357.III.23	whats	No contemporary evidence
357.III.26	shed,	No contemporary evidence
358.24	horn	CTS, NLI 30,200
358.25	hound	CTS, NLI 30,200
359.title	Cuchullain	Yeats's spelling since the 1904 *Poems*
359.12, 13	[no initial quotation mark]	TS, NLI 13,593 (50)

359.13	shroud/Mainly	TS, NLI 13,593 (50)
359.15	afraid	CTS, NLI 30, 132
359.16	needles	No contemporary evidence
359.16, 22	[no initial quotation mark]	No contemporary evidence
359.17	do!' [double quotation mark typed over period]	Typing error?
360.I.20, 30	And all that's	Cf. l. 10
360.II.17, 27	marches through the	Cf. l. 7
360.II.18	son not	Cf. l. 8
360.II.21	theres	No contemporary evidence
360.II.note	'airy'	No contemporary evidence
360.II.note	eary [no punctuation]	No contemporary evidence
360.III.title	Three Marching Songs/*(To the Tune of O'Donnell Abu)*	No contemporary evidence
361.12	haroow	No contemporary evidence
362.25	Cuchullain	Yeats's spelling since the 1904 *Poems*
362.26	intellect	No contemporary evidence
364.17	Practice	LM (March 1939); Yeats's usual spelling
365.7	Hysterico-passio	Cf. 304.I.21
365.20	itself,	ink correction, probably posthumous; page proofs for *Last Poems and Two Plays* (NLI 30,013)
365.22	supernatural;	ink correction, probably posthumous; page proofs for *Last Poems and Two Plays* (NLI 30,013)
365.26	stye	Cf. 273.6
365.27	revery	Cf. 212.29 and elsewhere
366.3	St	Cf. 262.80
366.4	like	TS, NLI 13,593 (38)
367.9	Voices	Cf. l. 7; TSS, NLI 13,593 (40) and Harvard University
369.4	fench	CTS, NLI 13,593 (41); *The Nation* (10 December 1938)
373.title	Animal's	TSS, NLI 13,593 (47)
373.10	Usheen	Yeats's spelling since CP
373.26	Cuchullain	Yeats's spelling since the 1904 *Poems*
375.III.169	And before I	All earlier printings
376.11	[no note on pronunciation]	Cf. 125 and 288
381.183	whirling dance	CPMBY
A1.I.i.63–64	[no space]	Cf. ll. 31–32, 50–51

A1.I.i.136	Oenone	Cf. A1.I.i.17
A1.I.ii.16	so.	No contemporary evidence
A1.II.iii.title	Island of Statutes./ A Fragment.	Only one scene from play included in WO
A1.II.iii.55	left the	DUR (July 1885)
A1.II.iii.132	all;	WOPM
A1.II.iii.213	fair years	DUR (July 1885)
A1.II.iii.239	things you speak. But what	WOPM
A1.II.iii.294	moon's	DUR (July 1885)
A3.II.11A–12	'Behold the Knight of the waterfall, whose heart/The spirits stole, and gave him in its stead	WOPM
A3.II.31A	*[Knight.]* I sought thee not. *Figure.* Men call me Infamy.	WOPM*
A7.epigraph	'And my Lord Cardinal hath had strange days in his youth.'—*Extract from a Memoir of the Fifteenth Century.*	WOPM [the epigraph is deleted]
A7.I.38	and comes	WOPM
A7.I.97	come; ha! ha! they	WOPM
A7.II.23	By the	WOPM
A7.II.24	Then he shouted	WOPM
A7.II.42	wages	WOPM, WOP, WOR
A7.II.42	use. No good.	WOPM
A7.III.5	long-lost	WOPM, WOR
A7.III.6	brothers will pass	WOPM, WOR
A7.III.7	Quite soon the	WOPM, WOR
A7.III.10	Will be the	WOPM, WOP, WOR
A7.III.12	is scarcely dawning	WOPM
A7.III.13	And Hassan will be with them—	WOPM, WOR
A7.III.[40A]	. . . . . Yonder a leaf	WOPM, WOP [the line is deleted]
A7.III.41	Of apple-blossom	WOPM, WOP
A7.III.57	the flags	WOPM*, WOR
A7.III.78	Afar along	WOR
A11.7	watch tor the	No contemporary evidence
A13.3	*To prisons go,*	WOPM
A13.20–21	The doves whose growing forms he'd watched. Not these/ He numbers.	WOPM
A13.65	off 'neath a	WOPM

A13.84	[no stanza break]	WOPM
A13.106	Assassin, my assassin	WOR
A13.118	Beside the	WOPM
A13.121–22	Where lies the cow at peace beside her calf,/ He rushes, rolling from his lips a mad-man's laugh.	WOPM
A14.9	the six feet	WOR
A14.11	four eyes	WOR
A15.11	fills full	WOPM
A16.1	Mat formed	MS, NLI 30,340
A16.2	Hurried . . . earth	MS, NLI 30,340
A16.7	pine wood	No contemporary evidence
A16.12	hoofs from	MS, NLI 30,340
A16.18	ebbs	MS, NLI 30,340
A16.19	luxurious in the slow;	MS, NLI 30,340
A16.24	den./To	MS, NLI 30,340
A16.38	came,	No contemporary evidence
A16.39	underneath,	No contemporary evidence
A16.42	we our	No contemporary evidence
A19.28	And rubbed along the rail his nose.	WOPM
A20.15s.d.	*bag.*]	WOPM
A20.15	Ha, ha! ha, ha, ha!	WOPM
A20.36s.d.	hour-glass. [*Pointing to the instruments of magic.*] You	WOPM
A20.58–59	I do miscalculate./ I am dull to-day, or you were now all lost.	WOPM
A23.27	yon newt	WOPM
A23.46	green.	No contemporary evidence
A24.48	Where the	WOPM
A24.69	lev'ret's	WOPM
A24.72	Upraised their	WOPM
A25.6	'mong the vapours	WOPM
A25.8	Hangs o'er all the	WOPM
A25.10, 23, 36, 62	Footing in the feeble glow,	WOPM
A25.11	Of a wide wood's starry leisure,	WOPM
A25.49	Dancing in the feeble glow,	WOPM
A.25.50	other's	Cf. ll. 24, 37
A25.60	Sorrows sapping brain	WOPM
A26.21	'Around	WOP, WOR
A26.24	hides.'	WOP, WOR
A31.8	true/When	No contemporary evidence

A33.67	dweft in	No contemporary evidence
A33.68	Kinsale,	No contemporary evidence
A34.17	Shee	Yeats's spelling since the 1899 *The Wind Among the Reeds*
A34.29	Niam	Yeats's spelling since CP
A44.7	*Diarmid*	Yeats's spelling since CP
A46.7	head,—	*United Irishman,* 5 May 1902; *Samhain,* October 1902; 1902 and first 1904 editions
A65.9, 23	Leagerie	Yeats's spelling since the 1910 *The Green Helmet*
A65.22	Conal	Yeats's spelling since the 1910 *The Green Helmet*
A67.17	another'	Cf. l. 9
A67.20	dear) [no punctuation]	No contemporary evidence
A105.III.19	walk,	Cf. ll. 9 and 19
A113.15, 20	Athene	Final page proofs for *New Poems* (NLI 30,008)
A122.1	MacCartan	Proper name
A127.17	Cuchullain	Yeats's spelling since the 1904 *Poems*
A128.6	troup	Cf. 338.17
A129.3	Conal	Yeats's spelling since the 1910 *The Green Helmet*
A129.3, 23	Cuchullain	Yeats's spelling since the 1904 *Poems*
A129.6	Adore	Typing error
A129.8	thighs/I	No contemporary evidence
A129.16	loathe/Are	No contemporary evidence

In addition, the following minor modifications and conventions have been adopted:

1. For convenience of reference in the Notes, the poems have been numbered.
2. Insofar as possible, the capitalization of titles follows that in the copy-texts. When the typography of a particular copy-text (including its Table of Contents) does not distinguish between capitals and lower-case letters, the capitalization has been regularized.
3. Periods found at the end of some titles have been deleted.
4. All poems open with a capital letter followed by lower-case letters.
5. All dashes, regardless of their length in the copy-texts, have been set as em-dashes.
6. Single and double quotation marks have been regularized according to British usage.
7. All indications of place and date of composition at the end of poems are in italic arabic.

8. The typographical format of all dramatic verse follows that of *The Shadowy Waters* in the 1933 *Collected Poems*.

9. In the Table of Contents to the 1933 *Collected Poems,* poems 112, 142, and 378 are called, respectively, 'Introductory Rhymes,' 'Closing Rhyme,' and 'Introductory Lines'; but the Index to Titles uses instead the first lines of the poems. On the assumption that Yeats is more likely to have seen proofs of the Table of Contents than of the Index to Titles, in the present edition the titles, in square brackets, are used in the Index to Titles.

10. Roman rather than arabic numerals have been used for Yeats's numbering of poems 309–20.

11. In incorporating Yeats's corrections from WOPM, four editorial emendations have been made: lower-case "what" (A1.II.iii.239) and "not" (A13.20) have been capitalized; a comma has been added in "come; they come, they" (A7.I.97); and "Over hangs" has been corrected to "Overhangs" (A25.8).

12. The indications 'End of Scene I' and 'End of Act I' in the copy-text of poem A1 have been deleted.

13. Poems A66, A68, and A111 have been set in roman rather than in the italic of the copy-texts.

14. Em-rules before the authors' names in some of the epigraphs have been deleted.

15. The poems in Part Two are presented in chronological order of first publication.

16. In songs taken from plays in Part Two, dialogue occurring between stanzas has not been cited, and the occasional repetitions of stanzas or parts of stanzas have been eliminated.

17. The frontispiece of the 1933 *Collected Poems,* a 1907 portrait of Yeats by the English artist Augustus John (1878–1961), has not been reproduced.

18. In the Notes to this edition, quotations from Yeats's prose have been corrected or emended (either silently or in square brackets) only when absolutely necessary for comprehension (e.g., 'anyrate' to 'any rate').

19. The music in Appendix B has been re-drawn.

*

A stanza break coincides with the end of the following pages. This list does not include such unambiguous breaks as numbered stanzas, regularly occurring stanzas, or, in dramatic verse, a change in speaker-tags.

12	33	103	115	121	141	148	153	183	188	254
266	281	368	371	377	595					

INDEX TO TITLES

Titles that have been editorially supplied from the first lines of poems are omitted from this index, since they can be found in the Index to First Lines on p. 742.

INDEX TO FIRST LINES